Here's What You Get on the CD:

The CD included with the first edition of the *MCSE: Windows 98 Study Guide* contains invaluable programs and information to help you prepare for your MCSE exams. You can access and install the files on the CD through a user-friendly graphical interface by running the CLICKME.EXE file located in the root directory.

NOTE *The Sybex CD interface is supported only by Windows 95/98 and Windows NT 4.*

Custom Exam Review Software

Test your knowledge with custom exam preparation software. Explanations of correct answers are also provided. To install the exam review program, run SETUP.EXE in the StudyGuide folder. (During installation you may be prompted to allow the program to update system files. The file that is updated is OLEPRO32.DLL. This is a Microsoft DLL and should not cause any problems; however, as a precaution, we recommend that you back up this file prior to installing the test program.)

MCSE: Windows 98 Study Guide—Electronic Copy

We've heard your requests, so here it is—the entire *MCSE: Windows 98 Study Guide* in searchable electronic format! Now you can study for the exam anytime, anywhere. Perfect for frequent business travelers. Just pop the CD into your laptop and those cross-country flights will pass by in no time. You'll need the Adobe Acrobat Reader installed on your system, which is included on the CD as well.

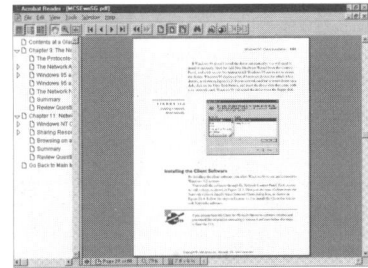

Network Press MCSE Study Guide Sampler

Preview chapters from the best-selling line of *MCSE Study Guides* from Sybex. We've also included a copy of the Adobe Acrobat Reader, which you'll need to view the various preview chapters. From the core requirements to the most popular electives, you'll see why Sybex's *MCSE Study Guides* have become the self-study method of choice for tens of thousands of individuals seeking MCSE certification.

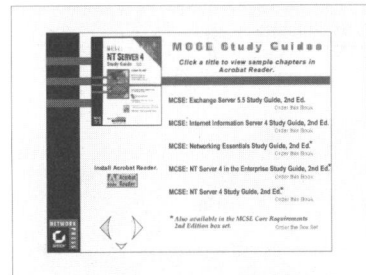

Microsoft Train_Cert Offline Update and Internet Explorer 4

Look to Microsoft's *Train_Cert Offline* Web site, a quarterly snapshot of Microsoft's Education and Certification Web site, for all of the information you need to plot your course for MCSE certification. You'll need to run *Internet Explorer 4* to access all of the features of the *Train_Cert Offline* Web site, so we've included a free copy on the CD. To install the *Train_Cert Offline* Web site to your system, run the SETUP file located in the Microsoft\Offline folder.

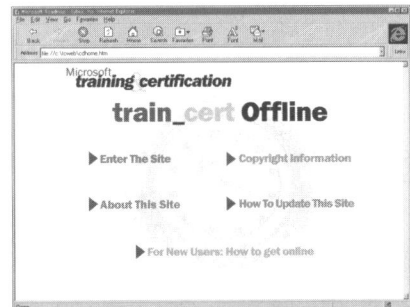

MCSE: Windows 98
Study Guide

MCSE: Windows® 98
Study Guide

Lance Mortensen
Rick Sawtell

NETWORK PRESS®
SYBEX

San Francisco • Paris • Düsseldorf • Soest

Associate Publisher: Guy Hart-Davis
Acquisitions Manager: Kristine Plachy
Acquisitions & Developmental Editor: Neil Edde
Editor: Kathy Grider-Carlyle
Project Editor: Emily K. Wolman
Technical Editors: Jon Hansen
Book Designer: Patrick Dintino
Graphic Illustrator: Tony Jonick
Desktop Publisher: Robin Kibby
Production Coordinator: Blythe Woolston
Indexer: Ted Laux
Cover Designer: Archer Design
Cover Illustrator/Photograph: The Image Bank

Screen reproductions produced with Collage Complete.
Collage Complete is a trademark of Inner Media Inc.

SYBEX, Network Press, and the Network Press logo are registered trademarks of SYBEX Inc.

TRADEMARKS: SYBEX has attempted throughout this book to distinguish proprietary trademarks from descriptive terms by following the capitalization style used by the manufacturer.

The CD Interface music is from GIRA Sound AURIA Music Library (NCP) GIRA Sound 1996.

The author and publisher have made their best efforts to prepare this book, and the content is based upon final release software whenever possible. Portions of the manuscript may be based upon pre-release versions supplied by software manufacturer(s). The author and the publisher make no representation or warranties of any kind with regard to the completeness or accuracy of the contents herein and accept no liability of any kind including but not limited to performance, merchantability, fitness for any particular purpose, or any losses or damages of any kind caused or alleged to be caused directly or indirectly from this book.

Microsoft® Internet Explorer ©1996 Microsoft Corporation. All rights reserved. Microsoft, the Microsoft Internet Explorer logo, Windows, Windows NT, and the Windows logo are either registered trademarks or trademarks of Microsoft Corporation in the United States and/or other countries.

SYBEX is an independent entity from Microsoft Corporation, and not affiliated with Microsoft Corporation in any manner. This publication may be used in assisting students to prepare for a Microsoft Certified Professional Exam. Neither Microsoft Corporation, its designated review company, nor SYBEX warrants that use of this publication will ensure passing the relevant Exam. Microsoft is either a registered trademark or trademark of Microsoft Corporation in the United States and/or other countries.

Library of Congress Card Number: 98-87090
ISBN: 0-7821-2373-2

Manufactured in the United States of America

10 9 8 7 6 5 4 3 2 1

November 1, 1997

Dear SYBEX Customer:

Microsoft is pleased to inform you that SYBEX is a participant in the Microsoft® Independent Courseware Vendor (ICV) program. Microsoft ICVs design, develop, and market self-paced courseware, books, and other products that support Microsoft software and the Microsoft Certified Professional (MCP) program.

To be accepted into the Microsoft ICV program, an ICV must meet set criteria. In addition, Microsoft reviews and approves each ICV training product before permission is granted to use the Microsoft Certified Professional Approved Study Guide logo on that product. This logo assures the consumer that the product has passed the following Microsoft standards:

- The course contains accurate product information.
- The course includes labs and activities during which the student can apply knowledge and skills learned from the course.
- The course teaches skills that help prepare the student to take corresponding MCP exams.

Microsoft ICVs continually develop and release new MCP Approved Study Guides. To prepare for a particular Microsoft certification exam, a student may choose one or more single, self-paced training courses or a series of training courses.

You will be pleased with the quality and effectiveness of the MCP Approved Study Guides available from SYBEX.

Sincerely,

Holly Heath
ICV Account Manager
Microsoft Training & Certification

MICROSOFT INDEPENDENT COURSEWARE VENDOR PROGRAM

This book is dedicated to Microsoft. May you play fair in your dealings with other companies and be allowed to continue to develop software without the interference of the government.

Acknowledgments

I'd like to thank Neil, Emily, Davina, Kathy, and Marilyn, along with all the others at Sybex, for being such a great crew to work with. I realize that this book, and the professional quality of it, wouldn't have been possible without you.

Thanks to Rick for plugging away at deadlines—I think your chapters changed more than mine did with Windows 98 versus Windows 95.

As always, thanks to Luann for being there and taking care of business when I have to write, travel, or do both. Thanks to Bryce, Jessany, Devin, and Logan for being the cutest, most fun kids a Dad could have.

—Lance

I would like to thank all of the wonderful people at Sybex. Working with the best in the industry has made the task of authoring a book much less difficult. You allow us to concentrate on the contents of the book rather than the formatting, spelling, grammar, and myriad other details about which I know nothing. Y'all are great! Of course, Lance, it's always a pleasure working with you on these books. Let's do some more.

Thanks to my wonderful wife and best friend, Melissa. I know that the long hours and late nights aren't what you signed up for, but thanks for the understanding. You are the best. I'll be available for snuggling again soon.

I should say thanks to Mom and Dad for making education such an important part of my life. I couldn't have done any of this without it. You did a wonderful job.

Of course, what acknowledgment would be complete without a special thanks to my intrepid pal Kenya (my cat), who has made many a sojourn into the wee hours of the morning. Thanks for tap-tap-tapping away at the keyboard while I dictated the text to you.

—Rick

Contents at a Glance

Table of Contents

Table of Exercises

Introduction

There's an old Army reserve commercial where a young man can't get employed because he has no experience, and he can't get experience because he can't get employed—a classic "Catch-22" situation. Although certification is best used in conjunction with real-life experience, it can go a long way toward making up for lack of experience.

The value of certification is undeniable. Many people get certified just to compete in the job market. For example, if you were an employer and you had two candidates with the same experience, but one was also certified, which one would you hire? The fact is that even though the number of certified professionals has grown tremendously, the demand has grown at least as fast as, if not faster than, the number of certified people.

Whether you are just getting started or are ready to move ahead in the computer industry, the knowledge and skills you have are your most valuable assets. Recognizing this, Microsoft has developed its Microsoft Certified Professional (MCP) program to give you credentials that verify your ability to work with Microsoft products effectively and professionally. The Microsoft Certified Systems Engineer (MCSE) certification is the premier MCP credential, designed for professionals who support Microsoft networks.

Is This Book for You?

If you want to become certified as an MCSE, this book is for you. The MCSE is *the* hot ticket in the field of professional computer networking. Microsoft is putting its weight behind the program, so now is the time to act. This book will start you off on the right foot.

If you want to learn techniques that you can apply in your day-to-day work as a systems engineer or administrator, this book is for you, too. You will learn about the fundamentals of Windows 98 operations, ranging from installation, to optimizing and monitoring performance, to running on a network. You will also find troubleshooting information for each topic.

MCSE: Windows 98 Study Guide provides clear explanations of the fundamental concepts you must grasp both to become certified and to do your job effectively and efficiently. Our intention in writing this book was not merely to help you pass the MCSE tests. We tried to make the book comprehensive and detailed enough that it will remain a valuable resource for you once you have passed your test and become a certified systems engineering professional.

What Does This Book Cover?

Think of this book as your complete guide to Microsoft Windows 98. It begins with an overview of the Windows family and continues with the following topics:

- Installing Windows 98
- Booting Windows 98
- Windows 98 architecture and memory
- The Windows 98 Registry
- Backing up and restoring data
- Running Windows and MS-DOS applications
- Managing disk resources
- Printing from Windows 98
- Communications features in Windows 98
- Mobile computing
- E-mail
- Plug-and-Play support
- Windows 98 and the Internet
- Troubleshooting Windows 98

This book (and the test) also heavily emphasize networking issues, including:

- Windows 98 networking components
- Installing and configuring TCP/IP
- Connecting to Windows NT networks
- Connecting to Novell NetWare networks
- Setting up user profiles
- Using system policies
- Remote administration with Windows 98

How Do You Become an MCSE?

Attaining MCSE status is a serious challenge. The exams cover a wide range of topics and require dedicated study and expertise. Many who have achieved other computer industry credentials have had troubles with the MCSE. This is, however, why the MCSE certificate is so valuable. If achieving MCSE status were easy, the market would be quickly flooded by MCSEs, and the certification would quickly become meaningless. Microsoft, keenly aware of this fact, has taken steps to ensure that the certification means its holder is truly knowledgeable and skilled.

To become an MCSE, you must pass four core requirements and two electives. Most people select the following exam combination for the MCSE core requirements for the 4.0 track, which is the most current track:

Client Requirement

70-098: Implementing and Supporting Windows 98

or

70-073: Implementing and Supporting Windows NT Workstation 4.0

Networking Requirement

70-058: Networking Essentials

Windows NT Server 4.0 Requirement

70-067: Implementing and Supporting Windows NT Server 4.0

Windows NT Server 4.0 in the Enterprise Requirement

70-068: Implementing and Supporting Windows NT Server 4.0 in the Enterprise

For the electives, you have about ten choices. The most popular elective is:

70-059: Internetworking with Microsoft TCP/IP on NT 4.0

Other electives include:

70-081: Implementing and Supporting Microsoft Exchange Server 5.5

70-026: SQL Server Administration for 6.5

70-018: SMS Administration for 1.2

70-087: Implementing and Supporting IIS 4.0

NOTE   For a complete description of all the MCSE options, see the Microsoft Train_Cert Offline Web site on the CD that comes with this book, or go directly to www.microsoft.com/train_cert.

Where Do You Take the Exams?

You may take the MCP exams at any of more than 800 Authorized Sylvan Testing Centers around the world. For the location of a testing center near you, call (800) 755-EXAM (755-3926). Outside the United States and Canada, contact your local Sylvan Registration Center.

To register for a Microsoft Certified Professional exam:

- Determine the number of the exam you want to take.

- Determine when and where you want to take the test. If you don't know where any testing centers are, you can ask Sylvan when you register.

- Register with the Sylvan Registration Center that is nearest to you. At this point, you will be asked for advance payment for the exam. At this writing, the exams are $100 each. Exams must be taken within one year of payment. You can schedule exams up to six weeks in advance or as late as one working day prior to the date of the exam. You can cancel or reschedule your exam if you contact Sylvan at least two working days prior to the exam. Same-day registration is available in some locations, although this is subject to space availability. Where same-day registration is available, you must register a minimum of two hours before test time.

NOTE   You can now register for tests on the Internet. The address at the time of this writing is www.slspro.com/msreg/microsoft.asp. If that doesn't work, try www.microsoft.com/mcp as a starting point.

When you schedule the exam, you'll be provided with information regarding appointment and cancellation procedures, ID requirements, and the testing center location.

MCSE and MCPS candidates in the U.S. and Canada will be able to sign up to take the exams from Virtual University Enterprises (VUE) as well as Sylvan Prometric. To enroll at a VUE testing center, call toll-free in North America: (888) 837-8616; or visit VUE's Web site at www.vue.com/student-services.

What the Windows 98 Exam Measures

The Windows 98 exam covers concepts and skills required for the support of Windows 98 computers running on a network. It emphasizes the following areas:

- Planning and installation
- Remote administration and system policies
- Printing on both the local computer and on a network
- Network protocols and their configurations
- Being a client and/or server in both the Windows NT and NetWare networking environments
- Backing up and restoring
- Troubleshooting

If we could rename the exam to be precisely descriptive, its new name would be "Installing, Backing Up, Restoring, and Supporting Windows 98 as a Client and as a File and Print Server on NetWare and Windows NT Networks, Using System Monitor, Remote Administration, and System Policies as Needed." Over half of the questions deal with Windows 98 connected to some sort of network. A thorough understanding of Chapters 7–15 are critical to passing the test.

The exam focuses on fundamental concepts related to Windows 98 operations, as well as how to make Windows 98 function in a networked corporate environment. Careful study of this book, along with hands-on experience with the operating system, will be especially helpful in preparing you for the exam.

Tips for Taking the Windows 98 Exam

Here are some general tips for taking the exams successfully:

- Arrive early at the exam center so you can relax and review your study materials, particularly tables and lists of exam-related information.

- Read the questions carefully. Don't be tempted to jump to an early conclusion. Make sure you know *exactly* what the question is asking.

- Don't leave any unanswered questions. They count against you.

- When answering multiple-choice questions you're not sure about, use a process of elimination to get rid of the obviously incorrect questions first. This will improve your odds if you need to make an educated guess.

- Because the hard questions will take up the most time, save them for last. You can move forward and backward through the exam, unless the question specifically states that you cannot go back. At this time the Windows 98 test allows you to go back and change previous answers, but that is always subject to change.

- This test has some exhibits (pictures). It can be difficult, if not impossible, to view both the questions and the exhibit simulation on the 14- and 15-inch screens usually found at the testing centers. Call around to each center and see if they have 17-inch monitors available (most don't). If they don't, perhaps you can arrange to bring in your own. Failing this, some have found it useful to quickly draw the diagram on the scratch paper provided by the testing center and use the monitor to view just the question.

- As mentioned previously, one of the keys to correctly answering Microsoft tests is figuring out just what it is that you are being asked. Most test questions are in the form of a story problem—cutting through the fluff and understanding the issue involved is most of the battle. You may want to look at the answer choices and "reverse-engineer" the question.

- Many of the Multiple Rating Items (MRI) questions that ask you "How well does this solution address the problem?" are very intimidating at first, because they are very long. One strategy is to look at the solution and compare it against each desired outcome, keeping track of whether it works or doesn't. The available responses will sometimes consist of a count or list of the items that were successfully accomplished. Sometimes the question will end with a list of the objectives, and you will be asked to specify if they were fulfilled or not. These questions seem to be much easier because you can look at the solution and see if it fulfilled each individual objective.

- This is not simply a test of your knowledge of Windows 98; you'll need to know how it is implemented in a network. You will also need to know about Windows NT, NetWare, protocols, and other networking issues in order to pass the test.

How to Use This Book

This book can provide a solid foundation for the serious effort of preparing for the Windows 98 exam. To best benefit from this book, you might want to use the following study method:

1. Study a chapter carefully, making sure you fully understand the information.

2. Complete all hands-on exercises in the chapter, referring back to the chapter so that you understand each step you take.

3. Answer the exercise questions related to that chapter. (You will find the answers to these questions in Appendix A and on the CD.)

4. Note which questions you did not understand, and study those sections of the book again.

5. Study each chapter in the same manner.

6. Before taking the exam, try the practice exams included on the CD that comes with this book. They will give you an idea of what you can expect to see on the real thing. Many additional questions were added to the Windows 98 edition of the book in order to help you better prepare for the test.

7. Use resources available on the Internet to help supplement and update your training preparation. The best place to start is the Certification area on Microsoft's Web page, `www.microsoft.com/mcp`. When you are ready to get more details about a particular test or objective list, the `www.microsoft.com/train_cert` Web site is another invaluable resource.

If you prefer to use this book in conjunction with classroom or online training, you have many options. Both Microsoft-authorized training and independent training are widely available. See Microsoft's Web site (www.microsoft.com/train_cert) for more information. The best place to start is the Certification area at www.microsoft.com/mcp.

To learn all the material covered in this book, you will need to study regularly and with discipline. Try to set aside the same time every day to study, and select a comfortable and quiet place in which to do it. If you work hard, you will be surprised at how quickly you learn this material. Good luck!

What's on the CD?

The CD contains several valuable tools to help you study for your MCSE exams:

- The review questions and answers from each of the chapters in this book are included in a simple-to-use exam preparation program.

- The entire *Windows 98 Study Guide* is now in electronic format! Now you can study for the exam anytime, anywhere. You'll need the Adobe Acrobat Reader installed to view the files, and that is included on the CD as well.

- Preview chapters from the best-selling line of MCSE Study Guides from Sybex are supplied.

- The Microsoft Train_Cert Offline Web site is a good place to start. It provides an overview of Microsoft's training and certification program and the process of becoming an MCSE.

How to Contact the Authors

We welcome any of your comments, suggestions, and feedback.
You can e-mail Lance Mortensen at:

LMWin95@aol.com

You can e-mail Rick Sawtell at:

Quickening@email.msn.com

CHAPTER

1

Windows 98 and the
Windows Family

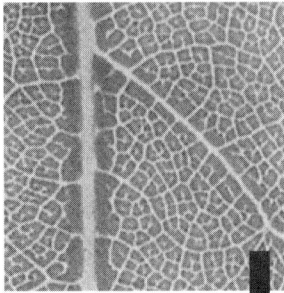

Understanding the history of the Windows operating system will help you to see where Windows development is going. With this knowledge, you will be able to better support the products your system currently uses and plan for the future.

Microsoft has split the Windows family into two distinct branches: the Windows 95/98 branch and the Windows NT branch. Microsoft has always excelled at coding software that was before its time. Remember when Windows NT was the butt of all the computer jokes? Now it is a force to be reckoned with, as it slowly takes over both the client and server roles.

Whether or not you use Microsoft Windows as your operating system is no longer the big decision it once was. The real decision is which version to use: Windows 95/98 or Windows NT. Both operating systems have their advantages and disadvantages. The key to deciding between them is knowing what those advantages and disadvantages are and predicting how your company will be affected.

Although no one can predict all the changes for the next release, the future of the Windows 95/98 platform is starting to become clearer. Windows 98 is more of an evolutionary product, rather than the revolutionary product that Windows 95 was. Microsoft has publicly stated that there will be no next version of the Windows 95/98 platform. The plan is to integrate the Windows 95/98 and Windows NT platforms together into possible Windows NT 6.0 or even 7.0.

Our best guess is that there could be a Windows NT 6.0 Consumer Edition and then Windows NT 6.0 Workstation and Windows NT 6.0 Server versions, although only the future knows for sure.

Even if Windows 98 is the end of the 95/98 product cycle, the product line has to go down in history as the best selling operating system so far, with over 100 million copies installed, and as the operating system that cemented Microsoft's dominance in the operating system market.

Whatever the future holds, it is always important to remember an ancient Chinese curse: "May you be born in interesting times."

This chapter begins with a brief history lesson and then explains the differences between Windows 98 and Windows NT. We will then look at how Windows 98 fits into a stand-alone or networking environment.

The History of Windows

The Windows family emerged in 1985 with the 1.0 16-bit version. In 1987, Windows 2.*x*, or Windows 286, was released. Although it supported Dynamic Data Exchange (DDE) and overlapping windows, it was still used as a glorified menu program. Windows 386 (version 2.10) added preemptive multitasking of DOS programs and the concept of virtual machines (see Chapter 4 for details about Windows and virtual machines).

Windows 3.0 was released in 1990. Its enhanced mode took advantage of the 386 protected architecture. Windows 3.0 was the operating system that convinced people to switch from DOS-based programs to native Windows programs because the new enhanced mode enabled applications to run much better than their DOS counterparts.

Windows 3.1 was released in 1992. The operating system was more stable in this version, which also included multimedia support. In the same year, Windows for Workgroups 3.1 was released, and then in late 1993, Windows 3.11 was released. These versions, especially Windows 3.11, added Microsoft Mail and better networking integration.

By this time, Microsoft knew that an entirely new operating system was required to take advantage of the power of the personal computer and to provide better multitasking and network functionality. Windows NT 3.1 was first released in 1993. Although this version looked like earlier versions of Windows (due to the similarity of the interfaces), Windows NT acted more like a mainframe operating system designed to replace the older DOS-based operating systems. The current version is NT 4.0, which has a Windows 95-type user interface. Windows NT is a fully protected-mode (32-bit) operating system, with compatibility sacrificed for new features.

Work on Windows 95 began in 1992, and it hit the market in August 1995. Windows 95 incorporates many features of the Windows 3.*x* family and features from the Windows NT family. Windows 95 continues to be the most popular of the Microsoft operating systems for many reasons, such as its ease of use, lower hardware requirements compared to Windows NT, and backward compatibility with DOS and Windows 16-bit applications.

Windows 95 was a revolutionary operating system. Support for 32-bit applications and preemptive multitasking proved far superior than Windows 3.*x* versions.

Windows 98 was released in June 1998 amid a flurry of lawsuits by various federal and state governments charging that Microsoft was illegally using its operating system monopoly to promote its own software—software that the government alleges is not integral to the operating system (like Internet Explorer).

Windows 98 professes to have over 3,000 bug fixes from the original version of Windows 95.

> **NOTE** Because this chapter discusses the history and details of the Windows operating systems, we will refer to both Windows 95/98 and just to Windows 98. When an item is virtually identical in both operating systems, we will list it as 95/98; when there is something unique to Windows 98, it will be referred to by just its name.

Windows 95 Design Philosophy

The Windows 95 programmers had some definite goals in mind when they created this operating system, including the following:

- **Compatibility:** Windows 95 was designed to run on existing hardware and to be able to run software better than Windows 3.*x*.

- **Speed:** Windows 95 was designed to be at least as fast as Windows 3.*x*, and considerably faster when given newer software and hardware. New 32-bit, protected-mode caching components were one of the reasons for better performance.

- **Reliability:** Windows 95 was designed to better recover from GPFs (General Protection Faults) and hung (nonresponding) programs.

- **Ease of use:** Windows 95 was designed to be easier to use than Windows 3.*x*. With Plug-and-Play support, less time and effort were required to configure hardware and software.

- **Robust, integrated networking:** Windows 95 was designed with 32-bit, protected-mode network drivers and protocols, making networking faster and more reliable.

Windows 95 was almost a clean break from earlier versions of Windows. As with all major upgrades, there was some hassle and pain involved in converting to the new product. However, after converting to Windows 95, many people actually admitted that all of those commercials were closer to the truth than they expected. Although Windows 95 didn't cure all of society's ills (it didn't increase gas mileage, after all), it was (and is) still a darn good product.

Windows 98 Design Philosophy

Windows 98 builds on the success of Windows 95. Although Windows 98 could be called Windows 95 version 2.0, the innovations and new, natively supported technologies add up to a great package. The design goals for Windows 98 included the following:

- Support the latest hardware and software innovations
- Make the work environment even easier to use
- Make Windows 98 even more stable and easier to troubleshoot
- Integrate Internet technologies into the operating system
- Support the latest multimedia and TV interfaces

Major New Features in Windows 98

Windows 98 has several major features that make it an almost required upgrade for many users:

- USB support
- DVD support
- FAT32 support and nondestructive upgrade option
- Better Registry tools
- Better disk defragmentation
- Better system tools

- Support for Windows NT DFS (Distributed File System)

- Multiple monitor support

- DIRECTV support

- Powerful enhancements to the work environment (e.g., being able to make a new shortcut by right-dragging an icon from the Start menu)

- Complete integration with the Internet and Internet Explorer 4.*x*

- Active Desktop support, which allows you to make the Desktop more "Internet-like" by adding support for single-click operations and active content

> **NOTE** Although almost all of the new features of Windows 98 will be covered in detail in their respective chapters, the Active Desktop will not be covered in this book for several reasons. First, none of the exam objectives cover the Active Desktop. Second, the Active Desktop is a user interface choice that doesn't affect the underlying technology and architecture of Windows 98. And finally, most people are not using the Active Desktop. There are several good books on the Active Desktop, including *Mastering Windows 98* (Sybex, 1998).

Windows 98 versus Windows NT Workstation

Many companies struggle with the decision of whether to use Windows 98 or Windows NT Workstation on the Desktop. You need to consider two overriding things when you look at the two operating systems:

- Windows 98 stresses compatibility and is usually a better choice for laptops because of its advanced power management capabilities.

- Windows NT Workstation stresses security and is usually a better choice for most businesses.

Windows 98 is a mixture of 32- and 16-bit components. It can even use 16-bit device drivers. Windows NT Workstation is a pure 32-bit operating system, and it controls all access to hardware resources. Applications are allowed access to hardware resources only through NT itself. If applications try to directly access hardware, NT will stop them. On the other hand, Windows 98 tries to control access to hardware resources, but if an application needs or wants to access hardware directly, it can. This makes Windows 98 inherently less stable than Windows NT Workstation, but much more compatible with older legacy applications and utilities.

Windows 98 and Windows NT Workstation have many things in common. Both systems have the following features:

- They can run 16-bit applications.
- They can run 32-bit applications.
- They use preemptive multitasking.
- They provide multithreaded support.
- They can share files.
- They can be personal Web servers.
- They have user profiles available.
- They can enforce system policies (NT 4.0 and later).
- They replace INI files with the Registry.
- They can be clients for Microsoft.
- They can be clients for NetWare.
- They run on Intel-compatible CPUs.
- They require over 100+ MB of free hard drive space to install.

However, there are also some big differences between the two programs. Table 1.1 lists the differences between Windows 98 and Windows NT Workstation.

The question is not, "Which one is better?" You need to ask, "Which one is right for my company and me?" Although Windows NT Workstation is positioned as the premier client platform, Windows 98 has some advanced capabilities, as you will discover in this book.

TABLE 1.1 Differences between Windows 98 and Windows NT Workstation	Item	Windows 98	Windows NT
	Can use 16-bit drivers	Yes	No
	Supports Plug and Play	Yes	No*
	Can run DOS applications	Yes	Most**
	Can run 16-bit applications in separate address space	No	Yes
	Supports multiple CPUs	No	Yes
	Certified for C2 security	No	Yes
	Requires secured logon	No	Yes
	Runs on Alpha, PPC, MIPS	No	Yes***
	Stated minimum RAM	16MB	12MB
	Realistic minimum RAM	32MB****	32MB

*NT 5.0 will add Plug-and-Play support.
**DOS applications that attempt direct access to hardware resources are not allowed by NT.
***Until NT 4.0. Although some OEM companies are still creating a MIPS version of NT, Microsoft only officially supports Alpha and Intel versions of NT.
****Windows 98 has higher RAM requirements than Windows 95, and although it will run in 16MB, you should plan on 32MB+ for best performance.

Integrating Windows 98 into an Environment

There are three general ways to integrate Windows 98 into an environment:

- As a stand-alone computer
- As a member of a workgroup
- As a member of a Windows NT domain or other type of server-based network

Each of these various ways to integrate Windows 98 will be discussed in the following text.

Microsoft *Exam* *Objective*	**Develop an appropriate implementation model for specific requirements in a Microsoft environment or a mixed Microsoft and NetWare environment. Considerations include:** • Choosing the appropriate file system • Planning a workgroup

---

> **NOTE** See Chapter 7 for an in-depth coverage of choosing the appropriate file system.

Stand-Alone Installations

The easiest way to install Windows 98 is as a *stand-alone installation*. Most home computers and many laptops are installed this way.

The major advantage of a stand-alone installation is that it doesn't rely on other computers, which means that any problems you encounter come from that one computer.

The major disadvantage is the lack of connectivity. Without a connection to other computers, you are dependent on the old "sneaker net," which means you copy data to floppies and run the floppies around with your sneakers. (There was an advanced version called "Frisbee net," where you could take the floppies and throw them back and forth, but it still wasn't very good.)

Workgroup Configurations

Windows 98 can participate in a *workgroup*, which is a grouping of computers with no central server. Windows 98 can connect to other computers via a network (be a client) and use resources on other computers as if those resources were its own. Windows 98 can also allow other computers to connect to it (act as a server) and can share both folders and printers to clients connected via a network.

The major advantage of a workgroup is that a dedicated, expensive computer is not required—Windows 98 comes with all the software you need to be both a client and a server. Each computer can be configured as a client and/or a server in the workgroup.

The major disadvantage of a workgroup model is that, because there is no central server, each Windows 98 computer may be set up slightly differently, thereby requiring clients to remember many passwords. For example, the password to use the laser printer hooked to the secretary's computer may be "rain," but the password required to print to the color printer hooked to the sales-rep computer may be "cowhands."

Workgroups, as well as the sharing of folders and printers, are covered in depth in later chapters.

> **WARNING** Workgroup security models are based on passwords (called *share-level security*), which means that anyone who knows the password can gain access to shared resources. This is inherently insecure because you *cannot* limit access to certain users—you can only hope that users you don't want to have access never learn the password.

Windows NT Domain or Other Server-Based Configurations

Windows 98 has the ability to join an existing Windows NT domain. This allows Windows 98 to still act as a client and/or server, with the added benefit of having a centralized database for users, passwords, and security. Windows 98 comes with the software to join a Windows NT domain and a NetWare server environment. Other types of server environments can also be supported by adding additional components to Windows 98. Joining a domain will be covered in later chapters.

The major advantage of joining an existing domain is that all security is centrally controlled. In a correctly configured environment, you will have only one username and password. Your single username can then be assigned rights to various printers and folders. Windows 98 can still operate as a client and/or a server in a domain environment.

The major disadvantage is that you will need a dedicated server computer, with Windows NT Server, NetWare, or some other type of high-end server software. Joining and maintaining a domain is also more complex than creating and maintaining a workgroup.

> **NOTE**
>
> Because the security model of a domain is based on users and groups (called *user-level security*), you can limit access to people based on their user account or on group membership. This is the best form of security available for Windows 98. Joining a domain is the preferred option for most businesses.

The Future of Windows 98

Although no one knows what will happen with Windows 98 and the Windows 9*x* line of operating systems, the overwhelming success of Windows 9*x* ensures that its various flavors will be around for a very long time.

Future upgrade paths from Windows 98 may include a pure 32-bit operating environment or possibly a Windows NT 6.0 Consumer Edition. Although Windows NT is the direction Microsoft would like the operating system to head, the Windows 9*x* platform is so successful that it may be years before everyone upgrades from Windows 9*x*.

Review Questions

1. Your company is upgrading its computers. The choice is between Windows 98 and Windows NT. You want to support user profiles, the Registry, and 32-bit applications, but you have many DOS applications that access the video card directly. Which operating system should you choose, and why?

   A. Windows 98 because you need to allow applications to access the video card directly.

   B. Windows NT because it runs DOS applications just fine.

   C. Both A and B would work fine.

   D. Neither A nor B would work.

2. How many CPUs can Windows 98 support?

   A. 1

   B. 2

   C. 4

   D. Unlimited

3. Which of the following support Plug and Play? Choose all that apply.

   A. MS-DOS 6.22

   B. Windows 98

   C. Windows NT Workstation 4.0

   D. Windows NT Server 4.0

4. Which of the following support multithreaded, multitasking applications? Choose all that apply.

   A. MS-DOS 6.22

   B. Windows 98

   C. Windows NT Workstation 4.0

   D. Windows NT Server 4.0

5. Which network model has no dedicated server?

   A. Stand-alone

   B. Networked

   C. Workgroup

   D. Member of an NT Domain

6. In which model can Windows 98 be both a client and a server? Choose all that apply.

   A. Stand-alone

   B. Networked

   C. Workgroup

   D. Member of an NT Domain

7. Which model would be appropriate for the home user with one computer?

   A. Stand-alone

   B. Networked

   C. Workgroup

   D. Member of an NT Domain

8. Which model would be most appropriate for a large company?

   A. Stand-alone

   B. Networked

   C. Workgroup

   D. Member of an NT Domain

9. Which model would be appropriate for a small office on a limited budget?

A. Stand-alone

B. Networked

C. Workgroup

D. Member of an NT Domain

10. You want to upgrade to Windows 98. Which of these computers can be upgraded without any hardware additions?

A. 486/66 CPU with 8MB of RAM and 150MB of free disk space

B. 486/66 CPU with 16MB of RAM and 150MB of free disk space

C. Pentium CPU with 32MB of RAM and 75MB of free disk space

D. Pentium CPU with 64MB of RAM and 150MB of free disk space

11. You have only Windows 98 at your office. You want to share files and folders but need as much security as possible. You want all users to be able to read the Memos folder but only the managers to be able to create new memos. How would you set up the sharing services?

A. Use share-level security. Share the Memos folder and give Read rights to The World and Full rights to the managers group.

B. Use share-level security. Share the Memos folder with a password for read-level access and a different password for full-level access. Give the appropriate password to the appropriate users.

C. Use user-level security. Share the Memos folder and give Read rights to The World and Full rights to the managers group.

D. Use user-level security. Share the Memos folder with a password for read-level access and a different password for full-level access. Give the appropriate password to the appropriate users.

CHAPTER

2

Deploying and Installing Windows 98

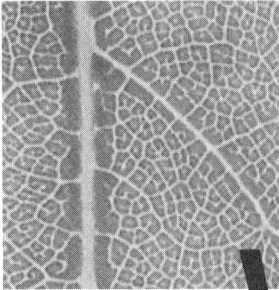

Windows 98 provides a wide array of installation and configuration options. It includes a simple and versatile installation program that installs Windows 98 on a new computer or upgrades an existing Windows 95 or Windows 3.*x* system.

This chapter provides an overview of the Windows 98 installation process, including how to prepare for installation and how to install Windows 98 in a stand-alone or networked environment. It also discusses how to automate the installation process, making it a "hands-off" procedure. Windows 98 is intended to operate singularly on a computer system; it can, however, coexist with Microsoft DOS, Caldera's Digital Research DOS (DR-DOS), IBM OS/2, Windows 3.*x*, Windows NT 3.5*x*, or Windows NT 4.0. This chapter also addresses the need for dual-boot combinations with various operating systems.

Microsoft
Exam
Objective

Install Windows 98. Installation options include:

- Automated Windows setup
- New
- Upgrade
- Uninstall
- Dual-boot combination with Microsoft Windows NT

Deployment Policies and Procedures

 T here is a something to be said about a carefully laid plan. Even more can be said about a carefully executed plan. Experience suggests that software can be installed in many different ways. Some methods are more appropriate than others in certain circumstances. As a systems engineer, you need to be aware of some of the variables that can exist when you install Windows 98.

> **NOTE** Although some of this information is not covered on the Windows 98 certification exam, it will provide you with practical ideas and real-life food-for-thought as you embark on your MCSE career.

Windows 98 can be deployed in an organization using any of several, different methods and strategies relating to the preinstallation, installation, and postinstallation phases. These strategies, which include defined policies and corporate procedures, are sometimes referred to as a *deployment guide*. They provide the blueprint for implementing and supporting new software in the Windows 98 environment.

Whether an entire deployment team or you alone are implementing the switch to Windows 98, the following issues must be addressed:

- How many users are involved and/or affected by this installation?

- Is this installation corporate-wide or for only a select department?

- What type of hardware is required? What type of hardware do you currently have?

- What considerations are there for Windows 98 and your system's BIOS, Plug-and-Play, and PCI capabilities?

- Will software applications be affected and will they still operate correctly after the installation?

- Who is going to perform the initial review, testing, installation, and support?

- What are the client configuration considerations? Are the computers stand-alone or networked? Is there a shared file system or shared workstations? Are 32-bit client-protocols, adapter drivers, and software used?

- What are the server configuration considerations? Are you connecting to a Microsoft NT, Novell NetWare, or some other network? Will you allow peer-to-peer sharing, access to the Internet, and use of home directories?

- Will user profiles be needed?

- Will user policies be needed?

- Will any users require Dial-Up Networking?

- Will users be allowed to use 98 Plus!, including themes, games, etc.?

- Will multimedia capabilities (i.e., support for sound cards, speakers, DVD drives, etc.) be needed?

- Will there be mobile users? What support strategy will be used for them? Will Briefcase be utilized?

- What security model (user-level or share-level) will be employed?

- Is remote administration needed?

- Who will document the deployment logistics?

- What naming conventions will be used for computers, file names, and folders? Will long file names be used?

- Who will work with the users?

- Will users need to be trained? How long will the training take? Where and when will it occur?

- Will there be lab testing or a pilot phase with user feedback?

- What automated setup scripts and tools will be used to install Windows 98?

- What installation medium (CD-ROM, floppy disk, or network download) will be used?

- Who will support the users after the installation takes place? How will this support occur?

Remember—a carefully laid plan usually yields a successful installation. You can't just wing it. By taking the time to plan and implement your changeover, you can avoid expensive, time-consuming "mop-up" situations.

The remainder of this book provides insights into the planning procedure. Microsoft has numerous case studies and deployment guides available to assist you and to make the installation and support of any product easier.

Take the time and have the determination to perform your installation correctly by preparing a thorough deployment guide.

Hardware Requirements

Before you install Windows 98, you must ensure that your system meets the minimum hardware requirements as set forth by Microsoft. Table 2.1 identifies the minimum and recommended hardware requirements for installing Windows 98.

T A B L E 2.1: Windows 98 Hardware Requirements

Hardware	Minimum	Recommended
Disk space to upgrade Windows 95	120MB	295MB
Disk space to upgrade Windows 3.x	120MB	295MB
Disk space for new install of FAT16	225MB	355MB
Disk space for new install of FAT32	175MB*	225MB
Floppy disk drive	One 3.5-inch high-density	One 3.5-inch high-density
Memory	16MB 16MB for Internet Explorer and Messaging	32MB is the de-facto standard 64MB or more is even better
Monitor	VGA (16-colors)	Super VGA 16- or 24-bit color
Processor	486DX-66MHz	Pentium 133 or higher

T A B L E 2.1: Windows 98 Hardware Requirements *(Continued)*

Hardware	Minimum	Recommended
Optional Components		
ATI All-in-Wonder card or compatible device		Required to watch TV using WebTV for Windows
Audio card and speakers	Sound Blaster or Sound Blaster-compatible device	Full-duplex sound card
CD-ROM	1x speed or faster	8x speed or faster
Modem	14.4 baud modem	28.8 baud modem or faster
Mouse	Windows 98-compatible device	Whatever works best for you
Network adapter card	NDIS 2.0 or MAC Driver Support	NDIS 4.0 or 5.0 with OnNow power management support

* A new installation could require up to 355MB. You also need to plan for a certain amount of disk space for the swap file, which is usually 25MB to 35MB but can go higher than 75MB. If you plan to save the previous file system, you will need between 50–75MB to save your current system to the uninstall files.

The Windows 98 CD-ROM comes with many hardware drivers, but it doesn't come with every driver. Most hardware vendors provide Web site posts of the files that are needed to support the Windows 98 operating system. But plan ahead, and test your hardware prior to performing a corporate roll-out.

Keep in mind that a specific driver may not be available for your older hardware devices; if this is the case, you must use the existing real-mode drivers. Also, when you purchase new hardware, you need to use the drivers that came from that vendor, as new drivers become available, you should be able to access them from the Windows Update page at the Microsoft Web site. Microsoft suggests that you choose hardware components that carry their "Designed for Microsoft Windows" logo to ensure optimal performance and experience.

Real-mode drivers are MS-DOS–based 16-bit drivers that are loaded in the CONFIG.SYS and AUTOEXEC.BAT files. Protected-mode drivers are 32-bit drivers that are loaded during the protected-mode boot phase. Windows 9x replaces 16-bit drivers with 32-bit drivers whenever possible.

Windows 98 does not support every CD-ROM drive. Make sure you keep your existing AUTOEXEC.BAT and CONFIG.SYS files (as well as the necessary drivers) to ensure you always have CD-ROM access and the real-mode network-connection drivers.

Software Requirements

According to Microsoft, your system must have MS-DOS 5.0 or later to install Windows 98. Previous versions of Windows depended on DOS 3.x versions. Because of the various OEM (Original Equipment Manufacturer) versions of DOS, installing Windows 98 using MS-DOS 5.0 or above is strongly recommended.

Windows 98 can be installed onto a system that is using disk compression drivers. Microsoft has many compression engines (DriveSpace and DriveSpace3 for Windows 95, DriveSpace for DOS 6.22, and DoubleSpace for DOS 6.00 and 6.20). When you install to a system that has a compressed drive, you will need at least 3MB of free uncompressed hard disk space on the host drive. If you are using a third-party compression utility, you should contact the product's support team to see what steps need to be taken to ensure compatibility with Windows 98 and the compression product.

Do not erase DRVSPACE.BIN or DBLSPACE.BIN if you have compressed your drive. Windows 98 uses DxxSPACE.BIN files to mount old volume files compressed with either DoubleSpace or DriveSpace.

Windows 98 can be installed on any drive that has enough available disk space and is FAT16 partitioned. If you plan to dual-boot Windows 98 with another operating system, the boot partition must be FAT16. Windows 98 cannot be installed on an NTFS (NT File System) partition. Likewise, Windows 98 cannot be installed on an HPFS (OS/2 File System) partition. Dual-boot configurations will be discussed later in this chapter.

New Windows 98 Installation Features

The Windows 98 setup process includes many new features and is now down to five simple phases. (The Windows 95 setup uses a twelve-phase process.) The new Setup utility makes the installation process faster and minimizes user input.

When you upgrade from a Windows 95 environment, the Windows 98 setup is optimized, and current Windows 95 system configurations and settings are used. This results in the overall improvement of the setup process and the least amount of user input. Here are some of the key changes and enhancements:

- Legacy settings are verified and maintained. Undetected legacy or undetermined legacy components require full hardware detection.

- Generic CD-ROMs are supported on the Startup disk.

- CAB files are grouped by function. Only the files needed by your specific setup are copied.

- Enumeration is performed before detection, thereby reducing errors.

- An option is available to run antivirus programs.

Remember, it is best to install from a Windows 95 environment.

WARNING Setup will not detect protected-mode drivers until after the first restart (when the hardware detection and device enumeration take place). We suggest that you keep real-mode drivers available throughout the installation process, especially if you are installing from a network connection or a CD-ROM.

Preinstallation Checklist

Before you begin the upgrade to Windows 98 in any environment, you should consider performing the following tasks:

1. Have a boot disk available. If problems occur, you will want to be able to access to your system. This disk should contain basic commands that are typically found on the Startup disk (created using the Windows 95 SETUP /F command or the DOS 6.*x* FORMAT /S command).

2. Back up your hard disk or important data files.

3. Back up your CONFIG.SYS and AUTOEXEC.BAT files (as well as any needed .INI, .DAT, .PWL, and .GRP files).

4. Run SCANDISK on your hard disk(s).

5. Run DEFRAG on your hard disk(s).

6. Remove or remark any TSR references (especially memory managers) in the CONFIG.SYS and AUTOEXEC.BAT files.

> **NOTE** TSRs are terminate-and-stay resident programs found in your CONFIG.SYS and AUTOEXEC.BAT files.

---

7. Remove or remark any RUN= or LOAD= references in the WIN.INI file.

8. Remove the items from the Start-up group.

9. Close all open applications.

10. If you are installing to a laptop, disable the suspend features.

These simple tasks ensure that you are prepared for the installation process and that it will run as smoothly possible.

Setup Switches

To install Windows 98, go to the Windows 95 Explorer, or the File Manager for Windows 3.*x*, and double-click the SETUP.EXE file in the root directory on the Windows 98 CD-ROM. There may be instances, however, when you'll need to specify certain installation parameters

Microsoft employs command-line switches to accomplish controlling tasks. In these cases, you can run Setup from a DOS prompt, from the Start ➤ Run command of Windows 95, or from the File ➤ Run command for Windows 3.*x*. Table 2.2 lists some of the key Setup switches that can be employed for installing Windows 98.

For a complete listing of Setup switches, see the *Windows 98 Resource Kit.*

T A B L E 2.2 Setup Command-Line Switches for Windows 98	**Switch**	**End Result**
	/?	Provides a list of Setup switches and the syntax to use.
	/c	Prevents SmartDrive from loading and creating a cache.
	/d	Prevents Setup from detecting or using any existing version of Windows (typically used in the DOS Setup on a Windows NT system).
	/ic	Ignore Configuration Files. Performs a clean boot.
	/id	Ignore Disk. Does not check for the minimum disk space.
	/ie	Ignore Emergency Disk Option. Skips the Startup disk screen.
	/ih	Ignore ScanDisk in the Background. Runs ScanDisk in the foreground.
	/im	Ignore Memory. Does not check for low conventional memory.
	/in	Ignore Network. Does not install the networking software. Does not use the Networking Wizard.
	/iq	Ignore Cross-Linked Files. Doesn't check for cross-linked files.
	/is	Ignore ScanDisk. Runs Setup without running ScanDisk first.

T A B L E 2.2 *(cont.)*	**Switch**	**End Result**
Setup Command-Line Switches for Windows 98	/iv	Ignore Verbose Ads. Advertisement graphics will not be displayed as Setup proceeds.
	/IW	Ignore Windows Agreement. Option must be uppercase. Skips the Windows licensing screen.
	/nf	No Floppy. Skips prompt to remove floppy Drive A. Use this option when installing from a bootable CD.
	/nr	No Registry Check. Skips the Registry check and analysis.
	Script *file-name*	Scripted file (MSBATCH.INF) will be used to automate installation process.
	/s *filename*	Specifies the SETUP.INF file when starting Setup.
	/SRCDir	Specifies the source directory in which the Windows 98 source files are located.
	/t:TempDir	Specifies the directory to which Windows 98 will copy the temporary Setup files. The directory must exist, and any existing files in this directory will be deleted.

Usually, you will install Windows 98 by double-clicking the SETUP.EXE file. Typically, only advanced users or situations require the use of the Windows 98 Setup switches.

Upgrading to Windows 98

As stated earlier, installing Windows 98 from a Windows 95 environment is the preferred procedure. Originally, Microsoft was not going to allow you to install Windows 98 from Windows 3.*x* or MS-DOS. However, because so many beta users complained, Microsoft relented and made a universal Setup utility. This section discusses the issues relating to the process of upgrading Windows 95 to Windows 98.

Five versions of Windows 95 are available in the wonderful world of Microsoft computing:

- Windows 95 (the first version)

- Service Pack 1 for Windows 95 (which essentially made OSR1 an OSR2 version)

- OSR2 (OSR1 with Service Pack 1 included in the software)

- OSR2.1 (Upgrade to IE 3.0)

- OSR2.5 (Upgrade to IE 4.0)

Just be aware that there are several versions of Windows 95 out there and that you are now heading to Windows 98. When you are finished upgrading, you will only have to worry about one version.

Microsoft ✓ *Exam* *Objective*

Install Windows 98. Installation options include:

- Upgrade

Upgrading from Windows 95 to Windows 98

You may think that the setup process is complicated, but it is not. Microsoft invested a great deal of time and testing to ensure that the setup and installation process is simple and straightforward. Most Windows 98 Setup dialog boxes contain Next and Back command buttons that allow you to easily progress or move back to review your selections. You can cancel the setup process at any time. Setup prepares the Windows 98 Setup Wizard, which in turn takes you through the simple five-phase process.

1. Preparing to run Windows 98 Setup

2. Collecting information about your computer

3. Copying Windows 98 files to your computer

4. Restarting your computer

5. Setting up hardware and finalizing settings

Phase 1: Preparing to Run Windows 98 Setup

When you start the Windows 98 CD-ROM, you will see the Introduction screen shown in Figure 2.1. This is where your installation process will begin.

When you select the Yes button, you are taken to the Windows 98 Setup screen. If any applications are still running, you will first see the warning screen shown in Figure 2.2.

As noted in the Preinstallation Checklist, you should close all open applications. After you close them, click the OK button to continue. (See Figure 2.3.)

This new Setup Wizard provides much more information about the setup process than did previous installation wizards. The information on the left side of the screen identifies which of the five Setup phases you are at, gives the time remaining to complete the setup process, and describes the current Setup activity.

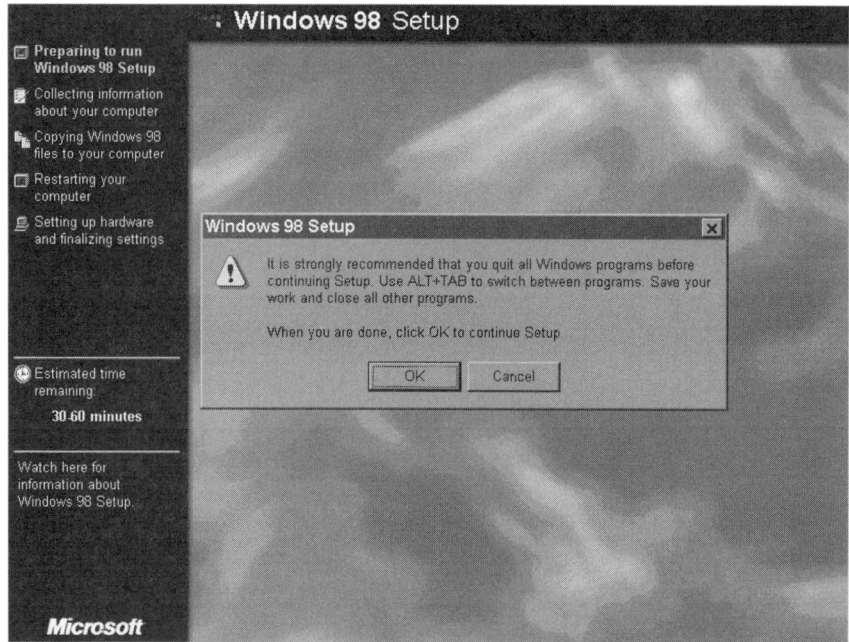

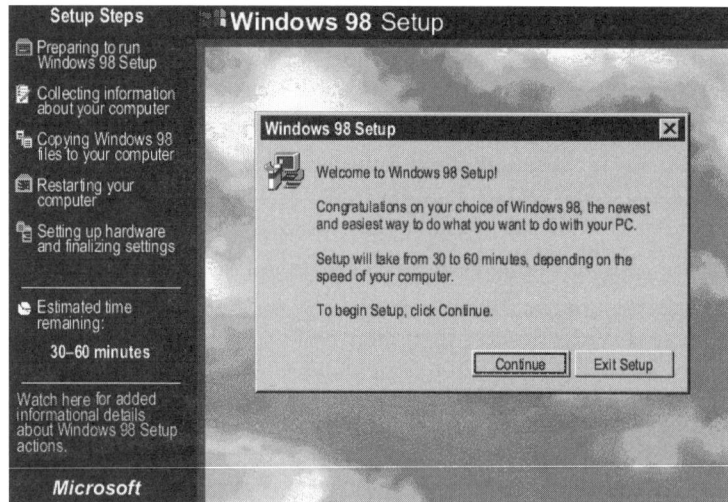

> **NOTE** The "Estimated time remaining" information is usually incorrect. One activity will complete ahead of the projected time, and the next activity will lag far behind its projected time. A typical Windows 98 installation can take between 30 and 60 minutes. Each installation is different, and the time will vary.

During this preparation phase, a temporary directory called Wininst0 .400 is created on drive C:. Windows 98 uses this directory to expand and copy the files required to run the Setup Wizard. MINI.CAB, PRECOPY1 .CAB, and PRECOPY2.CAB assist in the initial launch of the setup process.

A file called SETUPLOG.TXT is created in the root directory of drive C:. The SETUPLOG.TXT file is an ASCII text file that contains information about the setup process. Entries in this log document the installation steps and whether or not they were successful. During a recovery, Setup uses this file to determine where Setup should resume, preventing Setup from failing twice at the same location and/or problem.

During the first phase, Windows 98 also checks for antivirus software and systems that may have the CMOS with an enabled antivirus checker. An antivirus program will prevent Windows 98 from changing the Master Boot Record. If an antivirus program is detected, Windows 98 will ask you to restart the system and disable the software or CMOS setting. Windows 98 also adds an entry to the AUTOEXEC.BAT file, warning you that you need to disable all antivirus software.

> **NOTE** If you happen to see the \Wininst1.400 or \Wininst2.400 directories, the Setup has failed and the Recovery feature was not selected when the prompt appeared. If Windows 98 has installed and is functioning, you can delete these directories.

Phase 2: Collecting Information about Your Computer

After the Setup Wizard is loaded, the temporary directory is created, and the SETUPLOG.TXT file is enabled, Setup collects information about your system and prepares to copy the Windows 98 files. During this phase, the EULA (End User License Agreement) screen appears. (See Figure 2.4.)

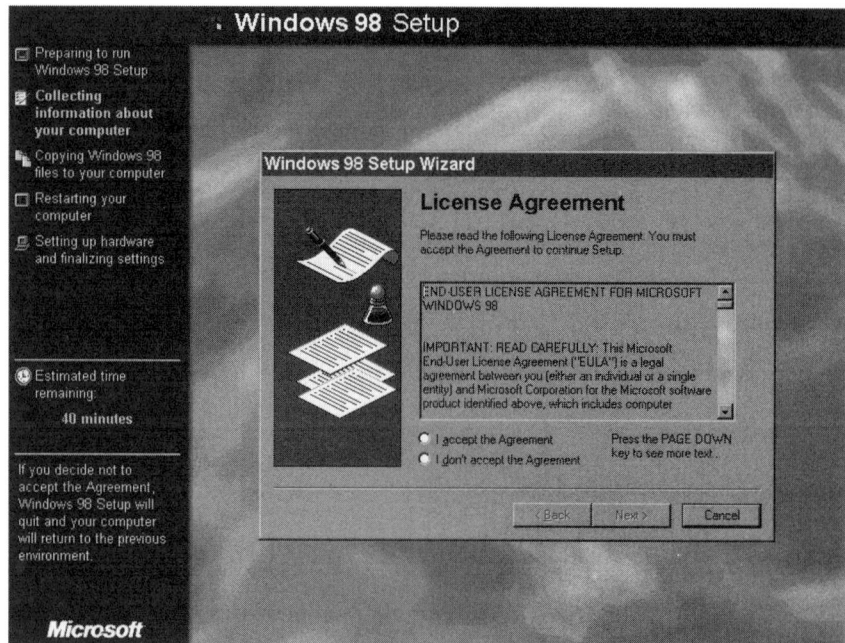

You must accept the terms of the license agreement to continue the setup process.

You will next be prompted to enter the Product Key (a 25-character alphanumeric code) as shown in Figure 2.5. This code is located either on the Certificate of Authenticity that shipped with your documentation or on the back cover of your CD case.

The Product Key is case sensitive. Make sure you use proper case when entering the 25-character alphanumeric key.

The Product Key dialog box may not appear if you are installing Windows 98 from a network, using a script, or using command-line switches.

FIGURE 2.5

The Product Key
dialog box

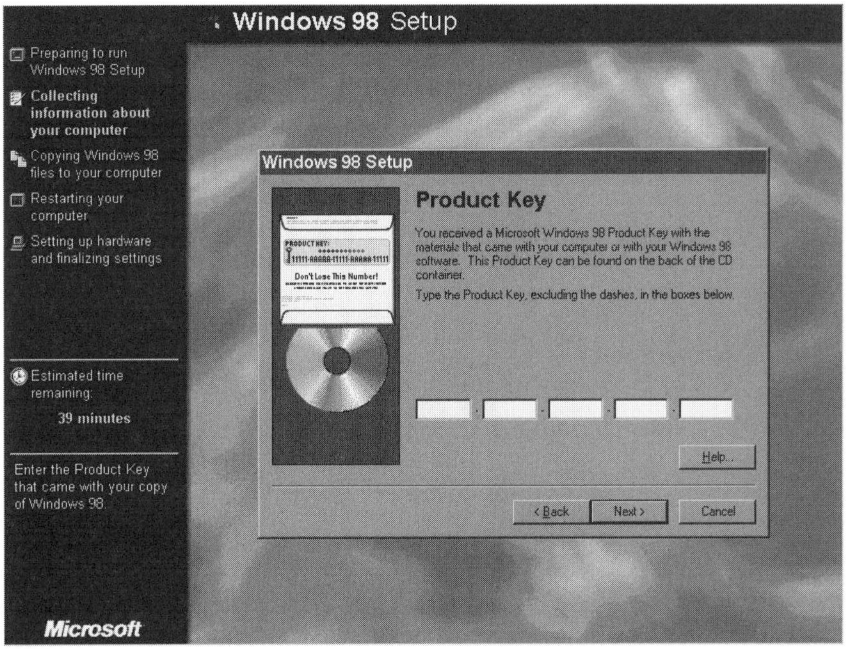

By default, Windows 98 will install to the directory where the Windows 95 files are located, typically this is C:\Windows. If you are prompted with a window that asks for a directory, accept the default directory of C:\Windows. However, if you plan to dual-boot Windows 98 with another operating system, indicate the directory into which Windows 98 should be installed (e.g., C:\Win98).

The Checking Your System dialog screen will appear next, as shown in Figure 2.6.

Setup checks your system at this point. ScanDisk runs in protected mode. If ScanDisk finds a problem, it will stop and allow you to run ScanDisk manually. Upon completion of the ScanDisk operation, Setup checks to see that the Registry settings are all right and are not corrupt. To do this, the Setup Wizard runs the ScanRegW utility, which checks the integrity of the Registry files. ScanRegW does not fix corrupted Registries, it just detects status (Okay or Not Okay). If there is a problem, you can run the ScanReg program from the command line. ScanReg will attempt to replace the corrupted Registry with a known valid backup. If ScanReg cannot do this, it will attempt to fix the corruption.

F I G U R E   2.6

Checking your system

When ScanDisk runs in protected mode, it does not check for physical errors or perform a surface scan. This is why you want to complete the ScanDisk task on the Preinstallation Checklist.

When your system checks out okay, Windows 98 verifies that the required disk space is available. You will see a Preparing Directory dialog box where Setup checks for installed components based on the Windows 95 system. Setup then creates the Windows 98 directory structure, typically C:\Windows and C:\Program Files folders.

The next step in the Collection phase is determining whether or not you want to save your existing MS-DOS and Windows system files. The Save System Files dialog box will appear, as shown in Figure 2.7.

When you choose to save your existing files, two files will be created: WINUNDO.DAT and WINUNDO.INI.

The WINUNDO.DAT file contains all the files necessary to restore your old system. This file ranges in size from 35MB to 75MB. The WINUNDO .INI file contains the information necessary to restore the files contained in the WINUNDO.DAT file. Typically, these files are located in the root of drive C: and are marked as read-only and hidden. (If you have more than one local hard disk drive, you will be prompted to select the drive to which information should be saved.)

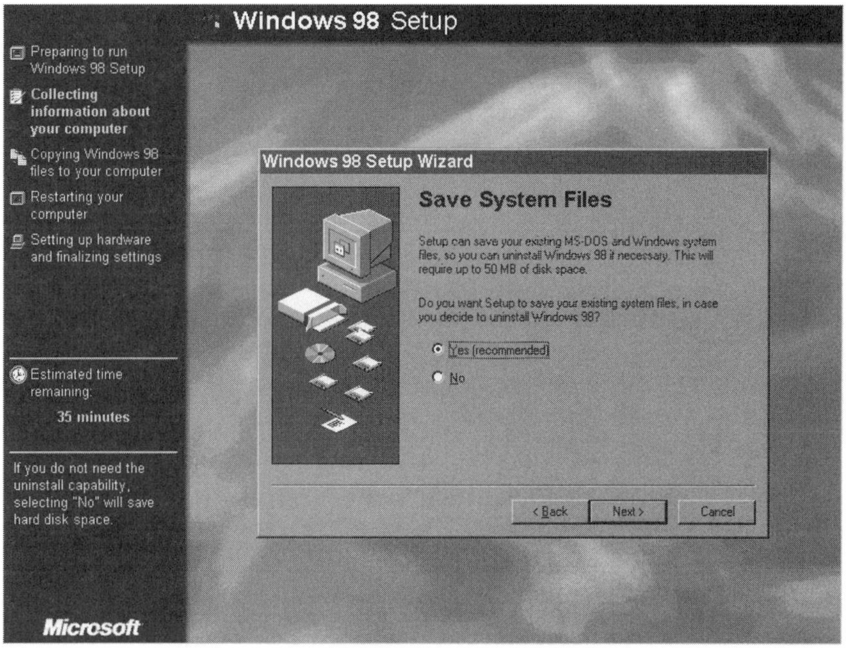

FIGURE 2.7

The Save System Files window

WARNING

If you are using a compressed drive or FAT32, you might be prompted to Save System Files. Windows 98 cannot be uninstalled from either of these environments, even if you are able to save your files.

If you are unsure of the Windows 98 setup process, select the Save System Files option. The two WINUNDO files are created and you can choose to uninstall Windows 98. (If you skip this section, you can always use the data you backed up per the Preinstallation Checklist.)

When all is said and done, Setup saves the current system files in the root directory. When you go to the Control Panel ➤ Add/Remove Programs applet, "Uninstall Windows 98" will be listed.

As you complete the Collection Phase process, you need to address a few items:

- The type of setup to be performed
- User information

- What medium to use to receive information

- The Startup disk

Once the Save System Files procedure is complete, you will then be asked to indicate from where you want to receive information. This feature provides the option of receiving information from *channels* (Web sites designed to deliver content from their site to you via the Internet). The Establishing Your Location dialog box will appear, giving you the option of choosing your source, as shown in Figure 2.8.

FIGURE 2.8

Establishing your channel location

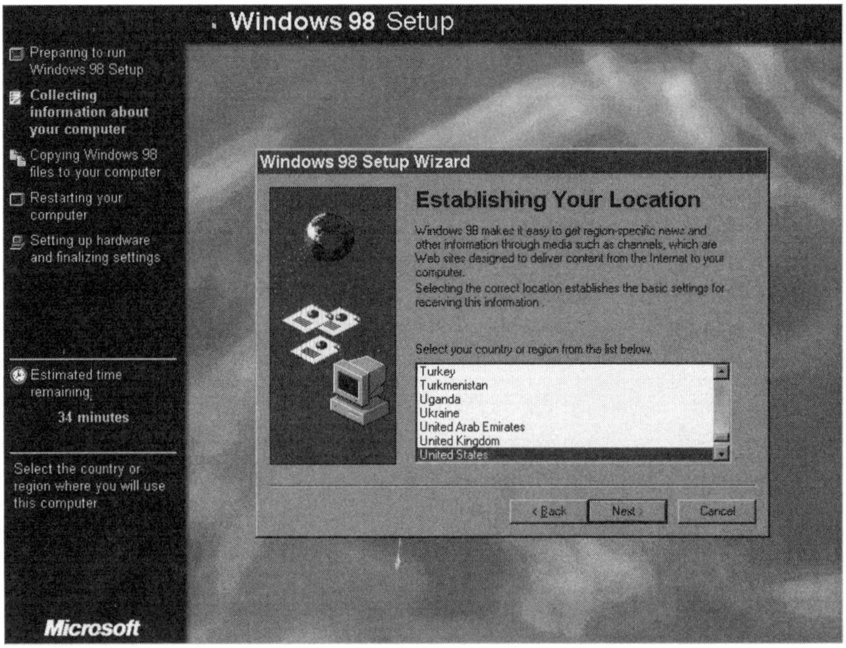

After you have established your channel location, Setup prompts you to create a Startup disk (often referred to as the Emergency Startup Disk). Because the Windows 98 and the Windows 95 Startup disks are not compatible, you should create a new Startup disk. The Startup Disk Wizard simplifies the task of creating a Startup disk as shown in Figure 2.9.

The Windows 98 Startup disk will enable you to effectively troubleshoot problems when the system does not boot.

FIGURE 2.9

The Startup Disk
Wizard

FIGURE 2.9

The Startup Disk
Wizard

> **WARNING**
>
> The Windows 98 Startup disk is very different from the Windows 95 Startup disk. Make sure you create the Startup disk while you are upgrading to Windows 98.

When you boot from the Windows 98 Startup disk, a menu will appear asking you if you want CD-ROM support. This is a new addition to the Startup disk. Support for generic CD-ROM drivers is based on the IDE and SCSI technologies. Keep in mind that these drivers will not work with all CD-ROMs; you may still need the real-mode drivers for your hardware devices. From the menu, make your decision to install support for the CD-ROM drive if you need it. The Startup disk will then create a RAM drive and expand a series of needed utilities.

Included with Windows 98 is a new batch file called BOOTDISK.BAT that will create a Windows 98 Startup disk. This utility was created for laptop users who must exchange drives (i.e., physically remove their CD-ROM drive and replace it with their floppy drive). Simply type **Bootdisk,** and a Startup disk can be created. You can also use the Add/Remove applet in the

Control Panel to create a new Startup disk. Start the applet and choose the Startup Disk tab. From there, click the Create Startup Disk button.

WARNING The CD-ROM that you use must be connected to the motherboard or a controller card. A CD-ROM connected to a soundcard will have problems and probably will not be recognized at startup. You should keep a backup copy of your MS-DOS drivers for your sound card and CD-ROM. You should also keep a backup copy of the original CONFIG.SYS and AUTOEXEC.BAT files as well as the drivers 16-bit drivers that are listed there.

Whether or not you load the CD-ROM real-mode drivers is up to you. After you make your menu selection as to whether you need CD-ROM access, the Startup disk creates a 2MB RAM drive. To contain multiple drivers on one disk, Microsoft elected to compress several files. A new file entitled EBD.CAB contains most of the MS-DOS diagnostic tools found on the Windows 95 Startup disk. Once the RAM drive is installed, the contents of the EBD.CAB file are extracted and placed on the RAM drive.

After the files are copied and the Startup disk is created, you will be prompted to remove the disk and continue the setup process.

TIP You are free to add additional files and tools to the EBD.CAB file using a utility called CABARC.EXE. This tool is available from the Microsoft Web site.

NOTE The files on the Startup disk are not copied to the \Windows\Command folder as part of the Copy process. They are copied to the \Windows\Command folder when you create a Startup disk during setup. Make sure this occurs when you set up Windows 98 for the first time. This will save you time and frustration in the future.

Phase 3: Copying Windows 98 Files to Your Computer

You have made it this far; now you can coast a little. After the Setup Wizard finishes with the Startup disk, you enter the third phase of the setup process. Setup has the information needed to proceed. No input is required during this phase. The last screen you see is Figure 2.10.

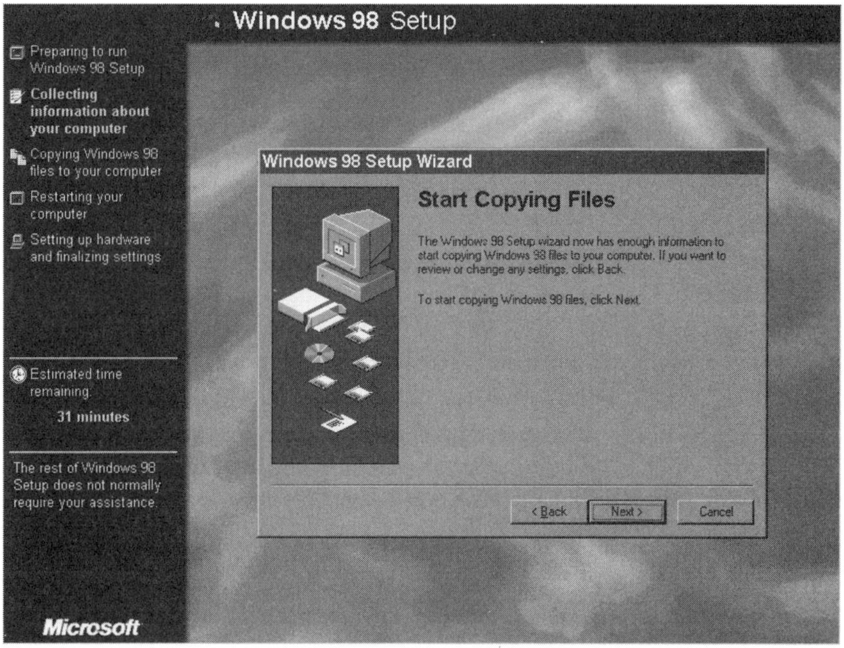

FIGURE 2.10

The Start Copying
Files screen

> **WARNING**
>
> Do *not* interrupt the copy process. If this process is stopped or interrupted, Windows 98 may not run correctly or at all when you restart your system. You probably will have to restart the setup process.

Phase 4: Restarting Your Computer

Now that the Windows 98 files have been copied to your computer, Setup prompts you to restart the computer. You can select the Restart Now button, or you can just watch and wait. After 15 seconds, the system will reboot automatically.

After Setup has restarted your computer, the following message appears briefly on your screen, "Getting ready to start Windows 98 for the first time."

The computer system starts as a Windows 98 operating system, and the following items occur:

- The WIN.INI and SYSTEM.INI files are modified to add Windows 98-specific settings.

- The Registry files are modified to add Windows 98-specific settings.

- The AUTOEXEC.BAT and CONFIG.SYS files are modified to reflect the Windows 98 environment.

Once these files are adjusted to Windows 98, it is time to move to the final phase of the installation process.

> **NOTE**
>
> During this phase, Windows 98 may REM (remark out) items in any of the mentioned files. Some programs require specific entry information in the CONFIG.SYS and AUTOEXEC.BAT files. After the Windows 98 Setup is complete, check these files to see that your needed device drivers still exist. If a problem exists, delete the REM statement or manually add the entry to ensure that you have full access to all of your resources. Under normal conditions, Windows 98 will only REM out the drivers for which it has a 32-bit version. Test your system before you "unremark" drivers. With newer computers, you may not even need your CONFIG.SYS and AUTOEXEC .BAT files.

Phase 5: Setting Up Hardware and Finalizing Settings

Unlike Windows 95, Windows 98 waits until this final phase to talk to your specific hardware devices. Because hardware detection is now placed at the end of the copy process, the setup process is more reliable and less problematic.

Setup attempts to retain and verify the settings used by Windows 95. If a problem or failure occurs, Setup will perform a full hardware detection. Once the hardware information has been internalized for the legacy devices and the Plug-and-Play devices have enumerated themselves, Windows 98 is ready to conclude with the final settings. Enumeration refers to the process by which Plug-and-Play devices notify the system of their resource requirements and are then assigned the requested resources.

The following are configured:

- Control Panel entries are added and updated.

- Programs items on the Start menu are created.

- The Windows Help file is established.

- Support for MS-DOS programs is installed.

- WALIGN (The Tuning Up application) is started.

- Time Zone and Date may be changed if necessary.

- The core system configuration files are modified and upgraded to reflect the Windows 98 operating system.

When Setup has finished setting up the hardware and finalizing the configuration settings, Windows 98 is restarted for the second time. When Windows 98 returns, you are asked to log on. If you have installed network software, you will be asked to log on to the network.

When you log on, Setup builds the information driver database, it updates the system settings, and it displays any personalized settings you might have selected during the setup process (e.g., viewing channels).

When all of these phases are completed and you have successfully upgraded to Windows 98, Setup displays the Welcome to Windows 98 dialog box.

Upgrading from Windows 3.*x* to Windows 98

The migration path for Windows 3.*x* users is very similar to the procedure for Windows 95 users. The main difference is that Windows 3.*x* still depends on real-mode drivers and does not have a Registry from which Windows 98 can glean and access data.

The points discussed in the previous section on deployment strategies, the Preinstallation Checklist, and whether any Setup Switches are needed still apply. Decisions still need to be made regarding these salient issues.

Phase 1: Preparing to Run Windows 98 Setup

These steps are virtually the same as the ones for upgrading from Windows 95. Start the Setup Wizard by double-clicking the SETUP.EXE file in the File Manager. Make sure that no antivirus software is running.

Phase 2: Collecting Information about Your Computer

This phase is also very similar to a Windows 95 upgrade. The differences are:

- You can select the installation directory.

- You can select the Setup mode: Typical, Compact, Portable, or Custom.

- You can specify user and computer information.

After you accept the EULA and input the correct Product Key, you are asked to identify and select the destination folder for the Windows 98 files. The default is C:\Windows, as you can see in Figure 2.11.

If you choose to install Windows 98 into a new directory, you must reinstall all Windows-based applications on this system to make sure they will run correctly. This task is not an easy one. At issue is "Do you really need to dual-boot with the Windows 3.*x* environment?"

Windows 98 will continue the setup process. It checks your system, grants you the ability to save all files, and continues to get ready for the Copy process.

A key difference between the Windows 3.*x* upgrade and the Windows 95 upgrade is that Windows 3.*x* allows you to choose the type of Setup installation to perform. This option isn't available with the Windows 95 upgrade because you have already decided what you want and are using the installed components. With the Windows 3.*x* upgrade to Windows 98, you are basically starting fresh. You must be able to choose the options and programs you need. After the Save System Files dialog box is completed, the Setup Options window appears as shown in Figure 2.12.

Table 2.3 explains the four Windows 98 installation types.

T A B L E 2.3

Setup Option
Types for
Windows 98

Option Type	Components Installed
Typical	This option installs all of the components that are usually installed in a Windows 98 Setup. This is similar to the Windows 3.*x* installation method known as "Express Setup." Most users select this option.
Portable	This option installs a smaller footprint of Windows 98. It is generally used for portable computers and laptops.
Compact	This option installs the smallest footprint of Windows 98. It is generally used when hard disk space is very limited and optional components are not needed.
Custom	This option allows you to choose explicitly which options you want to install during the setup process. This option requires more input from the user, but it grants greater control of what exactly is installed.

Choose Typical if you are new to Windows 98 and have limited experience. If you are a more-experienced user, you may want to choose Custom so you can make your own decisions.

If you choose Typical or Custom, you will be prompted to choose which Windows 98 components you want to install. If you select Typical, "Install the most common components" will appear on your screen. If you select "Show me the list of components so I can choose," you will be taken to the Select Components window, as shown in Figure 2.13. This window is automatically displayed without the questions for those who selected the Custom method.

F I G U R E 2.13

The Select Components window

Keep in mind that you can return to this window at any time after Windows 98 is installed. Go to Control Panel ➣ Add/Remove Programs and select the Windows Setup tab. You can select or deselect the items you need.

Windows 98 uses the networking components that you have installed in Windows 3.x. They could be a combination of real-mode drivers, protected-mode drivers, or combination drivers for both real and protected mode. If you don't have network software installed at this stage, you will be asked to enter computer network identity information, as shown in Figure 2.14. Enter the computer name, workgroup name, and computer description.

F I G U R E   2.14

Identify your computer on the network

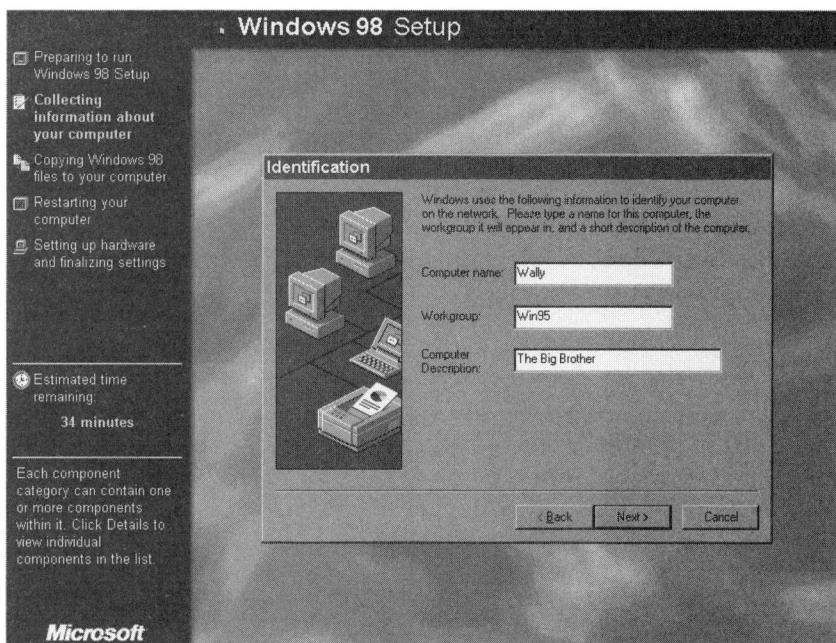

The computer name must be unique. Workgroup names are also unique. Multiple users can belong to a workgroup, but only one computer name is allowed for each computer in your organization. (If this window does not appear while you are upgrading Windows 3.x, this information was probably obtained from your system. This window will definitely appear during an MS-DOS to Windows 98 upgrade.)

The remaining procedures for this upgrade are similar to those of the Windows 95 upgrade. Make sure you establish your location and create the Startup disk. Once you have completed these tasks, you can move onto the third phase.

Phase 3: Copying Windows 98 Files to Your Computer

Follow the same installation upgrade steps as the ones for the Windows 95 upgrade.

Phase 4: Restarting Your Computer

Follow the same installation upgrade steps as the ones for the Windows 95 upgrade.

Phase 5: Setting Up Hardware and Finalizing Settings

The installation upgrade procedures are the basically the same as those for the Windows 95 upgrade. Depending on your hardware, Windows 98 will need to detect the legacy (non–Plug-and-Play) components and then enumerate the Plug-and-Play components.

When the upgrade is complete, the Welcome to Windows 98 dialog box appears.

> If you install Windows 98 in a new separate directory, you must reinstall your Windows-based applications because there are no shortcuts to their executables.

New Windows 98 Installation

You can also install Windows 98 from the MS-DOS prompt. There are two main reasons for you use this installation method:

1. You are installing Windows 98 on a new or recently formatted hard disk drive.

2. You want to dual-boot your system with another operating system, such as Windows NT or DOS 6.2*x*/Windows 3.*x* combination.

Microsoft
✓ Exam
Objective

Install Windows 98. Installation options include:

- New

This section identifies the steps that the Setup Wizard will follow during the installation of a new or recently formatted hard disk.

WARNING

When running the Windows 98 Setup Wizard from MS-DOS, you must have the real-mode network drivers and the real-mode CD-ROM drivers available and loaded. Otherwise, you will lose your network connection or the use of your CD-ROM. Make sure the appropriate drivers are on the local hard disk. The driver settings probably can be found in the CONFIG.SYS and AUTOEXEC.BAT files.

TIP

If you have an OEM Version of Windows 98, you can use it to update a DOS computer. If you have Microsoft's version, you will need to verify previous versions of a Windows operating system.

Phase 0: Start at the Ground Level

When you install from the MS-DOS prompt, Setup performs a routine check on your system to ensure that a Windows 98 environment can exist. You can think of this procedure as Phase 0.

Setup runs the real-mode version of ScanDisk, which checks the directory structure, file allocation table, and the file system. It does not check for physical errors, and long filename errors are not corrected.

The MINI.CAB file is expanded and a run-time version of Windows is loaded. If needed, a special Extended Memory Manager is loaded to run Windows during the setup process.

With the needed files to run Windows, the mini-Windows is loaded and the Setup Wizard can be started.

Phase 1: Preparing to Run Windows 98 Setup

Installing Windows 98 to a new or recently formatted disk uses almost the same procedures as the Windows 95 and the Windows 3.*x* installations. After typing **SETUP** and pressing Enter to activate the Setup Wizard, you begin Phase 1. The same tasks are performed during this setup process

- The Windows 98 Setup dialog box is displayed.

- SETUPLOG.TXT is created in the root of drive C:.

- The target drive (the drive you are installing to) and the source drive (the drive you are installing from) are identified. (This step is unique to this setup process.)

- The Wininst0.400 directory is created for temporary files.

- The MINI.CAB FILE, PRECOPY1.CAB, and PRECOPY2.CAB files are extracted. The needed files to run the Windows 98 Setup Wizard are loaded.

Phase 2: Collecting Information about Your Computer

This phase is very similar as the previously discussed Phase 2s. To recap this phase:

- You must complete the license agreement (EULA).

- You are asked to input the Product Key.

- You are asked to select the directory into which you want Windows 98 installed.

- You are asked to choose Typical or Custom installation.

- You are prompted for user information (name and company).

- You are asked to install the window components. You can select "Show me the list of components so I can choose." You are then taken to the Select Components window.

- You are asked to provide computer information for the network.

- You are asked to provide hardware component information about the keyboard and region.

- You are asked to choose the channel source.

- You are asked to create a Startup disk.

Phase 3: Copying Windows 98 Files to Your Computer

The steps for copying Windows 98 files to your computer are similar to those of the Phase 3 steps previously discussed. The copy process begins, and files are copied. Avoid any interruptions to this process, otherwise you probably will have to begin from the beginning of the setup process.

Phase 4: Restarting Your Computer

Again, the same process occurs. After 15 seconds, the computer is restarted and the message "Getting ready to start Windows 98 for the first time" is displayed. This phase is complete and you are ready for the final phase of the installation process.

Phase 5: Setting Up Hardware and Finalizing Settings

Windows 98 performs a complete hardware detection of Plug-and-Play components and attempts to correctly identify and install the legacy devices. If Windows 98 does not find a particular device, you will have to install it manually by selecting Control Panel ➢ Add/Remove Hardware.

After the hardware devices are identified, the Setup Wizard continues. The Control Panel entries are added. Programs on the Start menu are created. The Windows Help file is set up. Support for MS-DOS programs is installed. You are prompted for time zone and date verification. The driver database is built, and the core system configuration file is initialized and ready to roll.

You should be feeling very comfortable about the Windows 98 installation process. Exercise 2.1 walks you through the simple steps of upgrading to Windows 98 one more time.

EXERCISE 2.1

Upgrading to Windows 98

1. Insert the Windows 98 CD-ROM into your CD-ROM drive.

2. The Windows 98 CD-ROM window appears. Select Yes to continue. (See Figure 2.1.)

3. Begin Phase 1. The Windows 98 Setup window appears. (See Figure 2.2.) You should be able to see the five phases listed on the upper-left side of the screen. The time information appears on the lower-left side of the screen. Select OK to continue.

4. Begin Phase 2. At this point Windows 98 will begin checking your system. The Windows 98 Setup Wizard will appear. (See Figure 2.3.) The License Agreement will appear. (See Figure 2.4.) Click the radio button to accept the agreement. Click Next to continue.

5. The Product Key window will appear. (See Figure 2.5.) Enter your 25-character alphanumeric key. Click Next to continue.

6. Select the directory where you want Windows 98 to be installed. The default directory is usually C:\Windows. Click Next to continue.

7. You will now see a series of background tasks. Your system is checked. (See Figure 2.6.) ScanDisk and ScanRegW are executed. At the conclusion of these items, you will be asked to save the file system. Click Yes.

8. The Save File System windows will appear. If you are prompted to select a location, you probably have more than one local hard disk drive. Accept the default. Wait while the WINUNDO.DAT and the WINUNDO.INI files are created.

9. At this point, you probably will be asked to choose an installation method. Click Custom if you are prompted.

10. Input the requested user information (e.g., your name and company name). Click Next to continue.

11. The Select Components window will appear. Select all of the components. Make sure that you select 7 of 7 (or whatever the series of numbers may be) in the Description dialog box. You will be using several items in the following chapters, so make sure you install everything. Click Next to continue.

12. After you have identified the components to install, provide information about your system. Enter a computer name, workgroup name, and a description. Click Next to continue.

13. The Computer Settings screen will appear. Accept the defaults and click Next to continue.

14. The Location window will appear. Click Next to continue.

15. The Startup Disk window will appear. (See Figure 2.9.) You will be asked if you want to create a Startup disk. Select Yes. Click Next to continue.

16. Insert a blank disk when you are prompted. The Windows 98 Startup disk will be created, and you will be prompted to remove it.

17. Once the Startup disk is created, you are almost home free. At this point Phase 3 begins. Watch and wait as the Windows 98 copy process begins. (See Figure 2.10.)

18. The system will restart after Phases 3 and 4 complete. Various files will be modified, and you will move on to the next phase.

EXERCISE 2.1 (CONTINUED)

19. Phase 5 will begin. A variety of options will be installed, initialized, and set to the go position. Windows 98 will be restarted. Watch and wait. You are almost done.

20. You will be prompted for name and password verification. Enter the requested information. Click OK.

21. The "Building driver information database" prompt will appear. New hardware may be detected. Personalized settings will be initialized during this final phase. Finally, the Welcome to Windows 98 dialog box will appear. Windows 98 is now installed. You are ready to have a great time!

The individual steps for upgrading to Windows 98 may vary depending on what is installed on your computer and whether you are installing from MS-DOS or Windows 95. Some of the following steps may not appear during your system setup. If some options do not appear, continue with the next listed step.

Using Automated Setup Scripts and Tools to Install Windows 98

The procedures that have been discussed so far have dealt with upgrading issues regarding single, stand-alone systems. What happens when you must upgrade multiple computer systems to Windows 98? If you are going to upgrade three or more systems, you need to create a setup script or batch file to help expedite the installation process.

Microsoft *Exam* *Objective*

Install Windows 98. Installation options include:

▪ Automated Windows setup

This section deals with the issues surrounding automated setups and three specific tools that assist the setup process:

- Microsoft Batch 98 (BATCH.EXE)
- INFINST.EXE
- DBSET.EXE

Installation Sources

Windows 98 comes in two media forms: floppy disks and CD-ROMs. Like Windows 95 files, the Windows 98 installation files come in the form of .CAB files. (A *.CAB file*, or *cabinet file*, is actually a container file of several compressed files.) Both of these mediums can be used to upgrade your system to Windows 98.

When using Windows 95 with networked systems, most administrators either copied the .CAB files to a directory on the server or used the Windows 95 utility NetSetup to create an Administration installation source. Windows 98 has eliminated the Windows 95 utility NetSetup. Its functionality is now included in the Windows 98 utility *Microsoft Batch 98*. With this method, you merely copy the .CAB files to a shared folder on the network server. This folder becomes your Windows 98 installation source.

WARNING   Windows 98 does not support shared installations, nor does it support remote-boot options. This may affect your current network installations.

Installing from floppy disks will provide a functional Windows 98 installation. However, the floppy disks contain only the files needed for the basic installations. The Administration tools, the *Windows 98 Resource Kit*, Personal Web Server software, and a host of other CD-based tools and accessories are missing. The main disadvantage to a floppy disk upgrade is the speed factor. It takes significantly longer to upgrade Windows 95 to Windows 98 from floppy disks than from a CD. By choosing a floppy disk upgrade, you may be shortchanging yourself.

The CD-ROM is the most obvious medium choice for a stand-alone, single system upgrade. The CD-ROM contains the aforementioned software, and it is faster and more convenient.

If you are going to upgrade multiple systems, both the floppy disk and CD-ROM methods become impractical. The installation medium that is most frequently used is the network. Copy the Win98 folder from the CD-ROM to a location on the file server, then share this location so that you can access it. The Windows 98 files are still in a compressed format in the .CAB files. However, they can easily be accessed from computers on the company server. Some administrators actually copy the entire CD-ROM to a location on the server.

> **NOTE**
>
> A *push installation* can also be performed on a network. In a push installation, the server sends an automated upgrade of Windows 98 to client workstations. Windows 98 does not include the software for this method. A Microsoft BackOffice product called Systems Management Server (SMS) running on an NT server can perform a push installation.

Most companies use the administration installation method (Microsoft Batch 98) for networked systems and the CD-ROM method for systems that cannot connect to the network server.

Microsoft Batch 98

Automating the setup process of an operating system or an application can be a lot of fun and very satisfying. Sure there are some frustrating moments...all right, lots of frustrating moments, but when all is said and done, you have a scripted file that answers all of the setup questions and you can perform a hands-off installation. Seeing your creation work is a great feeling!

With Windows 98, you can use the scripted file if you are upgrading from the CD-ROM or are upgrading multiple systems on a company network. A setup script file allows you to include all the components that you want installed during the upgrade process. In Windows 95 a setup script file called MSBATCH.INF contains predefined settings for all the options to be selected. In Windows 98 the MSBATCH.INF file is used during a System Recovery situation. However, you can easily create a file using the Microsoft Batch 98 tool.

> **TIP**
>
> The *Microsoft Windows 98 Resource Kit* CD-ROM includes various examples of setup scripts. If you plan to use the Microsoft Batch 98 utility, refer to the Resource Kit for more information.

The Microsoft Batch 98 utility is a Windows-based program that makes it easy to create installation script files. You customize the Setup Wizard to accept EULA, to inhibit display of the Product Key, and to control all user input (including user, company, computer, and workgroup names). Batch 98 can also be used to install printers and network components, to select the optional components that you want, and to customize the Internet Explorer 4.*x* setup. In addition, Batch 98 can scan your computer's Registry to see what components you have installed, create an .INF file, and store your settings in the .INF file.

Microsoft Batch 98 is an improvement over the Windows 95 BATCH.EXE utility. Batch 98 offers a more intuitive interface and improved functionality, as shown in Figure 2.15.

F I G U R E 2.15

The Microsoft Batch 98 utility

When you use the Batch 98 utility, you work with seven key options:

Gather Now: Scans the local system for current settings

General Setup Options: Presents most of Windows 98 general settings

Network Options: Customizes network settings

Optional Components: Chooses which Windows 98 components to install

Internet Explorer Options: Customizes the Internet Browser and Shell options

Advanced Options: Presents Registry, Policy, and Windows Update options

Save Settings to INF: Saves the local settings or new MSBATCH.INF type file to a .INF file

Microsoft Batch 98 can be installed on a Windows 95 or a Windows NT computer; however, installing it on a Windows 98 computer system is preferred. Gather Now scans the existing Windows 98 system settings and configuration and collects information about the following:

- Microsoft 32-bit networking clients
- Microsoft 32-bit networking services
- Microsoft 32-bit networking protocols
- Installed printers
- Current time zone and time/date
- User-level security settings
- Windows directory
- User and machine information
- Network card
- Optional components installed

Information about all of these items will be collected. They can be saved using the Save Settings To INF option. Figure 2.16 illustrates some of the settings created from this process.

To fully enjoy the Microsoft Batch 98 tool, you must use it. Exercise 2.2 shows you just how easy it is to create a MSBATCH.INF file and to use the Batch 98 Windows-based program.

```
; MSBATCH.INF
;
; Copyright (c) 1995-1998 Microsoft Corporation.
; All rights reserved.
;

[BatchSetup]
Version=3.0 (32-bit)
SaveDate=08/24/98

[Version]
Signature = "$CHICAGO$"
LayoutFile=layout.inf

[Setup]
Express=1
InstallDir="c:\windows"
InstallType=3
EBD=0
ShowEula=0
ChangeDir=0
OptionalComponents=1
Network=1
System=0
CCP=0
CleanBoot=0
Display=0
DevicePath=0
NoDirWarn=1
TimeZone="Mountain"
Uninstall=0
NoPrompt2Boot=1

[System]
```

EXERCISE 2.2

Using Microsoft Batch 98

1. Installing this utility is simple. Make sure your Windows 98 CD-ROM is in the CD-ROM drive.

2. Right-click the Start button. Select Explore ➤ CD-ROM drive ➤ the \Tools\ResKit\Batch folder.

3. Double-click SETUP.EXE.

4. Select and accept all of the defaults. Batch 98 is now installed on your system.

5. Your system does not need to restart. Select Start ➤ Programs ➤ Microsoft Batch 98.

6. The Batch 98 program is loaded. Click Gather Now. Windows 98 will peruse the current Registry settings and collect all of the current Windows 98 settings and data.

7. Click through each of the five Batch 98 options: General Setup Options, Network Options, Optional Components, Internet Explorer Options, and Advanced Options. You should see information about you and your current Windows 98 installation.

8. Click Save Settings to INF.

9. Name the file **C:\Temp\MYBATCH.INF.**

10. Select File ➢ Exit.

11. Select Start ➢ Programs ➢ Accessories ➢ Notepad.

12. Select File ➢ Open ➢ C:\Temp\MYBATCH.INF. Press Enter.

13. Review the file and identify the various sections.

14. Select File ➢ Print. A sample script file will print.

15. Select File ➢ Exit.

As you can see, the Microsoft Batch 98 utility can enhance your ability to create and execute multiple script files. Your Windows 98 setup practices and methods will be greatly improved.

With the newly created setup script, you can run the Windows 98 setup with command-line parameter that uses the script filename (for example, D:\Win98\SETUP.EXE C:\Temp\MYBATCH.INF).

The D:\ is the CD-ROM drive letter with the setup executable specified. C:\Temp is the location of the script file MYBATCH.INF. As previously mentioned, MSBATCH.INF is a name that was used in Windows 95. You can use any name you want to use. Just make sure you use the .INF extension.

The Microsoft Batch 98 program makes it easy to create installation scripts through a Windows-based navigation program. This is one of the better tools to come from Microsoft.

When you use Microsoft Batch 98, the .INF file you create will contain a single computer name. As previously discussed, each computer on your network must have a unique name. The Multiple Machine-Name Save utility (which comes with Batch 98) allows you to create and incorporate a text file that contains unique machine names for use during the Windows 98 setup.

INF Installer for Windows 98

Even though you can automate the Windows 98 installation process, some files and drivers cannot be controlled by the Microsoft Batch 98 program. The INF Installer program, INFINST.EXE, allows you to add device drivers, network drivers, and other third-party software. (See Figure 2.17.) The neat thing about INFINST.EXE is that all of the drivers will be installed just as though they were part of the Windows 98 Setup program.

FIGURE 2.17

The INF Installer window

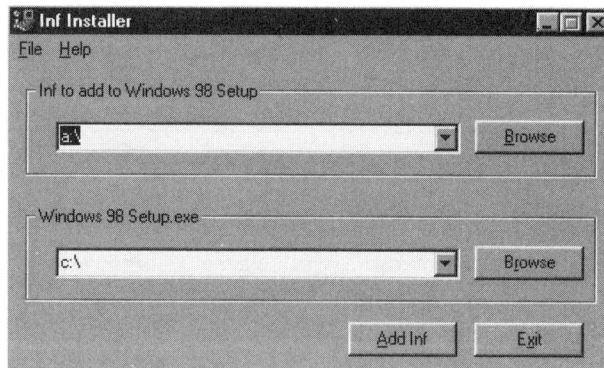

This is a great utility when you need to install more than just Windows 98 and you also need to control other setup functions. You can use this tool with the Microsoft Batch 98 utility to eliminate the need to manually install third-party drivers.

DBSET.EXE for Windows 98

DBSET.EXE is another new utility in the Windows 98 suite of tools. It allows you to personalize the setup process by creating a database. The information in this database can be used to change information on a system or systems from the server. An example option of DBSET is illustrated in Figure 2.18.

```
Microsoft (R) Front-end Application Tool - Version 1.0  (018) .. (03/18/98)
Copyright (c) Microsoft Corp 1998.  All rights reserved.

Writes from a text database appropriate DOS environment variables or to a
text file based on a template.

dbset [/s:delimiter] [/f [field_name]] [/d [database_file]] data
dbset [/o field_record] [/i [template_file]] [/r [output_file]] [/m] [data]

/i template_file          Specifies the name and location of the template file.
                          (default template.txt) The template file will be used
                          as the basis for the output file. Variable names in the
                          template file are denoted in %variable% format. Actual
                          % characters are denoted by %%. The variable names will
                          be matched with field names in the database file and
                          and replace with the values from the apropriate record.
Example:
      Registry file:
      [HKEY_CURRENT_USER\RemoteAccess\Profile\JohnD]
      "User"="JohnD"
      "MachineName"="dev_01"
      "IP"=145.25.12.1
      "Server"="msg-10"
```

With this tool, you can individualize setup scripts by creating a database file containing specific data for each user (e.g., username, computer name, IP address, etc.). This tool can also be used to customize Registry files and write environment variables.

> Other files can be modified to enhance the setup process. NETDET.INI is used to detect NetWare components and TSRs during the Windows 98 installation. You can use a file named WRKGRP.INI to specify a list of workgroups in which users can participate. APPS.INI lets you define information that completely takes care of the installation process. Using it, users can upgrade from Windows 95 to Windows 98 with a one-click installation.

Multiple installations require more work than single, stand-alone installations. Automated tools (like Microsoft Batch 98's Infinst, and Dbset) make the installation process easier.

In summary, automating is a three-step process.

1. Create a custom script with the needed configuration for your environment.

2. Set up an installation source that contains the Windows 98 .CAB files. Share this source so that it can be accessed from the network.

3. Use a login script that calls the Setup Wizard, an APPS.INI file that helps upgrade from Windows 95 to Windows 98 by simply clicking a button, or a system policy that calls the Setup Wizard that will use this script. You can also use the Microsoft tool SMS or some other product that allows you to install Windows 98.

Dual-Booting Options with Windows 98

There may be times when you or someone on your administration team needs two operating systems on the same machine. If you are currently running IBM OS/2, Microsoft Windows NT, or Caldera's DR-DOS on your system, you can install Windows 98 onto this system, and both operating systems can coexist.

Microsoft ✓ *Exam* *Objective*

Install Windows 98. Installation options include:

- Dual-boot combination with Windows NT 4.0

Here are a few points to consider about a dual-boot system:

- Typically, Windows 98 is going to be used to upgrade an existing Windows 95 or Windows 3.*x* system. If you are an advanced user who needs access to two operating systems, perhaps you are justified in having a dual-boot system but think carefully before you choose to dual-boot. If you are supporting multiple operating systems, then maybe you should have two separate machines so that your systems more closely resemble the systems of those you are supporting. Windows 98 is not intended to dual-boot. Windows 98 Plug-and-Play drivers can conflict with Windows NT drivers. So prior to initiating the installation process, ask yourself if you really need a dual-boot system.

- In order to dual-boot, the boot partition must be FAT16. Windows NT is not compatible with FAT32. Windows 98 is not compatible with NT's NTFS or OS/2's HPFS. (You always seem to return to your roots—FAT16. And you thought this was the 90s!)

- In order to dual-boot, you need to install Windows 98 into a folder other than C:\Windows (or other than the current location of your operating system files).

- You must be using MS-DOS 5.0 or later in order to dual-boot. (You may use any OS as long as it has a boot manager.)

- You really need to decide how a dual-boot configuration is going to help you. Microsoft has not made it easy to coexist with third-party operating systems. Not to mention that you must install your applications twice, once for each system.

Dual-Booting Windows 98 with Windows NT

The Windows NT Boot Loader tool will direct the flow of the boot process. When you boot your system, the Windows NT Boot Loader appears and allows you to choose between Windows NT and Microsoft DOS. Choose the MS-DOS option to install Windows 98. Once the Setup Wizard runs and your system has rebooted, you will need to select the MS-DOS option once again to finalize the Windows 98 setup.

You can install Windows NT onto a system that currently has Windows 98 on it, or you can install Windows 98 onto a system that currently contains Windows NT. Exercises 2.3 and 2.4 will assist you in either situation that you have.

If Windows 98 is already installed on your system, you can follow the steps in Exercise 2.3 to install Windows NT.

EXERCISE 2.3

Installing Windows NT onto a System Where Windows 98 Is Currently Installed

1. After you have booted into Windows 98, select Start ➢ Programs ➢ MS-DOS Prompt.

2. The MS-DOS prompt will appear. Switch to the directory that contains the Windows NT source files. (This directory usually will be a folder entitled \I386 on the Windows NT CD-ROM or a share installation source on your network.)

EXERCISE 2.3 (CONTINUED)

3. At the source folder location, type **winnt /b /w**. WINNT is the Windows NT Setup program. The NT files will be copied from the source to your local system. The /b option prevents the Setup program from creating the floppy disks. The /w option allows you to run WINNT in a Windows environment.

4. Follow and accept the prompts of the WINNT Setup Wizard. Windows NT will load the files that it needs, including the Boot Loader tool.

5. After the installation completes, your system will boot to the Windows NT Loader window. Make your selection from the various options. Now you can choose to go to the operating system you need.

If Windows NT is already installed on your system, you can follow the steps in Exercise 2.4 to install Windows 98.

EXERCISE 2.4

Installing Windows 98 onto a System Where Windows NT Is Currently Installed

1. Start the computer with a MS-DOS floppy disk; a Windows 95 or 98 Startup disk should work fine. The disk should contain the MS-DOS utility SYS.COM.

2. Once the system has booted successfully and you are at the command prompt, enter **A:SYS C:**. This operation will transfer the MS-DOS files needed to dual-boot with Windows NT. You should see the message "System transferred."

3. Remove the floppy disk and reboot the system. You should be at an MS-DOS prompt once the system starts.

4. Go to the folder location of the Windows 98 source files and type **Setup**. The Windows 98 Setup Wizard will appear. Make sure you install Windows 98 into a separate directory and do not delete the partition on which Windows NT is installed.

5. After all of the Windows 98 installation reboots are complete and Windows 98 appears to be working, reboot the system using the Windows NT Setup disks. Boot the system with the NT Setup disk in drive A:. The Windows NT Setup utility will start, and a list of menu options will appear.

6. At the Windows NT Setup options window, select R to repair Windows NT. This process repairs only the Windows NT boot sector. Do not choose to inspect the Registry or system files or the boot environment. Repair only the boot sector.

7. One more time, reboot the system and you should see the Windows NT multiboot option screen.

8. Edit the Windows NT BOOT.INI file. You may need to use the MS-DOS ATTRIB command to change the attributes of this file to allow changes. Once in the BOOT.INI file, add the following line to the [OPERATING SYSTEMS] section: **c:\=Windows 98**.

9. Save the file. Restore the attribute. Restart the system.

10. After you reboot the system, you will see the Windows NT boot-loader menu. One of the options is MS-DOS from which the Windows 98 program will load.

Dual-Booting Windows 98 with OS/2

Like Windows NT, the IBM OS/2 operating system has a boot loading tool, the Boot Manager. OS/2 must be set up to dual-boot to MS-DOS. You must run the Windows 98 Setup from the MS-DOS prompt.

Go to the folder location of the Windows 98 source files, and type **Setup** to start the Setup Wizard. Install Windows 98 as previously discussed, make sure to install Windows 98 into a separate directory, and do not delete the partition on which OS/2 is installed.

Upon completion, you may need to reenable the OS/2 Boot Manager by running the OS/2 command FDISK from the OS/2 boot disk. With the OS/2 Boot Manager reenabled, reboot the system. The Multiboot option window will appear; make your selection and you are ready to go.

WARNING Microsoft does not advise, nor do they support, a dual-boot environment with IBM's OS/2 or DR DOS. You are on your own. Good luck!

Dual-Booting Windows 98 with DR-DOS

Installing Windows 98 onto a computer that already has Calera's DR-DOS installed is very similar to the Microsoft DOS installation. Make sure that you REM any programs or TSRs in the CONFIG.SYS and AUTOEXEC.BAT files that could conflict with the Windows 98 setup process. If you have enabled the DR-DOS Volume Protection option, you need to disable it before you start the setup process.

At the DR-DOS prompt, switch to the directory that contains the Windows 98 source files, and install as usual. When Setup is complete, you are ready to go.

Troubleshooting the Windows 98 Installation

The Windows 98 setup process is not always going to come off as easily or as neatly as you would like. Setup uses different procedures to recover from setup failures. Some of the common installation problems are:

- System hangs during the setup process
- Hardware detection problems
- Software driver problems

System Hangs During Setup

If your computer system stops responding or hangs during the setup process, prior to the first restart, you must turn off your system, wait, and then run Setup again. When you rerun Setup, SETUPLOG.TXT and DETCRASH .LOG (files that assist in the setup process) determine that Setup previously failed. As a result, you will see a helpful message screen that indicates that you should use the "Safe Recovery" feature as illustrated in Figure 2.19.

FIGURE 2.19

The Safe Recovery
screen

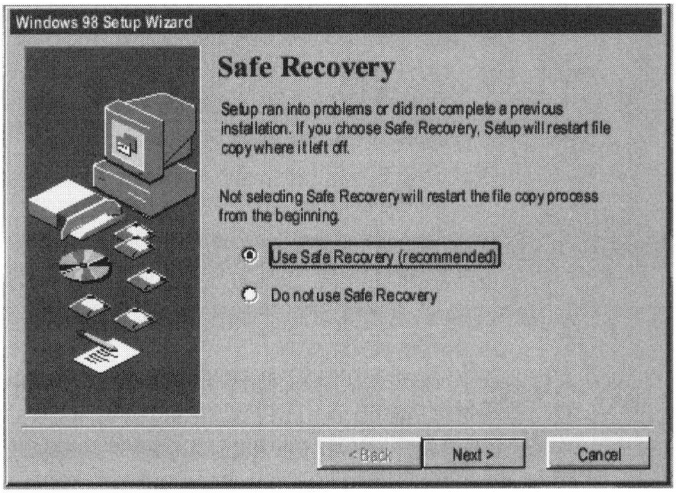

Using this recovery option is recommended. The SETUPLOG.TXT file contains information regarding Setup installation successes and failures. The Setup Wizard examines this file to determine where the failure or problem occurred, and then it resumes from that point. If you don't choose Safe Recovery, the installation process starts from scratch and you could potentially encounter the same problem again.

Hardware Detection Problems

When you run the Setup Wizard, Setup attempts to identify hardware based on information from the Registry for a Windows 95 to Windows 98 setup, or the Setup Wizard performs full hardware detection. Hardware detection of legacy devices will take place after the first reboot. During this phase, information is collected about the various hardware components. Like Windows 95, Windows 98 utilizes several key logs during the installation process. Table 2.4 details the log files and their role in the setup process.

> Do not delete the setup log files during the setup process. Once Windows 98 has successfully installed, you could delete these files.

T A B L E 2.4	**Log File Name**	**Role during the Setup Process**
Setup Log Files for Windows 98	DETLOG.TXT	This file keeps a record of devices found during the setup process. It records the start of a detection test and then the test outcome, i.e., the information about this particular piece of hardware. This file will be located on the root of the C: drive and is a hidden file.
	DETCRASH.LOG	This file keeps information about which components of the setup process loaded successfully or failed. If the component fails and you must restart the setup process, DETCRASH.LOG tells the Setup Wizard where the previous failure occurred and to skip that procedure during this installation process. Even though this file contains the .LOG extension (which suggests that this is a log file that can be viewed), it is not a log file and cannot be viewed. This is a binary file stored in the root of the C: drive and is a hidden file.
	SETUPLOG.TXT	This file actually identifies what took place during the setup process. This is the file that Safe Recovery uses to determine where it will resume the setup process. This is a regular read/write file located in the root of the C: drive.
	BOOTLOG.TXT	This file contains a record of the current startup processes involved in starting Windows 98. When you install Windows 98 for the first time, this file is created automatically. This file shows the components and the drivers that have been loaded and initialized, as well as the current state of said items. This file is located in the root of the C: drive and is a normal read/write file. (This file can be used after Windows 98 is installed to identify startup problems.)

Software Driver Problems

During the Setup Wizard process, Setup tries to determine any problematic software. If during the setup process it is unable to diagnose the cause of the problem or failure, the system may lock up or display an error message that Setup has failed. If this type of problem occurs, you must power off the system and restart the Setup Wizard from the beginning.

During the installation process, you need to ensure that you are using the most current driver. Using an incorrect driver will typically result in the inability to use the specific hardware device. You may need to install the driver for this device in Safe mode after the setup process is complete. You can use the Add New Hardware and Add/Remove Programs components of Control Panel to resolve these types of problems.

> Refer to Chapter 5 of the *Windows 98 Resource Kit* for more information about technical problems during the setup process.

Welcome to Windows

Once Windows 98 is installed, you will still need to deal with a few items, like registering. The Windows 98 Welcome screen (see Figure 2.20) identifies additional or follow-up issues you will need to handle.

FIGURE 2.20

Welcome to Windows 98!

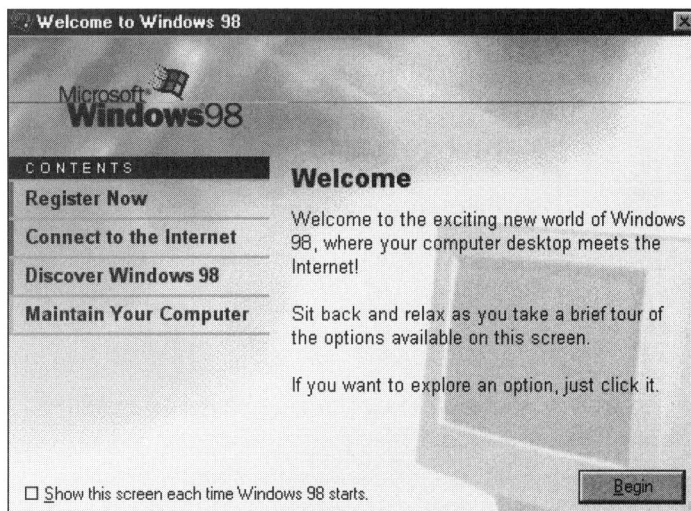

Uninstalling Windows 98

Installing a new operating system is a one way street. Because your software needs may change, Microsoft created a way to remove software by using the Uninstall feature.

Microsoft
✓ *Exam*
Objective

Install Windows 98. Installation options include:

- Uninstall

To Uninstall Windows 98, you must meet the following conditions:

- The system files must have been saved when you were prompted to save them. This operation produced two files: WINUNDO.DAT and WINUNDO.INI.

- The hard disk where Windows 98 is located cannot be compressed.

- The current file system cannot be Windows 98 FAT32.

If the previous conditions are met, you should be able to successfully uninstall Windows 98. Please keep in mind that this process does not always work and is not fail safe.

Figure 2.21 lists the two components that you should find in the list of items on the Install/Uninstall tab from the Add/Remove Programs item.

EXERCISE 2.5

Uninstalling Windows 98

1. Go to the Control Panel.

2. Select Add/Remove Programs.

3. Select the Install/Uninstall Tab (default view).

4. Select the Windows 98 Uninstall option.

5. Select Add/Remove.

EXERCISE 2.5 (CONTINUED)

6. A dialog box appears indicating what is happening. Click Yes to continue.
7. Another dialog box appears indicating that your disk will be checked for errors. Click Yes to continue.
8. The ScanDisk program runs, and yet another dialog box appears asking if you want to continue. Click Yes to continue.
9. The system restarts.
10. You should return to Windows 95.

FIGURE 2.21
The Uninstall options

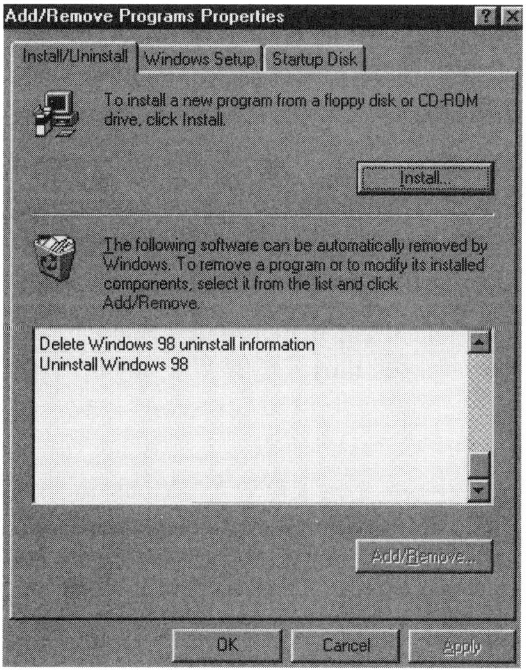

If you choose to keep Windows 98 as your installed operating system, you should remove the Windows 95 file system. You can manually delete the WINUNDO.DAT and the WINUNDO.INI files or following the steps in Exercise 2.6 to remove them automatically.

EXERCISE 2.6

Manually Deleting WINUNDO.DAT and WINUNDO.INI

1. Go to the Control Panel.

2. Select Add/Remove Programs.

3. Select the Install/Uninstall tab (default view).

4. Select Remove Windows 95 System Files.

5. Select Add/Remove.

6. A dialog box appears indicating that you will not be able to go back to the Windows 95 environment. Click Yes to continue.

7. A dialog box appears indicating that the files have been deleted. Click OK.

Administrative Tip

Having a Windows 98 Startup disk is always a good idea and is a requirement for most Windows 98 installations. You can create additional Startup disks. To create a Startup disk, go to the Control Panel and double-click Add/Remove programs. This will open the Add/Remove Programs dialog box. Select the Startup tab and then click the Create Startup Disk button. That's all there is to it.

For those of you who are interested, the Windows 95 and Windows 98 Startup disks have changed dramatically. Here is a list of changes between the two versions:

- New CONFIG.SYS file that contains a Multi-Configuration Menu that allows you to the option to load real-mode CD-ROM drivers

- Real-mode CD-ROM Drivers for IDE

- Real-mode CD-ROM Drivers for SCSI

- The RAM Drive installation and the extraction of MS-DOS applications from the EBD.CAB file

- New Extract utility

Table 2.5 provides a list of the file names and the accompanying information found on the Windows 98 Startup Disk.

T A B L E 2.5	**File Name**	**Function**
Windows 98 Startup Disk Files	ASPI2DOS.SYS	Real-mode Adaptec CD-ROM driver
	ASPI4DOS.SYS	Real-mode Adaptec CD-ROM driver
	ASPI8DOS.SYS	Real-mode Adaptec CD-ROM driver
	ASPICD. SYS	Real-mode Adaptec CD-ROM driver
	AUTOEXEC.BAT	File that automatically starts when you boot
	BTCDROM. SYS	Mylex/BusLogic CD-ROM driver
	BTDOSM. SYS	Mylex/BusLogic CD-ROM driver
	COMMAND.COM	MS-DOS Command Interpreter
	CONFIG.SYS	Configuration file that loads real-mode device drivers
	DRVSPACE.BIN	DriveSpace compression engine
	EBD.CAB	CAB file containing extract utilities
	EBD. SYS	File identifying the disk as the Startup disk for Windows 98
	EXTRACT.EXE	File to expand the EBD.CAB file
	FDISK.EXE	Disk partition tool
	FINDRAMD.EXE	Utility to find the RAMDrive during startup
	FLASHPT. SYS	Mylex/BusLogic CD-ROM driver
	HIMEM.SYS	XMS Memory Manager
	IO.SYS	System boot file

T A B L E 2.5 *(cont.)* Windows 98 Startup Disk Files	File Name	Function
	MSDOD.SYS	Boot option information
	MODE.COM	Allows you to change display parameters
	OAKCDROM.SYS	Generic device driver for ATAPI CD-ROM drives
	RAMDRIVE.SYS	Creates a Ramdrive during startup
	README.TXT	Information file about the Windows 98 Startup disk
	SETRAMD.BAT	Searches for first available drive to be a Ramdrive
	SYS.COM	System transfer utility

The compressed EBD.CAB file has the files listed in Table 2.6 compressed within it.

T A B L E 2.6 EBD.CAB Compressed Files	File Name	Function
	ATTRIB.EXE	Add or remove file attributes
	CHKDSK.EXE	MS-DOS tool to check disk status—use ScanDisk
	DEBUG.EXE	Debugging utility
	EDIT.COM	MS-DOS real-mode text editor
	EXT.EXE	New Windows 98 extract utility
	FORMAT.COM	Disk formatting tool
	HELP.BAT	Batch file to launch the README.TXT file on the disk
	HELP.TXT	Text document with trouble-shooting information
	MSCDEX.EXE	CD-ROM file extension for MS-DOS

T A B L E 2.6 *(cont.)* EBD.CAB Compressed Files	**File Name**	**Function**
	RESTART.COM	Utility to restart your system
	SCANDISK.EXE	Disk status tool
	SCANDISK.INI	Disk status tool configuration file
	SYS.COM	Transfers system files and make disk bootable
	UNINSTAL.EXE	Removes Windows 98 from the system

Table 2.7 lists some additional files that you may like to include on your Startup disks. These files are located in the \Windows\Command folder.

T A B L E 2.7 Additional Useful Files	**File Name**	**Function**
	CD-ROMDRIVER.SYS	16-bit real-mode driver for CD-ROM
	DELTREE.EXE	Allows you to delete multiple directory structures
	MEM.EXE	Allows you to identify your memory configurations
	MORE.COM	Allows you to display one page of information at a time
	XCOPY.EXE	The Extended Copy utility allows you to copy directories

Knowledge of these files is not tested on the exam; however, knowing what files are located on your Startup disk and what they do is a valuable troubleshooting tool.

Summary

You have covered a lot of ground in this chapter. Remember, the better your installation and configuration plans are, the better off you will be down the road.

The following list recaps what you need to do to have a successful Windows 98 installation.

- Make sure that your hardware and software are sufficient and that they meet the minimum requirements.

- Remember to create the Startup disk during the initial setup process. This gives you a great trouble-shooting resource, and it copies the Startup disk files to the C:\Windows\Command folder for future use.

- If possible, use automated setup scripts and tools.

- If a failure occurs during setup, use the Safe Recovery feature when you restart the setup process.

- Do not delete the various support log files (SETUPLOG.TXT, DET-CRASH.LOG, and DETLOG.TXT) until after the setup process has been successful and they are no longer needed.

- Make sure you have copies of your real-mode CD-ROM drivers and real-mode network drivers.

- Save the Windows 95 files system if you think you might uninstall Windows 98 some day.

Remember, the more you plan and the better your preinstallation configuration considerations are, the better off you will be in the long run. Take the time to do things right the first time!

Review Questions

1. What is a deployment guide?

    A. An automated script

    B. Part of the Uninstall process

    C. A carefully laid plan to install Windows 98

    D. Part of the DBSet file structure

2. What are some of the minimum hardware requirements for Windows 98? Choose all that apply.

    A. 120MB of free hard disk space

    B. 16MB of RAM

    C. Sound Blaster

    D. 14.4 baud modem

3. How much disk space will you typically need to save the existing file system?

    A. 35MB

    B. 40MB

    C. 50MB

    D. 75MB

4. Which version of MS-DOS is considered to be the bare basics?

    A. MS-DOS 7.0

    B. MS DOS 6.22

    C. MS-DOS 5.0

    D. MS-DOS 3.3

5. If you upgrade Windows 98 to a hard disk that is compressed, how much free noncompressed space must you have?

   A. 1MB

   B. 3MB

   C. 5MB

   D. 10MB

6. Windows 98 can be installed on which of the following file systems? Choose all that apply.

   A. NTFS

   B. FAT16

   C. FAT32

   D. HPFS

7. Windows 95 uses a 12-step installation process. How many steps does Windows 98 use?

   A. 5

   B. 8

   C. 10

   D. 12

8. The most optimized Windows 98 upgrade is from which operating system?

   A. MS-DOS

   B. Windows 3.*x*

   C. Windows 95

   D. Windows NT

9. The Windows 98 setup could require the use of which of the following? Choose all that apply.

   A. DR-DOS

   B. HPFS

   C. Protected-mode drivers

   D. Real-mode drivers

10. The Setup /d option prevents Windows 98 from doing what?

   A. Diagnosing real-mode problems

   B. Diagnosing hard-disk errors with ScanDisk

   C. Detecting virtual hard disks

   D. Detecting and using any previous version of Windows

11. Which of the following processors are required for Windows 98? Choose all that apply.

   A. Pentium/60MHz

   B. 386DX/25MHz

   C. 486SX/33MHz

   D. 486DX/66MHz

12. According to Microsoft, what is the minimum amount of RAM required to run Windows 98?

   A. 4MB

   B. 8MB

   C. 16MB

   D. 32MB

13. Which of the following are needed to perform a successful installation? Choose all that apply.

   A. A bootable floppy accessible

   B. A backup of CONFIG.SYS and AUTOEXEC.BAT

   C. ScanDisk must be run on your system

   D. Defrag must be run on your system

14. You want to install Windows 98, but you do not want it to perform the ScanDisk or Registry check. Which of the following switches should you use?

   A. Setup /is /ir

   B. Setup /is /nr

   C. Setup /ih /ir

   D. Setup /ih /is

15. If you want Setup to run automatically, what type of file could you use to assist in the setup process?

   A. SETUP.DAT

   B. MSBATCH.DAT

   C. SETUP.INF

   D. MSBATCH.INF

16. Which of the following is not one of the five setup phases?

   A. Preparing to run Windows 98 Setup

   B. Collecting information about your computer

   C. Compressing the source files on your computer

   D. Finalizing settings

17. What is Wininst0.400?

   A. A file needed for the installation process

   B. A folder on the Windows 98 CD-ROM that contains the installation instructions

   C. A temporary folder created to help facilitate the setup process

   D. A permanent folder used by Internet Explorer 4

18. What are the WINUNDO.DAT and WINUNDO.INI files?

   A. Compressed files stored on the Startup disk

   B. Compressed files stored on the Windows 98 CD-ROM that are used to install

   C. Hidden/read-only files stored on the local drive as a result of saving the previous file system

   D. Hidden/read-only files stored in the C:\Windows folder used to uninstall Windows 98

19. Which of the following statements are correct? Choose all that apply.

   A. The Startup disk contains drivers for generic CD-ROM readers.

   B. The Startup disk will create a RAM drive on your system.

   C. The Startup disk can be used to view files on a NTFS partition.

   D. Other files can be added to the Startup disk.

20. Which program can automate the Windows 98 setup process?

   A. DBSetup

   B. Microsoft Batch 98

   C. NetSetup

   D. Microsoft Information Installer

21. Which file allows you to add device drivers to the installation process?

   A. DBSet

   B. Microsoft Batch 98

   C. APPS.INI

   D. INFINST.EXE

22. BOOTDISK.BAT allows you to do which of the following?

   A. Create a Startup disk for Windows 98

   B. Create a Startup disk for Windows NT

   C. Format the existing drive and copy the system files to it

   D. Boot up with OS/2

23. To uninstall Windows 98, which of the following must be true?

   A. You did not select to Save File System during setup.

   B. You selected to Save File System during setup.

   C. You have a compressed drive.

   D. You have a FAT32 drive.

24. To dual-boot with Windows NT, which of the following must be true? Choose all that apply.

   A. The boot partition must be FAT16.

   B. The boot partition must be NTFS.

   C. You must install Windows 98 from MS-DOS shell while in NT.

   D. You must install Windows 98 from MS-DOS from the Boot Manager menu.

25. You can install Window 98 from a server using push technology if you are using which of the following? Choose all that apply.

   A. Channels from Internet partners

   B. Microsoft's BackOffice SMS

   C. Logon Scripts

   D. DBSET

C H A P T E R

3

Installing and Configuring Hardware Devices in Windows 98

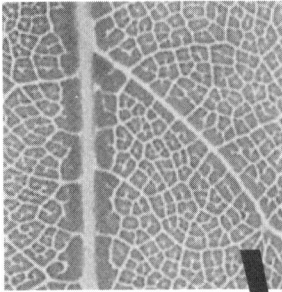

Windows 98 introduces some fantastic new technologies in the hardware arena. These technologies include the new Win32 Driver Model (WDM) used in Windows 98 and future releases of Windows NT and the new bus architectures supported by WDM (USB and IEEE 1394).

Microsoft
Exam
Objective

Install and configure hardware devices in a Microsoft environment and a mixed Microsoft and NetWare environment. Hardware devices include:

- Modems
- Printers
- Universal Serial Bus (USB)
- Multiple display support
- IEEE 1394 FireWire
- Infrared Data Association (IrDA)
- Multilink
- Power management scheme

NOTE

We will only be discussing the last six of the eight hardware devices listed above in this chapter. See Chapter 15, *The Internet and Dial-Up Networking*, for an in-depth discussion of modems, and Chapter 11, *Printing with Windows 98*, for complete coverage of printers.

This chapter will discuss the new WDM architecture and then take a closer look at both the Universal Serial Bus and the IEEE 1394 FireWire Bus. You will learn about the devices and features that each Bus supports, as well as the requirements for special connectors and cables. You will also learn about the extraordinary data transfer rates achieved with these new busses.

The chapter will conclude with a short discussion on installing and configuring multidisplay support, multilink capabilities with your dial-up adapters, power management schemes and infrared support in Windows 98.

Device Driver Architecture

A *device driver* is a piece of software that has been designed by the hardware manufacturer. This software is supposed to transfer information between a hardware device and the operating system. In the past, device drivers were written to specific operating systems on specific platforms. This was a proprietary model and was very inefficient. Hardware vendors had to write a different version of their device driver for each different platform and operating system.

With Windows 95, much of this problem was taken care of by the way Windows handles device drivers. Windows provides part of the device driver functionality in its architecture. Hardware vendors still write drivers for specific types of platforms (Intel, Alpha-AXP, RISC, etc.), but the operating system interface has become more or less standardized. This means that everyone can use the same Windows-side functionality, and vendors only provide the device-specific functionality. What does this mean? Let's go back to the old days and look at an example. Way back in olden times (you remember, six years ago, in a galaxy far, far away… ahem!) every device had its own special management interface and its own special drivers. Think about the old printers. Some manufacturers included software that would allow you to monitor the printer while others just provided the capabilities to print. With the advent of Windows 95, much of the administrative functionality was encapsulated in the operating system, which allowed hardware vendors to concentrate on building device drivers rather than device drivers and administration tools.

What does all of this have to do with Windows 98? Well, in Windows 95, you still have to provide device drivers specific to a particular platform and version of Windows. Now in Windows 98 and future releases of Windows NT, Microsoft has taken encapsulation of functionality a step further. The new

Win32 Driver Model (WDM) has been standardized in such a way that hardware vendors now only need to create one version of their device driver regardless of the platform upon which it will be running. Essentially, WDM is a common set of I/O functionality that is understood by Windows 98 and new versions of Windows NT.

Windows 98 supports both the new WDM and all of the old bus interfaces from Windows 95. These include PCI, PC Card, SCSI, ISA, and EISA bus architectures. These interfaces are provided for backward compatibility with Windows 95 and legacy devices. WDM supports two new bus architectures: USB and IEEE 1394. Let's take a closer look at what these new bus architectures support and what new features have been incorporated into them.

Universal Serial Bus (USB)

Universal Serial Bus is an external bus standard for computers. Its main advantage is that it takes the Plug-and-Play functionality of hardware devices outside of the computer. This means that that functionality must reside on the hardware rather than on a special card that needs to be installed into your PC.

Microsoft ✓ *Exam* *Objective*	**Install and configure hardware devices in a Microsoft environment and a mixed Microsoft and NetWare environment. Hardware devices include:** ▪ Universal Serial Bus (USB)

When you attach a USB-compliant device, it can be automatically configured as soon as it is attached to the PC. In most cases, this can be done without the need to reboot the PC or run through the setup sequence.

USB supports the following devices:

- Audio devices
- Data gloves
- Digital still cameras
- Digitizers

- ISDN and digital PBX systems

- Joysticks, keyboards, and mice

- Low bandwidth video

- Modems

- Monitor controls

- Printers and scanners

- Telephones

USB supports the following features:

- **Hot Plug and Play:** You can plug a USB device into your system at any time. It will be automatically configured and the operating system will be notified that it is present and available.

- **Power management support:** With a USB device, you can take advantage of three different power modes: Off, On, and Suspend. A nice feature of the Suspend mode is that the device has the ability to wake itself up and then wake up the system. For example, a USB modem might wake up when an incoming phone call is received. The modem might then determine that it is a fax and wake up the PC so that the fax software can receive the incoming fax.

USB also specifies a new standard for connectors, sockets, and the cables that a USB-compliant device may use. By taking advantage of this new standard, you will find that there is a lot less confusion than before. In the past, everything had its own special card, its own special connectors, sockets, and a special types of cables. By standardizing, hardware manufacturers can create a single device that will run on any computer that supports USB without making modifications to these three parts.

Let's finish up with a quick look at the four different data transfer modes supported by USB: isochronous, interrupt, bulk, and control.

Isochronous and *interrupt transfers* guarantee a particular transfer rate by reserving a certain amount of bandwidth. *Bulk* and *control transfers* take advantage of a best-fit scenario depending on how much bandwidth is available to them. Keep in mind, however, that 10 percent of the total bandwidth is reserved for bulk and control transfers. Isochronous and interrupt transfers with a guaranteed amount of bandwidth are really needed to support the demands of multimedia application where large streams of data need to be transferred.

USB supports the following transfer rates based upon the device's data requirements:

- **5Mbps:** Used for devices that do not require a large amount of data transfer (e.g., the mouse, keyboard, and joystick). These devices generally use the bulk and control transfers.

- **12Mbps:** Used for isochronous devices that require a guaranteed level of data transfer and a large amount of bandwidth (e.g., scanners, telephones, speakers, and printers).

IEEE 1394 Bus—FireWire

Windows 98 now supports the IEEE 1394 standard. Because of its extremely high bandwidth, it is sometimes called *FireWire*. It is used to support devices like cameras, videodisc players, and digital camcorders. FireWire is also supported by the new WDM.

Microsoft
✓ Exam
Objective

Install and configure hardware devices in a Microsoft environment and a mixed Microsoft and NetWare environment. Hardware devices include:

- IEEE 1394 FireWire

IEEE 1394 can support up to 63 devices on each bus. You can interconnect busses to support up to 1023 additional busses, each of which can support up to 63 devices. In other words, you can create a network with almost 64,500 devices attached to it. The bus also allows each device to address up to 256 terabytes (TB) of memory. This might seem overwhelming at first, but the topology of IEEE 1394 was designed to be scalable. Every device will have equal access to the bus itself.

IEEE 1394 is still in development and standards have not been reached. Proposals are on the table now that will standardize FireWire over the OpenHCI, SBP-2 (a general-purpose, command transport protocol), power management schemes, and Hot Plug-and-Play interoperability.

IEEE 1394 defines the Nintendo GameBoy connector as its standard connector and socket setup. (See Mom, playing games all the time does pay off in the long run!)

Isochronous and asynchronous data transfer are supported by the IEEE 1394 bus. An interesting attribute of the IEEE 1394 standard is that devices with different data transfer rates can still talk to each other. Two devices will connect at the highest speed that both devices support. IEEE 1394 supports three current transfer rates: S100 (98.3Mbps), S200 (196.6Mbps), and S400 (393.2Mbps). Additional standards with even faster rates are in the works.

Windows 98 Devices

In this section, we will discuss some of the new devices that are supported in Windows 98. This includes support for enlarging your desktop to span multiple monitors, multilink support, infrared technology, power management schemes, and modem installation and configuration.

Let's dive right in and take a look at a technology that has been around for a while in the Unix world and is now currently available in Windows.

Multiple Display Support

A really cool, new feature of Windows 98 is the ability to gain more screen real estate by adding additional monitors and "enlarging" the desktop to cover them. This larger virtual desktop can be spread across as many as nine different monitors.

Microsoft ✓ *Exam* *Objective*

Install and configure hardware devices in a Microsoft environment and a mixed Microsoft and NetWare environment. Hardware devices include:

- Multiple display support

The screen space on each monitor butts up against the screen space displayed by every other monitor. When your mouse moves to the edge of the desktop display on one monitor, it instantly appears at the appropriate location on the next monitor. This provides the appearance of a seamless desktop, as shown in Figure 3.1.

For this to work, the BIOS picks one of the monitors to be the primary display based on the PCI slot order. All other monitors are secondary monitors. The primary monitor has a coordinate system starting with 0,0 for the upper-left corner. The lower-right corner is specified by the screen resolution on the primary monitor. Let's say that the right monitor in Figure 3.1 is the primary monitor with a resolution of 800×600. The monitor on the left would then have an upper-left coordinate of –800,0 and a lower-right coordinate of –1,600.

You are not restricted by the resolution of the primary monitor. For example, if the primary monitor had a resolution of 1024×768 and the secondary monitor had a resolution of 800×600, you would still be able to use multidisplay. The virtual desktop is defined by coordinates of the monitors. It is possible to have some portion of the screen real estate that is not displayed on a monitor, as shown in Figure 3.2. You can still use that screen real estate by moving portions of open windows into it, but you just can't view it unless you change the resolution on your monitor or you adjust the coordinates of the secondary monitors.

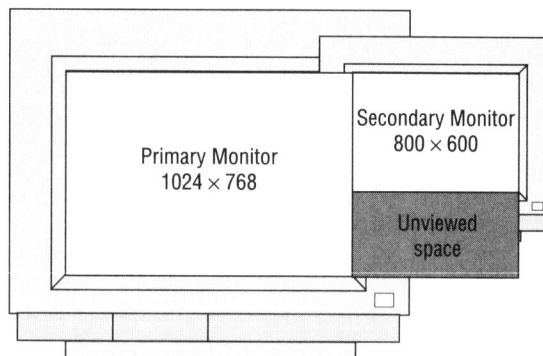

There are a couple of rules regarding the secondary monitor that you must adhere to if you want to take advantage of this new technology:

- It must be a PCI or AGP device.

- It must be able to run in GUI mode or support GUI mode without the use of VGA resources.

- There must be a Windows 98 driver that supports it as a secondary device.

Multilink

Multilink is a new technology that allows you to combine multiple dial-up adapters for a single session. To use multilinking, you must have the PPP Multilink protocol installed on both the client and the server.

Microsoft ✓ *Exam* *Objective*

Install and configure hardware devices in a Microsoft environment and a mixed Microsoft and NetWare environment. Hardware devices include:

- Multilink

In essence, multilink combines multiple physical links and aggregates them into a single "bundle." This increases your bandwidth and, therefore, your throughput. Bundling occurs most often over ISDN channels, but multilinking is also supported for modems or modem/ISDN combinations.

NOTE Multilink supports mixing ISDN and analog modems; however, you should try to use devices that connect at the same speeds.

Installing Multilink

In order to install and use multilink, you must first have at least one dial-up networking connection created. For more information on dial-up networking, see Chapter 15. These are the basic steps that you need to follow in order to install and use multilink:

1. Open My Computer.

2. Double-click Dial-Up Networking.

3. You can make a new connection or edit an existing connection. Once a connection has been created, right-click the connection icon and open the property sheet.

4. The property sheet will open. Select the Multilink tab as shown in Figure 3.3.

FIGURE 3.3

The Multilink tab

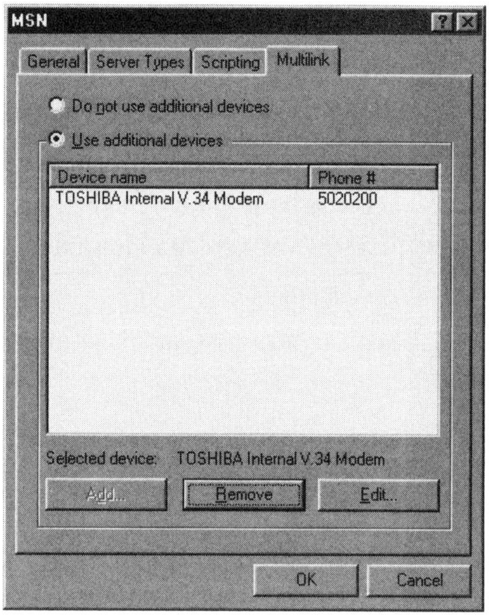

5. Select Use Additional Devices.

6. You will now be able to add additional devices to your bundle to create the multilink.

7. With the Add, Remove, and Edit buttons, you can modify the properties of each of these devices. This includes modifying the phone number that each device will dial.

Using Multilink

Now that you have configured your multilink bundle, it is time to use it. You simply double-click the Dial-Up Networking connection as you would normally for a single device dial-up. The number of the primary device will be called and a connection will be made. Once a connection has been established, Dial-Up Networking will then use the other devices one at a time until all devices have made a connection.

Once you have established your connections, you can view status information about your links by double-clicking the communicating computer's icon displayed in the taskbar. Status information will be displayed about the number of bytes sent and received, the protocols in use, and the additional devices that are in use.

When you select a device (not the primary device), you will be given a Suspend button and a Resume button. The Suspend button allows you to disconnect that device and remove it from the bundled connection. The Resume button, when clicked, will reconnect and become part of the bundle again. A nice feature of these Suspend and Resume buttons is that you can drop and connect without dropping the original connection.

This can be especially useful because you can use your bundled connections to increase your speed. When all of your dial-up adapters are used, you cannot send a fax or make a phone call on one of those lines. Simply suspend the connection, make your call, and then resume when you are finished with that particular line.

Power Management Schemes

Power management schemes allow you to set up energy-saving policies for your computers that support power management. With power management, you have the ability to turn off monitors and power down hard drives after a predetermined amount of time. If you are using a laptop computer, there are options to shut down after a predetermined amount of time and to notify you when your batteries are running low.

Microsoft ✓ *Exam* *Objective*

Install and configure hardware devices in a Microsoft environment and a mixed Microsoft and NetWare environment. Hardware devices include:

- Power management scheme

Power management is a part of Microsoft's SIPC (Simply Interactive Personal Computer) initiative. Microsoft wants computers to be as easy to use as any household appliance. Under SIPC, a user never needs to open up the box to install new hardware. As previously discussed, USB and IEEE 1394 technology means the hardware vendor no longer needs to create a special card to fit in a slot in your computer. That portion of the technology now resides on the device itself and connects to the computer through a standardized cable into a standardized port. Windows 98 uses OnNow power management in much the same way. With the OnNow power management initiative, you will be able to put your PC and all of the peripherals into low power modes when they are not in use. These power policies are called power schemes, and they can be manipulated through the Power Management icon in the Control Panel.

There are three predefined power management schemes and a custom option to create others:

- **Home/Office Desk:** This is ideal for desktop computers and is automatically installed when you install Windows 98.

- **Portable/Laptop:** This scheme is optimized for laptop users. It has additional settings for computers that sometimes run on battery power.

- **Always On:** This scheme is used primarily for personal servers. It is similar to the Home/Office Desk scheme, but the standby timer is not available and the hard disk timer is significantly increased. This is the default power scheme.

- **Custom:** You can create your own schemes. Simply set your timer values and then choose Save As.

If you activate the Power Management icon in the Control Panel, you should see something similar to Figure 3.4. If you are using a laptop computer, you will have the Alarms and Power Meter tabs in addition to the Power Schemes and Advanced tabs.

As you can see, there are options to put the computer in standby mode, turn off the monitor after a predetermined amount of time, and turn off the hard disks after a predetermined amount of time. Because Figure 3.4 was generated from a laptop computer, additional values are specified for shutdown times when the computer is running on battery power.

The Alarms tab allows you to set an alarm (both audio and textual) when the batteries are low or critical (see Figure 3.5).

FIGURE 3.4

Power Schemes
tab of the Power
Management
Properties window

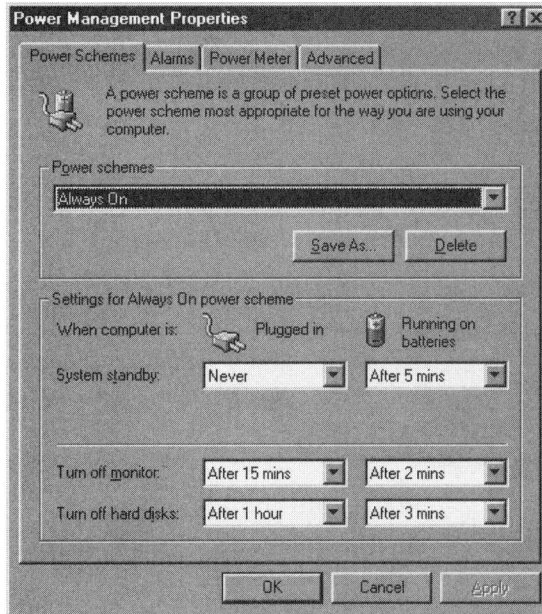

FIGURE 3.4

Power Schemes tab of the Power Management Properties window

FIGURE 3.5

Alarms tab

The Power Meter tab allows you to determine whether or not you want to display a power meter in the system tray of your taskbar and also determine what will it look like.

The Advanced tab is used to determine whether or not you want to show your power meter and if you would like to password protect your computer when it comes out of standby or sleep mode.

Infrared Data Association (IrDA)

Windows 98 supports all types of infrared devices. You can wirelessly connect a laptop to PCs, printers, and other devices like infrared cameras. Infrared supports file-and-printer sharing, as well as other utilities like Direct Cable Connection.

Microsoft ✓ *Exam* *Objective*	**Install and configure hardware devices in a Microsoft environment and a mixed Microsoft and NetWare environment. Hardware devices include:** • Infrared Data Association (IrDA)

Windows 98 supports these devices through the Microsoft Infrared 3.0 drivers. These drivers support the following formats:

- IrDA 1.0 for serial interfaces (SIR)
- IrDA 1.1 for fast infrared devices (FIR)

Using infrared technology, you can gain the following benefits from Windows 98:

- SIR can support transfer speeds of 115Kbps.
- FIR can support transfer speeds of 4Mbps.
- Microsoft Utilities can transfer files over infrared.

Infrared has high transfer rates and is a well understood technology (think of your TV remote control or your keyless entry for your car). This makes it the most widely accepted form of wireless communication currently available to the PC world.

Installing an Infrared Device

If your infrared device is Plug-and-Play–compliant, all you must do is install or attach the device to your computer, power on the device, and then turn on your computer. Windows 98 will recognize the device and automatically begin the installation process. If the device is not recognized, you may have to activate the Infrared icon in the Control Panel (see Figure 3.6). If the Infrared icon does not appear, press F5 to refresh the screen.

FIGURE 3.6

The Infrared icon

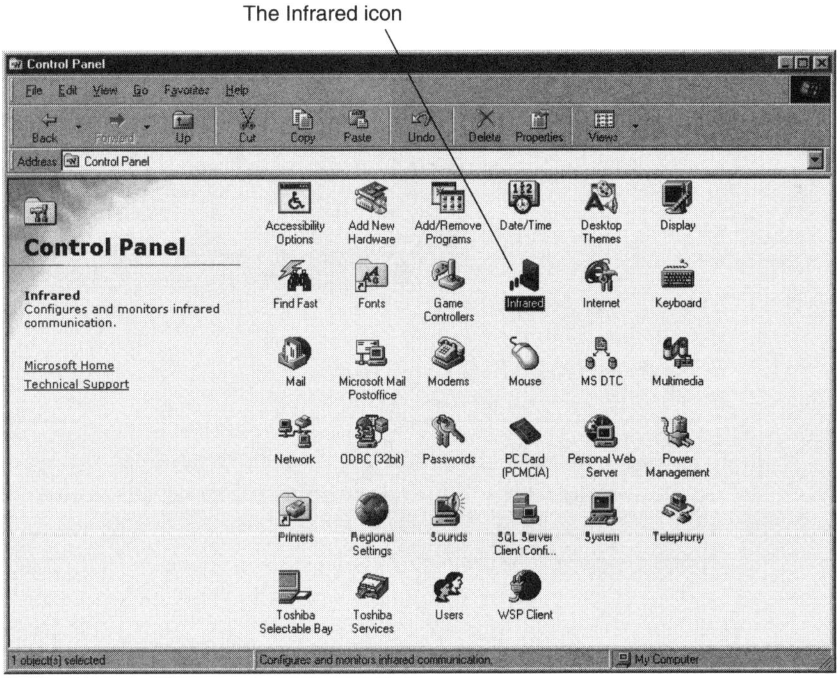

The Infrared icon

You can also use this icon to start the Infrared Monitor applet. This tool allows you to check the status of your infrared devices, enable and disable communication, set connection speeds, turn sounds on and off, and view the infrared device identification information.

If your infrared device is not Plug-and-Play–compliant, then you should use the Add New Hardware Wizard in the Control Panel. Select Infrared Device from the Hardware Types dialog box. For the device section, choose

"Generic Infrared Serial Port or dongle," as shown in Figure 3.7. All of the others are Plug-and-Play–compliant devices. Set any other parameters that are requested.

F I G U R E 3.7

Add Infrared Device
Wizard

Printing with Infrared

To print to an infrared-enabled printer, simply bring your computer within range of the printer. If the printer has been installed, Windows 98 should detect it and install the appropriate drivers. Otherwise, you may need to set up the printer manually as discussed in Chapter 11.

Once the printer is set up and Windows 98 recognizes it, you can choose to print as you would normally. This includes printing from within your applications and dragging-and-dropping a file onto the printer icon.

Transferring Files with Infrared

When you install an infrared device, Windows 98 will add the Infrared Transfer program, which you can use to move files back and forth between two infrared-enabled computers.

The Infrared Transfer program adds an icon to the My Computer screen and the Infrared Recipient menu item in the Send To menu. The Send To menu is activated when you right-click a file.

The first time you use the Infrared Transfer, a folder called "My Received Files" is created, and your transferred files will be placed there. There are a couple of methods you can use to send your files. Here are the steps quickly outlined:

1. Double-click the Infrared Recipient in My Computer.

2. Select an infrared recipient from the list of available recipients.

3. Click Send Files.

4. You will be presented with an Explorer where you can choose the files to send. Make your selections and choose Open.

You can also drag-and-drop files to the Infrared Recipient icon in the My Computer screen. Another method is to right-click a file and select the Send To menu item. You can then choose the Infrared Recipient submenu item to send your files.

If you like oxymorons, you're going to love this one. You can use the Direct Cable Connection program over the "cableless" infrared channel. You must set up a Direct Cable Connection host at the other PC. On the guest PC, you can then use the Direct Cable Connection applet to log in to the host computer. The connection will automatically be made over the infrared link, and you will see the shared folders and printers on the host PC. You can then transfer information as you would over a regular network connection.

The Device Manager

The *Device Manager* provides a graphical representation of devices connected to the system. From here, you can check the properties of different devices to determine whether they are functioning properly. You can also discover what may be wrong with devices that are not working properly. You can configure many devices with their Control Panel applets, but there are many other devices that you must configure using the Device Manager. To access the Device Manager, right-click the My Computer icon on the Desktop and choose Properties, or go to the System/Control Panel applet.

When you start up the Device Manager on a system with no hardware problems and select the View Devices By Type button, it looks something like the dialog box shown in Figure 3.8. All the main hardware devices are listed, each on a single line.

F I G U R E   3.8

The Device Manager

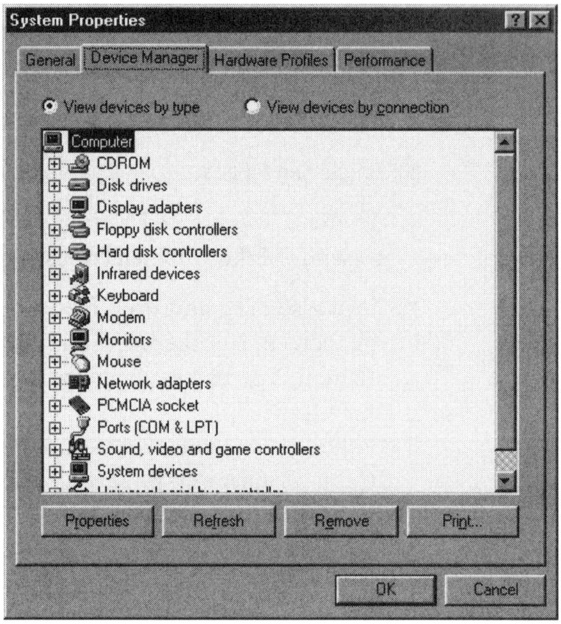

To look at specific devices listed under each main category, click the plus sign (+) to the left of the heading. Each main category heading now lists the individual devices below it. By double-clicking any specific device, or highlighting it and pressing the Enter key, you can see the properties for that device. Figure 3.9 shows an example of the property sheet for a Yamaha OPL3 sound card. You can obtain the following information from a device's property sheet:

- Device type
- Manufacturer
- Hardware version
- Supporting drivers installed
- Installed drivers configured properly
- Resources used by the device, including any conflicts that might be present

F I G U R E   3.9

Properties of a device

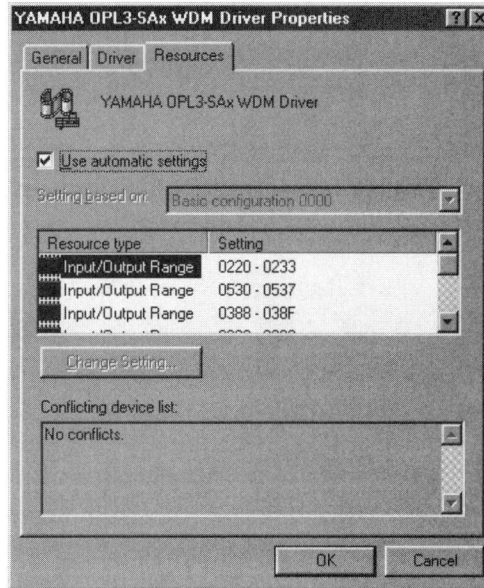

Clicking the View Devices By Connection option on the main Device Manager screen changes the view to show items listed under the device to which they are connected. For example, your CD-ROM will be listed under your sound card if it is using the sound card for its connection.

When you boot your system in Safe mode (press F5 after the "Starting Windows 98" message, or press F8 and choose Safe Mode from the Startup menu), you may see devices listed more than once. This is a fairly common occurrence, but it can cause problems. When you are working in Device Manager after a Safe-mode boot, you should always check for multiple instances of any device and remove any that you find. Even if this is not the cause of the current problem, it may save you further trouble.

Safe mode is a way of booting Windows 98 without the Registry, CONFIG .SYS, AUTOEXEC.BAT, or any protected-mode drivers. In this mode, you can work with system files, Device Manager, or anything else you suspect might be causing problems. See Chapter 2 on installing and configuring Windows 98 for more information about Safe mode and other startup options.

Hardware Profiles

Windows 98 allows you to keep different sets of hardware device settings called *hardware profiles*. For example, on a laptop with a docking station you may have one profile with additional network, video, and SCSI drivers for when you are docked and one profile for when your laptop is operating undocked.

Microsoft
✓ *Exam*
Objective

Create hardware profiles.

Specific device drivers (such as network cards, modems, video adapters, etc.) can be disabled for a particular profile. When a profile is created, the different sets of enabled and disabled devices are stored in the Registry in the Hkey_Local_Machine key.

Hardware profiles are created and managed using Control Panel ➤ System. Once hardware profiles are enabled, you select which profile to use when Windows 98 boots.

The steps for using a hardware profile are:

1. Create a new hardware profile by copying an existing one.

2. Reboot Windows 98 and select the new profile.

3. Disable drivers as desired—your configuration will automatically be saved to the current hardware profile.

4. Reboot Windows 98 and select, modify, and test various hardware profiles.

In Exercise 3.1 we will create and test a hardware profile.

EXERCISE 3.1

Creating Hardware Profiles

1. Go to Control Panel ➤ System.

2. Select the Hardware Profiles tab.

3. Highlight the Original Configuration profile and choose Copy.

4. Enter **No LPT Port** for the name of the new profile. Click OK to save the new hardware profile.

5. Reboot Windows 98 and select the No LPT Port profile.

6. Go to Control Panel ≻ System.

7. Go to the Device Manager tab, open the Ports icon, and highlight the Printer Port.

8. Click on Properties.

9. In the Properties windows, select "Disable in this hardware profile".

10. Select OK to save your settings. Notice that the Printer Port will now have a red X on it. Select Properties again to see that the device has been disabled.

11. Close the System applet.

12. Reboot and select Original Configuration. Your printer port should work.

13. Reboot and select No LPT Port. Your printer port should not work.

14. Reboot and select Original Configuration (you cannot delete the currently selected profile).

15. Go to Control Panel ≻ System.

16. Select the Hardware Profiles tab.

17. Delete the No LPT Port hardware profile. Close the System applet.

Summary

This chapter discussed some of the exciting new technology offered in Windows 98. The Win32 Driver Model (WDM) abstracts your hardware in such a way that the new USB and IEEE 1394 busses can take advantage of Microsoft SIPC.

Essentially, Microsoft wants to create computer software that will allow you to plug in new peripherals using a standard USB or IEEE 1394 connector and do nothing else. Windows 98 will automatically configure the new devices and allow you to begin using them without the need to run a setup program or reboot the system. Another advantage is that you will no longer have to install new cards into your system because the hardware that formerly resided on the card is now part of the device itself. This has advantages for hardware manufacturers as well. They no longer need to create multiple cards that fit into different computing platforms. A single device can now use the standard cables and connectors and be used by any operating system that supports USB or IEEE 1394.

Both USB and IEEE 1394 define a standard cable and connector type. These two new technologies support incredible data transfer rates ranging from 115Kbps to 400Mbps.

Some fantastic new features are included with Windows 98. These include the ability to expand your desktop across multiple displays. You can increase your dial-up networking speeds by bundling your dial-up connections using the PPP Multilink protocols. One multilink feature is the ability to suspend a connection and remove it from the bundle without losing your connection. You can then resume using that connection when you are done working with it from the suspended state.

Power management schemes have been added to Windows 98. These schemes allow you to determine when your monitor and hard disks go into a low-power standby mode. You can use one of several built-in schemes, or you can customize them and create your own scheme. Additional features have been added to the laptop scheme that are useful when you are running on batteries. Windows 98 has utilized forward-thinking in relation to the OnNow power management. In the future, peripheral devices will also be managed by a power policy that you implement from Windows 98.

With infrared technology, you can send output to a printer. You can also take advantage of networking features through your infrared connection. Windows 98 also supports the use of Direct Cable Connection over your infrared link.

Windows 98 can track various configurations of hardware devices in hardware profiles. To create a hardware profile, copy the existing profile to a new profile, reboot Windows 98, select the new profile, and use Device Manager to disable various device drivers for the given situation.

Windows 98 has a lot of new features; these are just a few of them. Enjoy your exploration!

Review Questions

1. Two modems are installed in your computer, and each one uses a separate phone line. You used the Windows NT RAS services to log in to Windows NT using PPP with multilink. While online with Windows NT, you want to send a fax from your computer, but you don't want to lose your connection. You decide to suspend one of your connections to the Windows NT server and use that modem to send your fax. When you are finished faxing, you resume your connection with the multilink. How would you rate this solution?

   A. This is an excellent solution and will work.

   B. This is a good solution, but you will lose your connection to your RAS session on both lines and will have to reinstate both of them.

   C. This is poor solution, but it appears to work.

   D. This is a poor solution and will not work as specified.

2. Your infrared printer is not automatically installing itself when you bring your laptop into range. You decide to manually install your infrared device. You start the Install New Hardware Wizard and choose the "Generic Infrared Serial Port or dongle device". How would you rate this solution?

   A. This is an excellent solution and appears to work.

   B. This is a good solution, but the Generic choice will not work with your printer.

   C. This is a poor solution, but it appears to work.

   D. This is a poor solution and will not work.

3. WDM (Win32 Device Manager) is built into the operating system of Windows 98. The WDM supports which of the following features?

   A. The WDM forces hardware vendors to create a single version of their hardware, but they must write platform-specific minidrivers.

   B. The WDM forces hardware vendors to create a single version of their minidriver software, but they must design platform-specific versions of their hardware.

    C. The WDM allows hardware vendors to create a single card that will fit into the motherboard of any computer.

    D. The WDM allows hardware vendors to create a single version of their hardware and minidriver software which will run on any platform.

4. IEEE 1394 FireWire supports which of the following? Choose all that apply.

    A. Low bandwidth connections

    B. High bandwidth connections

    C. Speeds in excess of 200Mbps

    D. Speeds around 115Kbps

5. Which of the following bus architectures are supported by WDM? Choose all that apply.

    A. PCI

    B. ISA

    C. SCSI

    D. IEEE 1394 FireWire

    E. USB

6. Which of the following support an isochronous connection where you have a guaranteed rate of data transfer? Choose all that apply.

    A. PCI

    B. ISA

    C. SCSI

    D. IEEE 1394 FireWire

    E. USB

7. Windows 98 has been installed on all of your office computers as well as on all of your laptop computers. You want to use power management schemes to reduce energy consumption costs and increase the lifespan of your hardware components. Which of the following are true regarding power management schemes? Choose all that apply.

   A. You can have the monitor and the hard drive turn off automatically after a predetermined amount of time.

   B. You can have either the monitor or the hard drive turn off automatically, but you can't have both of them turn off automatically.

   C. A device on standby can wake up the system if the need arises.

   D. When installed on a laptop computer, Windows 98 offers some additional options regarding battery use.

8. Your laptop computer is currently running the Windows 98 operating system. You want to be able to view information about your system, its resources, and its configuration settings. You decide to use the Device Manager. The Device Manager can be used for which of the following? Choose all that apply.

   A. Determining the devices currently attached to your PC

   B. Determining the resources with which each device is currently configured

   C. Modifying the configuration of your devices

   D. Installing new devices on your PC

9. Multidisplay is an exciting new feature of Windows 98 that allows you to spread a virtual desktop across multiple monitors. Which of the following are true regarding multidisplay? Choose all that apply.

   A. All monitors involved in multidisplay must have the same resolution.

   B. The primary monitor always has an upper-left coordinate of 0,0.

   C. Every secondary display has coordinates based on the primary display.

   D. Every display's coordinates butt up against each other.

10. Windows 98 supports several different bus architectures. In the past, these bus architectures required a hardware vendor to create a specialized card, a special type of socket, and cable to connect to the custom card. New emerging standards allow Windows 98 to take advantage of standard cables and sockets. Which of the following specifies a particular type of cable and socket for use as part of its bus architecture? Choose all that apply.

    A. WDM

    B. IEEE 1394 FireWire

    C. SCSI

    D. USB

    E. PCI

11. Infrared technology allows you to make all kinds of connections to various hardware devices without the need of a cable. Your current Windows 98 laptop is equipped with an infrared port. Which of the following can you do with this infrared-enabled laptop? Choose all that apply.

    A. Print to an infrared printer

    B. Send files to an infrared-enabled computer

    C. Use Direct Cable Connection software to make a network-style connection over infrared

    D. RAS into Windows NT

12. You have a manager who uses a laptop at work and at home. She has a docking station at work with a network card but uses an external modem at home to dial into the network. How would you set up the laptop so that she can use both configurations easily?

    A. Create two hardware profiles. Disable the network card for the work profile and disable the modem for the home profile.

    B. Create two hardware profiles. Delete the network card driver in the home profile and delete the modem driver in the work profile.

C. Create user profiles. Disable the network card driver in the home user profile and disable the modem driver for the work profile.

D. Create two hardware profiles. Disable the network card for the home profile and disable the modem in the work profile.

13. Where are hardware profiles stored?

    A. The Hkey_Local_Machine Registry key

    B. The Hkey_Users Registry key

    C. CONFIG.SYS

    D. The Hkey_Dyn_Data Registry key

CHAPTER

4

The Boot Sequence

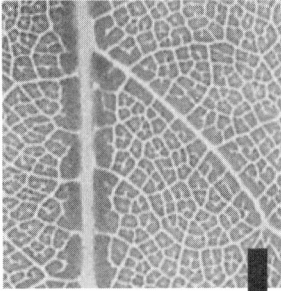

Understanding the boot sequence is essential in troubleshooting and fixing problems with Windows 98. Because many changes or additions you make take effect only at startup, some configuration problems don't appear until you restart Windows 98. Although the Windows 98 boot process is rather long, some very good troubleshooting tools are built into Windows 98 that can help you quickly isolate and solve problems.

In this chapter, you will first examine how Windows 98 boots, and you will take a detailed look at each of the steps. You will then examine how the boot process can be configured and controlled. You will then look at another way to control how Windows 98 starts up—through WIN.COM command-line switches.

After the boot process completes, you may have some devices that did not configure properly. You will finish this chapter by examining the System Information utility. With the System Information utility, you will be able to gather information about your configured devices and make modifications to those configurations.

Windows 98 Boot Process Elements

The Windows 98 boot process takes place in several discrete steps:

- BIOS bootstrap
- Master boot record and boot sector
- Real-mode boot
- Real-mode configuration
- Protected-mode boot

Each of these steps is described in the following sections.

BIOS Bootstrap

The *BIOS bootstrap* occurs right after you power your computer on, but before the actual boot process occurs. The bootstrap phase performs the following tasks:

- Identifies and configures any Plug-and-Play devices. If the system has a Plug-and-Play BIOS, it will look for and test any Plug-and-Play devices installed and assign them DMA channels, IRQs, and any other resources that they require.

- Performs the Power On Self Test (POST). The POST detects and tests memory, ports, and basic devices, such as the keyboard, video adapter, and disk drives. Newer versions on some systems even support CD-ROM drives.

- Locates a bootable partition on the boot drive. The BIOS has a setting for the order in which you want the system to look for the bootable partition. The default setting on most systems is floppy drive, then hard drive, and then CD-ROM (if supported). This order can be changed if you want to check the drives in a different order.

- Loads the Master Boot Record (MBR) and the partition table of the bootable drive, and executes the MBR.

MBR and Boot Sector

After the MBR finds the bootable partition on the hard disk, it passes control to the boot sector in that partition. The partition contains the boot program and a table of disk properties and characteristics. The root directory is located, and IO.SYS is executed. IO.SYS is basically DOS. In Windows 98, it takes over the functions of both IO.SYS and MSDOS.SYS from previous versions of MS-DOS.

WARNING Boot viruses affect the boot process at this point, which may cause Windows 98 and Windows NT to fail to load. Booting off a clean floppy (your emergency boot disk) and running the command FDISK /MBR *may* restore the master boot record and nondestructively eliminate the boot virus.

Real-Mode Boot

Once IO.SYS has been executed, the real-mode boot process begins:

- MSDOS.SYS is checked for boot configuration parameters. Keep in mind that MSDOS.SYS does not perform the same function as in previous versions of DOS. In Windows 98, MSDOS.SYS is a text file in which you can control certain options of the boot process, as explained later in this chapter.

- LOGO.SYS is displayed, if it exists. IO.SYS has a copy of the default Windows 98 image if LOGO.SYS cannot be found. The image can be disabled by pressing the Esc key.

- If DBLSPACE.INI or DRVSPACE.INI is present, DBLSPACE.BIN or DRVSPACE.BIN is loaded, respectively.

- SYSTEM.DAT is checked.

- SYSTEM.DAT is loaded if it is present and valid; otherwise, the backup of SYSTEM.DAT (SYSTEM.DA0) is loaded. After a successful boot, whichever file was loaded updates the other.

- If the system detects that double-buffering is necessary, it is loaded.

- Based on detected hardware, a hardware profile is chosen, or the user is prompted to choose one.

- IO.SYS reads CONFIG.SYS, if it exists, and processes its commands.

- IO.SYS reads AUTOEXEC.BAT, if it exists, and processes its commands.

Real-Mode Configuration

CONFIG.SYS and AUTOEXEC.BAT are not necessary with Windows 98; however, they will be processed by IO.SYS if they are present. If the CONFIG.SYS file does not exist, Windows 98 will automatically load HIMEM.SYS, IFSHLP.SYS, SETVER.EXE, and several environment variables. CONFIG.SYS (if it exists) will override these defaults.

Protected-Mode Boot

The protected-mode boot process proceeds as follows:

- While still in real-mode, WIN.COM is automatically executed after AUTOEXEC.BAT is run. WIN.COM loads VMM32.VXD and any other real-mode virtual device drivers which are referenced in the Registry, WIN.INI, and SYSTEM.INI. Note that Registry device options take precedence over configuration options found in the VMM32.VXD file. If a device is found to be conflicting, then the system will use information in the SYSTEM.INI to override the conflict.

- The processor is switched into protected mode, and the virtual device drivers are initialized and configured at the correct time and in the correct sequence. This is done by reading the hardware tree that was created by a Plug-and-Play BIOS. If there is no hardware tree, Windows 98 will create a new one by enumerating the devices and dynamically loading their drivers.

- The core Windows Kernel, GDI, and User libraries are loaded. WIN.INI is processed and then the shell (Windows Explorer) is loaded along with any network support (if present).

- Any programs in the Start Up group are executed.

- The last step is to run any programs located in the Registry at Hkey_Local_Machine\Software\Microsoft\Windows\CurrentVersion\RunOnce. After an item is successfully run from the RunOnce key, its entry is removed from this key.

Configuring and Controlling the Boot Process

Windows 98 takes care of the boot process for you, and most actions are executed in accordance with their default settings. However, Windows 98 provides some ways for you to control the boot process. The Windows 98 Startup menu offers options for various boot modes. Another way to set boot options is by editing the MSDOS.SYS file. The following sections explain both approaches.

Using the Windows 98 Startup Menu

To start Windows 3.*x*, you entered the WIN command after you booted to MS-DOS. If you had problems with Windows, you could return to a DOS prompt, fix the problem, and restart the system. Even if WIN.COM loaded in AUTOEXEC.BAT, you could bypass it for troubleshooting purposes by remarking it out.

Windows 98 still has WIN.COM but, because Windows loads automatically, you won't need to include it in the AUTOEXEC.BAT file and will rarely use it from the command line. So what do you do if you need to bypass loading the GUI (graphical user interface)? The easiest way to do this is with the Windows 98 Startup menu. This menu has various options for loading Windows, booting directly to a command prompt, or even loading a previous version of MS-DOS.

You can access the Startup menu by pressing the F8 key after the system POST beep signals, or you can hold down the Ctrl key while the system is booting. F8 is supported for backward compatibility.

You can use the MSCONFIG.EXE (System Configuration utility) and the Advanced option to force the Startup menu to appear each time you boot up the system. You may also edit the MSDOS.SYS file manually and add the BootMenu=1 line to it. The Startup menu will look something like this:

```
Microsoft Windows 98 Startup Menu
=================================
     1.  Normal
     2.  Logged (\BOOTLOG.TXT)
     3.  Safe Mode
     4.  Step-by-step confirmation
     5.  Command prompt only
     6.  Safe Mode command prompt only

Enter a choice:   1
```

The first option, Normal, loads Windows in the usual way. The other options are described in the following sections.

Windows 98 also has shortcut keys associated with several Startup menu options. Table 4.1 lists the key combinations you can press after the POST beep.

T A B L E 4.1	**Shortcut Key**	**Startup Menu Equivalent**
Startup Menu Shortcut Keys	F8 or CTRL	Startup menu
	F4	Previous version of MS-DOS (Only available if the BootMulti=1 is set in the MSDOS.SYS file.)
	F5	Safe mode
	Shift+F5	Safe mode command prompt only
	F6	Safe mode with network support
	F8	Step-by-step confirmation

The Logged (BOOTLOG.TXT) Option

BOOTLOG.TXT is a text file that can be created by Windows 98 during the boot process. This file records each of the devices and drivers, including all of the protected-mode (virtual) drivers, as the system attempts to load it, and whether the loading was a success or failure. BOOTLOG.TXT is automatically created during the first boot sequence following a successful setup. After that, Windows 98 creates this file when you choose the Logged option from the Startup menu.

You can use the information in the BOOTLOG.TXT file to diagnose driver loading failures, determine whether or not the driver was found, and learn about driver initialization failures. A typical BOOTLOG.TXT file may look something like the one shown in Figure 4.1.

The Safe Mode Option

Safe mode is a way of booting Windows 98 with the minimal set of drivers needed to function. Bypassing the normal loading of hardware and software is useful for troubleshooting. You can use the Device Manager or the System Conflict manager (later in this chapter) to troubleshoot suspected hardware problems and conflicts. You can also edit the *.INI files, or any other files, that may be causing problems.

F I G U R E 4.1

A BOOTLOG.TXT file

```
Bootlog.txt - Notepad
File  Edit  Search  Help
[0010F465] Loading Device = C:\WINDOWS\HIMEM.SYS
[0010F466] LoadSuccess   = C:\WINDOWS\HIMEM.SYS
[0010F466] Loading Device = C:\WINDOWS\EMM386.EXE
[0010F491] LoadSuccess   = C:\WINDOWS\EMM386.EXE
[0010F491] Loading Device = C:\WINDOWS\DBLBUFF.SYS
[0010F48A] LoadSuccess   = C:\WINDOWS\DBLBUFF.SYS
[0010F48A] Loading Device = C:\WINDOWS\PANNING.SYS
[0010F48A] LoadSuccess   = C:\WINDOWS\PANNING.SYS
[0010F48A] Loading Device = C:\WINDOWS\IFSHLP.SYS
[0010F48A] LoadSuccess   = C:\WINDOWS\IFSHLP.SYS
[0010F4E7] Loading Vxd = VMM
[0010F4E7] LoadSuccess = VMM
[0010F4E7] Loading Vxd = C:\WINDOWS\SMARTDRV.EXE
[0010F4E5] LoadSuccess = C:\WINDOWS\SMARTDRV.EXE
[0010F4E5] Loading Vxd = JAVASUP.UXD
[0010F4E5] LoadSuccess = JAVASUP.UXD
[0010F4E5] Loading Vxd = CONFIGMG
[0010F4E6] LoadSuccess = CONFIGMG
[0010F4E6] Loading Vxd = VSHARE
[0010F4E6] LoadSuccess = VSHARE
[0010F4E6] Loading Vxd = VWIN32
[0010F4E6] LoadSuccess = VWIN32
[0010F4E6] Loading Vxd = VFBACKUP
[0010F4E6] LoadSuccess = VFBACKUP
[0010F4E6] Loading Vxd = VCOMM
[0010F4E6] LoadSuccess = VCOMM
[0010F4E6] Loading Vxd = COMBUFF
[0010F4E6] LoadSuccess = COMBUFF
[0010F4E6] Loading Vxd = C:\WINDOWS\system\VMM32\IFSMGR.UXD
[0010F4E5] LoadSuccess = C:\WINDOWS\system\VMM32\IFSMGR.UXD
[0010F4E5] Loading Vxd = C:\WINDOWS\system\VMM32\IOS.UXD
[0010F4E5] LoadSuccess = C:\WINDOWS\system\VMM32\IOS.UXD
[0010F4E5] Loading Vxd = SPOOLER
```

> **NOTE**
> Windows 98 automatically boots to Safe mode if there is a drive failure or conflict, or if an application requests it.

When you choose to boot in Safe mode from the Windows 98 Startup menu, several things happen:

- Windows does not load the Registry, CONFIG.SYS file, or AUTOEXEC .BAT file. Windows also ignores most of the commands in the SYSTEM.INI and WIN.INI files.

- The HIMEM.SYS (high memory manager) and IFSHLP.SYS (install-able file system driver) files are loaded.

- Win /d:m, the WIN.COM switch for starting Windows 98 in Safe mode, is executed. (WIN.COM switches are discussed later in this chapter.)

When you boot Windows 98 in Safe mode, you will see a command line under the Startup menu reminding you that you are running in Safe mode. When you reach the Windows Desktop, you are again reminded by the words "Safe mode" appearing in each corner of the screen, as shown in Figure 4.2.

FIGURE 4.2

Windows 98 reminds you that it is running in Safe mode.

While Windows 98 is in Safe mode, you can remove hardware devices by using the Device Manager, but you cannot add hardware. This can be useful if you think a certain device is causing problems during bootup. Boot to Safe mode, remove the device, and reboot the system. This step can be repeated as many times as necessary to find the hardware causing the problem.

The Step-by-Step Confirmation Option

This option allows you see each item loaded in CONFIG.SYS and AUTOEXEC.BAT and to decide whether or not each command is executed. This is a very valuable tool for troubleshooting when you suspect that a command or driver is responsible for boot problems. By stepping through these commands, you can see which items execute properly, and which, if any, are not loading properly. The success or failure of each command will help you determine the command or driver that is not working correctly. As you step through each command, you will see:

```
[Enter=Y, ESC=N]?
```

To run the command or load the driver, press Enter or **Y**. To bypass the command or driver, press Esc or **N**.

In Exercise 4.1, you will select the Step-by-Step boot option so you can see Windows 98 load the various support files it needs to operate.

EXERCISE 4.1

Starting Windows 98 with Step-by-Step Confirmation

1. Restart Windows 98.

2. When you hear the POST beep (this only occurs if you powered off and powered on the system), or when the screen goes black after choosing Start ➤ Shutdown ➤ Restart, hold the Ctrl key down until the Windows 98 Startup menu appears.

3. Choose the Step-by-Step Confirmation option from the Startup menu.

4. At each prompt, press Enter or **Y** to run the command. This is the same as doing a normal boot. After Windows 98 has gone through all the steps and booted, you should notice no differences from when you boot normally.

The Command Prompt Only Option

This option boots you to the Windows 98 equivalent of a DOS prompt. The Windows 98 GUI is not loaded, and neither are protected-mode drivers. CONFIG.SYS and AUTOEXEC.BAT, if they are present, are executed.

The Command Prompt Only option boots quickly and can be useful if you need to edit a file before going into Windows or for running programs that will only run in DOS mode. You can also use this option to take advantage of the command-line switches available with WIN.COM, which are discussed later in this chapter. You can go to Windows from the command prompt by typing **WIN**.

The Safe Mode Command Prompt Only Option

This option is the same as Safe mode except that the GUI is not loaded. CONFIG.SYS and AUTOEXEC.BAT are bypassed, as is the Registry and any protected-mode drivers. This option can be useful if you need to get to a command prompt quickly and don't need to have drivers and devices loaded.

Previous Version of MS-DOS

This option, which loads a previous version of DOS if it is present on the system, is used for dual-booting. As explained in Chapter 2, you can boot to a previous operating system only under the following conditions:

- A previous version of DOS must be installed on the system.

- If you want to be able to run a previous version of Windows, it must be installed in a different directory from where Windows 98 resides.

- The option BootMulti=1 must be present in the MSDOS.SYS file.

WARNING
If you have formatted any of your hard disk partitions using the FAT32 file system, you will not be able to use those partitions with any operating system other than Windows 98.

If all of these conditions are met, you can access the previous version of MS-DOS by choosing Previous Version of MS-DOS from the Startup menu (or by pressing the F4 shortcut key). Several things happen in the system when this option is chosen:

- The Windows 98 versions of your AUTOEXEC.BAT and CONFIG.SYS are renamed. The old MS-DOS files are renamed back to CONFIG .SYS and AUTOEXEC.BAT. (This operation will reverse when you return to using Windows 98.)

- The Registry is bypassed.

Modifying the MSDOS.SYS File

With earlier versions of Windows, DOS used three core system files in the initial bootstrap process. IO.SYS provided the system initialization code and then called MSDOS.SYS, which loaded basic system drivers, determined equipment status, and performed other preliminary functions. COMMAND.COM was then loaded, which added functionality to the user interface.

With Windows 95 and now Windows 98, MSDOS.SYS performs a very different function. The tasks handled by MSDOS.SYS in previous versions of DOS have been transferred to IO.SYS, and MSDOS.SYS is now a text file that controls certain Windows 98 startup options, similar to the Windows NT BOOT.INI file. You can modify these parameters by adding, changing, or removing lines from MSDOS.SYS. You can edit this file manually or through the System Information utility.

MSDOS.SYS is a read-only, hidden, system file. Before you can make any changes, you need to change the attributes of the file. This can be done from the File Properties dialog box in Windows, or by using the ATTRIB command from a command prompt. To get to the Windows 98 File Properties dialog box, navigate to the file you want to edit, right-click it, and choose Properties. You can then clear the checkboxes for Hidden and Read Only. Be sure to change the attributes of MSDOS.SYS back to Read Only after you have finished editing. This will keep the file from being changed or deleted accidentally.

A typical MSDOS.SYS file will look something like the one shown in Figure 4.3.

FIGURE 4.3 An MSDOS.SYS file

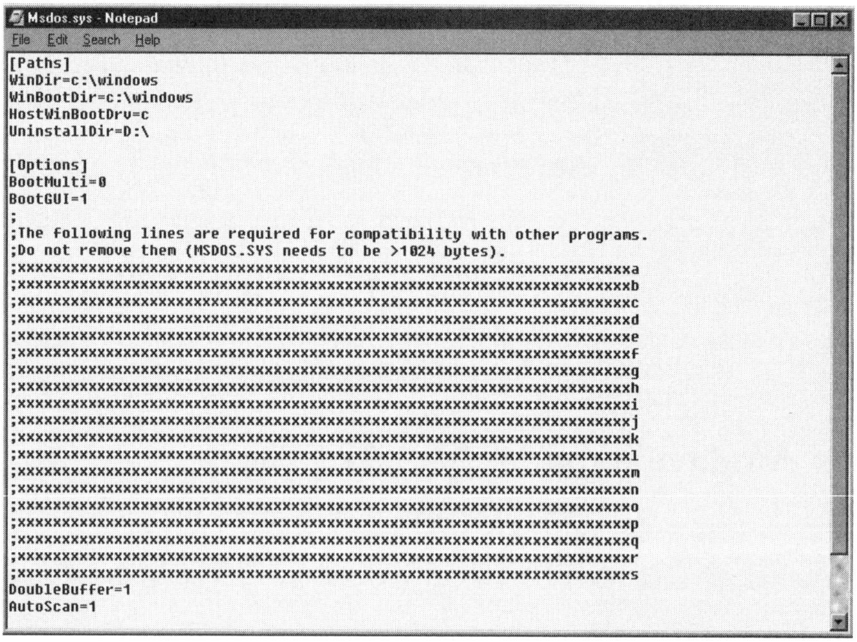


```
[Paths]
WinDir=c:\windows
WinBootDir=c:\windows
HostWinBootDrv=c
UninstallDir=D:\

[Options]
BootMulti=0
BootGUI=1
;
;The following lines are required for compatibility with other programs.
;Do not remove them (MSDOS.SYS needs to be >1024 bytes).
;xxxxxxxxxxxxxxxxxxxxxxxxxxxxxxxxxxxxxxxxxxxxxxxxxxxxxxxxxxxxxxxxxxxxxxa
;xxxxxxxxxxxxxxxxxxxxxxxxxxxxxxxxxxxxxxxxxxxxxxxxxxxxxxxxxxxxxxxxxxxxxxb
;xxxxxxxxxxxxxxxxxxxxxxxxxxxxxxxxxxxxxxxxxxxxxxxxxxxxxxxxxxxxxxxxxxxxxxc
;xxxxxxxxxxxxxxxxxxxxxxxxxxxxxxxxxxxxxxxxxxxxxxxxxxxxxxxxxxxxxxxxxxxxxxd
;xxxxxxxxxxxxxxxxxxxxxxxxxxxxxxxxxxxxxxxxxxxxxxxxxxxxxxxxxxxxxxxxxxxxxxe
;xxxxxxxxxxxxxxxxxxxxxxxxxxxxxxxxxxxxxxxxxxxxxxxxxxxxxxxxxxxxxxxxxxxxxxf
;xxxxxxxxxxxxxxxxxxxxxxxxxxxxxxxxxxxxxxxxxxxxxxxxxxxxxxxxxxxxxxxxxxxxxxg
;xxxxxxxxxxxxxxxxxxxxxxxxxxxxxxxxxxxxxxxxxxxxxxxxxxxxxxxxxxxxxxxxxxxxxxh
;xxxxxxxxxxxxxxxxxxxxxxxxxxxxxxxxxxxxxxxxxxxxxxxxxxxxxxxxxxxxxxxxxxxxxxi
;xxxxxxxxxxxxxxxxxxxxxxxxxxxxxxxxxxxxxxxxxxxxxxxxxxxxxxxxxxxxxxxxxxxxxxj
;xxxxxxxxxxxxxxxxxxxxxxxxxxxxxxxxxxxxxxxxxxxxxxxxxxxxxxxxxxxxxxxxxxxxxxk
;xxxxxxxxxxxxxxxxxxxxxxxxxxxxxxxxxxxxxxxxxxxxxxxxxxxxxxxxxxxxxxxxxxxxxxl
;xxxxxxxxxxxxxxxxxxxxxxxxxxxxxxxxxxxxxxxxxxxxxxxxxxxxxxxxxxxxxxxxxxxxxxm
;xxxxxxxxxxxxxxxxxxxxxxxxxxxxxxxxxxxxxxxxxxxxxxxxxxxxxxxxxxxxxxxxxxxxxxn
;xxxxxxxxxxxxxxxxxxxxxxxxxxxxxxxxxxxxxxxxxxxxxxxxxxxxxxxxxxxxxxxxxxxxxxo
;xxxxxxxxxxxxxxxxxxxxxxxxxxxxxxxxxxxxxxxxxxxxxxxxxxxxxxxxxxxxxxxxxxxxxxp
;xxxxxxxxxxxxxxxxxxxxxxxxxxxxxxxxxxxxxxxxxxxxxxxxxxxxxxxxxxxxxxxxxxxxxxq
;xxxxxxxxxxxxxxxxxxxxxxxxxxxxxxxxxxxxxxxxxxxxxxxxxxxxxxxxxxxxxxxxxxxxxxr
;xxxxxxxxxxxxxxxxxxxxxxxxxxxxxxxxxxxxxxxxxxxxxxxxxxxxxxxxxxxxxxxxxxxxxxs
DoubleBuffer=1
AutoScan=1
```

WARNING

Incorrect settings in MSDOS.SYS can prevent the system from booting properly. MSDOS.SYS must be at least 1024 bytes for backward compatibility. This is why you see all of the *x*'s. There is no limit to how big the file can be—only how small. Double-check your settings before saving and rebooting the system.

Table 4.2 shows the command options that can be entered into MSDOS.SYS and their default values.

T A B L E 4.2 MSDOS.SYS File Commands	**Command**	**Description**
	[Paths] section	
	HostWinBootDrv=	Defines the root directory of the boot drive, usually C.
	WinBootDir=	Specifies the location of the Windows 98 startup files, usually C:\Windows. This location is defined during setup.
	[Options] section	
	AutoScan=	Tells Windows 98 whether or not to run ScanDisk after an improper shutdown. The possible values are 1 (default), which notifies the user before running Scan-Disk; 2, which runs ScanDisk without notifying the user; and 0, which does not run ScanDisk.
	BootDelay=	Specifies the startup delay after "Starting Windows 98" is displayed, in *x* seconds. The default is 2. This delay is to allow the user time to press the F8 key to display the Setup menu (or any of the shortcut keys) before the boot continues. BootKeys=0 disables this delay.
	BootKeys=	Enables (1) or disables (0) the startup function keys (F8, F5, etc.). The default is 1 (enabled). When set to 0 (disabled), the BootDelay setting is also ignored. Disabling the startup function keys can provide tighter system security by not allowing users to bypass the normal boot process.

T A B L E 4.2 (cont.) MSDOS.SYS File Commands	**Command**	**Description**
	BootFailSafe=	Enables (1) or disables (0) starting the system automatically in Safe mode. The default is 0 (disabled).
	BootGUI=	Enables (1) or disables (0) starting the system automatically in the Windows 98 GUI. The default is 1 (enabled). A 0 allows booting to a command prompt with all drivers and the Registry loaded. Typing **WIN** at this command prompt takes you to the GUI.
	BootMenu=	Enables (1) or disables (0) automatically displaying the Startup menu without the user pressing F8. The default is 0 (disabled).
	BootMenuDefault=	Specifies the default option on the Startup menu when it is displayed. The default is 1, for a normal start.
	BootMenuDelay=	Specifies how long to display the Startup menu before executing the default menu item, in x seconds. The default is 30 seconds.
	BootMulti=	Enables (1) or disables (0) dual-boot capabilities if a previous version of MS-DOS is loaded on the system. The default is 0 (disabled). A 1 allows booting to the previous version by pressing F4 or choosing Previous Version of MS-DOS from the Startup menu.
	BootWarn=	Enables (1) or disables (0) the prompt for a Safe mode startup after a failed boot attempt or a corrupt Registry is found. The default is 1 (enabled).
	BootWin=	Enables (1) or disables (0) Windows 98 as the default operating system on bootup. The default is 1 (enabled). A 0 boots to a previous version of MS-DOS by default.
	DoubleBuffer=	Specifies loading a double-buffering driver for SCSI controllers. The possible values are 0, for disabled (default); 1, which allows for double-buffering if the SCSI controller requires it; or 2, which forces double-buffering.

TABLE 4.2 (cont.)	Command	Description
MSDOS.SYS File Commands	DrvSpace=	Enables (1) or disables (0) loading DRVSPACE.BIN automatically. The default is 1 (enabled).
	LoadTop=	Enables (1) or disables (0) COMMAND.COM or DRVS-PACE.BIN loading at the top of conventional (640KB) memory. The default is 1 (enabled). This should be set to 0 (disabled) if you are using software that uses specific memory settings.
	Logo=	Enables (1) or disables (0) displaying the animated startup screen. The default is 1 (enabled). This may be set to 0 (disabled) to accommodate certain third-party memory managers, or if you prefer to see what is loading and any error messages during the boot process. Pressing the Esc key when the logo screen appears will also do this on a less permanent basis.
	Network=	Allows you to boot in Safe mode with network support if network software is installed. On systems with network software installed, the default is 1 (enabled). The default should be 0 (disabled) on systems without network software installed.

Starting Windows 98 with Switches

Windows 98 has several command-line switches that can be used with WIN.COM to troubleshoot problems during the boot process. For example, if your problem is caused by memory address conflicts, you can use the switch win /d:x to prevent Windows 98 from using any of the expanded memory area. This is equivalent to the SYSTEM.INI file setting EMMExclude=A000-FFFF.

The command WIN /*switch* can be put into the AUTOEXEC.BAT file, and Windows 98 will load with the switches that are present.

The syntax is:

```
win /?
```

or

```
win /d:[f] [m] [s] [v] [x]
```

These options are described in Table 4.3.

T A B L E 4.3 WIN.COM switches	**Option**	**Action Taken**
	/?	Displays a list of available switches.
	/d:f	Disables 32-bit disk access. This option is useful if you believe that the hard disk may be having problems or if Windows 98 stalls during the boot process.
	/d:m	Starts Windows 98 in Safe mode.
	/d:n	Starts Windows 98 in the Safe mode with networking. This is automatically enabled during Safe startup by pressing function key F6.
	/d:s	Disables Windows 98 from using the ROM address space between F000:0000 and 1024K for a break point.
	/d:v	Tells the ROM routine to handle interrupts from the hard disk controller.
	/d:x	Disables Windows from scanning the entire adapter area when looking for used space; equivalent to the SYSTEM.INI setting EMMExclude=A000-FFFF. This may be helpful in troubleshooting upper-memory conflicts.

System Configuration Utility

The System Configuration utility (MSCONFIG.EXE) is used to automate many of the troubleshooting steps that are used to diagnose and fix Windows 98 configuration problems. One of the best features of this utility is the ability to use point-and-click methods to make changes to your configurations. This can significantly reduce the number of errors because you no longer use the Notepad or the SYSEDIT.EXE utilities to modify your system configuration.

Microsoft ✓ *Exam* *Objective*

Diagnose and resolve boot process failures. Tasks include:

- Editing configuration files by using System Configuration utility.

The System Configuration utility can also create backups of your system files before you start troubleshooting. This way you can always undo the changes that you make during the troubleshooting session.

Exercise 4.2 will walk you through the process of using the System Configuration utility.

EXERCISE 4.2

The System Configuration Utility

1. Start the utility. You can do this in two ways. Method one: Click Start ➢ Run. In the Run dialog box, type **MSCONFIG.EXE** and then click OK. Method two: Click Start ➢ Programs ➢ Accessories ➢ System Tools ➢ System Information.

2. This starts the System Information utility as indicated. Within the utility, click Tools ➤ System Configuration Utility. You should get a screen similar to the one shown here.

3. Before you begin making changes, you should back up your current settings. Click the Create Backup button and make a backup of your configuration.

4. You can now make modifications to your startup. Click the different tabs to see what options are available to you for troubleshooting.

5. When you are finished, click the Restore Backup button on the General tab and restore your previous configuration.

6. Close the System Configuration utility.

Version Conflict Manager

When you install Windows 98, older versions of your software files are detected by the installation process and are upgraded to newer versions. The old versions are backed up and saved on your hard drive. Once Windows 98 finishes its installation, you may find that some of your devices don't work properly. The newer versions of the software may conflict with your devices or software. You can go back to the older versions of your device drivers using the Version Conflict Manager.

Microsoft ✓ *Exam Objective*

Diagnose and resolve installation failures. Tasks include:

- Resolve file and driver version conflicts by using Version Conflict Manager and the System Information utility.

The Version Conflict Manager will list all of your backup files, the files that are currently in use, and both sets of file version numbers. Exercise 4.3 will walk you through the process of using the Version Conflict Manager.

EXERCISE 4.3

The Version Conflict Manager

1. Start the utility. Click Start ➤ Programs ➤ Accessories ➤ System Tools ➤ System Information.

2. This starts the System Information utility again. Within the utility, click Tools ➤ Version Conflict Manager. You should get a screen similar to the one shown here:

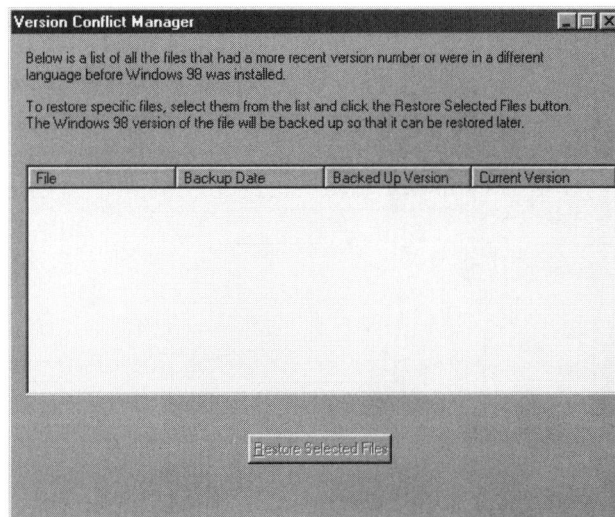

EXERCISE 4.3 (CONTINUED)

3. If there are old files, they will be listed here. In the graphic, Windows 98 was installed on a fresh new system and, therefore, no older files are listed. If files were available, you would only need to select the files and click Restore Selected Files. This would back up your current version of the files and then replace the current version with the old version.

4. Close the Version Conflict Manager.

5. Close the System Information utility.

Summary

Understanding the boot sequence is essential to troubleshooting and fixing problems with Windows 98. In this chapter, you learned about the steps in the Windows 98 boot process, which include BIOS bootstrap, master boot record and boot sector, real-mode boot, real-mode configuration, and protected-mode boot. You also reviewed the two main ways that you can control the boot process: through the Windows 98 Startup menu (press F8 or hold down the Ctrl key after the POST beep) or by editing the MSDOS.SYS file.

You studied the command-line switches that can be used with WIN.COM and can be helpful in tracking down problems during the boot process.

You concluded this chapter by looking at two utilities that can be used to troubleshoot your system. With the System Configuration utility, you can modify the way the boot process runs and what data will be made available to the boot process. You also worked with the Version Conflict utility, which allows you to manage different versions of your software components.

Review Questions

1. What is the first step in the Windows 98 boot process?

   A. BIOS bootstrap phase

   B. Master boot record and boot sector phase

   C. Real-mode boot phase

   D. Protected-mode boot phase

2. During what step of the boot process is VMM32.VXD loaded?

   A. BIOS bootstrap phase

   B. Master boot record and boot sector phase

   C. Real-mode boot phase

   D. Protected-mode boot phase

3. Your local PC has been upgraded from Windows 95 to Windows 98. You would like to configure changes to your boot process. Which of the following methods will allow you to configure the way in which Windows 98 boots? Choose three.

   A. Using the Startup menu

   B. Editing BOOT.SYS

   C. Editing IO.SYS

   D. Editing MSDOS.SYS

   E. Using the System Configuration utility

4. You have recently upgraded your Windows 3.*x* computer to Windows 98. When you were using Windows 3.*x*, you had no problems with your old two-speed CD-ROM player. When you boot to Windows 98, the player doesn't seem to work properly. Because you are using real-mode drivers to work with your CD-ROM, which Startup menu option should you choose to see which real-mode driver(s) might be giving you trouble?

   A. Previous Version of DOS

   B. Safe Mode with Network Support

   C. Safe Mode

   D. Step-by-Step Confirmation

5. After the real-mode boot sequence occurs, Windows 98 begins its protected-mode boot phase. You want to determine which virtual device drivers and 32-bit protected mode drivers are loaded during the startup process. Some of these drivers appear to be giving you problems, but you are not sure which ones. What Startup menu option should you choose to see which protected-mode driver(s) might be giving you trouble?

   A. Logged (to create BOOTLOG.TXT)

   B. Step-by-Step Confirmation

   C. Command Prompt Only

   D. Previous Version of DOS

6. Your Windows 98 machine seems to be having all kinds of problems during the boot phase and won't start. You have recently updated several drivers on your system and are confident that these new drivers are causing the problems. You decide to do a Safe-mode boot of Windows 98 so that you can actually get into Windows 98 and make the appropriate changes. During a Safe-mode boot, which of the following drivers are loaded? Choose all that apply.

   A. Mouse driver

   B. Keyboard driver

   C. Standard VGA device driver

   D. Network drivers

7. Windows 98 supplies you with additional startup switches when you run the WIN.COM program. You can't remember what these switches do. What can you use to find out which switches are available with WIN.COM?

A. `Win /?`

B. `Win /help`

C. `Win /switches`

D. `Help /Win`

8. Windows 98 has been installed on your desktop PC. Since its installation, you have installed new network drivers and new sound card drivers. Windows 98 recognizes these new drivers and allows them to be installed. A new feature of Windows 98 automatically backs up the old drivers in case you want to use them again. Which of the following utilities will allow you to specify which version of a driver (the original or a newer one that has been installed) is to be used?

A. System Information utility

B. System Configuration utility

C. Version Conflict Manager

D. MSDOS.INI

9. You can alter the boot sequence on your Windows 98 machine by making modifications to the MSDOS.SYS file, the SYSTEM.INI file, the Registry, and the WIN.INI files. You can use the Notepad program and the Regedit programs to make these modification to each file, one at a time. Which of the following Windows 98 utilities will allow you to specify which values are processed during the boot sequence from a single program?

A. System Information utility

B. System Configuration utility

C. Version Conflict Manager

D. MSDOS.INI

CHAPTER

5

The Registry

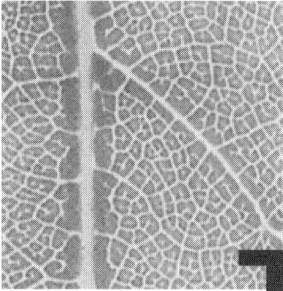

The Registry is a central database of settings and configurations that Windows 98 uses to hold both hardware configurations and software settings. Windows 98 introduced the Registry as a way of bringing the chaos of INI files and the settings they contain into control. The Registry also overcomes some of the limitations of the INI files of previous Windows versions.

Most users will seldom, if ever, need to worry about the Registry, let alone edit it directly. As an administrator or technical support professional, you will find that understanding and being able to troubleshoot and edit the Registry is vital to your success as a "miracle worker."

The Registry is used by almost every aspect of Windows 98:

- **Hardware:** Stores Plug-and-Play data

- **Applications:** Store settings, paths, and DLL information

- **Device drivers:** Store settings, versions, and filenames

- **Operating system:** Tracks installed software, drivers, settings, and associations

Although INI files worked well in the past, their limitations quickly became evident. INI files are important to understand, not only because the Registry solves most, if not all, of the limitations of INI files, but also because Windows 98 still supports INI files for backward compatibility.

This chapter begins with a review of INI files, and then moves on to Registry-related topics: using the Registry Editor program, Registry components, backing up and restoring the Registry, modifying the Registry, and troubleshooting Registry problems.

Understanding INI Files

Both the operating system and applications previously stored their information in the SYSTEM.INI file, the WINDOWS.INI file, or any other INI file they chose. Types of information stored in INI files included paths, DLLs and their paths and versions, settings that the user had saved, and various drivers and their configurations. Finding and changing values in the INI files was somewhat difficult, if not impossible. However, users and administrators quickly found that editing the INI files manually was not only possible, but sometimes it was the only way a problem could be fixed or advanced functionality could be addressed.

INI Files Limitations

For simple purposes, the INI files were adequate, but the limitations of INI files soon became apparent when more than one user wanted to use a computer. INI files could hold only a single value for any variable, which meant that every user on a particular system shared the same settings. In order for users to share a computer and utilize different settings, elaborate batch files were necessary. These batch files copied an individual's version of the INI files into the Window's directory before that user loaded Windows.

Also, INI files did not provide a built-in way of allowing administrators to troubleshoot and edit them remotely. Administrators would almost always need to physically visit a computer to diagnose and fix problems with INI files and settings. INI files were limited to 64KB in size, which was usually adequate for the common user. Users who installed a lot of software might find problems later, however, because they couldn't add any more entries to their INI files.

One of the most important limitations that administrators faced daily was the lack of standards for INI files. Software companies pretty much did their own thing. INI files were never guaranteed to be consistent, which meant that wise users backed up their INI files before attempting to edit them.

INI Files under Windows 98

INI files are still used by, and acceptable to, Windows 98 for compatibility reasons. This is because 16-bit programs may not know to save their settings in the Registry.

The SYSTEM.INI and WIN.INI files are still present in Windows 98, and settings in those files can affect the way Windows 98 behaves. If Windows 98 is installed on top of an older version of Windows 3.*x*, most settings from the SYSTEM.INI, WIN.INI, CONTROL.INI, and PROGMAN.INI files migrate to the Registry. Some settings, however, are left in the SYSTEM.INI and WIN.INI files for backward compatibility.

Viewing and Editing INI Files

You can see and edit the old INI files by running the System Configuration Editor (Sysedit), shown in Figure 5.1. Exercise 5.1 shows the steps for viewing and editing the INI files. You will add a line to WIN.INI that will start Solitaire when Windows 98 boots.

FIGURE 5.1

Using Sysedit to view and edit INI files

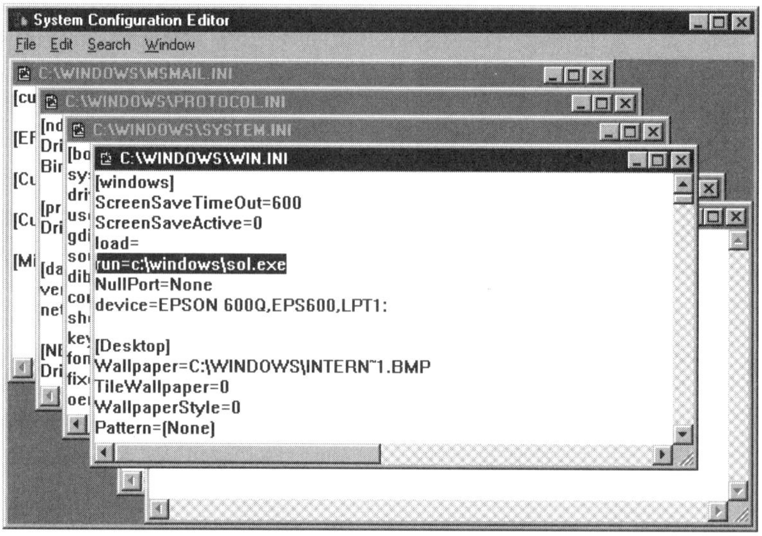

EXERCISE 5.1

Examining INI Files with Sysedit

1. Select Start ➢ Run to open the Run dialog box.

2. Type **SYSEDIT** and click OK. Your INI files and the AUTOEXEC.BAT and CONFIG.SYS files will open (see Figure 5.1).

3. Make the WIN.INI window active.

4. Look for a RUN command.

   - If there already is a RUN command, add a space to the current command and add the path to the Solitaire program, such as **C:\Windows\Sol**.

   - If there are no RUN entries, add **Run=** and the path to the Solitaire program, such as **Run=C:\Windows\Sol** (as shown in Figure 5.1).

5. Close the System Configuration Editor, saving WIN.INI when prompted.

6. Reboot and see if Solitaire loads.

7. After you get Solitaire to load automatically, you will probably want to return to the System Configuration Editor and remove the RUN command.

Using the Registry Editor

Normally, the Registry works in the background, tracking configurations and settings that the user makes. Occasionally, you may need to look at the Registry and possibly edit it directly, in order to provide advanced functionality and customization of Windows 98. The Registry Editor (Regedit) is the program used to examine and edit the Registry.

By default, the Registry Editor does not appear on either the Desktop or anywhere in the Start menu.

After you start the Registry Editor (REGEDIT.EXE), you will see the entire Registry opened by default—all six keys will appear. You can search the Registry for keys, text strings, or numeric data. If you know what key or value you are looking for, the Find feature of the Registry Editor is invaluable. As you can see in Figure 5.2, the Registry Editor is made up of the menu bar; the left pane, which shows what section or subkey of the Registry you are looking at; the right pane, which shows the contents of the section or subkey (it will be blank until you open a key by clicking on the + symbol); and the status bar, which tells you what part of the Registry you are looking at. Follow the steps in Exercise 5.2 to start the Registry Editor and find a value.

F I G U R E   5.2

The Registry Editor

EXERCISE 5.2

Finding Registry Values with Regedit

1. Select Start ➤ Run to open the Run dialog box.

2. Type **Regedit** and click OK. The Registry Editor will open, and the six keys will be visible (see Figure 5.2).

3. Select Edit ➤ Find to get to the Find submenu.

4. Type in the key or value you are looking for (try **background**).

5. It may take a few seconds, but the Registry Editor should find the key and display its associated value.

WARNING Although the Registry Editor is easy to use, the main drawback to using it is that it doesn't check any changes you make for their effect on Windows 98 or your applications. It is all too easy to change or delete something vital and not even know it! You should *always* back up the Registry before attempting direct edits on it.

Registry Components

The Registry uses a very organized and flexible system to store a lot of information. The following sections describe how the Registry is organized, the types of values it contains, and the Registry files.

Registry Organization by Keys

The Registry is organized into six different sections, or *keys*. Some keys have to do with hardware configurations; others deal with software and configurations the user may have set. There are six main keys:

- Hkey_Local_Machine: Hardware settings
- Hkey_Current_Config: Hardware profiles
- Hkey_Classes_Root: Associations and file linkings
- Hkey_Dyn_Data: Hardware settings in RAM for fast access
- Hkey_Users: Software settings for all users
- Hkey_Current_User: Software settings for the current user

These keys can contain *subkeys* that help organize data according to category or user. The following sections describe each main key and the major subkeys.

NOTE The Registries of Windows 95/98 and Windows NT look very similar on the outside, but they share few specific settings within the Registry. The six general keys are about the same, with computer-specific information held in Hkey_Local_Machine and user information held in Hkey_Users. In Windows NT, the name of the editor is Regedt32.exe, although regedit.exe can also be used. Specific keys and values will be different, and just because a setting works in one operating system doesn't mean it will work in the other. The Registries for Windows 95 and Windows 98 are also similar, but different enough that specific settings that used to work in Windows 95 may not work in Windows 98.

The Hkey_Local_Machine Key

The *Hkey_Local_Machine* key holds the hardware settings for the computer, such as IRQs, network cards, video devices, and other hardware-specific information. It also holds settings that are common for all users, such as local printers, protocols, and computer identifications. Figure 5.3 shows this key displayed in the Registry Editor.

FIGURE 5.3

The Hkey_Local_Machine key

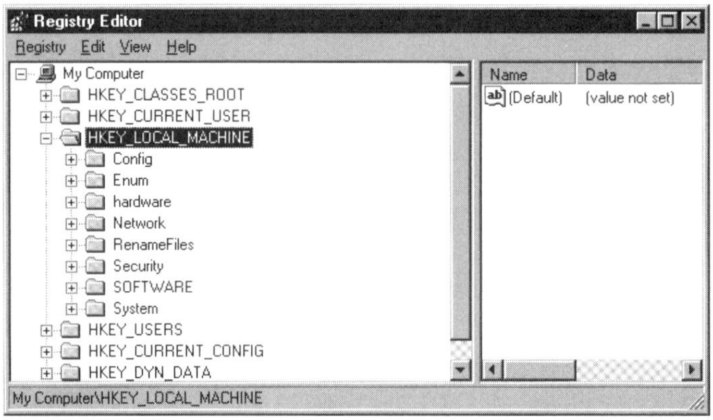

All users who log on to this computer will use the settings from this Registry key. The following summaries briefly describe the Hkey_Local_Machine key's subkeys.

The Config Subkey The *Config* subkey tracks different hardware configurations that the computer may need. For example, a laptop that is used by itself and at a docking station would have two configurations: one for undocked mode and one for docked mode. Each configuration would appear in the Control Panel, under the System icon, under the Hardware Profiles tab, as shown in Figure 5.4. Each configuration would have a corresponding entry in the Config subkey, as shown in Figure 5.5.

F I G U R E 5.4

The Hardware Profiles tab of the System Properties window

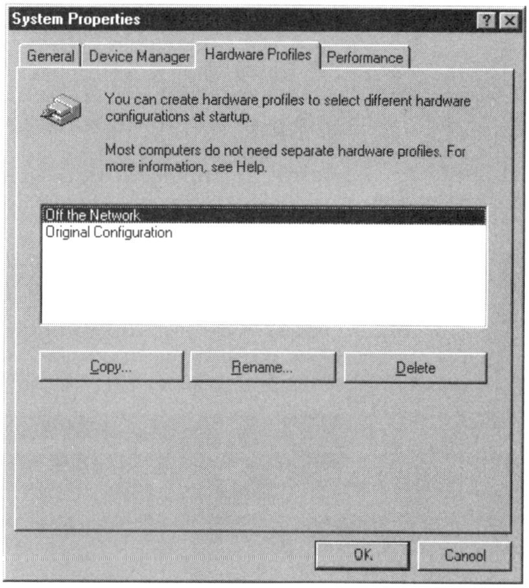

F I G U R E 5.5

The Config subkey in the Registry contains entries for each hardware profile.

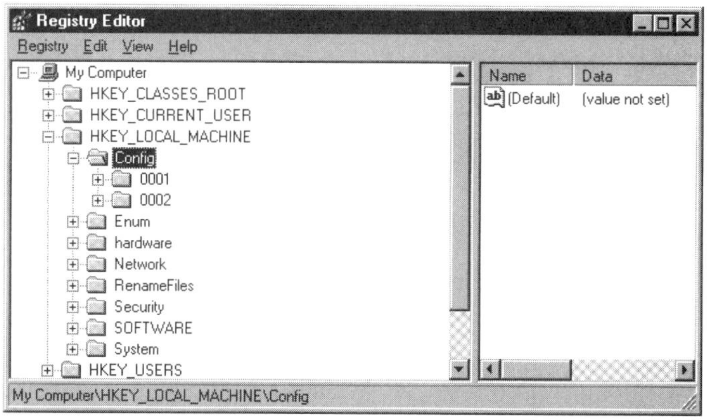

The Enum Subkey   The *Enum* subkey contains information about hardware devices and bus enumeration that Windows 98 uses to build and store the hardware tree. Different types of busses and their keywords in the Registry include the following:

- BIOS for BIOS-supported devices
- ESDI for hard drives
- PCI for the PCI bus
- ISAPNP for the Plug-and-Play bus
- FLOP for the floppy interface
- Monitor for monitor devices
- Network for the network devices
- ROOT for legacy devices
- SCSI for SCSI devices

Figure 5.6 shows the Enum subkey entries.

FIGURE 5.6

The Enum subkey in the Registry contains entries for different types of busses.

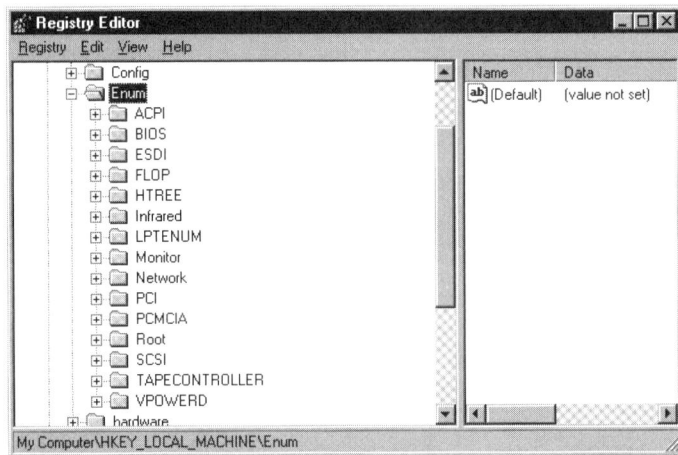

The Software Subkey   The *Software* subkey contains information about all software that is compatible with the Registry, as shown in Figure 5.7. All 32-bit software should register itself in this subkey, and some 16-bit software may also enter values into the Software subkey. Whether or not software registers itself in the Registry is determined by the software programmers. If an application doesn't register itself or registers itself in a way you don't agree with, there is not much (if anything) you can do about it.

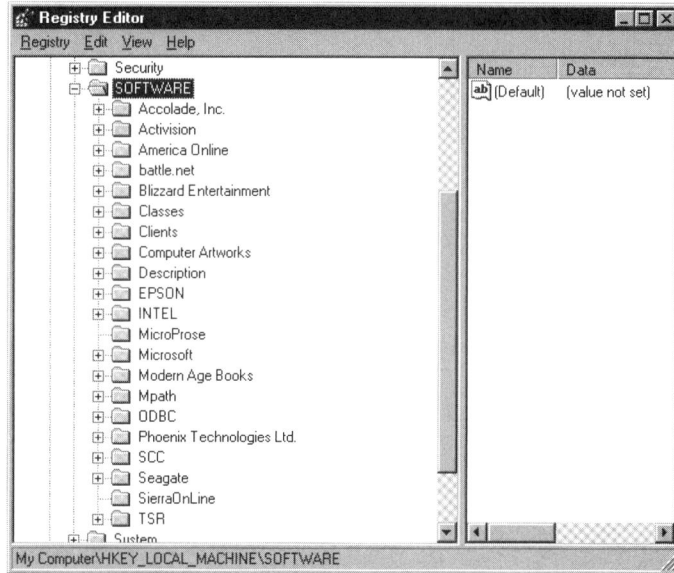

F I G U R E 5.7

The Software subkey in the Registry contains entries for compatible software.

Applications will use this information to store their configurations and paths, and any preferences the user may set. This key may be changed by the applications as options are selected, preferences changed, and setups reconfigured.

The *Classes* subkey under the Software heading contains the OLE and extension information that Windows 98 needs to function. The Hkey_Classes_Root key points to this subkey.

The *Description* subkeys under the Software heading are usually associated with particular manufacturers, and contain information specific to their products.

WARNING   Data within these subkeys should be edited only with the help of technical support from that particular software company.

The System Subkey The *System* subkey contains configuration information that Windows 98 uses on startup and that helps determine how the various pieces of Windows 98 interact with each other.

The *Control* subkey under the System heading contains startup parameters, as well as printing engine parameters, as shown in Figure 5.8.

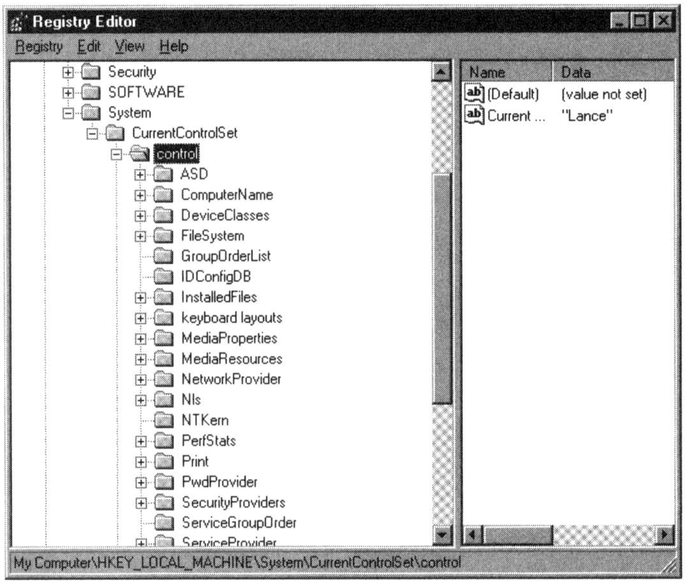

FIGURE 5.8

The Control subkey under the System subkey contains entries for startup parameters.

The *Services* subkey contains information that the various services of Windows 98 use to determine how and in what order the various device drivers and services will load.

The Hardware Subkey The *Hardware* subkey holds information about the CPU and serial ports. You should never need to edit it manually.

The Network Subkey The *Network* subkey holds information about the username and what server (if any) the user is logging on to. The best way to edit this key is through the Network Control Panel applet.

The Security Subkey The *Security* subkey is where the server name and type are stored when user-level security is configured. (User-level security is covered in Chapter 10.) Like the Network subkey, the Security subkey should be changed through the Network Control Panel rather than edited directly.

The Hkey_Current_Config Key

The *Hkey_Current_Config* key is just a pointer that refers back to the current configuration, which is stored in the Config subkey of Hkey_Local_Machine. Figure 5.9 shows this key displayed in the Registry Editor. This key is used to track hardware profiles and changes that might occur on a regular basis with the hardware.

FIGURE 5.9

The Hkey_Current_
Config key

The Hkey_Current_Config key

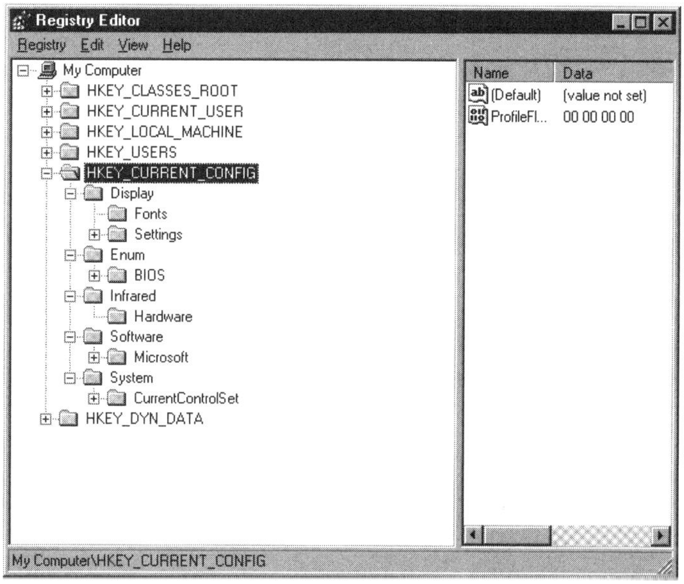

The Hkey_Classes_Root Key

The *Hkey_Classes_Root* key deals with OLE and associations that accompany file extensions. This key deals primarily with Windows 3.*x* Registry information—it was added to Windows 95 for backward compatibility. Figure 5.10 shows this key displayed in the Registry Editor. Windows 98 uses these settings for shortcuts and parts of the user interface.

Windows 98 is highly dependent on correct file associations, and it uses this key to help keep track of how all of its pieces and files interact and work together. This key ensures that when you double-click on a file, the correct application automatically opens it.

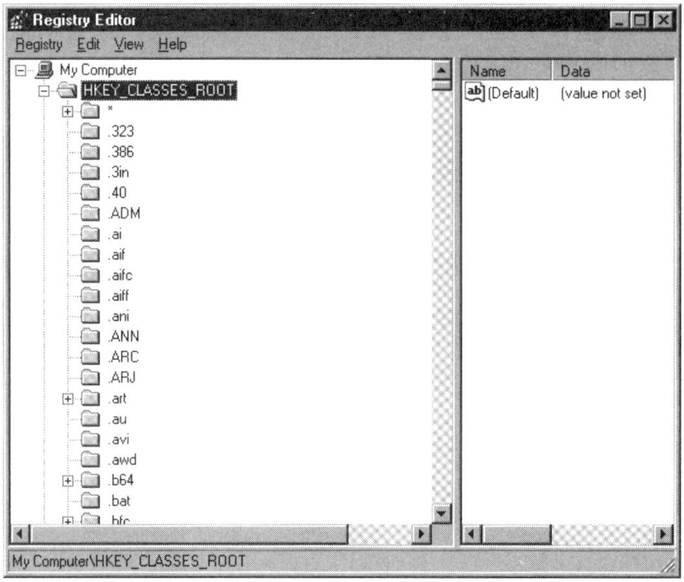

FIGURE 5.10

The Hkey_Classes_
Root key

The Hkey_Dyn_Data Key

The *Hkey_Dyn_Data* key resides in RAM for fast access, and it contains information about hardware devices, including Plug-and-Play devices. The Config Manager subkey deals with hardware configurations, and the Perf-Stats subkey maintains statistics for network components.

The Hkey_Users Key

The *Hkey_Users* key has the configurations for all of the users who have ever used the system, as well as default user settings. Hkey_Current_User points back to this key to the corresponding user who is currently logged in. Because you usually look at and make changes to the Hkey_Current_User key (to ensure that your changes are made to the correct user), details about the Hkey_Users key are covered in the next section.

The Hkey_Current_User Key

The *Hkey_Current_User* key points to the specific subkey of the user contained in Hkey_Users who is logged in at the present time. Figure 5.11 shows this key displayed in the Registry Editor.

F I G U R E   5.11

The Hkey_Current_
User key

F I G U R E   5.11

The Hkey_Current_
User key

> **NOTE**
>
> If there is ever a conflict between subkeys in Hkey_Current_User and Hkey_
> Local Machine, the settings in Hkey_Current_User will override those of
> the Hkey_Local_Machine. The Software subkey is especially prone to this
> effect because it exists in both keys.

This is one of the more important keys because it holds settings for the current user. You will usually be in one of the following subkeys when you are diagnosing or fixing problems:

- **AppEvents subkey:** Contains sound file and theme settings (if and when themes are installed) for Windows 98.

- **Control Panel subkey:** Contains Control Panel settings, including settings that may have been stored in the WINDOWS.INI and CONTROL .INI files in older versions of Windows.

- **Install LocationsMRU subkey:** Tracks most recently used installation paths. You can change the default location of the Windows 98 Source files in Hkey_Local_Machine\Software\Microsoft\Windows\ Current-Version\Setup\SourcePath.

- **Keyboard Layout subkey:** Contains the keyboard layout. This setting should be changed only by using the Keyboard Control Panel applet.

- **Network subkey:** Contains information about recent and persistent network connections.

- **RemoteAccess subkey:** Contains information about any remote-access connections that have been defined by the user.

- **Software subkey:** Contains software configuration information that is unique to this particular user. Sometimes software may register itself in both the Hkey_Local_Machine key and in the Hkey_Current_User key.

Keep in mind that settings that are in Hkey_Local_Machine are available to everyone who uses the computer, while settings found in Hkey_Current_User apply to only the user who is logged in.

Values in the Registry

A Registry entry consists of a value that has a name and some data associated with it. The entry itself can be no larger than 64KB, although the entire Registry is limited only by the amount of hard drive space available. There are three generic types of data:

- **Binary:** This is for numeric data stored as hexadecimal data (a-h, 0-9).

- **String or Text:** This data is a variable-length character field enclosed in quotation marks.

- **Dword:** This is a binary value that can be up to four bytes in length.

Files Comprising the Registry

Although the Registry is logically one database, it has been physically divided into two files for ease of administration and use. It has a third, optional file used to store system policy settings. The three files are:

- **USER.DAT:** User-specific settings

- **SYSTEM.DAT:** System-specific settings
- **CONFIG.POL:** The optional, system policy file

The only real drawback to splitting up the Registry is that you need to back up all three files in order to have a complete backup of the Registry.

Usually, both of the DAT files are in the Windows directory, but Windows 98 allows the USER.DAT file to be placed on a server in a user's home directory so that user's unique settings are available from whatever Windows 98 machine he or she may log on to. This is called a *roaming profile*, which is covered in more detail in Chapter 12.

Backing Up and Restoring the Registry

Because the Registry contains all of the settings for your computer, it is essential that it does not become corrupt or erased. Because the Registry is constantly being changed and added to by applications and hardware configurations, it is more likely to become corrupted or damaged than other, more static, files on your computer. By backing up the Registry, you can ensure that the latest changes and configurations can be restored in case of corruption or damage.

Microsoft ✓ *Exam* *Objective*	**Back up data and the Registry, and restore data and the Registry.**

Another reason you may want to restore your Registry to an earlier state is if an application installs incorrectly, thereby damaging your Registry.

The Windows 98 designers realized that the Registry is extremely important, so they programmed Windows 98 to automatically back up the Registry. You can also manually back up the Registry to further ensure recoverability.

Automatic Registry Backup

Windows 98 includes a new utility called the *Registry Checker* which automatically runs at bootup. The Registry Checker scans the Registry for corruption and backs up the Registry if there are no errors. The Registry backup is stored in a file called RBXXX.CAB, with the five most recent backups being kept, by default.

The Registry Checker consists of two programs:

- **ScanReg:** A real-mode version of the Registry Checker that allows you to restore the Registry from a command prompt.

- **ScanRegW:** A protected-mode version of the Registry Checker that allows you to scan the Registry for errors and create a new backup of the Registry from within Windows 98.

Manually Backing Up and Restoring the Registry with Registry Checker

The Registry Checker can also be started manually by going to Start ➤ Run and typing **SCANREGW**.

In Exercise 5.3 you will run the Registry Checker and perform a new backup of the Registry.

EXERCISE 5.3

Backing Up the Registry with Registry Checker

1. Go to Start ➤ Run and type **SCANREGW**, and then choose OK to start the Registry Checker. Your Registry will be scanned for errors. If errors are found, either they will be fixed or you will have to boot to MS-DOS mode to load an old copy of the Registry using SCANREG.EXE.

2. If the Registry Checker has already backed up the Registry today, you will get a screen like this.

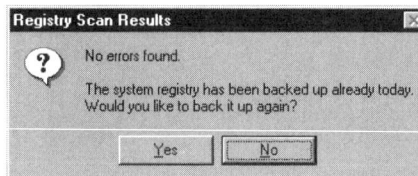

3. Choose Yes to make a new backup.

4. If the Registry Checker has not already backed up the Registry today, you will get a screen like this one.

5. Choose Yes to make a new backup.

If you need to restore the Registry, you must boot to MS-DOS mode or boot with the Windows 98 Startup disk. Run the SCANREG.EXE program, which will present you with a list of the last five backups of the Registry. Choose the backup you want to restore. Reboot Windows 98 to use that copy of the Registry.

Backups of the Registry will be labeled "Started" or "Not Started." "Started" simply means that Windows 98 was successfully started using that copy of the Registry. "Not Started" means that, although the copy may be good, it has not actually been run, so Windows 98 is not sure if it is good or not.

Manually Backing Up and Restoring the Registry with Regedit

You can use the Regedit command to back up and to restore the Registry manually while within Windows 98. The Regedit program is contained on the Windows 98 Startup disk, so that if the Registry becomes corrupted, it can be restored.

To export the Registry to an ASCII text file, enter this command at the command prompt:

Regedit /e *file.txt*

To overwrite the current Registry with the file that you indicate, use this command at the command prompt:

Regedit /c *file.txt*

Follow the steps in Exercise 5.4 to run the command that will back up your Registry, and then open your backup file to see what it looks like.

EXERCISE 5.4

Backing Up the Registry from a Command Prompt

1. Start a command prompt by selecting Start ➣ Programs ➣ MS-DOS Command Prompt.

2. Type **REGEDIT /e regback.txt**. This backs up your Registry to a file called regback.txt.

3. Type **EDIT regback.txt**. This calls up the editor and allows you to look at the backup file.

4. When you are finished looking around, close the editor (press Alt+F, then choose Exit) and command prompt (type **EXIT**).

WARNING The Windows 95 Resource Kit came with a program named CFGBACK.EXE (Configuration Backup) that could be used to back up and restore a Windows 95 Registry. If CFGBACK is used to restore a Windows 95 Registry to a Windows 98 computer, Windows 98 will not boot! CFGBACK seems to work when backing up and restoring the Windows 98 Registry, but it doesn't appear to be supported by Microsoft at this time.

For more details about backing up and restoring individual pieces of the Registry, see the section on "Troubleshooting the Registry," later in this chapter.

Checking the Registry for Corruption

Windows 98 automatically checks the Registry for corruption in case of an improper shutdown. You can also scan the Registry for corruption at any time by using the ScanRegW program.

Microsoft
Exam
Objective

Diagnose and resolve hardware device and device driver problems. Tasks include:

- Checking for corrupt Registry files by using ScanReg and ScanRegW

Whenever Windows 98 boots, the Registry Checker is run, which scans the Registry for errors and performs a backup. You can also scan the Registry for errors by starting the ScanRegW program from within Windows 98 (as in Exercise 5.3) or the ScanReg program from MS-DOS mode.

Modifying the Registry

As you use Windows 98 and your applications, the Registry is constantly being added to and changed. Applications will add subkeys to the Registry when you install them, and each will change its particular settings when you change settings within the application. Adding new hardware to the computer will also cause changes as configurations and driver information are written to the Registry.

WARNING

Under most circumstances, you should not change Registry entries directly; instead, you should rely on your applications to edit the Registry as needed.

There are two basic ways to modify the Registry:

- Make changes within an application and let the application modify the Registry. All 32-bit programs should keep their settings in the Registry, but some are specifically designed to change the way Windows 98 works. The Control Panel and Power Toys (a freeware program from Microsoft) are examples of such programs.

- Edit the Registry directly (manually). This requires knowledge of the specific subkey and value you want to edit, and the value you need to change it to.

There are times when you may need to edit the Registry directly. One reason you would edit the Registry is to add functionality to Windows 98 (see Exercise 5.5) or change the way Windows 98 works (see Exercises 5.6. and 5.7). Another common reason to edit the Registry directly is to trouble-shoot—either by replacing a deleted section or by changing bad values in an existing subkey.

> Windows 98 allows the Registry to be administered and edited remotely. Chapter 14 provides details on how to do this.

Using Programs to Modify the Registry

Many changes that you make in Windows 98 are best made using the Control Panel. Applets exist for changing items like your mouse and cursors, as well as all of your networking components.

Other programs that let you change how Windows 98 works are available. For example, Microsoft's Power Toys for Windows 98 contains a useful applet called Tweak UI, shown in Figure 5.12. This applet allows you to modify the Windows 98 interface.

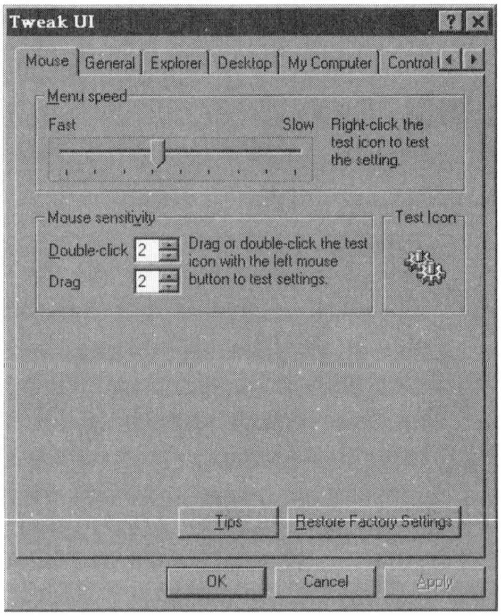

FIGURE 5.12

The Tweak UI applet

Power Toys is a set of applets that Microsoft has released into the public domain for convenience (but doesn't support in any way). You can obtain the Tweak UI applet from the Windows 98 CD-ROM in the tools\tweakui folder. You can also obtain Tweak UI from the Windows 98 Resource Kit or download Power Toys from the Microsoft Web site at www.microsoft.com. Some of the Registry changes presented in the following exercises in this chapter can be made by using the Power Toys utility rather than by using the Registry Editor to make them manually. Note that although the Windows 98 version of Tweak UI looks slightly different than the Windows 95 version, both versions seem to work on both Windows 95 and Windows 98. It is, however, always best to upgrade to the latest versions of utilities when a new operating system is installed, and Tweak UI is no exception.

Using the Control Panel is the safest way to make changes to the Registry. Similarly, all the changes you can make through the Tweak UI applet are also possible by directly editing the Registry, but using this type of application is a much safer way to modify the interface.

Using the Registry Editor to Modify the Registry

As mentioned earlier in the chapter, the Registry Editor lets you directly edit the Registry, as well as view its contents. With the Registry Editor, you can make real-time edits of keys and values in the Registry. Just be sure to always double-check your edits for accuracy because the Registry Editor has no safeguards built into it to check for bad data.

You may need to edit the Registry in order to get Windows 98 to behave exactly as you want. For example, you may want to disable animations or speed up the menus. These and some other useful Registry entries are described in the following sections.

You will use the Registry Editor to modify the Registry directly in the upcoming exercises. Make sure you carefully read and understand the exercises before attempting them. Be sure you have a current backup of the Registry before attempting any direct modifications! You should back up your Registry before trying these exercises—just in case you make a mistake in editing.

Adding a Viewer for Unregistered Files

Whenever you try to open a file that Windows 98 does not have registered, it will prompt you for an application to use to open the file. You can adjust the Registry so that an option to open the document with Notepad appears when you right-click the document.

Follow the steps in Exercise 5.5 to edit the Registry so that Open With Notepad appears as a pop-up menu option, both when you right-click an unknown file type and when you Shift+right-click on known file types. To do this, you need to add a key named Open With Notepad and another new key named Command, below that, as shown in Figure 5.13.

F I G U R E 5.13

Editing the Registry to add Open With Notepad

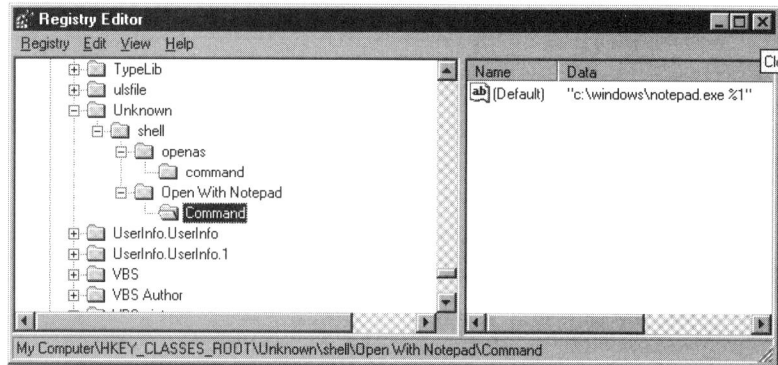

EXERCISE 5.5

Adding a Default Application for Opening Files

1. Start the Regedit program.

2. Open the Hkey_Classes_Root\Unknown\Shell subkey.

3. To add a new key, select Edit ➤ New ➤ Key. Type **Open With Notepad** as its name.

4. To add a new key below that called Command, open your new key. Then choose Edit ➤ New ➤ Key.

5. Right-click Default in the right pane, and select Modify.

6. Change the value for the command to match the path for Notepad, and add **%1** after Notepad; for example, change it to **C:\Windows\ Notepad.exe %1** (see Figure 5.13).

7. To test the change, close the Registry Editor and return to the Desktop.

8. Create a new file with the extension of .XYZ (an unregistered extension).

9. Right-click the file to display the pop-up menu.

10. Choose your new Open With Notepad option, as shown here. Notepad should open the file.

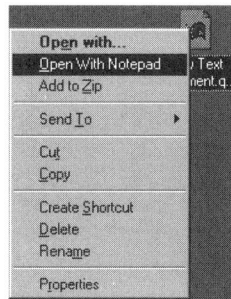

Disabling Windows Animations

Windows 98 animates the minimizing and maximizing of windows to help users visualize where their work has gone. On slower machines, the animations may be so slow as to be distracting. You can disable animations by editing the Registry and adding a value, as shown in Figure 5.14. Follow the steps in Exercise 5.6 to disable these animations.

Disabling Windows Animations

1. Start the Regedit program.

2. Open the Hkey_Current_User\Control Panel\Desktop\WindowsMetrics subkey.

EXERCISE 5.6 (CONTINUED)

3. Add a new string value called MinAnimate with a value of 0 for no animations (see Figure 5.14). To turn animations back on, you can change this value to 1 by highlighting it and choosing Modify.

4. Restart Windows 98.

FIGURE 5.14

Adding value to disable animations

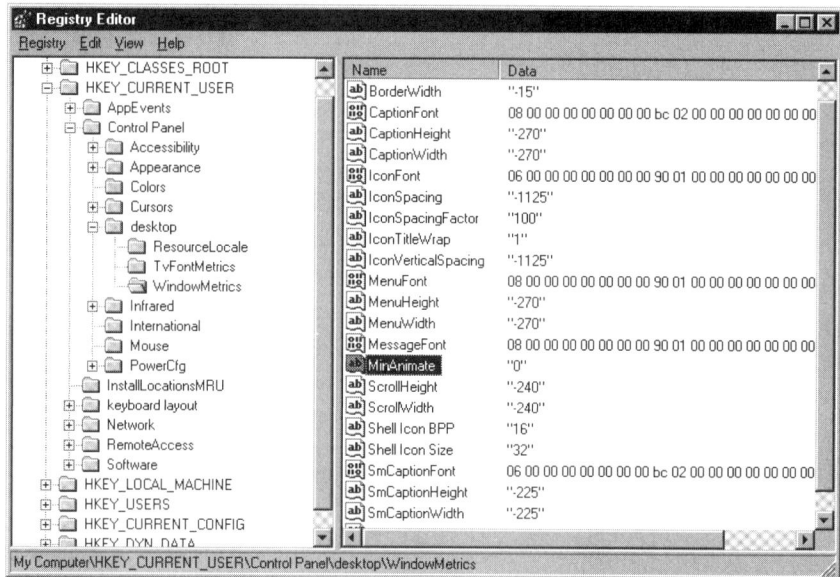

Increasing Menu Speed

Whenever you click the Start button, the first level of menus pops up. As you move your mouse over the different menu items, the submenus pop up. The default speed at which menus pop up from the taskbar is too slow for most people. You can increase the pop-up speed by by editing the Registry and adding a value, as shown in Figure 5.15. Follow the steps in Exercise 5.7 to adjust the speed of the pop-up menus so they will appear much more quickly. Of course, you can also enter a different number to slow them down.

F I G U R E   5.15

Adding a value to
speed up menus

EXERCISE 5.7

Increasing the Speed of the Taskbar's Pop-Up Menus

1. Start the Regedit program.

2. Go to the Hkey_Current_User\Control Panel\Desktop subkey.

3. Add a new string value called MenuShowDelay.

4. Highlight the new value, and select Modify.

5. Set the value from 0 to 10, with 0 being the fastest (see Figure 5.15).

6. Restart Windows 98.

Troubleshooting the Registry

Troubleshooting the Registry has many aspects, such as backing up the entire Registry, exporting certain sections of the Registry, importing either the entire Registry or certain parts, and printing the Registry to help pinpoint differences between subkeys and between computers. If you have planned ahead and have a current backup of the Registry, a corrupt Registry file is nothing more than an inconvenience. If you have no backups, a failure of your Registry could be catastrophic—you may need to reinstall applications and even Windows 98 itself.

Exporting the Registry

There are two reasons that exporting the Registry might help you trouble-shoot problems:

- If you are prepared for (or expecting) trouble, you can export the Registry in order to have a current backup.

- You can export the subkey in question from a computer that works, and import it into the computer that is having problems.

The Registry can be exported in its entirety by using the /e switch with the Regedit command from the command prompt, as explained earlier in the chapter.

Creating a Startup Disk

Windows 98 comes with a feature that allows you to create what is called a *Startup disk*. The option is on the Startup Disk tab of the Add/Remove Programs Properties dialog box, shown in Figure 5.16. The Startup disk that Windows 98 creates contains several programs you can use to help recover from disasters that may prevent Windows 98 from booting. One of the files that is copied onto the disk is the real-mode Registry Checker (ScanReg). Follow the steps in Exercise 5.8 to make a Startup disk.

FIGURE 5.16

Creating a Windows 98
Startup disk

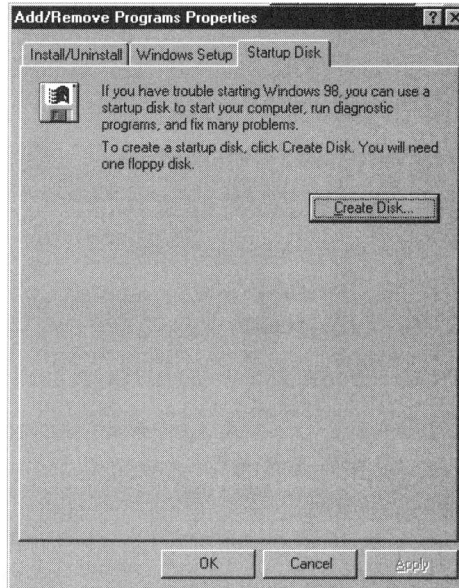

FIGURE 5.16

Creating a Windows 98
Startup disk

EXERCISE 5.8

Making a Startup Disk

1. Obtain a blank, formatted floppy disk.

2. Go to Control Panel ➢ Add/Remove Programs.

3. Go to the Startup Disk tab (see Figure 5.16).

4. Insert the Windows 98 CD if prompted.

5. When the Startup disk is completed, check out the files on the disk. Regedit should be there, along with other utilities.

Exporting the Registry from the Registry Editor

You can also export the Registry from within the Registry Editor by selecting Registry ➢ Export. You are then presented with the Export Registry File dialog box, which includes a choice between exporting the entire Registry and exporting just a part of the Registry. Figure 5.17 shows this dialog box with an export range specified.

When you export the Registry, Windows 98 writes the saved file as an ASCII text file. If necessary, you can edit the file before importing it back.

F I G U R E 5.17

Exporting a piece of the Registry

Importing a Copy of the Registry

There are three basic ways to import into the Registry using Regedit. The first is called *real-mode importing using Registry Checker*. The second is *real-mode importing using the Registry Editor* because you run them both in MS-DOS mode at a command prompt. The third way is to use Regedit by selecting the Import command and then specifying the import file.

Real-Mode Importing Using the Registry Checker

Backups of the Registry made using the Registry Checker can be imported by booting to MS-DOS mode and running the ScanReg program. A list of backups will be presented. After the Registry is restored, reboot Windows 98 to have the new Registry take effect.

Real-Mode Importing Using the Registry Editor

The Regedit program has command-line switches that allow you to easily back up and restore the entire Registry. As mentioned earlier, Regedit /e will back up the Registry to an ASCII file.

If you are lucky enough to have a backup of the Registry that has been created this way, you can also restore the Registry from a command prompt. The command is:

`Regedit` /c *name_of_backup_file*

The /c switch replaces the entire contents of the Registry with the file you specify. You may need to run Regedit from a floppy disk if Windows 98 has been damaged badly.

> **WARNING**
>
> If you ever have to restore the Registry (using the Regedit /c command) from a previous backup that was made using the Regedit /e command, be aware that the file is not checked by the system before it is restored in place of your current Registry. Make sure that the file you are restoring is a complete, bug-free text version of the Registry because it completely overwrites (and does *not* merge with) your old Registry.

Importing the Registry Using the Registry Editor

From within the Registry Editor, you can import either the entire Registry or a select piece of the Registry by choosing Registry ➤ Import Registry File.

If you import pieces of the Registry, it adds to your current Registry. This is extremely helpful when you are replacing pieces of the Registry that have been deleted by mistake or when you are adding the same variable repeatedly. In order to import a piece of the Registry, it must have been exported first, or be an ASCII file created by hand.

Printing the Registry

You may want to print parts of the Registry so you will have a hard copy of your settings and to help you better understand the format of the Registry. Printing the Registry is also useful in troubleshooting because you can compare printed subkeys of two computers (one that is working and one that is not).

To print the Registry from within the Registry Editor, select Registry ➤ Print. Just as when you are exporting the Registry, you will be given the choice between printing the entire Registry or printing only certain keys.

NOTE If you print the entire Registry, you may be looking at 100 or more pages!

Summary

The Registry represents a dramatic change in the way configuration information is kept compared to older versions of Windows. The limitations of old INI files have been overcome with the Registry, although Windows 98 still supports INI files for backward compatibility.

The Registry contains settings for both hardware and software, and it is very flexible. It is composed of various keys, subkeys, and values. Multiple subkeys can be kept under each key, allowing for multiple configurations for both hardware and users. This allows Windows 98 to natively support hardware and user profiles.

The Registry can be backed up and restored by various methods. Windows 98 scans the Registry for errors whenever you boot, and it keeps an automatic backup in the files RBXXX.CAB. The Registry Editor can also be used to back up and restore the Registry.

The best way to make changes to the Registry is to use the appropriate program, which is usually a Control Panel applet. However, sometimes the only way to make a program or Windows 98 behave the way you want is to make changes directly to the Registry. The Registry can be edited directly by using the Registry Editor (Regedit). However, use extreme caution when you edit the Registry directly because modifications are not checked for compatibility by the editor.

This chapter covered techniques for troubleshooting the Registry, including exporting all or parts of the Registry, importing Registry information, and printing a copy of the Registry.

Review Questions

1. What is the name of the Registry key that holds user settings?

    A. Hkey_Local_Machine

    B. Hkey_Users

    C. Hkey_Dyn_Data

    D. Hkey_Current_Config

2. What is the name of the Registry key that holds Plug-and-Play settings?

    A. Hkey_Local_Machine

    B. Hkey_Users

    C. Hkey_Dyn_Data

    D. Hkey_Current_Config

3. What is the name of the Registry key that holds generic hardware information?

    A. Hkey_Local_Machine

    B. Hkey_Users

    C. Hkey_Dyn_Data

    D. Hkey_Current_Config

4. What is the name of the Registry key that holds hardware profile information?

    A. Hkey_Local_Machine

    B. Hkey_Users

    C. Hkey_Dyn_Data

    D. Hkey_Current_Config

5. What is the name of the Registry file that holds system settings?

   A. USER.INI

   B. USER.DAT

   C. SYSTEM.DAT

   D. SYSTEM.INI

6. What is the name of the Registry file that holds user settings?

   A. USER.INI

   B. USER.DAT

   C. SYSTEM.DAT

   D. SYSTEM.INI

7. What is the name of the Registry editor for Windows 98?

   A. REGEDT32.EXE

   B. REGISTRY EDITOR.EXE

   C. REGEDIT.EXE

   D. REGISTRY.EXE

8. What is the name of the real-mode Registry Checker that must be run from MS-DOS mode?

   A. REGCHECK.EXE

   B. REGCHECKW.EXE

   C. SCANREG.EXE

   D. SCANREGW.EXE

9. What is the name of the protected-mode version of the Registry Checker that can be run from within Windows 98?

   A. REGCHECK.EXE

   B. REGCHECKW.EXE

   C. SCANREG.EXE

   D. SCANREGW.EXE

10. What is the name of the backup Registry file that is automatically created by the Registry Checker?

   A. RBXXX.CAB

   B. USER.BAK

   C. SYSTEM.BAK

   D. REGISTRY.BAK

11. You need to edit the Registry on a user's computer. You want to back it up first. What Windows 98 tool should you use to back up the Registry?

   A. ScanDisk

   B. Disk Defragmenter

   C. WALIGN.EXE

   D. Registry Checker

12. A user dual-boots Windows 98 and Windows NT. He or she wants to keep the Registries in sync so that applications will run on both operating systems. You are asked for advice. How can this be done?

   A. Run Registry Checker on one system to back up the Registry, and Registry Checker on the other system to restore it.

   B. Run Regedit on one system to back up only the changes in the Registry, and use Regedit to import those changes to the other operating system.

   C. Run Cfgback on one operating system to make a backup, and run Regedit on the other operating system to restore the Registry.

   D. Because the Registries are incompatible, you can't use any automated method to synchronize them.

6

Managing Applications

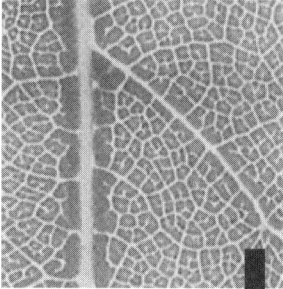

In this chapter, you will learn how different types of applications behave and interact in the Windows 98 environment. You will begin by studying general protection faults and nonresponding programs and how to deal with them. Then you will learn how system resources (User, GDI, and Kernel) are used and subsequently returned to the system. Although Windows 98 is considered a 32-bit operating system, it still uses some 16-bit code for processing. You will look at why it still uses 16-bit code and how it might affect your applications.

Tune and optimize the system in a Microsoft environment and a mixed Microsoft and NetWare environment. Tasks include:

- Optimizing the hard disk by using Disk Defragmenter and ScanDisk

- Compressing data by using DriveSpace3 and the Compression Agent

- Updating drivers and applying service packs by using Windows Update and the Signature Verification tool

- Automating tasks by using Maintenance Wizard

- Scheduling tasks by using Task Scheduler

- Checking for corrupt files and extracting files from the installation media by using the System File Checker

Of all the sub-objectives listed above, we'll only be discussing Windows Update and the Signature Verification tool in this chapter. The System File Checker is covered in Chapter 16 with the remaining topics covered in Chapter 7.

You will also spend some time studying how to set up Program Information Files (PIFs), which allow MS-DOS–based programs to coexist with Windows programs. You will learn about the options for customizing your PIFs for individual MS-DOS programs so that they run more efficiently.

You will then delve into some Windows 98 administrative features, including how to update drivers and apply service packs using the Windows Update. You can also check for digital signatures on files that you download from the Internet using the Signature Verification tool.

Let's get started with a look at general protection faults (GPFs), including why they occur and how you can deal with them.

General Protection Faults

An understanding of what causes *general protection faults* (GPFs) and how to deal with them can be very beneficial to the systems administrator who must spend time troubleshooting these problems. A GPF occurs when a program violates the integrity of the system. This often happens when a program tries to access memory that is not part of its assigned memory address space. The GPF is a defense mechanism employed by the operating system. When a program attempts to do something that could corrupt the operating system, the operating system halts the program before it can do any damage.

Let's look at how the different types of programs handle GPFs in Windows 98.

GPFs in MS-DOS–Based Programs

If an MS-DOS–based program fails, only that program is affected. This is because the MS-DOS program is running in its own virtual machine. A Windows 98-style GPF message will be displayed to the user, indicating that the program failed. When you click the OK button in the GPF dialog box, the MS-DOS program will be terminated along with the virtual machine in which it was running.

If you click the Details button, you will get the stack dump. A *stack dump* is the information stored in the system registers at the time the program crashed. This information is generally useful only to the person who wrote the program.

GPFs in 16-Bit Windows Programs

When a 16-bit Windows program fails, the operating system will again issue a GPF dialog box indicating the failed program. This dialog box will have the old Windows 3.*x*-style dialog box with a Close button and an Ignore button. After you select the Close button, you will see the Windows 98 GPF dialog box.

Because all other 16-bit programs share the same address space, they will be halted until the 16-bit program that caused the GPF is cleared. Once the program is cleared, the other 16-bit applications should be able to resume reading their messages in the thread and continue to operate normally. The failed program generally will not return its resources back to the operating system due to the shared address space and shared thread. To return resources, you must close all 16-bit Windows-based programs.

GPFs in 32-Bit Windows Programs

When a 32-bit Windows-based program fails, it does not affect other programs because each 32-bit program receives its own virtual address space.

You will see the Windows 98 GPF dialog box. When you click the OK button, Windows 98 will remove that failed program and return its resources back to the operating system.

GPFs in Device Drivers

You might encounter a GPF with a driver program. Because drivers can access hardware directly and run as part of the base operating system, you should take a GPF with a driver very seriously.

Driver failures can affect the ability of the entire operating system to continue functioning properly. A little later in this chapter, you will learn how to find and replace a corrupted driver.

Nonresponding Programs

Nonresponding, or *hung*, programs are still running, but they are not responding to the system. *Program hangs* can happen for many reasons. Your 16-bit programs can hang when they do not have access to the message queue. This can be caused by a poorly written program that doesn't voluntarily share resources with other 16-bit programs. Program hangs can also occur when a GPF hasn't been cleared. Your 32-bit programs can hang when a resource they need is being used by some other program.

If any program hangs while it is using a critical resource, any other program that needs that resource will hang also. The hung program will need to be restarted so that the other programs can continue execution.

This is a nice upgrade from Windows 3.*x*, in which you were required to restart the entire Windows 3.*x* operating system.

Hung MS-DOS–Based Programs

When an MS-DOS–based program hangs, you need to perform a local restart of the program. To run a local restart, press the Ctrl+Alt+Del key combination (press all three keys at the same time). This will bring up the Close Program dialog box, shown in Figure 6.1.

F I G U R E   6.1

The Close Program dialog box

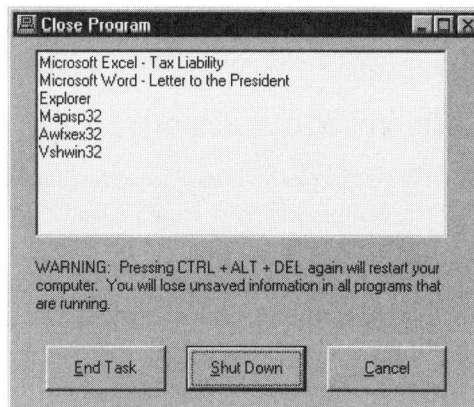

As you can see, you can make several choices. If you choose End Task, the selected program will shut down immediately. If you choose Shut Down, all active programs will shut down and Windows 98 will close. Pressing the Cancel button cancels this window without changing anything. Occasionally, a program won't respond to the End Task messages being sent to it when you click the End Task button. After a few seconds, a secondary dialog box will pop up and give you two options: End Task and Cancel, as shown in Figure 6.2. The titlebar for the End Task dialog box will display the application's titlebar. (In Figure 6.2, the Microsoft Excel - Tax Liability program is the program in question.) If you choose Cancel, the program will wait for a few seconds and try to end the program again. If you choose End Task from this dialog box, whatever the program is doing (or not doing) will be overridden, and the program will close.

FIGURE 6.2

The End Task
dialog box

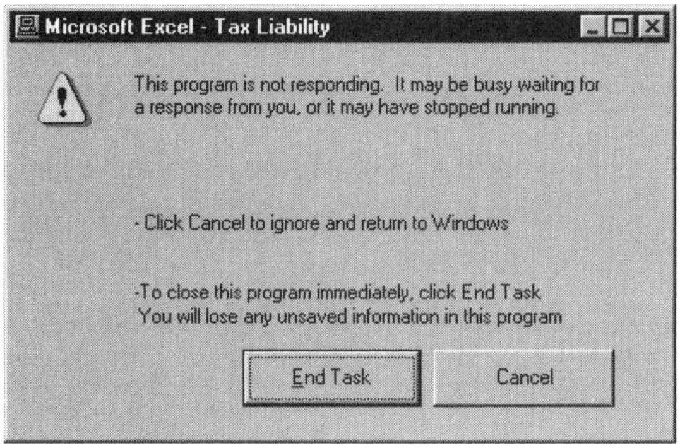

Hung 16-Bit Windows Programs

When 16-bit Windows programs hang, they might not release control of the thread or other system resources. This will cause all other 16-bit programs to hang also.

You should perform a local restart and terminate the hung program. After termination, the other programs should resume operating normally because they again have access to their messages in the thread.

Hung 32-Bit Windows Programs

If a 32-bit Windows program hangs, you can terminate it with a local restart. This should not affect any other running programs because the 32-bit program has its own threads and doesn't share them. Exercise 6.1 simulates 16-bit and 32-bit program hangs and GPFs.

EXERCISE 6.1

Simulating General Protection Faults and Program Hangs

1. You will first simulate a 16-bit Windows GPF. Navigate to the \Labs\ Crash16 folder on the CD-ROM that accompanies this book and run the SETUP.EXE program to install the Crash16 application. Then select Start ➢ Programs ➢ Crash16.

2. Click the Crash button. This forces the program to create a GPF, and the Windows 3.x GPF dialog box appears.

3. Select Close from the GPF dialog box. You now see the Windows 98 GPF dialog box.

4. Select Close from the Windows 98 GPF dialog box. This terminates your Crash16 program.

5. Let's do the same thing with a 32-bit application. From the \Labs\ Crash32 folder on your CD-ROM, run the SETUP.EXE program to install the Crash32 application. Then select Start ➢ Programs ➢ Crash32.

6. Click the Crash button. This forces the program to create a GPF, and you see only the Windows 98 GPF dialog box.

7. Choose Close to terminate your Crash32 program.

8. Now let's simulate a program hang in the 16-bit Windows environment. Open Crash16, and then open a second instance of Crash16. These instances will be referred to as App A and App B, respectively. From App A, click the Hang button.

9. App A has now been hung. Note that the other 16-bit application (App B) is hung also. They are both hung because they share the same thread, and App B cannot get to its messages in the thread because of App A. To resolve this problem, press Ctrl+Alt+Del to open the Task Manager dialog box.

10. In the list of running applications, you should see "Crash16 (Not Responding)." Click on that line, and then choose End Task. This pops up another dialog box indicating that the program is still not responding. Click End Task again. Once you have done this, App B will begin running again because it can now read the thread.

11. Close App B.

12. Follow the same procedures outlined in Steps 8 through 10 for Crash32. You will find that App B continues to run despite App A's hung status.

Resource Usage in Windows 98

In Windows 3.x, you may have had problems with Out of Memory errors caused by memory leaks in those 16-bit programs and the resource architecture of Windows 3.x. Because 16-bit programs share the same memory address space, these problems can still happen in Windows 98, especially if you have 16-bit programs that crash. Losing all of your resources while using 32-bit programs is much more difficult. Remember, every 32-bit Windows program gets its own separate address space and system resources.

Let's look at how and when system resources (User, GDI, and Kernel) are used and returned to the system.

- **MS-DOS–based programs:** When an MS-DOS program is terminated, all of the resources it was using, as well as the virtual machine it was running in, are returned to Windows 98.

- **16-bit Windows programs:** These programs may use resources that the operating system doesn't know about. They might also share resources used by other 16-bit programs. Because of this, when a 16-bit program is closed, its resources will not be returned to the operating system. This can eventually cause an Out of Memory error. To fix this error, close all 16-bit programs. Resources used by 16-bit programs will be returned after all 16-bit applications are closed. This will include any orphaned resources that were once attached to a 16-bit program. Resources are handled this way for backward compatibility.

- **32-bit Windows programs:** Resources used by 32-bit programs can be tracked in their entirety by the operating system. When a 32-bit application is closed, it will return all resources.

> Resources returned to the system may not affect your resource counts. This is due to the fact that Windows 98 will cache frequently used and shared resources. This allows programs in Windows 98 to start up and run more quickly.

Resource Architecture

Windows 98 is considered a 32-bit operating system, but it still uses a lot of 16-bit code at the system level. This was done for several reasons. One reason is that 32-bit code takes up more memory than an equivalent amount of 16-bit code. Windows 98 was built for efficiency. Many functions don't need the larger 32-bit memory areas. For example, would you rent an 18-wheel tractor trailer to move a one bedroom apartment? Probably not. A smaller truck would be much more efficient and cost-effective.

Also, in certain instances, 16-bit code runs faster than 32-bit code. Compatibility with existing programs is another reason Windows 98 still uses 16-bit code fragments.

> Under normal circumstances, a 32-bit program cannot use 16-bit code and vice versa. Think of them as two different languages. To translate between these languages and get the benefits previously outlined, Windows 98 employs a procedure called *thunking* in which the code is redirected and translated from one version to the other.

Here is how 16-bit and 32-bit code are used in Windows 98 system components:

- **User interface:** The user interface in Windows 98 is almost totally written in 16-bit code. This was done to keep this component as small and fast as possible.

- **GDI:** The GDI (graphical device interface) uses a fairly even mix of 16-bit and 32-bit code. The GDI will use 16-bit code when compatibility is necessary. It will use 32-bit code for speed or when precise floating-point measurements are necessary (such as rendering a high-resolution graphic).

- **Kernel:** The Kernel uses all 32-bit code. When a program makes a call to a 16-bit procedure, that call is thunked to the 32-bit version.

16-Bit versus 32-Bit Code

There are different rules for using 16-bit and 32-bit code. For example, 16-bit code is *non-reentrant*. This means that while a particular thread is using a 16-bit piece of code, no other programs can be using that same 16-bit piece of code. Because it is reentrant, 32-bit code does not have this problem, which means that many threads can be processing the same procedures at the same time.

Windows 98 uses a Win16Mutex flag to indicate to other programs that this particular 16-bit section of code is currently in use. This blocks other programs from using that same procedure. If a program hangs and the Win16Mutex flag is set, you must perform a local restart on the hung program, which will then release the Win16Mutex flag. An interesting side effect of the Win16Mutex flag is that a 32-bit program that uses a 16-bit code fragment could be hung by other programs that are trying to use the same 16-bit code fragment.

> Because the Kernel uses only 32-bit code, it cannot be blocked by the Win16Mutex flag.

Tracking Resource Usage with Resource Meter

***Microsoft
Exam
Objective***

Monitor system performance by using Net Watcher, System Monitor, and Resource Meter.

You can track resource usage using the Resource Meter. Select Start ➢ Programs ➢ Accessories ➢ System Tools ➢ Resource Meter. This will place the Resource Meter icon on your taskbar. Right-click the icon (it should look like three horizontal bars) and choose Details. You should see a dialog box similar to the one shown in Figure 6.3.

FIGURE 6.3

The Resource Meter monitors the System, User, and GDI resources.

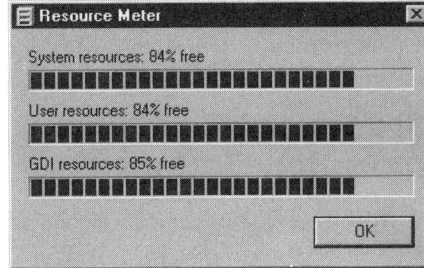

Configuring PIFs for MS-DOS Programs

Windows-based programs keep information about resources and memory in their headers, which allows them to coexist with other running Windows applications. MS-DOS–based programs were designed to use whatever resources were in the system. For MS-DOS–based programs to comfortably coexist with Windows programs, they need to have a header information file. This file is called a *Program Information File*, or *PIF*.

If an MS-DOS–based application doesn't have its own PIF, one can be created for it. Windows 95 provided default properties for most MS-DOS–based applications. These properties were stored in the file APPS.INF. The first time the MS-DOS–based application was run, the properties from APPS .INF were loaded. If the MS-DOS application behaved poorly, or if it was not listed on the APPS.INF list, you went to the property sheets of that MS-DOS–based application to refine the performance. This is still true of Windows 98. The APPS.INF file is still used, and it acts as the master list of settings for MS-DOS–based applications. The PIF95 section of the APPS.INF file contains the necessary information about running a specific MS-DOS–based application.

> **NOTE**
>
> If you upgraded Windows 3.1*x* to Windows 98, a _DEFAULT.PIF file remains in the directory and can be used to create PIFs for DOS-based applications. The _DEFAULT.PIF is similar to the APPS.INF; that is, it has default settings that work with most MS-DOS–based programs too. Regardless of which file is used, all MS-DOS–based applications can easily be adjusted by going to the Properties sheet of that application.

In short, a PIF is really a configuration header file for the MS-DOS virtual machine. You can customize PIFs for individual MS-DOS programs so they will run more efficiently. The following sections describe how to customize a PIF for a particular MS-DOS program

PIF Customization Options

When you complete a customized PIF, the PIF itself will be stored in the same folder where the MS-DOS file is located. It will also have the same eight-character filename, followed by .PIF. For example, if your MS-DOS file is located and named C:\Games\DOOM.EXE, then your PIF file would be C:\Games\DOOM.PIF.

You use the property sheets of an MS-DOS–based program to customize its PIF. Property sheets can be accessed by right-clicking the MS-DOS–based .EXE or .COM file and then selecting Properties from the pop-up menu. The Properties dialog box is divided into several tabs. In the following sections, you will go through the features of each tab. At the end of this section, you will be able to customize your own PIF (see Exercise 6.2).

The General Tab

The General tab of the DOS Properties dialog box, shown in Figure 6.4, shows general-purpose information about the MS-DOS program. It includes the file's location, size, PIF name, creation date, modification date, last accessed date, and file attributes.

You can modify the following file attributes from this screen:

- **Read Only:** When this attribute is set, the file becomes Read Only. This means that the file cannot be overwritten or accidentally deleted.

- **Archive:** Some programs use this attribute to decide whether or not the program should be backed up.

- **Hidden:** This attribute will hide the file from view. You will not be able to use the file unless you know its exact filename.

- **System:** This attribute normally will be disabled. When it is checked, it means that this file is required for use by the system. This file will also be hidden automatically. You should not delete system files.

The Program Tab

The Program tab of the DOS Properties dialog box, shown in Figure 6.5, is used to specify how this MS-DOS program will start up. The first line shows the program or shortcut name.

The following options are available on the Program tab:

- **Cmd line:** Allows you to type the path and command needed to start an MS-DOS application. You can enter any information on this command line, including command-line parameters that the program might need to run.

- **Working:** Allows you to specify a working directory. The working directory is where the MS-DOS program will store its data. Normally, the working directory is the same as the directory where the MS-DOS program is stored. The path statement you place here can be a UNC name for a network location. For example, your MS-DOS program may reside in C:\Games\Doom, but you might want to store data associated with that program on the network at \\MainServer\Games\DoomData.

F I G U R E 6.5

The Program tab of
the DOS Properties
dialog box

- **Batch file:** Allows you to specify a batch file that will run before the MS-DOS program starts. This is a nice way to start a terminate-and-stay-resident (TSR) program that the MS-DOS program might need. You might also use this to log on to a network server from which the MS-DOS program will pull data.

- **Shortcut key:** Allows you to specify a shortcut key to start this application. The shortcut keys will be reserved for the entire system; no matter where you are, if you hit that shortcut key, this program will start executing.

WARNING Be careful when you assign shortcut keys, because they are reserved for the entire system and will overwrite any other shortcut keys that have been created within applications. For example, if you assign the shortcut key Ctrl+C to an MS-DOS application, you will no longer be able to use that shortcut to copy selected information to the Clipboard.

- **Run:** A list box that allows you to change the default window in which the MS-DOS program will start. Your choices are Normal window, Minimized, and Maximized. The Normal window opens up a full-screen MS-DOS window. Minimized will start the program and then run it minimized on your taskbar. Maximized will place the program in an MS-DOS window, which will take up roughly three-quarters of your screen.

> You can force a normal full-screen MS-DOS window into a windowed MS-DOS window and vice-versa by pressing Alt+Enter.

- **Close on exit:** If you run the MEM command from an MS-DOS command prompt, it will write data to the MS-DOS screen about the current memory configurations and then close the window before you have a chance to read it. To avoid this problem, make sure that the Close on Exit checkbox is not selected. This will force the MS-DOS window to stay open until you close it by clicking the X in the upper-right corner.

- **Change Icon:** Allows you to change the icon shown for the MS-DOS program for which you are creating this PIF. Normally, you will see the MS-DOS icon with your filename listed below it.

- **Advanced:** Most MS-DOS programs will run without forcing you to make the modifications available when you click the Advanced button. The Advanced options are discussed next.

Advanced Program Settings   When you click the Advanced button in the Program tab of the DOS Properties dialog box, the Advanced Program Settings dialog box appears, as shown in Figure 6.6.

The following settings are available in this dialog box:

- **Prevent MS-DOS–based programs from detecting Windows:** Some MS-DOS programs can detect whether or not they are running within a Windows virtual machine or in the native MS-DOS environment. Many of these programs will issue an error message telling you that they cannot be run from Windows. Selecting this option will prevent those programs from detecting that they are running in a Windows virtual machine.

- **Suggest MS-DOS mode as necessary:** Allows Windows to decide whether or not the MS-DOS program will run best from a Windows virtual machine or in the native MS-DOS environment. If the program requires the native MS-DOS environment, Windows will automatically run a wizard to create a custom icon that you can select to run the program.

> **WARNING**
>
> If the program needs to run in the native MS-DOS environment and the Suggest MS-DOS mode as necessary option is not selected, the program may run poorly or could fail completely. Some MS-DOS programs, like flight simulators and graphic design programs, are resource-intensive and should be run only in MS–DOS mode. If you are having problems because an MS-DOS application crashes when running in a window, switch it to MS-DOS mode.

- **MS-DOS mode:** Forces the program to be run in the native MS-DOS environment. It does this by unloading the Windows 98 Desktop. You will see the normal Windows 98 shutdown screens. Once Windows 98 is unloaded, the program will reboot your system, and then run in the MS-DOS environment.

- **Warn before entering MS-DOS mode:** Displays a warning message when Windows 98 is about to shut down and restart in MS-DOS mode.

- **Use current MS-DOS configuration:** Forces the MS-DOS program to use the current AUTOEXEC.BAT and CONFIG.SYS files to load environment settings for the MS-DOS program about to start.

- **Specify a new MS-DOS configuration:** Allows you to specify AUTOEXEC.BAT and CONFIG.SYS settings for your program.

- **Configuration:** Brings up a checklist of items that can be added to your CONFIG.SYS and AUTOEXEC.BAT programs, as shown in Figure 6.7. The checklist is nice because you don't need to remember all of the syntax to properly set up these files. Just click on a choice, and it will be added.

FIGURE 6.7

MS-DOS configuration options

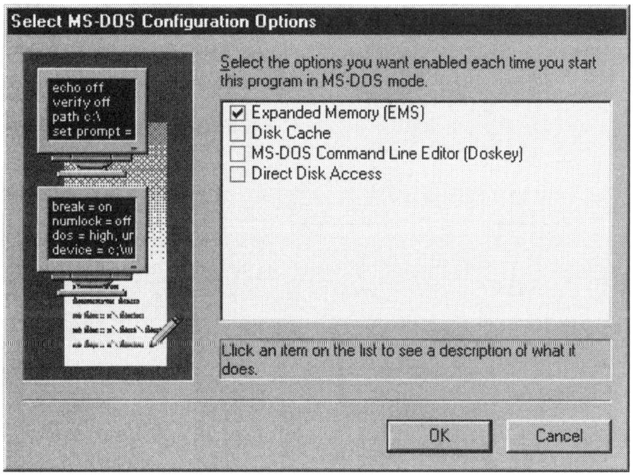

When you specify a new MS-DOS configuration, you can also copy and paste settings from a DOS boot disk. This procedure will essentially replace the need for your boot disk, and it is especially useful when your program needs specific DOS drivers or other TSRs to be loaded.

The Font Tab

The Font tab of the DOS Properties dialog box, shown in Figure 6.8, allows you to specify what font type you want your MS-DOS window to display.

FIGURE 6.8

The Font tab of the DOS Properties dialog box

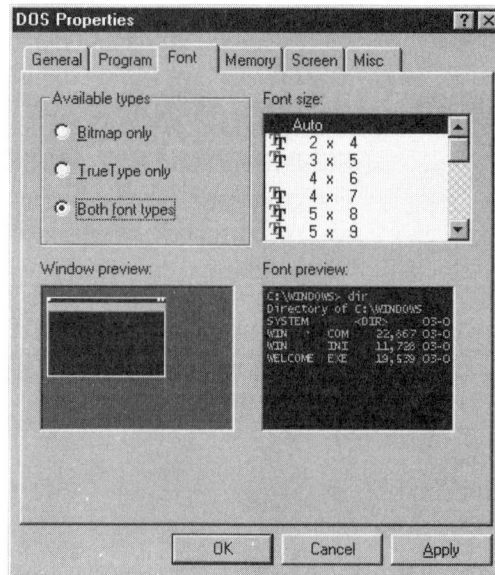

Bitmap fonts take up more space than TrueType fonts. Bitmap fonts are saved as bitmap images; every font size must be rendered and saved as a bitmap image.

TrueType fonts are stored as a set of instructions on how to render the image. As each TrueType letter is rendered, the instructions are modified appropriately. This is similar to following a cookie recipe. The recipe might call for one egg and one cup of sugar for 10 cookies. To make 100 cookies, you would increase all the recipe specifications 10 times (that is, add 10 eggs and 10 cups of sugar). Some printers don't support TrueType fonts and require bitmap fonts to be downloaded to them.

You can also alter the font size. The Auto setting will adjust the size of the font based on the size of the window in which it will be displayed.

You will find it much more convenient to view MS-DOS windows if you leave the Font Size setting as Auto. This is especially true if you resize an MS-DOS window.

The Memory Tab

The Memory tab of the DOS Properties dialog box, shown in Figure 6.9, is used to adjust how the different types of memory available to an MS-DOS program should be used.

The following options are available on the Memory tab:

- **Conventional memory:** Conventional memory is considered the first 1MB of memory (640KB of conventional memory and 384KB of high memory). Within the conventional memory area, the following items can be modified:

  - The Total box indicates how much conventional memory is set aside for this program. In most cases, the Auto setting will be best.

  - The Initial Environment box is used to set aside some conventional memory for use by the COMMAND.COM MS-DOS interpreter and variable settings like PATH statements in an AUTOEXEC.BAT file.

> **NOTE** If you increase the initial environment amount, you will decrease the amount of conventional memory set aside for this program.

- The Protected checkbox can increase the memory protection for your application. When this checkbox is selected, the memory set aside for this program will not be swapped to a swapfile. This can impact the performance of your entire system.

- **Expanded (EMS) memory:** Specifies the maximum amount of expanded memory to allocate to this program. The numbers are in kilobytes. If you set this to Auto, no limit is imposed on the program.

> **NOTE** Older MS-DOS programs have difficulty with large amounts of expanded and extended memory. If this is the case, try setting the values of the Expanded Memory and Extended Memory options to 8192 or 8MB.

- **Extended (XMS) memory:** Specifies the maximum amount of extended memory to allocate to this program. The numbers are in kilobytes. If you set this to Auto, no limit is imposed on the program.

- **MS-DOS protected-mode (DPMI) memory:** Specifies the maximum amount of DPMI memory to allocate to this program. The numbers are in kilobytes. Setting this value to Auto allows Windows to choose limits based on current system configuration settings.

> **WARNING** If you have a DEVICE=C:\DOS\EMM386.EXE NOEMS parameter in your CONFIG.SYS file, Windows cannot provide you with DPMI memory. You can use the RAM parameter with $x=mmmm\text{-}nnnn$ statement to allocate enough space in upper memory for Windows 98 to create an EMS page frame for your DPMI memory.

The Screen Tab

The Screen tab of the DOS Properties dialog box, shown in Figure 6.10, is used to determine how the MS-DOS program will start up, such as whether it will be in a full screen or a window, if it will have toolbars, and so on.

The following options are available on the Screen tab:

- **Usage:** Determines how the MS-DOS application will be viewed. Within the Usage area, the following items can be adjusted.

  - The Full-screen setting specifies that the program will run in a full screen. This uses the least memory and CPU cycles and is used to run many graphics-based MS-DOS programs. This is faster for graphical applications because the processor doesn't need to re-render an image into a smaller version that would be displayed in a Window.

  - The Window setting specifies that the application should run in a window. This makes it easier to share information with other Windows programs through cut-and-paste operations. This is used primarily with text-based applications.

  - The Initial Size setting specifies a certain number of lines to display on the screen when you start this program. Many programs will override this setting and set it back to the default.

- **Window:** Modifies how the MS-DOS window will be displayed.

  - The Display Toolbar option adds a toolbar to the MS-DOS window. The toolbar has features like Cut and Paste buttons.

  - The Restore Settings on Startup checkbox resets all the changes you have made after the program finishes executing. This includes things like position, font, and window size.

- **Performance:** Affects the way MS-DOS windows use video drivers.

  - The Fast ROM Emulation option allows the system to emulate video ROM drivers while in protected mode. This allows the system to write to the screen faster. If your program is having difficulty writing text to the screen or other video problems, try disabling this option.

  - The Dynamic Memory Allocation option allows the program to hold memory for video display. This is useful for programs that switch between text and graphics modes, such as when a word processing program switches from text view to a print preview. If this option is not set, the memory needed to switch displays must be reallocated every time you switch modes.

NOTE

If you want to ensure that there is always enough memory for Windows 98 to correctly display this program, be sure that the Dynamic Memory Allocation option is not selected.

The Misc Tab

The Misc tab of the DOS Properties dialog box, shown in Figure 6.11, is the catch-all for the options that don't fit neatly into the other categories. This includes things like shortcut keys and mouse interaction.

This tab includes the following options:

- **Foreground:** When the Allow Screen Saver checkbox is selected, the Windows 98 screen saver will be allowed to display even when the MS-DOS program is running in the foreground. When deselected, the screen saver will be prevented from running when the MS-DOS application is in the foreground.

F I G U R E   6.11

The Miscellaneous tab
of the DOS Properties
dialog box

- **Mouse:** Affects how the mouse is used within an MS-DOS window.

  - The QuickEdit option allows the mouse to be used to highlight text within the MS-DOS window. This should not be used when the MS-DOS application itself supports a mouse.

  - The Exclusive Mode option confines the mouse within the MS-DOS window. This can be useful with programs that lose mouse synchronization between the MS-DOS window and the Windows 98 environment.

- **Background:** The Always Suspend option forces the MS-DOS application to pause when it has been minimized or placed in the background.

- **Termination:** The Warn If Still Active choice displays a dialog box warning you that the MS-DOS application is about to close when you try to close it. This will give you a chance to cancel the program termination and save any work you might have forgotten to save from the MS-DOS application. This is especially useful if the MS-DOS application opens up sensitive files. If the MS-DOS application terminates, those files may become corrupted.

- **Idle Sensitivity:** Determines when the system suspends a program. A program will be suspended after a certain length of inactivity. This can be caused by the program waiting for some user input. This slider control is useful when a program is using the math coprocessor. Even though the program is running (using the math coprocessor), Windows 98 might think it is idle.

- **Other:** Fast Pasting allows pasting from the Windows 98 Clipboard into the MS-DOS–based program. If you are having trouble doing this, try deselecting this option.

- **Windows Shortcut Keys:** When these shortcut key options are selected, you can use them within the MS-DOS window. The keystrokes themselves will bypass the MS-DOS program and be sent directly to Windows 98. If you need to have the MS-DOS program receive any of the keystrokes, deselect the appropriate option.

Configuring a PIF for an MS-DOS Program

Now that you know about all the properties you can set for your MS-DOS programs, you are prepared to create a PIF. Follow the steps in Exercise 6.2 to configure a PIF. For this exercise, you will use the MS-DOS Prompt program, which is stored in the Programs folder beneath the Start Menu folder, as shown in Figure 6.12.

EXERCISE 6.2

Configuring a PIF

1. Locate an MS-DOS–based program.

2. To get to Windows Explorer, select Start ➢ Programs➢Explorer.

3. From Explorer, "drill down" (either double-click on the folders in the left pane of the window or click on the + symbols next to the folders in the left pane) to the Start Menu folder.

EXERCISE 6.2 (CONTINUED)

4. You should see the Programs folder. Click on the Programs folder in the left pane. You should see the contents of this folder (see Figure 6.12).
5. Right-click the MS-DOS prompt and choose Properties. You should now see the General tab displayed (see Figure 6.4).
6. Click on the different tabs to see the information displayed.
7. If you want further detail on any option, click the question mark in the upper-right corner of the Properties dialog box, and then click the option that interests you.
8. When you are finished, close the Properties dialog box.

FIGURE 6.12

Contents of the Programs folder

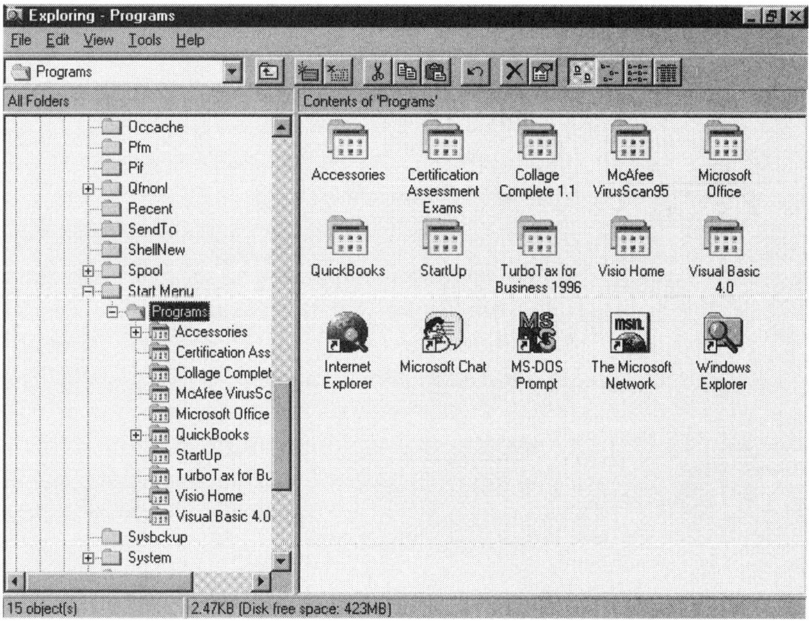

Using the Windows Update Utility

Microsoft periodically releases service packs for different software programs. The service packs are used to do any of the following:

- Fix problems with current drivers, DLLs, and other files

- Add new features to drivers, DLLs, and other files

- Add new components to take advantage of more of the features already included in the current drivers, DLLs, and other files.

Microsoft ✓ *Exam* *Objective*

Tune and optimize the system in a Microsoft environment and a mixed Microsoft and NetWare environment. Tasks include:

- Updating drivers and applying service packs by using Windows Update and the Signature Verification tool

The Signature Verification tool is discussed later in this chapter.

Keeping track of all of these modified files can be cumbersome. Windows 98 has a utility called Windows Update that provides a central location where you can find product enhancements, new system files, device drivers, and any other features that have been added.

If you skipped the Microsoft's Registration Wizard when you installed Windows 98, the Windows Update Wizard won't work.

Running the Microsoft Registration Wizard changes two lines in the Windows 98 Registry. You can easily make those changes yourself by creating text with the following information:

1. Load Notepad.

2. Type **REGEDIT4.** Press Enter.

3. On the next line type: [**Hkey_Local_Machine\Software\Microsoft\ Windows\CurrentVersion**].

4. Press Enter, and on the next line type **"RegDone"="1"**.

5. Press Enter, and on the next line type: [**Hkey_Local_Machine\ Software\Microsoft\Windows\CurrentVersion\Welcome\ RegWiz**].

6. Press Enter, and on the next line type **"@"="1"**. Press Enter.

7. Save the files as UPDATE.REG.

8. Now go to Windows Explorer, locate the UPDATE.REG file, right-click the UPDATE.REG file and then select Merge. This then updates the Registry, and you can now run the Update Wizard.

To update files on your system with the most recent versions, run the Windows Update program. Click Start ➣ Settings ➣ Windows Update. An Internet connection to the Microsoft Web site will be initiated as shown in Figure 6.13.

F I G U R E   6.13

The Windows Update utility

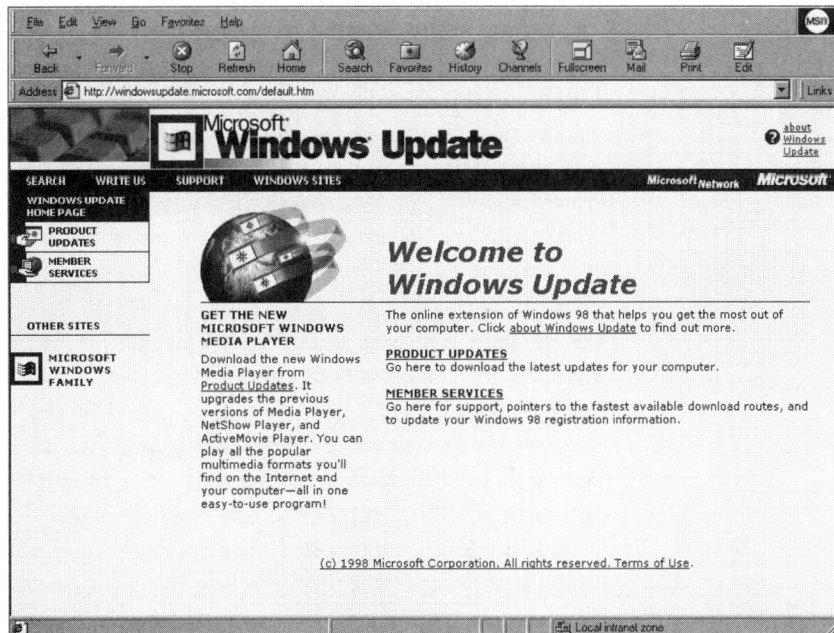

From here you should select the Product Updates icon on the left side of the screen or from the hyperlink in the middle of the page. You will be asked to allow a program to scan your system to determine what products you currently have (see Figure 6.14). The information gained by the program is not sent to Microsoft. Once the program determines what has been installed on your system and what service packs, if any, are there, it will generate a list of available downloads from which you can choose. Some of these items will be listed in a Critical Update, Pick of the Month Update, Recommended Updates, and Additional Files.

F I G U R E   6.14

Scan System
dialog box

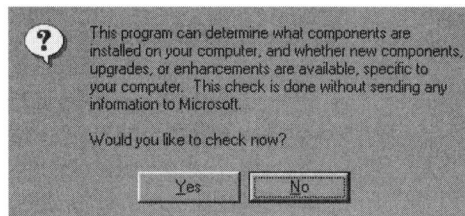

As you can see in Figure 6.15, the Outlook Express service pack was chosen to be downloaded. Once you have made your update choices, click the Download Now item at the bottom of the Web page. This will begin the download and installation process.

The download process will provide feedback in the form of a download and installation dialog box shown in Figure 6.16. If you have chosen to download and install multiple files, you may be asked to reboot your system during the installation portion of the dialog. Normally, you should choose No. This will allow the other programs to continue to do their installations as well. Once all of the installations have completed, then you can reboot your system. This will save you time because there may be several programs that require you to reboot your system. It's better to reboot once than to reboot several times.

Once you are finished downloading and installing, you will be presented with a dialog box that summarizes the downloaded programs and whether or not they were successfully installed (see Figure 6.17).

If you want to view which files you have downloaded and used for updates, you can rerun the Windows Update utility. Once the main Web site appears, click the History item. You should see a list and description of the files you downloaded and when that was done (see Figure 6.18).

F I G U R E   6.15

Select updates to
download

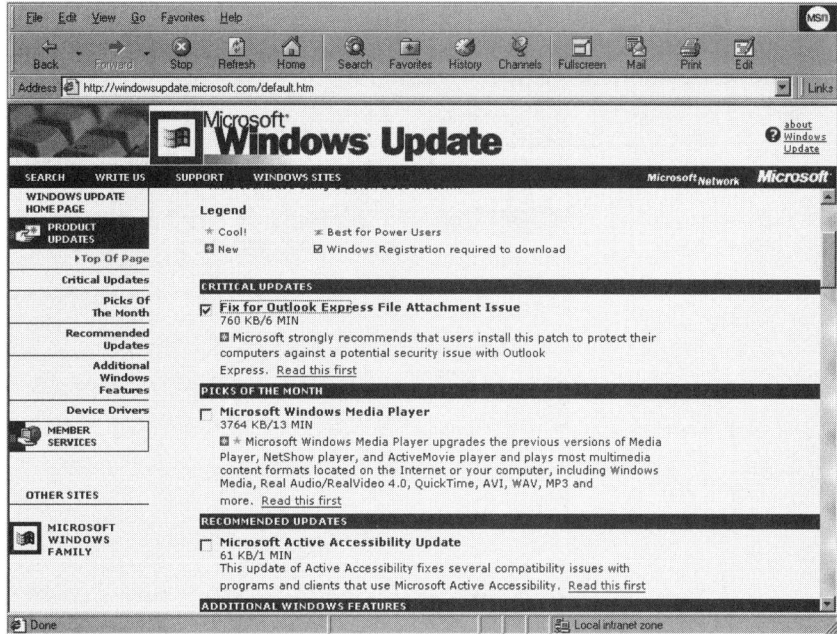

F I G U R E   6.16

The Download/
Installation progress
dialog box

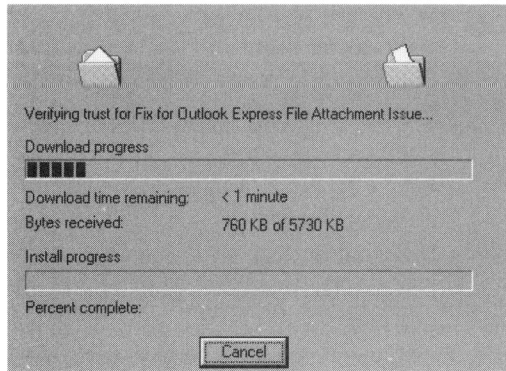

F I G U R E   6.17

Installation Summary
dialog box

F I G U R E 6.18

Windows Update
History window

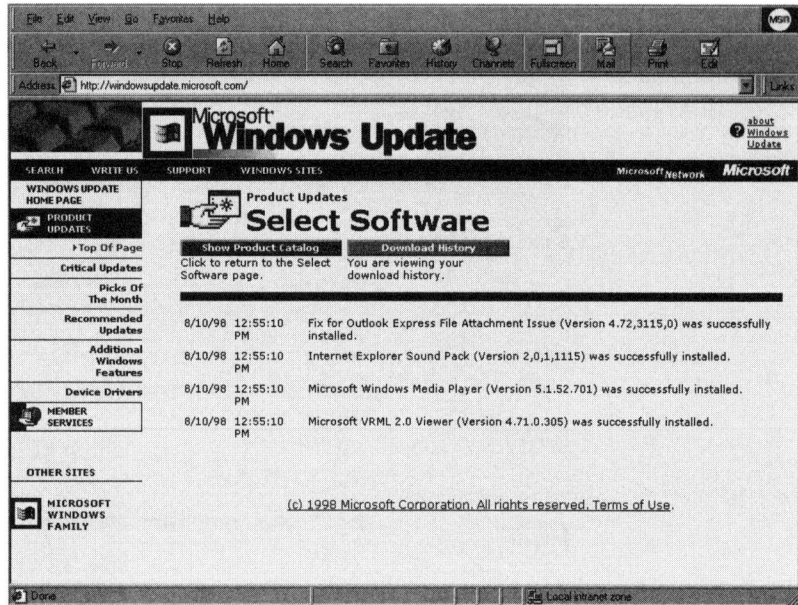

F I G U R E 6.18

Windows Update
History window

The way you remove updates from Windows 98 depends on whether or not you have a connection to the Internet. If you have a connection, you can do the following.

Start the Windows Update utility by selection Start ➢ Settings ➢ Windows Update. You will be presented with the Windows Update dialog box. Choose the Program Updates and then choose the Device Driver item from the list of choices on the left. This will open another Window as shown in Figure 6.19. Click the Restore button. This will allow you to select updated drivers from the left panel. Once you have made your selections, click the Uninstall button, and your new drivers will be replaced with your old drivers. Your old drivers are saved to a backup folder when they are updated.

If you don't have an Internet connection, you can use the Update Wizard Uninstall utility. Click Start ➢ Programs ➢ Accessories ➢ System Tools ➢ System Information Utility. This will start the System Information utility. From the Tools menu, select Update Wizard Uninstall. This will start the Wizard. In the Wizard, choose which files you want to uninstall and then choose OK. The current files selected will revert to their previous versions.

FIGURE 6.19

Restoring updates

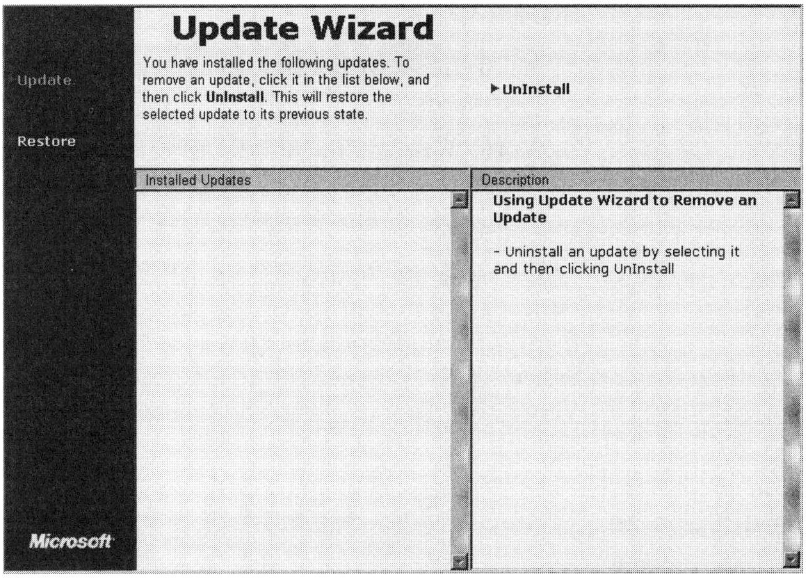

Signature Verification

With all of the information and files available on the Internet, the security of your system is quickly becoming a task that needs to be monitored closely. Using digital signatures is one method of guaranteeing that files downloaded from the Internet or elsewhere are from whom they are supposed to be.

Microsoft Exam Objective

Tune and optimize the system in a Microsoft environment and a mixed Microsoft and NetWare environment. Tasks include:

- Updating drivers and applying service packs by using Windows Update and the Signature Verification tool

NOTE

The Windows Update program is discussed earlier in the chapter.

When a digital signature is applied to a file, that file has the following characteristics:

- The files have not been tampered with since the digital signature was applied.

- The author of the file(s) is known. To gain a digital certificate, you must apply for one through a Certificate Authority (CA). The CA verifies the author of the work and provides other services.

The Signature Verification tool allows you to search for both signed and unsigned files in your system. To start the Signature Verification tool, open the System Information utility by clicking Start ➢ Programs ➢ Accessories ➢ System Tools ➢ System Information Utility. From there, choose Signature Verification Tool from the Tools menu (see Figure 6.20).

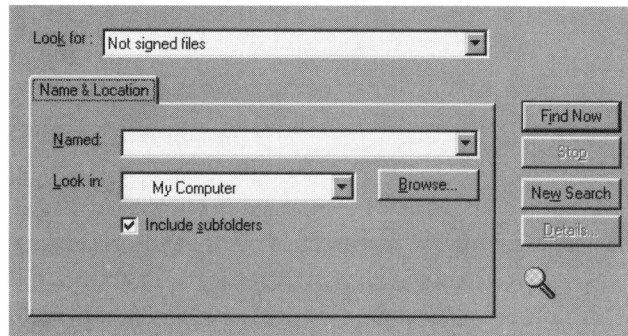

FIGURE 6.20

The Signature Verification tool

You can use the tool to search for signed files in a particular folder. The system will display the signed files that it finds. If you select a particular program and click the Details button, you can see general information about the file. If you click the Fine Print button (see Figure 6.21), you will get the copyright information for this file. Other tabs will give you additional information about a file and its digital certificate.

F I G U R E   6.21

General tab of the
digital certificate

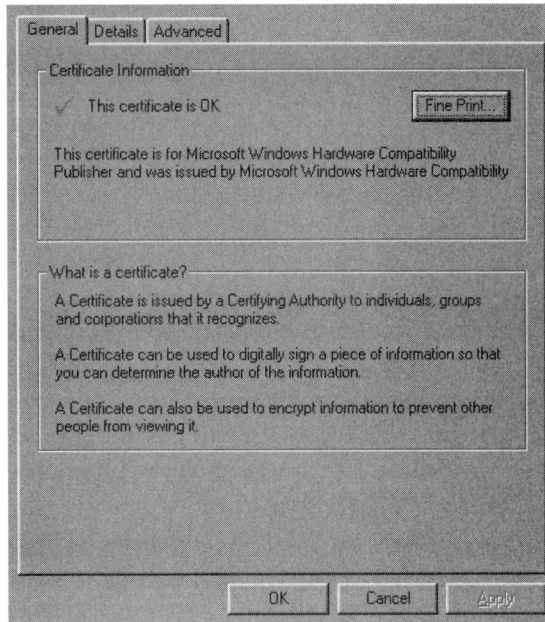

Summary

In this chapter, we discussed how different types of applications behave and interact in the Windows 98 environment. Because 16-bit Windows programs cooperatively multitask and share a single thread of execution, they can step on each other's resources. They are also less efficient than 32-bit programs, which don't share address space and can have multiple threads of execution. Because of this sharing, 16-bit resources are not returned to the system until all 16-bit Windows applications are terminated.

GPFs are handled differently for these different types of programs also. When a 16-bit program is hung or crashed, it will hang all of the other 16-bit programs. MS-DOS programs just terminate. The 32-bit Windows programs also terminate, but generally don't hang other running applications.

There are still portions of 16-bit code in the Windows 98 operating system. They were retained for speed and backward compatibility. The Win16Mutex flag is used to keep different programs from trying to use the same non-reentrant 16-bit procedures.

MS-DOS–based programs use PIFs to configure the virtual machine in which they run. Many options can be changed from the DOS Properties dialog box, including window type, font size, and toolbars, as well as behind-the-scenes instructions, like memory management features.

You can use the Windows Update utility to manage different versions of the files that make up your Windows 98 operating system. With this tool, you can have a program scan your computer for current configurations and then download the appropriate upgrades and service packs. The tool also allows you to revert to older versions of your files. This is possible because the old versions are not deleted; they are simply moved to a backup folder.

Protecting yourself on the Internet is always a good idea. Companies doing business on the Internet have developed a method of digitally signing your files. Once a digital signature has been applied to a file, that file can be verified as untampered with and uncorrupted. You can use the Signature Verification utility to locate and view files with digital signatures.

Review Questions

1. Which of the following are virtual machines used in Windows 98? Choose all that apply.

    A. System VM

    B. Core VM

    C. W98 VM

    D. MS-DOS VM

> **NOTE** For the next three questions, please use this scenario. You have three 16-bit applications, one 32-bit application, and two MS-DOS–based applications running.

2. If one of the 16-bit applications is hung, how many programs will be hung including the hung application?

    A. 1

    B. 2

    C. 3

    D. 5

3. If one of the 32-bit applications has hung, how many programs will be hung including the hung application?

    A. 1

    B. 2

    C. 3

    D. 5

4. If an MS-DOS application has a GPF, how many programs will be affected including the crashed MS-DOS application?

    A. 1

    B. 2

    C. 3

    D. 5

5. You want to run a batch file to log on to a network server before your MS-DOS application runs. What is the easiest method to accomplish this?

    A. Build a shortcut to the batch file and to the MS-DOS program; double-click on the batch shortcut first, and then run the MS-DOS program.

    B. Go to a command prompt and run the batch file before running the MS-DOS program.

    C. Add the batch file to the Batch File parameter in the property sheet for the MS-DOS program.

    D. You don't need to run the batch file because Windows 98 will automatically detect that the MS-DOS program needs access to the server and will log you in.

6. Your MS-DOS program is named FOO.EXE. You create a PIF file for your MS-DOS program. What is the name of the PIF file?

    A. MS-DOS.PIF

    B. PIF.EXE

    C. _DEFAULT.PIF

    D. FOO.PIF

7. In the Working parameter of an MS-DOS property sheet, you specify C:\Temp. What, if anything, will be placed in the C:\Temp directory?

    A. Output files used by your MS-DOS program

    B. The files used by Windows 98 to track program performance

    C. The .INI files used by all the Windows programs running at the same time your MS-DOS program is running

    D. Nothing

8. You are editing a document in Microsoft Word. You highlight a line of text and press Ctrl+C to copy it to the Clipboard. Suddenly your MS-DOS application starts up. What could cause this?

    A. The OLE functionality of Microsoft Word is linked to your MS-DOS program.

    B. You have chosen Ctrl+C as a shortcut for your MS-DOS–based application.

    C. Ctrl+C always starts up the last used MS-DOS program.

    D. This is a glitch in the computer system and should never happen.

9. When you are in your MS-DOS program, you want to be able to press Alt+Enter to switch to another running application. How could you enable this feature?

    A. In the Misc tab of the MS-DOS property sheet, click on the Alt+Enter checkbox.

    B. You don't have to do anything—this functionality always exists for MS-DOS applications.

    C. This is not an available feature and can't be implemented.

    D. You must edit the Registry in order to do this.

10. Because 16-bit code is non-reentrant, how does Windows handle multitasking procedures that require the same DLL function usage?

    A. Windows employs a Win16Mutex flag to signal other programs that a particular 16-bit procedure is currently in use.

    B. Windows employs a 16- and 32-Mutex flag to signal other programs that a particular procedure is currently in use.

    C. Windows does not need to worry about this because it is a cooperatively multitasked environment.

    D. Windows uses thunking to work with all 32-bit code instead of working with flags to signal 16-bit DLL usage.

CHAPTER

7

Managing Disk Resources and Utilities

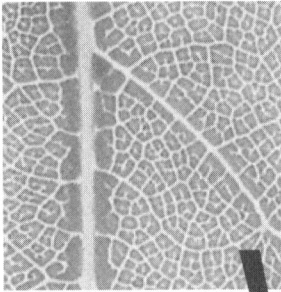

Windows 98 has many built-in utilities for managing your hard drive and files. Support for 32-bit disk drivers has also been enhanced from previous versions of Windows.

Microsoft ✓ *Exam Objective*

Tune and optimize the system in a Microsoft environment and a mixed Microsoft and NetWare environment. Tasks include:

- Optimizing the hard disk by using Disk Defragmenter and ScanDisk
- Compressing data by using DriveSpace 3 and the Compression Agent
- Updating drivers and applying service packs by using Windows Update and the Signature Verification tool
- Automating tasks by using Maintenance Wizard
- Scheduling tasks by using Task Scheduler
- Checking for corrupt files and extracting files from the installation media by using the System File Checker

NOTE See Chapter 6 for complete coverage of Windows Update and the Signature Verification tool, and Chapter 16 for details on the System File Checker.

Microsoft ✓ Exam Objective

Configure hard disks. Tasks include:

- Disk compression
- Partitioning
- Enabling large disk support
- Converting to FAT32

This chapter begins with a discussion of the disk drivers supported by Windows 98 and how to troubleshoot problems with your disk drivers. Then it covers long-filename support, as well as how to troubleshoot problems with long filenames. You'll then learn about the integrated tools and utilities, including the disk compressor, disk defragmenter, disk-error checker, and backup and restore programs. Finally, we'll cover all the other disk-management tasks, such as partitioning the hard drive, formatting floppy drives, managing the hard drive cache, and optimizing your cluster size.

> **NOTE** Both the Tune and Optimize objective will be broken down, and only the pertinent subobjective will be shown in its respective place in this chapter.

Windows 98 Disk Drivers

To understand how Windows 98 handles requests to and from the hard disk, you need to understand the driver architecture, as well as the advantages of 32-bit disk drivers. As explained in Chapter 4, *device drivers* are the software that Windows 98 uses to communicate with the hardware. Drivers are a "middleman" of sorts—they interpret commands from Windows 98 and pass the commands along to the hardware.

Like other types of device drivers, disk drivers can be categorized as being *real-mode (16-bit)* or *protected-mode (32-bit)*. Protected-mode drivers are used by Windows 98 and Windows NT. Protected-mode drivers are usually superior in both their stability and performance compared to real-mode drivers (created to be used in the MS-DOS environment). The term protected comes from the fact that applications can be protected from each other, so if one application locks up, it does not affect other applications.

Windows 98 uses 32-bit disk drivers that have been enhanced over the 32-bit versions used in earlier Windows versions. The new disk drivers are capable of supporting large hard drives (LBA mode drives). They also have real-mode (16-bit) versions that can be enabled for compatibility.

Types of Devices and Drivers

The types of disk drives supported by Windows 98 are listed in Table 7.1. Table 7.2 lists the bus adapters that Windows 98 supports.

T A B L E 7.1 Disk Drives Supported by Windows 98	Disk Drive	Description
	IDE	The new standard for most hard drives based on the MFM and RLL standard.
	IDE-LBA	A mode where the motherboard BIOS translates drive parameters to maintain compatibility because IDE drives that are larger than 512MB have a hard time being recognized by both software and hardware.
	Ultra-IDE or Ultra-DMA	This new standard for IDE drives doubles the theoretical throughput of the hard drive from 16.67Mbps to 33.33Mbps. You will need both a UDMA hard drive and a UDMA controller to take advantage of UDMA.
	MFM	The old standard for hard drives—rarely seen anymore.
	SCSI	A standard that allows greater flexibility than IDE (but at a higher cost).
	SCSI 2	The newer SCSI standard that offers (among other things) faster data transfers.

	Bus Adapter	Description
T A B L E 7.2 Bus Adapters Supported by Windows 98	EISA	An early standard for a 32-bit bus.
	PCI	The current 32-bit standard for desktops.
	PCMCIA (PC Card)	The current standard for laptops.
	ISA	The old 16-bit standard.
	MCA (Microchannel)	A 32-bit standard from IBM.
	RLL	A hard drive standard that squeezed 50 percent more drive space from MFM drives with the same physical drive. This technology has been incorporated into the IDE standard.
	VLB	A 32-bit standard especially good for fast video cards, mostly used for 486 computers.
	SCSI2 PCI	A 32-bit *de facto* standard for expansion cards for Pentium-based computers.
	AGP	A 32-bit standard which stands for Advanced Graphics Port—a new standard for high-end video cards.

Windows 98 uses a 32-bit virtual file allocation table file system (VFAT) as the primary file system. VFAT is enabled by default and cannot be turned off. VFAT handles all disk requests and operates in protected mode (32-bit). VFAT communicates with both 32-bit disk drivers (preferred) and with 16-bit disk drivers (for compatibility).

IDE Devices and Drivers

Windows 98 provides protected-mode (32-bit) drivers for the following IDE disk drives:

- LBA (logical block addressing) IDE drives

- Alternate IDE disk drives such as found in docking stations
- IDE-based CD-ROMS
- Bus-mastering IDE chip sets
- SMART (Self-monitoring analysis and reporting technology) hard drives
- Tape backup drives
- CD-ROM changers

SCSI Devices and Drivers

Windows 98 provides 32-bit driver support for SCSI, which earlier versions of Windows 3.x did not. Windows 98 includes drivers for some of the most common SCSI manufacturers, such as Adaptec, Future Domain, and others.

The SCSI drivers included with Windows 98 also support common SCSI specifications, such as Advanced SCSI Programming Interface (ASPI) and Common Access Method (CAM).

DVD Drives

Windows 98 supports both the UDF (Universal Data Format) format, as well as the Mt. Fuji (SFF80980) format. DVD drives under Windows 98 must support DMA. To check on or enable DMA support for DVD drives, go to Control Panel ➤ System ➤ Device Manager, highlight the DVD drive and examine its properties.

Floppy Devices and Drivers

Windows 98 provides a protected-mode (32-bit) driver for the floppy drive. This means that all of the advantages of protected mode (multitasking, performance, and reliability) are now available when using or formatting floppy disks. Note that support for the LS-120 (the 120MB floppy disk drive) has also been added.

Removable Media Drivers

Most removable media have new protected-mode drivers. Windows 98 supports floppy drives, CD-ROM drives, and other removable media, such as Iomega's Zip and Jaz drives. Windows 98 allows you to lock the media so it cannot be ejected during your session. Windows 98 also supports software-controlled ejection of your media.

Improved support for docking stations has also been added. Windows 98 can detect when your docking status has changed, and it can work in *hot docking* (where the computer is on when docking or undocking) or c*old docking* (where the computer is turned off before docking or undocking). Windows 98 can even help resolve hot undocking problems by asking the user to save files that would be lost after the undocking.

Troubleshooting Windows 98 Disk Drivers

Windows 98 sometimes has problems with older hard drives and controllers. You can do several things to troubleshoot a disk driver problem. Most of the solutions entail turning off features of Windows 98 so that it operates in an older, more compatible mode.

Occasionally, you might want to disable certain features of Windows 98, including some features of the 32-bit disk drivers (even though they are working correctly) because they are not what the user wants. For instance, users may want to disable the write-behind cache because they have been losing data during power outages (or just when the user turns the power off without shutting down Windows 98 properly).

Disabling the 32-Bit Mode Drivers

Some older hard drive controllers or older motherboards may have a difficult time using 32-bit drivers. If this is the case, you can set Windows 98 to disable 32-bit mode operation to the hard drive. You can disable the 32-bit mode drivers through the Troubleshooting tab of the File System Properties dialog box, shown in Figure 7.1. Exercise 7.1 shows the steps involved.

FIGURE 7.1

Disabling the 32-bit disk drivers

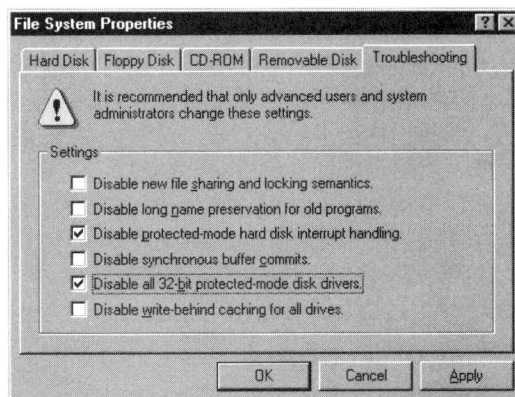

EXERCISE 7.1

Disabling the 32-Bit Mode Drivers

1. Go to Control Panel ➤ System and choose the Performance tab.

2. Click the File System button at the bottom of the dialog box.

3. Choose the Troubleshooting tab in the File System Properties dialog box.

4. Select the two checkboxes to disable 32-bit mode: Disable all 32-bit protected-mode disk drivers, and disable protected-mode hard disk interrupt handling (see Figure 7.1). This will cause 16-bit drivers to be used.

NOTE Installing old DOS drivers directly in the CONFIG.SYS or AUTOEXEC.BAT file can sometimes automatically "trip" the switches in this trouble-shooting exercise.

Disabling the Write-Behind Cache

Earlier versions of DOS introduced the concept of a *hard drive cache,* which is used to read data into RAM before the CPU requests it, hoping that the CPU can get the data from the cache instead of the hard disk.

DOS 6.0 introduced the write-behind cache as an extension of the read cache. A *write-behind cache* fools applications by writing their changes into RAM, and eventually flushing the changes to the hard disk (usually within a couple of seconds). The application will behave as though the data had been written, when the data is actually in volatile RAM. If the computer is turned off for any reason before the data is flushed to disk, the data is gone. Write-behind caching is a default feature of Windows 98 that was designed with performance (not safety) in mind. Exercise 7.2 shows you how to disable the write-behind cache.

EXERCISE 7.2

Disabling the Write-Behind Cache

1. Go to Control Panel ➤ System and choose the Performance tab.

2. Click on the File System button at the bottom of the dialog box.

EXERCISE 7.2 (CONTINUED)

3. Choose the Troubleshooting tab in the File System Properties dialog box (see Figure 7.1).

4. Select Disable Write-Behind Caching For All Drives. Now only the read cache is enabled.

Long Filenames

As explained in Chapter 5, Windows 98 has added the ability to save files with names up to 255 characters long.

> Although filenames can be 255 characters long, the entire path of a file can only be 260 characters.

Spaces in filenames are supported now. All 32-bit programs should be able to recognize, use, and save files with long filenames.

Older 16-bit programs use the older file system API, which does not recognize long filenames. For compatibility purposes, Windows 98 constructs an 8.3 name whenever a long filename is saved.

> When Windows 98 truncates a long filename to make an 8.3 name, it uses the first six characters and then a tilde (~) and then a number from 1 to 9. If there are more than nine files with the same 8.3 alias, then the first five characters are used, then a ~, then the number of the file (11-99). You can see the 8.3 names from the MS-DOS prompt or by viewing the properties of a file.

Once you start using long filenames, you will wonder how you ever got along with just the 8.3 convention. The only problems you will probably face will be exchanging files with people who are not using Windows 95 or Windows 98 (they will see the 8.3 alias) and who are using applications or utilities (older 16-bit applications like Word 6.0 or Office 4.3) that don't recognize the long filenames. The following sections describe how long filenames work on servers and the problems you may encounter with long filenames.

Long Filenames on Servers

Windows 98 can save files with long filenames on networks if the servers support long filenames. Microsoft's Windows NT versions 3.5 and higher support long filenames natively. Novell's NetWare needs to have support for OS/2 installed before Windows 98 can use long filenames on the server.

Microsoft
✓ *Exam*
Objective

Diagnose and resolve resource access problems in a Microsoft environment or a mixed Microsoft and NetWare environment.

If you have DOS clients on the network, they will see the long filename files as 8.3 files. Macintosh clients will see the long filename if it is less than 34 characters (the Macintosh limit). Otherwise, the Macintosh client will see the 8.3 name.

Problems Associated with Long Filenames

You may come across programs, such as applications, backup programs, or utilities, that don't recognize long filenames. Another problem you may encounter with long filenames is that they take up more directory entries, therefore limiting the number of files that may be stored in a root directory. The following sections discuss these issues and suggest how to troubleshoot and fix problems.

Programs That Don't Recognize Long Filenames

The main category of programs that won't recognize long filenames are older, 16-bit programs. These programs will show only the 8.3 alias for both folders and files when you go to open or save a file. The solution to this problem is quite simple—upgrade to the 32-bit, Windows 95/98 version of the software.

Older backup programs may not recognize long filenames (LFNs). If you use older backup programs, or programs that are not certified to work with Windows 98, you probably will be able to back up your files, but only the 8.3 names will be saved. If you do restore your files and find you have only 8.3 names, there is no way to fix the problem—the long filenames will be permanently gone.

Older versions of utility programs such as Norton Disk Utilities and PC Tools are not compatible with Windows 98. These older disk utilities will not only report errors when they encounter long filenames, but they may also cause long filenames and even data files to be erased if you have them "fix" the long filenames. Using compression in Windows 98 also raises your risk of incompatibilities with older utilities.

WARNING   Make sure that any backup or utility program you run under Windows 98 has been certified for Windows 98.

The 512 Directory Entry Limit in Root Directories

A file is normally allocated 13 spaces (one directory entry) for the filename. Long filenames work by being assigned one directory entry for every 13 spaces of the filename. For example, if the long filename is composed of 27 to 39 characters, it takes three directory entries, and so on.

By default, the root of any volume is limited to 512 directory entries. Under DOS, that would mean you were limited to 512 files in the root directory, no matter how much hard drive space you had left. Under Windows 98, if each file takes five directory entries (names of 53 to 65 characters on average), then there are only enough directory entries for a little more than 100 files. The solution is either to use shorter names for files in the root directory or keep as few files as possible in the root of any volume.

NOTE   The 512 FAT entry limitation applies only to FAT16 volumes, not FAT32 volumes.

Turning Off Long Filenames

If you have an application that is incompatible with long filenames, you can temporarily disable long filenames, run your application, and re-enable long filenames again. You can also disable long filenames on a permanent basis.

To temporarily back up and remove long filenames, you can run the LFNBK utility, which copies all of the long filenames to a file and then renames the files to match their 8.3 aliases. Exercise 7.3 shows the steps for backing up your old filenames, deleting them, and then restoring your saved filenames.

WARNING You should just read through Exercise 7.3 or perform the steps on a non-critical computer. LFNBK is an advanced utility and should be run only by people with a very good working knowledge of Windows 98.

EXERCISE 7.3

Backing Up, Deleting, and Restoring Long Filenames

1. Go to Control Panel ➢ System and choose the Performance tab.

2. Click the File System button at the bottom of the dialog box.

3. Choose the Troubleshooting tab in the File System Properties dialog box (see Figure 7.1).

4. Check the Disable Long Name Preservation For Old Programs option.

5. Close all applications and files.

6. At a command prompt, type **LFNBK /b** *drive*, where *drive* is the drive from which you want the long filenames removed. LFNBK will back up the long filenames to a file on the root of the drive called LFNBK.DAT, and it will remove long filenames from your drive by renaming all your files to their 8.3 alias.

7. Restart your computer and run your application that is incompatible with long filenames.

8. At a command prompt, type **LFNBK /r** *drive*, where *drive* is the drive to which you want to restore long filenames.

9. Return to the Troubleshooting tab of the File System Properties dialog box and uncheck the Disable Long Name Preservation For Old Programs option.

10. Restart your computer.

WARNING If your directory structure changes for any reason (such as defragmentation, adding and deleting folders, and so on), the LFNBK.DAT file will no longer precisely correspond to your drive, and your long filenames cannot be restored.

To permanently disable long filenames, you need to first remove long filenames using the LFNBK /b option. You can also use the Scandsk /o option to remove long filenames. You will then need to go to the Registry in Hkey_Local_Machine\System\CurrentControlSet\Control\FileSystem and set the Win31FileSystem value to 1 (see Chapter 5 for more information about modifying the Registry). After your next reboot, your file system will use the 8.3 DOS naming conventions.

Disk Compression

Disk compression has been around for many years. Some early versions of disk compression required that a hardware compression board be installed in the computer; eventually disk compression became software-based.

Microsoft ✓ *Exam* *Objective*

Configure hard disks. Tasks include:

▪ Disk compression

The primary benefit of using disk compression is that you can store more on a hard drive. The two disadvantages of using compression are a speed decrease and a chance for the entire drive to become corrupted. With prices of hard drives dropping rapidly the last couple of years, compression makes more sense for computers that are hard to upgrade to larger hard drives (such as laptops) than for computers easily upgraded (such as desktops).

Windows 98 supports and comes with software-based, real-time compression of volumes and disk drives by using the program called DriveSpace 3. By using compression, you can gain anywhere from 10 percent to 100 percent or more disk space. Windows 98 has new protected-mode compression drivers, but is also backward compatible with older compression programs from Microsoft. Because compression is now an integral part of Windows 98, both the paging file and Windows 98 itself can be kept on a compressed drive.

WARNING   Drives compressed under Windows 98 are unavailable to both OS/2 and to Windows NT. If you are dual-booting Windows 98 and NT, you should not use compression. Although compressed removable drives created under Windows 98 have a README file that says that they require Windows 98, floppies compressed with Windows 98 have been read successfully on a Windows 95B (OSR2) computer.

Windows 98 is compatible with DOS compression programs, including DBLSPACE (DOS 6.0 and 6.20) and DRVSPACE (DOS 6.22). Windows 98 replaces the DBLSPACE.BIN or DRVSPACE.BIN files in the root directory with ones that it can unload, so that the new 32-bit version (DBLSPACX .VXD) can be loaded.

The version of compression that comes with Windows 98 is fully integrated into the operating system. This means that Registry files, page files, and system files can all reside on a compressed drive. Compressed drives can hold long filenames and can be cached by Vcache.

When you compress a volume, you have two choices:

- Compress the entire volume.

- Use some of the free space on the volume to make a new, compressed volume.

For example, if you had a 2GB drive (your E: drive) with 500MB of free space, you could compress the entire E: drive, giving you approximately 1GB of free space, or you could use part of the 500MB (let's say 150MB) to create a new drive (call it H:) that would have approximately 300MB of free space.

NOTE

Although DriveSpace 3 will recognize FAT32 volumes, FAT32 volumes cannot be compressed by DriveSpace 3.

Compressing a Drive Using DriveSpace 3

When you compress a drive, you are actually taking the contents of an entire drive and putting them into one large file. The file is called a *compressed volume file (CVF)*. The CVF usually has a filename such as DRVSPACE.000 or DBLSPACE.000. DBLSPACE.000 appears if Windows 98 reads an older compressed drive, and DRVSPACE.000 appears when Windows 98 reads a newer compressed drive or creates a new one.

Microsoft ✔ *Exam* *Objective*

Tune and optimize the system in a Microsoft environment and a mixed Microsoft and NetWare environment. Tasks include:

- Compressing data by using DriveSpace3 and the Compression Agent

When you compress a drive, the CVF is stored on the host drive, which is the original drive. The host drive letter is then changed to a higher letter, usually *H*. Programs see the compressed drive normally, but Windows 98 is actually compressing and decompressing files into and out of the CVF (which is on the H: drive) and displaying the uncompressed files as the C: drive. You can choose to hide the host drive, which is a good option for users with less experience; they will hve less chance of damaging or deleting the CVF.

WARNING

It is absolutely *essential* that the CVF is not modified or edited by hand. Doing so could cause the entire compressed volume to become corrupt.

Compressing a Floppy Disk Drive

Compressing a drive under Windows 98 is a simple process. When you run the DriveSpace program and choose to compress a drive, it will show you before and after compression information, as shown in Figures 7.2 and 7.3. Follow the steps in Exercise 7.4 to compress a floppy disk drive.

FIGURE 7.2

Confirming the compression

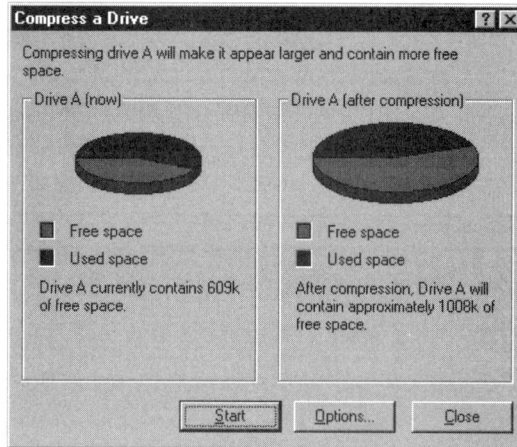

Compress a Drive

Compressing drive A will make it appear larger and contain more free space.

Drive A (now)

- Free space
- Used space

Drive A currently contains 609k of free space.

Drive A (after compression)

- Free space
- Used space

After compression, Drive A will contain approximately 1008k of free space.

Start   Options...   Close

FIGURE 7.3

Post-compression status screen

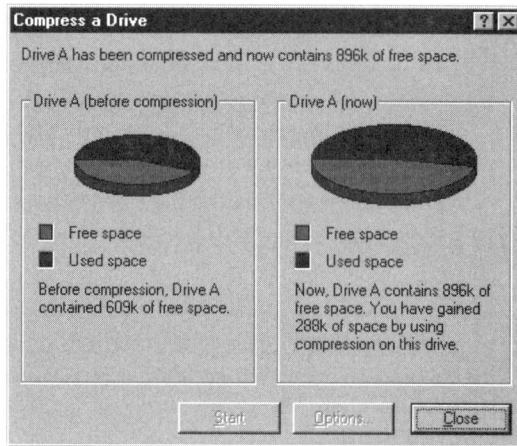

Compress a Drive

Drive A has been compressed and now contains 896k of free space.

Drive A (before compression)

- Free space
- Used space

Before compression, Drive A contained 609k of free space.

Drive A (now)

- Free space
- Used space

Now, Drive A contains 896k of free space. You have gained 288k of space by using compression on this drive.

Start   Options...   Close

EXERCISE 7.4

Compressing a Floppy Disk

1. Format a floppy disk, or find one that still has some room on it.

2. Select Start ➢ Run and type **drvspace**, or go to Start ➢ Programs ➢ Accessories ➢ System Tools ➢ DriveSpace.

3. From the DriveSpace menu, highlight the floppy drive and choose Drive ➢ Compress. DriveSpace will then show you the estimated size of your new drive and ask you to confirm before it actually does the compression (see Figure 7.2).

4. Click the Start button to start the compression. It may take a while (up to 5 minutes).

5. After compressing your floppy, you should get a status screen, reporting on the compressed floppy drive (see Figure 7.3).

6. Click the Close button to close the window.

Compressing a Hard Disk Drive

The steps in Exercise 7.4 will also work on your hard drive, but you should back up any critical data before compressing or decompressing a hard drive. If you are compressing a hard drive, you can choose to compress the entire volume or just a part of the volume. If you choose to take part of the free space to make a new compressed drive, Windows 98 will prompt you for a size to make the new drive.

As you copy data to your new drive, you can check the status of your compressed files on the Compression tab of the drive's Properties dialog box, as shown in Figure 7.4. If there are many uncompressed files, you can run the Compression Agent manually. Click the Run Agent button in the Compression tab to see the Compression Agent dialog box, shown in Figure 7.5. You can either cause compression to happen with your current settings or you can change your compression settings by choosing the Settings button, as shown in Figure 7.6.

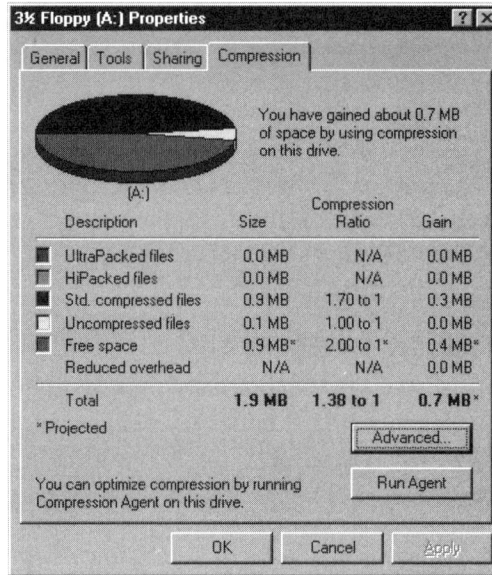

3½ Floppy (A:) Properties

General | Tools | Sharing | Compression

You have gained about 0.7 MB of space by using compression on this drive.

(A:)

Description	Size	Compression Ratio	Gain
UltraPacked files	0.0 MB	N/A	0.0 MB
HiPacked files	0.0 MB	N/A	0.0 MB
Std. compressed files	0.9 MB	1.70 to 1	0.3 MB
Uncompressed files	0.1 MB	1.00 to 1	0.0 MB
Free space	0.9 MB*	2.00 to 1*	0.4 MB*
Reduced overhead	N/A	N/A	0.0 MB
Total	**1.9 MB**	**1.38 to 1**	**0.7 MB***

* Projected

Advanced...

You can optimize compression by running Compression Agent on this drive.

Run Agent

OK | Cancel | Apply

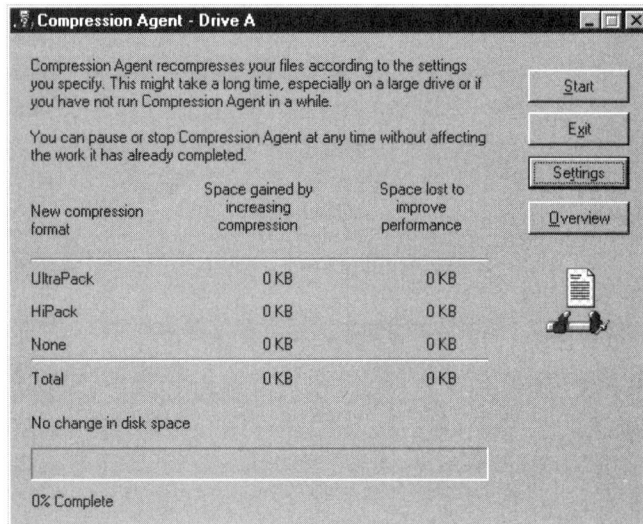

Compression Agent - Drive A

Compression Agent recompresses your files according to the settings you specify. This might take a long time, especially on a large drive or if you have not run Compression Agent in a while.

You can pause or stop Compression Agent at any time without affecting the work it has already completed.

New compression format	Space gained by increasing compression	Space lost to improve performance
UltraPack	0 KB	0 KB
HiPack	0 KB	0 KB
None	0 KB	0 KB
Total	0 KB	0 KB

No change in disk space

0% Complete

Start

Exit

Settings

Overview

FIGURE 7.6

Changing the Compression Agent Settings

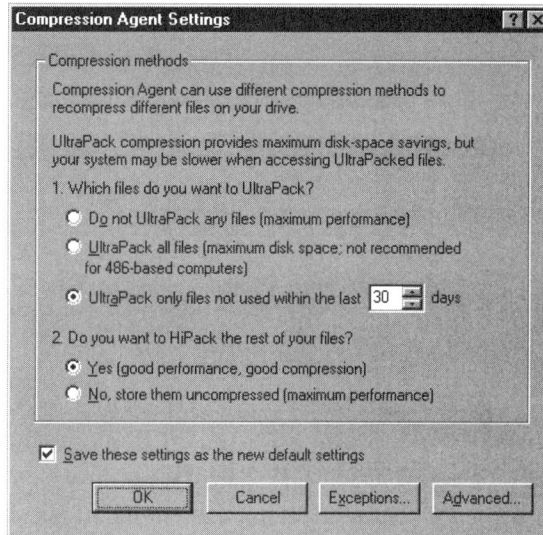

Decompressing a Drive

You may want to *decompress* your drive at some future date. Windows 98 supports nondestructive decompression of the hard drive. When you run DriveSpace and choose the Uncompress option, you will see before and after decompression status screens, similar to the compression status screens (see Figures 7.2 and 7.3). In Exercise 7.5, you will decompress the floppy you compressed in Exercise 7.4.

EXERCISE 7.5

Decompressing a Drive

1. Make sure your disk (floppy or hard drive) is large enough to hold the files it may contain after it has been decompressed by checking the Properties dialog box for your disk. Make sure that used space is less than the capacity of your drive after decompression.

2. Select Start ➢ Run and type **drvspace**, or go to Start ➢ Programs ➢ Accessories ➢ System Tools ➢ DriveSpace.

3. Highlight the drive you want to decompress and choose Uncompress. Windows 98 will show an Uncompress screen, with estimates for how much free space your drive will have after decompressing it.

EXERCISE 7.5 (CONTINUED)

4. Click the Start button to begin the decompression process.

5. After successfully decompressing your drive, you will see a final status screen, with your new used and free space for that drive.

6. Click the Close button to close the window.

Disk Fragmentation

Over time, you may find that your computer doesn't perform as fast as it once did. Fragmentation of your files may have occurred. *Fragmentation* is a natural phenomenon that occurs during normal disk usage and can easily be fixed.

Microsoft ✓ *Exam Objective*

Tune and optimize the system in a Microsoft environment and a mixed Microsoft and NetWare environment. Tasks include:

- Optimizing the hard disk by using Disk Defragmenter and ScanDisk

---

Fragmentation occurs as files are deleted and their space is used by new files. When files are saved, they are saved in sequential order on your hard drive. If a 10MB file is being saved, it will use free space as it finds it, not bothering to look for a contiguous 10MB spot it can use. By being scattered all over the hard drive, the file is harder to find and put back together. Finding it may take twice the number of hard drive revolutions it would take if it were contiguous.

Windows 98 Disk Defragmenter not only defragments the hard drive, it also puts EXE and DLL files from the same application together, cutting load times as much as 50 percent, especially when combined with FAT32 volumes.

Defragmenting the Hard Drive

Windows 98 includes a disk defragmentation program. The default settings will defragment your drive both by making sure that files are stored in contiguous clusters and by consolidating free space so fragmentation is less likely to happen in the future. The defragmentation program will also run ScanDisk to check for errors before defragmenting.

The defragmentation program is available from the Tools tab of any drive's Properties dialog box, as shown in Figure 7.7.

FIGURE 7.7

The Defragment option in the Tools dialog box

The Disk Cleanup program can be started from the General tab and Scan-Disk or the Backup program from the Tools tab of the Properties of a hard drive.

You can also start the defragmentation program by going to Start ➤ Programs ➤ Accessories ➤ System Tools ➤ Disk Defragmenter. If you start the disk defragmentation program this way, you can change the settings for the program and specify which drive to defragment (see Figure 7.8).

The Settings dialog box, shown in Figure 7.9, changes the way the defrag-mentation program will work, but the default options are probably the best. The options you can set are:

- **Rearrange Program Files So My Programs Start Faster:** This puts EXE and DLL files from the same application together to speed loading times as much as 50 percent.

- **Check The Drive For Errors:** This runs ScanDisk before the disk defragmenter program runs.

- **This Time Only:** The settings you picked are only used once.

- **Every Time I Defragment My Drive:** The settings are saved as the default.

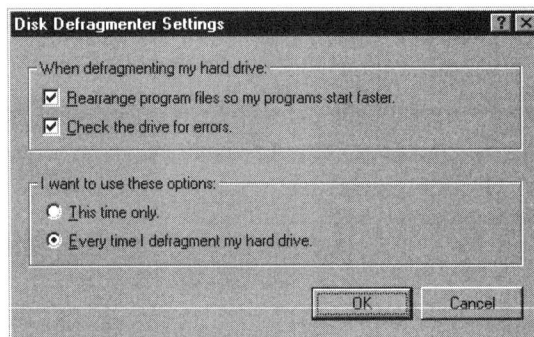

You can also see a graphical display of the defragmentation process, as shown in Figure 7.10. In Exercise 7.6, you will run the defragmentation program and look at the settings options as well as the graphical display.

FIGURE 7.10

Disk defragmentation in progress

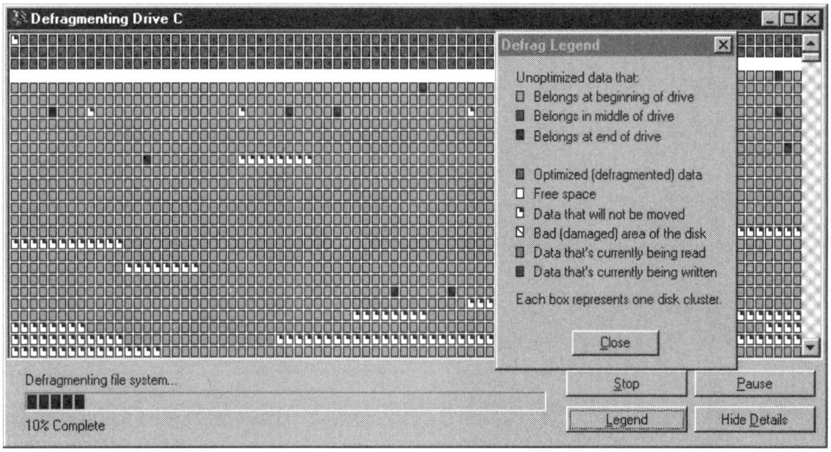

EXERCISE 7.6

Defragmenting a Hard Drive

1. Start the disk defragmentation program by going to Start ➤ Programs ➤ Accessories ➤ System Tools ➤ Disk Defragmenter. Note that if you start the disk defragmenter by going to the Properties dialog box for any drive and choosing the Tools tab, you cannot change any settings—it just runs using the default settings.

2. Click the Settings button to see how you can change the way defragmentation works (see Figure 7.9). The default settings are recommended.

3. Start the defragmentation process by making sure the hard drive you want to defragment is selected and clicking on the Start button.

4. While your disk is defragmenting, click the Show Details button to get a graphical representation of your drive. Then click the Legend button to see the Defrag Legend box (see Figure 7.10).

5. After defragmentation is complete, close the window.

> **TIP** If you run the Maintenance Wizard, Disk Defragmenter and ScanDisk will be run on a regular basis.

Checking for Disk Errors Using ScanDisk

Although there is no software fix for your hard drive if the drive is failing because of physical defects, some problems that occur on a hard drive can be repaired with software. Windows 98 comes with a program called *ScanDisk*, which can diagnose and fix many problems with either floppy drives or hard drives.

Microsoft ✔ *Exam* *Objective*	**Tune and optimize the system in a Microsoft environment and a mixed Microsoft and NetWare environment. Tasks include:** • Optimizing the hard disk by using Disk Defragmenter and ScanDisk

Microsoft ✔ *Exam* *Objective*	**Diagnose and resolve file system problems.**

Common Disk Problems

Several things can happen to files on your hard drive that might make them unusable. Some problems are easily fixed; others can be very serious. Here are some occurrences that could cause problems on your drive:

- **Crosslinked files:** This can happen when two or more files have become confused as to where their data resides. The crosslinked files both point to the same data area, as illustrated in Figure 7.11. This is one of the more serious errors because one of the two files no longer points to the correct data area, and it will probably not be recoverable.

F I G U R E 7.11

Crosslinked files

Data Clusters

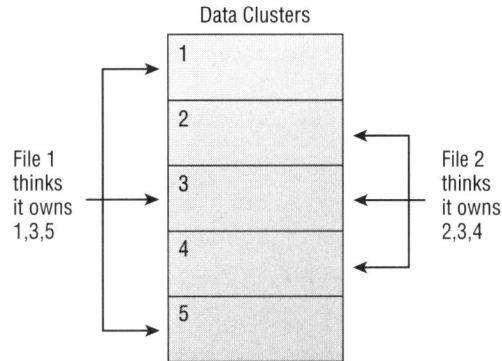

- **Bad spots:** These can occur on either a floppy disk or a hard drive. They can prevent programs or data files from working correctly. Bad spots can happen naturally because of wear and tear on a drive. The surface of a floppy drive can be scratched by touching it. A hard drive can be damaged if the drive head hits the platter (usually because the drive is dropped or banged while in use). Bad spots can sometimes be read, and the data moved to a good spot, but sometimes a bad spot can be completely unrecoverable. If the latter happens, the affected file is probably unrecoverable.

- **Lost clusters:** These appear when data areas have not been correctly identified as either in use or available for use by a new file. Lost clusters cannot be used for files until their status is resolved. Lost clusters can either be correctly marked as deleted, or they can be recovered as files in case something valuable was in them. This is usually the least damaging problem that you will encounter on your hard drive.

Fixing Problems Using ScanDisk

ScanDisk can fix all three of these problems. As with any kind of troubleshooting, success is never guaranteed, but ScanDisk has a relatively good chance:

- **Fixing crosslinked files:** Because ScanDisk can't tell which crosslinked file is the original and which one was attached by mistake, by default it fixes crosslinked files by taking the crosslinked data area and attaching it to both files. One of your files will be good, while the other one will be corrupted. You can have ScanDisk copy the crosslinked data to both files, delete both files, or ignore any crosslinked errors by using the Advanced button.

> If you have crosslinked files, one of the two files is bad. The best thing to do is to save both files, carefully go through each file, find the bad one, copy out all the good data still in the file, and then delete and re-create the file. (Hopefully, you have a backup of some sort.)

- **Fixing bad spots:** Files that happen to be on bad spots can sometimes be read by ScanDisk and moved to a safe area. The bad area is then marked so that future files will not be saved there.

> If you have bad spots on your drive, you have about a 50/50 chance of reading the data and moving it to a good spot. This means there is a 50 percent chance that the bad spot has completely destroyed your data. Anything critical will, hopefully, have been backed up.

- **Fixing lost clusters:** Lost clusters can either be erased or saved as a file. If you save the lost cluster as a file, you can later look at the file and see if it contains any data that you still need. Seldom, if ever, do these files contain anything of use. You can change this option by using the Advanced button.

> Experienced computer professionals rarely, if ever, find something useful after choosing to save a lost cluster file. Many people automatically delete them.

The ScanDisk program is available from the Tools tab of the drive's Properties dialog box, as shown in Figure 7.12. Click on the Advanced button while in ScanDisk if you want to configure the way ScanDisk will run, and how it will deal with any errors it may find. Figure 7.13 shows the ScanDisk Advanced Options dialog box. In Exercise 7.7, you will run ScanDisk to check the C: drive for errors.

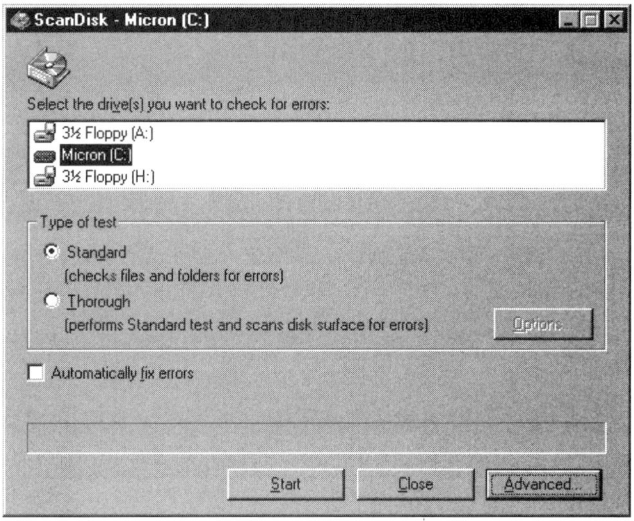

F I G U R E   7.12

Starting ScanDisk

F I G U R E   7.12

Starting ScanDisk

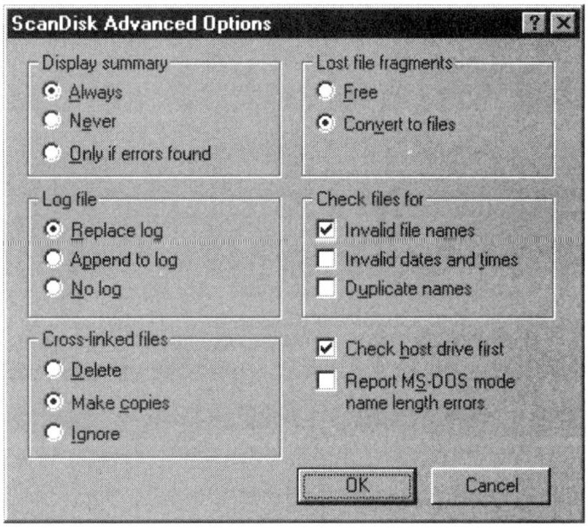

F I G U R E   7.13

The ScanDisk
Advanced Options
dialog box

EXERCISE 7.7

Checking a Drive for Errors with ScanDisk

1. Go to the Properties dialog box for the C: drive, choose the Tools tab, and select Check Now from the Error checking status section of the dialog box (see Figure 7.12).

EXERCISE 7.7 (CONTINUED)

2. Click on the Advanced button to see the default options (see Figure 7.13). Click Cancel to go back to the main ScanDisk dialog box.

3. If you are in a hurry, choose Standard for the type of test and check the Automatically Fix Errors checkbox. If you have a while, choose the Thorough Test and deselect Automatically Fix Errors.

4. Wait for ScanDisk to finish. If there are any errors, ScanDisk will automatically fix them (if selected) or it will prompt you on how to fix them.

5. If you selected a Thorough test, ScanDisk will check your current files and then check the entire hard drive for bad spots—this takes a while.

6. When ScanDisk is finished, close its information box.

The Maintenance Wizard automatically schedules ScanDisk (as well as the Disk Defragmenter) to run at regular intervals.

Disk Cleanup

Windows 98 includes a new wizard (called *Disk Cleanup*) designed to help you delete files from your hard drive that you no longer need (see Figure 7.14). The Disk Cleanup Wizard runs automatically when your hard drive runs low on space.

The Disk Cleanup Wizard makes it easy to delete the following (presumably) temporary files:

- **Temporary Internet files:** These are cached WWW pages.

- **Downloaded program files:** These are ActiveX and Java applets that have been downloaded to your computer probably during a WWW session.

- **Recycle Bin:** This contains files you have deleted but have been saved in case you want to get them back.

- **Temporary files:** Programs that have created temporary files as part of their installation and have not correctly deleted those temporary files.

F I G U R E 7.14

The Disk Cleanup
Wizard

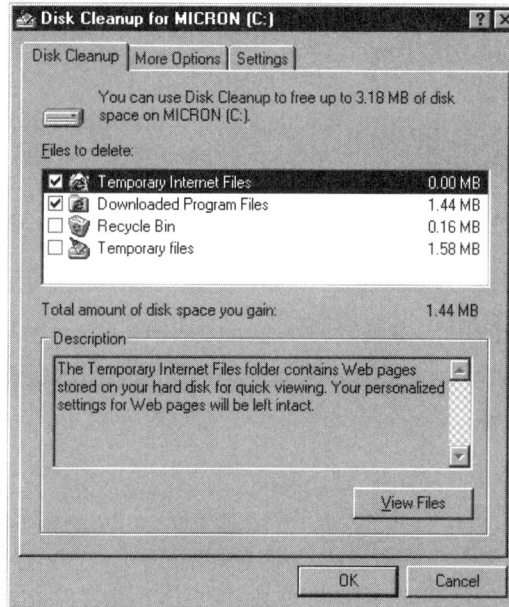

The More Options tab basically takes you to either Control Panel ➣ Add/ Remove Programs applet or to the Drive Converter (FAT32) utility. The Settings tab allows you to have the Disk Cleanup Wizard run automatically when the drive gets full (the default) or not.

The Disk Cleanup Wizard can be started by going to Start ➣ Programs ➣ Accessories ➣ System Tools and choosing Disk Cleanup. It can also be started by going to My Computer, highlighting a drive, choosing Properties, and then selecting the Disk Cleanup button. In Exercise 7.8, you will run the Disk Cleanup Wizard.

EXERCISE 7.8

The Disk Cleanup Wizard

1. Start the Disk Cleanup Wizard by going to the properties of one of your hard drives and selecting the Disk Cleanup button, or go to Start ➣ Programs ➣ Accessories ➣ System Tools ➣ Disk Cleanup.

2. Tag the types of files you want to delete (see Figure 7.14).

3. Choose OK to have the Wizard delete those files.

4. Answer Yes to the confirmation prompt.

Backing Up and Restoring Data

$\mathbf{T}$oday's hardware has become so reliable that people expect it to work forever. When a hard drive fails, it is usually catastrophic because most people don't expect hard drives to fail anymore. Viruses are another reason to back up your data because certain viruses can cause data loss. Data can also be lost because of accidental or malicious deletions by users.

Microsoft
✓ *Exam*
Objective

Back up data and the Registry and restore data and the Registry.

Windows 98 includes a backup and restore program that lets you easily back up and restore files on your hard drive. Although there are many different programs you could use to back up your hard drive, the program that comes with Windows 98 has the advantage of being able to save long filenames. Other programs may not preserve long filenames if they are not certified for Windows 98.

Installing Backup Hardware and Software

Before you can use the Backup program, you will need to install your hardware and software. The Backup application supports backing up to a wide variety of hardware devices. You can back up to floppy disks, other hard disks, a network drive, or a tape drive. Tape drives are probably the most difficult type of devices to install, but they offer an inexpensive backup solution so they are in wide use.

Microsoft
✓ *Exam*
Objective

Install and configure Microsoft Backup.

Installing Tape Devices

Tape drives fall into three generic categories: those that work with Windows 98 software, those that install their own software, and those that won't work under Windows 98 at all.

Native Windows 98 Tape Drives   Native Windows 98 tape drives are few and far between. The Help files for the Backup program list compatible tape drives, which mostly consist of QIC 80, and 3010 tape drives. These types of tape drives have become relatively obsolete in recent years. If you have one of these tape drives, it is probably connected to the floppy controller or connected through the parallel port. The Backup program should detect these tape drives automatically when it starts. You can force a scan for compatible tape drives by going to Tools ➤ Redetect Tape Drive from within the Backup program.

Third-Party Tape Drives   Most newer tape drives come with their own software. Newer tape drives are capable of backing up 10GB of data and cost only $200 or so. Some tape drives and the software they come with can simulate a (very slow) hard drive, in that you can drag-and-drop files onto the tape drive to perform your backups.

Incompatible Tape Drives   Older tape drives may not even be compatible with Windows 98. If your local computer store is going out of business and has a bargain-priced tape drive, ask about compatibility. You may find that it only works under plain MS-DOS and won't work even in MS-DOS mode in Windows 98. Needless to say, don't buy it if it isn't Windows 98 compatible.

Backup Techniques

There are various techniques you can use when performing backups in order to shorten the time it takes to back up or restore data. There are three general techniques.

Full Backup   Doing a full backup entails backing up every folder and file on the computer system. Although this is the slowest method to perform backups, it is the fastest method when doing a restore because only the most recent tape needs to be used. The archive bit is reset on every folder and file after performing a full backup.

Incremental   Performing an incremental backup only backs up the folders and files that have changed since the last backup session, making it the fastest way to back up a computer (assuming a full backup is done occasionally). The archive bit is reset after an incremental backup is performed. Restoring data takes the longest, because the full set must be restored first, and then each and every incremental set must be restored in its proper order.

Differential   Differential backups are similar to incremental backups in that only the data that has changed since the last full backup is saved. The archive bit is not reset after a differential backup, which means that the backup set is a cumulative set of changes since the last full backup. Differential backups are slow to do but are fast to restore, because only the most recent set has to be restored after the full backup set is restored.

Installing the Software

When you install the backup software, you have two choices as to how your computer will be backed up.

- The Backup program allows you to make local backups.

- Backup agents allow a network server to back up your computer.

Installing the Backup Program   Installing the Backup program is done via the Add Software applet in the Control Panel. The Disk Tools category contains only one entry—that of the Backup program. After you install the Backup program you will be able to run it from Start ≻ Programs ≻ Accessories ≻ System Tools ≻ Backup.

Installing Backup Agents   Windows 98 doesn't come with any backup agents, but many backup programs come with Windows 98-compatible agents that allow a workstation to be backed up to a network server.

By installing these agents, you allow a network server (with a really big tape drive) to back up your computer to the network. Of course, your network server will need to be running the appropriate backup application in order to use its respective agent installed on your computer, and the computer needs to be left on the night it will be backed up.

> **NOTE**   Windows 95 came with native agents for Arcada and Cheyenne backup programs, but they are no longer present in Windows 98.

Backing Up Your Data

The Windows 98 Backup program was designed to be easy to use. The Backup program can back up to any valid device, including floppies, hard drives, tape drives, removable media (such as Zip drives), or network drives. When you start the Backup program, the Microsoft Backup introduction screen prompts if you want to Create a new backup job, Open an existing backup job, or Restore backed-up files (see Figure 7.15). If you choose to

Create a new backup job, the Backup Wizard starts and you are asked to choose to do a full backup or just selected files, as shown in Figure 7.16. The next screen allows you to select whether to do a full backup or to just backup the files that have changed (see Figure 7.17). The next screen allows you to choose the file and folder that will contain your backup (see Figure 7.18). The next screen allows you to verify the backup and compress the backup (see Figure 7.19). The last screen allows you to save your job and start the backup.

FIGURE 7.15

Choosing to create a new backup job

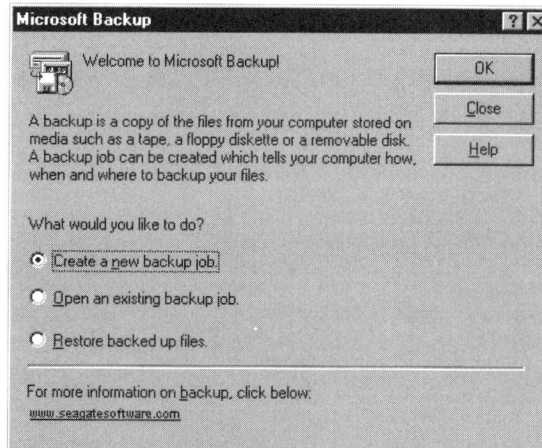

FIGURE 7.16

The Backup Wizard

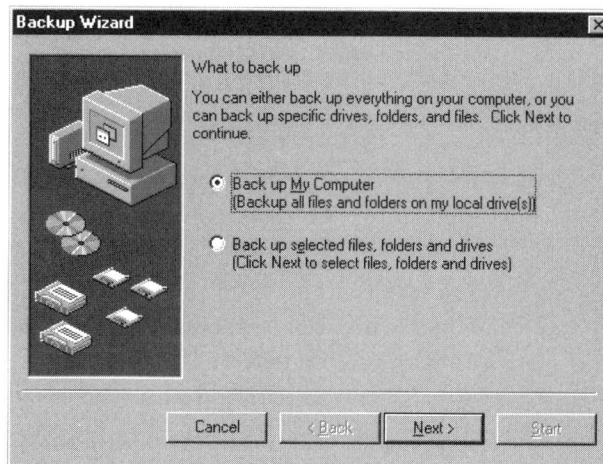

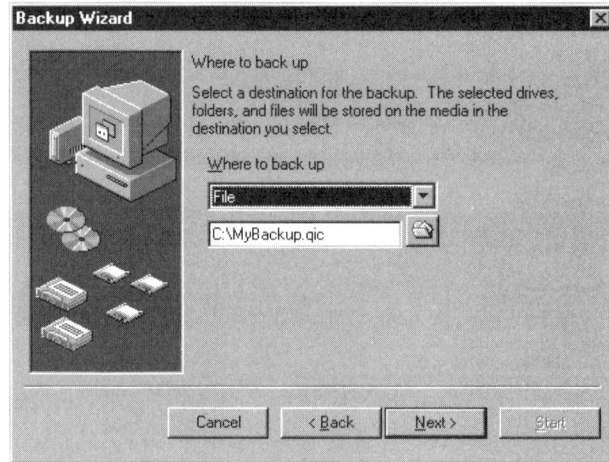

If you don't use the Backup Wizard, the Backup program is relatively intuitive (see Figure 7.20), allowing you to specify what to backup or restore, and allowing you to set various options for the backup or restore, including verification, compression, and overwriting on restoration. In Exercise 7.9, you will create a backup directory and back up the Windows 98 cursors to it.

F I G U R E 7.19

Setting backup
options

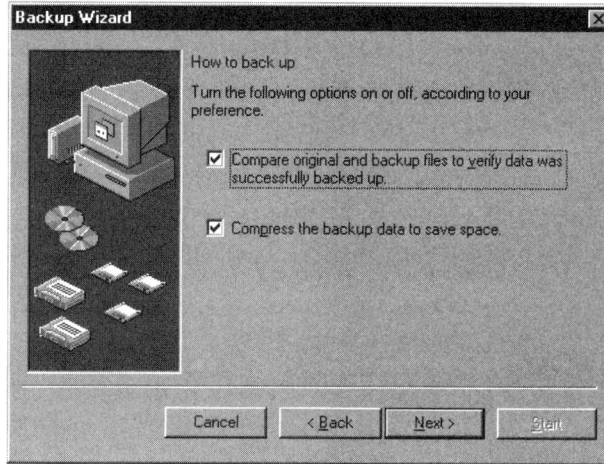

F I G U R E 7.19

Setting backup
options

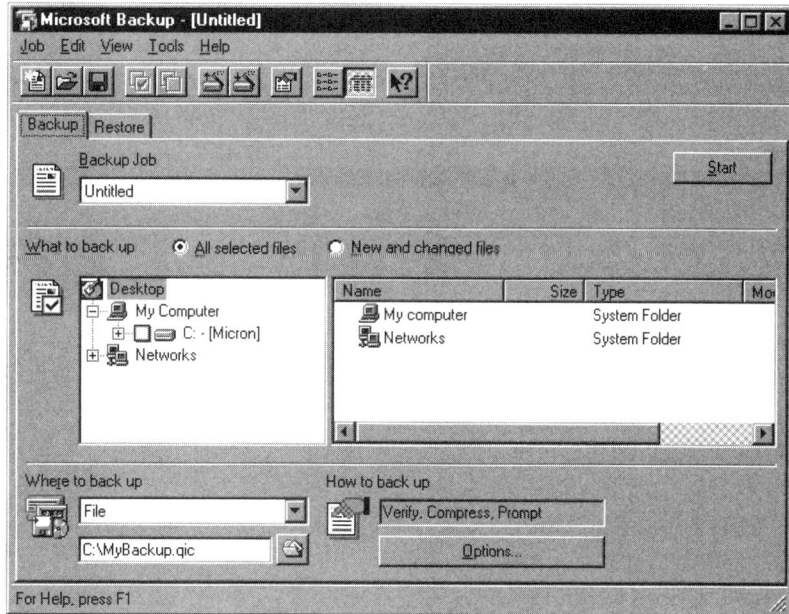

F I G U R E 7.20

The Backup program

EXERCISE 7.9

Backing Up Data

1. Create a folder on your C: drive called Backups.

2. Start the Backup program by going to the Properties dialog box of the C: drive and choosing Backup Now from the middle pane, or by going to Start ➢ Programs ➢ Accessories ➢ System Tools ➢ Backup. The Backup Wizard will start, allowing you to create a new backup job, which starts the Backup Wizard.

3. Select Backup selected files, folders, and drives (see Figure 7.16), and choose Next.

4. Open the C: drive and go to your Windows 98 directory. You should find a Cursors folder. Click on the Cursors folder to mark it for backup as shown here.

5. Click the Next button, choose All selected files, and then choose Next.

6. Click the browser button next to the filename and browse to the C:\backup folder so that the file will be saved as C:\backups\ MYBACKUP.QIC. Click Next.

7. Leave both of the next options selected in order to verify and compress the backup (see Figure 7.19). Click Next.

8. Give the backup set a name (such as Test), and click Start. After a few seconds, the backup should finish. Click OK to close the prompt, but keep the main backup screen open.

9. Click the Report button to see a report of the backup. The report should look something like this.

```
test1.txt - Notepad
File  Edit  Search  Help
Start Job Report


    Job Name: test1

    Backup Job Started - 7/17/98 10:11:59AM
    Processed File Count: 60
    Total Bytes After Compression: 71,482
    Total Bytes Before Compression: 160,892
    Operation Completed - Yes
    Backup Job Ended - 7/17/98 10:12:05AM
    Compare Job Started - 7/17/98 10:12:05AM
    Processed File Count: 60
    Total Bytes Before Compression: 160,892
    Operation Completed - Yes
    Compare Job Ended - 7/17/98 10:12:06AM



End Job Report
```

10. Close the Report window, and click OK to close the Backup window.

> **NOTE** If you do not have the Backup program installed, use the Add/Remove programs applet of the Control Panel to install it.

Restoring Your Data

There are several reasons you may need to restore data:

- Accidental erasure or editing of data
- Malicious erasure or editing of data
- Viruses
- Failure of a hard disk
- Archive data loading

There are several questions to ask yourself before you can restore your data:

- Do I have a valid backup?

- Have I solved the problem that is requiring me to restore my data?

- Where do I want to restore my data to?

If you don't have a valid backup, you may need to send your hard drive to a professional repair service. This can get quite expensive. (Recovering your data could cost you thousands of dollars.) If you have a valid backup and you have fixed your problem, then restoring your data is relatively simple.

To restore your data, run the Backup program and choose the Restore tab, shown in Figure 7.21. You can select to restore to the same drive and directory, or you can specify a different drive and directory to which to restore. If you suffer a complete failure of your hard drive, but you have a backup on tape, you will need to reinstall Windows 98 and then use the Restore program to restore your drive the way it was.

FIGURE 7.21

Choosing files to restore

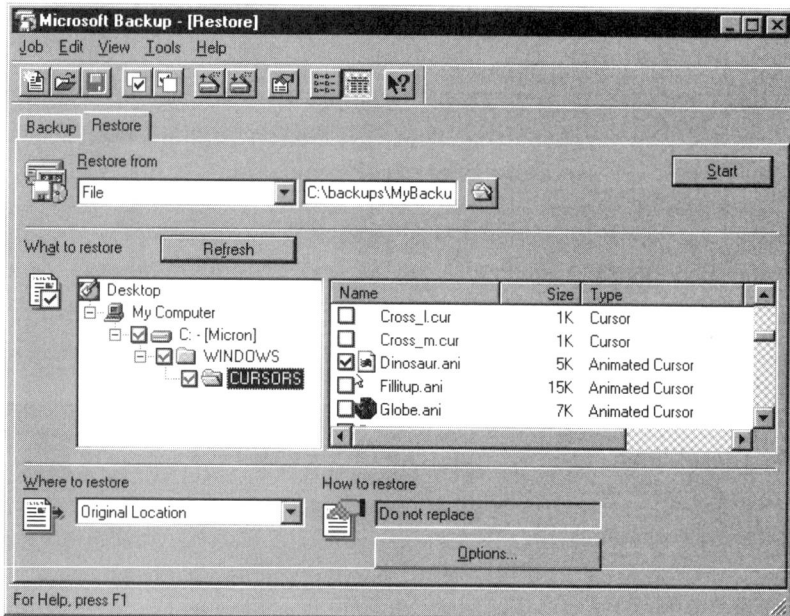

In Exercise 7.10, you will rename one of the cursor files you backed up in Exercise 7.9. You will then restore from your backup, which will let you recover the file you renamed. Note that you will not use the Restore Wizard for this demonstration of the Backup program.

EXERCISE 7.10

Restoring Files

1. Go to the C:\Windows98\Cursors folder, and rename the Dinosaur.ani animated cursor to something else (like T-REX.ANI).

2. Start the Backup program by selecting Start ≻ Programs ≻ Accessories ≻System Tools ≻Backup. Choose the Close button to close the Backup Wizard.

3. Choose the Restore tab. Open the C: drive and highlight your Backups directory. The backup set you saved in Exercise 7.9 should show up. If you cannot find your backup, repeat Exercise 7.9.

4. Highlight your backup set, and choose Refresh.

5. Open your backup set and deselect everything. Open the Windows folder, and go to the Cursors folder.

6. Scroll down in the right pane until you find the Dinosaur animated cursor. Put a check in the appropriate box (see Figure 7.21).

7. Click on the Start Restore button. Click on OK to start the restoration. After a few seconds, the restore process should finish successfully.

8. Go back to your Cursors folder and make sure the Dinosaur cursor is back (you may need to refresh with F5).

If you want your restored files to overwrite existing files, you need to change the default setting using the Options button before you start the restore.

The Backup program that is included with Windows 98 is not compatible with any earlier versions from MS-DOS. If you have backup files that were made with an MS-DOS version of a backup program, you will not be able to restore them with Windows 98.

Other Disk Management Tasks

Windows 98 includes other tools and utilities that help you manage your hard drive and files. The major tasks and tools required for each are detailed in the following sections.

The Recycle Bin

In versions of Windows prior to Windows 95, a file was gone when you deleted it. If you discovered that you deleted the wrong file (something very easy to do considering the cryptic nature of eight-character filenames), you could take your chances with the Undelete feature in Windows for Workgroups 3.11, or you could use a third-party utility like Norton Utilities.

Windows 98 is much more forgiving. Instead of deleting a file, Windows 98 simply moves it to the Recycle Bin. The Recycle Bin resides on your Desktop. Double-clicking on it will list all the files you have deleted since the Bin was last emptied. If you've accidentally deleted a file, open the Recycle Bin. Simply click on the file to select it, and choose Restore from the File menu (or right-click the file and choose Restore). The file will be restored to where it was when you deleted it.

There is one caveat, however. If you are deleting files in order to free up hard disk space, you must empty the Recycle Bin before that space is freed. Simply sending a document to the Recycle Bin does not free up hard disk space. To empty the Recycle Bin, either right-click the Recycle Bin icon and choose Empty Recycle Bin, or open the Recycle Bin and choose Empty Recycle Bin from the File menu.

If you want to delete an item and bypass the Recycle Bin, hold down the Shift key while deleting. Also, you can remove the confirmation warning and allocate how much hard drive space the Recycle Bin is allowed to use by right-clicking the Recycle Bin and choosing Properties.

Scheduled Tasks

Windows 98 includes a task-scheduling component that allows you to automate certain tasks on a preset schedule.

NOTE Windows 95 users had to purchase and install Microsoft Plus! in order to get the scheduling component, which was called the System Agent.

Microsoft Exam Objective

Tune and optimize the system in a Microsoft environment and a mixed Microsoft and NetWare environment. Tasks include:

- Automating tasks by using Maintenance Wizard
- Scheduling tasks by using Task Scheduler

You can add, edit, or delete scheduled tasks by opening the Scheduled Tasks folder now located in My Computer. To create a new task, simply choose Add a New Task, which starts the Scheduled Task Wizard (see Figure 7.22). You will then be presented with a list of the applications installed on your computer and prompted through scheduling them to automatically start.

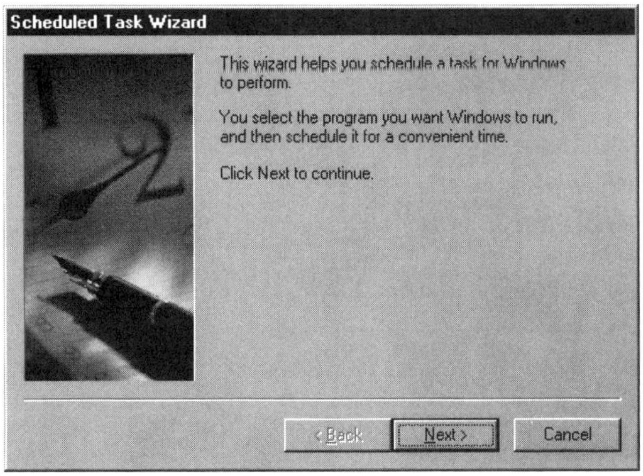

FIGURE 7.22

The Scheduled Tasks Wizard

The Maintenance Wizard

Windows 98 comes with a Maintenance Wizard that builds disk-maintenance tasks including the Disk Defragmenter, Disk Cleanup, and ScanDisk that will be performed on a regular basis.

NOTE

The Microsoft Plus! Pack for Windows 95 contained the System Agent, which basically has become the Maintenance Wizard and Scheduled Tasks in Windows 98. (As an added bonus the Maintenance Wizard and Scheduled Tasks come with the Windows 98 CD-ROM—you don't need to purchase the Plus! Pack for Windows 98 to get it.)

In Exercise 7.11 you will use the Maintenance Wizard to build tasks to help maintain the file system.

EXERCISE 7.11

The Maintenance Wizard

1. Start the Maintenance Wizard by going to Start ➢ Programs ➢ Accessories ➢ System Tools ➢ Maintenance Wizard.

2. Choose Change my maintenance settings or schedule (as shown here) and click OK.

3. Select Custom and then Next so you can selectively set up maintenance options.

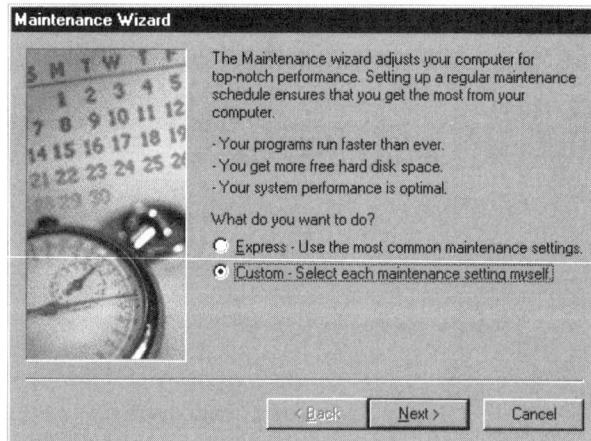

4. You then are prompted for a time to run the tasks. Pick the time most appropriate for your computer and click Next.

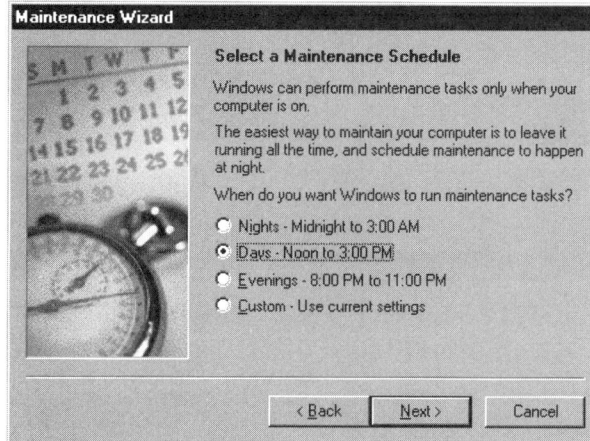

5. The next screen shows you which programs are started automatically by Windows 98. It allows you to select or deselect a program. Choose Next when you are done.

6. The next screen prompts for a time to run the Disk Defragmenter. Select Yes to have it run, and use the Reschedule button to change the time or the Settings button to change how the Disk Defragmenter program runs. Click Next when you are done.

7. The next screen prompts for a time to run ScanDisk. Select Yes to have it run, and use the Reschedule button to change the time or the Settings button to change how ScanDisk will run. Click Next when you are done.

8. The next screen prompts for a time to run Disk Cleanup. Select Yes to have it run, and use the Reschedule button to change the time or the Settings button to change how Disk Cleanup will run. Click Next when you are done.

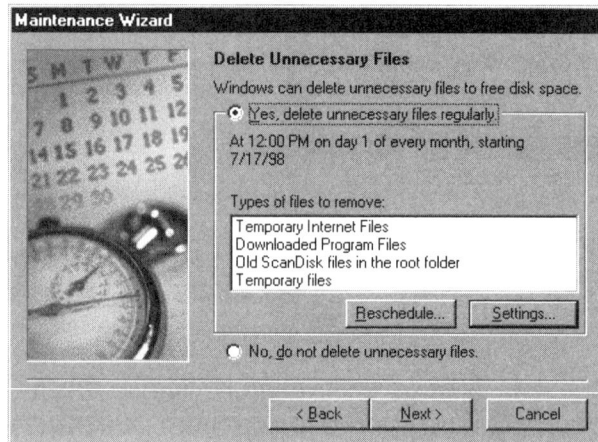

9. You should now see a completed list of your new schedules maintenance tasks. Choose Finish to save the tasks.

Editing Tasks

Once an application is scheduled, it is easy to change the schedule for the application. Simply go to the Scheduled Tasks folder and double-click the task you want to edit. If you did Exercise 7.11, you should have some scheduled tasks such as the ScanDisk task as shown in Figure 7.23. The Schedule tab lets you change the schedule for a task (see Figure 7.24) and the Settings tab lets you set various options for running the task (see Figure 7.25).

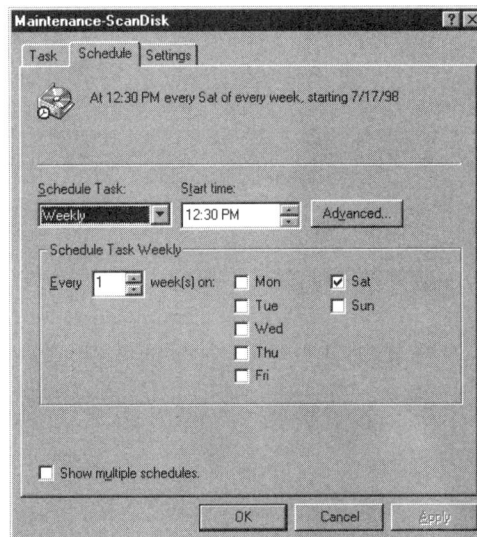

F I G U R E   7.25

Changing the options of an existing task

Disk Partitioning

Before you can format a hard drive, it must be *partitioned*. Windows 98 supports two versions of partitions: FAT16 and FAT32.

- **FAT16:** The original partitioning scheme for MS-DOS and Windows 95 partitions. FAT16 partitions are limited to 2GB in size.

- **FAT32:** A new partitioning scheme that allows for much larger partitions at the expense of some backward compatibility.

Microsoft Exam Objective	**Configure hard disks. Tasks include:** - Partitioning

You can make three types of partitions using the Fdisk utility: primary, extended, and logical. Each of these partition types is described in detail in the following sections.

Primary Partition

The first partition you create on a hard disk is almost always a *primary partition*. A primary partition is required to be bootable in DOS. This is generally how the C: drive is partitioned. Older versions of DOS (5.0 and earlier) would allow only one primary partition per hard drive, but DOS 6.0 and higher allow up to four.

Extended and Logical Partitions

An *extended partition* can hold logical partitions within it, and these can be formatted as separate drives. Extended partitions exist because of the limitations that older versions of DOS (5.0 and earlier) had regarding the number and sizes of partitions. Older versions of DOS allowed only two partitions: one primary and one of another type. Older versions of DOS (4.01 and earlier) allowed partitions of only 32.5MB or less. If you had a hard drive that was 80MB, without extended partitions, you could have only 65MB of your hard drive in use (32.5MB on each of the two allowed partitions).

Extended partitions can fill the remainder of the space left after the primary partition is created. Within the extended partition, logical drives can be created (each adhering to the 30MB size restriction).

By using logical partitions within extended partitions, DOS can get around its limitations of number of partitions (two—the primary and extended) and size of partition. Size restrictions affect only primary and logical partitions, so the extended partition can be as large as is needed to fill the hard drive.

With DOS version 6.2x, FAT16 still has a size restriction of 2GB partitions, so being able to use primary, extended, and logical partitions is still useful. Figure 7.26 shows a typical hard drive, with a primary partition (C:), and an extended partition that has been divided into a D: and an E: by using logical partitions.

FIGURE 7.26

Disk partitions

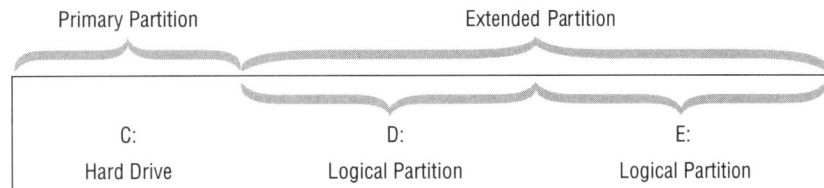

Partitioning a Disk with Fdisk

Windows 98 does not provide a graphical partition manager. You must still use the DOS-based partition manager called *Fdisk*, shown in Figure 7.27.

Microsoft
Exam
Objective

Configure hard disks. Tasks include:

- Enabling large disk support

When Fdisk starts, if it detects a hard drive larger than 512MB you will be prompted if you want to enable large disk support. Choosing (Y)es enables FAT32 support. If you choose (Y)es, then all partitions larger than 512MB will be created using the FAT32 scheme instead of the FAT16 scheme. If you choose (N)o, then you will be limited to FAT16 partitions.

When you choose to display the partition information, you'll see a screen similar to the one shown in Figure 7.28. Fdisk also allows you to change your current hard drive, as shown in Figure 7.29. In Exercise 7.12, you will use Fdisk to look at the disk partition on the drive.

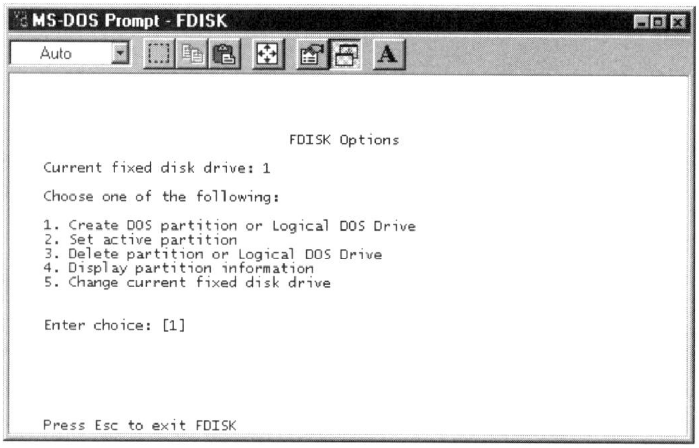

FIGURE 7.27

The Fdisk menu

FIGURE 7.28

Fdisk partition
information

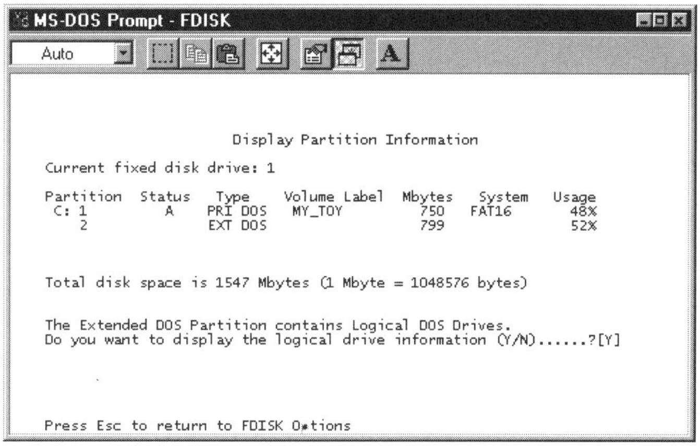

```
MS-DOS Prompt - FDISK
Auto

                      Display Partition Information
  Current fixed disk drive: 1

  Partition  Status   Type    Volume Label  Mbytes   System   Usage
     C: 1       A     PRI DOS  MY_TOY          750    FAT16     48%
        2             EXT DOS                  799              52%


  Total disk space is 1547 Mbytes (1 Mbyte = 1048576 bytes)


  The Extended DOS Partition contains Logical DOS Drives.
  Do you want to display the logical drive information (Y/N)......?[Y]



  Press Esc to return to FDISK Options
```

FIGURE 7.28

Fdisk partition
information

FIGURE 7.29

Choosing a hard drive
to change

```
MS-DOS Prompt - FDISK
Auto

                       Change Current Fixed Disk Drive
  Disk  Drv   Mbytes   Free   Usage
    1          1547            100%
        C:      750
        E:      799
    2          2012            100%
        D:      801
        F:      801










  (1 MByte = 1048576 bytes)
  Enter Fixed Disk Drive Number (1-2).......................[1]

  Press Esc to return to FDISK Options
```

FIGURE 7.29

Choosing a hard drive
to change

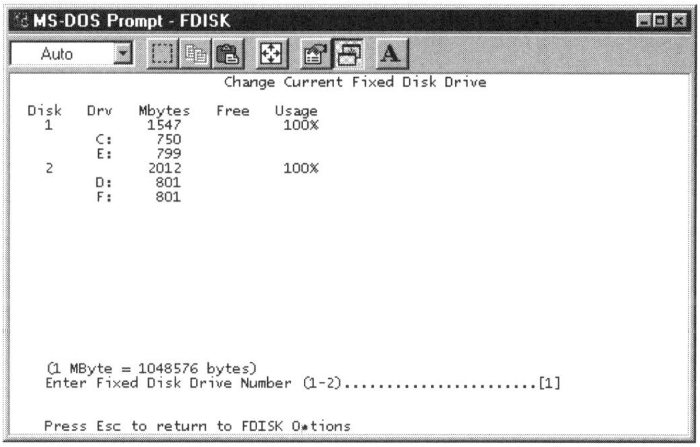

EXERCISE 7.12

Looking at Partitions with Fdisk

1. Open a DOS screen by selecting Start ➤ Programs ➤ MS-DOS
   Prompt.

2. Type **Fdisk**. If you are prompted to enable large disk support, say
   (Y)es. You should see the FDISK Options screen (see Figure 7.27).

3. Choose 4. Display partition information.

EXERCISE 7.12 (CONTINUED)

4. From the information screen (see Figure 7.28), press Y to see your logical drive partitions (if applicable).

5. Press the Esc key when you are finished looking.

6. If you have more than one hard drive, go back to the main menu and choose 5. Change current fixed disk drive. The next screen will show your hard disks (see Figure 7.29).

7. Repeat Steps 3–6 for each drive.

8. Press Esc when you are finished looking around.

WARNING
Any changes you make with Fdisk will destroy all of your data on that partition. To nondestructively change your partitions, use a product like Partition Magic from PowerQuest Corporation in Orem, Utah (the company's Web site is `www.powerquest.com`).

Formatting Drives

Before a floppy or hard drive can be used, it must be *formatted*. You can format a drive from a DOS prompt, or use the Windows 98 Format feature, shown in Figure 7.30. The options in the Format dialog box let you do a quick format (which reformats just the header part of the disk), make a system disk (equivalent to the old SYS command or FORMAT /s command), or do a full format (equivalent to the FORMAT command). In Exercise 7.13, you will format a floppy using the mouse.

EXERCISE 7.13

Formatting a Floppy

1. Insert a floppy that it is safe to format (no essential data is on the disk).

2. Go to My Computer.

3. Highlight the floppy and right-click it.

4. Choose Format from the pop-up menu.

5. You will be presented with the Format dialog box, which lets you choose how to format the disk (see Figure 7.30). Choose Quick Format.

6. In a few seconds, the disk will be formatted.

7. Close the Format dialog box.

FIGURE 7.30

The Windows 98 Format dialog box

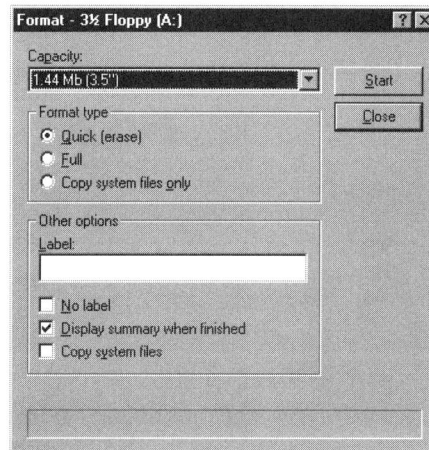

Managing the Hard Drive Cache

A caching program uses RAM to store information to and from the hard drive, so that the CPU can get the information from RAM instead of from the hard drive. When caching is enabled, the CPU checks the cache for any data it might need. If the data is in cache, it can be quickly grabbed by the CPU. If the data is not in cache, the CPU will read the data from the hard drive, as shown in Figure 7.31. Because RAM is rated in nanoseconds, and hard drives in milliseconds, it is easy to see that using RAM to temporarily cache data can significantly speed up access to data on the hard drive.

FIGURE 7.31

A hard drive cache

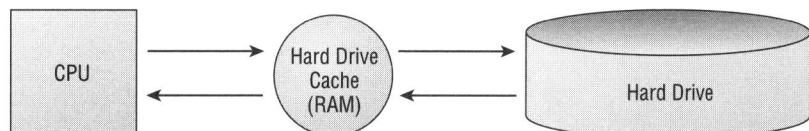

Running Vcache and the Role of Your Computer

Windows 98 uses a 32-bit program called *Vcache* to manage the caching of data from the hard drive. (Vcache was introduced in Windows for Workgroups 3.11. The Installable File System [IFS] supported this new 32-bit disk caching technology.)

You can adjust the size of Vcache to increase performance if you have enough RAM for your applications. There is also a setting that affects the way your computer reserves memory for use. You can set your computer for the role it plays: as a server, workstation, or laptop. These settings are located on the Hard Disk tab of the File System Properties dialog box, shown in Figure 7.32. In Exercise 7.14, you will look at the Vcache settings and the role of your computer.

FIGURE 7.32

Adjusting the
Vcache size

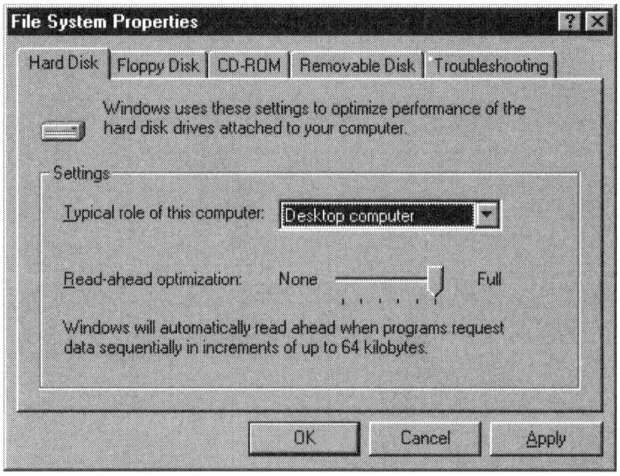

EXERCISE 7.14

Adjusting the Size of Vcache and Setting the Role

1. Select Control Panel ➤ System ➤ File System ➤ Hard Disk tab.

2. Choose the role that your computer will function as most of the time (probably Desktop computer).

3. Adjust Vcache to its maximum size by sliding the Read-Ahead Optimization slider to the right to the Full setting (see Figure 7.32).

4. Click OK to close the dialog box and save your changes.

If your computer has plenty of RAM, you may increase its performance by selecting Network server, as this leaves more RAM for caching data. By selecting the Mobile system role, you lower the amount of time data is in the write-back cache, therefore lowering the chance of lost data if your batteries run down.

Running CDFS

You must set the size of the CD-ROM cache separately from the size of the hard drive cache. Caching is built into the CD-ROM driver, which is called *CDFS*. This keeps the CD-ROM and hard drive from competing with each other and increases performance. The CD-ROM cache settings are located on the CD-ROM tab of the File System Properties dialog box, shown in Figure 7.33. Follow the steps in Exercise 7.15 to adjust this cache's settings.

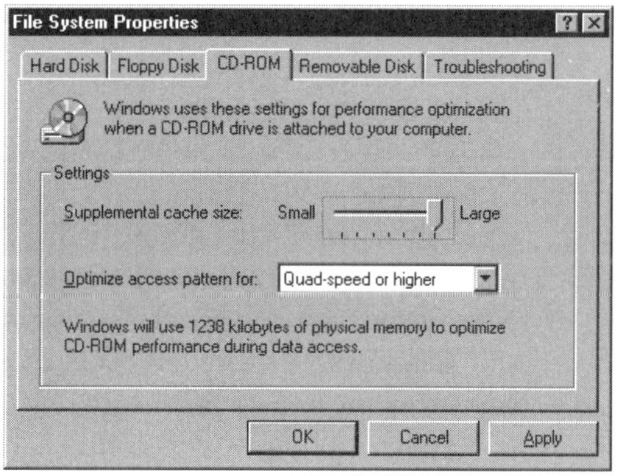

FIGURE 7.33
Adjusting the CD-ROM cache

EXERCISE 7.15

Adjusting the Size of the CD-ROM Cache

1. Select Control Panel ➢ System ➢ File System ➢ CD-ROM tab.

2. If you have 32MB or more of RAM, adjust the size of the cache to its largest size (Figure 7.33). If you have 16MB of RAM, adjust the size of the cache to about the halfway point. If you have less than 16MB, go get some more RAM!

EXERCISE 7.15 (CONTINUED)

3. Make sure the speed setting is also correct for your CD-ROM.

4. Click OK to close the dialog box and save your changes.

> **TIP** If you need to use a real-mode driver (a 16-bit driver) for your CD-ROM, you must use SMARTDRV (a 16-bit caching program) to cache your CD-ROM. When you run in a real-mode MS-DOS environment or even when you run Windows 98 in Safe mode, FAT32 is considerably slower than FAT16. (SMARTDRV.EXE is not completely dead.)

FAT16 versus FAT32

Hard drives are organized by sectors, with clusters as groups of sectors. The cluster is the smallest size that a file uses when it is saved; clusters can't be subdivided between files.

The FAT file system that is used to format floppy disks and hard drives has been with us since DOS 1.0. It was never intended for huge partitions such as those we are seeing now. Because DOS and Windows 98 must remain backward compatible with older versions of DOS, newer operating systems (including Windows 98) must find ways to extend the operating system while adhering to the restrictions of previous versions of DOS. DOS and Windows 98 overcome the FAT's limitations in the partition size by increasing the size of each cluster as the partition grows bigger. This older way of partitioning drives is referred to as FAT16. Table 7.3 lists the sizes of partitions and their cluster sizes in FAT16.

T A B L E 7.3 FAT16 Cluster Sizes	Size of Partition	Size of Clusters in FAT16
	1–15 MB*	4KB
	16–127MB	2KB
	128–255MB	4KB
	256–511MB	8KB

T A B L E 7.3 *(cont.)* FAT16 Cluster Sizes	Size of Partition	Size of Clusters in FAT16
	512–1023MB	16KB
	1024–2047MB	32KB

*The FAT for 1-15 MB partitions is a 12-bit FAT. All others are 16-bit FAT.

As you can see, when partitions become bigger, the cluster size also becomes bigger. Any time a file is saved, it uses at least one cluster, so files saved on large partitions have more wasted space than those on smaller partitions. In other words, a file that contains only one sentence still takes 32KB if saved on a partition larger than 1,023MB.

> **NOTE** Windows NT can create 4GB partitions using FAT16. Dual-booting such a system with Windows 98 should work fine, but is not recommended because of various, noncritical compatibility issues (such as programs reporting 0 bytes free, etc).

The FAT32 Solution

Microsoft's response to the problem of large cluster sizes has been to release a partitioning scheme that supports partitions up to 8GB with a cluster size of only 4KB and supports a maximum volume size of 2 terabytes (TB)! This new FAT scheme is called FAT32.

> **NOTE** FAT32 first made its appearance with Windows 95B, also called OSR2, but if you had FAT16 volumes there was no conversion tool available from Microsoft, until Windows 98.

Table 7.4 lists the sizes of partitions and their cluster sizes in FAT32.

TABLE 7.4 FAT32 Cluster Sizes	Size of Partition	Size of Clusters in FAT32
	1–512MB	FAT116 is used
	513MB–8GB	4KB
	8GB–16GB	8KB
	16GB–32GB	16KB
	32GB–2TB	32KB

The only problem is that FAT32, which comes with Windows 98, is no longer backward compatible with DOS or with some third-party utilities that were compatible with the original version of Windows 95.

> **WARNING**
>
> FAT32 partitions are not visible to NT 4.0 or MS-DOS, but they will be visible to Windows NT 5.0.

Follow the steps in Exercise 7.15 to determine if your drives have been partitioned with FAT32.

> **NOTE**
>
> Just because you have Windows 98 doesn't necessarily mean you have the benefit of decreased cluster size. Use Exercise 7.15 to determine your partition status. If your hard drive was partitioned and formatted with MS-DOS or Windows 95(A) Fdisk and format, your partitions will be in the old FAT16 style. You can convert to FAT32 with the new Drive Converter program.

EXERCISE 7.16

Determining If Your Drives Are FAT16 or FAT32

1. Go to My Computer.

2. Highlight a drive, right-click, and choose Properties.

3. If the drive says Local Drive (FAT), it is a FAT16 partition.

4. If the drive says Local Drive (FAT32), it is a FAT32 partition, as shown here.

Converting to FAT32

Windows 98 comes with a program that will nondestructively convert a FAT16 partition to FAT32.

Microsoft *Exam* *Objective*	**Configure hard disks. Tasks include:** • Converting to FAT32

Microsoft *Exam* *Objective*	**Develop an appropriate implementation model for specific requirements in a Microsoft environment or a mixed Microsoft and NetWare environment. Considerations include:** • Choosing the appropriate file system • Planning a workgroup

You must understand several "gotchas" before you convert a partition to FAT32.

- The name of the protected-mode drive converter program is CVT1.EXE, and the name of the real-mode program is CVT.EXE. Normally, you would use the protected-mode program.

- Windows 98 comes with a one-way conversion program. If you want to convert a FAT32 partition back to a FAT16 partition, you will need to use a third-party utility such as Partition Magic from Power Quest.

- Most third-party compression programs are incompatible with FAT32. If you are using such a program, you will be unable to convert to FAT32.

- If you convert a removable media drive such as a Zip or Jaz drive, that drive can be used only by Windows 98 or by Windows 95B (OSR2).

- You cannot uninstall Windows 98 after converting to FAT32 (unless you use a third-party utility to first go back to FAT16).

- You cannot dual-boot with MS-DOS or Windows NT 4.0 or earlier after converting to FAT32.

- FAT32 is considerably slower than FAT16 when running in MS-DOS mode or Safe mode.

- Many older third-party disk utilities are not compatible with FAT32 and may need to be upgraded.

- Many programs (such as setup programs for various applications) will not show available space past 2GB on a FAT32 volume. This is a cosmetic bug and should not affect the operation of the program.

- Many laptops will have "hibernate" software installed, which may cause the Drive Converter program to either suggest not converting the drive or may cause the conversion process to be automatically canceled. To override the defaults, run the CVT.EXE with the /HIB switch to delete any hibernation programs it finds.

- The conversion program may take an hour or more. After the conversion, you should run the disk defragmentation program which may take 2 or more hours to run.

In order to convert to FAT32, run the Drive Converter program as shown in Exercise 7.17.

WARNING You may not want to actually perform this exercise; you may want to just read it. Converting to FAT32 could have undesirable results on your computer and older applications. As with any major system modifications, backup any critical data!

EXERCISE 7.17

Converting a Drive to FAT32

1. Go to Start ➤ Accessories ➤ System Tools, and run the Drive Converter (FAT32) program.

2. Choose Next from the opening screen (shown here). Note that you can get more information about FAT32 by selecting the Details button.

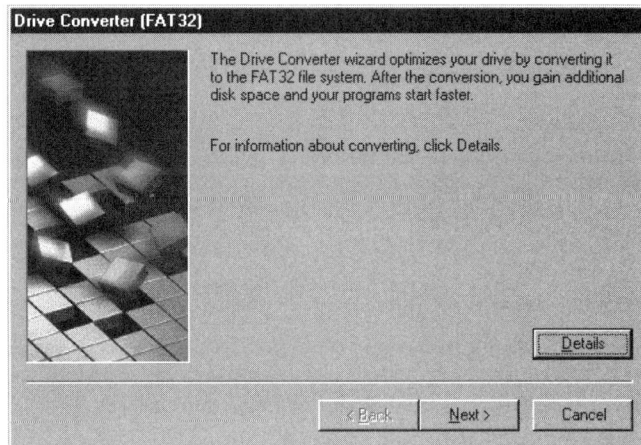

3. Select the drive you want to convert.

4. Choose Next to start the conversion process. Answer Yes to any prompts verifying the conversion.

Summary

Windows 98 has various programs and utilities to help you manage your hard drive and files. New protected-mode drivers support almost any kind of hard drive and CD-ROM.

This chapter began with a summary of the types of disk drives and bus adapters supported by Windows 98. You then learned how to troubleshoot disk driver problems by disabling features such as 32-bit mode drivers and the write-behind cache.

Our next topic was long filenames and how to handle problems associated with them, including programs that don't recognize long filenames and the 512 directory entry limit in root directories. You learned how to turn off and restore long filename support.

Next, you learned about the built-in tools for managing disk resources:

- *Compression* is now natively supported by Windows 98. To compress a drive, run the DriveSpace 3 program and choose which drive to compress. Remember you cannot compress a FAT32 volume.

- The *defragmentation* program is available from the Tools tab of any drive's Properties dialog box.

- *ScanDisk* is the main utility used to fix minor problems on your hard drive.

- *Disk Cleanup* helps get rid of old temporary file.

- The *Backup program* provides a quick and easy way to back up and restore both the Registry and files. Files can be backed up to tape or to a local or network drive.

- *Scheduled Tasks* shows any tasks you have created to run automatically on your computer.

- The *Maintenance Wizard* helps you easily build new scheduled tasks to help maintain your hard drive.

The final sections of the chapter described how to accomplish other disk-management tasks:

- Fdisk is used to partition a drive.

- Format is used to format a drive.

- SYS can restore the boot files to a drive without destroying the data on the drive.

- An improved version of the 32-bit program called *Vcache* is used to manage the caching of data from the hard drive.

- Caching is built into the CD-ROM driver, which is called *CDFS*.

- A new FAT scheme called *FAT32* supports partitions up to 8GB with a cluster size of only 4KB, with a maximum of 2TB of volume size supported with 32KB clusters.

- Windows 98 comes with a *Drive Converter* program that will allow you to convert FAT16 volumes to FAT32 volumes (but not the other way around).

Review Questions

1. What is the name of the program that can fix minor errors on your hard drive?

   A. Format

   B. Fdisk

   C. ScanDisk

   D. Vcache

2. What is it called when files get scattered over a hard drive?

   A. Compression

   B. Corruption

   C. Clustering

   D. Fragmentation

3. What is the name of the new 32-bit caching tool of Windows 98?

   A. Format

   B. Fdisk

   C. ScanDisk

   D. Vcache

4. Does Windows 98 include a native antivirus program?

   A. Yes, but only on the CD-ROM version of Windows 98

   B. Yes, but you have to pay for it before you can install it

   C. Yes, but it only comes with the upgrade version

   D. No

5. Windows 98's Backup program can restore backups made from which operating system? Choose all that apply.

    A. MS-DOS 5.0

    B. MS-DOS 6.22

    C. Windows 3.11

    D. Windows 95

6. Is creating smaller partitions a more efficient way to format your hard drive if you have to use FAT16 partitions?

    A. Yes, because files take up less room on your disk.

    B. Yes, because the hard drive works faster.

    C. Yes, because the hard drive spins less often, saving wear and tear.

    D. No, there is no difference.

7. The long filename "This is a company memo about the party for.1997.doc" would have which 8.3 name created for it?

    A. This is .doc

    B. Thisis~1.199

    C. Thisis~1.doc

    D. Thisisal.doc

8. Disabling the write-behind cache is done with which program?

    A. Control Panel ➤ System

    B. Control Panel ➤ Devices

    C. Control Panel ➤ Drives

    D. My Computer ➤ Properties of the Drive

9. You can restore deleted files in Windows 98 due to which program?

  A. Vcache

  B. Recycle Bin

  C. Trash Can

  D. Undelete

10. Which program can be used to schedule tasks such as ScanDisk and Disk Defragmenter in Windows 98?

  A. My Computer ➤ Properties

  B. Shortcuts

  C. Scheduled Tasks

  D. The AT command

11. How do you enable FAT32 support?

  A. Run FAT32.EXE.

  B. Run Fdisk with the /FAT32 switch.

  C. It is always enabled.

  D. Run Fdisk, and answer Yes to the Large Disk Support prompt.

12. What is the easiest way to create tasks to do regular hard drive maintenance?

  A. Create the tasks by hand.

  B. Copy the tasks from another computer.

  C. Use the Maintenance Wizard.

  D. Use the Create Scheduled Tasks Wizard.

13. A user comes to you and says he has compressed his C: drive on his Windows 98 computer and wants to install Windows NT so that he has a dual-boot system. How can you do this?

    A. Install Windows NT normally. It will automatically set up dual-booting.

    B. Convert to FAT32, and then perform the Windows NT installation.

    C. Use FDISK to mark the partition as Other, and then install Windows NT.

    D. Decompress the drive, and then install Windows NT.

14. A user wants to know what is the tightest compression level she can pick. She is running Windows 98 with a FAT16 partition. What sd you tell her?

    A. Hipack

    B. Ultrapack

    C. Default

    D. Compression is not supported for FAT16 partitions.

15. A user wants to know what is the tightest compression level he can pick. He is running Windows 98 with a FAT32 partition. What do you tell him?

    A. Hipack

    B. Ultrapack

    C. Default

    D. Compression is not supported for FAT32 partitions.

16. You want to back up your drive so that it is quick to restore in case of a hard disk failure. You don't plan on doing full backups every night. What method would you choose when backing up your drive?

   A. Partial

   B. Incremental

   C. Differential

   D. Saved

17. Which types of partitions can be marked active (bootable)? Choose all that apply.

   A. Primary

   B. Extended

   C. Logical

   D. Expanded

18. You upgraded a Windows for Workgroups computer to Windows 98. You want to minimize the space wasted on your hard drive. Which utility should you run?

   A. Disk Defragmenter

   B. ScanDisk

   C. Fdisk

   D. FAT32 Converter

19. A user comes to you and explains that she wants to uninstall Windows 98 and go back to Windows for Workgroups. She has a FAT32 partition with 1GB of free space. How can you uninstall Windows 98 without losing her data?

A. Convert the FAT32 partition to FAT16 by using the FAT32 conversion program, and run uninstall.

B. Run uninstall. The FAT32 partition will automatically revert to FAT16.

C. Run Fdisk. Choose No when asked if large disk support should be enabled. Then run uninstall.

D. Back up the data, run Fdisk, delete the partition, and create a FAT16 partition, reinstall Windows, and restore the data.

CHAPTER

8

Networking Protocols and Windows 98

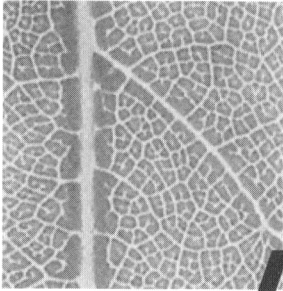

Almost every company is using one or more types of networks. Windows 98 was "born to network" and makes an excellent network client because of its flexibility and security. The improvements in Windows 98 over earlier versions of Windows may be most remarkable in the networking area.

Microsoft ✓ *Exam Objective*

Install and configure the network components of Windows 98 in a Microsoft environment or a mixed Microsoft and NetWare environment. Network components include:

- Client for Microsoft Networks
- Client for NetWare Networks
- Network adapters
- File and Printer Sharing for Microsoft Networks
- File and Printer Sharing for NetWare Networks
- Service for NetWare Directory Services (NDS)
- Asynchronous Transfer Mode (ATM)
- Virtual private networking and PPTP
- Browse Master

> **NOTE** Of the items listed above, only ATM will be addressed in this chapter. We'll discuss network clients, adapters, and NDS in Chapter 9; File and Printer Sharing topics and the Browse Master in Chapter 10; and virtual private networking and PPTP in Chapter 15.

In this chapter, you will look at the major network protocols that Windows 98 supports. Next, you will examine the network architecture of Windows 98, explaining how it corresponds with the OSI (Open Systems Interconnection) reference model. Then you will learn how Windows 98 can function as a network client or server. Finally, you will be introduced to the Network Neighborhood, which provides easy access to network resources.

If you are fairly new to networking, you probably want to review *MCSE: Networking Essentials Study Guide* (published by Sybex) for a complete, in-depth look at networking protocols, configurations, and implementations.

The Protocols—An Overview

Networks must use some kind of protocol to communicate. The three major protocols that Windows 98 supports are TCP/IP (Transmission Control Protocol/Internet Protocol), IPX/SPX (Internet Packet Exchange/Sequenced Packet Exchange), and NetBEUI (Network Basic Extended User Interface). Support for DLC (Data Link Control) and NetBIOS (Network Basic Input/ Output System) is also available.

Microsoft Exam Objective

Install and configure network protocols in a Microsoft environment or a mixed Microsoft and NetWare environment. Protocols include:

- NetBEUI
- IPX/SPX-compatible protocol
- TCP/IP
- Microsoft DLC
- Fast Infrared

Here is a brief overview of these protocols, which are each discussed in more detail later:

- **TCP/IP:** This protocol is popular for many reasons, including its open design, its nonproprietary heterogeneous support, and the Internet. TCP/IP, and how it is installed and configured on a Windows 98 computer, is covered in the following section. Every network administrator needs to be at least familiar with, if not an expert in, TCP/IP.

- **IPX/SPX:** This is a proprietary protocol that Novell developed for use in its NetWare networks. In the past, Microsoft called its compatible protocol NWLink; now it is called by the very inventive name "IPX/SPX-compatible protocol." Almost every application that works with, and expects, NetWare's IPX/SPX will also work with Microsoft's IPX/SPX-compatible protocol. In order to communicate with NetWare servers, the IPX/SPX-compatible protocol must be installed. Installing and configuring IPX/SPX are covered in the following section.

- **NetBEUI:** This protocol was developed by IBM for small interoffice networks. NetBEUI has severe limitations because it was designed for up to only 254 nodes and can't be routed. Interoffice mail may be a good analogy for NetBEUI: Interoffice mail is quick and cheap inside your company, but if an envelope is put in the regular mail bin, there is no way of delivering it, because it has no address (other than the person's name) on it. This protocol is almost never used as a regular protocol in a large company, but it can be useful as a dial-up protocol or in very small environments.

- **DLC:** This protocol must be used in conjunction with another protocol (e.g, TCP/IP, IPX/SPX, or NetBEUI). DLC is used to communicate with IBM mainframe computers and Hewlett-Packard (HP) JetDirect adapters. Because Windows 98 includes the lastest HP JetAdmin utility to install and configure HP printers, the use of DLC to communicate with printers will probably be limited.

- **NetBIOS:** This is not a protocol per se, but is a specification that protocols and applications can be designed to support. IPX/SPX adds support for NetBIOS via TSRs (terminate-and-stay resident programs), but Microsoft's IPX-compatible protocol, TCP/IP, and NetBEUI come with native NetBIOS support. Microsoft's networking, as well as many applications, requires NetBIOS support in order to function correctly.

- **Fast Infrared:** This is a relatively new protocol designed for communication between devices that have infrared ports (like laptops and certain printers).

- **Asynchronous Transfer Mode (ATM):** ATM technology is the result of the efforts of the International Telecommunication Union Telecommunication Standardization Sector (ITU-T) Study Group XVIII (formerly known as CCITT) to develop Broadband Integrated Services Digital Network (BISDN) for the high-speed transfer of data, image, video, text, and voice through public networks. ATM is the transfer mode of choice for BISDN networks. An ATM cell (packet) is always comprised of 53 bytes of which the first 5 bytes are the header and the last 48 bytes are payload. By using a fixed-length cell, ATM can easily be routed and multiplexed on a network and various services can have their bandwidth usage tightly controlled. Microsoft ATM services support LAN emulation so that protocols such as TCP/IP or IPX/SPX can be used across an ATM connection.

- **Virtual Private Networking (VPN)/Point-to-Point Tunneling Protocol (PPTP):** PPTP is used to make a secured, encrypted connection via the Internet. In other words, the Internet can function as a WAN link for a secured, virtual connection. It is virtual in the sense that if you reestablish the connection, it may follow a different path through the Internet—it is not limited to a single physical connection.

TCP/IP

TCP/IP (Transmission Control Protocol/Internet Protocol) has become one of the most (if not the most) widely used protocols in today's computing environments. Its popularity is due to many things, including its availability on almost every hardware platform, its support of open standards, and the explosion of the Internet. TCP/IP allows the operation of various network applications, from FTP clients to Web browsers. TCP/IP will be covered in more detail than the other protocols because of both its popularity and its importance on the test.

A Brief History of TCP/IP

Originally developed in 1969 for the Department of Defense Advanced Research Project Agency (ARPA), TCP/IP was part of a resource-sharing experiment called ARPANET. The original motivation was to design a communications protocol that could be implemented independently of the various existing hardware systems the government possessed. This would allow these systems to exchange data, regardless of their hardware makeup.

Eventually, ARPANET and the network infrastructure provided by the National Science Foundation (NSFNET) grew into the worldwide community of networks now known as the Internet. Because ARPA provided the standards for the protocol free of charge to government agencies and universities, the protocols were further developed. The public universities became great contributors to the development of TCP/IP. Many of the higher-level protocols for such things as e-mail (SMTP), newsgroups, printing, and file transfer (FTP) came from those working in the universities.

The initial fuel for this growth began when TCP/IP was included with Berkeley Standard Distribution (BSD) Unix, and it has been a standard feature of Unix almost ever since. Now TCP/IP can be found in just about every other operating system, from Macintosh to mainframes to Windows. The most explosive growth, however, has come with the development of HTTP (Hypertext Transfer Protocol) for the sharing of HTML (Hypertext Markup Language) documents, which has evolved into the Internet's World Wide Web.

One feature of TCP/IP that makes it popular in its use across hardware platforms and software vendors is that it's an "open" protocol—*open* meaning that not just one organization has input into its design. Ideas for its improvement can be offered via documents called Requests for Comments (RFCs). More than 2000 RFCs have been submitted to date that, directly or indirectly, define the current standards for TCP/IP.

RFCs can be submitted to the Internet Activities Board (IAB), where they will be debated, considered, and assigned a priority level or classification that determines whether they should be used for future implementations. There are five possible classifications:

- Required (must be used for TCP/IP hosts)

- Recommended (encouraged but not required)

- Elective (optional—agreed upon but not in wide use)

- Limited Use (not recommended for general use)

- Not Recommended (not meeting any usage requirements)

TCP/IP Addresses

Unlike IPX or NetBEUI, TCP/IP requires each node or host to be assigned a unique address to participate on the network. This can require much more administrative work than other protocols because each host (which includes desktop computers, printers, routers, and any other device that needs to communicate on the network) needs to have an address assigned to it. The address, commonly referred to as an *IP address*, looks similar to this:

131.107.2.200

An IP address is a 32-bit address, where each of the four sets of numbers presented is actually an octet, or contains eight bits of data. For example, the above address is actually:

10000011.01101011.00000010.11001000

or four eight-bit numbers (octets). Because this binary format is not easily read by humans, it is converted into decimal format as first shown.

In determining IP addresses, several factors must be considered:

- Class of address

- Address uniqueness

- Restricted addresses

TCP/IP Address Classes

The *class of address*, along with the subnet mask (explained later in the chapter) determines which part of the IP address is used for network identification (net ID) and which part is used for host identification (host ID). Although five address classes are defined, only three can be used for host addressing: Class A, Class B, and Class C.

> **NOTE** The first octet in the address determines whether an address is a Class A, B, or C address.

Table 8.1 provides a summary of the properties for each class of address. They are discussed in more detail in the following sections.

T A B L E 8.1 IP Address Class Summary	**Address Class**	**Range of Network IDs**	**Number of Networks**	**Hosts per Network**
	Class A	1–126	126	16,777,214
	Class B	128–191	16,384	65,534
	Class C	192–223	2,097,152	254

The separation between net ID and host ID in an IP address helps define the subnet mask. In this example of a Class A address, because the first octet is taken to identify the network, it is "masked out" from being used for host IDs. The default subnet mask with a Class A address is 255.0.0.0, signifying that the first octet is unavailable for host IDs. The default subnet mask for a Class B address is 255.255.0.0 because the first two octets are masked out from being used as host IDs. The default subnet mask for a Class C address is 255.255.255.0 because these octets are used for the net ID and are unavailable for use as host IDs.

TCP/IP Address Restrictions   IP addresses must be unique for every host on the network. This means that there must be a unique combination of net ID and host ID for every host. Also, every host on the same network segment must have the same net ID. This is because local communication is established through a series of broadcasts that are for that network only. These broadcasts will not cross a router (which connects the different networks). So, if a host with the same net ID is across a router, it will never be reached. (In TCP/IP terminology, *router* and *gateway* mean the same thing.)

Subnets and Subnet Masks

Before studying subnet masks, it is important to understand what a subnet is. Simply put, a *subnet* is a network segment. However, from an IP perspective, it is a segment in a multiple-segmented network that has been given a net ID derived from a "parent" net ID. For example, in Figure 8.1, a Class B parent net ID of 131.107.0.0 is the assigned address and has been subnetted into smaller networks.

FIGURE 8.1

Subnets are segments
of multiple-segmented
networks.

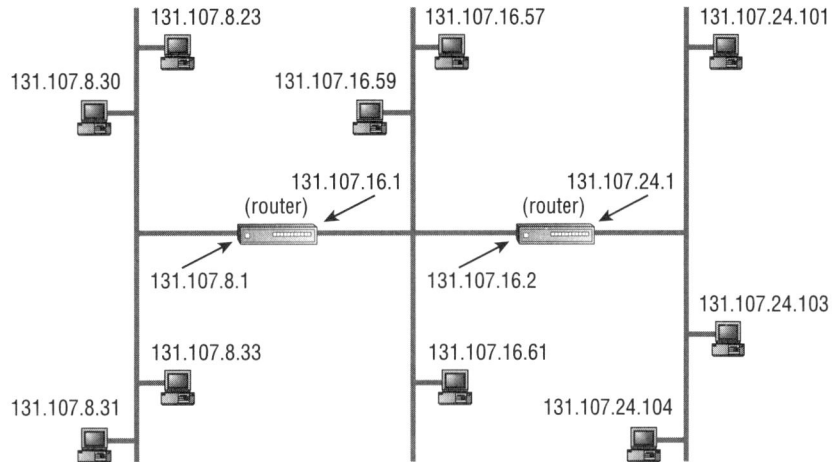

FIGURE 8.1

Subnets are segments of multiple-segmented networks.

In the example in Figure 8.1, three subnets are connected by routers:

- 131.107.8.0
- 131.107.16.0
- 131.107.24.0

Because the parent address has been subnetted, it is no longer used as a single network; but all the subnets together are the network of 131.107.0.0.

The subnet mask used determines how many subnets have been created. Whatever the subnet mask is, it must be the same for all the subnets created, even though they will each have their own unique net IDs. The subnet mask not only determines what part of the IP address belongs to the host (host ID) and what part belongs to the network (net ID), it also determines what is local or remote to a subnet.

> The subnet mask is frequently the component that is incorrectly defined and set up. Of the three, this is the one where most errors/mistakes occur.

> Each subnet must be connected by a router (or gateway) to the other subnets in order to communicate.

The Default Gateway

The *default gateway* is the way out of a subnet. It is the router that connects one subnet to another so that hosts can communicate with hosts on other interconnected networks. The default gateway has its own IP address, which the hosts on its subnet must know to use.

When a host determines that a destination host is not local, it sends its data to its configured default gateway. The router then refers to its route table to determine if it has a direct connection to the destination network or if it must send the data on to another router that can deliver the data to the destination host.

DHCP and TCP/IP

Microsoft bundles a service called *DHCP* (Dynamic Host Configuration Protocol) with Windows NT Server that allows you to preconfigure TCP/IP addresses, subnet masks, and default gateway settings (as well as other settings), so that clients can ask for and automatically receive their settings.

Your configuration choices are whether to use DHCP to dynamically assign addresses and subnet masks or to manually assign addresses and subnet masks. The addresses of DNS servers, WINS servers, and default gateways can also be assigned manually or by DHCP.

TCP/IP Improvements in Windows 98

TCP/IP in Windows 98 has some improvements over earlier versions that include:

- Automatic private IP addressing in case of DHCP failure using the 169.254.*x.x* range

- Support for more than one address (multihomed)

- Support for IP multicasting

- Support for Windows Sockets 2.0

- DHCP enhancements, including address conflict detection and longer time-out periods

- WINS enhancements including the querying of multiple WINS servers (persistent connections)

NOTE

If a computer uses automatic private addressing, it can only communicate with other computers that also used private addressing. Note also that only those computers on the local subnet can be seen. When the DHCP server comes back on line, the correct (DHCP) addresses will be used instead of the private addresses. Automatic private addresses make it possible for small companies to operate without a DHCP server because all computers would use private addressing.

Installing TCP/IP in Windows 98

Microsoft *Exam* *Objective*

Install and configure network protocols in a Microsoft environment or a mixed Microsoft and NetWare environment. Protocols include:

- TCP/IP

Three major configuration items must be set for TCP/IP:

- **IP Address:** This is the address of the computer. Addresses must be unique.

- **Subnet Mask:** This shows which part of the address connotes the network versus the client.

- **Default Gateway:** This tells the computer how to reach an outside network.

You can add a protocol through the Network Control Panel, as shown in Figure 8.2. Windows 98 offers TCP/IP as a choice in the Select Network Protocol dialog box, as shown in Figure 8.3. Follow the steps in Exercise 8.1 to install TCP/IP.

NOTE

If you already have TCP/IP installed and you want to practice reinstalling it, remove TCP/IP first. If you are not using DHCP (Dynamic Host Configuration Protocol), you should record your settings so you can reenter them later.

FIGURE 8.2

The Select Network
Component Type
dialog box

FIGURE 8.3

The Select Network
Protocol dialog box

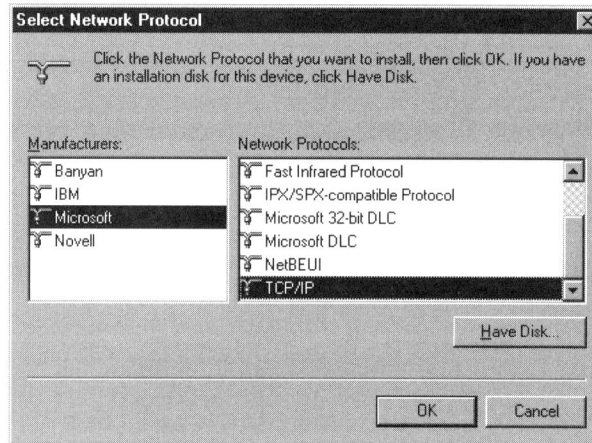

EXERCISE 8.1

Installing TCP/IP

1. In the Control Panel, double-click the Network icon to open the Select Network Component Type dialog box (see Figure 8.2).

2. Click Add, select Protocol, and click Add again. This brings up the Select Network Protocol dialog box (see Figure 8.3).

3. Select Microsoft in the list of Manufacturers.

4. Select TCP/IP in the list of Network Protocols.

5. Click OK. Windows will prompt you for the location of the Windows 98 distribution files.

6. Indicate the location of the files. After Windows 98 finishes copying files, you will be prompted to restart your computer, as shown here.

7. Click Yes to reboot your computer and have the changes take effect.

Microsoft ✓ *Exam* *Objective*

Diagnose and resolve connectivity problems in a Microsoft environment and a mixed Microsoft and NetWare environment. Tools include:

- WinIPCfg
- Net Watcher
- Ping
- Tracert

Using TCP/IP Utilities

Several utilities and applications are installed with TCP/IP that can help with diagnostic functions:

- **WinIPCfg:** A GUI utility for verification of IP settings, such as IP address, subnet mask, default gateway, WINS server address, MAC address, DHCP server address, and DHCP lease status. WinIPCfg was introduced with Windows 95.

- **IPCONFIG:** A command line program with the same functionality as WinIPCfg. IPCONFIG was first introduced with Windows NT and was not present in Windows 95 or earlier versions of Windows.

- **Ping:** For verification of configuration and connections.

- **Tracert:** For verification of the route taken to reach another host.

- **Route:** For viewing or editing a local route table.

- **NetStat:** For viewing protocol statistics and connections.

- **FTP:** A command-line FTP client.

- **Telnet:** A GUI Telnet client.

The Winsock interface (version 2.0) will automatically be available, so it is not necessary to install a third-party Winsock utility such as Trumpet. If DHCP is not configured on the network, you may need to open the TCP/IP property sheet and fill in the IP address information manually, as discussed in the "TCP/IP Configuration" section later in this chapter.

See Chapter 10 for complete coverage of Net Watcher.

In Exercise 8.2, you will use WinIPCfg to look at the TCP/IP settings, Ping to test your settings, and Tracert to look at the patch to another computer.

EXERCISE 8.2

Using WinIPCfg, Ping, and Tracert

1. Select Start ➤ Run and type **WINIPCFG**.

2. Click the More Info button. You should see something like this:

IP Configuration

Host Information
Host Name | LBMLAPTOP
DNS Servers |
Node Type | Broadcast
NetBIOS Scope Id |
IP Routing Enabled | WINS Proxy Enabled
NetBIOS Resolution Uses DNS |

Ethernet Adapter Information
PPP Adapter.
Adapter Address | 44-45-53-54-00-00
IP Address | 131.107.2.155
Subnet Mask | 255.255.255.0
Default Gateway |
DHCP Server |
Primary WINS Server |
Secondary WINS Server |
Lease Obtained |
Lease Expires |

OK | Release | Renew | Release All | Renew All

3. Click OK to close WinIPCfg.

4. Open a command prompt.

5. Run the utility IPCONFIG.EXE. The results should be the same as you got with WinIPCfg.

6. Select OK to close WinIPCfg.

7. From the command prompt, type **Ping 127.0.0.1**. This will test the connectivity to yourself. You can also substitute the address or name of a computer on the network.

8. From the command prompt, type **Tracert 127.0.0.1**. This will show you the route to yourself. You can also substitute the address or name of a computer on the network.

9. Close the command prompt.

> **NOTE** When using WinIPCfg the Release All button gives back an automatic address to the DHCP server and the Renew All address attempts to contact a DHCP server for a new address. When using IPCONFIG, the /release switch gives back an automatic address, the /renew switch attempts to get a new address, and the /all switch shows detailed information.

Changing TCP/IP Settings

Configure the TCP/IP settings by going to the properties of the protocol. Figure 8.4 shows the IP Address tab where you can either choose to manually assign an address and subnet mask, or you can have DHCP automatically do the assignment. The default gateway is set using the Gateway tab.

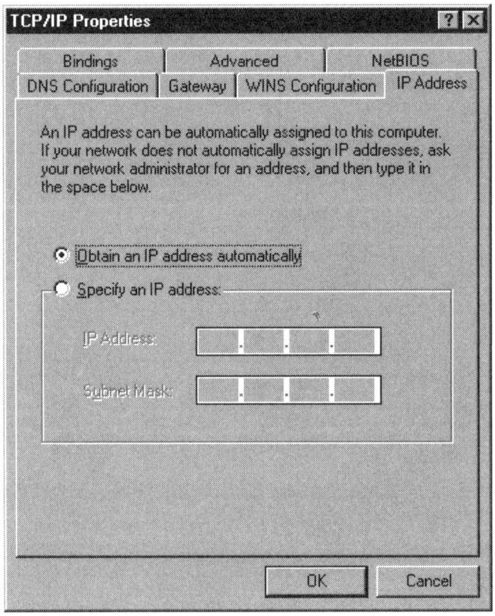

FIGURE 8.4

The TCP/IP Properties page

Using DHCP to Configure TCP/IP   DHCP was developed to help with the administration of TCP/IP. DHCP allows for centralization of TCP/IP management. An administrator does not need to individually configure each host with its IP parameters. This configuration can be done automatically with a DHCP server.

NOTE
Although Microsoft has been one of the first to implement DHCP, it was not developed by Microsoft. Like the other TCP/IP protocols, DHCP was developed through RFCs. DHCP is defined in RFCs 1533, 1534, 1541, and 1542. It is an extension of the BOOTP protocol (RFC 951), which automatically assigns IP addresses to diskless clients.

The DHCP server can assign an IP address, a subnet mask, a default gateway, and a WINS server address to hosts. A client needs to specify that it will use DHCP (Automatic Settings) instead of being manually configured with IP information. In Windows 98, this is done via a radio button in the TCP/IP Properties dialog box (see Figure 8.4).

NOTE
The DHCP server software can run only on Windows NT Server (not Windows 98 or Windows NT Workstation). Once the server software is installed, an icon called DHCP Manager is added to the NT Administration Tools group. This is what the interface administrators use to define the pool of IP addresses. DHCP clients (those that receive an IP address from the DHCP server) can be any of several operating systems, including Windows 98. Refer to Sybex's *MCSE: Windows NT 4 Server* or *MCSE: TCP/IP* books for more information about installing and configuring DHCP.

There is a four-step process for a host to receive IP configuration through DHCP:

1. The DHCP client boots up and broadcasts a DHCP Discover message looking for a DHCP server.

2. Any DHCP server that received the broadcast responds with a DHCP Offer (which includes the IP address of the offering server). This message has the IP address being offered.

3. The client broadcasts a DHCP Request for the first offer received (in a case where multiple servers responded with offers) to accept.

4. The DHCP server broadcasts a DHCP Acknowledgment to confirm the assignment.

The address is assigned on a lease basis (usually somewhere between 72 and 96 hours, but this can be changed by the administrator). When half of the lease time expires, the client renews the lease to full time again. In this way, the lease will never run out unless the client could not find the server to renew, or the client was shut down and could not renew.

Using WINS for NetBIOS Communication

WINS (Windows Internet Name Service) is another NT Server service that helps lower administrative overhead. WINS is an enhanced NetBIOS Name Server (NBNS) designed by Microsoft to perform two main tasks:

- To help eliminate broadcast traffic associated with resolving NetBIOS names over TCP/IP

- To help facilitate NetBIOS communication between subnets

Most of the applications that are native to Windows and Windows NT (such as File Manager and Explorer) are NetBIOS-based. One of the requirements for a NetBIOS session to be established is that each side has a NetBIOS name to reference. In Windows, this is accomplished by assigning a computer name. The computer name is a NetBIOS name that can be used to establish a NetBIOS session.

When running over TCP/IP, an IP address is also required for communication. This means that a NetBIOS name must be resolved to an IP address. This can be done by means of a broadcast (which works only if the computers are on the same subnet), a WINS server, or a local LMHOSTS file (which is an ASCII file that has computer names listed along with their IP addresses) that has been configured at each host. The LMHOST is usually used to map servers across remote networks connected by routers or gateways. You use the LMHOST file when or if the WINS server is not available on the network.

To configure a host to be a WINS client in Windows 98, the client needs to have the IP address of the WINS server. This can either be done manually by entering the address by hand or automatically by using DHCP.

WINS works dynamically by registering computer names and IP addresses of clients as they boot up and become active on the network. Because each WINS client knows the IP address of the WINS server, it can communicate directly with a WINS server to register its computer name and IP address instead of using a broadcast. When a WINS client needs to resolve a computer name to an IP address, such as when a net use \\computer\share is used, the WINS client sends a direct request to the WINS server (again saving the broadcast traffic) for the IP address of the requested computer name.

If you have enabled the DNS (Domain Name Service), this is an additional global database based on a hierarchical naming system. If you haven't correctly defined the DNS data, the WINS and the DNS compete to find the name in their respective databases, therefore slowing the process and creating possible time-out scenarios. Make sure your DNS is correctly defined or it could conflict with the WINS.

Installing and Configuring IPX/SPX

Microsoft
Exam
Objective

Install and configure network protocols in a Microsoft environment or a mixed Microsoft and NetWare environment. Protocols include:

- IPX/SPX-compatible protocol

Installing IPX/SPX is relatively straightforward. Simply select IPX/SPX from the list of protocols provided by Microsoft.

There are only a couple of settings you may need to change on a regular basis when using the IPX/SPX protocol: selecting the frame type and enabling NetBIOS support.

The most important setting to check when using the IPX/SPX protocol on an Ethernet network is the frame type. Four basic frames can be run under Ethernet:

- Ethernet 802.2

- Ethernet 802.3

- Ethernet_II

- Ethernet_Snap

Microsoft's IPX/SPX default frame selection is Automatic, which means that Windows 98 will try to determine the frame type being used and match itself to that. If a frame cannot be determined, it will default to 802.2 (which is the default for NetWare 3.12 and higher).

> If you use IPX/SPX from Novell and have different frame types on two computers, the two computers will not see each other at all. If you select the wrong frame type when you are using Microsoft's version of IPX/SPX, the computers may still connect, but the communication will be extremely slow. You may be able to see servers with different frames, even though Windows 98 is using only one, because a server is routing, or converting, to the other frame type. For the best performance, you should run the same frame type on all your computers.

The Automatic setting will bind to the frame it finds most on the network. If you have multiple frames on your network, Windows 98 may bind to the wrong one. If you have servers with various frame types, you should specify the frame for the client software so it will see the correct servers. The Frame Type setting is on the Advanced tab of the IPX/SPX-Compatible Protocol Properties dialog box (see Figure 8.5).

FIGURE 8.5

The Advanced tab of the IPX/SPX-Compatible Protocol Properties box

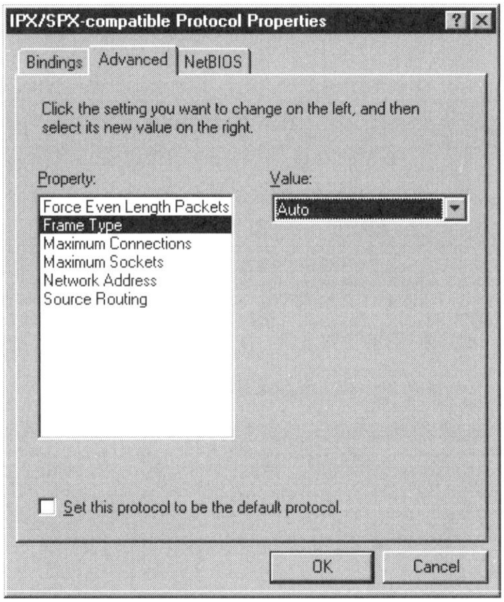

Another parameter you may need to set is whether to support NetBIOS over IPX/SPX. NetBIOS is a specification that some programs require in order to work on a network. The documentation for the network application should specify which protocol is are supported and if NetBIOS support is required. Older network applications often require NetBIOS support; newer applications seldom do. If you have applications that require NetBIOS support, you will need to select the option. This setting is on the NetBIOS tab of the IPX/SPX-Compatible Protocol Properties dialog box. (See Figure 8.6.)

FIGURE 8.6

Enabling NetBIOS support using IPX/SPX

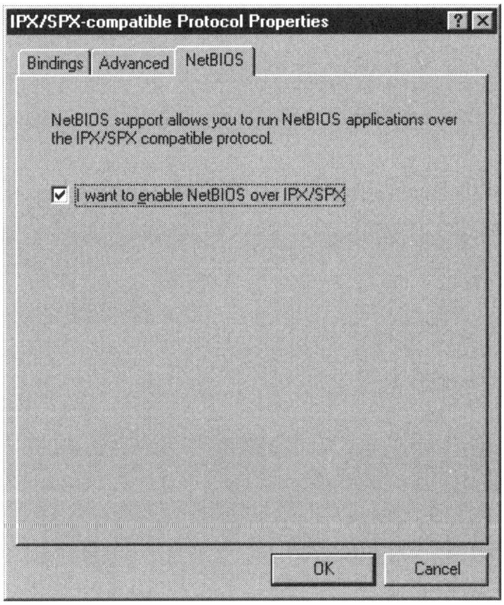

Installing and Configuring NetBEUI

Microsoft
✓ *Exam*
Objective

Install and configure network protocols in a Microsoft environment or a mixed Microsoft and NetWare environment. Protocols include:

- NetBEUI

NetBEUI parameters will rarely, if ever, need to be changed. Changing these settings affects only real-mode NetBEUI. Windows 98 dynamically adjusts the protected-mode NetBEUI parameters.

Remember, NetBEUI can handle only up to only 254 nodes, and NetBEUI packets cannot cross a router. Although this protocol is rarely used as a regular protocol, it can be useful as a dial-up protocol.

Protected-mode NetBEUI is totally self-tuning, and the administrator will not need to change any of its parameters. Only two parameters can be changed for real-mode NetBEUI: maximum sessions and NCBs (Network Control Blocks). These settings are on the Advanced tab of the NetBEUI Properties dialog box, as shown in Figure 8.7.

FIGURE 8.7

Real-mode NetBEUI parameters

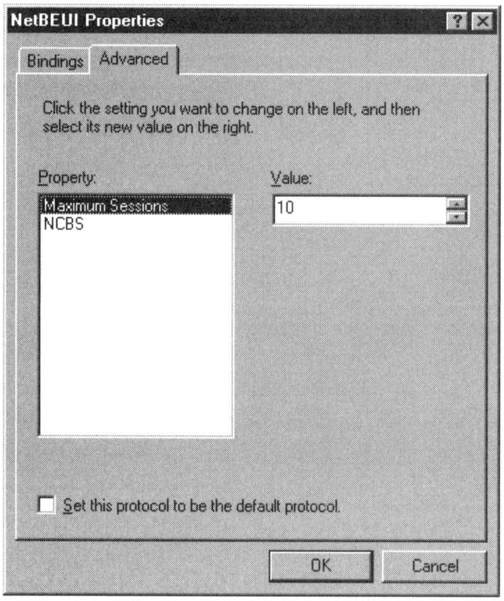

Installing and Configuring DLC

Microsoft Exam Objective

Install and configure network protocols in a Microsoft environment or a mixed Microsoft and NetWare environment. Protocols include:

- Microsoft DLC

The DLC protocol can be used for direct communication and connection with mainframe computers that support DLC, as well as PC-based peripherals like HP printers that have an HP JetDirect network card installed. The JetDirect card allows you to connect your printer directly to the network rather than to a printer port on a PC.

To use an HP printer with an HP JetDirect card on your network, you must have the following configuration:

- An HP printer with an HP JetDirect card installed and connected to the network

- Microsoft DLC installed and running on the PC that is to be the Print Server

- A network printer in the Printers folder on the Print Server

To install the DLC protocol, follow the steps outlined in Exercise 8.1. substituting the 32-bit DLC protocol for TCP/IP.

> **NOTE** Only the Print Server needs to have the DLC protocol installed. All other computers can send print jobs to the Print Server using any available protocol that has been configured.

Windows 98 comes with a native HP JetAdmin program, which can be used to install and manage HP JetDirect network printers. Note that if you use the HP JetAdmin program the DLC protocol is not required.

To use the HP JetAdmin program, you must install the HP JetAdmin Network Service by going to Control Panel ➣ Network ➣ Add ➣ Service ➣ Hewlett-Packard ➣ HP JetAdmin. Once you have rebooted, the JetAdmin icon will appear in your Control Panel.

> **NOTE** Windows 98 includes a 32-bit DLC protocol and a 16-bit DLC protocol (for backward compatibility). Microsoft recommends using the 32-bit DLC protocol if possible.

Installing and Configuring Fast Infrared (FIR)

Microsoft Exam Objective

Install and configure network protocols in a Microsoft environment or a mixed Microsoft and NetWare environment. Protocols include:

- Fast Infrared

Windows 98 includes the Microsoft Infrared version 3.0, which allows you to connect to and use devices such as printers, computers, and cameras. Fast Infrared installs like any other protocol under Windows 98. Simply go to the Add ➤ Protocols ➤ Microsoft and choose Fast Infrared from the Network Applet (see Figure 8.8).

F I G U R E 8.8

Installing the Fast Infrared Protocol

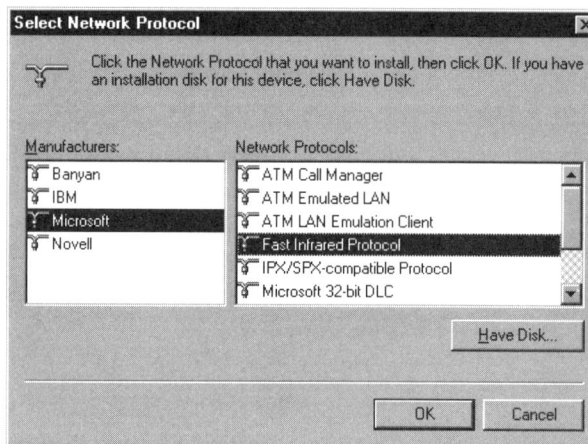

Once the protocol is installed, you can configure it by highlighting it and choosing Properties.

Installing and Configuring ATM Services

Microsoft ✓ *Exam* *Objective*

Install and configure the network components of Windows 98 in a Microsoft environment or a mixed Microsoft and NetWare environment. Network components include:

- **Asynchronous Transfer Mode (ATM)**

Support for ATM services is easy to install with Windows 98. After installing the ATM support services, you will also need to install and configure the protocol (TCP/IP or IPX/SPX) you will use across the ATM connection. There are three separate protocols that must be individually installed for ATM support (shown in Figure 8.8). To install ATM support do the following:

1. Go to Control Panel ➤ Network; choose Add, highlight Protocol; choose Add, highlight Microsoft; and choose ATM Call Manager.

2. Select OK to add the protocol.

3. Repeat Step 1, highlighting ATM Emulated LAN.

4. Select OK to add the protocol.

5. Repeat Step 1, highlighting ATM LAN Emulation Client.

6. Select OK to add the protocol.

7. Install any protocols you need that are not already installed (TCP/IP, IPX/SPX).

8. Select OK from the main Network Properties screen to save your changes.

9. Reboot Windows 98.

Once the ATM services are installed, you will need to specify the name of the emulated LAN. To configure the ATM services do the following:

1. Go to Control Panel ➤ Network.

2. Highlight the ATM LAN Emulation Client.

3. Select Properties.

4. Enter the name of the emulated LAN in the Value box.

5. Select OK to save your changes.

Windows 98 Network Architecture

Networking is a very complex matter. Fortunately, it can be broken down into smaller parts to make it easier to understand.

> **NOTE** This section is presented to help "fill in the gaps" that many administrators have when it comes to networking. If you are already quite comfortable with networking models, you can skip to the next section, "Windows 98 as a Client."

The OSI model is one of the most prevalent models used to break down networking. First, this section will review the OSI model, and then it will match the Windows 98 components to their respective layers. This approach will help you understand how Windows 98 implements networking and where the various pieces fit.

The OSI Model

There are several different ways of looking at networking, just as there are several ways of looking at building a house. The OSI model is presented here because it is a popular and well-defined model for breaking down networking into more manageable pieces.

Just as a set of blueprints for a house can be read and used by any competent contractor, the *OSI model* provides a blueprint for networking that can be (and usually is) followed (to one degree or another) by most major software and hardware companies. If you build a house, you should be able to hire any plumbing subcontractor and any electrical subcontractor, and your plumbing and electricity should be installed to standard specifications and function as you expect. The OSI model, and the standards built around it, has the same goal; that is, you should not be forced into using equipment from a particular manufacturer—you should be able to use software and hardware from any company and make them communicate. (It's a nice idea in theory, but sometimes you can still get tied to a proprietary solution.)

> **NOTE** The OSI model, developed by the ISO (International Standardization Organization), is a conceptual framework used to describe how to connect any combination of devices for purposes of communication. Although there are other networking models developed by other organizations, the OSI model is the standard for network layered architecture and the most widely accepted model for understanding network communications. The OSI model does not perform any functions in the communication processes; this work is done by the appropriate software and hardware. The model's purpose is to define the tasks that need to be done and which protocols will handle those tasks.

The OSI model has seven layers:

- **Application:** The layer with which the user's applications communicate. This layer consists of API (Application Programming Interface) calls that applications can make. Its purpose is to allow transparent access to operating system or networking functions. For instance, an application shouldn't need to know which protocol or brand of network card is being used, as long as that protocol or card is compatible with Windows 98.

- **Presentation:** The layer that is responsible for translating the input from the application (and therefore the user) into a form that can more easily be transmitted across the network. ASCII and EBCDIC are two methods of translating the alphabet into bits and bytes. This layer is also responsible for data encryption and compression.

- **Session:** The layer that is in charge of the big picture. It makes the overall networking session happen by synchronizing and sequencing the elements (packets) in a network connection. This layer also deals with any errors that are not caused by the network or a protocol (such as running out of paper), makes sure that the transmission is complete, and ensures that appropriate security measures are taken during the connection.

- **Transport:** The layer that makes sure the packets are delivered correctly. This layer is where the connection is made for the TCP and SPX protocols.

- **Network:** The layer that is in charge of addressing the packets so they are delivered to the correct network. Network routers work at this level. Routers examine the destination network address and pass the packet along on its way.

- **Data Link:** The layer that consists of the driver for the network card. This layer, often split into two sub-layers called the Data Link and MAC (Media Access Control) layers, helps watch for errors in the transmission and conversion of signals, and it is responsible for delivering packets between computers without errors. Network bridges function at this layer. A bridge put in between two segments of the same network will examine each packet, and if the destination is on the other side of the bridge, it will let it pass; otherwise, the bridge keeps the traffic local.

- **Physical:** This layer consists of the network card, which is in charge of translating bits and bytes to and from electrical impulses. Network repeaters operate at this level; their job is to boost the network signal (without doing any analysis on the signal).

One way to help remember the OSI model layers (and their order) is the saying **A**ll **P**eople **S**eem **T**o **N**eed **D**ata **P**rocessing.

Data is passed from applications down through the layers of communications until it reaches the network card and cabling system. It is then transmitted back up the network layers until it reaches the appropriate application on the receiving side. Figure 8.9 illustrates communication through the OSI model's layers.

Windows 98 and the OSI Model

Microsoft presents its networking components in a model that is similar to the OSI model. The OSI layers, corresponding Microsoft layers, and Windows 98 implementation are shown in Figure 8.10.

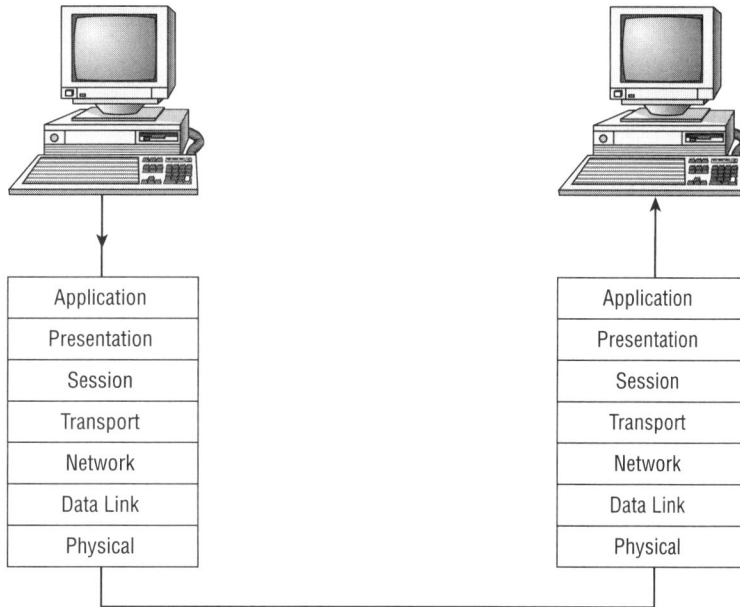

FIGURE 8.9

Communication through the OSI model's layers

| Application |
| Presentation |
| Session |
| Transport |
| Network |
| Data Link |
| Physical |

| Application |
| Presentation |
| Session |
| Transport |
| Network |
| Data Link |
| Physical |

This figure shouldn't be taken too literally, because the layers don't match exactly with each other due to differences in definitions.

FIGURE 8.10

The OSI and Microsoft models, and the respective Windows 98 implementations

OSI Layers	Microsoft Layers	Windows 98 Implementation
Application	Application Interface	Win32 WinNet APIs / Win32 Print APIs
Presentation	Network Providers	WinNet16 / NetWare/Windows
Session	File System Interface	IFS Manager
Transport	Redirectors and Services	Redirector/Services
Network	Transport Driver Interface	NETBIOS / Windows Sockets
Data Link	Transport Protocols	TCP/IP / IPX/SPX / NetBEUI
Physical	Device Driver Interface	NDIS 3.x / ODI / NDIS 2.x

Microsoft's model includes the following seven layers:

- **Application Interface:** Like the OSI model's Application layer, this layer is where the API calls are made by user applications. Windows 98 provides APIs for file access as well as printing.

- **Network Providers:** Like its OSI model counterpart, this layer translates the API calls into a language that other computers can understand. Windows 98 has support for 16-bit networking calls (for compatibility) as well as 32-bit providers for Microsoft, NetWare, and other servers.

- **File System Interface:** This layer provides a "railroad switch" function—it figures out whether a request can be fulfilled locally or needs to come from across the network. The IFS (Installable File System) manager is the Windows 98 component that fulfills this role. Windows 98 was designed so that resources look the same whether they are local or across the network.

> **NOTE** You can see how the transparency of network access works in Windows 98 by going into Network Neighborhood and showing the resources on your machine (something that Windows for Workgroups couldn't do). Network Neighborhood is discussed later in the chapter.

- **Redirectors and Services:** Redirectors function when Windows 98 acts like a client, and services are used when Windows 98 is acting like a server or providing a function on the network. The redirectors and services are discussed in more detail in Chapters 11, 12, and 13.

- **Transport Driver Interface:** This layer allows applications, redirectors, and services to communicate via NetBIOS or socket connections. The Transport Driver Interface ensures that applications have transparent access to network resources.

- **Transport Protocols:** This layer is where TCP/IP, IPX/SPX, and/or NetBEUI are implemented.

- **Device Driver Interface:** This layer is where the software driver that comes with the network card operates. Windows 98 can use drivers written to the ODI (Open Data-Link Interface, for NetWare) specification, but ODI drivers are real-mode (16-bit). Microsoft uses the NDIS (Network Driver Interface Specification) standard for network card adapters. Windows 98 also supports the Windows Driver Model (WDM), which means that the same driver should work with both Windows 98 and Windows NT 5.0

> There are five versions of NDIS for Windows. Version 2.0, real mode (16-bit), is the lowest type usable by Windows 98. Version 3.0, protected mode (32-bit), is the lowest type usable by Windows NT 3.x. Version 3.1, protected mode, adds Plug and Play for Windows 98. Version 4.0 added PPTP (Point-to-Point Tunneling Protocol), better network monitor support, and better network monitoring for Windows NT 4.0. Version 5.0 adds the Windows Driver Model (WDM) support.

Windows 98 as a Client

Windows 98 excels as a networking client. In order to understand your options when installing client software for Windows 98, it is important to know how networking works for both Novell and Microsoft networks.

Various new features in Windows 98 offer compelling reasons to upgrade from earlier versions of MS-DOS or Windows 3.x software. Windows 98 also works very well in mixed environments; it can easily handle two or more different types of servers concurrently.

Windows 98 Networking Features

Windows 98 has many more networking features than earlier versions of Windows, including the following:

- **Graphical, standardized way of making networking changes:** All networking functions can be changed from one spot—the Network Control Panel. Using the Network Control Panel to make changes is much easier than using the methods available in previous versions of Windows. Use of the Network Control Panel is covered in Chapters 9 and 10.

- **Simultaneous client connections to dissimilar servers:** Although Windows 3.*x* could connect to different types of networks, it wasn't designed from the ground up for networking, and conflicts often resulted. With the appropriate software, Windows 98 can connect to and be a client to both NetWare and Microsoft servers.

- **Plug-and-Play support for network adapters:** Windows 98 adds this support, which makes installing and configuring network cards easier. The procedures for installing and configuring network cards are discussed in Chapters 9 and 10.

- **Automatic reconnection of lost connections:** Windows 98 will attempt to reconnect if a connection is broken. Often, the user doesn't even know the connection was broken and reestablished.

- **Client-side caching of network data:** Windows 98 uses Vcache (the protected-mode cache program) to cache data from the network to increase performance.

- **Long filename support:** Long filenames can be stored on both Microsoft and NetWare servers. NT servers automatically save long filenames. NetWare servers need the OS2 support enabled, as explained in Chapter 10.

- **Support for user profiles and system policies:** User profiles allow more than one user to save user settings on a computer. System policies allow administrators to enforce rules on the network. User profiles are covered in Chapter 12, and system policies are the topic of Chapter 13.

- **Real-mode (16-bit) network driver support:** Windows 98 can use older real-mode (16-bit) drivers if 32-bit drivers are not available. This will affect performance, but at least the drivers will function. Real mode versus protected mode is explained in Chapter 4.

- **Protected-mode (32-bit) network driver support:** Windows 98 can use all protected-mode drivers for network connectivity. In this mode, networking components use no conventional memory. This allows DOS programs that are run under Windows 98 to have much more conventional RAM than they would have under DOS.

- **Windows Driver Model (WDM) support:** NDIS 5.0 specifications allow the same driver and should work with both Windows 98 and Windows NT 5.0.

Communicating with Servers

Novell NetWare servers communicate using a language called *NCP* (Net-Ware Core Protocol). This language is spoken by both the NetWare clients and servers. When you install the Client for NetWare Networks, you are enabling Windows 98 to communicate (using NCP) with NetWare servers, as illustrated in Figure 8.11. See Chapter 9 for details on networking with NetWare servers.

FIGURE 8.11

Windows 98 communicating with NetWare servers

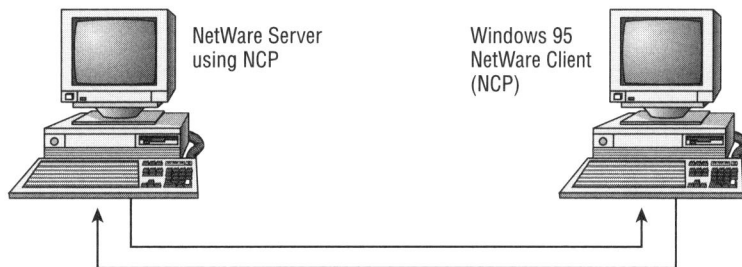

NetWare Server using NCP

Windows 95 NetWare Client (NCP)

Microsoft servers communicate using a language called SMB (Simple Message Blocks). By installing the Client for Microsoft Networks, you enable Windows 98 to communicate with Microsoft (Windows NT) servers, as illustrated in Figure 8.12. See Chapter 9 for details on networking with NT servers.

FIGURE 8.12

Windows 98 communicating with Windows NT Servers

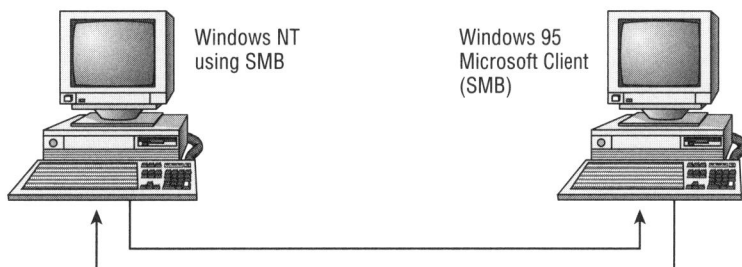

Windows NT using SMB

Windows 95 Microsoft Client (SMB)

Windows 98 is flexible enough to have both client languages (NCP and SMB) installed at the same time. This allows Windows 98 to simultaneously communicate with both NetWare and Microsoft servers, as illustrated in Figure 8.13.

FIGURE 8.13

Windows 98 and simultaneous connections to NetWare and NT

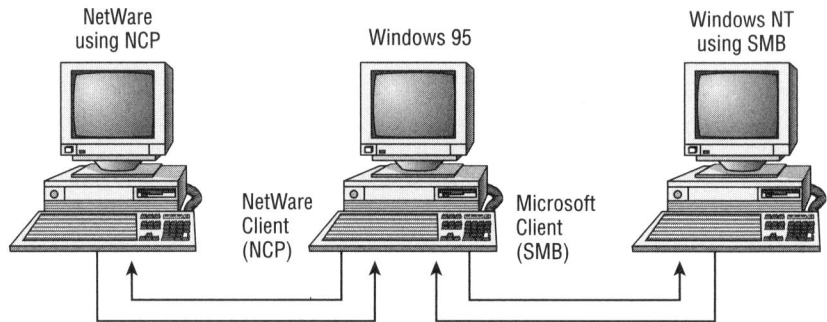

Using SMB or NCP is independent of which network protocol is in use. SMB and NCP are used at a higher level of the OSI model (the Application layer); protocols are used at a lower level (the Data Link layer).

Another way to allow Windows 98 to communicate with both NetWare and Microsoft servers is to have both servers speak a common language, and install just one client on Windows 98. A product from Microsoft called File and Print Services for NetWare (FPNW) makes this possible. With this product installed, Windows NT servers speak the NCP language as well as their own native SMB language, as illustrated in Figure 8.14.

FIGURE 8.14

Windows 98 using a NetWare client to communicate with both NetWare and NT servers

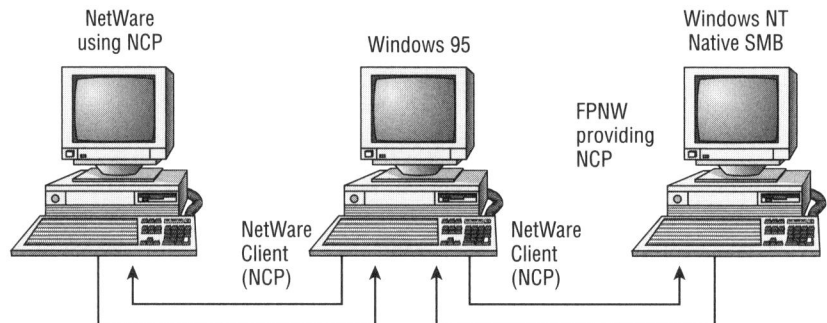

Getting Windows 98 to communicate with other types of servers (such as Banyan Vines) is basically done in the same way. By installing the appropriate client software, you allow Windows 98 to communicate with almost any server.

Computer Names and Usernames

Because Microsoft follows the NetBIOS specifications, and all Windows 98 computers could possibly be servers as well as clients, *all* computers are required to have a unique computer name, even if they are participating only on a NetWare network (where names are ordinarily required only for servers). Computer names must be unique, and they can be up to 15 characters long.

If your computer name is not unique, upon booting your computer you will get an error message stating that networking services have not been started because of a duplicate computer name. You will need to either change your computer name or find the duplicate and change that computer name.

Usernames don't need to be unique. However, any pop-up message or notification will be sent to all users who are logged in as the target recipient.

> **WARNING** Computer and workgroup names can include the % symbol. However, using this symbol is not recommended because it is used in the MSBATCH .INF file as a variable code. You should also avoid using spaces and hyphens, as these characters can cause problems with certain applications (like SQL Server 7.0).

Accessing Resources with UNC

UNC (Universal Naming Convention) is a NetBIOS specification that lets you easily specify the computer and shared resource you want to access. The format of a UNC is:

```
\\Server\Shared_Resource
Here is a typical command:
Net Use S: \\Server\Shared Folder-
Net Use S: \\SLC\AcctData
```

This would connect the S: to the shared folder, and whenever the S: is used, it would actually be the shared folder. For example, if you typed **DIR S:**, you would get a directory listing of the shared folder.

> **NOTE**   Connecting a drive via a UNC is like mapping a drive under NetWare.

Most applications are now UNC-aware; that is, you can use a UNC where you would normally use a local drive and directory (when saving files, inputting the path to new software, and so on).

Windows 98 as a Server

Besides functioning as a client, Windows 98 can also function as a server, allowing others to connect to shared drives or shared printers. Such an arrangement is called a *peer-to-peer network*, which is illustrated in Figure 8.15. Windows 98 can perform both client and server functions simultaneously, but larger networks tend to have dedicated servers for security and performance reasons. However, small offices may have neither the budget nor the need for a dedicated server. Windows 98 operates as a peer-to-peer server when it uses share-level security (the default). Windows 98 can also act like a dedicated server when it uses user-level security. Both of these security options are discussed in Chapter 10.

FIGURE 8.15

A peer-to-peer network

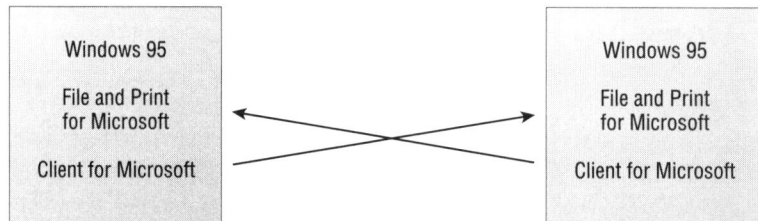

Windows 98 can act as a server; however its intended role is that of a client. Windows 98 can only service or be a server to one client set; that is, it can be installed as either a Microsoft or a NetWare server—not both. Only Windows NT can be simultaneously both a Microsoft and NetWare server (by using File and Print Services for NetWare to provide NCP support).

You can have Windows 98 share its resources as a Microsoft server by installing file and printer sharing for Microsoft Networks, as illustrated in Figure 8.16. This allows both folders and printers to be shared. Installing and configuring sharing are covered in detail in Chapter 10.

FIGURE 8.16

File and printer sharing installed for Microsoft networks

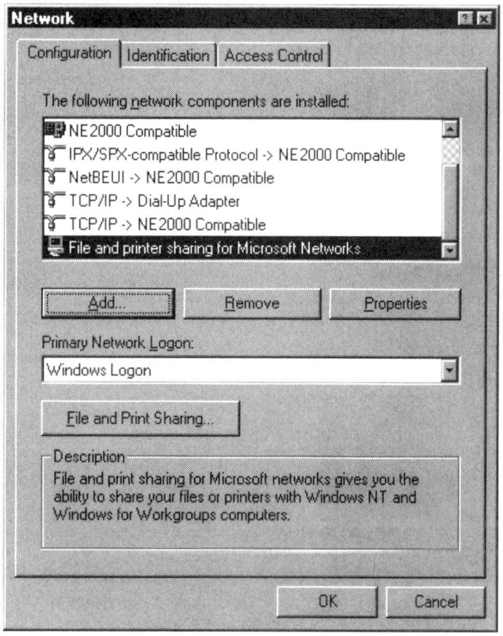

For Windows 98 to act like a NetWare server, you need to install file and printer sharing for NetWare Networks, as shown in Figure 8.17. This allows NetWare clients to use the server's folders and printers. The major restriction is that a NetWare server must already be in place on the network before you can set up a Windows 98 server. Details on installing and configuring the service are in Chapter 10.

F I G U R E   8.17

File and printer sharing installed for NetWare networks

The Network Neighborhood

The Network Neighborhood in Windows 98 introduces an integrated way of looking at network resources as if they were merely an extension of your local computer's resources. The Network Neighborhood presents network resources from a hierarchical viewpoint, starting with the domain or workgroup of which you are a member. Network Neighborhood can be found on the Desktop. When Explorer is open, the Network Neighborhood is shown at the same level as My Computer, as you can see in Figure 8.18. You can view other domains or workgroups by choosing Entire Network.

> In order to see Microsoft servers, you need to have the Microsoft client installed (covered in Chapter 9). To see NetWare servers, you need the NetWare client installed (also covered in Chapter 9).

F I G U R E   8.18

The Network Neigh-
borhood in Explorer

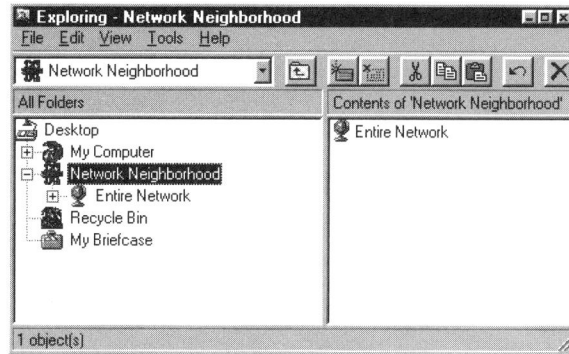

The Network Neighborhood's context menu (which appears when you highlight the Network Neighborhood and right-click) has the following options:

- **Open:** Presents the servers in your domain or workgroup in a folder format. You can then open a server to see the shared folders available.

- **Explore:** Presents the network in an Explorer fashion, and also shows My Computer and the Recycle Bin.

- **Find Computer:** Bypasses the browser and allows you to see the server you are searching for, regardless of the state of the browsing service. This command is very valuable, because servers do not always register themselves with the browser service, which is responsible for maintaining the Network Neighborhood lists.

- **Map Network Drive:** Lets you connect a drive letter to a shared folder on the network. The drive letter will then appear in My Computer. This is the same as using the Net Use command from a DOS prompt.

- **Disconnect Network Drive:** Lets you disconnect a drive letter from a network folder.

- **Create Shortcut:** Makes a shortcut to the Network Neighborhood. You can also make shortcuts to a server or a shared folder by right-dragging the server or folder to your Desktop and choosing Create Shortcut.

- **Rename:** Lets you rename the Network Neighborhood.

- **Properties:** Brings up the Network Control Panel (same as selecting Control Panel ➢ Network).

Summary

Windows 98 comes with full TCP/IP, IPX/SPX, NetBEUI, and DLC protocol support, which makes hooking it to existing networks, and to the Internet, a breeze. This chapter provided an introduction to the use of these protocols.

TPC/IP is the most popular protocol in use. TCP/IP is an open protocol that was jointly developed and enhanced over time by the Internet community through a series of documents called RFCs. It is a routable protocol that is used for connecting dissimilar hardware platforms and for connecting to the Internet. There are also many other protocols commonly associated with TCP/IP for higher-level functions such as e-mail and file transfer.

Three classes of IP addresses are available for networking: Class A, Class B, and Class C. Each of these varies in the number of hosts and networks supported. Custom subnet masks can be used to alter the number of networks and host addresses available for an address.

Windows 98 provides a 32-bit TCP/IP protocol and built-in dial-up connectivity software. It also comes with several TCP/IP utilities and applications, including Ping, WinIPCfg, and a Web browser.

DHCP and WINS can be used to ease administrative overhead on a TCP/IP network. DHCP is used to automatically configure hosts with IP settings. WINS is used to provide a dynamic, centralized database for resolving NetBIOS names to IP addresses.

Understanding the process of networking will help you in both supporting and troubleshooting Windows 98 systems. As you learned in this chapter, the OSI model was developed to break networking down into its basic components. Analyzing networking functions based on the OSI model is a popular way to help isolate functions and understand how networks work. Microsoft has a networking model similar to the OSI model. Windows 98 networking components match up well to the OSI model.

Windows 98 can function as a network client in Novell NetWare, Microsoft, and other types of networks, and can do it simultaneously and without any conflicts. Configuring Windows 98 as an NT client and configuring Windows 98 as a NetWare client are covered in Chapter 9.

Windows 98 can also act like a server, allowing either Microsoft or NetWare clients access to its resources. Windows 98 can be a server for only one type of network at a time. Configuring Windows 98 as a Microsoft network server is covered in Chapter 9. Installing NetWare server support is also described in Chapter 9.

Whatever type of network you are connected to, the Network Neighborhood provides easy access to available resources. The Network Neighborhood presents network resources in a hierarchical structure, starting with your domain or workgroup.

Review Questions

1. Which Microsoft layer talks to the network card?

   A. Device Driver Interface

   B. Physical Driver Interface

   C. Transport Driver Interface

   D. Session Driver Interface

2. Which of the following is not a protocol that Windows 98 supports?

   A. IPX/SPX

   B. Frame0

   C. NetBEUI

   D. TCP/IP

3. Which NDIS specification was designed for Windows 98 and for Windows NT 5.0?

   A. NDIS 2.0

   B. NDIS 3.0

   C. NDIS 4.0

   D. NDIS 5.0

4. Does Windows 98 support auto-reconnect for both Windows NT and NetWare environments?

   A. Yes, for both environments

   B. No, only for the Windows NT environment

   C. No, only for the NetWare environment

   D. No, for neither environment

5. What does UNC stand for?

    A. Universal Network Convention

    B. Universal Naming Convention

    C. Universal NetBIOS Convention

    D. Universal NetWare Convention

6. Microsoft servers communicate natively with which language?

    A. NCP

    B. MMP

    C. BTT

    D. SMB

7. Can Windows 98 be both a Microsoft and a NetWare client simultaneously?

    A. Yes, it can be both.

    B. No, it can only function as a Microsoft client.

    C. No, it can only function as a NetWare client.

    D. No, it can do both but not simultaneously.

8. Can Windows 98 be both a Microsoft and NetWare server simultaneously?

    A. Yes, it can be both.

    B. No, it can function only as a Microsoft server.

    C. No, it can function only as a NetWare server.

    D. No, it can function as one or the other but not both simultaneously.

9. Which protocols can cross routers (under normal conditions)? Choose all that apply.

   A. TCP/IP

   B. NetBEUI

   C. IPX/SPX

   D. Fast Infrared

10. What feature of Windows 98 lets you see network resources?

    A. My Computer

    B. Network Resources

    C. Network Servers

    D. Network Neighborhood

11. Refer to Figure 8.1. You are configuring a computer with the address of 131.107.8.31. What should you enter for the default gateway?

    A. 131.107.24.1

    B. 131.107.16.1

    C. 131.107.8.1

    D. 127.0.0.1

12. Your computer has an address of 131.107.8.31. What class of address is it?

    A. Class A

    B. Class B

    C. Class C

    D. Class D

13. Your computer has an address of 131.107.8.31. What is the network address where your computer resides?

   A. 131

   B. 131.107

   C. 131.107.8

   D. 127.0.0.1

14. You have a network across five routers that consists of NetWare and Windows NT servers. You also have HP printers with JetDirect cards in them. You want your clients to be able to get to the Internet. Which protocol(s) should you install? Choose all that apply.

   A. DLC

   B. TCP/IP

   C. IPX/SPX

   D. NetBEUI

15. You have an application that uses NetBIOS computer names. The application works for computers on the local subnet, but it fails to connect to computers across the router. Which service do you need to install?

   A. DHCP

   B. DNS

   C. WINS

   D. MSNDS

16. Some of your users complain that they can connect to some servers but not to others. You find that the affected users can connect to servers in their department but not to those in other departments. You are using TCP/IP. What parameter is probably set up wrong?

   A. Subnet mask

   B. Default gateway

   C. TCP/IP address

   D. DNS address

17. You want users to be able to connect to Microsoft and NetWare servers. The Microsoft servers are using TCP/IP, and the NetWare servers are using IPX/SPX. You want TCP/IP addresses to be automatically assigned. Here is your proposed solution: Install TCP/IP and IPX on each client. Install DHCP on a fast Windows 98 computer. Configure the DHCP server to give out addresses. Does your solution work?

   A. Yes, it works perfectly.

   B. Yes, it will work after you install WINS as well.

   C. Yes, it will work after you install DNS as well.

   D. No, the proposed solution won't work.

18. You want users to be able to connect to Microsoft and NetWare 4.11 servers. The Microsoft servers are using TCP/IP, and the NetWare servers are using their default protocols. You want TCP/IP addresses to be automatically assigned. Here is your proposed solution: Install TCP/IP on each client. Install DHCP on a Windows NT Server. Configure the DHCP server to give out addresses. Does your solution work?

   A. Yes, it works perfectly.

   B. Yes, it will work after you install WINS as well.

   C. Yes, it will work after you install DNS as well.

   D. No, the proposed solution won't work.

19. Which protocol is used to connect to cameras, laptops, and personal devices.

   A. ATM

   B. NetBEUI

   C. TCP/IP

   D. Fast Infrared

CHAPTER

9

Windows 98 as a Network Client

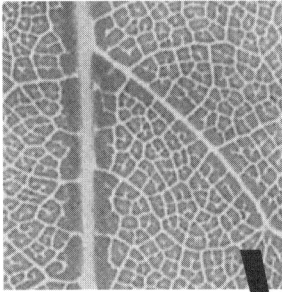

Windows 98 makes a great networking client. It can simultaneously connect to the two leading providers of network servers: Microsoft and NetWare.

Of all the sub-objectives listed above, only those pertaining to the network client, adapters, and NDS are covered in this chapter. We'll discuss ATM in Chapter 8; printer sharing and the Browse Master in Chapter 10; and VPN and PPTP in Chapter 15.

First, this chapter will cover networking with Microsoft servers, including installing and configuring the various Microsoft clients. Then it will cover networking with NetWare clients. Various clients can be used to connect to various servers. Table 9.1 lists the possible choices for Windows 98.

T A B L E 9.1: Clients That Windows 98 Can Use

Manufacturer	Name	Server Support	Versions
Microsoft	Client for Microsoft	Microsoft (SMB)	All
Microsoft	Client for NetWare	NetWare (NCP)	2.*x*, 3.*x*, (Bindery Modes in 4.*x*, 5.*x*)
Microsoft	Service for NDS	NetWare (NCP)	4.*x*, 5.*x*, (NDS)
NetWare	NETX, VLM*	NetWare (NCP)	2.*x*, 3.*x*, /4.*x*, 5.*x*
NetWare	Client for Windows 95**	NetWare (NCP)	All

*These are real-mode clients and are not recommended for use with Windows 98.
**This client can be downloaded from www.novell.com.

Networking with Microsoft Servers

Connecting a Windows 98 computer to a Windows NT network is fairly straightforward. All of the software needed to connect Windows 98 to an NT computer is included on the Windows 98 CD-ROM and is relatively easy to install. The major decision that must be made is whether to allow each Windows 98 computer to share its resources (acting like a server) as well as being a client on the network.

Microsoft
✓ *Exam*
Objective

Install and configure the network components of Windows 98 in a Microsoft environment and a mixed Microsoft and NetWare environment. Network components include:

- Client for Microsoft Networks
- Network adapters

As explained in Chapter 8, when computers act as both clients and servers they form a *peer-to-peer network*. Peer-to-peer networks are great for small offices (such as a dentist's or doctor's office). However, when you have more than about six to eight computers, keeping track of all of the shares and passwords on the network can get rather confusing and time-consuming. After a network grows to ten or more machines, companies often find it easier to dedicate one computer to being a server (even if it can still perform client functions), and let the rest of the clients be just plain clients.

In this chapter, you will learn how to install and configure the Client for Microsoft Networks software so that Windows 98 can connect to Windows NT servers. You will also learn how to allow a Windows 98 computer to share its resources. This chapter will discuss setting up shares and selecting a security level. Finally, it will cover the network browsing service, which allows users to see the shared resources on the network; Windows 98 can act as a browser client and/or browser server.

Windows NT Client Installation

Microsoft servers communicate using a language called *SMB* (Server Message Blocks). By installing the Client for Microsoft Networks, you enable Windows 98 to communicate with Microsoft (Windows NT) servers.

Several steps are involved in installing the client software for Windows NT:

- Check licensing agreements to ensure legality.
- Install the network card and drivers.
- Install the client software.
- Configure the network card.
- Configure the protocols.
- Configure the client software.

Each of these steps is explained in the following sections.

Licensing the Client

By purchasing Windows 98, you have bought a license to use it on a single computer, but not necessarily on a network. If you connect the Windows 98 computer to an NT server, you will need to make sure you have a Client Access License (CAL) for each client attached.

There are two different client licensing schemes:

- **Per Server:** Licenses are purchased with the Windows NT Server package. They allow a certain number of simultaneous connections to that server.

- **Per Seat:** Licenses are purchased for each client that needs to connect to NT servers. These licenses allow the client to connect to any NT server on the network.

When you buy additional licenses, you usually just get a piece of paper that proves you are legal, in case of an audit.

> For more information about the licensing schemes, see *MCSE: NT Server Study Guide*, published by Sybex.

Installing a Network Card and Driver

The first step in installing network support in Windows 98 is to install the physical card in the computer. If the card is an older, legacy card (its settings are made by jumpers and/or switches), you should make a note of its settings. If the card is a Plug-and-Play variety, Windows 98 should be able to automatically detect and configure the card to the correct settings.

If Windows 98 can auto-detect the card, it may install the driver automatically. You can force Windows 98 to search for new hardware by starting the Add New Hardware Wizard from the Control Panel, as shown in Figure 9.1. Once the new hardware is found, you may be prompted to insert a disk containing the correct driver, or Windows 98 will find the driver in the CAB files.

FIGURE 9.1

Searching for new hardware

If Windows 98 doesn't install the driver automatically, you will need to install it manually. Start the Add New Hardware Wizard from the Control Panel. After the automatic detection, click the No button to tell Windows 98 not to try to detect the device. Then click No again to select the hardware from a list. Windows 98 displays a list of hardware devices for which it has drivers. Select Network adapters, and you will be presented with a list of network cards to choose from, as shown in Figure 9.2. If your network card has a newer driver on a disk, click the Have Disk button, and insert the driver disk that came with your network card. Windows 98 will install the driver from the floppy disk.

F I G U R E 9.2

Installing a network driver manually

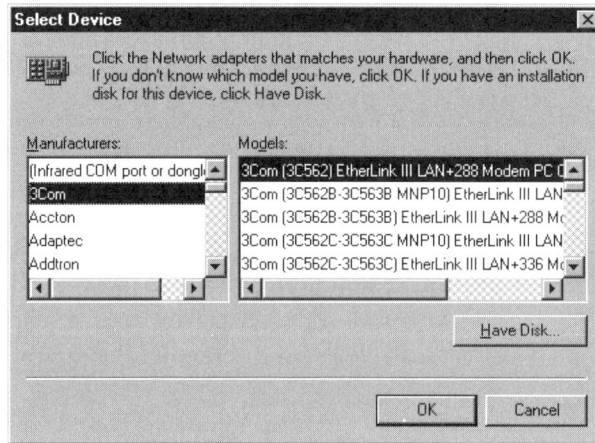

Installing the Client Software

By installing the client software, you allow Windows 98 to see and connect to Windows NT servers.

You install the software through the Network Control Panel. First choose to add a client, as shown in Figure 9.3. Then pick the type of client from the Network Control Panel's Select Network Client dialog box, as shown in Figure 9.4. Follow the steps in Exercise 9.1 to install the Client for Microsoft Networks software.

NOTE

If you already have the Client for Microsoft Networks software installed and you would like to practice reinstalling it, remove it and then follow the steps in Exercise 9.1.

FIGURE 9.3

Adding a new client

FIGURE 9.4

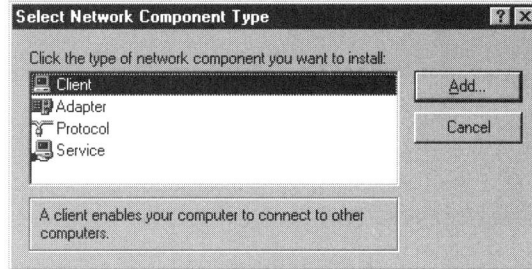

Choosing the Client for
Microsoft Networks

EXERCISE 9.1

Installing the Client for Microsoft Networks

1. Go to Control Panel ≻ Network and choose Add.

2. Highlight Client and choose Add (see Figure 9.3).

3. Highlight Microsoft in the list of Manufacturers.

4. Highlight Client for Microsoft Networks in the list of Network Clients
   (see Figure 9.4).

5. Click OK.

6. Reboot Windows 98.

Configuring the Network Card

Windows 98 should detect and install the correct drivers for your network card. Every device connected to your computer needs to be assigned a unique IRQ, I/O port, and memory address (if used):

- **IRQ or interrupt:** This is like a doorbell that devices use to get the attention of the CPU. Every device needs a unique IRQ or your accessories may not be able to talk to the CPU. IRQs range from 0 to 15. IRQs 5, 10, 11, and 12 are commonly used for accessories.

- **I/O port:** This is like a doorway that data travels through to get to and from the CPU. Every device needs a unique I/O port assigned to it. The I/O port ranges are from 200 to 3E0. I/O ports 210, 220, 300, and 310 are often used by accessories.

- **Memory address:** This is like a waiting room outside the CPU. Older network cards (especially older Token Ring cards) may require a memory address, which must then be excluded from the range that Windows 98 is using (see Chapter 4 for switches to use to exclude memory addresses from Windows 98). CC00 to FF00 is a common range that accessories use (if they need one).

- **Slot number:** This specifies the slot in which the card is installed. The driver almost always auto-detects the correct setting for the slot number and will seldom (if ever) have to be changed. Note that many cards do no use or need a slot address assigned to them.

If more than one device is assigned a particular setting, you will need to resolve the conflict before Windows 98 will work properly.

How you change the settings of your network card depends on whether it is a Plug-and-Play card or a legacy (jumpered or set by software) card. If it is a Plug-and-Play card, you should be able to change its settings in Device Manager by going to the property sheet for the card and choosing Change Setting, as shown in Figure 9.5. After you reboot, the card should be set to the new settings.

Device Manager is one of the best utilities included in Windows 98 because it allows you to see, troubleshoot, and control your hardware settings. To open Device Manager, go to Control Panel ➤ System and choose the Device Manager tab. See Chapter 16 about using the Device Manager and troubleshooting problems.

F I G U R E 9.5

Changing network
card settings in Device
Manager

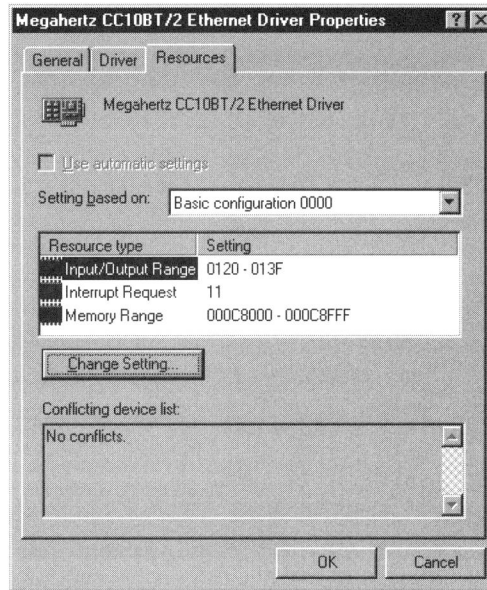

Megahertz CC10BT/2 Ethernet Driver Properties

General | Driver | Resources |

Megahertz CC10BT/2 Ethernet Driver

☐ Use automatic settings

Setting based on: Basic configuration 0000

Resource type	Setting
Input/Output Range	0120 - 013F
Interrupt Request	11
Memory Range	000C8000 - 000C8FFF

Change Setting...

Conflicting device list:

No conflicts.

OK   Cancel

If your card is a legacy card, you will need to power off the computer and then change the jumpers or switches on your card or use a software setup program (sometimes called *softset*) to change to the new settings. When you are finished, turn on your computer and start Windows 98, and then make the changes in Device Manager. Reboot for the changes to take effect.

Configuring the Client

Several options can be configured for the client software, including the protocols bound to the network card and which client (NetWare, NT, or another client) software will be the primary one (the one that Windows 98 loads and logs in to first). These settings are usually set during installation of the computer, when the client is first set up, and rarely need to be changed.

Microsoft
Exam
Objective

Configure a Windows 98 computer as a client computer in a network that contains a Windows NT 4.0 domain.

The user password may need to be changed on a regular basis (if the security policy of the server requires it). Windows 98 will cache usernames and passwords that you use to connect to various shared resources so it can automatically reconnect to those resources after you log in. You may want to disable the password cache for security reasons.

Choosing a Primary Network Logon

Windows 98 keeps a local database of usernames and passwords. If you are logging on to a domain or another type of server, you must choose whether to have Windows 98 first log you in to the domain and then the local computer, or first log in to the local computer and then the domain.

You have the following choices for primary logon:

- **Windows Logon:** When you use this logon, you supply a single name and password into Windows, which is then passed to any servers to which you attempt to connect.

- **Microsoft Family Logon:** This new feature for Windows 98 (if installed) will present a list of enabled profiles from which you can select.

- **Client for Microsoft Networks:** Selecting this client (if installed) will log you directly into the configured Microsoft server or domain.

- **Client for NetWare:** Selecting this client (if installed) will log you directly into the configured NetWare server or NDS tree.

- **Other clients:** You may be able to choose other clients, such as Banyan VINES or DECNET (if installed).

You should set the client that you use most often as your primary client. Some features of Windows 98 (such as roaming user profiles, described in Chapter 12) work only if the Client for Microsoft Networks is set as the primary client.

If security is not an issue, you may not want to be prompted for a password. To keep Windows 98 from prompting you for a password, set Primary Network Logon to Windows Logon, don't enable profiles, and make your password blank. Although this is not secure, it is convenient.

The Primary Network Logon setting is on the Configuration tab of the Network Control Panel, as shown in Figure 9.6. Follow the steps in Exercise 9.2 to choose your primary logon.

F I G U R E 9.6

Choosing a primary
network logon

EXERCISE 9.2

Changing Your Primary Network Logon

1. Go to Control Panel ≻ Network.

2. From the Primary Network Logon drop-down list, choose where you want to log on first. Select Windows Logon for a peer-to-peer network (see Figure 9.6), or select Client for Microsoft if you log in to an NT domain.

3. Click OK.

4. Reboot Windows 98.

Logging In to an NT Domain

Another logon option you have is whether you log in to a workgroup or a domain. If you choose to log in to a domain, you must already have an account on that domain (usually created by a network administrator).

> **NOTE**
> A *workgroup* is a loose association of computers that has no central database of users, groups, or passwords. A *domain* has one or more Windows NT servers acting as controllers. Each controller has a copy of a user database and can validate logon requests.

The benefit of logging in to a domain is that once you are validated, you should never need to enter your username and password again (during your session) to access resources on the network. The controllers on the domain create an access token when you log in, and that token is used by all the servers in the domain. It is much like getting your ticket stamped at an amusement park and being able to go on any of the rides (because you have been authenticated at one of the ticket windows).

The option to log on to a Windows NT domain is in the Client for Microsoft Networks Properties dialog box, as shown in Figure 9.7. Follow the steps in Exercise 9.3 to set up Windows 98 to log on to an NT domain.

FIGURE 9.7

Setting Windows 98 to log on to an NT domain

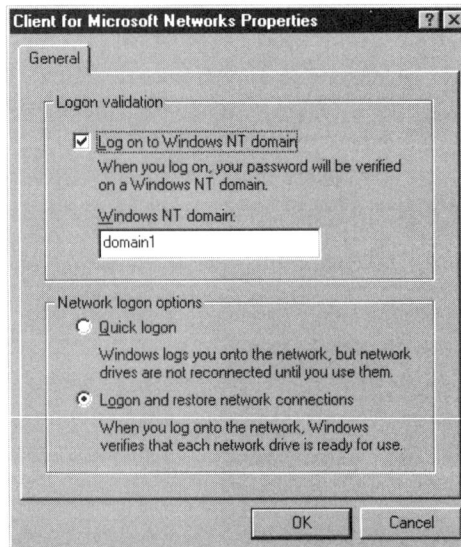

EXERCISE 9.3

Setting Windows 98 to Log On to an NT Domain

1. Go to Control Panel ➢ Network.

2. Highlight Client for Microsoft and choose Properties.

3. Put a checkmark in the Log On To Windows NT Domain box.

4. Type the name of the domain in the text box. If you don't currently have a real domain, enter **domain1** (see Figure 9.7).

5. Click OK.

6. Reboot Windows 98.

Changing Your Password

You can change both your Windows 98 local password and your NT password from the Password Properties dialog box, shown in Figure 9.8. Windows 98 will also allow you to change other passwords, such as those for screen savers, from the same Properties dialog box.

F I G U R E 9.8

The Password Properties dialog box

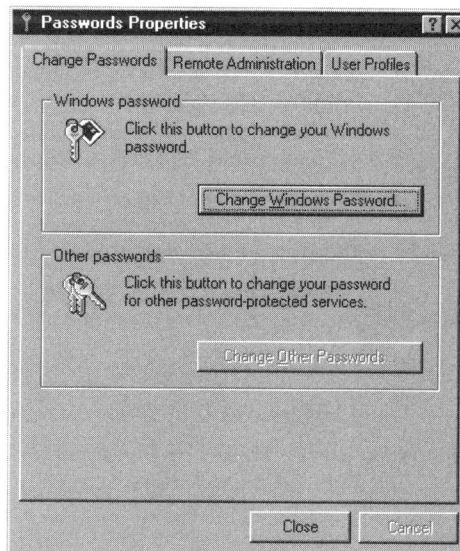

Exercise 9.4 shows the steps for changing the Windows password, as well as the NT domain and screen saver passwords (if those passwords are enabled).

EXERCISE 9.4

Changing Your Passwords

1. Go to Control Panel ➤ Passwords.

2. Click Change Windows Password (see Figure 9.8).

3. In the Change Windows Password dialog box, select the Microsoft Networking (to change your NT domain password) and the Windows Screen Saver boxes, as shown here.

Change Windows Password

You may also change other passwords at the same time as your Windows password.

Check the other passwords you would like to change to use the same password as your Windows password.

☑ Microsoft Networking
☑ Windows Screen Saver

[OK] [Cancel]

4. Click OK.

5. In the next dialog box, change your password by typing the old one once and the new one twice.

6. Click OK.

7. Reboot Windows 98 to use your new password.

Password Caching

Windows 98 can *cache*, or remember, the usernames and passwords with which you connect to shared resources. While convenient, caching passwords poses a security risk if the password file is decrypted. Passwords are cached if you select the Reconnect at Logon box when using a network resource. When you log in to Windows 98, the system uses the cached passwords to automatically reestablish all the drive connections you had the last time you logged off.

Password caching can be disabled by using a system policy. See Chapter 13 for more information.

Networking with NetWare Servers

Windows 98 makes an excellent client for NetWare networks. The Windows 98 CD-ROM comes with everything you need to connect to a NetWare server, including a NetWare client from Microsoft. Windows 98 can be a client to NetWare 2.*x*, 3.*x*, 4.*x*, and 5.*x* servers. NetWare also supplies a client that can be installed in Windows 98 to provide connectivity to NetWare servers.

Microsoft
✓ *Exam*
Objective

Install and configure the network components of Windows 98 in a Microsoft environment and a mixed Microsoft and NetWare environment. Network components include:

- Client for NetWare Networks
- Network adapters
- Service for NetWare Directory Services (NDS)

Windows 98 can also act as a NetWare server, by sharing its files and printers using the NetWare Core Protocol (NCP) standard. Chapter 10 will explain how to install and configure the File and Printer Sharing for NetWare Service. As explained in Chapter 8, Windows 98 can share files and printers as *either* a NetWare server or as a Microsoft server—not both.

NetWare Client Installation and Configuration

NetWare servers communicate using a language called *NCP* (NetWare Core Protocol). By installing the NetWare client software, you enable Windows 98 to communicate with NetWare servers.

Before you begin client installation, you should check to make sure that you have enough NetWare client licenses for all of your clients. NetWare will not allow more than the licensed number of clients to connect to a server.

In order for Windows 98 clients to save files on NetWare servers using long filenames (LFNs), you need to install NetWare's OS2 support for the server volumes. See your NetWare documentation for instructions.

To set up the client software for NetWare on a Windows 98 machine, you need to install and configure the network card and drivers, the client software, and the protocols. These procedures are described in the following sections.

Installing and Configuring the Network Card and Drivers

When installing the network card, you have two basic choices for the drivers you can use:

- ODI real-mode drivers
- NDIS 3.1/5.0 protected-mode drivers

If you choose to use NDIS 3.1/5.0 protected-mode drivers, you follow the same procedures for installing a network card and drivers as you use for a Microsoft client. All of the protected-mode clients mentioned in this chapter can use the NDIS drivers for the network card.

If you choose to use the older ODI drivers, which are necessary for NETX or VLM (real-mode) client software, you load the drivers from the AUTOEXEC.BAT file. A sample way of doing this is by adding the following commands to your AUTOEXEC.BAT:

LSL	The supporting driver
NE2000	This is the driver for an NE2000-compatible card; other cards would have a differently named driver
IPXODI	The protocol driver
VLM or NETX	The client software

Windows 98 reads your AUTOEXEC.BAT file during the boot process and opens an MS-DOS window to load the drivers. You are then prompted to log in at the MS-DOS screen. After you log in, Windows 98 continues loading.

Configuring the network card to avoid hardware conflicts was covered earlier in this chapter (network card configuration is the same whether you are connecting to NetWare or Microsoft servers). As a general rule, you should always install your actual hardware first, and then use the Add New Hardware Wizard from the Control Panel to install the drivers and support files.

Installing and Configuring the Client Software

Once the network card and driver are installed, you will need to install client software. You can choose from various client software options:

- **Microsoft Client for NetWare Networks:** This is a 32-bit, protected-mode client that can connect to NetWare servers. It is a bindery-emulation client, however, and connects to NetWare 4.x servers in bindery mode (it does not support NDS).

- **Microsoft's Service for NetWare Directory Services:** This is a true, protected-mode NDS client with a terribly long name. This client is listed with the various services (instead of clients) and requires the Microsoft Client for NetWare to function.

- **Novell's VLM or NETX:** NETX is a real-mode MS-DOS client that was used extensively to connect to NetWare 2.x and 3.x servers. NETX is a bindery client and does not provide true NDS support. VLM came out when NetWare 4.x did, and it is a real-mode, true NDS client. NETX and VLM are loaded from the AUTOEXEC.BAT file as Windows 98 boots. As mentioned in the previous section, if you're using NETX or VLM, you must use ODI drivers (which also load from the AUTOEXEC.BAT file). Note that VLM and NETX do not come with Windows 98—you must obtain them from Novell.

- **Novell's Client for Windows 95:** This is a 32-bit, protected-mode client that provides true NDS support. The Novell Client v2.5 for Windows 95 is also compatible with Windows 98 and supports the following versions of NetWare: 3.11, 3.12, 3.2, 4.10, and 4.11. The Novell Client v2.5 for Windows 95 can be downloaded from www.novell.com/download.

- **Other Clients:** Windows 98 supports client software from Digital and Banyan, among others, that allow connection to various types of servers such as Pathworks and VINES servers. Note that the only clients that come on the CD-ROM are the Microsoft Client for Microsoft (including MS-NDS) and Microsoft Client for NetWare.

First, you will learn how to install and configure Microsoft's client for NetWare. Then you will learn how to install and configure Novell's native client.

NetWare 2.*x* and 3.*x* servers rely on a bindery to hold all user, group, password, and printer information. The bindery is essentially a flat-file database and is server specific. NetWare 4.*x* and 5.*x* use NDS (NetWare Directory Services), which holds the users, groups, printers, and other resources in a hierarchical tree. The same NDS tree can link many servers, and is not server specific. Because many applications are not yet NDS-aware, the NDS tree supports bindery emulation, which makes the 4.*x* and 5.*x* servers look and function like 3.*x* servers. True NDS support is preferred to bindery emulation because NDS is more flexible than bindery emulation.

Installing the Microsoft Client for NetWare Networks

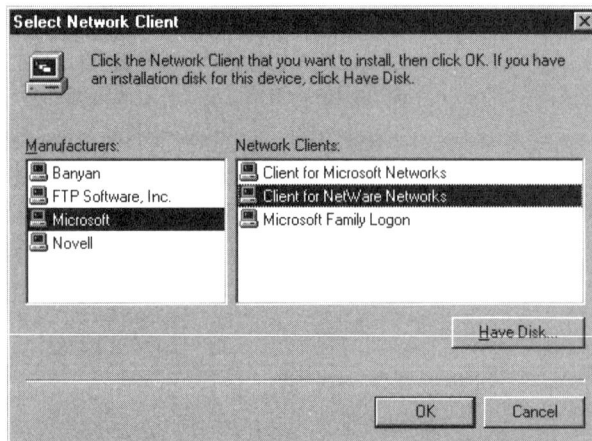

You install the Microsoft Client for NetWare Networks by adding a client using the Network Control Panel, as shown in Figure 9.9. Follow the steps in Exercise 9.5 to install this client.

FIGURE 9.9

Installing the Microsoft Client for NetWare Networks

EXERCISE 9.5

Installing the Microsoft Client for NetWare Networks

1. Go to Control Panel ≻ Network and choose Add.

2. Highlight Client and choose Add.

3. Highlight Microsoft in the list of Manufacturers.

4. Highlight Client for NetWare Networks in the list of Network Clients (see Figure 9.9).

5. Click OK.

6. Reboot Windows 98.

Installing the Microsoft Service for NDS Client

You install the Microsoft Service for NetWare Directory Services (MS-NDS) client software by adding it as a service using the Network Control Panel, as shown in Figure 9.10. Follow the steps in Exercise 9.6 to install this client.

FIGURE 9.10

Installing the Microsoft Service for NetWare Directory Services (MS-NDS) client

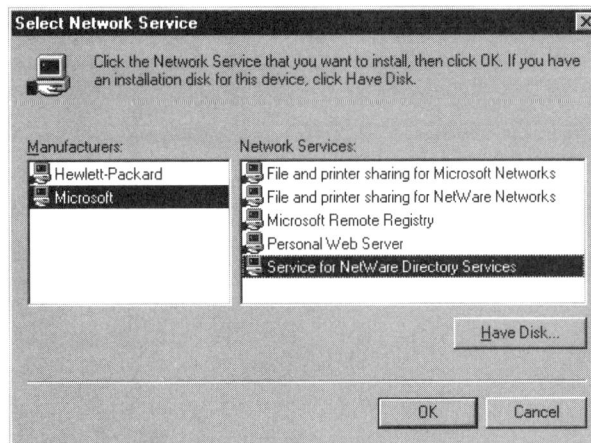

EXERCISE 9.6

Installing the Service for NetWare Directory Services (MS-NDS)

1. Go to Control Panel ➢ Network and choose Add.

2. Highlight Service and choose Add.

3. Select Microsoft.

4. Select Service for NetWare Directory Services (see Figure 9.10).

5. Choose OK. The Service for NetWare Directory Services should load. You may be prompted for the Windows 98 CD-ROM.

6. Choose OK in the Network Control Panel to save your changes.

7. Reboot Windows 98.

Configuring the Protocols

NetWare uses the IPX/SPX protocol to communicate between the servers and clients. There are several parameters that may need to be adjusted for IPX/SPX protocol. The main parameters are frame type and NETBIOS support.

As explained in Chapter 8, different frame types can be run on your network. A frame type can be considered a *dialect*. Ethernet has four possible frame types or dialects; Token Ring has two possible frame types.

> **NOTE** IPX/SPX is the name of the protocol because the IPX piece is connectionless, while the SPX part is connection-oriented. Connectionless protocols can be compared to first-class mail, while connection-oriented protocols are like registered mail. We send the bulk of our mail first class, even though there is no guarantee of delivery. Only valuable documents are worth sending as registered mail.

If IPX/SPX doesn't seem to work, check your frame type. Automatic is the default setting for the frame type, and it may not correctly detect the frame type that you are running. If the Automatic setting fails to find a frame, it will default to the 802.2 frame type.

The procedures for changing the frame type and adding NetBIOS support are explained in Chapter 8.

Configuring a Microsoft NetWare Client

Various options can be set for the client software to modify how the connections to the NetWare servers will be made.

Microsoft
Exam
Objective

Configure a Windows 98 computer as a client computer in a NetWare network.

You can set the preferred server and enable login script support in the Client for NetWare Networks property sheet, as shown in Figure 9.11.

FIGURE 9.11

Options for setting the preferred server and enabling login script support

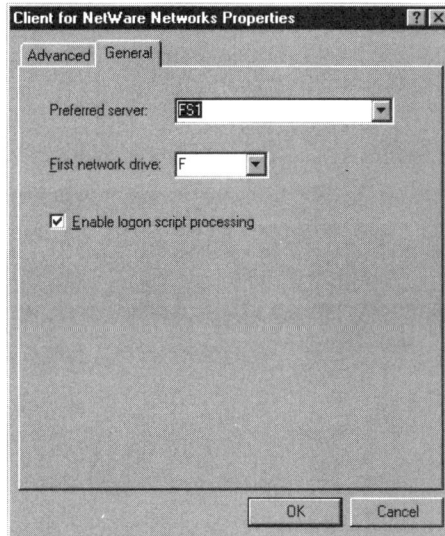

If you are using the MS-NDS client, it will also be listed in the Configuration tab of the Network Control Panel, as shown in Figure 9.12. Its property sheet includes settings for the preferred tree and context, as shown in Figure 9.13. In Exercise 9.7, you will configure the Microsoft NetWare and MS-NDS clients.

F I G U R E 9.12

Selecting the Service
for NetWare Directory
Services

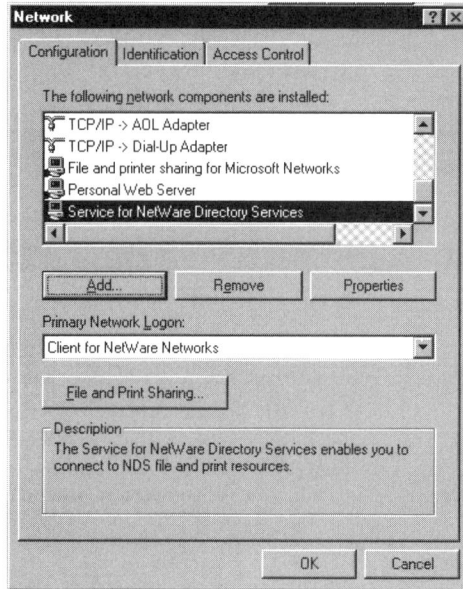

F I G U R E 9.12

Selecting the Service
for NetWare Directory
Services

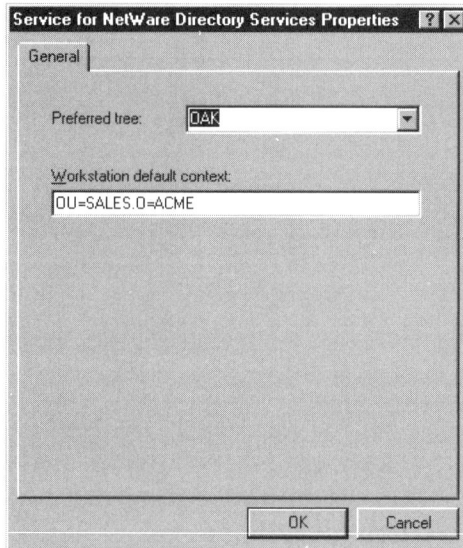

F I G U R E 9.13

Setting the preferred
tree and context

EXERCISE 9.7

Configuring the Microsoft NetWare and MS-NDS Clients

1. Go to Control Panel ➤ Network.

2. Highlight the Client for NetWare Networks and choose Properties.

3. Enter the preferred server. Use the name FS1 if you don't have one.

4. Turn off login script processing.

5. Choose OK to save your changes.

6. Highlight the Services for NetWare Directory Services, and choose Properties.

7. Enter your preferred tree and context. Use OAK and OU=SALES.O=ACME if you don't have them (see Figure 9.13).

8. Choose OK twice.

9. Reboot Windows 98 to have your changes take effect.

Installing and Configuring Novell's Client for Windows 95

Client for Windows 95 is Novell's protected-mode Windows 95/98 client that has native NDS support. Client for Windows 95 comes in two flavors: a smaller version that is designed for basic server support and the full version, designed to support new, optional components of 4.11 and 5.0 servers. You will need to download (from Novell's Web site—www.novell.com) and decompress the software before you can install and configure it.

> **NOTE**
>
> Client for Windows 95 was previously called Client32. The most recent version is 2.5, and it has been tested for compatibility with both Windows 95 and Windows 98.

> **WARNING**
>
> The Novell Client v2.5 for Windows 95 uninstall program will not completely remove all files when executed on Windows 98. Novell and Microsoft are currently trying to identify the cause of this so it can be corrected.

The NetWare Client32 Installation screen is shown in Figure 9.14. The tabs in the Novell NetWare Client32 Properties dialog box are shown in Figures 9.15 through 9.19. Follow the steps in Exercise 9.8 to install and configure Novell's Client32.

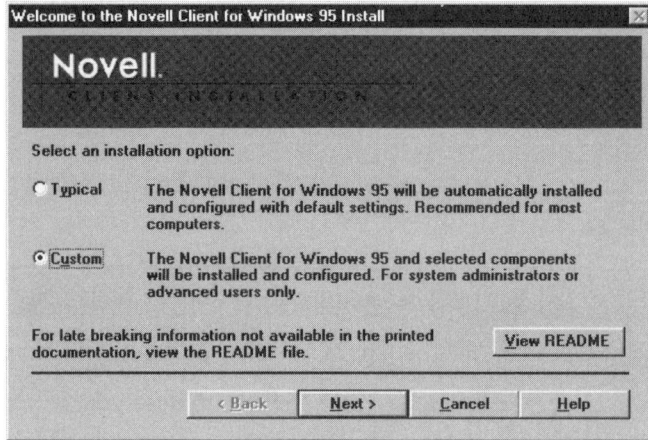

F I G U R E   9.14

Installing Novell's Client32

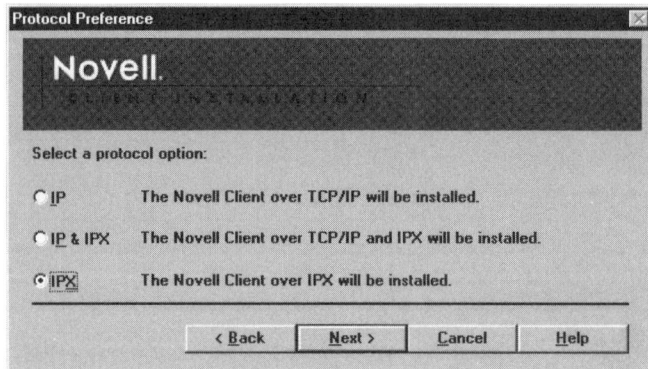

F I G U R E   9.15

Selecting supported protocols

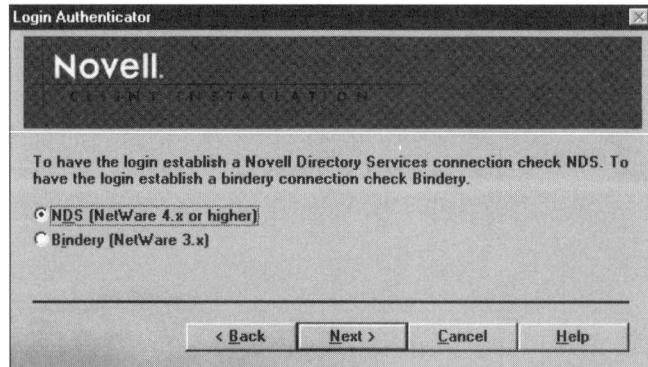

F I G U R E   9.16

Selecting NDS or Bindery mode

F I G U R E   9.17

Selecting optional
client components

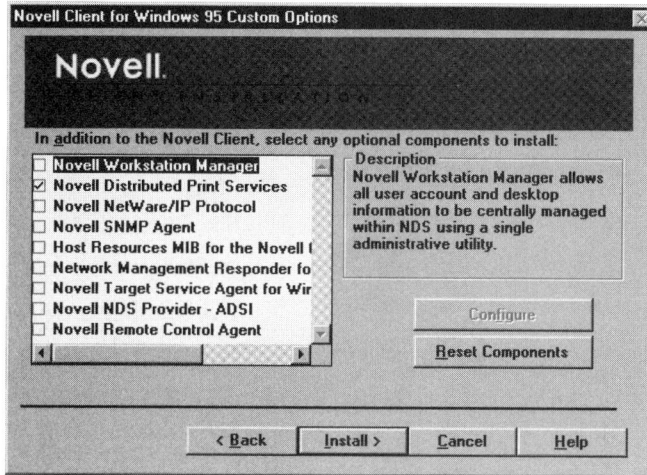

F I G U R E   9.18

Entering the preferred
server and tree

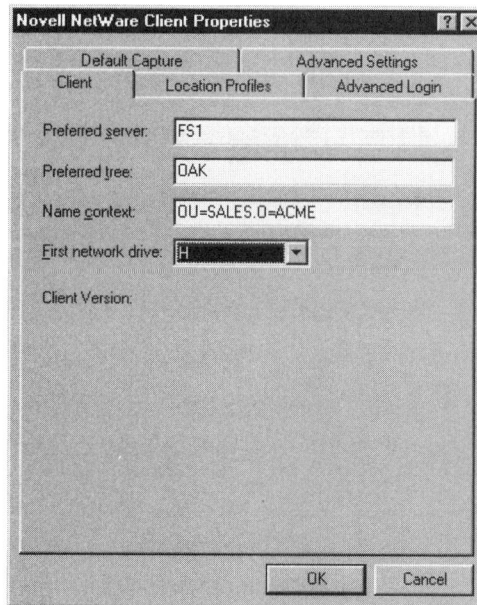

F I G U R E   9.19

Configuring printer
capture support

F I G U R E   9.19

Configuring printer
capture support

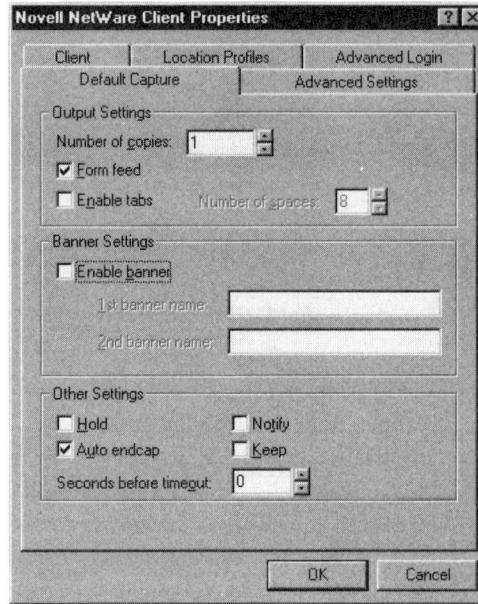

EXERCISE 9.8

Installing and Configuring Novell's Client32

1. Go to the folder where Client for Windows 95 has been decompressed.

2. Start the Setup program.

3. Answer Yes to the licensing question.

4. Choose Typical or Custom to begin the installation process (see Figure 9.14). Click Next.

5. Select the protocols with which you want the client to communicate. NetWare 5.0 will support a pure TCP/IP environment, otherwise select IPX (see Figure 9.15). Click Next.

6. Select the type of servers you will be connecting to, Bindery (3.*x*) or NDS (4.*x* and up) (see Figure 9.16). Click Next.

7. Select any optional components you want and click Next. (See Figure 9.17.)

8. After the installation (before rebooting), choose to customize your settings. This will allow you to change your server and context (see Figure 9.18) as well as your printer settings (see Figure 9.19). Click Next to continue the setup.

9. Reboot Windows 98 to have the changes take effect.

Summary

As you learned in this chapter, connecting a Windows 98 computer to a Windows NT network is fairly straightforward. Installing the Client for Microsoft Networks software allows Windows 98 to connect to Windows NT servers and use their shared resources as if they were its own. A network usually consists of a few servers, with the majority of computers configured as clients.

Before you install the client, you need to install the network card and drivers. Windows 98 can automatically detect and configure Plug-and-Play cards. You can configure the network protocols and client software through the Network Control Panel.

In this chapter, you learned how to set up a Windows 98 machine as a NetWare client. Several NetWare clients are available from Microsoft and Novell. Microsoft's Client for NetWare is a bindery-compatible client, and the MS-NDS client is a true NDS client. Novell's NETX client is a real-mode bindery client; VLM is a Real-mode NDS client. Client for Windows 95, which also works on Windows 98 and is available from Novell's Web site, is a Protected-mode NDS client.

Like any other machine on a network, the NetWare client requires a properly configured network card. Once hardware conflicts have been eliminated, the correct protocol and frame type must be selected.

Review Questions

1. When installing a network card, you may need to configure which items? Choose all that apply.

   A. Interrupt

   B. I/O port

   C. Memory address

   D. Slot number

2. You can use which program(s) to configure the network card?

   A. Control Panel ➤ Network ➤ Properties of the card

   B. Network Neighborhood ➤ Properties ➤ Properties of the card

   C. Control Panel ➤ Devices ➤ Properties of the card

   D. Control Panel ➤ System ➤ Device Manager ➤ Properties of the card

3. By installing the Client for Microsoft Networks, you allow Windows 98 to understand which language?

   A. NCPs

   B. MMPs

   C. NTBs

   D. SMBs

4. If Windows 98 is set up to use IPX/SPX and it cannot auto-detect a frame type, what frame will it pick?

   A. No frames

   B. All frames

   C. Ethernet_802.2

   D. Ethernet_II

5. Which service allows automatic assignment of TCP/IP addresses?

 A. DHCP

 B. WINS

 C. DNS

 D. DXNP

6. Can NetBEUI packets cross a router?

 A. Yes, always

 B. Only if the router is connected to the Internet

 C. Only if the router is the latest model

 D. No, they can't

7. True or False: You can change your NT password from within Windows 98.

 A. True, but not your screen saver

 B. True, and also your screen saver at the same time

 C. True, and all other passwords (including NetWare)

 D. False

8. NetWare servers communicate using which language?

 A. SMB

 B. PPP

 C. NDS

 D. NCP

9. Windows 98 can communicate with which NetWare servers? Choose all that apply.

   A. 2.*x* (bindery)

   B. 3.*x* (bindery)

   C. 4.*x* (NDS)

   D. 5.*x* (NDS)

10. Which clients are real-mode clients? Choose all that apply.

   A. NETX

   B. VLM

   C. Microsoft's Client for NetWare

   D. Novell's Client for Windows 95

11. Which clients are true NDS clients? Choose all that apply.

   A. NETX

   B. Service for NetWare Directory Services

   C. Microsoft's Client for NetWare

   D. Novell's Client for Windows 95

12. A user complains that sometimes she can connect to a certain NetWare 4.11 server but at other times the connection doesn't work. She is using Service for NetWare Directory Services. What could be the problem?

   A. The NetWare server could be out of licenses.

   B. The client and the server could be using different frame types.

   C. The client needs to install the Microsoft Client for NetWare.

   D. The client needs to install IPX/SPX.

13. Your network consists of Windows 98 clients and Windows NT servers. Which networking clients do you need installed on your clients? Choose all that apply.

   A. Microsoft Client for Microsoft

   B. Microsoft Client for NetWare

   C. Service for NetWare Directory Services

   D. Microsoft Family Logon

14. Your network consists of Windows 98 clients and NetWare 3.12 servers. Which networking clients do you need installed on your clients? Choose all that apply.

   A. Microsoft Client for Microsoft

   B. Microsoft Client for NetWare

   C. Service for NetWare Directory Services

   D. Microsoft Family Logon

15. You have Windows NT servers running TCP/IP and NetWare servers running IPX. You are running the Client for Windows and the Client for NetWare clients. What can you do to optimize your connections?

   A. Unbind TCP/IP from the NetWare client and IPX/SPX from the Windows client

   B. Unbind TCP/IP from the Windows client and IPX/SPX from the NetWare client

   C. Run the Network Optimization Wizard

   D. Nothing, because there are no options to help optimize performance

CHAPTER

10

Sharing Resources with Windows 98

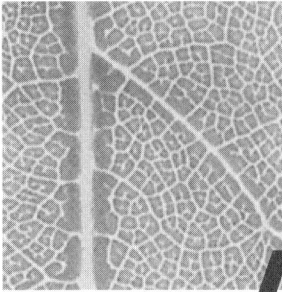

Although Windows 98 functions primarily as a client on most networks, it also has the ability to share local resources such as folders and printers with the network, just like any other network server.

When sharing local resources, Windows 98 can still function as a network client to different types of servers, making it a very flexible operating system. One of the few limitations Windows 98 has when operating as a network server is its inability to support Microsoft-type networks (speaking the SMB language) and NetWare-type servers (speaking the NCP language) simultaneously. It can do either but not both. (The client side has no such restriction.)

In this chapter, you will look at installing the file and printer services for Microsoft and share folders using the default share-level security settings. You will then switch to user-level security and share resources under that system. The browser service will then be discussed and configured.

You will uninstall File and Printer Sharing for Microsoft so that you can install File and Printer Sharing for NetWare. You will then learn how to enable browser support for various NetWare clients.

You will complete the chapter with a discussion of Net Watcher, a utility that monitors and manages shared resources.

Sharing Resources on a Microsoft Network

Windows 98 computers can have an additional service installed that allows them to share resources and act like Windows NT file and print servers. Allowing users to share their resources makes sharing information more convenient. However, it also makes more work for those who maintain and administer the network, and it decreases security. By sharing resources, you have many administrators to train and supervise, instead of just a few. Problems can arise if users share their drives incorrectly and sensitive information gets out. Problems can also arise if users have too many rights and delete files they shouldn't.

Microsoft Exam Objective

Develop a security strategy in a Microsoft environment or a mixed Microsoft and NetWare environment. Strategies include:

- System policies
- User profiles
- File and printer sharing
- Share-level access control or user-level access control

Microsoft Exam Objective

Install and configure the network components of Windows 98 in a Microsoft environment or a mixed Microsoft and NetWare environment. Network components include:

- Client for Microsoft Networks
- Client for NetWare Networks
- Network adapters
- File and Printer Sharing for Microsoft Networks
- File and Printer Sharing for NetWare Networks
- Service for NetWare Directory Services (NDS)
- Asynchronous Transer Mode (ATM)
- Virtual private networking and PPTP
- Browse Master

NOTE

See Chapter 9 for details on Windows 98 as a Microsoft and NetWare client, including the NDS client, and installing network adapters. See Chapter 8 for details on ATM and Chapter 15 for details on PPTP and VPN. See Chapter 13 for details on system policies and Chapter 12 for details on user profiles. We will be breaking down the objectives and only show the pertinent subobjective where it is discussed in the chapter.

Many smaller companies love the fact that they don't need a dedicated, expensive computer in order to share a few files and printers. Larger companies tend to have more resources for both hardware and administrators, so they usually don't allow users to share their local resources on the network. Restrictions can be enforced with system policies, which are discussed in Chapter 13.

TIP

When all is said and done, Windows 98 is a great PC operating system and network client, but it's much better to leave the role of a server to Windows NT or NetWare.

The steps to set up and manage shared resources are:

- Choose a security model (share-level versus user-level).
- Install File and Printer Sharing for Microsoft Networks.
- Configure file and printer sharing.
- Create shared resources.
- Modify shared resources.

These steps are discussed in detail in the following sections.

Choosing a Security Model

Windows 98 can use two types of security systems to share resources: share-level and user-level.

Microsoft
Exam
Objective

Assign access permissions for shared folders in a Microsoft environment or a mixed Microsoft and NetWare environment. Methods include:

- Passwords
- User permissions
- Group permissions

The way you create and modify shared resources depends on whether you set share-level or user-level security.

> **NOTE**
>
> You will need to "reshare" all your resources if you switch between the two security types. When you switch, Windows 98 will turn off sharing of all folders and printers. Windows 98 cannot convert rights from one scheme to another, so it doesn't even try.

Share-Level Security

Share-level security is the same as it is in Windows for Workgroups. A password is assigned to a shared resource when the shared resource is created. This is the default level of security.

With share-level security, a user who knows the passwords can access the resources, even if the original owner did not intend for that particular user to have access to those shared resources.

Using share-level security is easy and fast. However, it has the following disadvantages:

- It is not secure.
- Specific users cannot be blocked.
- The passwords may be discovered by someone you don't want to use the shared resource.
- There is no centralized control (i.e., Central Information Systems is no longer in charge).
- Changing passwords requires informing all intended users.

> Share-level security is the default security setting for the sharing service for Microsoft networks.

User-Level Security

Because of the limitations of share-level security, Microsoft added a more advanced option to Windows 98 (first included in Windows 95) that is much more secure. The user-level system bases its security on an existing server of some sort, either a Windows NT server (NT Workstation, NT Server, or a domain controller) or a NetWare server. User-level security works best in a Microsoft environment using a Windows NT domain controller. Although the other NT systems can be used, and NetWare is an acceptable alternative, Windows 98 networking is optimized in a domain environment. After a new share is made, existing users or groups are then given rights to the share. This means that you must have some kind of server in place before you can switch to user-level security.

User-level security has the following advantages:

- Rights can be assigned to a user or group.

- It allows centralized control of users and groups.

- It's more flexible than share-level security (custom rights can be assigned).

However, using user-level security has a few disadvantages, including:

- Some kind of server must be in place.

- It's more complex than share-level security.

- A live network connection to the server must be maintained when rights and shares are assigned and used.

You can switch to user-level security when you configure the sharing services, as described later in this chapter.

Installing File and Printer Sharing for Microsoft Networks

A Windows 98 computer can have many different client pieces installed simultaneously, but it can have only one sharing service installed at a time.

Microsoft
✓ Exam
Objective

Install and configure the network components of Windows 98 in a Microsoft environment and a mixed Microsoft and NetWare environment. Network components include:

- File and Printer Sharing for Microsoft Networks

Installing File and Printer Sharing is quite easy. This is a network service, which you can install from the Network applet of the Control Panel using the Add ➤ Service button, as shown in Figure 10.1.

F I G U R E 10.1

Adding File and Printer Sharing for Microsoft Networks

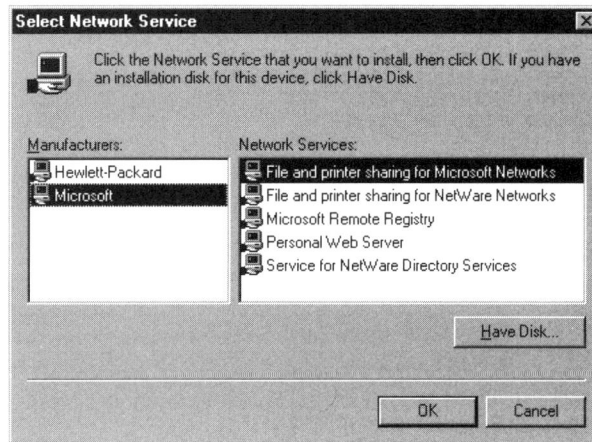

TIP Another way to access the network configuration dialog box is by right-clicking on Network Neighborhood and selecting Properties.

Follow the steps in Exercise 10.1 to install the sharing service for Microsoft Networks.

EXERCISE 10.1

Installing File and Printer Sharing for Microsoft Networks

1. Go to Control Panel ➣ Network.

2. Choose Add in the Select Network Component Type dialog box.

3. Highlight Service and choose Add.

4. Highlight Microsoft and choose File and Printer Sharing for Microsoft Networks (see Figure 10.1).

5. Click OK.

6. Reboot Windows 98.

Configuring File and Printer Sharing for Microsoft Networks

The major decision when configuring file and printer sharing is which security model to use. If you are in a workgroup, without any central server, share-level security is probably your best (if not only) option. If you have a central server (either NetWare or NT), user-level security is probably the better option. In either case, the mechanics of sharing resources is the same, but the security options are different.

Enabling Sharing

A global setting determines whether or not folders and printers may be shared on a computer (see Figure 10.2). Follow Exercise 10.2 to make sure that sharing is allowed (the default is to allow both resources to be shared).

FIGURE 10.2

Enabling resource sharing

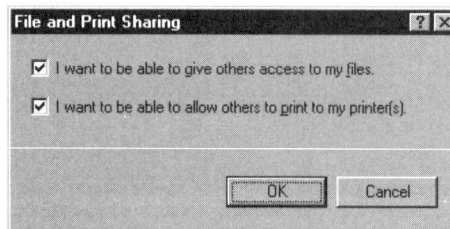

EXERCISE 10.2

Enabling Resource Sharing

1. Check to see if sharing is enabled by going to Control Panel ➤ Network and choosing the File and Print Sharing button.

2. Make sure that "I want to be able to give others access to my files." and "I want to be able to allow others to print to my printer(s)." are both checked to enable folder sharing and printer sharing (both boxes are selected by default).

3. Click OK twice to save your changes.

Changing the Security Model

As explained earlier, the default security model is share level, which allows you to put passwords on shared resources. User level is more secure, and is, therefore, preferred when users will be allowed to share their resources. Before you can change to user level, you need a server (either NetWare or Windows NT) in place.

You switch to user-level security through the Access Control tab of the Network Control Panel, as shown in Figure 10.3. If you set the access control to an NT server that is not a domain controller you will need the server name. If you set the access control to an NT domain, you will need the domain name. Exercise 10.3 shows the steps for switching the security model to user level, based on an NT domain.

EXERCISE 10.3

Switching to User-Level Security

1. Got to Control Panel ➤ Network.

2. Choose the Access Control tab.

3. Select User-Level Access Control.

4. Enter the name of the NT server or domain. Use **Domain1** if you don't have a real domain to use (see Figure 10.3).

5. Click OK.

6. Reboot Windows 98.

F I G U R E 10.3

Changing to user-level security

To switch back to share-level security, follow the steps in Exercise 10.3 to return to the Access Control tab and select Share-Level Access Control.

Sharing Resources

The process of creating shared folders is similar for both share-level and user-level security settings, but the types of security settings you can pick are different. The following sections describe the procedures for sharing folders and managing shares for both share-level and user-level sharing.

> **NOTE** Installing local and network printers is discussed in more detail in Chapter 11.

Creating Shares Using Share-Level Security

When you share a folder using share-level security, you have three basic security options:

- **Read Only:** Allows users on the network to see and run applications in that folder and to see and open files.

- **Full:** Allows all of the read-only rights. It also gives users the right to modify and delete programs and files and allows them to create new files.

- **Depends on Password:** Allows you to set different passwords for Read Only and Full access. You then give the appropriate password to users based on which rights you want them to have.

WARNING

If you select Read Only or Full access and don't enter a password, users don't need to use a password to connect to the shared resource. The shares are wide open to any and all users on your network—even those who have not been authenticated by a server!

These options are listed on the Sharing tab of a folder's Properties dialog box, as shown in Figure 10.4.

F I G U R E   10.4

Setting up a new share with share-level security

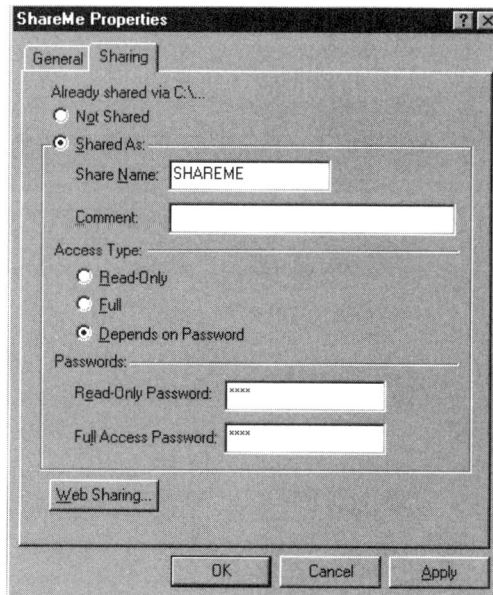

Follow the steps in Exercise 10.4 to share a folder and set the security using passwords.

EXERCISE 10.4

Creating a Share Using Share-Level Security

1. Create a folder called "ShareMe."

2. Highlight the folder and right-click. If you installed the Sharing service correctly (refer to Exercise 10.1), Sharing should appear in the pop-up menu, as shown here.

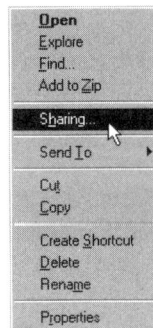

3. Select Sharing to display the Sharing tab of the ShareMe Properties dialog box.

4. Select the Shared As button.

5. Leave the default name SHAREME, or you may enter another name.

6. Select Depends on Password.

7. Enter **Read** in the Read Only Password box.

8. Enter **Full** in the Full Access Password box (see Figure 10.4).

9. Retype the passwords when prompted.

10. Click the Web Sharing button. You will then see the Web Sharing Folder Properties window.

11. Notice that the default is for the folder to be shared for HTTP access but not for FTP access. Click Cancel to close the screen.

12. Click OK to save your new share.

13. You should now see the folder with a hand under it, signifying that it is shared, as shown here.

If your share name ends with a $ (dollar sign), the share will be hidden from the browser. The only way to connect to this share is to use the UNC syntax, *computer name**share name*. To do this, map a network drive and enter the UNC for the path or use the File ➣ Run command, enter the UNC information, and hit Enter. If you want a permanent connection, use the Map Network Drive option.

You can check all of your shares by going to the Network Neighborhood. All of the shares should be listed under your computer name (unless they end with a $). If you have installed the Net Watcher utility, you can view your normal shares there. You can also go to the DOS prompt and use a Lan Manager command, Net View *computer name*.

Creating Shares Using User-Level Security

When you share folders with user-level security, you are able to grant rights to users or groups. The Sharing tab of the shared folder's Properties dialog box looks different than one that has share-level security, as shown in Figure 10.5.

F I G U R E 10.5

Setting up a new
share with user-level
security

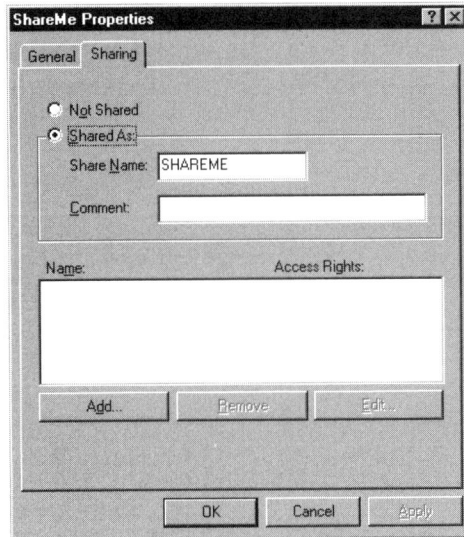

The rights you can grant are Read Only, Full Access, or Custom, as shown in Figure 10.6. You can grant rights to users or groups from the domain, or you can grant rights to "The world," which consists of all users on the network.

Microsoft
Exam
Objective

Diagnose and resolve resource access problems in a Microsoft environment or a mixed Micrososft and NetWare environment.

If you choose Custom, you can set individual rights, as shown in Figure 10.7. These include the following:

- **Read Files:** Allows the user to open or run files or applications
- **Write to Files:** Allows the user to edit existing files

F I G U R E   10.6

Assigning rights using
user-level security

F I G U R E   10.6

Assigning rights using
user-level security

- **Create Files and Folders:** Allows the user to create new files or folders

- **Delete Files:** Allows the user to delete files or folders

- **Change File Attributes:** Allows the user to change file or folder attributes

- **List Files:** Allows the user to show files and folders

- **Change Access Control:** Allows the user to change security settings

F I G U R E   10.7

Assigning custom
security rights

Follow the steps in Exercise 10.5 to create a new share using user-level access and assign rights to users and groups. Note that this exercise assumes you are using a Windows NT domain as your user-level security provider.

EXERCISE 10.5

Creating a Share Using User-Level Security

1. Make sure you are using user-level security (see Exercise 10.3).

2. Create a folder called "ShareMe."

3. Select the ShareMe folder, right-click it, and choose Sharing.

4. Choose the Shared As button.

5. Leave the default name of ShareMe as the Share Name, or enter a different name.

6. Click the Add button.

7. In the Add Users dialog box, highlight the Domain users group and click the Read Only button.

8. Highlight the Domain Admins group and click the Full Access button.

9. Highlight the Administrator user and click the Custom button.

10. Click OK. The Change Access Rights dialog box for the Administrator user appears.

11. Choose all custom access rights except Delete Files.

12. Choose OK twice to save your new share.

Managing Existing Shared Folders

To modify the properties of existing shares, return to the Sharing tab of the shared folder's Properties dialog box by right-clicking on the folder and choosing Sharing from the menu. From the Sharing tab of a shared resource that was created using share-level security, you can change the share name, how it is shared, or the passwords. From the Sharing tab of a user-level security share you can change the share name, how it is shared, or which users and groups have rights to the share.

Sharing Printers on a Microsoft Network

Although Chapter 11 covers printing in detail, the process of creating a shared printer will be covered here. Sharing a printer using share-level security allows you to assign a password to the printer, while sharing a printer using user-level security allows you to assign Print rights to various users and groups.

Microsoft
Exam
Objective

Create, share, and monitor resources. Resources include:

- Remote computers
- Network printers

NOTE

Creating remote shares and monitoring remote computers are covered in Chapter 14.

Sharing a printer on a Microsoft network consists of the following steps:

1. Verify that File and Printer Sharing for Microsoft is installed (see Exercise 10.1).

2. Verify that Printer Sharing is enabled (see Exercise 10.2).

3. Verify that share-level or user-level security is configured properly (see Exercise 10.3).

4. Create a local printer (see Exercise 11.1).

5. Share the local printer.

Sharing Printers Using Share-Level Security

Share-level security allows you to put passwords on your shared printers so that only those with the password can connect and use the shared printer. In Exercise 10.6, you will share a local printer using share-level security.

EXERCISE 10.6

Sharing Printers on the Network

1. Go to My Computer ➤ Printers (or Control Panel ➤ Printers).

2. Highlight a local printer, right-click the mouse, and choose Sharing (or go to the Properties of the printer and select the Sharing tab).

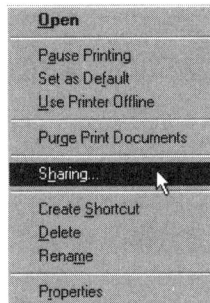

3. Select the Share As button, and enter a name for the shared printer (such as HP4).

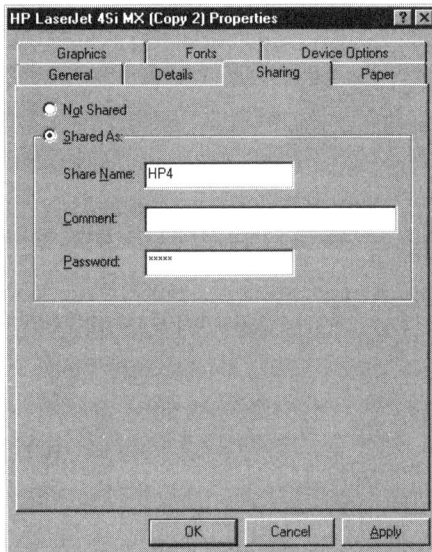

4. Note that if there is a field in which to enter a password, you are running in share-level security (as shown above). Enter a password.

5. Click OK to save your changes.

6. Enter the password again, and choose OK to share the printer.

Sharing Printers Using User-Level Security

If your computer is running with user-level security, you can assign print rights to the users and groups associated with the server or domain you have specified.

> **NOTE** Windows 98 can grant either no rights or full rights to the shared printer. Windows NT, when using shared printers, can grant more specific rights (for example, allowing users to modify their print jobs but nothing else).

In Exercise 10.7, you will share a printer using user-level security.

EXERCISE 10.7

Sharing Printers with User-Level Security

1. Go to My Computer ➤ Printers (or Control Panel ➤ Printers).

2. Highlight a local printer, right-click the mouse, and choose Sharing (or go to the Properties of the printer and select the Sharing tab).

3. Select the Shared As button, and enter a name for the shared printer (such as HP4).

4. Note that if there are fields for names and access rights you are running in user-level security. Select Add to add users to the printer.

5. Select Domain Users and yourself, and click the Full Access button. This will give all authenticated users (including you) full access to the shared printer.

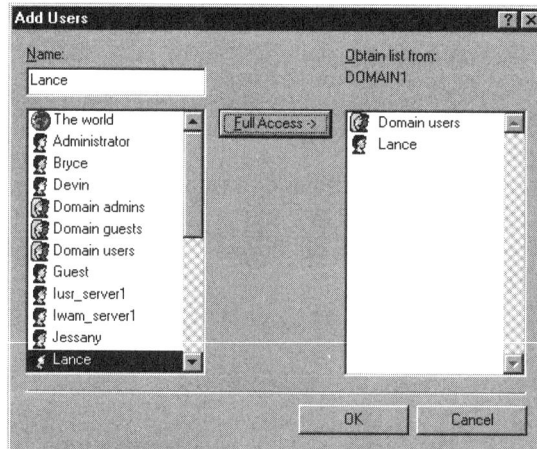

6. Click OK twice to save your changes.

> **NOTE**
>
> The workgroup that a computer is assigned to controls which servers are shown by Network Neighborhood. When Network Neighborhood is opened, only those servers in your workgroup are shown by default. In order to see servers outside of your workgroup, you need to select Entire Network and then choose to see the entire Microsoft or NetWare list of servers. To change your workgroup, go to the Identification tab of the Network applet in Control Panel.

Browsing on a Microsoft Network

The network browsing service is designed to allow clients to access a complete list of available servers, shared folders, and shared printers, without needing to keep their own copy of the list. When a computer browses the network, it downloads a list of available servers and shares from a central computer that maintains the list. As the number of clients increases, Windows (both NT and 98) will increase the number of servers keeping lists. The default number of browse servers is one server for every 32 clients.

Microsoft
✓ Exam
Objective

Install and configure the network components of Windows 98 in a Microsoft environment or a mixed Microsoft and NetWare environment. Network components include:

- **Browse Master**

If Windows 98 is part of a domain, the Primary Domain Controller (PDC) of the domain will be the *Browse Master* for the entire domain, and will have helper servers (backup browsers) to give lists to clients. When a Browse Master or backup browser is turned off, an "election" is held to pick a new Browse Master. The order of precedence is as follows:

- Windows NT Domain Controller

- Windows NT Server

- Windows NT Workstation

- Windows 95/98

- Windows for Workgroups

You can "stuff the ballot box" by editing the Registry to make one server take precedence over another to become Browse Master. For example, you may have two Windows 98 computers—one is a 486 with 8MB of RAM, and the other is a Pentium II 450 with 128 MB. Obviously, the Pentium computer would make the faster Browse Master.

Browse Master is a property of File and Printer Sharing for Microsoft Networks, as shown in Figure 10.8. There are three settings for this property:

- **Automatic:** This is the default. It means that the computer can be elected to become a Browse Master if it is needed.

- **Enabled:** This means that the computer will always be a Browse Master.

- **Disabled:** This means the computer will never become a Browse Master.

F I G U R E   10.8

Enabling the Browse Master property

Follow the steps in Exercise 10.8 to make a Windows 98 computer a preferred Browse Master.

> **EXERCISE 10.8**
>
> **Setting Windows 98 as a Preferred Browse Master**
>
> **1.** Go to Control Panel ≻ Network.
>
> **2.** In the Configuration tab, highlight File and printer sharing for Microsoft Networks and choose Properties.
>
> **3.** Highlight Browse Master and choose Enabled (see Figure 10.8).
>
> **4.** Choose OK twice to save your changes.
>
> **5.** Reboot Windows 98.

Sharing Resources on a NetWare Network

Windows 98 has the unique ability to imitate a NetWare server. A NetWare client can log in to and copy files to and from a Windows 98 computer as though it were a real NetWare server.

Once File and Printer Sharing for NetWare Networks is installed, you can share files and printers so that NetWare clients can connect to your resources.

> **NOTE**
>
> NetWare networks have no support for share-level security. Therefore, if a Windows 98 computer wants to share its resources on a NetWare network, it must be configured for user-level access with the list of users on an existing NetWare server.

When a client connects to the Windows 98 machine and tries to log on to it, Windows 98 doesn't actually authenticate the request—it passes it to the server assigned for user-level security.

> *Microsoft*
> *Exam*
> *Objective*
>
> **Install and configure the network components of Windows 98 in a Microsoft environment or a mixed Microsoft and NetWare environment. Network components include:**
>
> - File and Printer Sharing for NetWare Networks

Setting user-level security and creating shares have already been discussed (see Exercises 10.3 and 10.5). You also need to enable SAP (Service Advertising Protocol) support so that non-Windows 98 clients can see the Windows 98 machines as servers.

WARNING   Novell's Client for Windows 95 does not work with Microsoft's File and Printer Sharing for NetWare.

Windows 98 can also function as a NetWare print server, much like the PSERVER.EXE program that came with NetWare 2.*x* and 3.*x*. This allows Windows 98 to pull print jobs from a NetWare print queue and feed those jobs to a local printer. Windows 98 also has the ability to edit the printer information on NetWare servers so that the path for printer drivers exists with the printer. See Chapter 11 for more information about setting up Windows 98 as a NetWare print server and Point-and-Print installation for NetWare machines.

Installing File and Printer Sharing for NetWare Networks

Installing File and Printer Sharing for NetWare Networks is a simple matter of adding a network service. Of course, if you already have File and Printer Sharing for Microsoft installed you must uninstall it, because you can have only one sharing service installed at a time. Install the service from the Network Control Panel, as shown in Figure 10.9. Follow the steps in Exercise 10.9 to install File and Printer Sharing for NetWare Networks.

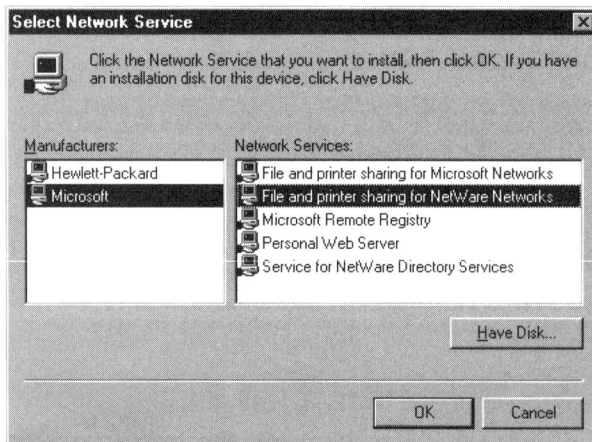

F I G U R E   10.9

Installing File and Printer Sharing for NetWare Networks

EXERCISE 10.9

Installing File and Printer Sharing for NetWare Networks

1. Go to Control Panel ➢ Network.

2. If you have File and Printer Sharing for Microsoft Networks installed, highlight it and choose Remove.

3. Choose Add, and then select Service.

4. Choose Microsoft in the Manufacturers list, and choose File and printer sharing for NetWare Networks in the Network Services list (see Figure 10.9).

5. Choose OK to install the service.

6. Choose OK in the Network Control Panel to save your changes.

7. If user-level security is not set, you will see the warning shown in the following graphic. Choose OK. This takes you to the Access Control tab, where you can enter the name of the NetWare server that will be used to authenticate the users (use FS1 if you don't have one). Choose OK twice to save your changes.

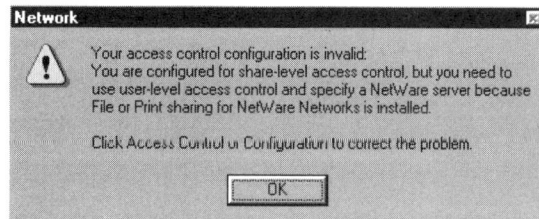

8. Reboot Windows 98.

Enabling SAP Support

Every 60 seconds, NetWare servers broadcast a SAP packet, which contains the server name and the shared resources it has. If you want to allow non-Windows 98 clients to see your Windows 98 server, the Windows 98 machine must also generate SAP packets.

Microsoft
Exam
Objective

Diagnose and resolve resource access problems in a Microsoft environment or a mixed Microsoft and NetWare environment.

SAP Advertising is a property of the file and printer sharing service, as shown in Figure 10.10. Follow the steps in Exercise 10.10 to enable SAP support.

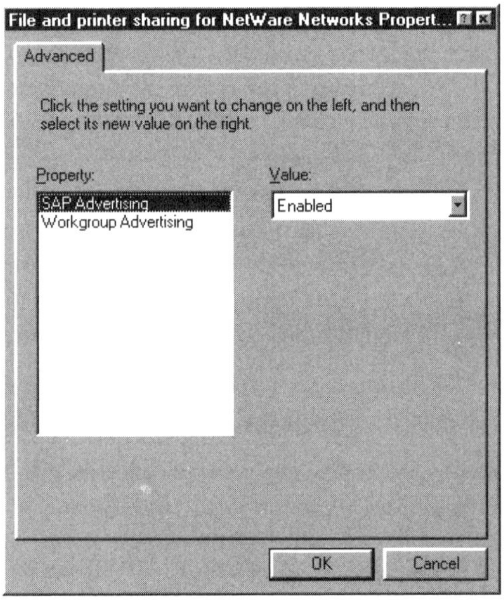

FIGURE 10.10

Enabling SAP
Advertising

EXERCISE 10.10

Enabling SAP Advertising

1. Go to Control Panel ➤ Network.

2. Highlight File and Printer Sharing for NetWare Networks and choose Properties.

3. Highlight SAP Advertising and select Enabled (see Figure 10.10).

4. Choose OK twice to save your changes.

5. Reboot Windows 98.

WARNING

If File and Printer Sharing for NetWare is installed on all of your Windows 98 computers and SAP support is enabled, there will be a large amount of background traffic generated from just the SAP broadcasts alone.

Browsing the NetWare Network

Once you have installed any of the NetWare clients, the Network Neighborhood will also include NetWare servers. Right-click on Network Neighborhood and choose the Who Am I option from the context menu. This brings up a list of all of the servers to which you are connected and as whom you are connected.

Double-clicking on any of the NetWare servers will prompt you to log in, if you haven't done so already. Once you have been authenticated, you can use NetWare volumes and printers just like any other NetWare client.

TIP

Who Am I is installed only for NetWare support. A number of shareware and freeware programs provide a similar command for Microsoft servers.

Monitoring Shared Resources

Having users connected to your computer can be scary for a couple of reasons. First, you want to make sure that only those users you want connected are connected. Second, you should always warn connected users before you reboot your computer. If a connected user has a file open, rebooting unexpectedly could cause a corrupt file if you don't give her a chance to save her work.

Windows 98 comes with a good utility you can use to monitor your shared resources—NetWatcher.

Microsoft ✓ Exam Objective

Monitor system performance by using Net Watcher, System Monitor, and Resource Meter.

> **NOTE** For details on System Monitor, see chapter 14; for coverage of Resource Meter, see Chapter 6.

Monitoring Shared Resources with Net Watcher

> ***Microsoft*** ✓ ***Exam Objective***
>
> **Diagnose and resolve connectivity problems in a Microsoft environment and a mixed Microsoft and NetWare environment. Tools include:**
>
> - WinIPCfg
> - Net Watcher
> - Ping
> - Tracert

The Net Watcher is an interactive tool for creating, controlling, and monitoring shared resources. Net Watcher can run locally on your system or it can be run on remote computers using either share-level or user-level security. If the remote PC is using user-level security, the administrating PC must also be using user-level security. The Net Watcher tool is similar to Caller ID. You are able to see what resources are being utilized, who is connected to the system, and what files are in use.

As an administrator, you can create, add, and delete shares; change resource properties; and monitor who is connected to which resource. Figure 10.11 shows an example of a Net Watcher screen.

FIGURE 10.11

The Net Watcher tool allows you to manage shares.

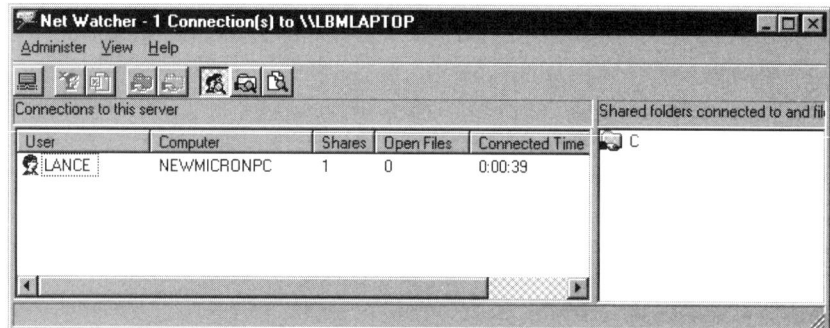

Using Net Watcher   Follow these steps to use the Net Watcher tool. Of course, the remote workstation must be sharing resources, folders, and/or printers for this tool to be useful. If it is not sharing resources, nothing will show up in the Net Watcher window.

1. Double-click the Network Neighborhood icon on your Desktop.

2. Navigate to a Windows 98-based computer involved in remote administration and right-click its icon.

3. From the context menu, choose Properties to open the Properties dialog box for that PC.

4. Choose the Tools tab.

5. Click the Net Watcher button. The Net Watcher application starts and shows you the status of shared resources on the remote PC (see Figure 10.11).

NOTE   When you use the Net Watcher, two special shares are created: Admin$ gives administrators access to the \Windows folder on the remote PC. IPC$ is an interprocess channel between the two computers. This is a buffer area for RPCs (remote procedure calls) to move between the workstations.

If you disconnect a user from a shared resource, the user will reconnect to the resource immediately. To prevent this if you are using share-level security, you need to change the password on the resource. If you are using user-level security, you need to remove the user from the users list. This is also true when you are closing a file. The user will still have access to the shared folder but will be momentarily disconnected from the file. The user will immediately reconnect to the file unless you do something to prevent it.

WARNING   If you are using share-level security and you change a password on a shared resource, everyone who is currently using that resource will be thrown out. They will need to supply the new password in order to reconnect.

Summary

Windows 98 can be set up to share its local resources on a network. When a Windows 98 computer shares its resources, it can use either share-level security (the default that puts passwords on the shared resource) or user-level security (which grants rights to existing users and groups from an NT or NetWare server). User-level security is tighter than share-level security, but it does require an existing NT or NetWare server to link to.

Browsing allows Windows 98 to see the servers and shared resources available on the network. By default, there is one browser server for every 32 clients. When Windows 98 is part of a domain, there is a Browse Master for the entire domain. Using the Browse Master property for a Windows 98 machine (through its File and Printer Sharing for Microsoft Networks property sheet), Windows 98 computers can belong to a workgroup. A workgroup is an association of computers, mainly used by Network Neighborhood. When Network Neighborhood is opened, only the servers in the workgroup are shown. In order to see all of the servers on the network, the Entire Network needs to be chosed from within Network Neighborhood you can designate that a specific machine is always the Browse Master.

For a Windows 98 machine to act as a NetWare server, it needs the File and Printer Sharing for NetWare Networks service installed. If Windows 98 is configured as a NetWare server, SAP must be enabled in order for non-Windows 98 (MS-DOS, WFW) NetWare clients to see the Windows 98 computer.

Review Questions

1. Which of the following are true? Choose all that apply.

   A. Windows 98 can be a client to an NT server while it is also acting as an NT server.

   B. You can set read-only rights using just share-level security.

   C. A stand-alone Windows 98 computer can use user-level security.

   D. A stand-alone Windows 98 computer can use share-level security.

2. Windows 98 must use which type of security to share files on a NetWare network?

   A. Share-level security

   B. User-level security

   C. Default-level security

   D. Secure-level security

3. You have a mixture of new, fast computers with lots of RAM and older computers with a minimum of RAM. All of them run Windows 98 in your peer-to-peer network. At times browsing seems slower. What can you do to help keep the speed of the browsing fast?

   A. Set the browser service to disabled on the fast computers and enabled on the slow computers.

   B. Set the browser service to automatic on the fast computers and enabled on the slow computers.

   C. Set the browser service to enabled on the fast computers and automatic on the slower computers

   D. Set the browser service to enabled on the fast computers and disabled on the slow computers.

4. You have a mixture of MS-DOS, WFW, and Windows 98 computers on your NetWare network. Some of the users who have Windows 98 are allowed to share their files with the others. The people on older computers are complaining that they cannot see the Windows 98 computers. What must you enable on the Windows 98 computers?

   A. SAP

   B. RIP

   C. HTTP

   D. VMS

5. Joe was sharing three folders when he switched from share-level security to user-level security. Now no one seems to be able to see the shares. What must Joe do to get the shares back?

   A. Reboot, then the shares will come back.

   B. He has to re-create all the shares because he switched security modes.

   C. The shares are still there, they are just hidden.

   D. The share are still there; however, the clients need to view them differently.

6. Which of the following types of servers can be security providers for user-level security? Choose all that apply.

   A. Windows 98

   B. Windows NT Server

   C. Windows NT Workstation

   D. NetWare Server

7. Sue is using default security settings on Windows 98 and is sharing office memos. She wants to be certain that the sales team can read the memos, but only the sales manager can make new memos. How can she do this?

   A. Share the folder as Full control, and mark the memos Read-only.

   B. Share the folder as Read-only, and then make a second Full control share.

   C. Share the folder as Depends On Password.

   D. Switch to user-level security.

8. Net Watcher allows you to do which of the following? Choose all that apply.

   A. Create new shares for folders

   B. Delete shares based on folders

   C. Disconnect users from shared folders

   D. Monitor shares on remote computers

9. Certain people should never be allowed to use a new color printer. What is the best way to secure it?

   A. Switch to user-level security and give access rights to the printer rights to the printer only to those who need it.

   B. Switch to user-level security and give everyone No Access. Then give the Print right only to the specific users and groups you want to be able to print.

   C. Switch to share-level security and share the printer with a password.

   D. Switch to share-level security and share the printer with Depends On Password.

10. Which of the following must be unique? Choose all that apply.

    A. Computer name

    B. Workgroup name

    C. Username

    D. Domain

11. You have three workgroups (Sales, Marketing, and Accounting) and two domains (Headquarters and Branch1). The Headquarters domain has two servers, HQ1 (the PDC) and HQ2 (the BDC). All users at your location log in to the Headquarters domain. You want your Windows 95 clients to switch to user-level security in the Headquarters domain. What do you enter for the security provider?

    A. HQ1

    B. HQ2

    C. HQ1 or HQ2

    D. Headquarters

12. You have three workgroups (Sales, Marketing, and Accounting) and two domains (Headquarters and Branch1). All users at your location log in to the Headquarters domain. The users from sales would like to see the computers in their sales group when they first open Network Neighborhood. How do you set their computers?

    A. Have their computers be members of the Headquarters domain, and set Network Neighborhood to the Sales workgroup.

    B. Have their computers be members of the Sales workgroup.

    C. Have their user accounts in the Sales workgroup.

    D. Have their user accounts in the Branch1 domain, and set Network Neighborhood to the Sales workgroup.

MCSE: Windows 98 Study Guide

Official Microsoft Objectives for Exam 70-098: Implementing and Supporting Windows® 98

Objective	Page
PLANNING	
Develop an appropriate implementation model for specific requirements in a Microsoft environment or a mixed Microsoft and NetWare environment. Considerations include choosing the appropriate file system and planning a workgroup.	9, 263
Develop a security strategy in a Microsoft environment or a mixed Microsoft and NetWare environment. Strategies include system policies, user profiles, file and printer sharing, and share-level access control or user-level access control.	355, 426, 444
INSTALLATION AND CONFIGURATION	
Install Windows 98. Installation options include automated Windows setup, New, Upgrade, Uninstall, and dual-boot combination with Microsoft Windows NT.	16, 26, 44, 49, 58, 66
Configure Windows 98 server components. Server components include Microsoft Personal Web Server 4.0 and Dial-Up Networking server.	524, 534
Install and configure the network components of Windows 98 in a Microsoft environment or a mixed Microsoft and NetWare environment. Network components include Client for Microsoft Networks, Client for NetWare Networks, network adapters, File and Printer Sharing for Microsoft Networks, File and Printer Sharing for NetWare Networks, Service for NetWare Directory Services (NDS), asynchronous transfer mode (ATM), virtual private networking and PPTP, and Browse Master.	276, 299, 322, 323, 335, 355, 359, 373, 375, 523
Install and configure network protocols in a Microsoft environment or a mixed Microsoft and NetWare environment. Protocols include NetBEUI, IPX/SPX-compatible protocol, IP, TCP/IP, Microsoft DLC, and Fast Infrared.	277, 285, 293, 295, 296, 298
Install and configure hardware devices in a Microsoft environment or a mixed Microsoft and NetWare environment. Hardware devices include modems, printers, Universal Serial Bus (USB), multiple display support, IEEE 1394 FireWire, Infrared Data Association (IrDA), multilink, and power management scheme.	80, 82, 84, 85, 87, 89, 92, 395, 500, 501
Install and configure Microsoft Backup.	236
CONFIGURING AND MANAGING RESOURCE ACCESS	
Assign access permissions for shared folders in a Microsoft environment or a mixed Microsoft and NetWare environment. Methods include passwords, user permissions, and group permissions.	357
Create, share, and monitor resources. Resources include remote computers and network printers.	369, 476
Set up user environments by using user profiles and system policies.	427, 447
Back up data and the Registry and restore data and the Registry.	149, 236

NETWORK PRESS
SYBEX

Objective	Page
CONFIGURING AND MANAGING RESOURCE ACCESS (cont.)	
Configure hard disks. Tasks include disk compression, partitioning, enabling large disk support, and converting to FAT32.	209, 219, 252, 254, 263
Create hardware profiles.	98
INTEGRATION AND INTEROPERABILITY	
Configure a Windows 98 computer as a client computer in a network that contains a Windows NT 4.0 domain.	329
Configure a Windows 98 computer as a client computer in a NetWare network.	341
Configure a Windows 98 computer for remote access by using various methods in a Microsoft environment or a mixed Microsoft and NetWare environment. Methods include Dial-Up Networking and Proxy Server.	509, 532
MONITORING AND OPTIMIZATION	
Monitor system performance by using Net Watcher, System Monitor, and Resource Meter.	178, 379, 480, 564
Tune and optimize the system in a Microsoft environment and a mixed Microsoft and NetWare environment. Tasks include optimizing the hard disk by using Disk Defragmenter and ScanDisk, compressing data by using DriveSpace3 and the Compression Agent, updating drivers and applying service packs by using Windows Update and the Signature Verification tool, automating tasks by using Maintenance Wizard, scheduling tasks by using Task Scheduler, and checking for corrupt files and extracting files from the installation media by using the System File Checker.	170, 194, 199, 208, 221, 226, 230, 247, 557
TROUBLESHOOTING	
Diagnose and resolve installation failures. Tasks include resolving file and driver version conflicts by using Version Conflict Manager and the Microsoft System Information utility.	127, 555, 563
Diagnose and resolve boot process failures. Tasks include editing configuration files by using the System Configuration utility.	125
Diagnose and resolve connectivity problems in a Microsoft environment or a mixed Microsoft and NetWare environment. Tools include WinIPCfg, Net Watcher, Ping, and Tracert.	287, 380
Diagnose and resolve printing problems in a Microsoft environment or a mixed Microsoft and NetWare environment.	416, 576
Diagnose and resolve file system problems.	230
Diagnose and resolve resource access problems in a Microsoft environment or a mixed Microsoft and NetWare environment.	216, 366, 378
Diagnose and resolve hardware device and device driver problems. Tasks include checking for corrupt registry files by using ScanReg and ScanRegW.	153

NETWORK ® PRESS SYBEX

13. Your network consists of MS-DOS NetWare and Windows Microsoft clients. You want all of the clients to access your computer so that they can look at old company memos. You intend to install the following components: File and Printer Sharing for Microsoft, File and Printer Sharing for NetWare, Service for NetWare Directory Service, IPX/SPX, and TCP/IP. Will this installation fulfill the requirements?

   A. Yes, all requirements are fulfilled.

   B. Yes, but only if you enable SAP advertising.

   C. Yes, but only if you enable the browser service.

   D. No, this installation will not work.

14. Your network consists of MS-DOS NetWare and Windows NetWare clients. You want all of the clients to access your computer so that they can look at old company memos. You intend to install the following components: File and Printer Sharing for NetWare, Service for Net-Ware Directory Service, and TCP/IP. Will this installation fulfill the requirements?

   A. Yes, all requirements are fulfilled.

   B. Yes, but only if you enable SAP advertising.

   C. Yes, but only if you enable the browser service.

   D. No, this installation will not work.

15. Your network consists of a domain (SALES) with a Windows NT PDC (PDC1) and a Windows NT BDC (BDC1) as well as threee application servers (UT, ID, CA). You are allowing users to share folders on their local workstations. Your domain covers three states. You want users to only see the shared resources from their state. How would you do this?

   A. Make three NT groups, one for each state. Assign the appropriate users to each group, give the appropriate group rights to the appropriate computers.

   B. Make three workgroups, one for each state. Assign the appropriate computers to the appropriate workgroups.

   C. Name each of the computers in the state after the state (UT, ID, CA).

   D. Make three workgroups and set Network Neighborhood to the preferred workgroup in the Registry.

11

Printing with Windows 98

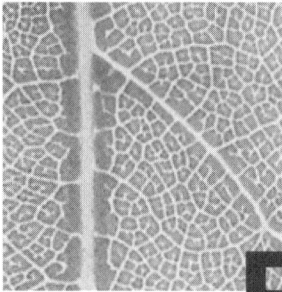

Because printing is such a common task, installing, administering, and troubleshooting printers are key areas of interest for most system engineers. This chapter will discuss the printing features in Windows 98, the printing architecture, the printing process, printer installation, printer configuration, and printer administration. Some troubleshooting tips for dealing with printer problems are also included.

Windows 98 Printing Features

Windows 98 supports several enhanced printing features:

- **Plug and Play:** If your motherboard is Plug-and-Play compliant, all you need to do to install a printer is to plug it in. Windows 98 should recognize the printer and install the appropriate drivers.

- **Drag and drop:** You can place printer shortcuts, to both local and network printers, on your Desktop and then drag files to be printed onto the printer icon. Your print jobs will be sent to that printer.

- **Extended Capabilities Port (ECP):** ECP allows you to add ECP-compliant cards to your PC. The additional cards will become ECPs and can be used to attach both ECP and non-ECP–compliant devices like printers.

- **Improved color management:** Windows 98 supports Image Color Matching (ICM) version 2.0 standards. This support allows you to maintain an image's original color from its source (scanner, digital camera, Internet, etc.) through your editing tools and finally as output. In other words, you get device-independent WYSIWYG color.

- **Point-and-Print setup:** Windows 98 uses a special Point-and-Print setup feature for installing networked printers. To install a printer, you only need to navigate to the printer or print queue and double-click its icon. Windows 98 will then begin the printer installation.

- **Microsoft Print Server for NetWare:** Windows 98 can be configured to act as a NetWare print server and despool (remove) print jobs from a NetWare print queue.

- **Working offline:** Windows 98 can print documents to a temporary queue while your computer is not hooked up to any printer. When Windows 98 detects that a printer has been attached, it will print the queued documents.

- **Font loading:** Unlike Windows 3.*x*, Windows 98 will load font files only as it needs them, therefore saving valuable memory space.

- **HP JetAdmin 2.54 utility:** This is an updated version of the Hewlett Packard JetAdmin utility which comes on the Windows 98 CD-ROM. HP JetAdmin allows you to manage HP-compatible printers that are connected to your enterprise through a network cable.

Printing Architecture

The following sections discuss how Windows 98 applies its modular approach to printing; this involves the universal driver and minidriver combinations, as well as the Windows metafiles. Then you will see where the interchangeable printing components are located in the network architecture.

Print Drivers

Windows 98 uses a set of universal drivers and minidrivers to handle the complex tasks of rendering and printing. *Minidrivers* are printer-specific chunks of code that can speak directly with the printer and also speak the common universal driver language.

You can download many of the latest printer drivers from Adobe's Web site: www.adobe.com.

There are currently three different types of minidrivers and one universal driver. The universal printer driver includes the following functionality:

- 600 dpi support

- Monochrome HP GL/2 support for compatibility with the LaserJet 4 standard

- Generic text that supports the TTY.DRV drivers

- Epson ESC P/2 raster graphics that can print directly thorough the universal driver and bypass minidriver support.

The following minidrivers are also supported:

- **Regular:** This is used for all black-and-white printers that do not use PostScript. (Some Hewlett-Packard inkjet printers will not use this driver either.) Regular universal drivers use a printer-specific minidriver.

- **PostScript:** This is used for all black-and-white PostScript printers. PostScript drivers will use PostScript minidrivers that adhere to the Adobe PPD (PostScript Printer Description) and SPD (Standard Printer Description) formats.

- **HP Color Inkjet:** This is used for inkjet printers and nearly all color printers. This special case uses a monolithic driver, which means that the minidriver code that would normally be in the minidriver is part of the universal driver itself.

These minidriver/universal driver combinations allow for device independence. In other words, you can have any program send output to any printer, and Windows 98 will be able to print it.

Printer drivers are stored in the \Windows\System directory on your hard drive. Printer Registry entries are stored in the Hkey_Local_Machine\System\CurrentControlSet\Control\Print folder.

Windows Metafiles

Windows *metafiles* (*.WMF) are files that contain the Windows internal graphics language. Windows 98 supports both the old WMF format and a new enhanced metafile format (EMF). These metafiles are basically a collection of internal commands that Windows 98 uses to render graphics to the screen. Metafiles are generally not device specific, which makes it easy to send them to other computers for printing. When a metafile is converted for output to a specific printer, it becomes a *raw file*. The raw file contains printer-specific codes that tell the printer how to print the images in the file.

Another advantage of using EMF files for printing is that they can be spooled to a hard disk location rather than being printed directly. This means that when a program prints a job, you can start working with the program again as soon as the file has been spooled. You no longer need to wait for the print job to be sent to the printer and for the printer to finish receiving the entire print job. This can return control of your system to you as much as four times more quickly. Spooled print jobs are located in the \Windows\Spool\Printers directory.

The Windows 98 Printing Process

The following sequence of events takes place when you send a print job from an application to the printer:

1. The printer driver is located. If the driver is on a network printer and you do not have a local copy of the driver, it will be copied from the network print server. If you have a local copy that is older than the driver on the network print server, again the newer driver will be copied to your machine. The printer driver is then loaded into RAM.

2. The application uses the current printer settings from the drivers (fonts, resolution, orientation, and so on) to build a WYSIWYG enhanced metafile (EMF).

3. The program creates a description of the output using the GDI (graphical device interface). The GDI will specify everything Windows 98 needs to know about the content and formatting of the image, but it does not tell the printer how to print the document. You are building the EMF.

4. If you have EMF spooling turned on, the GDI writes the EMF to the EMF spooler and returns control to the application. If you do not have EMF spooling turned on, the program must wait until the print job has completed before regaining control.

5. The spooler passes the document back through the drivers with a pass through the minidriver. The minidriver embeds printer-specific commands into the file and converts it to a raw printer file. The file is then submitted to the print spooler.

6. The spooler passes the document to the spooler on the print server through the router software. If the client PC and the print server are the same machine, this step is bypassed.

> **WARNING** If the router software fails for any reason, you will not receive any error messages regarding the lost print job.

7. When the print server spooler receives the document, it passes it on to the printer monitor, which will write the data to the appropriate printer destination (LPT1, or *servername**printername*, or directly to a network adapter card if it is installed on a printer).

8. The printer prints the document. The monitor will display a message letting the user know that the document is printing.

> **NOTE** The printer monitor can use bidirectional communications in nibble mode to inform the application of printer-related information (e.g., the printer is printing, low on toner, jammed, etc.).

Figure 11.1 illustrates the steps in the printing process.

FIGURE 11.1

The Windows 98
printing process

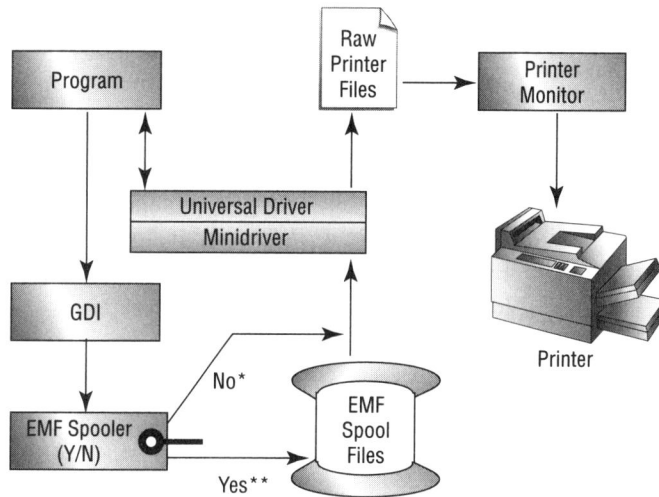

*Prints one page at a time. Control is returned after the last page has printed.
**Printing begins when spooled. Control is returned to the program.

Printer Installation

The procedure you use for installing a printer depends on whether or not you install a printer locally or across the network. The following sections discuss how to set up local printers and networked printers, including Point-and-Print setup.

Microsoft
Exam
Objective

Install and configure hardware devices in a Microsoft environment and a mixed Microsoft and NetWare environment. Hardware devices include:

- Modems
- Printers
- Universal Serial Bus (USB)
- Multiple Display Support

NOTE

Installing and configuring printers is covered in this chapter. Installing and configuring modems is covered inChapter 15. Installing an configuring all other devices are covered in Chapter 3.

Printer installation and management is handled through the Windows Explorer or the Printers folder, located under Start ➤ Settings ➤ Printers. From the Printers folder, shown in Figure 11.2, you can perform the following tasks:

- Install a printer

- Share a printer

- Administer both local and remote printers and print queues

- Control printer configurations, such as which printer is the default printer, font selections, spooler considerations, and orientation

FIGURE 11.2

The Printers folder allows you to install and administer printers.

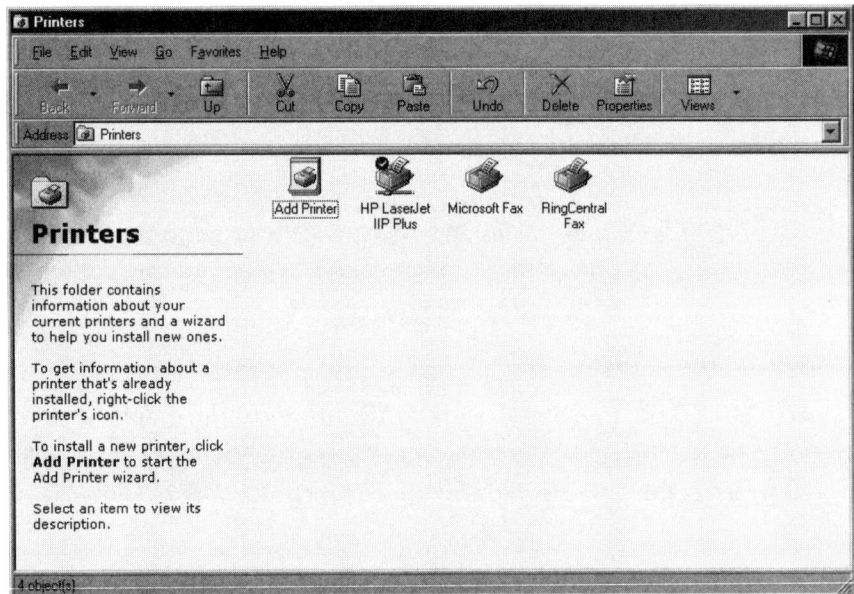

Installing Local Printers

If you have a Plug-and-Play printer, local installation is a snap. Simply attach the printer cables and turn on your printer. When you restart Windows 98, it should recognize the new printer and install the appropriate printer drivers for you.

If you do not have a Plug-and-Play printer, you can easily install a local printer from the Printers folder. The Add Printer Wizard allows you to select the printer manufacturer and model, as shown in Figure 11.3. Follow the steps in Exercise 11.1 to install a local printer through the Printers folder.

> **NOTE**
> If you don't see your printer in the Add Printer Wizard's list, check the printer manufacturer's documentation to see if there is a compatible driver you can select.

FIGURE 11.3

Selecting a manufacturer and printer model

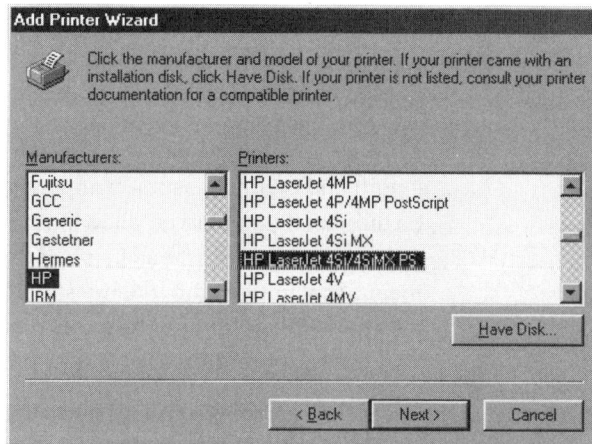

EXERCISE 11.1

Installing a Local Printer

1. Open the Printers folder by selecting Start ➤ Settings ➤ Printers.

2. Double-click the Add Printer icon (see Figure 11.2) to start the Add Printer Wizard.

3. You will be presented with a Welcome screen. Click Next to begin the installation process. This brings up a screen asking you whether this is a local printer or a network printer.

4. Choose the local printer option and then click Next. Windows 98 builds a driver information database and loads it into memory. The driver information database is a list of manufacturers, their printers, and the drivers needed to support those printers (see Figure 11.3).

5. Choose the manufacturer of your printer in the Manufacturers list, and then choose the printer in the Printers list. If you do not see your printer listed, click the Have Disk button. The Wizard will ask you to put the floppy disk that shipped with your printer into the floppy drive. The next screen asks you to select the port where your printer is located

6. Choose your printer port. In most cases, your printer will be hooked up through a parallel port to LPT1. If you want to configure your ports from here, click the Configure button. When you have made your selection, click the Next button to move to the screen that asks for a printer name.

7. Enter a name for this printer. This name can be up to 31 characters in length and is known as the "friendly name." Your friendly name must be unique. If you plan on allowing others access to your printer from across the network, it may be safer to use a UNC name, which means means that your friendly name should be 15 or fewer characters. You also have the option to make this printer the default printer for your Windows programs. Click Next when you are finished.

8. The last screen of the Wizard gives the option to print a test page. This is a good idea. The test page will show you that the printer is hooked up and running properly, and it will tell you which printer drivers your printer is using and their version numbers. It will also print a sample graphic. If you are using a color printer, the Windows logo graphic will be in color. When you are finished, click Finish. Your new printer icon will show up in the Printers folder.

Installing Network Printers Manually

Two types of installation methods are used for network printers. The first method is a *manual installation*, which follows essentially the same steps outlined in Exercise 11.1. The second method is called *Point-and-Print*, which allows you to browse the network for a printer or print queue and then double-click on that printer or queue; the driver files and printer information are then copied directly to your workstation.

An advantage of Point-and-Print installation is that you copy the current printer configurations over to your workstation. With manual installation, you are using fresh, unmodified drivers and configurations. You may need to make changes to these configurations for paper size, fonts, orientation, and so on.

Exercise 11.2 shows the steps for a manual network printer installation.

EXERCISE 11.2

Installing a Network Printer Manually

1. Open the Printers folder by selecting Start ➢ Settings ➢ Printers.

2. Double-click the Add Printer icon to start the Add Printer Wizard.

3. Click Next to begin the installation process. A screen appears asking you whether this is a local printer or a network printer.

4. Choose the Network printer option and then Next. The next screen asks you for the network path or queue name.

5. You can type in a UNC name, or you can click the Browse button to browse the network and locate the printer or queue. You also need to specify whether or not you print from MS-DOS–based programs. If you choose Yes to print from MS-DOS–based programs, you will be presented with a screen that has a Capture Printer Port button. Click this button to capture the printer port. In the Capture Printer Port dialog box, select the port to capture from the Device list (usually, you will choose LPT1), and then click OK.

6. Click Next to move to the manufacturers and printers screen (see Figure 11.3). Select the manufacturer and the appropriate printer from the lists. Click Next to move to the screen that asks for a printer name.

EXERCISE 11.2 (CONTINUED)

7. Enter a name for the printer. This name can be up to 31 characters in length and is known as the "friendly name." Your friendly name must be unique. If you plan on allowing others access to your printer from across the network, it might be safer to use a UNC name. This means that your friendly name should be 15 characters or fewer. You also have the option to make this printer the default printer for your Windows programs. Click Next when you are finished.

8. The last screen of the Wizard gives the option to print a test page. This is a good idea. The test page shows you that the printer is hooked up and running properly. It will also tell you which printer drivers and versions your printer is using and print a sample graphic. If you are using a color printer, the Windows logo graphic will be in color. When you are finished, click Finish. Your new printer icon will show up in the Printers folder.

If you are manually installing a printer from a Novell NetWare network, you should designate the print queue rather than a printer. This is because printers are not shared under NetWare.

Installing with Point-and-Print

With Point-and-Print, you can install driver files for a networked printer in several ways:

- Drag the Point-and-Print printer icon from the networked PC to your Printers folder or Desktop.

- Select the Install option from the context menu of the networked printer.

- Double-click the networked printer icon and begin the Point-and-Print installation.

You can also print to a networked printer by simply dragging-and-dropping documents onto the printer icon. If the printer hasn't been installed yet, this will initiate the installation process and then send the print job to the printer.

> **NOTE** For a machine with a printer to support Point-and-Print, it needs to know the printer name, printer configuration, which printer driver files are needed, and the location of those files.

Point-and-Print from a Windows 98 Machine

Point-and-Print is automatically supported by Windows 98 machines and requires very little setup. All you need to do to set up Point-and-Print on a Windows 98 server is to install the printer and then share it.

> **NOTE** The printer drivers needed for a Windows 98 machine to support Point-and-Print are specified in the MSPRINT.INF, MSPRINT1.INF, MSPRINT2 .INF, and PRNTUPD.INF files located in the hidden directory C:\Windows\Inf.

When you share a printer on a Windows 98 machine, Windows 98 will create a special hidden share called PRINTER$. This hidden share is used by other Windows 98 machines to copy the driver and configuration files from the server. The hidden share PRINTER$ has no password. It can be mapped through a network drive connection as *servername*\Printer$.

Point-and-Print from an NT Machine

The Point-and-Print installation for a Windows 98 client from a Windows NT machine is supported a bit differently than from a Windows 98 to Windows 98 configuration. This is because of the way Windows NT handles printing.

Printer drivers are downloaded to your Windows 98 machine from the NT machine in their original format. This means that you will not inherit the current printer configurations on your Windows 98 machine. You may need to make modifications locally to match the current printer configuration.

To install the network printer, follow the steps outlined in Exercise 11.2. If the .INF file on the NT machine is the same as the .INF file on the Windows 98 machine, you will not be prompted for a printer manufacturer and model, but you will still need to supply a friendly name.

> **NOTE** Point-and-Print from a Windows 98 print server to a Windows NT client is currently not supported.

Point-and-Print from a NetWare Machine

To use a Point-and-Print setup from a Novell NetWare machine, the NetWare server must be running bindery emulation or Novell Directory Services (NDS). A NetWare *bindery* is similar to the Windows 98 and Windows NT Registry. The bindery is composed of three parts:

- **Objects:** These are identified by their name and type of object. Objects are things like print queues, users, and file servers. Objects have properties associated with them.

- **Properties:** These are attributes that describe the object. For example, a user object might have properties for username, user password, and user e-mail directory. Properties have values.

- **Values:** These are the actual settings of particular properties. For example, the username property of a user object might have the value Dooless N. Seymore.

Before Point-and-Print can be used from the NetWare bindery-based server, the bindery needs to be updated with the printer name, driver files, and the driver file locations. To add these entries to the NetWare bindery, follow the steps in Exercise 11.3.

EXERCISE 11.3

Adding Printer Information to a NetWare Bindery

1. Log in to the NetWare server as a Supervisor or equivalent. (You need to have Supervisor privileges to modify a NetWare bindery.)

2. From your Windows 98 machine, navigate to a NetWare print queue and right-click the queue. This brings up a context menu with a Point-and-Print Setup menu item.

3. Click the Point-and-Print Setup menu item to see a submenu with two options: Set Printer Model and Set Driver Path.

4. Select the Set Printer Model menu item to display the standard Printer Manufacturer and Printer Model dialog box. Select your manufacturer and the printer from the lists, and then select OK. This adds an entry to the NetWare bindery.

EXERCISE 11.3 (CONTINUED)

5. Return to the Point-and-Print Setup submenu and select the Set Driver Path option. This brings up the Printer Driver Directory dialog box. Add a UNC path (in the format *server**volume**path*, such as \\NW312\Sys\Public) where the drivers can be found.

6. Manually copy the printer drivers to this directory on the NetWare server. To figure out which files you need, check for the appropriate drivers listed in the MSPRINT.INF file located in the \Windows\Inf directory.

7. Grant at least Read and File Scan rights to the directory on the Net-Ware server where you placed the driver files.

After you have added Point-and-Print information to the NetWare bindery, you can install printers simply by navigating to the NetWare print queue and double-clicking its icon. The driver files and the printer information will be downloaded to your local Windows 98 machine. You will still need to set printer specific options like font, orientation, etc.

To install Point-and-Print support using Microsoft Service for NDS follow the steps outlined in Exercise 11.4.

EXERCISE 11.4

Adding Printer Information to a Novell NDS tree

1. Log in to the NetWare server as a Supervisor or equivalent. You need to have Supervisor privileges to modify a Root object on the NDS tree the first time you implement Point-and-Print. You must also be a trustee for the printer object and have Supervisor Object and Supervisor Property rights for the printer.

2. From your Windows 98 machine, navigate to a NetWare print queue and right-click on the queue. This brings up a context menu with a Point-and-Print Setup tab.

3. Click the Enable Point-and-Print checkbox. This will enable the other boxes on the screen. In the textbox, type the UNC path to a directory where the drivers are located. (You must have Write access to this directory, and clients must have Read access to it.)

4. Click Set Printer Model, and select your manufacturer and printer model.

5. Click OK when you are finished.

6. Manually copy the printer drivers to the directory tree on the NetWare server. To figure out which files you need, check for the appropriate drivers listed in the MSPRINT.INF file located in the \Windows\Inf directory.

Installing Microsoft Print Server for NetWare

Microsoft Print Server for NetWare (MSPSRV.EXE) runs on a Windows 98 machine that has been set up with the Microsoft Client for NetWare Networks (see Chapter 10 for details on how to install and set up this network client). You enable the Microsoft Print Server for NetWare through the Print Server tab of the printer's Properties dialog box, as shown in Figure 11.4.

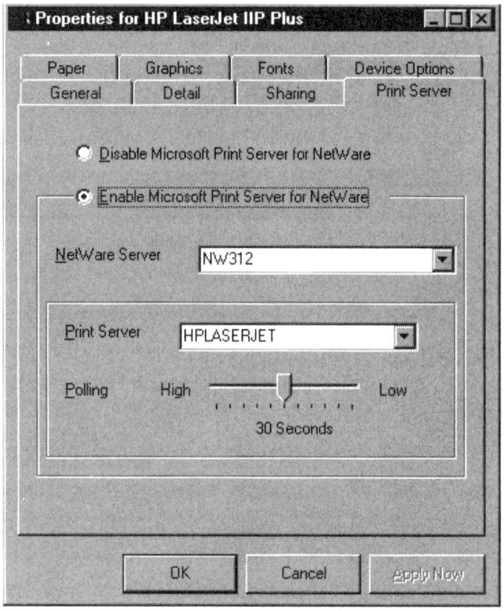

FIGURE 11.4

Enabling the Microsoft Print Server for NetWare

When you install the Print Server for NetWare, you will be able to despool print jobs from a NetWare print queue and print them on your local printer. The print server basically becomes just another program on the network, submitting print jobs to your local printer. Follow the steps in Exercise 11.5 to enable a print server for NetWare.

EXERCISE 11.5

Enabling Microsoft Print Server for NetWare

1. Verify that a print server object has been created and that the print queue object is configured to print on Printer 0–Remote, LPT1. (For more information about this setup, refer to your Novell NetWare manuals.)

2. In your Printers folder, select your printer and open its property sheet. Select the Print Server tab (see Figure 11.4).

3. Select the Enable Microsoft Print Server for NetWare option.

4. Select a server from the NetWare Server list box, which shows all of the available NetWare servers.

5. In the Print Server list box, choose the printer object that you would like. These printer objects are the available printers as defined by the NetWare server that you chose in Step 4.

6. Adjust the polling interval for your print queue. Polling checks the print queue for waiting jobs at the interval you specify. To maximize print queue performance, set the polling to 15 seconds. To maximize local printer performance, change this setting to 3 minutes.

Installing the Microsoft Print Server for NetWare does not hinder your ability to print directly to your locally installed printer. You can still administer your local printer in the same way that you have in the past. This includes the ability to share your printer on the network.

Administrative control of the print queue is shared by both the Windows 98 machine and the NetWare server. Your administrative privileges depend on what the NetWare administrator has allowed. If the NetWare administrator has not given you any administrative privileges on the print queue, when you attempt to administer the queue using Windows 98, your administrative options will be grayed out.

Printer Configuration

You can modify a printer's configuration through its property sheet. To open a printer property sheet, navigate to the Printers folder and right-click on an installed printer. Choose Properties from the context menu. You will see a dialog box similar to the one shown in Figure 11.5. This dialog box has the following tabs (the exact contents of the tabs depend on the specific printer):

- **General:** Lists the printer's name and any comments that you would like to add. You can specify a separator page to be printed between print jobs and even send a test page to the printer.

- **Details:** Allows you to specify a printer location and the drivers. You can also change the configuration of the printer port and the settings for spooling of print jobs, as shown in Figure 11.5.

FIGURE 11.5

The Details tab

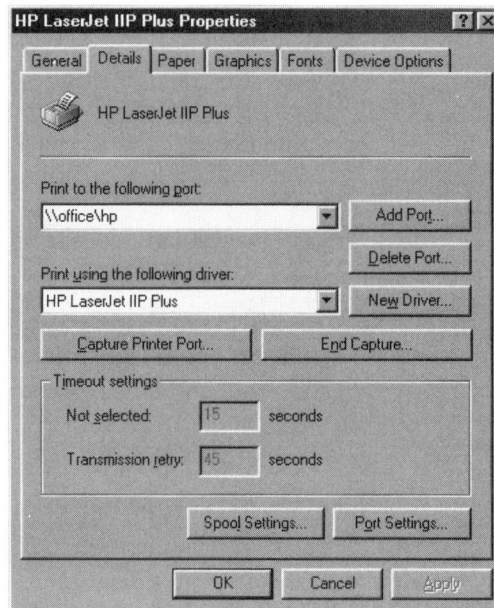

Additional settings displayed in this dialog box depend on the type of printer. You may have the following settings available:

- **Print To The Following Port:** Allows you to select a different port to send your printouts. This includes the ability to print to a file. The file will have a .PRN extension. To print this RAW file, simply COPY it to an LPT port on your local machine or save it to disk and print it on another computer. For example:

  ```
  COPY FOO.PRN LPT1
  ```

  Note that the file is in RAW format and will print only on a printer that uses the same minidrivers that were used to create the RAW file.

- **Print Using The Following Driver:** Allows you to select a different printer driver for this printer.

- **Add Port:** Allows you to specify a local port or a network port.

- **Delete Port:** Allows you to remove an existing port.

- **New Driver:** Allows you to implement a new printer driver.

- **Capture Printer Port:** Allows you to redirect printed output from an MS-DOS application to this printer.

- **End Capture:** Allows you to stop redirecting printed output from an MS-DOS application.

- **The Timeout Settings:** Allow you to specify wait times for Windows 98.

- **Not Selected:** Specifies how long Windows 98 will wait for this printer to come on-line before reporting error messages.

- **Transmission Retry:** Specifies how long Windows 98 will attempt to send data to a printer that is not responding before reporting an error message.

- **Spool Settings:** Allow you to specify how your print job will be spooled and whether or not to use RAW format or EMF. The spool settings will be covered a little later in this chapter.

- **Port Settings:** Allow you to specify any additional settings required for this port. In many cases, this option will display a message stating that there are no additional setting available for this port.

- **Paper:** Contains settings for paper size, orientation, paper source, and number of copies (see Figure 11.6). This tab may have an Advanced button, which offers advanced options, such as duplexing (printing on both sides of the paper).

F I G U R E   11.6

The Paper tab

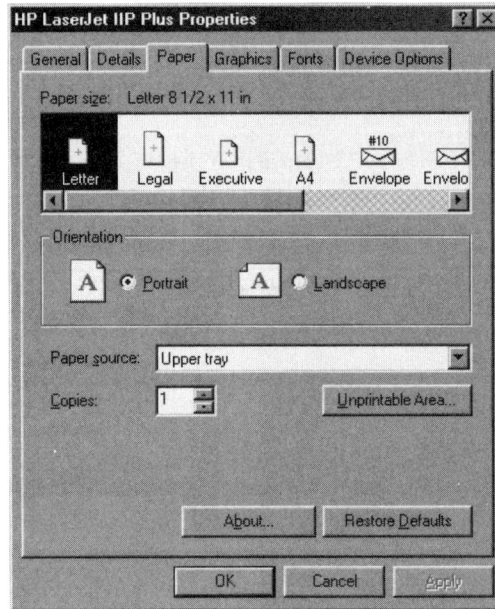

- **Graphics:** Allows you to modify detail or resolution described in dots per inch (dpi) as shown in Figure 11.7. High-quality printers print at a minimum of 600dpi. This tab may contain options for halftoning (which determines how graphics are rendered and printed), scaling, and mirroring. Color printers might have a setting for color calibration.

- **Fonts:** Determines how TrueType fonts are printed. Many PostScript printers print faster when the fonts used are native to the printer. (See Figure 11.8.)

  You have two options that will allow you to adjust how these fonts are used (other printers might have different or additional settings located here):

  - **Download TrueType Fonts As Bitmap Soft Fonts:** This is the default setting and is generally the fastest way to print your documents. If your document contains graphics or there are many different fonts on your document, you might be better off choosing the Print TrueType as graphics option.

F I G U R E 11.7

The Graphics tab

F I G U R E 11.8

The Fonts tab

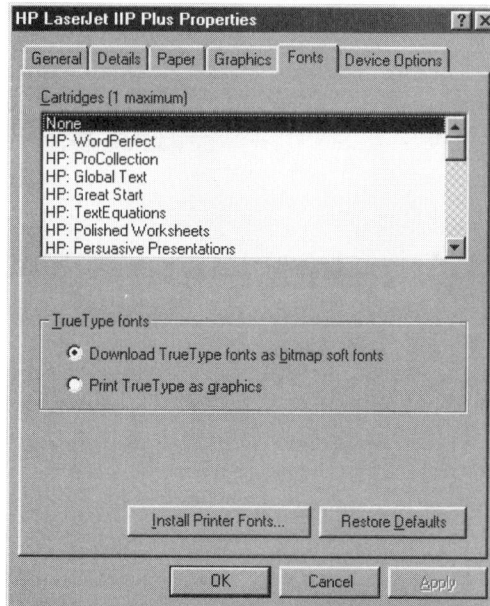

- **Print TrueType As Graphics:** This option may be quicker when you have many different fonts on your document or when your document contains graphics.

- **Device Options:** Contains settings that involve things like printer memory, installable fonts, and anything else that the manufacturer included in the minidriver for this printer (see Figure 11.9).

F I G U R E 11.9

The Device
Options tab

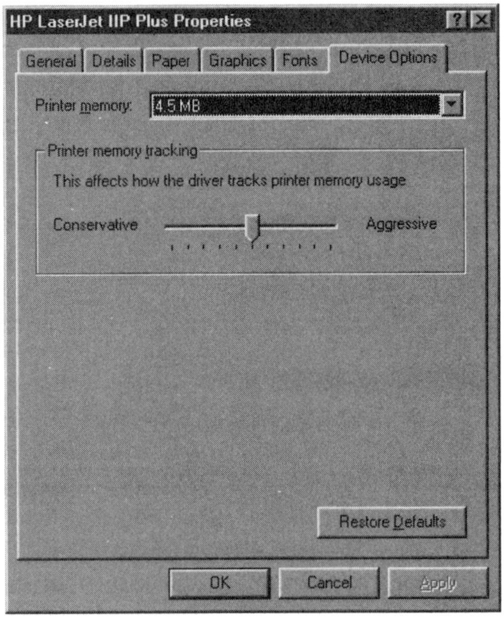

Printer Administration

All printer administration is handled through either the Printers folder or Windows Explorer. To manage a printer, you need to select it, and then right-click the printer to alter its properties or double-click the printer to manage the print queue as shown in Figure 11.10.

FIGURE 11.10

Print Queue window

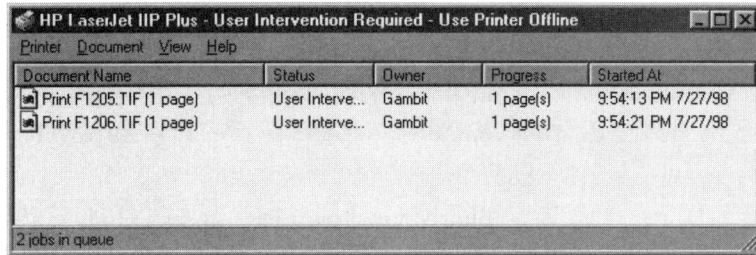

Printer administrative options vary depending on the location of the printer (network or local) and the options that the administrator of the printer allows you to have. For local printers, you can pause and resume print jobs, cancel any print job by deleting it from the list, add separator pages, work offline, or designate the default printer. You can also drag-and-drop print jobs within the Print Queue window to force a particular job to run sooner.

Your remote print queue management options are limited by the capabilities of the network operating system that you are using, the components installed, and your level of access to the print queue as specified by the network administrator. The following are the maximum network printer administrative capabilities:

- Pause current job

- View the queue

- Resume printing the current job

- Pause the entire queue

- Resume the entire queue

- Delete any or all jobs from the queue

Let's take a closer look at some of the additional printer enhancements and support that has been implemented in Windows 98.

Printing Enhancements

Several printing enhancements have been implemented in Windows 98. These include bidirectional printing support, ECP (extended capabilities port) support, spooler settings, and deferred printing.

Hardware Enahncements

Let's begin with a look at the enhancements made to the hardware. This includes the ability to utilitize bidirectional printing and ECPs.

Bidirectional printing allows your printer to give status information to your computer. For you to take advantage of bidirectional printing, you must have the following:

- Bidirectional parallel port set to bidirectional or PS/2 mode

- IEEE 1284-compliant printer cable

- Bidirectional printer

If you have all of these items, you can enable bidirectional printing on your computer by following the steps listed in Exercise 11.6.

EXERCISE 11.6

Enabling Bidirectional Printing

1. Open the Printers folder by selecting Start ➢ Settings ➢ Printers.

2. Right-click the icon of the printer with which you want to work. Choose Properties from the context menu.

3. Click the Details tab.

4. Click the Spool Settings button.

5. Click Enable bidirectional support for this printer.

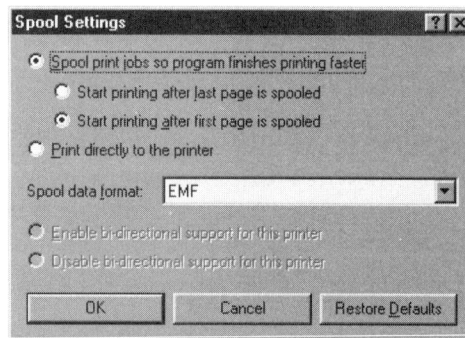

Extended capabilities ports allow improved I/O performance for ECP-compliant devices that are attached to it. You can connect both ECP and non-ECP devices to an ECP port. To take full advantage of the increased I/O performance of ECP, you must use an IEEE 1284-compliant cable. Because we are talking about printers here, an ECP-compliant printer will also add some additional efficiency. ECP ports are automatically configured in the BIOS of your system. If your BIOS recognized your ECP port but didn't enable it, you can follow the steps outlined in Exercise 11.7 to do so yourself.

EXERCISE 11.7

Enabling an ECP Port

1. Start the Device Manager, using any of several methods. You can use the System icon in the Control Panel, or you may prefer to right-click the My Computer icon and choose Properties.

2. Double-click Ports (COM & LPT).

3. Select the ECP device and open its properties.

4. Make changes to the IRQ, DMA channel, and I/O range.

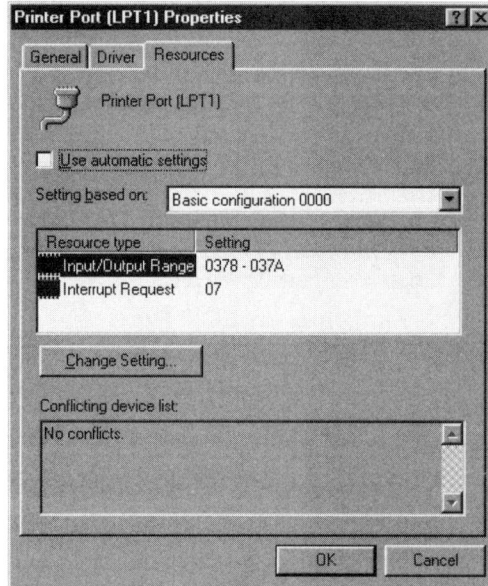

5. Close the property pages and the Device Manager.

6. You must restart the computer for these changes to take effect.

Spooler Options

The *spooling* options allow you to control the speed at which control returns to your program once spooling and printing begins. Figure 11.11 shows the spooling options available in Windows 98. To get to this screen, right-click on a printer from the Printers folder and choose properties. Select the Details tab and then click the Spool Settings button.

The Spool Print Jobs So Program Finishes Printing Faster option includes:

- **Start Printing After First Page Is Spooled:** This is the default setting, and it begins the printing process after the first page has spooled to disk. That page then despools to the printer and begins printing. This option uses less hard disk space, but your program will have to wait a little longer to have control passed back to it.

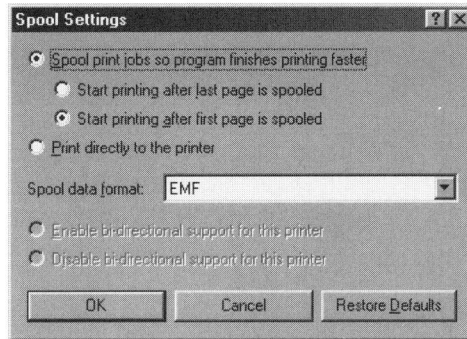

FIGURE 11.11

Spooler options

- **Start Printing After Last Page Has Spooled:** This option waits until the entire document has been spooled to hard disk before it begins the printing process. This takes up more hard disk space, but control is returned to your application more quickly.

- **Spooling Format:** This option allows you to specify whether or not you are spooling RAW files or EMF files. EMF files spool and print more quickly; however, RAW files may be required for certain types of printers.

The other option is Print Directly To The Printer. When this option is invoked, spooling is disabled. In other words, the print job is sent directly to the printer and control is not passed back to your application until the print job completes. The upside is that the document may print a bit more quickly.

Deferred Printing

Windows 98 allows you to *defer* printing until a later time. This feature can be useful if you are working with a laptop and are not currently connected to a network printer or to your docking station. This can also be useful if your printer is not available at the current time. When a printer is unavailable, its icon will be lightly shaded when viewed in the Printers folder.

Deferred printing files will be stored in the spooler directories until the printer is reattached. At that time, you can re-enable printing and send the deferred jobs to the printer.

When you are using a laptop computer, deferred printing is turned on automatically. When the laptop is docked or otherwise reconnected to the printer, you will be notified that deferred print jobs are waiting.

You can manually configure deferred printing by opening the print queue for a particular printer and then selecting Work Offline from the File menu. To open the print queue, double-click the printer icon in your Printers folder.

Troubleshooting Windows 98 Printing Problems

Microsoft ✓ *Exam Objective*

Diagnose and resolve printing problems in a Microsoft environment and a mixed Microsoft and NetWare environment.

The following steps can help you troubleshoot printing problems in Windows 98.

1. Check the cable connections between the printer and the computer.

2. Verify that you have the correct printer configuration settings.

3. Verify that you have installed the correct printer driver and it is configured properly.

TIP

When dealing with printer driver problems, it may be simplest to reinstall the printer driver.

4. Verify that enough hard disk space is available to generate your print jobs. Remember that print jobs get spooled to your \Windows\Spool directories.

5. Try printing from other programs in Windows 98. This will let you know whether the printer is causing the problem or if it is the program.

6. Try printing your output to a file and then copying that file to a printer port. This can be done by dragging-and-dropping the file on the printer icon, or from an MS-DOS prompt by typing **Copy** *filename* **LPT1**. If this works, your problem is with the spooler or data transmission. If it doesn't work, your problem is with the program or a printer driver.

Administrative Dos and Don'ts

Here is a short list of useful administrative hints:

- Create shortcuts for your printers on your desktop and use them for quick access to printer management, print queue management, and for drag-and-drop printing.

- If you have a printer that supports multiple configurations (PostScript and non-PostScript), add one printer with one configuration and add another with the same hardware settings, but a different configuration.

- If your printer supports ECP or bidirectional printing, take advantage of these higher-speed printing options.

- When your printer is configured and working properly, make a record of the printer settings and driver information.

Summary

In this chapter, you studied many printing-related issues. You began with the new printing features in Windows 98. Then you learned about the modular approach that Windows 98 takes to the printing architecture. The interchangeable components allow third-party developers to concentrate on building their printers, not on the code necessary to make those printers available on a particular network or platform.

Next, you reviewed the steps in the printing process. Then you got down to the business of installing printers. Local printers can be installed automatically if they are Plug-and-Play devices. Otherwise, you can use the Add Printer Wizard (accessed through the Printers folder) to install a local printer manually. A new Windows 98 feature, Point-and-Print, supports drag-and-drop printing and installation for network printers. Point-and-Print installations differ for Windows 98, Windows NT, and Novell NetWare servers

Printer configuration was another area of interest. Properly configuring printers is a relatively simple task, but one that might be beyond the ability of the users you support. Remember that you can take advantage of hardware enhancements like ECP and bidirectional printing. You can also set your spooling options to return control to your program more quickly. You learned how to defer printing until the printer becomes available. You also reviewed queue management and administration. You finished the chapter with some real-world troubleshooting techniques that have been found to be the most effective.

Review Questions

1. You have 30 Windows 98 computers installed on your network. You have an HP LaserJet IIP Plus printer attached to your local Windows 98 computer. You have shared this printer with others on the network. How can you check the status of your print queue in Windows 98? Choose all that apply.

   A. Select Start ➤ Run ➤ CheckQueue.

   B. Double-click the printer icon in the system tray.

   C. Go to the Printers folder, find your printer, and double-click it.

   D. Both A and C.

2. Windows 98 supports several methods to reference your shared resources in a networked environment. You browse the network and install the HPLaserJet printer located on the Frogger computer to your local PC. Once you have installed this Point-and-Print printer on your Desktop, how does Windows 98 reference the networked printer?

   A. Using a mapped drive letter (for example, P:)

   B. Using mapped ports (for example, LPT2:)

   C. Using a special printer reference tool (for example, MyPrinter)

   D. Using the UNC name (for example, "\\Frogger\HPPrinter")

3. Windows 98 allows several different methods for you to install a networked printer on your machine. Which of the following should you do to *install* and *configure* a printer from a Windows 98 machine? Choose all that apply.

   A. Browse the network until you find the shared printer, and then double-click its icon. Do nothing else. All options will be inherited.

   B. Browse the network until you find the shared printer, and then double-click its icon. You will then have to create new configuration options because they will not be inherited.

   C. Drag-and-drop the shared printer icon. Do nothing else. All options will be inherited.

   D. Drag-and-drop the shared printer icon, and then make your configuration changes because options will not be inherited.

4. Windows 98 allows several different methods for you to install a networked printer on your machine. When you install a Point-and-Print printer from a Windows NT server, which of the following must be true?

   A. The NT machine will download the files as well as the current printer configurations.

   B. The NT machine will download the files, but they will not have the current configuration information.

   C. The NT machine will not download the files. You must manually drag-and-drop the files and then set the configurations.

   D. The NT machine will not download the files. You must manually drag-and-drop the files. The files will have the current configuration.

5. Novell does not support Point-and-Print printers by default. You are working on a Windows 98 computer that is using a Novell server for login validation. Which of the following is true about setting up Novell for Point-and-Print? Choose all that apply.

   A. You must have a bindery or NDS tree.

   B. You must be the Supervisor or equivalent.

   C. You must copy the file to the location specified by the bindery or the NDS Root object that you altered.

   D. Clients must have read permissions on the directory where the files are stored.

6. In order for Windows 98 to actually take advantage of Point-and-Print, Windows 98 needs some information. Which of the following are required to set up a printer for Point-and-Print? Choose all that apply.

   A. The printer manufacturer's name and printer model

   B. The network that you are using

   C. The driver names

   D. The driver locations

7. What is the maximum number of printers Windows 98 can support?

　A. 1

　B. 2

　C. 6 (LPT1, LPT2, COM1–COM4)

　D. There is no predefined maximum

8. You have a printer attached to your Windows 98 machine, and it is shared across your Microsoft Windows NT network. You want to install a second printer on your computer and share that one as well. Which of the following is the best solution?

　A. Add a second parallel card to your computer. The BIOS will recognize it as LPT2, and you can now attach a second printer to your system.

　B. Use one of the SCSI adapters already on your computer and purchase a printer that can use the SCSI cable for support rather than a parallel port.

　C. If your computer supports infrared, just place a new infrared enabled printer in the computer's line of sight.

　D. Add a new parallel card to your computer that supports the ECP standard. Connect a printer that supports ECP to the new parallel port.

9. Which of the following should you check if your printer is not printing? Choose all that apply.

　A. The amount of hard disk on the computer

　B. The cable connections

　C. Whether the printer is on

　D. The \Windows\Spools directory to be sure that print jobs are being spooled properly

10. A user complains that his print jobs come out at the wrong printer if he forgets to change the printer before he prints a job. What can you do to fix it?

   A. Set the printer to offline.

   B. Change the printer device type.

   C. Change the default printer to the one he prints to most often.

   D. Install a new local printer on his computer and set it to offline.

11. Your printer is sending you a message that it is low on toner. You have printed the first 60 pages of a 200-page document and don't want to rerun the entire print job. You decide to cancel the print job and then resubmit the print job from your application, beginning with page 60. How would you rate this solution?

   A. This is an excellent solution and will work.

   B. This is a good solution and will work.

   C. This is a poor solution, but it appears to work.

   D. This is a poor solution and will not work.

12. When you turn on your printer, it takes about five minutes to finish its warm up routines before it comes online. Print jobs that were submitted receive error messages. Which of the following is the best choice to alleviate this problem?

   A. Set the printer to Offline and use deferred printing.

   B. Increase the timeout settings in the Details tab of the printer's property sheets.

   C. Change the default printer to a printer other than this one.

   D. Change the spool settings to print directly to the printer in RAW format.

13. Which of the following must you have to take advantage of ECP printing in Windows 98? Choose all that apply.

   A. ECP-compliant printer

   B. IEEE 1284-compliant cable

   C. ECP card in your computer

   D. ECP enabled

14. You are low on disk space and have a large document that needs to be printed. What can you do to ensure that the document will print properly and will not generate spooling errors? Choose the best answer.

   A. Set the spooler options to print after the first page has spooled.

   B. Set the spooler options to print after the last page has spooled.

   C. Set the spooler options to print directly to the printer.

   D. You don't have to do anything. It will print normally.

CHAPTER

12

User Profiles

Windows 98 was designed to be able to track individual preferences and settings. These preferences and settings are stored in a *user profile*. Profiles can track things such as wallpaper, Desktop, persistent network connections, shortcuts, and other various settings a user can choose.

Microsoft ✓ *Exam* *Objective*

Develop a security strategy in a Microsoft environment or a mixed Microsoft and NetWare environment. Strategies include:

- System policies
- User profiles
- File and printer sharing
- Share-level access control or user-level access control

> **NOTE** System policies are discussed in Chapter 13. File and printer sharing and share-level and user-level access control are discussed in Chapter 10.

This chapter describes how to enable local user profiles for the local computer and roaming user profiles for networks. It also offers some suggestions for troubleshooting problems with user profiles.

Understanding User Profiles

As you learned in Chapter 5, system settings are held in the SYSTEM.DAT file, and user settings are held in the USER.DAT file. Windows 98 creates user profiles by making a unique USER.DAT file for each user of the system and by making a personal folder for each user. This folder contains personal shortcuts, document history, and Start menu settings.

There are two types of user profiles:

- **Local profiles:** These profiles are stored only on the local computer. If a user logs on to one computer, makes changes to the environment, and then logs on to another computer, the changes from the first computer are not reflected on the second computer.

- **Roaming profiles:** These profiles are stored on either a NetWare or Microsoft NT server. When a user logs on to the server, that user's profile is downloaded to his or her computer. When the user logs off, any changes are then saved back to the copy on the server. When the user logs on to a different computer, the profile (and any changes) are downloaded to the new local computer again.

Enabling Local Profiles

User profiles are not enabled by default. Everyone uses the same settings on a computer until profiles are enabled. Once profiles are enabled, everyone on that computer will be asked to log in, so that Windows 98 will know who the user is and can load the appropriate profile.

The user will be prompted the first time he or she logs in and a profile is not found. If the user chooses not to create a profile, the default profile will be used.

Microsoft
✓ *Exam*
Objective

Set up user environments by using user profiles and system policies.

System policies are discussed in Chapter 13.

You can enable user profiles from the User Profiles tab of the Password applet, shown in Figure 12.1. The first two options disable or enable profiles:

- **All users of this computer use the same preferences and desktop settings:** This is the default option. Windows 98 uses the same settings for everyone. Choose this option to turn off profiles.

- **Users can customize their preferences and desktop settings. Windows switches to your personal settings when you log on:** Choose this option to enable profiles. You need to restart Windows 98 after you select this option to have profiles take effect.

F I G U R E   12.1

Enabling user profiles through the User Profiles tab of the Password applet

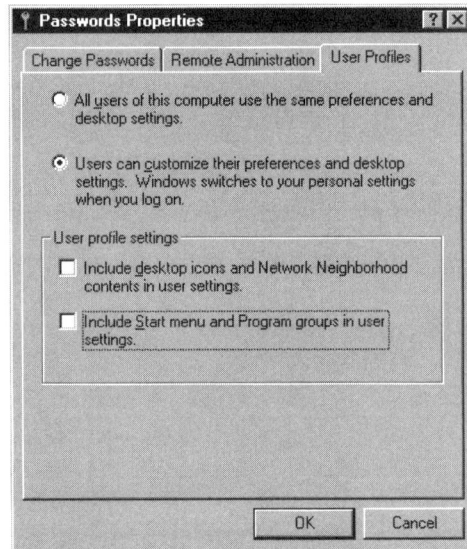

Profiles always contain the USER.DAT file, with unique user Registry settings. In addition to those settings, you can choose the following options in the User Profiles tab of the Password applet:

- **Include desktop icons and Network Neighborhood contents in user settings:** Choose this setting to create folders called Desktop, Recent, and NetHood under the user's unique profile folder. The Desktop folder contains shortcuts from the common Desktop, and it changes the common Desktop to a unique one for each user. The Recent folder keeps track of the documents the user has recently opened. The Net-Hood folder contains any network shortcuts.

> **WARNING** Folders and files stored on the original Desktop are not included in profiles once profiles are enabled. If you store folders or files on the Desktop, you should move them to a different folder and create shortcuts to the folder. By doing so, you can still see the files and folders when profiles are enabled. If you are a roaming user, these folders and files need to be stored on the network server in your home directory. When you log on from another machine, these folders and files will not be available for your use if you leave them on a local hard drive.

- **Include Start menu and program groups in user settings:** Choose this setting to create a folder called "Start Menu" under the user's unique profile folder. This folder is used as the Start menu for the user, instead of the common one found under <Windows Root>\Start Menu. Note that applications installed when saving the Start menu in profiles will be available only to the user who installed the program, because that user is the only one who will have the program group and icon in his or her unique Start Menu folder.

In Exercise 12.1, you will enable user profiles and log in as two different users with different settings.

> **NOTE** In Exercise 12.1, you will make new shortcuts on the Desktop, change the wallpaper and color scheme, and add an item to the Start menu. See Bob Cowart's *Mastering Windows 98* (Sybex, 1998) if you need a refresher on performing these tasks.

EXERCISE 12.1

Enabling Local Profiles

1. Go to Control Panel ➤ Passwords.

2. Go to the User Profiles tab.

3. Choose Users can customize their preferences and desktop settings.

EXERCISE 12.1 (CONTINUED)

4. Choose the "Include Desktop Icons..." option.

5. Choose the "Include Start Menu..." option.

6. Choose OK.

7. Restart Windows 98.

8. Log in as yourself. Use a blank password.

9. Answer Yes when prompted if you want to save a profile.

10. Make two new shortcuts on the Desktop.

11. Change your wallpaper and color scheme.

12. Add an item to the Start menu.

13. Select Start ➣ Log Off (your logged in username).

14. Choose Yes, and then log back in as "Bigfoot."

15. Check to see if your changes are present (they shouldn't be).

16. Log out as Bigfoot and log back in as yourself. Your changes should now be there.

If you want to disable user profiles, return to the User Profiles tab of the Password applet and choose "All users of this computer use the same preferences and desktop settings", and then restart Windows 98.

How Profiles Work

Before you enable profiles, user configurations are stored in the USER.DAT file, and in the Desktop, Start Menu, Recent, and NetHood folders located in the root of the Windows installation folder. User settings in the Registry are held in the USER.DAT file, which makes up the Hkey_Current_User key.

After you enable profiles, Windows 98 will create a Profiles folder and hold settings for each user in a folder named after that user. A unique copy of USER.DAT will be saved in the user's folder as well. Figure 12.2 shows an example of a user's folder within the Profiles folder. (Note that USER.DAT is a hidden file.)

F I G U R E   12.2

Storing the USER.DAT
file in the local profile

The various files and folders are:

- **Application Data:** Holds software and user-specific settings

- **Cookies:** Holds Internet browser cookies (files that track the status and history of certain WWW pages)

- **Desktop:** Holds files and shortcuts contained on the Desktop

- **History:** Holds browser history files

- **NetHood:** Holds Network Neighborhood custom icons and shortcuts

- **Recent:** Holds shortcuts to the most recently used documents

- **Start Menu:** Holds the personalized Start Menu folders and shortcuts

- **StartUp:** Holds shortcuts placed in the Startup folder

- **USER.DAT:** Holds the unique Registry settings for the user

Enabling Roaming Profiles

User profiles are *local* when they are created (i.e., they reside on the local hard drive). You can enable *roaming profiles* by configuring profiles to reside on a server, making the user profile available to the user no matter from which computer that user logs in.

Roaming profiles are stored on a central server and are loaded into the workstation to which a user is currently logged. You can enable roaming user profiles on Windows NT and NetWare servers.

> A user profile can be changed so that it is read-only; that is, the profile can be used by a user, but no changes are allowed. This is called a *mandatory profile* and is discussed later. Mandatory profiles work only with roaming user profiles.

Roaming Profiles on an NT Server

Roaming profiles are held in the NT server's home folder. When a user logs in to an NT domain and profiles are enabled, Windows 98 will ask the user if he or she would like to enable profiles. If the user answers No, the default profile will be used for that user. If the user answers Yes, Windows 98 will do one of four things:

- If Windows 98 can't find a profile for the user, the default profile is copied into the user's profile.

- If there is a profile both locally and on the server, Windows 98 compares the date and time of the profiles and loads the most recent one.

- If there is no profile on the server but there is one locally, the local profile will be used and then saved to the server when the user logs out.

- If there is a profile on the server but not one locally, Windows 98 copies the profile from the server to the local computer.

> Profiles are unique for each operating system. Profiles from Windows 98 and Windows NT (all versions) are not compatible. Any changes made to one will not be reflected if the user logs in from another type of operating system.

Follow the steps in Exercise 12.2 to enable user profiles on an NT server.

Enabling Roaming Profiles on an NT Server

1. Enable user profiles through the User Profiles tab of the Password applet (see Exercise 12.1).

2. Synchronize the clocks of the client and server. You can put the following command into the logon script to synchronize the workstation clock to the server:

   Net Time *Server* /set /y

   (In place of server, substitute the name of the server with which you want to synchronize the clock.)

   Alternatively, you could use a time synchronization program to keep the workstation clock in sync with the server.

3. Make sure you are using a 32-bit client. The Client for Microsoft Networks is a 32-bit client, and it works when roaming profiles are in use.

4. Make the Microsoft client the primary network logon. In the Network Control Panel, the Client for Microsoft Networks needs to be selected for the Primary Network Logon option for the Windows 98 client.

5. Assign the user a home directory on the NT server. In NT's User Manager, choose Properties ➢ Profile. Choose a drive letter and enter the UNC to the path, as shown in the following example.

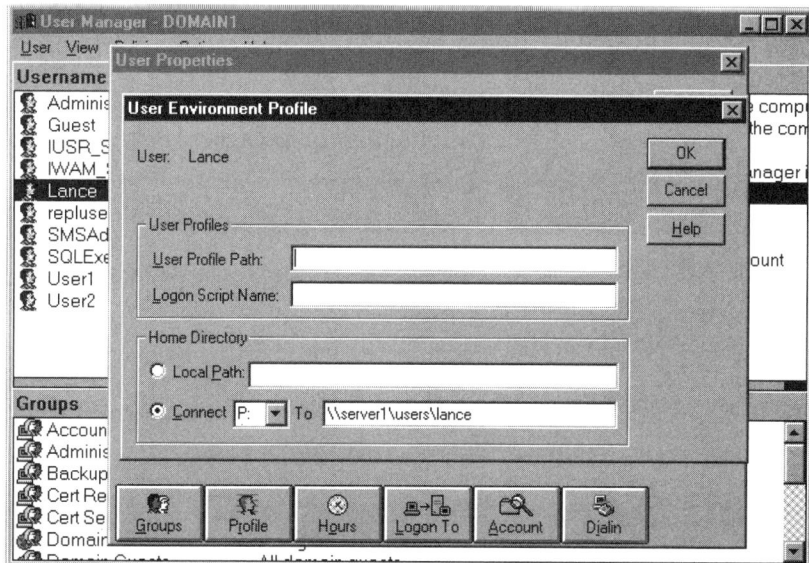

The easiest way to organize your home directories is to make a folder called "Users" on the NT server, share the folder, and create home folders beneath, as shown here.

If you are using NTFS security on your volume and you use User Manager to create the home folders, NT will create the home folder and it will assign rights only to that user.

After you enable roaming profiles, the user's home directory on the NT server should look something like the example shown in Figure 12.3. If the home directory does not contain the profile, either the home directory hasn't been assigned correctly or profiles haven't been enabled correctly.

FIGURE 12.3

Roaming profiles stored on the NT server

Roaming Profiles on a NetWare Server

If you have NetWare servers as your main servers, you can enable the NetWare servers to store user profiles. On a NetWare server, roaming profiles are stored in the Mail\User_Id directory on Bindery servers (NetWare 2.*x*, 3.*x*,) or in the user's home folder on NDS servers (NetWare 4.*x*, 5.*x*).

The procedure is essentially the same as the one for enabling roaming profiles on an NT server (see Exercise 12.2):

- Enable profiles through the Password applet, User Profiles tab (see Exercise 12.1).

- Synchronize the clocks of the client and server.

- Make sure you are using a 32-bit client.

- Make the NetWare client the primary network logon.

- Make sure the user has a directory under the Mail directory that corresponds to his or her ID number for NetWare 2.*x* and 3.*x* servers.

- Make sure a home folder has been assigned to the user for NetWare 4.*x* and 5.*x* servers.

- Make sure the NetWare server supports long filenames (the default on NetWare 4.11 and 5.*x*).

When Windows 98 looks for a profile from a NetWare server, it compares date and time stamps and loads the most recent one (much as it does on an NT server).

Disabling Roaming Profiles

If the Windows 98 computer is on a network, roaming profiles are automatically used. To disable roaming profiles, go to the Registry and add a new value. Go to the Hkey_Local_Machine\Network\Logon key and add a DWORD value called "UseHomeDirectory" with a value of 0 (see Figure 12.4).

FIGURE 12.4

Disabling roaming
profiles

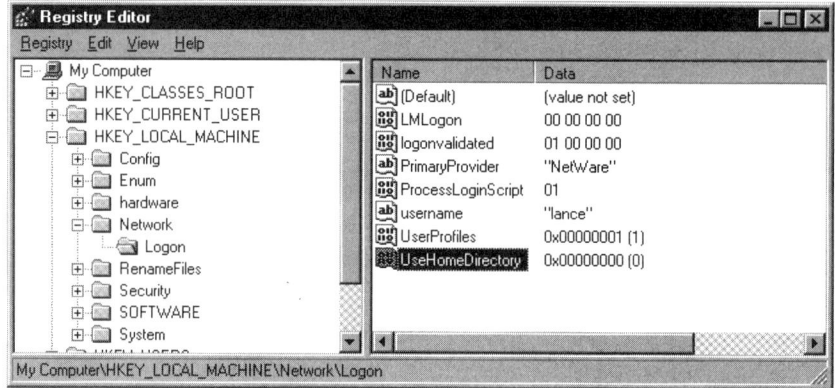

```
Registry Editor
Registry  Edit  View  Help
My Computer                              Name              Data
  HKEY_CLASSES_ROOT                     (Default)          (value not set)
  HKEY_CURRENT_USER                     LMLogon            00 00 00 00
  HKEY_LOCAL_MACHINE                    logonvalidated     01 00 00 00
      Config                            PrimaryProvider    "NetWare"
      Enum                              ProcessLoginScript 01
      hardware                          username           "lance"
      Network                           UserProfiles       0x00000001 (1)
          Logon                         UseHomeDirectory   0x00000000 (0)
      RenameFiles
      Security
      SOFTWARE
      System
My Computer\HKEY_LOCAL_MACHINE\Network\Logon
```

Mandatory Profiles

Mandatory profiles allow a single group of settings to be used for multiple users, with the users unable to save changes to the profile. To make mandatory profiles work, perform the following steps.

1. Enable profiles normally.

2. Copy the desired profile folders to the selected user's home directory on the network.

3. Rename the USER.DAT file to USER.MAN.

4. Change the attributes of USER.MAN to Read Only.

Although users can still make changes to their session (unless restricted via a System Policy, as detailed in Chapter 13) the changes will not be saved to the profile stored on the server.

Installing the Microsoft Family Logon

One of the problems people (especially children) have when using profiles is remembering exactly what logon names they used. Windows 98 has a new feature called Microsoft Family Logon that, after installed, lists all of the profiles held on the computer, making selection easy.

To install Microsoft Family Logon, go to Control Panel ➢ Network ➢ Add ➢ Client ➢ Microsoft and choose Microsoft Family Logon (see Figure 12.5). Select the Microsoft Family Logon as the Primary Network Logon as shown in Figure 12.6. Click OK and reboot to finish the installation.

F I G U R E 12.5

Installing Microsoft Family Logon

F I G U R E 12.6

Selecting the Microsoft Family Logon as the Primary Network Logon

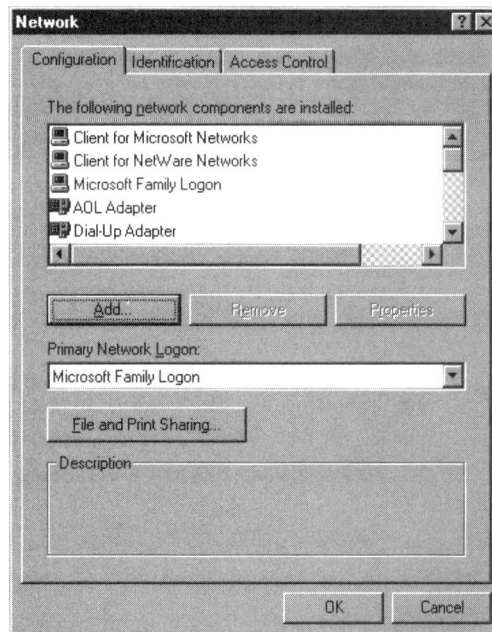

After rebooting, a list of all installed profiles will be presented, allowing you to easily pick from an existing profile (you should create the separate profiles before selecting Microsoft Family Logon as the Primary Network Logon).

> **NOTE** The Microsoft Family Logon is a wonderful addition for Windows 98 at home, but it is not a very good feature for Windows 98 at work. Choosing the Microsoft Family Logon displays all available profiles, and it also disables roaming profiles.

Troubleshooting User Profiles

If user profiles are not working correctly, here are some steps to take to see where the problem lies:

- Check to make sure profiles are enabled on the workstation.

- Check to make sure the appropriate client is picked as the default.

- Check the date/time/time zone of the workstation and server. Incorrect time zone settings are a major source of time synchronization problems under both Windows 98 and Windows NT.

- Check the NT server to ensure home directories have been assigned.

- Check the NetWare server for Mail\User_Id directories.

- Check the directories on the NT server for the folders and files to see if profiles are being saved to the server.

> **WARNING** If a user is logged on to more than one computer, when they log off from the first computer, the profile will be saved to the server. Changes made at this logoff are then lost when the user logs off from the second computer (and the profile is once again saved to the server).

- Any Briefcases that were created prior to enabling profiles will need to be re-created, because the links in the Briefcase are not updated to reflect the profile.

- Programs that do not record their information in the Registry (such as 16-bit programs) will probably record their information in the WIN.INI or another INI file.

Summary

Windows 98 stores settings and preferences in a profile. By default, all users on the same computer use the same profile. Windows 98 has the ability to track individual profiles for different users, so preferences and settings can be maintained by multiple users of a computer. You can enable user profiles (they are not enabled by default) through the Password applet, User Profiles tab.

Local profiles are stored on the local computer, and they don't follow the user around. Local profiles are held in the <Windows Root>\Profiles folder.

Roaming profiles are stored on a central server and are loaded into the current workstation a user logs on to. To enable roaming profiles, you must be using a 32-bit client (such as the Client for Microsoft Networks or the Client for NetWare Networks), and that client must be selected as the Windows 98 client's primary network logon. Roaming profiles are held in the home folder of an NT server, or in the Mail\User_Id directory of a NetWare server.

Profiles from Windows 98 and Windows NT are not compatible. You will need to create profiles for each if you log in to both of them.

Review Questions

1. To make profiles work, a unique copy of which Registry file is saved?

   A. REG.DAT

   B. REGISTRY.OUT

   C. SYSTEM.DAT

   D. USER.DAT

2. Roaming profiles (with all options) are enabled. You are logged in at two computers. You add a shortcut to your Desktop and log out from the first computer. You log out of the second computer. You log in at the first, but your shortcut isn't there. Why?

   A. Your local profile is not enabled.

   B. The profile from the second computer overwrote the profile from the first.

   C. The roaming profile is cached and isn't available for immediate loading.

   D. Profiles don't track shortcuts.

3. Which of the following is required to enable roaming profiles on an NT server? Choose all that apply.

   A. Users must have a home folder.

   B. Users must use TCP/IP.

   C. Usernames must be eight characters or less.

   D. The Client for Microsoft Networks must be the default logon.

4. Roaming profiles (with all options) are enabled. Profiles are being saved locally. They are present on the Windows NT server, but after a user logs into the domain, the profile does not always work. You set up profiles using Windows 98, but you also have Windows NT workstations in your company. What could be the cause? Choose all that apply.

   A. The time on the problematic workstations is ahead of the time of the server.

   B. The problematic workstations are not using the same protocol as the server.

   C. The problematic workstations don't have profiles enabled.

   D. The problematic workstations are NT workstations.

5. You want the local profile to include the Start menu but not the Desktop. Is that possible? If so, which option do you pick?

   A. Yes, enable profiles normally (with no options picked).

   B. Yes, enable profiles with the "Include Desktop Icons..." option.

   C. Yes, enable profiles with the "Include Start Menu..." option.

   D. No, this is not possible.

6. If you are using a Windows 98 client and Windows 98 is installed in the C:\Windows folder, where are roaming profiles stored on a NetWare 3.12 network?

   A. On the local computer, in the C:\Windows folder

   B. On the local computer, in the C:\Windows\System32 folder

   C. On the NetWare server, in the Public folder

   D. On the NetWare server, in the \Mail\Userid folder

7. How do you make a mandatory profile?

   A. Create a new group called "Mandatory" and assign the user to the group.

   B. Check the box "Create Mandatory Profile" when initially creating the profile.

   C. Set USER.DAT to hidden.

   D. Rename the USER.DAT to USER.MAN

8. What is required to enable roaming profiles on a NetWare 3.12 server? Choose all that apply.

   A. The IPX/SPX protocol

   B. Microsoft Client for NetWare

   C. Default Login set to Microsoft Client for NetWare

   D. Profiles enabled on the Windows 98 client

9. When can the same roaming profile be used on Windows NT workstations and Windows 98 clients?

   A. Never, they are incompatible.

   B. If you rename the profile to USER.NT, it will also work for Windows NT.

   C. If you place the profile in the NETLOGON share, both operating systems can use it.

   D. If you check the box "Create NT Compatible Profile" when initially setting up the profile.

10. How can you disable a person's ability to enable or disable profiles?

   A. Set the security on the profile to Administrators Only.

   B. Edit the Registry and add the Admin Edit Only value.

   C. Create a system policy that blocks normal users from the Password applet.

   D. Create a system policy that blocks normal users from the Profile applet.

CHAPTER

13

System Policies

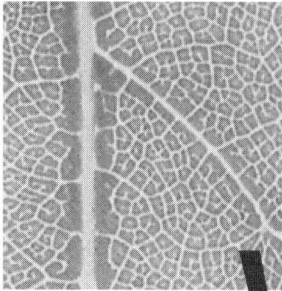

Windows 98 allows you to decide on a set of restrictions that your users must adhere to, and it gives you the power to enforce those via *system policies*. By enabling system policies, you can decide what is or is not allowed on a computer and what various users can do.

Microsoft Exam Objective	Develop a security strategy in a Microsoft environment and a mixed Microsoft and NetWare environment. Strategies include:
	• System policies
	• User profiles
	• File and printer sharing
	• Share-level access control or user-level access control

NOTE User profiles are discussed in Chapter 12. File and printer sharing and share-level and user-level access control are discussed in Chapter 10.

System policies allow network administrators to define guidelines that protect local or network resources based on restrictions defined in the policy. System policies work by selectively editing the Registry when a user logs in. Policies can be based on specific users, groups, and computers, or generic policies can be created that affect all users or computers.

You create policies through the System Policy Editor administration tool. In this editor, you load a template, make the desired changes, and then save the template as a policy file. This chapter describes how to install the System

Policy Editor and support for group policies; create policies for groups, users, and computers; and use the System Policy Editor to edit the Registry directly.

The System Policy Editor can be run in two basic modes:

- **Policy file mode:** In this mode, policies are saved to a file, which is later loaded by Windows 98 at startup in order to enforce the restrictions you have built via the policy file.

- **Registry edit mode:** In this mode, the (local or a remote) Registry is directly edited, but edits can only take place as the loaded policy template allows.

> **NOTE** Microsoft is emphasizing its new Zero Administration Initiative for Windows (ZAW), which is a system methodology that will heavily rely on implementing system policies in order to prevent users from changing their configurations (thereby requiring administration).

Understanding Policies and Templates

System policies are simply an automated way to enforce certain restrictions on certain users or computers. System policies work by selectively editing the Registry when a user logs in. You can set policies that not only restrict the user when he or she logs in, but that also restrict the user from making changes during their session by not allowing the Registry Editor to be run.

Two types of files are used in creating system policies:

- **Template (.ADM) files:** ASCII files that are filled in and modified

- **Policy (.POL) files:** The files that template files are saved as, which are read by Windows 98

Template files can be thought of as source code (which can be changed and added to), and the policy files can be looked at as compiled code (which is loaded and executed on a computer). When the policies are read and applied by Windows 98, they edit the Registry to enforce one or more restrictions. Figure 13.1 shows how the two types of files are used, and Figure 13.2 illustrates how Windows 98 processes policy files.

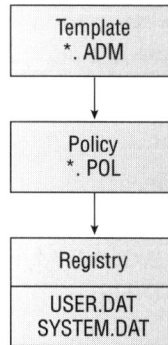

```
         ┌──────────────┐
         │   Template   │
         │   *. ADM     │
         └──────┬───────┘
                │
                ▼
         ┌──────────────┐
         │   Policy     │
         │   *. POL     │
         └──────┬───────┘
                │
                ▼
         ┌──────────────┐
         │   Registry   │
         ├──────────────┤
         │  USER.DAT    │
         │  SYSTEM.DAT  │
         └──────────────┘
```

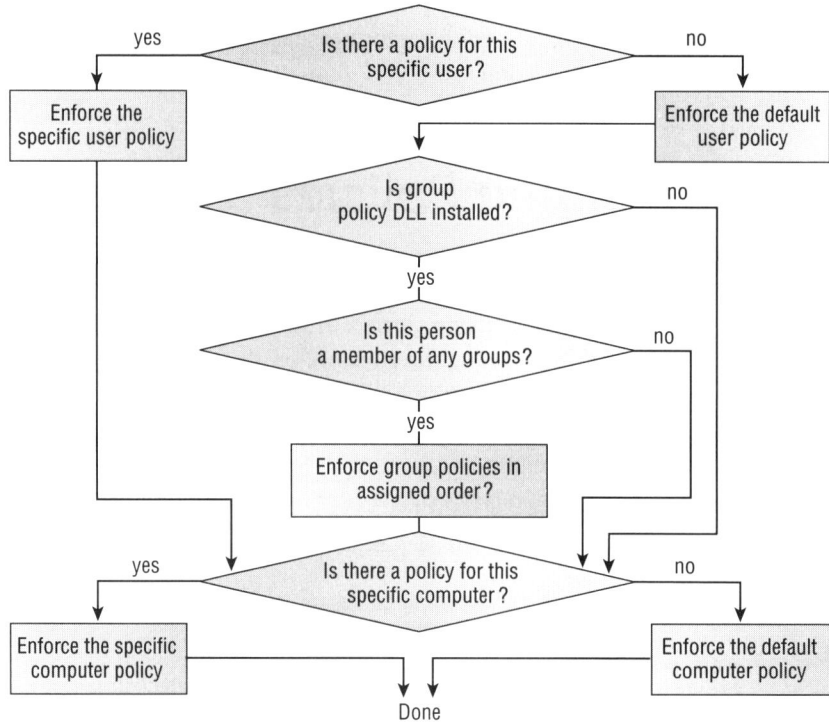

Is there a policy for this specific user?
- yes → Enforce the specific user policy
- no → Enforce the default user policy

Is group policy DLL installed?
- no
- yes

Is this person a member of any groups?
- no
- yes → Enforce group policies in assigned order?

Is there a policy for this specific computer?
- yes → Enforce the specific computer policy
- no → Enforce the default computer policy

Done

Creating Policies

Microsoft supplies templates that allow you to easily set up policies for your network. As with many network functions, creating policies is much easier if you have spent the time to plan which policies you want to implement.

Microsoft Exam Objective

Set up user environments by using user profiles and system policies.

> **NOTE**
>
> User profiles are discussed in Chapter 13.

The process for creating policies involves loading a template, modifying it to suit your needs, and saving it so Windows 98 can find it. This process can be broken down into the following steps:

- Enable user profiles.

> **NOTE**
>
> User profiles must be enabled (through the User Profiles tab of the Passwords Control Panel) before any restrictions based on Users (Default User or specific user settings) can be used. For more information about enabling profiles, see Chapter 12.

- Decide on the appropriate policies for your company.
- Decide if policies will be based on individual or group membership.
- Install the System Policy Editor and support for group policies (if you decided to base policies on group membership).

> **NOTE** Although these steps don't have to be done in order, many of the later steps rely on earlier steps.

- Load or create the appropriate template.
- Create policies for groups (if you decided to take this approach).
- Configure the order in which groups will take effect.
- Create default settings for users via the Default User.
- Create default settings for computers via the Default Computer.

> **NOTE** The Default User and Default Computer are part of a default template, made from COMMON.ADM and WINDOWS.ADM, supplied by Microsoft. This template is discussed later in the chapter.

- Create exceptions for users via unique user settings.
- Create exceptions for computers via unique computer settings.
- Save the policy as CONFIG.POL (the default name of the policy file that Windows 98 will automatically look for) where Windows 98 will find it (the location depends on the type of network you are on, and is explained later in the chapter).

Deciding How to Use Policies

Policies are so flexible that they can do almost anything you want, with respect to enforcing restrictions that may be required for your network. Some companies have even formed committees to look at the various restrictions available using policy files and decide which restrictions should be enforced. If your network requires restrictions that are not present in the default templates, you can edit the templates or create a new one.

Policies can be based on group membership. Groups can come from either a Windows NT server or a NetWare server. Support for group policies is not installed on local workstations by default; you must install this support for every computer that is expected to load group policies.

Installing the System Policy Editor and Group Policy Support

Policies are created using the System Policy Editor. Because this program is an administration tool, it is not installed by default. You must install it from the Windows 98 distribution CD-ROM before you can create or edit policies. If you plan to use group policies, you must also install group policy support on the computer that creates the policy, as well as each client workstation involved in the group. The System Policy Editor is located in the Tools\Reskit\Netadmin\Poledit folder of the CD-ROM, as shown in Figure 13.3.

FIGURE 13.3

Locating the System Policy Editor

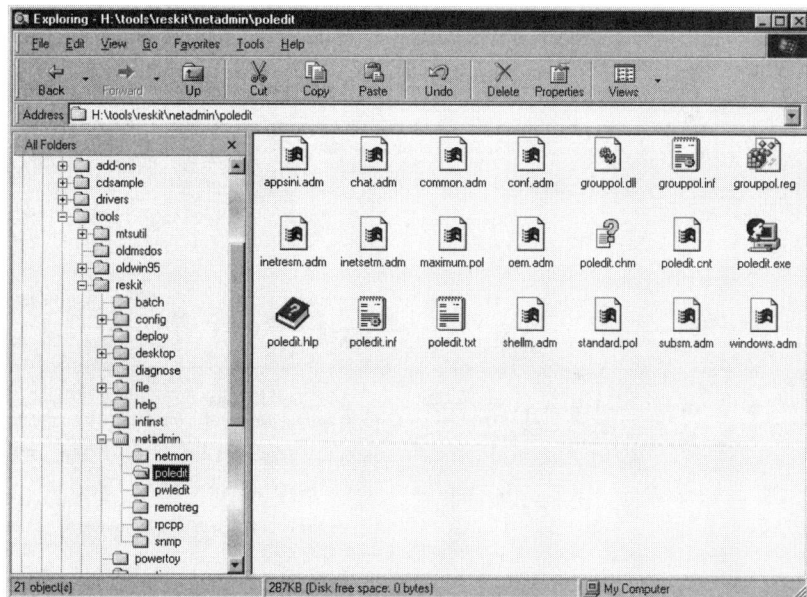

> **TIP**
>
> You can install group policies at the same time you install the System Policy Editor. For those computers that will be using group policies but will not be running the System Policy Editor, you still need to install group policy support. You can verify that group policy support is installed by searching for the file called "GROUPPOL.DLL."

Follow the steps in Exercise 13.1 to install the System Policy Editor and/or group policies.

EXERCISE 13.1

Installing the System Policy Editor and Group Policies

1. Go to Control Panel ➢ Add/Remove Programs.

2. Select the Windows Setup tab.

3. Choose Have Disk.

4. Type the path to the folder (**Tools\Reskit\Netadmin\Poledit**), or use the Browse button to point to the Poledit folder. If you use the Browse button, both the GROUPPOL.INF file and POLEDIT.INF file appear in the Open dialog box, as shown below. Windows 98 lets you select only the GROUPPOL.INF file (because it is the first INF file in the list). Choose OK after indicating which folder to open.

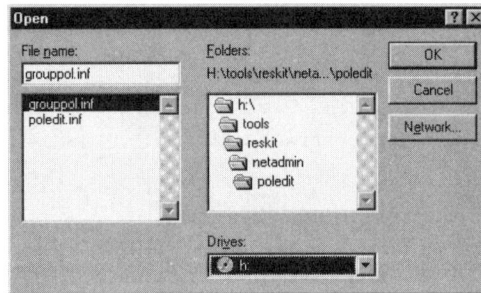

5. In the Have Disk dialog box, shown below, choose which components you want to install: Group Policies and/or System Policy Editor. Then click Install. Click OK to close Control Panel.

6. If you installed the System Policy Editor, verify that it is installed correctly by checking in the \Windows (or wherever Windows 98 is installed) folder for POLEDIT.EXE. You may want to make a shortcut to the editor if you use it a lot.

Loading Templates

Microsoft supplies default templates called COMMON.ADM and WINDOWS .ADM, which contain many popular Registry settings. These files are located in the (hidden) INF folder located in the Windows installation folder after the System Policy Editor is installed. There are two major sections to the templates: the Default Computer (which pertains to the Hkey_Local_Machine Registry key) and the Default User (which pertains to the Hkey_Users Registry key). You can view the Default Computer and Default User entries in the System Policy Editor by double-clicking their icons in the System Policy Editor window. These parts of the templates are described in the following sections.

Default Computer Settings

The Default Computer section of the templates includes Windows 98 Network and Windows 98 System entries. You can see these entries by using the System Policy Editor, as shown in Figure 13.4. Through the System entry, you can enable profiles and set paths for things such as a Start menu, Desktop, and other items.

The Network entry is divided into the following elements:

- **Access Control:** Allows you to assign user-level security and enter the server upon which to base security.

- **Logon:** Allows you to make a logon banner and require a valid logon before Windows 98 will let the user into the system (selecting Cancel to bypass the network logon and still be able to use the local computer, will not work).

- **Password:** Allows you to set a minimum length for the Windows password, disable password caching, and set other password options.

F I G U R E   13.4

The Default Computer
Windows 98 Network
settings

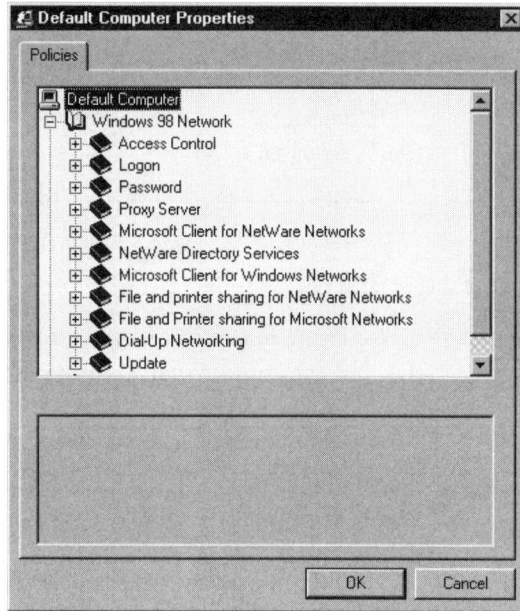

- **Proxy Server:** Disables the automatic search for a proxy server.

- **Microsoft Client for NetWare Networks:** Allows you to set the preferred server and other various options for a NetWare client machine.

- **NetWare Directory Services:** Allows you to customize NDS server
  settings.

- **Microsoft Client for Windows Networks:** Allows you to assign the
  workgroup name or enter the NT domain to which the user will log on.

- **File and printer sharing for NetWare Networks:** Allows you to set
  whether or not SAP (Service Advertising Protocol) will be sent out.

- **File and Printer Sharing for Microsoft:** Allows you to disable folder
  sharing and/or printer sharing.

- **Dial-Up Networking:** Allows you to disable the dial-in client.

- **Update:** Allows you to set the path for future system policy updates.

The Windows 98 System settings allow you to change the way Windows 98 works and upgrades itself. The various categories (see Figure 13.5) are:

- **User Profiles:** Allows you to enable profiles.

- **Network Paths:** Allows you to set the path to Windows 98 installation and tour files.

- **SNMP:** Allows you to set where the SNMP (Simple Network Management Protocol) error codes will go.

- **Programs to Run:** Allows you to specify programs to run at every startup or just once.

- **Install Device Drivers:** Allows you to specify whether or not non-Microsoft drivers will generate a prompt.

- **Windows Update:** Allows you to specify whether or not Windows 98 gets its updates automatically, and if so from which URL.

F I G U R E   13.5

The Default Computer Windows 98 System settings

Default User Settings

The Default User part of the template is shown in Figure 13.6. It also has a Windows 98 Network and Windows 98 System section.

The Windows 98 Network section has the following entry:

- **Sharing:** Allows you to disable folder sharing and/or printer sharing.

The Windows 98 System section has the following entries:

- **Shell:** Through the Custom Folders subentry, you can set various parts of Windows 98 (such as the Start menu or Desktop) to reside on places other than the local hard drive. Through the Restrictions subentry, you can shut down most of the functionality of Windows 98; for example, you could disable the Run command or hide the drives in My Computer and Network Neighborhood.

- **Control Panel:** Each one of these entries allows you to restrict various tabs of the Control Panel applet's dialog box—Display, Network, Passwords, Printers, and System.

- **Desktop Display:** This entry allows you to set various items dealing with the Desktop, including the wallpaper and color scheme.

- **Restrictions:** These settings allow you to disable MS-DOS mode, disable the Registry Editor, and create a list of approved programs so that Windows 98 will run only those programs.

Setting Policy Restrictions

Along with the templates that are loaded with the System Policy Editor, you can find other templates and policies in the *Windows 98 Resource Kit* or on Microsoft's Web site (www.microsoft.com).

After you've loaded a template, you can set various restrictions by filling out the template. You generally have three choices:

- A gray setting is the default. No change is made by the policy—the restrictions are left as they were.

- A checked setting means that the policy is enforced—the restrictions are put in place.

- A blank, or white, setting means that the policy is reset—the restrictions are removed.

When you leave a policy gray (which is the default), Windows 98 doesn't change whatever is currently recorded in the Registry. Although leaving boxes gray is faster (because nothing is being changed), Windows 98 will not reset a restriction to an earlier version. For example, if you had a restriction set (checked) for a low-security person, that restriction remains in place on the computer until someone who has the restriction reset (set to white) logs in.

Creating Policies for Groups

You can create policies for either NetWare or Windows NT groups by adding a group and assigning policies to it. You can also change the order in which Windows 98 implements groups so that users who belong to more than one group can have one group's right override an earlier group's restrictions.

WARNING Windows 98 does not support group policies by default. Group policy support must be installed on the computer that creates group policies and on every computer that will implement policies based on groups.

After you have installed group policy support for all the computers that will be using group policies (see Exercise 13.1), you can create and modify group policies. In Exercise 13.2, you will create a policy for a group so that its members cannot see the virtual memory settings. You do this by restricting the Windows 98 System Control Panel, as shown in Figure 13.6.

NOTE In Exercises 13.2 and 13.3, you will build policies for the Sales and Management groups. You can change those names to match the groups on your network.

EXERCISE 13.2

Creating a Group Policy

1. Start the System Policy Editor by selecting Start ≻ Programs ≻ Accessories ≻ System Tools ≻ System Policy Editor.

2. Create a new policy by choosing File ≻ New File.

3. Create a new group policy by choosing Edit ≻ Add Group.

4. Type Sales for the group. If user-level security is installed (see Chapter 10), you can browse for the group name.

5. Choose OK. Your policy should appear in the System Policy Editor window, as shown here.

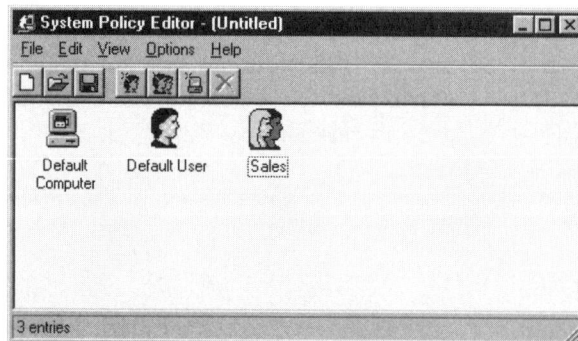

6. Highlight the Sales group and select Edit ≻ Properties, or double-click the Sales group.

7. Choose Control Panel ≻ System ≻ Restrictions, check Restrict System Control Panel, and check the Hide Virtual Memory button box as shown here.

8. Save the policy as CONFIG.POL (if you already have such a file save it as CONFIG2.POL) and close the editor.

Setting Group Priority

When you use group policies, the policies for groups that come later will override those for groups that come earlier. For example, suppose that Phil is a member of both the Sales and Management groups. The Sales group is restricted from sharing folders; the Management group has no such restriction. If the Sales group is processed first (Phil is a member, so he loses the right) and then the Management group is processed (Phil is a member so he gains the right), Phil will end up being able to share his folders. If the Sales group is processed last, the restrictions of the Sales group will take precedence, and Phil won't be able to share his folders. To make sure that the desired group policy is applied, you can specify group priority, as shown in Figure 13.7.

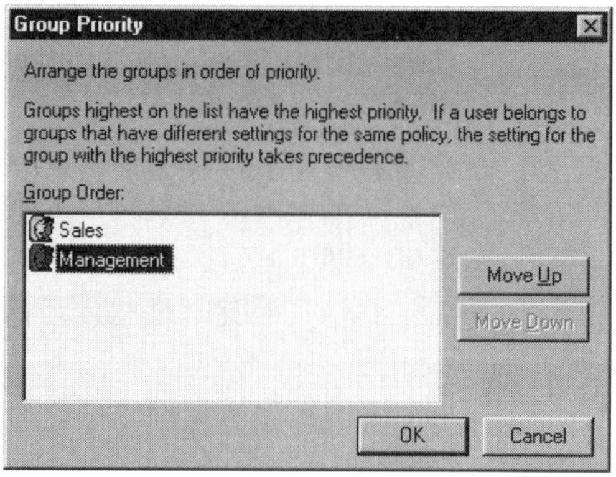

FIGURE 13.7

Specifying group
priorities

FIGURE 13.7
Specifying group
priorities

In Exercise 13.3, you will resolve the conflicts in the example by giving the Management group priority.

EXERCISE 13.3

Specifying Group Order

1. Start the System Policy Editor and load the policy CONFIG.POL (created in Exercise 13.2).

2. Create a new group policy for the Management group by choosing Edit ➢ Add Group and specifying the Management group.

3. To set the order of the groups, select Options ➢ Group Priority.

4. Make the Management group have priority over the Sales group by highlighting Management group and choosing Move Up until Management is on top (see Figure 13.7).

5. Save the policy as CONFIG.POL, and close the editor.

NOTE If a policy exists for a specific user, group policies are not applied for that user.

Creating Policies for Users

Policies set for the Default User apply to everyone except those who have a specific user policy. In Exercise 13.4, you will make a policy that sets a default wallpaper for users. You can do this through the Desktop settings for Default User properties, as shown in Figure 13.8.

F I G U R E 13.8

Setting the default wallpaper

EXERCISE 13.4

Creating a Default User Policy

1. Start the System Policy Editor and load the policy CONFIG.POL (created in Exercises 13.2 and 13.3).

2. Select Default User ➣ Desktop, and check the Wallpaper box.

3. Choose the BUBBLES.BMP for the wallpaper and select Tile Wallpaper (see Figure 13.8).

4. Choose OK to save the setting.

5. Save the policy as CONFIG.POL and close the editor.

All exceptions to the Default User policies must be specified by adding a policy for each specific user or group you want excluded.

Adding Specific Users

By creating entries for specific users, you can override both the Default User settings and any group policies that would have been enforced for that user. In Exercise 13.5, you will create a policy for a user called Phil that is different than the Default User policy.

Creating a Specific User Policy

1. Start the System Policy Editor and load the policy CONFIG.POL (created in previous exercises).

2. Create a user policy for Phil by choosing Edit ≻ New User, entering Phil for the username, and clicking OK. Your policy file should look like this:

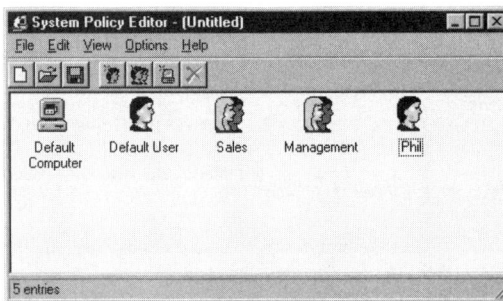

3. Open the policy for Phil (you can double-click Phil or highlight Phil and go to Edit ≻ Properties) and select Desktop. There should be a check in the Wallpaper box, and BUBBLES.BMP should be selected.

4. Change the wallpaper by selecting STRAW MAT.BMP (instead of BUBBLES.BMP).

5. Choose OK to save your changes.

6. Save the policy as CONFIG.POL.

Creating Policies for Computers

Policies can be set for all computers using the Default Computer specifications. Specific exceptions can be made by creating a separate computer entry for each excepted computer. Computer policies are based on the computer name.

In Exercise 13.6, you will make a policy that disables the password caching for computers. You can do this through the Network ➤ Password settings for the Default Computer properties, as shown in Figure 13.9.

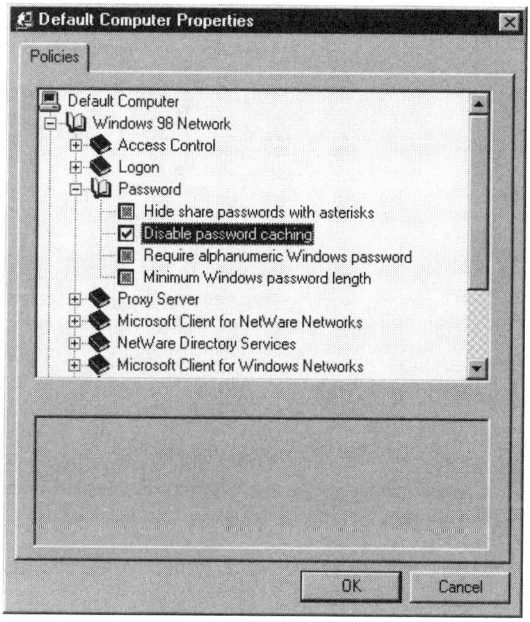

FIGURE 13.9

Disabling password caching

EXERCISE 13.6

Creating a Default Computer Policy

1. Start the System Policy Editor and load the policy CONFIG.POL (created in previous exercises).

2. Select Default Computer ➤ Windows 98 Network ➤ Password.

3. Check the Disable Password Caching box (see Figure 13.9).

4. Choose OK to save the setting.

5. Save the policy as CONFIG.POL and close the editor.

Adding Specific Computers

By creating entries for specific computers, you can override the Default Computer settings. In Exercise 13.7, you will create a policy that will set the access control to a Windows NT domain for a specific computer called Win95Server. You can do this through the Windows 98 Network ➤ Access Control settings for the Default Computer properties, as shown in Figure 13.10.

FIGURE 13.10

Setting user-level access via a policy

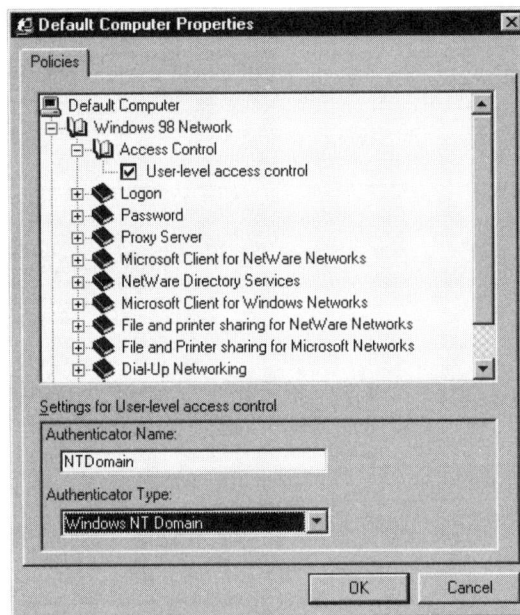

```
Default Computer Properties                          [X]

Policies

  Default Computer
  ⊟ Windows 98 Network
    ⊟ Access Control
        ☑ User-level access control
    ⊞ Logon
    ⊞ Password
    ⊞ Proxy Server
    ⊞ Microsoft Client for NetWare Networks
    ⊞ NetWare Directory Services
    ⊞ Microsoft Client for Windows Networks
    ⊞ File and printer sharing for NetWare Networks
    ⊞ File and Printer sharing for Microsoft Networks
    ⊞ Dial-Up Networking

Settings for User-level access control
Authenticator Name:
NTDomain
Authenticator Type:
Windows NT Domain

                         OK        Cancel
```

EXERCISE 13.7

Creating a Specific Computer Policy

1. Start the System Policy Editor, and load the policy CONFIG.POL (created in Exercise 13.6).

2. Create a new computer account by selecting Edit ➤ Add Computer.

3. Enter Win98Server as the computer name and click OK. (Notice the Browse button, which allows you to browse the Network Neighborhood to find a computer name.) Your policy file should look like this:

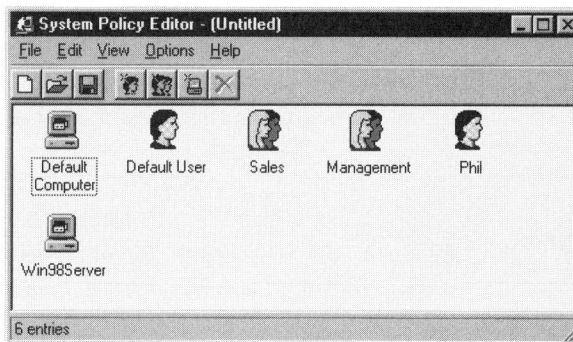

4. Open the Win98Server computer and select Windows 98 Network ➤ Access Control.

5. Check the User-Level Access Control box, type **NTDOMAIN** for the Authenticator name, and choose Windows NT Domain for the type (see Figure 13.10).

6. Choose OK to save your changes.

7. Save the policy as CONFIG.POL.

NOTE Entries for the computer are based on the computer name, and, therefore, will not work if the computer name changes.

Saving Policies

After making the appropriate changes in the System Policy Editor, you can save the policy and put it in the appropriate location.

Windows 98 looks for the file CONFIG.POL in one of two places:

- \\NT Server\NETLOGON share
- NetWare Server:Sys\Public directory

If the Client for Microsoft Networks is the primary logon, Windows 98 will look in the NETLOGON share of the PDC (Primary Domain Controller) of the domain. The NETLOGON share is usually the *<NT Root>*\System32\Repl\Import\Scripts folder, which is also where logon scripts are stored by default. Windows 98 loads policies only from the PDC by default, which could cause a bottleneck in a large environment. To avoid such a bottleneck, you can enable load balancing, which forces Windows 98 to look on domain controller servers other than the PDC for the policy file. For this to work, all of the controllers in the domain must have a current copy of the profile.

> You can use replication to automatically synchronize policy files. See *MCSE: NT Server 4 Study Guide* and *MCSE: Windows NT in the Enterprise* (both published by Sybex) for more information.

If the Client for NetWare Networks is chosen as the primary network logon, Windows 98 will look for the policy file in the public directory of the preferred NetWare server.

Windows 98 can also be directed to load a policy by specifying the path and filename of the policy. This is called Manual Update mode, and the procedure is explained in the next section.

> If you want a stand-alone computer to load a policy file, you must enable Manual Update mode and enter the path to the policy file.

Specifying a Policy Path

You can specify a path to a local computer through the Windows 98 Network ➤ Update settings for the Local Computer properties, as shown in Figure 13.11. In Exercise 13.8, you will set up Windows 98 to use policies on a stand-alone computer and test the policy file we have built so far.

EXERCISE 13.8

Setting the Policy Path Manually

1. Start the System Policy Editor.

2. Select File ➤ Open Registry. This will open the local Registry for editing, instead of making changes to a policy file.

3. Select Local Computer ➤ Windows 98 Network ➤Update.

4. Check the Remote Update box, change the type to Manual, and add the path, including the policy name, to your policy file (see Figure 13.11).

5. Choose OK to save your changes.

6. Exit the System Policy Editor. When you are asked if you want to save your Registry changes, answer Yes.

7. Restart Windows 98.

8. Log in as Phil. You should see the straw mat wallpaper.

9. Log in as anyone else. You should see the bubbles wallpaper.

F I G U R E   13.11

Specifying the policy file

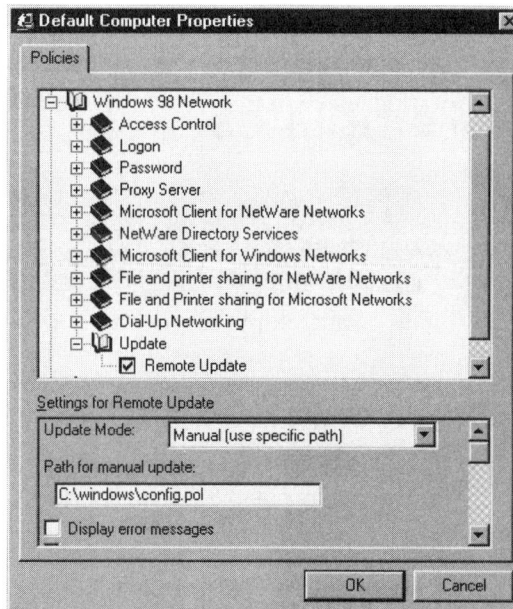

Windows NT 4.0 also uses system policies. The default filename that NT uses is NTCONFIG.POL. Windows NT 4.0 policies are incompatible with Windows 98 policies. If you have both types of workstations, you will need to make two sets of policies.

Specifying Load Balancing

By default, Windows 98 checks for and loads only the policy file from the PDC of a Windows NT domain. This can cause bottlenecks on the network from increased traffic to and from the PDC. The PDC may also reside across several slow routers or WAN connects. To fix bottlenecks these problems cause, you need to ensure that the policy file is on all controllers in the domain, and enable load balancing. Load balancing is enabled at the bottom of the update box, as shown in Figure 13.12.

FIGURE 13.12

Enabling load
balancing

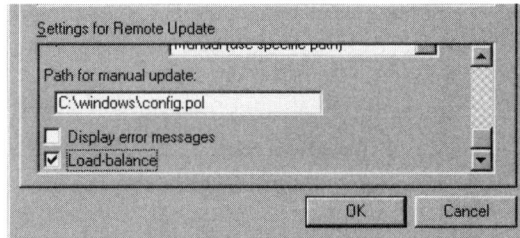

Creating Templates

Microsoft has supplied other templates and policies for use with the System Policy Editor. They can be found on the *Windows 98 Resource Kit* CD-ROM, and on Microsoft's Web site (www.microsoft.com). The great thing about templates is that they are written in ASCII, so they can be edited.

> **WARNING** Be careful when you create or edit templates. Because templates are used to create the system policies that edit the Registry, any mistake in the original template could have severe repercussions in the Registry.

Looking at a piece of the Registry and at a portion of a template written to modify it will help you to understand how templates are created. Figure 13.11 (in the previous section) shows the System Policy Editor opened to the Local Computer ➤ Windows 98 Network ➤Update ➤ Remote Update page. Now take a look at the actual template (WINDOWS.ADM) in Figure 13.13, and you will see how it was constructed.

Examining the Registry reveals the final piece of the puzzle. In the Registry, you can see the actual subkey that will be modified if the policy is

enforced, as shown in Figure 13.14. You know that this is under Hkey_
Local_Machine because you are looking at the local computer (not the local
user), and it will take effect under Hkey_Local_Machine\System\Current-
ControlSet\Control\Update.

F I G U R E 13.13

The Update options
and path inside the
template

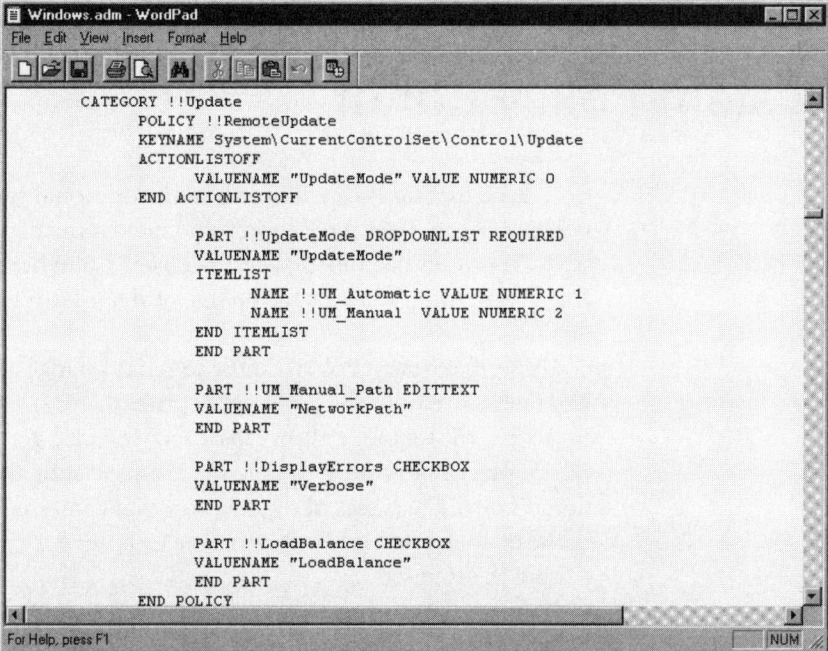

F I G U R E 13.14

The Registry update
options and path

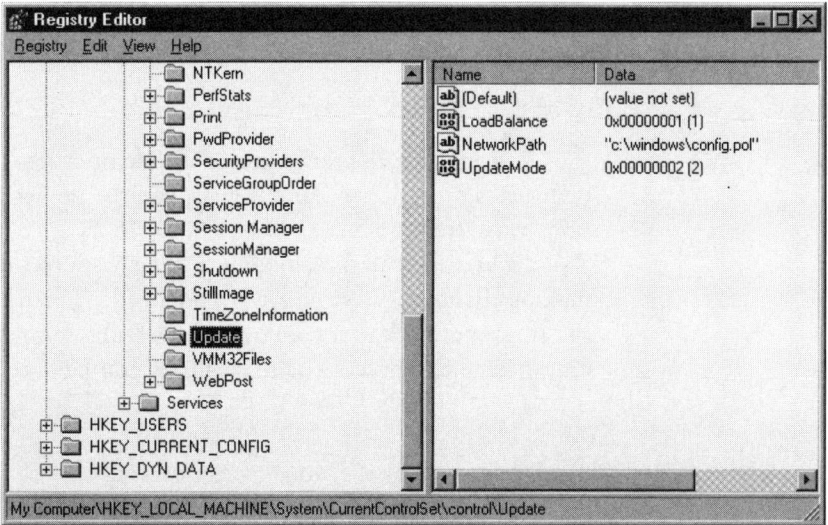

> **TIP** For more details about creating and editing templates and a list of all the keywords used in templates, refer to the *Windows 98 Resource Kit.*

Editing the Registry Directly Using the System Policy Editor

The System Policy Editor has an additional function besides creating policies: It can open the Registry and make direct edits of the Registry database. You used this function in Exercise 13.8, when you modified the local Registry to find the policy file on the local hard drive instead of on a network drive.

Using the System Policy Editor to make changes to the Registry is a safe and fast way to edit the Registry, because the only values that can be set are those that the template allows to be set. You also get prompted when closing the Registry if you want to save the changes (something the Registry Editor doesn't do). The pieces of the Registry that can be edited are directly related to the template that is being used. (See Chapter 5 for more information about editing the Registry.)

If remote administration is also enabled (see Chapter 14), the System Policy Editor can also open and make changes to remote registries.

Summary

Windows 98 allows you to decide on a set of restrictions to which your users must adhere, and it gives you the power to enforce those restrictions via system policies.

Policies are created by loading a template into the System Policy Editor, making changes, and saving it as a policy file. There is only one policy file for the entire network that contains the Default Computer, Default User, and any specific computers and user entries you have created.

You must install the System Policy Editor from the Windows 98 CD-ROM before you can create or edit policies. You must also enable user profiles (discussed in Chapter 12) in order for system policies based on username or group to take place.

Templates are ASCII files that correspond to subkeys and values in the Registry. Microsoft supplies the default COMMON.ADM and WINDOWS .ADM templates. Policies are powerful vehicles for enforcing policies that your company may have in place concerning how Windows 98 will operate on the network.

Windows 98 looks for policy files in either the NETLOGON share of the NT server acting as the PDC or in the PUBLIC directory of a NetWare server. You can also specify where the policy file will be held, and set up load balancing across the NT servers.

Along with creating and editing policies, the System Policy Editor can also open and edit the local and remote registries directly.

Review Questions

1. The System Policy Editor is installed by which method?

   A. It is installed by default.

   B. It is installed when you perform a "Custom" installation.

   C. It is installed automatically when you log on to a Windows NT server with Administrator rights.

   D. You must install it manually.

2. Policies can be used to enforce restrictions based on which of the following? Choose all that apply.

   A. Users

   B. Groups

   C. Time of Logon

   D. Computers

3. Templates end with which extension?

   A. .TEM

   B. .FIL

   C. .ADM

   D. .POL

4. Policies end with which extension?

   A. .POL

   B. .ADM

   C. .DLL

   D. .SEC

5. Group policies are not working. What steps should you check? Choose all that apply.

   A. Group policy support must be installed on every computer that will load policies based on groups.

   B. Users may not be assigned to the correct groups.

   C. The policy file should be named GROUPPOLICY.POL.

   D. The policy file should be named CONFIG.POL.

6. Phil is a member of both the Management and Sales groups. You want the Management group to take precedence over the Sales group. How would you set this up?

   A. Make the Sales group higher in the list.

   B. Make the Management group higher in the list.

   C. You can't control it—it goes alphabetically.

   D. Set Phil's primary group to the Management group.

7. Sally and Phil share a computer. Sally will have a restriction in place, but Phil shouldn't. How should you set Phil's checkbox for that restriction?

   A. Leave it gray (default).

   B. Put a check in it.

   C. Uncheck it (make it white).

   D. Leave Phil's checkbox alone; set Sally's checkbox to gray.

8. Windows 98 looks for the policy file in which NT share by default?

   A. The NETLOGON share of all domain controllers

   B. The NETLOGON share of the primary domain controller

   C. The USERS share of all domain controllers

   D. The USERS share of the primary domain controller

9. Templates can be stored as which type of files? Choose all that apply.

   A. ASCII text files

   B. Compressed binary files

   C. Word (.doc) files

   D. Policy Editor (.pol) files

10. You want to enable system policies on a NetWare network. You have 3.12 servers and 4.0 servers running in Bindery Emulation. Where do you need to put the system policy file so that your clients will find it?

    A. In the PUBLIC folders of the 3.12 servers, and the POLICY folders of the 4.*x* servers

    B. In the PUBLIC folders of all of the NetWare servers

    C. In the POLICY folders of all of the NetWare servers

    D. In the POLICY folders of the 3.12 servers, and the PUBLIC folders of the 4.*x* servers

11. You have a group created for your temporary employees called temp_ users. You don't want them to be able to share their folders or printers. How would you set your policy file?

    A. Create a policy file that selects "Disable file sharing" and "Disable printer sharing" and assign it to the temp_users group.

    B. Create a policy file that selects "Disable file sharing" and "Disable printer sharing" and name it TEMP_USERS.POL.

    C. Edit your existing policy file. Create a new group policy for the temp_users group, and select the "Disable file sharing" and "Disable printer sharing" options.

    D. Edit your existing policy file. Create user policies for all of the temporary employees and select the "Disable file sharing" and "Disable printer sharing" options.

12. You need to save your policy file on a NetWare server. What do you name it so that your Windows 98 clients can find it by default?

   A. CONFIG.POL

   B. NWCONFIG.POL

   C. NTCONFIG.POL

   D. 98CONFIG.POL

13. You have 10,000 clients (both Windows NT and Windows 98) in one large Windows NT domain. You have a large PDC in the central office, with a BDC in each of your 30 regional offices. Users complain that logging in from the Windows 98 clients take twice as long as logging in from the Windows NT clients. What steps do you need to take in order to speed up the login process? Choose all that apply.

   A. Make sure the policy file is on all the BDCs.

   B. Enable Manual Updates, and specify load balancing on the Windows 98 clients.

   C. Copy the policy file to the local hard drives of all of the Windows 98 clients.

   D. Set the policy file to only test for user configurations.

14. Your policy file is working for the Default Computer restrictions but not for the Default User restrictions. What is probably the cause?

   A. The users are not logging into the network.

   B. The users have blank passwords.

   C. The workstations do not have File and Printer Sharing installed.

   D. The workstations do not have profiles enabled.

CHAPTER

14

Remote Administration

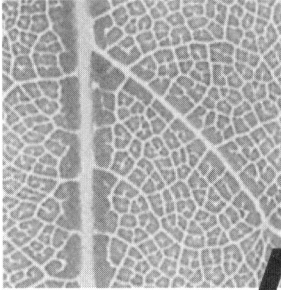

An old systems engineering law states that a warm administrator's seat is a happy administrator's seat. This means that the less running around you do, the more content (and efficient) you will be. Windows 98 allows the administrator to become an invisible noncorporeal being who is available only through corporate e-mail or 16 levels of a seemingly innocuous voice-mail system. Once a user has left a request for service, that request is either summarily denied or miraculously granted to the user. The user will never actually see the administrator come to fix his machine, but will assume that he just missed the administrator while taking a break from his nonfunctioning workstation. He doesn't know that the administrator, sitting comfortably in her ergonomically correct chair, has used her remote administrator's capabilities to fix the problem.

Microsoft ✓ *Exam Objective*

Create, share, and monitor resources. Resources include:

- Remote computers
- Network printers

NOTE   Creating, sharing, and monitoring network printers are covered in Chapters 10 and 11.

Several tools are available that you can use for remote administration of Windows 98 computers on your network. They include the Net Watcher, System Monitor, Administer, and Remote Registry Editor utilities. Before these tools can be used, the networked Windows 98 machines must be configured to accept *RPCs* (remote procedure calls) from the administrator's machine. Your administrative capabilities are also affected by the security level (share or user) that has been configured on both the remote PC and the administrating PC.

In this chapter, you will begin with a look at how remote administration is accomplished and then look at how it is related to security levels. Next, you will learn how to enable remote administration and use each of the remote administration utilities.

Remote Administration Architecture

Remote administration uses RPCs. Every Windows 98 machine that has been configured to participate in remote administration has a set of DLLs (dynamic link libraries) installed.

The administrator's machine will send an RPC to the client PC and run a particular procedure within the remote PC's local DLL files. The DLL file will run that procedure on that remote machine. This is analogous to you calling a friend across town and having him turn on a television. He is doing the work at his house, but you are telling him what to do.

Remote Administration and Security

Your level of access to remote workstations is affected by the security level that has been configured on both the remote PC and the administrating PC. These security levels are described in detail in Chapter 10. Here is a brief review:

- *Share-level security* is normally used in small peer-to-peer networks. Users assign passwords to shared folders and printers. Other users have access to those shared resources as long as they know the password.

- *User-level security* is used in larger enterprise networking environments. The Windows 98 machine assigns sharing to resources based on a user account. The user accounts are stored on a validation server (such as an NT or a NetWare server).

Share-level security is the default. You can enable user-level security through the Access Control tab of the Network Control Panel (see Chapter 12 for more information).

How the security level in use affects what you can do with the Windows 98 remote administration tools will be explained in the discussion of those tools, later in this chapter.

Enabling Remote Administration

You enable remote administration through the Remote Administration tab of the Passwords Properties dialog box, shown in Figure 14.1. (As an end-user, you probably won't see the Remote Administration tab. This tab is an Administration tool, and if used incorrectly, your computer might suffer unexpected problems. The Administrator probably will be using a system policy that does not allow this tab to be viewed and changed.) Follow the steps in Exercise 14.1 to enable remote administration on your Windows 98 machine.

F I G U R E   14.1

The Remote Administration tab

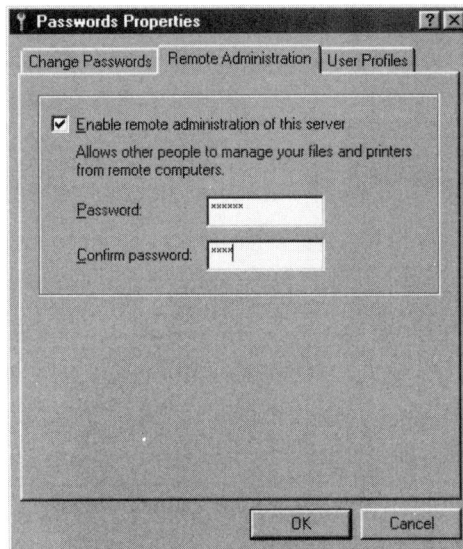

EXERCISE 14.1

Enabling Remote Administration

1. Go to Control Panel ➢ Passwords.

2. Choose the Remote Administration tab.

3. Click the Enable Remote Administration Of This Server checkbox.

4. If this PC is using share-level security, set a password and then confirm the password. If the PC is using user-level security, select the users and groups who have permission to administer this PC.

5. Click OK when you are finished.

When you make someone an administrator, you have given them full administration privileges, including the ability to add and remove other administrators.

Remote Administration Tools

Four Windows 98 tools are useful for remote administration:

- **Net Watcher:** Allows you to administer shared resources on a remote workstation. This tool can also be used locally. This tool includes the ability to view who is accessing those shared resources. This function is similar to "Caller ID"; you are able to see who is calling/connected to the system.

- **System Monitor:** Allows you to view performance statistics of a remote workstation. This can also be run locally.

- **Administer:** Allows you to access a special hidden share. This is an Administration share that Microsoft uses for all of its networking clients and servers. The share name is the drive letter of the local drive, typically called C$, D$, etc. C$ is the root directory of a remote workstation. The administrative shares are automatically enabled in the

Windows NT environment. In Windows 98, they must be manually turned on if they were not automatically installed during the installation process. (CD-ROM drives are not included in the scheme of the administrative share; they must still be shared manually.)

- **Remote Registry Editor:** Allows you to edit and modify a remote workstation's Registry.

Microsoft
✓ *Exam*
Objective

Monitor system performance by using Net Watcher, System Monitor, and Resource Meter.

NOTE Resource Meter is covered in Chapter 6.

Because the System Monitor and the Remote Registry Editor need access to a workstation's Registry database, they can be used only when user-level security has been enabled on both the remote workstation and the administrating computer. They also require Remote Registry Services to be installed.

The Net Watcher, System Monitor, and Administer tools are accessed from the Tools tab of the Properties dialog box for the Windows 98-based computer that you want to remotely administer, as shown in Figure 14.2. You can access the Remote Registry Editor from the Registry Editor program (Regedit). The following sections describe the use of each of these tools in more detail.

Using the Net Watcher for Resource Management

The Net Watcher is an interactive tool for creating, controlling, and monitoring shared resources. Both local and remote resources can be viewed. Net Watcher can be run on remote computers using either share-level or user-level security. If the remote PC is using user-level security, the administrating PC must also be using user-level security.

As an administrator, you can create, add, and delete shares; change resource properties; and monitor who is connected to which resource. Figure 14.3 shows an example of a Net Watcher screen.

F I G U R E   14.2

The Tools tab

F I G U R E   14.2

The Tools tab

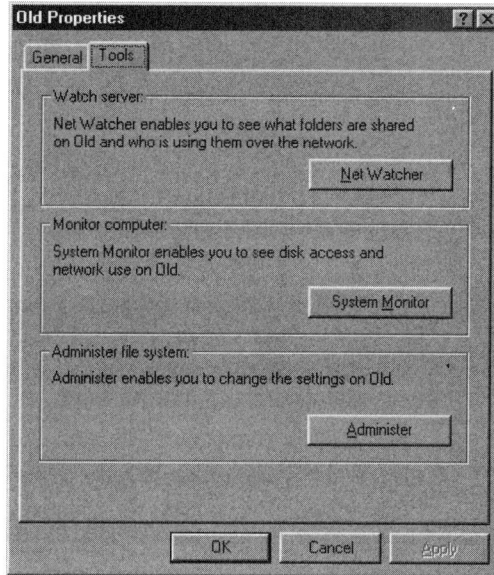

F I G U R E   14.3

The Remote
Administrator

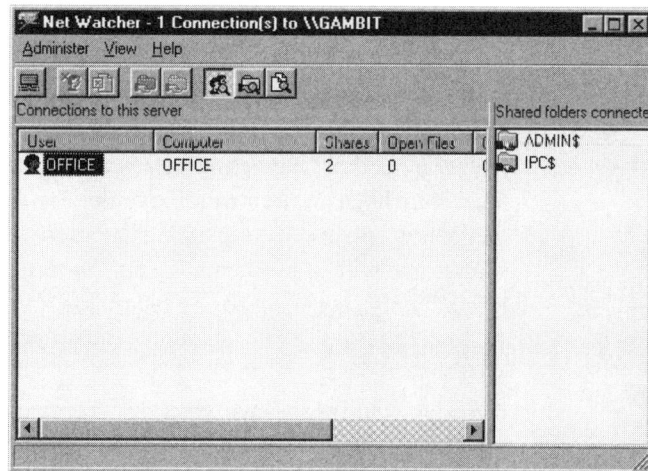

Follow the steps in Exercise 14.2 to use the Net Watcher tool. Of course,
the remote workstation must be sharing resources, folders, and/or printers
for this tool to be useful. If it is not sharing resources, nothing will show up
in the Net Watcher window.

EXERCISE 14.2

Using the Net Watcher Utility

1. Double-click the Network Neighborhood icon on your Desktop.

2. Navigate to a Windows 98-based computer involved in remote administration and right-click its icon.

3. From the Context menu, choose Properties to open the Properties dialog box for that PC.

4. Choose the Tools tab (see Figure 14.2).

5. Click the Net Watcher button. The Net Watcher application starts and shows you the status of shared resources on the remote PC (see Figure 14.3).

When you use the Net Watcher, two special shares are created:

- Admin$ gives administrators access to the \Windows folder on the remote PC.

- IPC$ is an interprocess channel between the two computers. This is a buffer area for RPCs to move between the workstations.

If you disconnect a user from a shared resource, the user will reconnect to the resource immediately. To prevent this, if you are using share-level security, you need to change the password on the resource. If you are using user-level security, you need to remove the user from the users list. This is also true when you are closing a file. The user will still have access to the shared folder, but will be momentarily disconnected from the file. The user will immediately reconnect to the file unless you do something to prevent it.

WARNING If you are using share-level security and you change a password on a shared resource, everyone who is currently using that resource will be thrown out. They will need to supply the new password in order to reconnect.

The Remote System Monitor

The Remote System Monitor tool can be used to monitor performance statistics on the remote workstation. The System Monitor uses values stored in the Hkey_Dyn_Data key in the Registry to get its information. To access the Registry on a remote computer, both the remote workstation and the administrating workstation must be using user-level security as well as have the Remote Registry Services service installed.

Installing Remote Registry Services

Because the Remote System Monitor must pull information from the Registry, you must install Remote Registry Services on both workstations to allow remote administrators to see the Registry. Installing Remote Registry Services is also necessary for using the Remote Registry Editor. Figure 14.4 shows the screens involved in this procedure. Follow the steps in Exercise 14.3 to add Remote Registry Services.

FIGURE 14.4

Installing Remote Registry Services

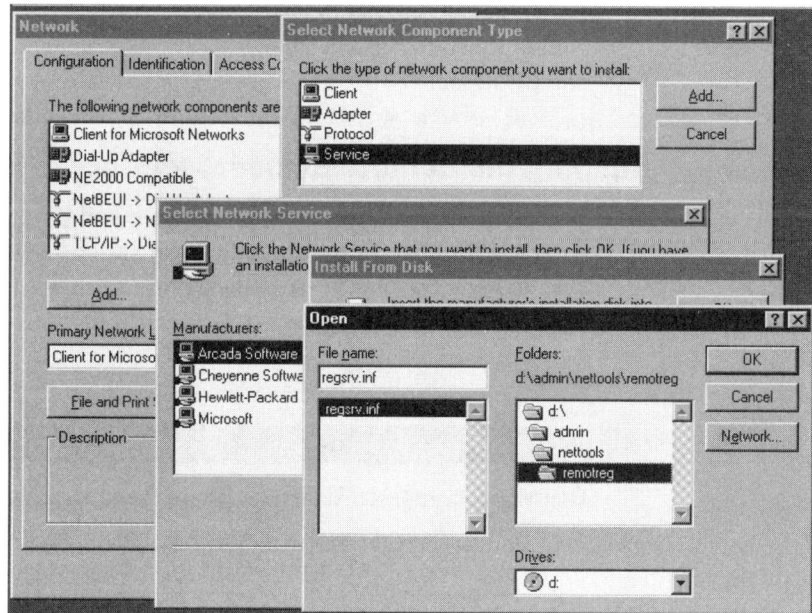

EXERCISE 14.3

Installing Remote Registry Services

1. Go to Control Panel ➢ Network.

2. From the Configuration tab, click the Add button.

3. Select Service, then Add, and then Have Disk.

4. Insert the Windows 98 CD-ROM and go to the \Admin\Nettools\ Remotereg folder (see Figure 14.4).

5. Click OK in the dialog boxes. You are told that you must reboot your system before these changes will take effect.

6. Click OK and let the system reboot.

WARNING Do not install Remote Registry Services unless you *need* it. Workstations with this installed take a slight performance hit in the memory, disk space, and CPU areas.

Running the Remote System Monitor

With Remote Registry Services installed, and both the remote workstation and the administrating workstation using user-level security, you can run the System Monitor. Figure 14.5 shows an example of the CPU utilization statistic on a remote workstation. Follow the steps in Exercise 14.4 to use the monitor.

EXERCISE 14.4

Running System Monitor on a Remote Workstation

1. Double-click the Network Neighborhood icon on your Desktop.

2. Navigate to a Windows 98-based computer involved in remote administration and right-click its icon.

3. From the Context menu, choose Properties to open the Properties dialog box for that PC.

4. Choose the Tools tab (see Figure 14.2).

5. Click the System Monitor button. The System Monitor starts and shows performance statistics for the other workstation (see Figure 14.5).

6. To look at different statistics, select Edit ➤ Add Item, choose a category, and click OK.

FIGURE 14.5

The Remote System Monitor utility

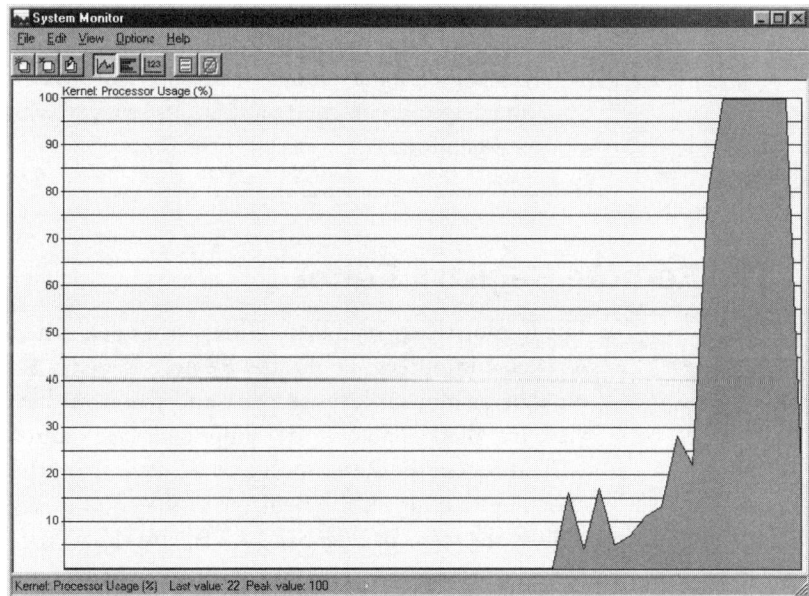

The Administer Utility

The Administer utility gives an administrator access to the hard disks on the remote workstation. From the local computer, you can administer the file system as if you were sitting at the remote workstation. The Administer tool can be used with both user-level and share-level security. Follow the steps in Exercise 14.5 to use Administer.

EXERCISE 14.5

Using the Administer Utility

1. Double-click the Network Neighborhood icon on your Desktop.

2. Navigate to a Windows 98-based computer involved in remote administration and right-click its icon.

3. From the Context menu, choose Properties to open the Properties dialog box for that PC.

4. Choose the Tools tab (see Figure 14.2).

5. Click the Administer button. The Administer utility starts and allows you to look at the remote workstation's C: drive. You can share resources and delete, create, and modify files as if you were sitting at that remote workstation.

The Remote Registry Editor

The Remote Registry Editor allows you to edit the Registry database on networked computers. To use the Remote Registry Editor, both computers must be using user-level security and you must have Remote Registry Services installed as a network component (see Exercise 14.3).

You access the Remote Registry Editor from the Registry Editor by choosing to connect the Registry of the computer you want to administer. Follow the steps in Exercise 14.6 to run the editor.

EXERCISE 14.6

Using the Remote Registry Editor

1. Select Start ➤ Run.

2. In the Run program dialog box, type **Regedit** to start the Registry Editor.

3. Select Registry ➤ Connect Network Registry to open the Connect Network Registry dialog box.

4. Type in the name of the computer you want to remotely administer, or click on the Browse button to browse the network and find the desired machine.

5. Click the OK button and close the dialog box. You can view and edit the Registry on the remote machine.

> **NOTE** For more information about the Registry and using the Registry Editor (Regedit) see Chapter 5.

Summary

Using the remote administration utilities included with Windows 98 allows systems engineers and network administrators to accomplish more work with less running around. While not as robust as the utilities available in Windows NT or Novell's NetWare, they are powerful nonetheless.

Remote administration takes place through the use of RPCs (remote procedure calls). These procedures are implemented as *.DLL files and allow you to track system performance statistics, manage and monitor shared resources, manipulate the file structures, and edit the Registry on remote workstations without ever leaving your chair.

Different levels of remote administration are available depending on the security level (share or user) and installed components (like Remote Registry Services) of both the administering workstation and the remote workstation. The four remote administration tools are the Net Watcher, System Monitor, Administer, and Remote Registry Editor. The Remote Registry Editor is accessed from the Registry Editor (Regedit). The other tools are available from the Tools tab of the remote machine's property sheet (accessed from the Network Neighborhood).

Table 14.1 summarizes the requirements for running the remote administration utilities.

T A B L E 14.1: Remote Administration Security Summary

Tool	Remote Workstation			Administering Workstation	
	User/Share	File & Printer Sharing Enabled	Remote Registry Services	User/Share	Remote Registry Services
Net Watcher	Share	Yes	N/A	Either	N/A
	User	Yes	N/A	User	N/A
Administer	Share	Yes	N/A	Either	N/A
	User	Yes	N/A	User	N/A
Remote System Monitor	User	Yes	Yes	User	Yes
Remote Registry Editor	User	Yes	Yes	User	Yes

Review Questions

1. In Windows 98, remote administration is accomplished through the use of which mechanism?

   A. Named pipes

   B. RPCs

   C. IPX/SPX

   D. TCP/IP

2. You have 15 Windows 98 computers on your network. You want to remotely administer the file structure on these Windows 98 computers from your own Windows 98 computer. All of the PCs have File and Print Sharing installed, and they all have the Remote Administration option enabled from the Passwords applet in the Control Panel. Which utility do you use to administer the file structure on a remote computer?

   A. Net Watcher

   B. Remote System Monitor

   C. Administer

   D. Remote Registry Editor

3. You want to view which resources are shared and who is using them on computers in your Windows 98 network. All 20 Windows 98 machines have been installed with File and Printer sharing. All of them use Windows NT Server for logon validation. Share-level security has been implemented on all of the PCs, and the Remote Administration option has been enabled. Which utility can you use to view resources that are shared on your PC and who is sharing them?

   A. Net Watcher

   B. Remote System Monitor

   C. Administer

   D. Remote Registry Editor

4. In this scenario, all 50 computers on your network have been configured with Windows 98. They are using Novell NetWare 4 as a logon validation server. User-level security has been enabled on all 50 PCs, and the Remote Registry Service has been installed as well. Which utility do you use to view performance statistics on a remote workstation?

    A. Net Watcher

    B. Remote System Monitor

    C. Administer

    D. Remote Registry Editor

5. You are attempting to modify the Registry database on a client Windows 98 machine from your administering Windows 98 machine. You have installed user-level security on both machines and have enabled remote administration from the Passwords applet in the Control Panel. You can work with the remote Net Watcher and the Administer features, but you cannot seem to get the Remote Registry Editor or the Remote System Monitor utilities to work. Which of the following could solve your problem?

    A. Install Net Watcher Services

    B. Install Remote Registry Services

    C. Install Client Services for Remote Administration

    D. Install Novell NetWare Client32 for Windows 98

6. You have 30 Windows 98 computers in your network. Each server is configured with user-level security and is gaining logon validation from a NetWare 3.12 server. You want to use some of the remote administrative utilities that come bundled with Windows 98. Which of the following utilities require user-level security on both the remote workstation and the administering workstation? Choose all that apply.

    A. Net Watcher

    B. Remote System Monitor

    C. Administer

    D. Remote Registry Editor

7. To enable remote administration of a client PC, you must first enable remote administration. From where is this accomplished?

   A. Network property sheets

   B. Add/Remove Programs icon in the Control Panel

   C. Passwords icon in the Control Panel

   D. Remote Administration icon in the Control Panel

8. Which of the following is true about Installing Remote Registry Services and your PC's performance?

   A. The 32-bit software makes your system run faster and makes access to the Registry quicker.

   B. The entire Registry will now be loaded into memory for quick access by any administering PC.

   C. The Service requires memory, CPU cycles, and hard disk space and will, therefore, slow your system down.

   D. The Service has no impact either way on your system's performance.

9. You are working in a mixed Windows 98 and Novell NetWare environment. The Novell server is performing all user validation. You have installed the Remote Registry Services on all of your PCs. They are all set up with user-level security, and you have enabled File and Print Sharing. You have also shared several folders on each of your PCs. When you try to use the Remote System Monitor, it fails to allow you access. Which of the following could be the cause?

   A. You cannot use Remote System Monitor when you are being validated by a Novell server.

   B. You have not yet assigned users the ability to remotely administer your computer from the Control Panel/Passwords tool.

   C. Remote System Monitor is available only when both PCs are using share-level security.

   D. There is no Remote System Monitor utility.

10. The following tuples (sets of elements) indicate what levels of security have been assigned on the remote PC and the administrating PC. Which of the following will support the Administer option? Choose all that apply.

   A. User – Share

   B. Share – Share

   C. User – User

   D. Share – User

11. The following tuples indicate what levels of security have been assigned on the remote PC and the administrating PC. Which of the following will support the Remote System Monitor option?

   A. User – Share

   B. Share – Share

   C. User – User

   D. Share – User

12. Your Windows 98 machine is currently set up with user-level security and TCP/IP. A NetWare server is providing your login validation. You have installed File and Printer Sharing for NetWare networks and have shared your printer and several folders. None of the other machines in your network have enabled remote administration. Using the Net Watcher utility, which of the following things can you accomplish?

   A. Create new shares for folders

   B. Delete shares based on folders

   C. Disconnect users from shared folders

   D. Monitor shares on remote computers

13. You have installed a new 32-bit program on your Windows 98 machine. You want to make sure that the program is operating properly, so you run the System Monitor utility. With the System Monitor running, you view the number of threads in the system. At program startup, approximately 10 threads are running. After 10 minutes, the program shows 30 threads running. You have not started any other programs during this time. Looking back through the graphic history shown in the System Monitor, you notice that the threads were steadily added. You check the System Monitor again after 30 minutes and now see that the threads have steadily continued to increase. Which of the following is true about this 32-bit program?

A. The program is running normally.

B. The program is not releasing memory properly.

C. The System Monitor cannot show this type of information.

D. The ReleaseMem Agent isn't installed on this computer.

14. You have been using the Remote Administration tool on your Windows 98 machine to administer other network client PCs. You have just added an additional 10 PCs to the network. You have enabled File and Printer Sharing on the 10 new PCs and have shared various folders and printers. You do have access to these shares from all of the different computers on the network. When you attempt to remotely administer the new PCs, you find that you cannot. What else do you need to do to enable remote administration of these 10 new client PCs?

A. Add a new protocol to the Network property sheets.

B. Add the Net Watcher program from the Add/Remove Programs icon in the Control Panel.

C. Enable remote administration from the Passwords icon in the Control Panel.

D. Run the Remote Administration icon in the Control Panel.

15. You have 25 Windows 98 computers in your network. They are all currently configured to use Windows NT Server for logon validation. You want to use the Remote System Monitor to gather performance statistics on the remote computers. Which of the following must be installed in order to use Remote System Monitor?

A. Remote Registry Services on the remote PC

B. Remote Registry Services on the administrating PC

C. User-level security on the remote PC

D. User-level security on the administering PC

CHAPTER

15

The Internet and Dial-Up Networking

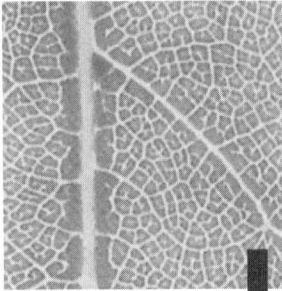

In the expanding world of high-speed communications (the World Wide Web, the Internet, and corporate intranets and extranets), understanding how Windows 98 handles telephony is a necessity. Modems provide a single, asynchronous data stream for sending and receiving information across a telephone line.

This chapter provides an overview of how Windows 98 can interoperate with the Internet. We will start with some general information about the Internet, including how to make Internet connections and how to extend Internet technology to intranets and extranets. Then we will describe the Internet-related features of Windows 98, with some details on using Internet Explorer and the Personal Web Server as well as Front Page.

In this chapter, we will also discuss the communications architecture of Windows 98 and how it impacts your computer system. We will then look at Dial-Up Networking and how to create and configure a connection. We will also look at the Telephony Application Programming Interface (TAPI), including special dialing properties that can be set for location-specific information as well as handling calling cards. We will finish the chapter with a look at dial-up security and performance.

The Internet

The Internet is defined as a matrix of networks that connects computers around the world. Since it began, the Internet has continued to grow rapidly. In the first months of 1998, access was available to approximately 180 countries, and there were around 100 million users. About 500 million computers are expected to be connected via the Internet by the twenty-first century, and even more will be in use via smaller intranets. The Internet now supports global information exchanges among individuals and organizations while being the driving force for hardware innovations.

The development of the global World Wide Web has made the Internet accessible to everyone. The Web has generated many new and innovative businesses, which in turn have produced billions of dollars in new business and created many new jobs.

The Internet uses the TCP/IP protocol, which is required in order to connect to the Internet. The most popular type of servers on the Internet are World Wide Web (WWW) servers, which use the HTTP (Hypertext Transfer Protocol) type of packet. The HTTP language allows *browsers*, such as Internet Explorer (IE) or Netscape Navigator and Communicator, to interpret formatting commands in order to present data in a friendly, easy-to-read format.

> **NOTE**   The Web was developed by University of Illinois student Marc Andreesen. Marc and others began building the Web and a Web browser called Mosaic. When Marc graduated, he added functionality to his browser and created Netscape Navigator, one of the most popular Web browsers on the market.

Look at the Internet as if it were your local telephone system connecting all of your friends and family together. It allows all of you to simultaneously talk and exchange information and video pictures (with the appropriate hardware) globally. And to think that not so long ago we marveled at the idea of Dick Tracy communicating with other people on a watch that could not only send voice but could also send pictures!

With the use of the Internet, you now have the ability to communicate with virtually anyone, anytime, anywhere, all over the world. When you visit Microsoft's Web site (`www.microsoft.com`), for example, you are instantly transported into the center of what is happening at Microsoft. Whether you are interested in the latest beta versions of your favorite software or the latest technical information about Windows NT and what's planned for the future, you will quickly realize you are in the right place.

You can keep up with business information, stock quotes, and even book your travel reservations—all from your personal computer over the Internet. Need to know what your bank balance is? Many banking institutions allow you to access your bank account and make transactions via the Internet.

The list of what you can do on the Internet is huge and continues to grow. Suffice it to say that as a systems engineer or administrator, you need to know about connecting to the Internet and other Internet-related functions.

Intranets and Extranets

With Internet technology abounding, companies can implement their own internal, independent internets called *intranets*. An intranet is a network of computers within the confines of an individual company, and it is meant to be private. This is in contrast to the Internet, which is designed to be public. The layout for an intranet is much the same as that of the Internet, but it is applied on a much smaller scale. One advantage of an intranet is that it can be local as well as global, depending on the size of the individual company.

For years, companies have been trying to set up company communications to share interdepartmental information, ranging from news about the company ball team to the latest financial statistics. Many different systems, some ingenious, have been put into place to facilitate this need to move large amounts of information throughout thousands of computers. The problem was that it required many different programs to make this happen. Some people run MS-DOS–based programs, some run Mac-based programs, and many run Windows-based software.

The great thing about an intranet is that you can use a Web browser, such as Internet Explorer, to cruise the internal network (the intranet) as well as the outside network (the Internet). Intranets can be designed so that workstations running any type of operating system can see the data exactly the same way. Macintosh, MS-DOS, Windows 3.*x*, Windows 95/98, Windows NT, and even Unix workstations can get to the company data.

As the popularity of the Internet has spread since the early 1990s, so has the popularity of intranets. One of the most important issues facing many companies is the problem of administration and management of their internal networks. By using the intranet philosophy, that job can be made much simpler. Network administrators do not need to spend all of their time helping users reset their Desktops and find their lost applications. They can have more time to do their necessary day-to-day tasks.

Extranets are the next generation in intranets. They are intranets that are shared among partner companies. Extranets promise increased communication and information flow among companies that work together. Just like intranets, extranets are designed to be private and for company (rather than personal) use.

Connecting to the Internet

Now that the price of hardware has dropped drastically, almost one out of every two homes in the United States has access to some kind of computer system—a laptop from work or a home system ranging from an older 386 to the new Pentium II machine. The only thing left to do is download the software (which is usually available free from companies such as Microsoft), find yourself an ISP (Internet service provider), and get online. Dial-Up Networking comes with Windows 98 and allows you to make connections to a remote computer using a standard modem.

People usually connect to the Internet through an ISP, or through one of the major online services such as America Online, MSN (Microsoft Network), CompuServe, or Prodigy. There are advantages to either choice—an ISP may have faster Internet connections, but the online services are usually easier to use and may have more native content.

Windows 98 Internet-Related Capabilities

You will find that Windows 98 has been designed with the Internet in mind. It allows even the most non-technical people to fire up their computers and, within minutes, start cruising the Web.

Windows 98 includes the following Internet-related pieces:

- TCP/IP support, including a DHCP client

- Dial-Up Networking

- Internet Explorer

- Internet Mail Client
- Internet News Reader
- Internet Meeting Software
- Personal Web Server

Windows 98 can be a client on the Internet by using Internet Explorer (or any other browser software), and it can be a server by installing Personal Web Server (PWS). PWS is available as a free download from Microsoft for Windows 95. Windows 98 comes with Internet Explorer (IE) and PWS built into it, although you may have to install PWS (which will be explained later in the chapter).

Connecting to the Internet becomes a simple matter of adding the Dial-Up Networking component and creating a connection to your local ISP if you are using a modem or using IE to directly connect to the Internet if you are on an office computer.

Microsoft Exam Objective

Install and configure hardware devices in a Microsoft environment and a mixed Microsoft and NetWare environment. Hardware devices include:

- Modems
- Printers
- Universal Serial Bus (USB)
- Multiple display support
- IEEE 1394 FireWire
- Infrared Data Association (IrDA)
- Multilink
- Power management scheme

NOTE Installing and configuring modems is covered in this chapter. For complete coverage of printers, see Chapter 11. The remaining hardware devices listed above are discussed in Chapter 3.

Modems

Because many connections to both dial-up servers and to the Internet are through modems, this section will show you how to install and configure a modem using Windows 98.

Windows 98 supports a wide variety of modems and makes it relatively simple to install them. The best way to add a new modem is to have Windows 98 automatically detect it using the Add New Hardware applet from Control Panel. Modems can be tested and configured from the Modems applet of the Control Panel once they are installed. Procedures for installing and configuring modems are shown in the following sections.

Microsoft
Exam
Objective

Install and configure hardware devices in a Microsoft environment and a mixed Microsoft and NetWare environment. Hardware devices include:

- Modems

Installing Modems

If you have a Plug-and-Play–compliant computer and a Plug-and-Play–compliant modem, Windows 98 should auto-detect the modem when your system is booted. Windows 98 will then install the appropriate drivers.

> **NOTE**
>
> *Modem* is short for modulate/demodulate. Modems work by converting binary electrical signals into acoustic signals for transmission over telephone lines (called *modulation*), and then converting these acoustic signals back into binary form at the receiving end (*demodulation*).

If you don't have a Plug-and-Play system, you can easily install a modem (or install a modem mini driver) through the Modems applet of the Control Panel. When you click on the Add button, the Install New Modem Wizard takes you through a series of steps for installing the modem.

In Exercise 15.1 we will have Windows 98 search the computer for a new modem.

EXERCISE 15.1

Installing a Modem

1. Go to Control Panel ≻ Modem.

2. Select Add. You should see a screen that looks like this. It is usually best to have Windows 98 detect your modem.

3. Select Next.

4. When the detection is completed, highlight the found modem and choose Next. You may be prompted for the Windows 98 CD-ROM or the driver disk that came with your modem.

5. Select Finish to end the process.

Modem Configuration

You can make changes to your modem's default settings through its Properties sheet. You can change things like the speaker volume and connection settings.

To begin, go to the Modems Control Panel (double-click the Modems icon in the Control Panel), select the modem that you want to configure, and click the Properties button. The modem's Properties dialog box has two tabs: General and Connection. The following sections describe the options available for most modems.

Some modems may have a third tab called Distinctive Ring. If your modem supports distinctive ring, you can program the modem to correctly answer the phone based on the type of ring.

General Modem Settings   The General tab of the modem's Properties dialog box, shown in Exercise 15.1, allows you to modify the general features that are part of all modems.

This tab includes the following settings:

Port: Allows you to change to a different communications port.

Speaker volume: Allows you to change the setting for the speaker volume. Normally, you will hear your modem dialing out, which sounds like a regular telephone call. Once the other modem answers, there will be a "handshake" period in which the modems try to synchronize themselves and let each other know how fast they want to communicate. This will sound like a high-pitched whine that may change in tone several times. Once the modems have synchronized, you will be connected, and the speakers will shut themselves off.

Maximum speed: Allows you to specify the maximum speed at which your modems will communicate. In the past, some manufacturers' modems were not compatible with other manufacturers' modems at high speeds. To avoid this problem, you could connect at a slower speed. If you have purchased a new modem since mid-1994, you should not have this problem. Set your maximum speed to the speed that is greater than or equal to your modem's speed. For example, if you have a 28,800bps modem, you should choose 28,800 or 38,400.

Connection Preferences   You can control the way connections are made with the modem setting the data, parity, and stop bits. The default settings will probably work best, unless you have an unusual situation.

Call Preferences   These options allow you to determine how your modem will behave. You can set the modem to wait for a dial tone before dialing, cancel the call if it's not connected within the specified number of seconds, and disconnect if the connection is idle for more than the specified number of seconds.

These settings are especially useful for dealing with unattended modem activity. For example, you might like to use a batch file that will run at midnight, connect to your network using Dial-Up Networking, and download some information.

Port Settings   Clicking the Port Settings button in the Connection tab brings up the Advanced Port Settings dialog box, shown in Exercise 15.2. These settings allow you to decide how your FIFO (First In-First Out) buffers are used. These buffers are temporary storage areas for transmitting and receiving packet information through your modems. You should set them to their maximum levels for the best throughput of information.

There are two types of FIFO buffers: the 16550 UART (Universal Asynchronous Receiver/Transmitter), which is standard on all 486 and later computers, and the 8250 UART. The 8250 is a much older standard, which allows a maximum rate of only 9600bps.

> **NOTE**   16550 UARTs provide larger and faster buffers than their 8250 counterparts. UART chips are found in many different places in your system. They can be located on modem hardware, parallel port boards, hard disk controllers, and other locations where communications are taking place.

Advanced Connection Settings   Clicking the Advanced button in the Connection tab brings up the Advanced Connection Settings dialog box, shown in Exercise 15.2.

These settings allow you to modify what type of error control and flow control you use, as well as set a modulation type and enter extra settings:

Use error control: Allows you to specify whether or not you use error control and compression. Windows 98 can support v42.bis compression and MNP/5 error correction.

Use flow control: Allows you to specify whether or not the modem or the software handles flow control between the modem and your computer. The default is for the hardware to do this. (XON/XOFF may not work with certain programs.)

Modulation type: Must be the same on both modems in order for them to communicate. If you are having trouble communicating with an older modem, try using the Non-standard setting.

Extra settings: Allows you to enter special modem initialization strings that older modems require in order to connect and communicate. These are strings like "AT&FE=S0." They tell the modem exactly how to behave.

Record a log file: Allows you to record a modem log file called MODEMLOG.TXT, which will be placed in your \Windows folder. You can use this file to monitor the modem and for troubleshooting. You can choose to overwrite or append to the log file.

Modem Diagnostics

To find out which drivers are installed for which modems and to test your modems, use the Diagnostics tab of the Modems Properties dialog box. This box shows all of the currently installed serial ports and what is attached to them.

Clicking the Driver button pops up a dialog box that will tell you what driver that particular port is using.

If you have selected a port with a device installed on it and you click on the More Info button, you will see information about that port. Windows 98 will send a standard set of AT commands to the port and then display your modem's response. You can compare the responses with the documentation supplied with your modem to make sure that everything is working properly. The More Info dialog box also shows which IRQ (interrupt) channel that port is using, its base address expressed as a hexadecimal value, and the type of UART it is using. You may also see information about the highest speed available on that port. If you choose a port that does not have a device attached to it and select More Info, you will get to the same dialog box, but it will not display any of the AT commands.

> The standard set of AT commands run from AT1 through AT17. AT+FCLASS=? will display a list of fax modem classes supported by this modem.

Clicking the Help button brings up troubleshooting information to walk you through some diagnostics.

In Exercise 15.2 we will examine the settings of the modem so that a custom configuration can be chosen.

EXERCISE 15.2

Configuring a Modem

1. Go to Control Panel ➤ Modems.

2. Highlight an installed modem and choose the Diagnostics tab.

3. Highlight the port the modem is on and choose More Info. You should get a screen that looks like this.

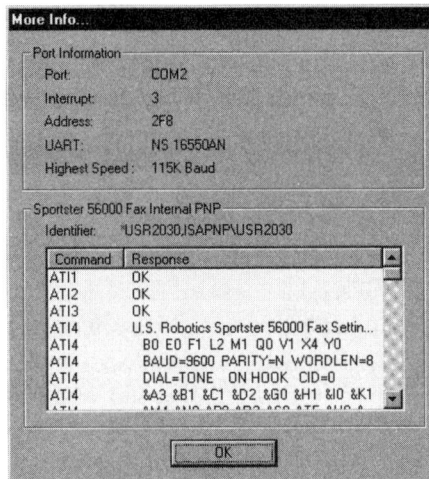

4. Choose OK to close the screen.

5. Choose the General tab, highlight the modem, and choose Properties. It should look something like this. Notice how you can change the speaker volume and maximum speed of the modem.

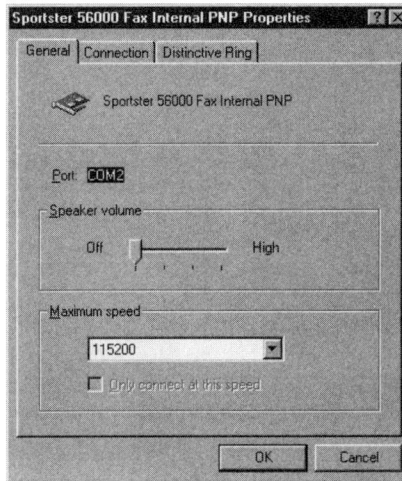

6. Select the Connection tab. Notice how you can change the way the modem will connect to and call other modems.

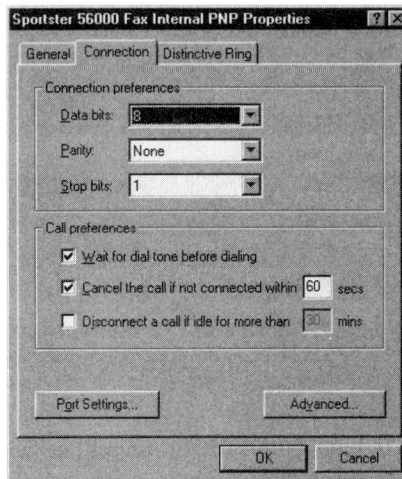

7. Select the Port Settings button. Notice how you can change the UART settings for the modem. Select Cancel to go back one screen.

8. Select the Advanced button. Notice how you can change the error and flow control, and how you can view the log file for the modem.

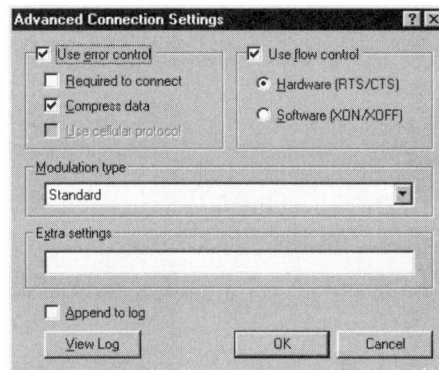

9. Select Cancel, Cancel, Close to close the applet.

Dial-Up Networking

With faster modems and the increasing popularity of laptop computers, doing work from a hotel room or any other off-site location has become more and more common. In 1980, approximately 100,000 people telecommuted in the United States; in 1995, an estimated 12 million telecommuted at least once during the week. If these numbers are extrapolated, 1998 should have approximately 30 million telecommuters.

Windows 98 allows you to remotely connect to your computer at the office and have the machine sitting in front of you share resources as if you were on the network. The modems at both computers act as the network cable. You can download e-mail, get those Microsoft Excel files that you forgot at the office, play a networked computer game like Hearts or Diablo, or do anything else that you would normally do on the network.

Microsoft
Exam
Objective

Configure a Windows 98 computer for remote access by using various methods in a Microsoft environment or a mixed Microsoft and NetWare environment. Methods include:

- Dial-Up Networking
- Proxy Server

Configuring Windows 98 to use a proxy server will be covered later in this chapter.

Dial-Up Networking allows you to access all the available resources on a network from a remote location like your home. The remote location essentially becomes a node on the network utilizing a "slow link." Modem connections to a network are considered slow links because they generally run between 28.8Kbps to 56Kbps on an analog modem and up to 128.8Kbps on a digital modem using ISDN (Integrated Services Digital Network) connections or even 2.5 megabits (roughly 2.5 million bps) on a cable modem. A standard 10 megabit network cable in your office can run between 4.2 million to 10 million bps, and is 65 to 200 times faster than a standard modem connection. New modem standards such as ADSL will help to increase the speed of telecommuting.

Dial-Up Networking Features

Dial-Up Networking encompasses many features found only in Windows 98 and Windows NT, including the following:

- **Compatibility:** As a dial-up server, Windows 98 can support Microsoft Windows NT, LAN Manager, Windows for Workgroups,

LAN Manager for Unix, IBM LAN servers, and Shiva LanRover protocols. When running as a dial-up client, Windows 98 can connect to systems supporting Microsoft RAS, Novell NRN, SLIP, or servers running PPP. (See the discussion of line protocols, under "Dial-Up Networking Architecture," for definitions of these protocols.)

- **LAN topology independent:** As a dial-up server, Windows 98 supports Ethernet, Token Ring, FDDI, and ARCnet.

- **Advanced security:** Dial-Up Networking allows the use of encrypted passwords to prevent their capture and use over public telephone lines.

- **Advanced modem support:** Dial-Up Networking supports all modems that work with the Windows 98 Unimodem driver system. This system includes support for flow control and both software and hardware compression.

- **Slow links:** Dial-Up Networking exposes the slow link API to indicate to programs that they are running over a slow link. This is useful because programs will wait for a predetermined amount of time to receive data across the network. Because networks are so much faster than modems, most programs would issue a timeout error while waiting for the information to come across a slow link. Because programs know that they are using a slow link, the timeout waiting period is much longer.

- **Dial-up server:** Windows 98 can be used as a dial-up server. As such, Windows 98 can support one connection. Note that although this software comes on the CD-ROM, it may have to be specifically installed. (Exercise 15.3 will walk you through the installation of Dial-Up Networking server software.) Note also that you can disable this feature by the use of a System Policy.

NOTE If you install RAS (Remote Access Service) on a Windows NT Server machine, it can support up to 256 simultaneous connections.

Dial-Up Networking Architecture

Like the other parts of Windows 98, the Dial-Up Networking architecture is based on a networking model that uses multiple layers and interchangeable components. The layers for Dial-Up Networking include the Network Interface, Network Protocol, and Line Protocol layers. Each layer communicates with the layer above it and the layer below it, as illustrated in Figure 15.1.

F I G U R E   15.1

Dial-Up Networking architecture

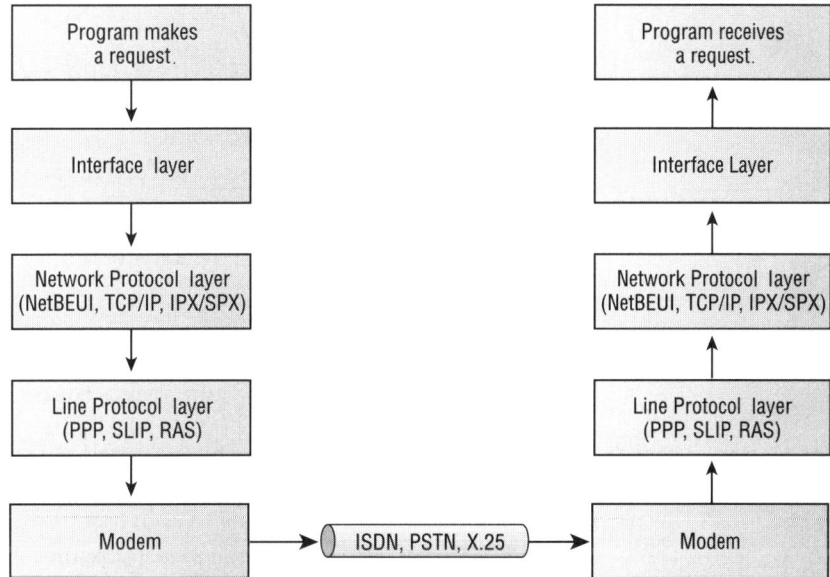

In the following sections, we will take a look at the different layers and their architecture, the different types of networks Dial-Up Networking can connect through, and an example of how the various parts of the architecture interact.

The Network Interface Layer   A *network interface* (also known as a *LAN adapter driver* or *network driver*) is the software that lets your network card talk to the network protocol. Dial-Up Networking supports the following network interfaces:

- **NetBIOS (Network Basic Input Output System):** Establishes sessions in which computers talk with each other. Computers will acknowledge receipt of messages from other computers in a two-way communication scheme.

- **Mailslots:** One-way communications, which do not establish sessions. Using mailslots is like writing a note on a paper airplane and then throwing it to someone else. You don't know whether or not the other person received the message.

- **Named pipes:** Another way to establish one-to-one connections with another computer.

- **RPCs (remote procedure calls):** Send messages to another computer telling it what to do. For example, you might tell another computer to start a particular program. For RPCs to work, the computer receiving the RPCs must be configured to receive them and use the calls.

- **LAN Manager APIs:** Calls to an API, which then executes those calls. They are similar to RPCs, but they do not use the RPC interface.

- **TCP/IP tools:** A set of protocols and interfaces for session-based communications.

- **WinSockets:** A library of support procedures for TCP/IP.

The Network Protocol Layer   As explained in Chapter 8, *network protocols* are like languages (English, German, French, and so on), which allow two computers to communicate with each other across the network. Dial-Up Networking is protocol independent and supports the same standard protocols as other networking features in Windows 98: NetBEUI, IPX/SPX, and TCP/IP. (See Chapter 9 for more information about these protocols.)

The Line Protocol Layer   *Line protocols* are used to encapsulate data into a format suitable for transmittal over telephone lines or null-modem cables. Dial-Up Networking supports the following line protocols:

- **Windows NT RAS (Remote Access Server):** An older protocol developed for Windows NT 3.1. It has been carried forward and is still available under NT 4.0. RAS uses asynchronous NetBEUI. This protocol is slower and less compact than SLIP and PPP, but it has the added advantage of being well tested. It runs with few errors and even fewer opportunities for improper configuration.

- **SLIP (Serial Line Internet Protocol):** A subset of the tools and utilities included with TCP/IP. SLIP should be used in a networking environment that requires machines to have their own unique IP addresses. SLIP is not installed automatically with Windows 98 because it is an older protocol that has been replaced with the more reliable PPP protocol. To add SLIP, use the Add/Remove Programs Control Panel. The files are located on your Windows 98 CD-ROM in the \Admin\Apptools\SLIP folder.

- **PPP (Point-to-Point Protocol):** A standard low-speed protocol that originated from TCP/IP. It has become the most widely used protocol because it is very flexible. Dial-Up Networking is compliant with the industry-standard PPP communications protocol. SLIP requires a pre-assigned IP address, whereas PPP can use a DHCP server and "lease" an IP address for a short period of time. (See Chapter 9 for more information about IP addresses and DHCP.)

- **PPTP/VPN:** Point-to-Point Tunneling Protocol/Virtual Private Network is a new standard. This new protocol allows a user to dial up an Internet service provider (ISP) and then use the PPTP to tunnel into an office network using the VPN protocol for secure communications.

- **NRN NetWare Connect:** A proprietary connection protocol that allows a Windows 98 machine to directly connect with a NetWare Connect server. Novell's IPX/SPX network protocol must be used for this type of connection.

WARNING NetWare Connect clients cannot connect to a Windows 98 dial-up server.

Wide Area Network Support   Dial-Up Networking can use the modem and TAPI (Telephony Applications Programming Interface) components to work over different types of wide area networks (WANs):

- **Public-switched telephone networks (PSTNs):** The regular telephone lines that you use every day to make phone calls. The modem in your computer can use these same telephone lines to transmit and receive data.

- **X.25:** A special packet-switching network. An X.25 packet is delivered to another X.25 node on a worldwide X.25 network. That node then forwards the packet to the next node, and so on until the packet finally reaches a packet assembler/disassembler (PAD) at the other machine. The PAD takes the place of your standard modem.

- **Integrated Services Digital Network (ISDN):** A standard for digital telephony. ISDN offers faster communications than you can get with a standard analog telephone line. ISDN speeds range from 64,000 to 128,800bps. ISDN requires a special digital modem and an ISDN telephone line to your home and office.

How Dial-Up Networking Works

Let's go through an example of what happens when you use Dial-Up Networking. After dinner, you decide to do some work on a Microsoft Word document. You fire up the computer and use Dial-Up Networking to log in to your computer at the office. You start up Microsoft Word on the client (your home PC) and then open a document located on the host (your computer at the office). When you open that document, Word is making a request for service at the top layer in the Dial-Up Networking architecture (see Figure 15.1).

The Network Interface layer will then format your request into a packet that the Network Protocol layer can understand. Essentially, you have a core piece of data that will get successive layers added around it. This process is called *encapsulation*. The packet is then passed to the Network Protocol layer, which will encapsulate your packet with the appropriate network protocol (like NetBEUI or TCP/IP). In a normal networked environment, your packet would then be sent across the wire to the appropriate server. Because you are using a dial-up interface, your network packet is passed on to the Line Protocol layer. This layer encapsulates the packet into a format that can be transmitted across the telephone lines (such as SLIP or PPP).

After the packet has been encapsulated for transmittal, it is sent through your modem to the telephone lines, where it travels through an ISDN, a PSTN, or an X.25 telephone service. Once the other modem receives the packet of information, it is passed up through the layers, where each layer of encapsulation is removed at the appropriate level. After all of the layers are removed, the host machine can then act upon the request, which was "give me this file."

> **NOTE**   You can use Dial-Up Networking over a telephone line or through a null-modem interface, using a serial cable or parallel cable linked between the two computers.

Dial-Up Networking Installation and Configuration

The requirements for Dial-Up Networking include one or more compatible modems. You also need 2MB of free hard disk space to install the client, server, and administrative utilities. The installation process consists of four parts:

- Install and configure your modem.
- Install Dial-Up Networking.
- Create a client connection to a server.
- Create a dial-up server.

The procedures for installing and configuring a modem were covered earlier in this chapter.

You install Dial-Up Networking using the Internet Connection Wizard (Dial-Up Networking will be installed if it hasn't been already) or through the Add/Remove Programs (in the Communication section) of Control Panel. The following sections describe how to create dial-up connections and a dial-up server.

Creating Dial-Up Connections

Creating a connection places a connection object in your Dial-Up Networking folder. The connection object is analogous to an index card. It tells Windows 98 where to go to connect to the host computer and can provide details like a user ID and password to the host system that it is attempting to log on to.

Setting up a connection involves specifying the computer you are dialing, the type of modem you are using, and the telephone number to dial. The New Connection Wizard steps you through the procedure, as shown in Figures 15.2 and 15.3.

Exercise 15.3 will take you through the steps for creating a dial-up connection.

Exercise 15.3 uses a sample computer name and telephone number. Substitute your own information if you want to set up an actual connection.

F I G U R E   15.2

Specifying the computer name and modem

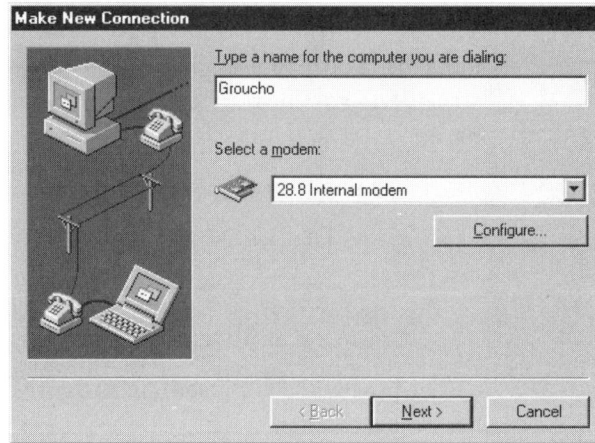

F I G U R E   15.3

Entering the telephone number information

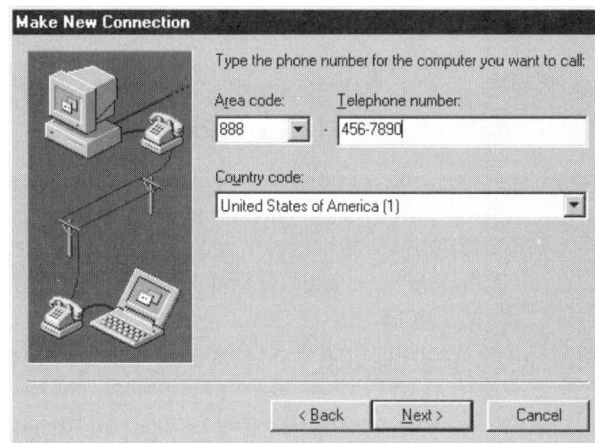

EXERCISE 15.3

Creating a Dial-Up Connection

1. Select Start ➢ Programs ➢ Accessories ➢ Dial-Up Networking to open the Dial-Up Networking folder.

2. Double-click the Make New Connection icon to start the New Connection Wizard.

3. If you see the Welcome To Dial-Up Networking screen, click the Next button. (Your version of Windows 98 might bypass this screen.) This takes you to the first Make New Connection dialog box.

4. In the "Type a name for the computer you are dialing" box, enter a name for this connection: **Groucho** (see Figure 15.2).

5. Select your modem. If you haven't installed your modem yet, review the beginning section of this chapter. (The Configure button allows you to make configuration changes to your currently selected modem.) Then click Next to move to the screen requesting the telephone number that you want to call.

6. Type in the area code **888** and the telephone number **456-7890** (see Figure 15.3). Then click Next to go to the Confirmation screen.

7. If everything looks correct on the final screen, click the Finish button. Your Dial-Up Networking folder now has a new icon in it called "Groucho."

Dial-Up Networking will treat your modem as a network card. This will require the PPP protocol to be installed. If you have not already installed PPP, don't worry—the Wizard will automatically install it for you.

Modifying Dialing Settings   The location settings in the Dialing Properties dialog box allow Windows 98 to analyze different telephone numbers and then decide how to dial them. For example, if your area code is 602 and you decide to send a fax from Microsoft Word, Word will fire up the fax service. The fax service will eventually ask you to type in a fax number. When you type in that number—(602) 555-4567, for example—TAPI will compare the 602 entries and will recognize that the number is a local call rather than a long-distance call.

You can add many different locations in the "Where I am" section. This is especially useful if you travel a lot and are in different area codes or even different countries.

The "To access an outside line" boxes are useful for dialing through PBX-type systems, which require dialing a number to get an outside line. For example, you may need to dial 9 and wait a second or two to get an outside line. If you place a comma in the telephone numbers, or in the Outside line box, this tells the computer to pause for one second before it continues dialing. If you placed **9,,** in the first dial box, this would dial the number 9, pause for two seconds, and then proceed to dial the rest of the number.

If you choose Dial Using Calling Card, your system will use your calling card to dial out. To set up a calling card, click the Dial Using Calling Card option and then click the Change button. You will see the Change Calling Card dialog box, shown in Figure 15.4. Choose your calling card from the list box. If you do not see your calling card in the list, choose New and add a new calling card. The Dialing Rules dialog box will be displayed, as shown in Figure 15.5. The text boxes can be filled with information from another calling card by choosing the Copy From button. Each box uses special letters and dollar signs ($) to denote different things. For instance, the G might signify "Wait for the dial tone before dialing." A *T* might signify "Wait until you hear the bong before proceeding."

F I G U R E 15.4

The Change Calling Card dialog box

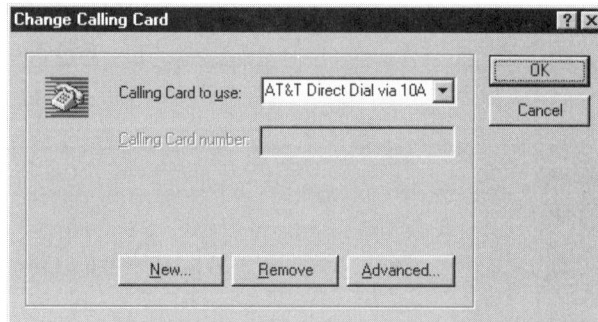

F I G U R E 15.5

The Dialing Rules dialog box

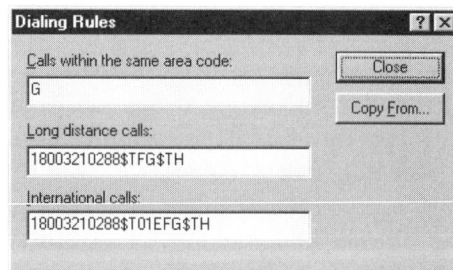

For more information about calling card codes, contact your calling card company.

If you have call waiting, you can disable it by selecting the "This location has call waiting..." option in the Dialing Properties dialog box. The standard is *70, which will disable call waiting for the duration of this call. Once you hang up, call waiting will automatically re-enable itself. If for some reason it does not, pick up your telephone and dial *71.

Connecting via Dial-Up Networking

When you select your connection icon in the Dial-Up Networking folder, Windows 98 presents the Connect To dialog box, shown in Figure 15.6. The Dial Properties button in this dialog box will take you to the Dialing Properties dialog box, which is discussed in the "Viewing TAPI Settings" section.

FIGURE 15.6

The Connect To
dialog box

While you are connected, you can see what type of server you have connected to and which protocols you are currently using. In the example shown in Figure 15.7, the connection is to a Windows for Workgroups and Windows NT server using the NetBEUI protocol.

F I G U R E   15.7

Viewing connection
details

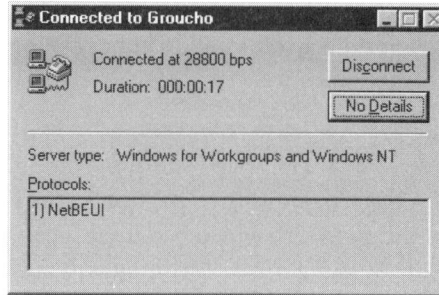

Once you have connected, you can use the resources on the dial-up server just as if you were working at the office. You can go to your Network Neighborhood and see the server there. If you have mapped drive letters to network resources, these should now be accessible through Windows Explorer or My Computer.

Follow the steps in Exercise 15.4 to make a connection and view connection details. (In order to complete this exercise, you need a dial-up server to connect to.)

EXERCISE 15.4

Connecting to a Dial-Up Server

1. Double-click the Groucho icon in your Dial-Up Networking folder (created in Exercise 15.3).

2. Enter a username and password that the dial-up server will recognize (see Figure 15.6). Make sure that the telephone number is correct.

3. Click the Connect button. Your computer dials the telephone number and attempts to connect to the server, displaying the message shown here.

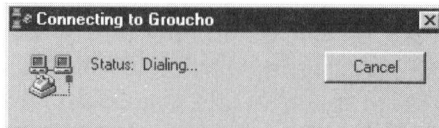

4. Once you have connected to the server, it will verify your username and password. The Connected To box, shown below, indicates the speed of your connection and the duration of time that you've been connected.

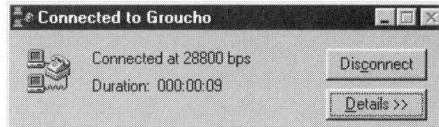

5. Click Details to see the type of server you are connected to and which protocols you are currently using (see Figure 15.7).

6. To disconnect and end your dial-up session, click the Disconnect button.

> **NOTE** If you do not have a dial-up session currently running and you try to access one of your mapped drive letters, the computer will try to connect to the network via the dial-up connection by starting the Dial-Up Networking program on your PC. This is called a *ghosted*, or *implicit, connection*. The ghosted connection is not really established until you log in and connect, but a ghost of the connection will be in your folder in the form of a mapped drive icon.

Telephony Application Programming Interface (TAPI)

TAPI (Telephony Application Programming Interface) is a standard way for programs to interact with the telephony functionality in Windows 98. TAPI works much like the Unimodem driver discussed earlier.

All programs that want to use telephony can do so through a standard set of calls to the TAPI interface. This makes it easier for third-party developers to create programs that are modem- and fax-ready. All the programmers must do is invoke the TAPI functionality to achieve a standard interface with which the user is already familiar. If this were not the case, every program a developer created would need to have its own dialing properties, location settings, and access to the modem hardware.

Viewing TAPI Settings   You can view the TAPI settings through the Modems Control Panel. In the General tab, click the Dialing Properties button to see the Dialing Properties dialog box, shown in Figure 15.8.

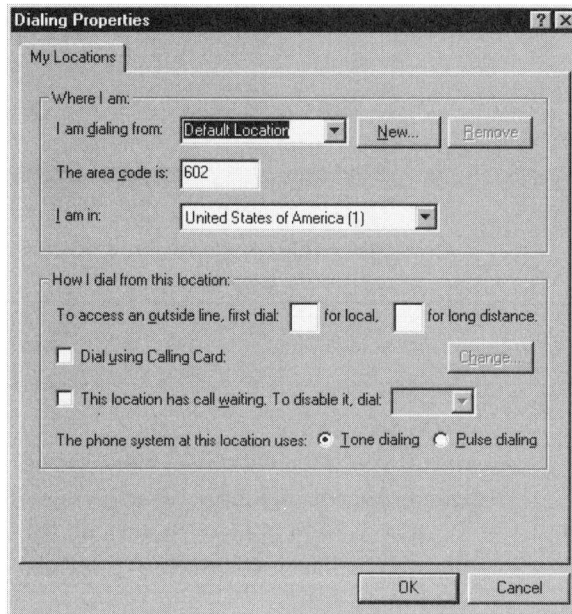

The Dialog Properties dialog box

VPN/PPTP

VPN/PPTP stands for Virtual Private Network/Point-to-Point Tunneling Protocol. It allows you to make secure, encrypted connections via the Internet. An example of its use would be a company that has branch offices but no company WAN. Each office (including the corporate headquarters) could connect to the Internet via a local ISP, and then to the company network using a secured connection via PPTP.

NOTE   Your dial-up server must also be configured for VPN/PPTP support in order for VPN/PPTP to work correctly.

Microsoft ✓ **Exam** **Objective**

Install and configure the network components of Windows 98 in a Microsoft environment or a mixed Microsoft and NetWare environment. Network components include:

- Client for Microsoft Networks
- Client for NetWare Networks
- NetWare adapters
- File and Printer Sharing for Microsoft Networks
- File and Printer Sharing for NetWare Networks
- Service for NetWare Directory Services (NDS)
- Asynchronous transfer mode (ATM)
- Virtual private networking (VPN) and PPTP
- Browse Master

NOTE: ATM is discussed in Chapter 8; the Microsoft and NetWare clients and network cards are discussed in Chatper 9; File and Printer Sharing for both Microsoft and NetWare and the Browse Master are discussed in Chapter 10.

Installing and Configuring VPN/PPTP

VPN/PPTP is installed using the Add/Remove Programs applet of Control Panel. VPN/PPTP is listed in the Communication section.

After installing VPN/PPTP support, you will see another adapter called "Dial-Up Adapter #2 (VPN Support)" in your list of network adapters.

Once you have installed the Dial-Up Networking 1.2 code, you can create a VPN/PPTP connection by specifying the VPN adapter instead of your regular modem when defining a dial-up networking connection.

Dial-Up Networking Server

Windows 98 can also install software that allows it to become a Dial-Up Networking server. When used as a Dial-Up server, Windows 98 allows a single connection to its resources. Windows 98 supports other Windows 95/98 machines, LAN Manager, Windows for Workgroups 3.11, Windows NT, and any PPP-based remote client.

Microsoft
✓ *Exam*
Objective

Configure Windows 98 server components. Server components include:

- Microsoft Personal Web Server 4.0
- Dial-Up Networking server

The Microsoft Personal Web Server 4.0 is discussed later in the chapter.

The Dial-Up Networking server is installed using the Add/Remove Programs applet of the Control Panel and is listed in the Communication section.

To set up a Dial-Up server, you need to enable caller access by opening the Dial-Up Networking window and going to Connections ➤ Dial-Up Server, as shown in Figure 15.9. You can also choose the server type and set password encryption and software compression options, as shown in Figure 15.10.

FIGURE 15.9

The Dial-Up Server dialog box

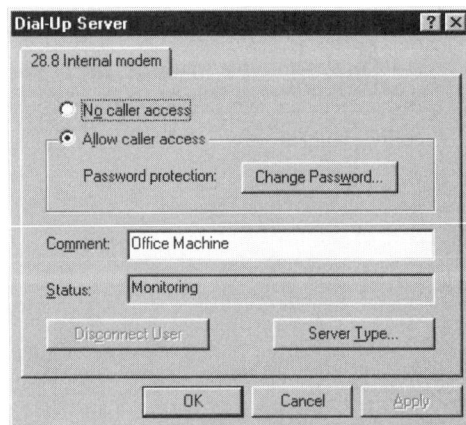

FIGURE 15.10

Selecting the
server type

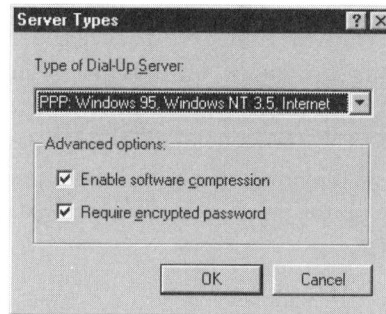

Follow the steps in Exercise 15.3 to turn your Windows 98 machine into a Dial-Up server.

EXERCISE 15.5

Setting Up a Dial-Up Server

1. Install the Dial-Up Networking server software (if it isn't already) by going to Control Panel ➤ Add/Remove Programs and selecting Dial-Up Server from the Communications section. Close the applet.

2. From the Dial-Up Networking folder, select Connections ➤ Dial-Up Server to bring up the Dial-Up Server dialog box (see Figure 15.9).

3. To make your Windows 98 machine a Dial-Up server, click the "Allow caller access" option.

4. If you want to create a password that a client must use to access your Dial-Up server, click the Change Password button.

5. Click the Server Type button to bring up the Server Types dialog box (see Figure 15.10). Choose a server type from the drop-down list and click the Enable Software Compression and/or Require Encrypted Password checkboxes if you want to use these options. Then choose OK.

6. In the Dial-Up Server dialog box, click Apply or OK to complete the setup. Your Windows 98 machine is now ready to accept calls from clients.

Internet Explorer 4

From the moment you click the Internet Explorer (IE) icon on your Desktop, its ease of operation is quite evident. IE is designed with the user in mind.

> **NOTE** At the time this book was written, Internet Explorer 4.02 was the current version on the market with IE 5 in early beta testing.

IE makes even the novice surfer feel right at home, with its built-in Help screens and its ability to remember all the Web sites you have visited. It allows you to create a "hot list" of all your favorite sites so that, the next time you log on, with a click on the Favorites button you can pick up right where you left off in your last session.

Installing Internet Explorer 4.0*x*

You may have to install IE 4.0 either to upgrade an existing version of IE or as part of a new installation of Windows 98.

If you install the latest version of Internet Explorer, you will be prompted to install either the standard or full installation of IE 4.02 (see Figure 15.11). The standard version includes the Web browser, Outlook Express, and various other multimedia enhancements, while the full version adds Net-Meeting, FrontPage Express, NetShow, Web Publishing Wizard, and Microsoft Chat 2.0.

The next major decision you will have to make during the installation is whether you want Active Desktop installed (see Figure 15.12).

By installing the Active Desktop, you dramatically change the way you work with your computer—instead of the Explorer, you basically use IE to view and manage your local hard drives as well as Internet resources. If you are very comfortable with the current interface, say "No" to the Active Desktop. If you love the look of the Internet, have a powerful computer with lots of spare CPU cycles and RAM, and wish that everything on your computer was more consistent, go ahead and try the Active Desktop.

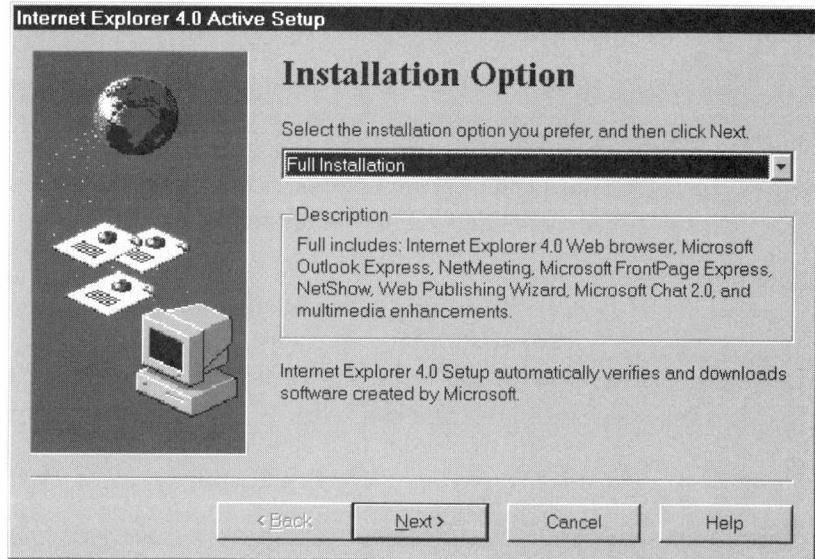

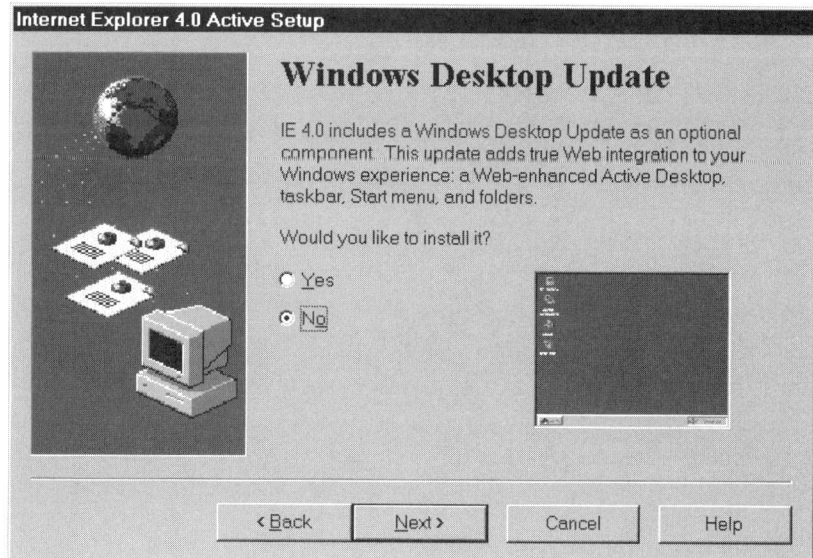

TIP

Installing the Active Desktop can consume up to 16MB more RAM than the plain, default Desktop. If your computer seems to be slow running Windows 98, installing the Active Desktop will probably make it slower. Also, the Active Desktop is most useful when you have a constant connection to the Internet. Home computers that use a dial-up connection to the Internet may not find the Active Desktop as useful.

The first time you run IE 4.02, it prompts you for connection setup options via the Internet Connection Wizard (see Figure 15.13). It can also be run manually at a later time if you want to set up a new connection, such as when you switch ISPs. If you already have an Internet account set up, or if you are connecting to the Internet at work, you should probably choose "I already have an Internet connection set up on this computer and I do not want to change it."

FIGURE 15.13

Connection Setup
Options

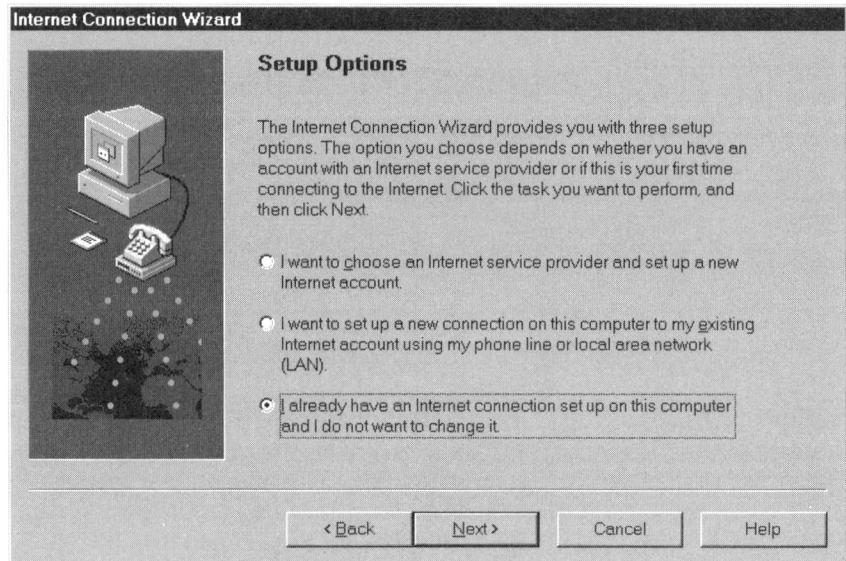

Internet Connection Wizard

Setup Options

The Internet Connection Wizard provides you with three setup options. The option you choose depends on whether you have an account with an Internet service provider or if this is your first time connecting to the Internet. Click the task you want to perform, and then click Next.

○ I want to choose an Internet service provider and set up a new Internet account.

○ I want to set up a new connection on this computer to my existing Internet account using my phone line or local area network (LAN).

⦿ I already have an Internet connection set up on this computer and I do not want to change it.

< Back   Next >   Cancel   Help

Internet Explorer will go to a startup page that will prompt for your time zone and zip code, after which you will go to a customizable start page.

As you can see in Figure 15.14, IE has all the familiar pull-down menus that you are accustomed to using in Microsoft products. It allows you to quickly access links and information that you can customize to fit your needs in the business, education, and just-plain-fun categories.

F I G U R E   15.14

Internet Explorer 4.02 main screen

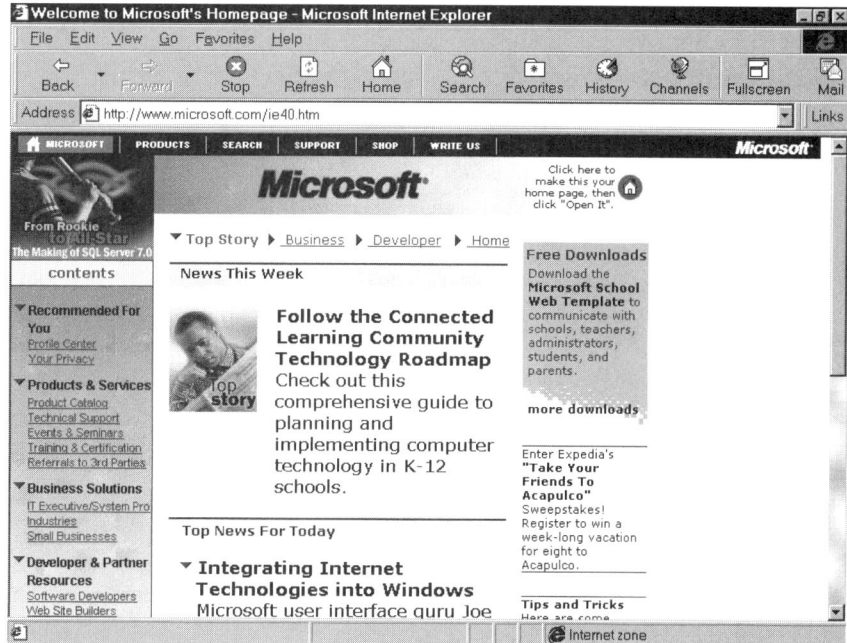

You can usually refer to WWW servers by their "friendly" name instead of their TCP/IP address because the Domain Name Service (DNS) resolves the name into the address. DNS works like a directory listing for phone numbers. If you are unable to connect to sites using friendly names but can still connect using the actual TCP/IP addresses, you may have a misconfigured DNS.

IE and E-Mail

IE makes sending and receiving e-mail simple. It is not necessary to go through all the Microsoft Mail or Exchange settings within Windows 98. You just need to fill in a few simple pieces of information and Outlook

Express can then send and receive e-mail. Figure 15.15 shows the Internet Mail screen.

F I G U R E   15.15

E-mail using IE 4.02 and Outlook Express

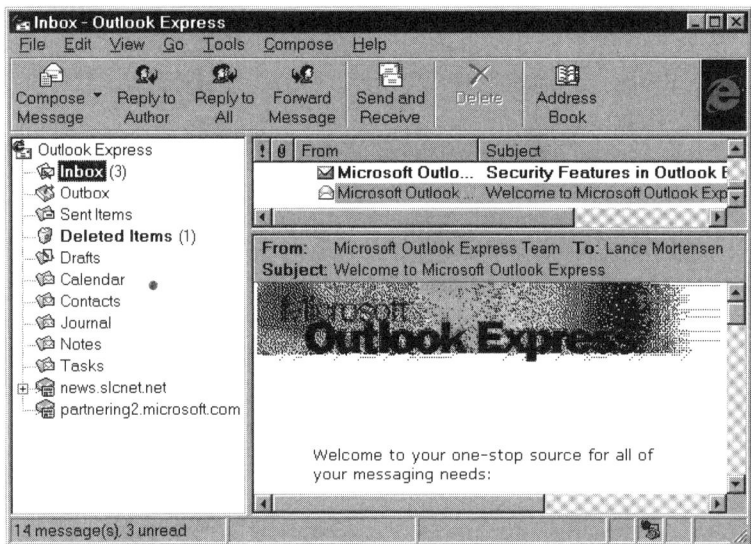

When you click the Mail button, your Internet e-mail shows up. Through the Tools ≻ Options menu, you can select the exact setup you need. You can also choose to send your message immediately or save a batch of messages to send the next time you log on to your mail connection service.

Ratings and IE

A big concern of most parents is what their children will find while surfing the Internet. IE has a built-in security feature that virtually eliminates this worry. When properly set up, IE will not allow users to venture into any area where they should not be.

To enable the ratings system, click the View menu and choose Internet Options. Then go to the Content tab, shown in Figure 15.16.

Click the Enable Ratings button and enter a password. Then click the Settings button to set the scale of different items that can be viewed, such as Language, Nudity, Sex, or Violence, as shown in Figure 15.17.

FIGURE 15.16

The Content tab of the Internet Explorer Internet Options dialog box

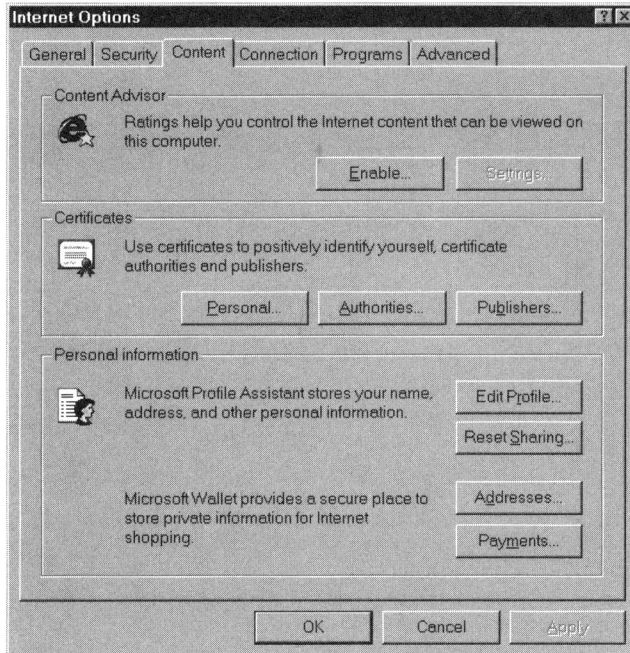

FIGURE 15.17

The Internet Explorer ratings scales

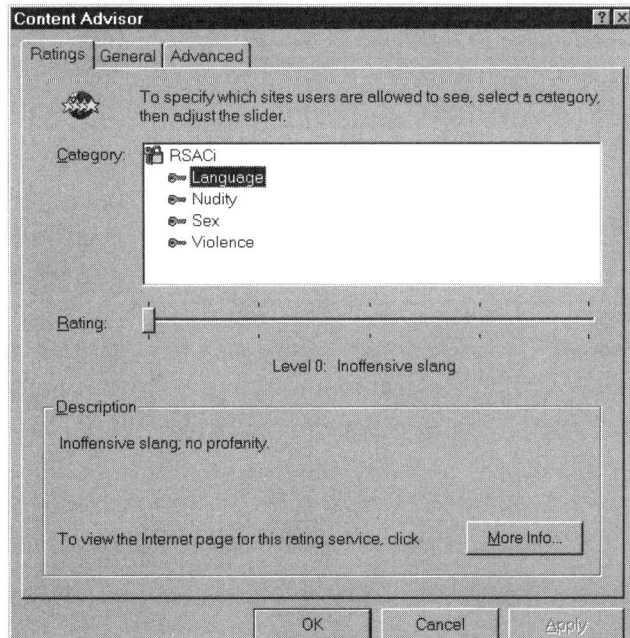

The General tab lets you specify whether IE will display pages that are not rated and if the password can be entered to bypass the ratings system. This tab is shown in Figure 15.18.

F I G U R E   15.18

The General tab of the Internet Explorer Content Advisor dialog box

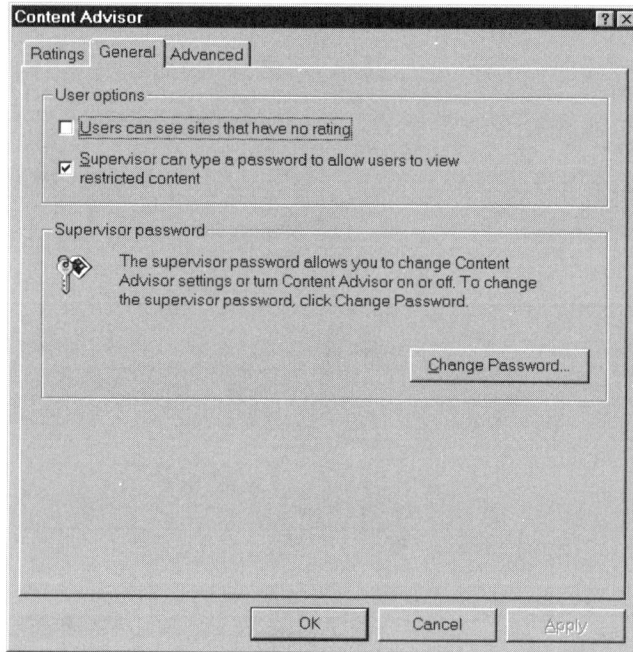

Proxy Server and IE

A *proxy server* is designed to act as a middle man between WWW servers and browsers so that it can cache frequently used WWW pages. Other uses of proxy servers are for firewalls and protocol conversions.

Microsoft Exam Objective

Configure a Windows 98 computer for remote access by using various methods in a Microsoft environment or mixed Microsoft and NetWare environment. Methods include:

- Dial-Up Networking
- Proxy Server

Dial-up Networking is discussed earlier in the chapter.

Proxy Server 2.0 for Windows NT is the current version out from Microsoft. IE can be configured to use a proxy server via the Connection tab of the Internet Options window (see Figure 15.19). Several options can be set for proxy server connections, including when to bypass the proxy server to connect to intranet servers as shown in Figure 15.19.

FIGURE 15.19

Configuring IE to use a proxy server

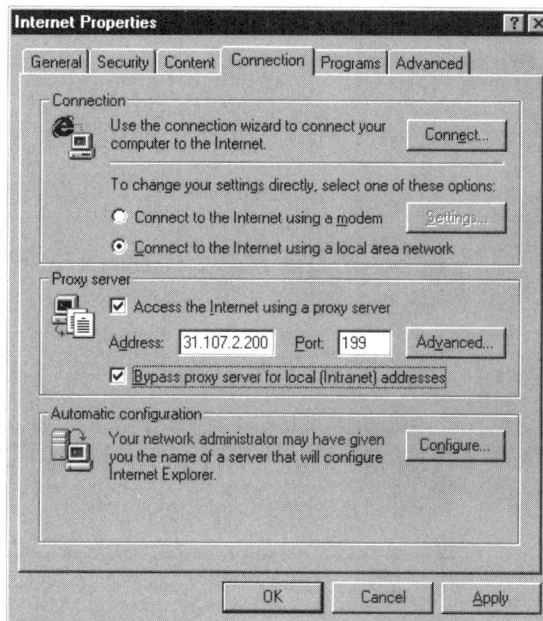

Advanced proxy server settings allow you to enable different proxy servers and ports for different applications, as well as build a list of sites and addresses that will cause the proxy server to be bypassed (see Figure 15.20).

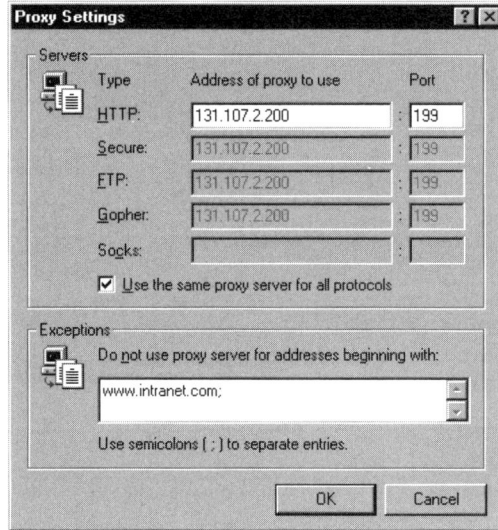

Personal Web Server for Windows 98

Microsoft ✓ *Exam* *Objective*	**Configure Windows 98 server components. Server components include:** • Microsoft Personal Web Server 4.0 • Dial-Up Networking Server

> **NOTE** The Dial-Up Networking server is discussed earlier in the chapter.

If you are considering putting your own Web page on the World Wide Web, using Personal Web Server (PWS) is an alternative to paying someone to create your page for you. With a copy of PWS and Microsoft FrontPage or Microsoft Publisher, you can create your own professional-looking Web page documents.

Installing PWS

Installing PWS into Windows 98 is quick and simple. Go to Control Panel ➤ Network, choose Add, highlight Service, pick Microsoft, highlight Personal Web Server (see Figure 15.21), and choose OK.

FIGURE 15.21

Installing Personal Web Server

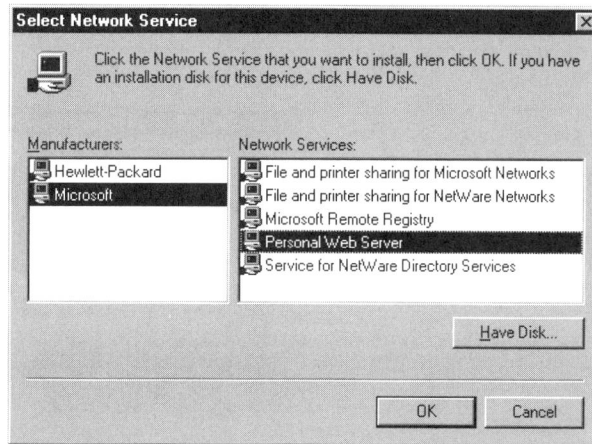

PWS version 4.0 has been released and can be downloaded for no charge from www.microsoft.com. PWS 4.0 also comes as part of the NT 4.0 Option Pack CD-ROM.

If you install Microsoft FrontPage, PWS will be installed automatically as one of the add-on items. Whichever way you install it, with PWS your Windows 98 machine has now been turned into a fully operational Web server.

Although Windows 98 can operate as an HTTP server, it was not designed for heavy-use, mission-critical production environments. For a heavy-use informational HTTP server, you should use Windows NT server, coupled with Internet Information Server (IIS). For a mission-critical electronic commerce HTTP server, Site Server for Windows NT should be used. Note that IIS is available for no additional charge, while Site Server is an add-on product for Windows NT and, therefore, costs extra. Details about IIS and Site Server can be found in *MCSE: IIS 4.0 Study Guide,* published by Sybex.

Configuring PWS

You configure PWS by clicking on the PWS icon that is added to your Control Panel or by going to Start ➤ Programs ➤ Microsoft Personal Web Server ➤ Personal Web Manager (for version 4.0). This brings up the Personal Web Server Properties dialog box (for older versions) or the Personal Web Manager (for 4.0). Either program allows you to start, configure, and stop the HTTP and FTP services as shown in Figure 15.22.

F I G U R E 15.22

Starting and stopping the HTTP and FTP services of PWS

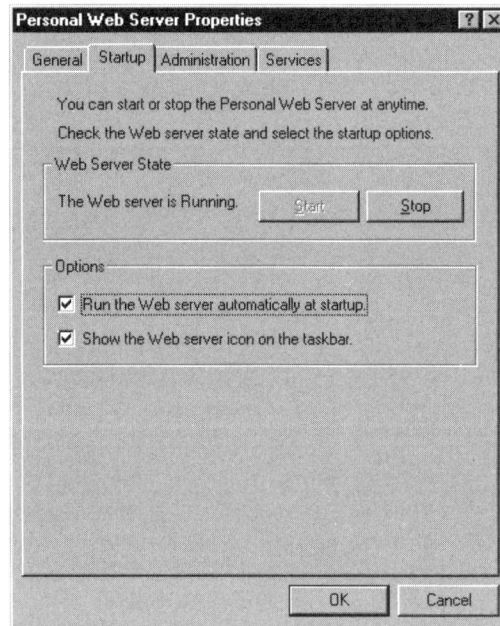

> **NOTE** Please refer to *MCSE: IIS Study Guide* (Sybex) for more information on installing, configuring, and administering HTTP servers.

Creating a Web Page

Perhaps the idea of creating a Web site that may be seen by millions of people makes you nervous. The plain and simple truth is that this should not be the case any longer. With Microsoft products, even a person with only basic word processing skills can create professional-looking Web pages. You don't even need to take an HTML programming course.

If you have Office 97, you basically have all you need. Word 97 allows you to create a document and insert all kinds of clip art, which can be supplied from its built-in clip art gallery. After you have finished, you simply save the document in the HTML format, and it is ready to go to your Web site.

The newest version of Excel is designed in the same way as all the new Office 97 products. Do you need to publish a spreadsheet on your Web site? Create it in Excel, save it as an HTML document, and you are ready to publish it on your Web site.

All of the Office 97 products, even PowerPoint, will let you save and publish HTML documents. However, if you are still using the Office 95 product line, don't despair—there is an add-on for Word 7.0 that you can download from the Microsoft Web site. This add-on gives Word 7 the ability to edit and save HTML documents.

As mentioned earlier, Microsoft FrontPage and Microsoft Publisher are products that make it simple to create Web pages. Both are driven by built-in wizards that give you a multitude of choices for Web page design. You can instantly transform your screen into a Web page that compares to those created by even the most advanced HTML expert. With FrontPage Editor, you can open Web pages that were previously created by anyone, edit them, and add background sounds, pictures, videos, and even hyperlinks—just by a click of your mouse.

If you are into Web page development and are running your own Web site, Microsoft has come up with a great add-on for IE that lets you edit your Web pages. If you have a copy of Microsoft FrontPage, it automatically adds Edit to the menu bar. Simply go to your Web site and click Edit. You can make live changes to your Web site and then save those changes without stopping to run additional software to download the changes to your site.

Security for Mobile Computing

Anytime you open up your computer system to the outside world, you take a chance that someone will try to break in and destroy information. When setting up your computers for dial-up access, you should consider implementing the following security strategies to prevent unauthorized access to your systems:

- Use user-level security on the server side. This forces the server to check both the user ID and the password before allowing access.

- Use system policies in conjunction with dial-up access. Windows 98 system policies can implement different levels of access to the computer resources based upon the login.

- Use encrypted passwords. This keeps outsiders from getting your password as it is passed along the telephone networks.

- Use firewalls for large servers that allow Internet access. A *firewall* is a set of multiple layers of security strategies to keep outsiders out of your system.

- You might want to encrypt sensitive documents that you will be sending over the Internet. Encryption software is available from a variety of sources, including the Internet.

Data-Transfer Performance

You can take a few simple steps to improve your data-transfer performance. Here are just a couple of things you might try:

- Use compression. Windows 98 supports both hardware and software compression. This setting is available from the Modems dialog box.

- Use the System Monitor to check your performance. Look at the bytes read per second and bytes written per second under the Microsoft Client.

Summary

Mobile computing allows you to connect a client computer to a host computer without the aid of a network cable. In this chapter, you learned about the Windows 98 support for mobile computing, including the Dial-Up Networking, Direct Cable Connection, and Briefcase features.

Windows 98 supports a wide variety of modems. The best way to install a new modem is to allow Windows 98 to automatically detect it. You can manually install, configure, and troubleshoot modems from the Modems applet of the Control Panel.

Windows 98 has many new features that are part of the Dial-Up Networking interface, including compatibility with many existing networks and protocols, security in the form of encryption and system policies, the VPN/PPTP protocol, and advanced modem support for today's latest and greatest. The Dial-Up Networking architecture comprises several layers that support network interfaces, network protocols (including NetBEUI, IPX/SPX, and TCP/IP), and line protocols (like PPP and SLIP). To use Dial-Up Networking, you need to set up both the dial-up client and server components.

The Internet is a public network that offers information, entertainment, and commercial activities to anyone connected to it. In this chapter, you learned about Windows 98's ability to connect to the Internet, its modem support, its dial-up networking support as both a client and as a server, its ability to see HTML pages using an Internet browser, and its ability to share HTML pages as a WWW server.

The Internet consists of World Wide Web servers and clients running a browser. These communicate using the HTTP language, which piggybacks on the TCP/IP protocol.

Intranets are for internal company use only, while an extranet is designed for use by partner companies to exchange data.

Windows 98 can be both an HTTP server (when Personal Web Server is installed) and a client (when a browser such as Internet Explorer is used).

The latest version of both PWS and IE are at version 4, and can be downloaded for free from Microsoft's Web site (`www.microsoft.com`). Internet Explorer 4.0x also includes an option to install Active Desktop, which makes your desktop, and all the resources on your computer, appear as Internet-type resources. If you install Active Desktop, Internet Explorer replaces My Computer and Explorer as the way you look at resources.

IIS (Internet Information Server) and Site Server are high-level HTTP server products, designed for mission-critical servers using Windows NT.

E-mail, newsgroup, and netmeeting client software is also freely available from Microsoft.

Publishing your own Web pages is relatively simple with today's software, as Office 97 and FrontPage 9.0x have been designed to help you easily save your work in HTML format, the format of the Internet.

Review Questions

1. What three network protocols are supported by Dial-Up Networking?

   A. NetBEUI

   B. PPP

   C. IPX/SPX

   D. TCP/IP

2. What can you do to increase security when using mobile computing? Choose all that apply.

   A. Utilize user-level security on the host computer.

   B. Use password encryption.

   C. Encrypt your data files when transferring them.

   D. Use a system policy.

3. A Windows 98 dial-up server can support all of the following except:

   A. Windows 98 client

   B. PPP-based client

   C. Windows NT client

   D. Macintosh client using AppleTalk

4. Which dial-up line protocol is the most flexible and is the default used by Windows 98?

   A. SLIP

   B. PPP

   C. NRN NetWare Connect

   D. NT RAS

5. What protocol is required in order to use Internet Explorer?

   A. TCP/IP

   B. IPX/SPX

   C. NetBEUI

   D. DLC

6. Can Windows 98 run Internet browsers?

   A. Yes, but only Microsoft's Internet Explorer.

   B. Yes, but only if you have the latest version of Internet Explorer.

   C. Yes, it can run any Internet browser written for Windows 98.

   D. No.

7. What is Active Desktop?

   A. It turns your computer into a Personal Web Server.

   B. It converts your Desktop into an ActiveX object.

   C. It converts your Desktop into HTTP objects, which means that IE is then used to manage local as well as Internet resources.

   D. It changes the Explorer to more of a file-manager type interface.

8. What do WWW servers and browsers use to communicate?

   A. DLC

   B. TCP/IP

   C. FTP

   D. HTTP

9. Which HTTP server would be the best fit for a small doctor's office intranet server?

    A. Personal Web Server on Windows 98

    B. IIS on Windows NT Server

    C. Peer Web Services on Windows NT Workstation

    D. Site Server on Windows NT Server

10. Which HTTP server should be used for a large, informational HTTP server?

    A. Personal Web Server

    B. IIS on Windows NT Server

    C. Peer Web Services on Windows NT Workstation

    D. Site Server on Windows NT Server

11. Which HTTP server should be used for a mission-critical electronic commerce server?

    A. Personal Web Server

    B. IIS on Windows NT Server

    C. Peer Web Services on Windows NT Workstation

    D. Site Server on Windows NT Server

12. If you are accessing the Internet using a dial-up connection, which protocol is required? Choose all that apply.

    A. NetBEUI

    B. IPX/SPX

    C. TCP/IP

    D. DLC

13. To access the WWW sites on the Internet as a client, you need to run which type of software?

   A. An HTTP server

   B. An HTTP browser

   C. Explorer will work fine

   D. My Computer will work fine

14. To connect to an HTTP server running on a NetWare 3.12 server, you will need which protocol(s)? Choose all that apply.

   A. NetBEUI

   B. IPX/SPX

   C. TCP/IP

   D. DLC

15. If you can connect to a Unix HTTP server by address, but not by name, which software program is probably at fault?

   A. WINS

   B. DNS

   C. DHCP

   D. NetBIOS

16. Which type of computers can be HTTP servers? Choose all that apply.

   A. Windows 98

   B. Windows NT

   C. NetWare

   D. Unix

17. In order to bypass security restrictions on a local network, proxy server settings should be configured to access an intranet as which of the following?

   A. Allow access to local intranet

   B. Bypass proxy server for local (intranet) addresses

   C. Don't allow access to local intranet

   D. Bypass security for local (intranet) addresses

18. What program comes with Windows 98 that allows you to easily edit and create Web pages?

   A. Notepad

   B. Word

   C. FrontPage Express

   D. Access

19. Some users are worried about security when they access the Internet using Dial-Up Networking because they have some shared folders. What is one method can you use to help secure their system when they access the Internet?

   A. Don't allow them to use Dial-Up Networking.

   B. Have them use PPTP to access the Internet.

   C. Have them unbind the Dial-Up Networking adapter from their File and Printer Sharing service.

   D. Have them use modem compression.

20. A user wants to make a newsletter available to the entire company. What service can she install in Windows 98?

   A. An Internet browser

   B. IIS

   C. FPNW

   D. PWS

21. A user has a hard time connecting to one particular dial-up server. How can log files can be created for a dial-up session?

   A. They can't be created.

   B. Log files must be enabled globally for every dial-up connection.

   C. Log files can be enabled individually for dial-up connections.

   D. Log files are enabled by default.

16

Troubleshooting Windows 98

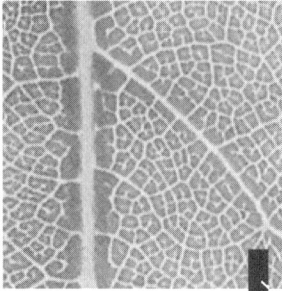

Using a multifaceted approach is the best way to troubleshoot any problem. Most of this chapter focuses on a general approach to troubleshooting, including initial diagnosis of the problem, troubleshooting resources, and Windows 98 troubleshooting tools. It also offers suggestions for monitoring the system, auditing Windows 98, optimizing Windows 98 memory usage, and optimizing the swap file. Finally, this chapter reviews some techniques for troubleshooting applications, printing, and a few other areas. For more details on troubleshooting particular situations, see the chapter in which the individual topic is covered. Of course, you should also check your online Help programs, online troubleshooters, and the documentation for specific troubleshooting steps.

> **NOTE** Troubleshooting in Windows 98 may involve several different tools and several different pieces of information. Although the exam objectives list different topics, this chapter will present the different troubleshooting methodologies and let you decide which one is best for a given situation. Although the exam objectives do not lend themselves well to a simple section-by-section breakdown, *all* of them are covered in this and other chapters. Please read the entire chapter because understanding how the different tools and utilities are interconnected will help you pass the exam and become an accomplished Windows 98 administrator.

Initial Diagnosis

There are several basic steps you can follow in troubleshooting Windows 98 problems:

- **Diagnose specific symptoms and factors.** Start by analyzing the symptoms to determine a strategy for finding a resolution. Here are some things you might consider:

  - Has the current configuration ever worked? If so, what has changed?

  - Is it reproducible?

  - Is it specific to a certain system or application?

  - Does the problem occur when you boot in Safe mode?

  - Is specific hardware involved?

  - Are any real-mode drivers or TSRs (terminate-and-stay resident programs) involved?

- **Find out if it is a common issue.** Has the problem been documented in any Help or any .TXT files? These types of files may note many common issues along with their solutions. Some good places to start are any README.TXT, README.1ST, and SETUP.TXT files. Other technical resources, some of which will be discussed later, can also provide information about common issues and resolutions.

- **Isolate error conditions.** Try to determine the specifics of a problem. Have you added anything to the CONFIG.SYS or AUTOEXEC.BAT file? If so, remove your changes and see if the issue continues. Have you loaded any new drivers? If so, replace them with the original driver and retest. The more specific you can get in determining any changes made since the system worked the last time, the sooner you can solve the problem.

- **Consult technical support resources.** Use Help files and documentation whenever available. Many online areas are available for seeking technical solutions. These include Internet pages, online forums, chat rooms, and BBS (bulletin board system) services.

Resources for Troubleshooting

Microsoft offers some very good resources to help you troubleshoot and fix problems that you may encounter with Windows 98. The following sections describe three of these resources: TechNet, Microsoft's Web site, and the *Windows 98 Resource Kit*.

Microsoft TechNet

Microsoft TechNet is a comprehensive worldwide information service designed for those who support or educate users, administer networks or databases, create automated solutions, and recommend or evaluate information-technology solutions.

For an annual TechNet subscription fee, subscribers receive two CDs per month containing Microsoft Knowledge Base, Resource Kits, up-to-date drivers, and other information. TechNet also maintains a CompuServe forum (GO TECHNET) for up-to-the-minute news. To subscribe in the United States and Canada, using your credit card, call (800) 344-2121, weekdays between 6:30A.M. and 5:30P.M., Pacific Standard Time. For international orders, call (303) 684-0914 (in the United States) for contacts in your area.

Microsoft's Web Site

Microsoft's Web site (www.microsoft.com) has many valuable resources, most of which are available for just the cost of your Internet connection. The page is full of news articles, product releases, device drivers, and other valuable tools and information. Subpages (which are available as links from the main page) contain up-to-date device drivers and software. You can use the Windows Update tool to look for new device drivers and patches. Other subpages contain links for contacting Microsoft Technical Support. You can reach this page by choosing the Support link at the top of the main page. From there, you have several options for contacting Microsoft to get answers to your questions or suggestions for solving problems.

Many other options are available from the Microsoft Web page. It is a fine resource. The best way to become acquainted with it is to actually visit the site and explore it yourself.

The Windows 98 Resource Kit

The *Windows 98 Resource Kit* (Microsoft Press) is written for administrators and MIS professionals; it provides the information required for rolling out, supporting, and understanding Windows 98. The *Resource Kit* is a technical resource that supplements the documentation included with the Windows 98 product.

The *Resource Kit* covers the details of planning and implementing Windows 98. The *Kit* is broken down into seven main sections, each with several subsections:

1. Deployment and Installation

2. System Configuration

3. Networking and Intranets

4. Internet and Communication Tools

5. System Management

6. Architecture

7. Appendices

The *Resource Kit* is available at all major bookstores. It is an excellent resource to keep around for reference and research. An online edition can be found on the CD included with the *Windows 98 Resource Kit* and on the Windows 98 CD. Look in the \Tools\ResKit folder.

Windows 98 Tools for Troubleshooting

Many different tools and methodologies are used for troubleshooting in the Windows 98 environment. In this section, you will walk through many of these different tools and utilities. Many of them have been examined closely in other chapters and will receive only a cursory inspection here. Others will receive a more-detailed look. In addition to the tools included with Windows 98, there are shareware or freeware tools that are available from a variety of sources including the Internet.

Let's get started with the Device Manager. As its name suggests, this tool is very useful when you are tracking down hardware problems.

The Device Manager

The Device Manager provides a graphical representation of devices connected to the system. From here, you can check the properties of different devices to determine whether they are functioning properly. You can also discover what may be wrong with devices that are not working as they should. To access the Device Manager, right-click the My Computer icon on the Desktop or go to the System/Control Panel applet.

When you start up the Device Manager on a system with no hardware problems and select the View Devices By Type button, it looks something like the dialog box shown in Figure 16.1. All the main hardware devices are listed, each on a single line.

To look at specific devices listed under each main category, click on the plus sign (+) to the left of the heading. Each main category heading now lists the individual devices below it. By double-clicking any specific device, or highlighting it and clicking the Properties button, you can see the properties for that device. Figure 16.2 shows an example of the Properties page for a Yamaha OPL3-SAx sound device. You can obtain the following information from a device's property sheet:

- Device type

- Manufacturer

- Hardware version

- Supporting drivers installed

- Whether or not the installed drivers are functioning properly

- Resources used by the device, including any conflicts that might be present

Clicking the View Devices By Connection button on the main Device Manager screen (see Figure 16.1) changes the view to show items listed under the resource to which they are connected. For example, your CD-ROM will be listed under your sound card if it is using the sound card for its connection.

When you boot your system in Safe mode (press F5 after the "Starting Windows 98" message, or hold the Ctrl key during bootup and choose Safe Mode from the Startup menu), you may see devices listed more than once. This is a fairly common occurrence, but it can cause problems. For this reason, when you are working in Device Manager after a Safe-mode boot, you should always check for multiple instances of any device, and remove

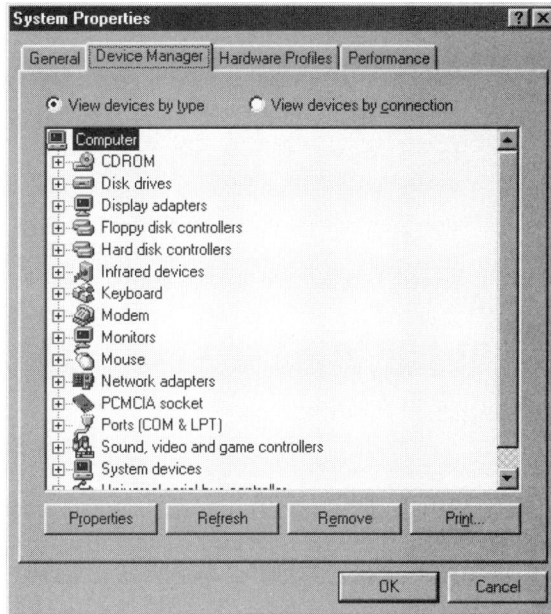

any that you find. Even if this is not the cause of the current problem, it may save you further trouble.

> *W 98*
>
> Safe mode is a way of booting Windows 98 without the Registry, CONFIG.SYS, AUTOEXEC.BAT, and any protected-mode drivers. In this mode, you can work with system files, Device Manager, or anything else you suspect might be causing problems. See Chapter 4 for more information about Safe mode and other startup options.

Other Control Panel Tools

As in previous versions of Windows, you can configure components of the system using the Control Panel. The Windows 98 version, however, is much more powerful than the one in previous versions.

The System /Control Panel's Device Manager was explained in the previous section. Here are some explanations of other Control Panel applets that can be useful for problem solving:

- **Add New Hardware:** Used to add new hardware to the system. This option is not available during a Safe-mode boot. (See Chapter 4 for details.)

- **Add/Remove Programs:** Used to add or remove software from the system and create a Startup disk. Only 32-bit applications will be registered in the remove section.

- **Display:** Used to change the display settings, including resolution and number of colors displayed. This can also be accessed by right-clicking an empty area of the Desktop.

- **Modems:** Used to add or remove modems and perform modem diagnostics.

- **Network:** Used to modify your network related settings.

- **Power Management:** Used to modify your power management schemes. This includes low battery warnings and powering down your hard disks and monitor after a preset length of time and others.

The System Information Utilities

The System Information utility (see Figure 16.3) is a suite of tools that allow you to gather information and make modifications to your system in many different areas. The System Information utility includes the following tools:

- Windows Report tool
- Update Wizard Uninstall
- System File Checker
- Signature Verification tool
- Registry Checker
- Automatic Skip Driver Agent (ASD)
- Dr. Watson
- System Configuration utility
- ScanDisk
- Version Conflict Manager

Microsoft ✓ *Exam Objective*

Diagnose and resolve installation failures. Tasks include:

- Resolve file and driver version conflicts by using Version Conflict Manager and the Microsoft System Information utility

NOTE
The Version Conflict Manager will be discussed later in the chapter.

Windows Report Tool

The Windows Report tool is a method for you to submit bugs in Windows 98. (See Figure 16.4) When you submit a report, the Report tool will gather your current computer settings and some of your system and application settings and send those to Microsoft's tech support.

F I G U R E   16.3

The System Informa-
tion utility

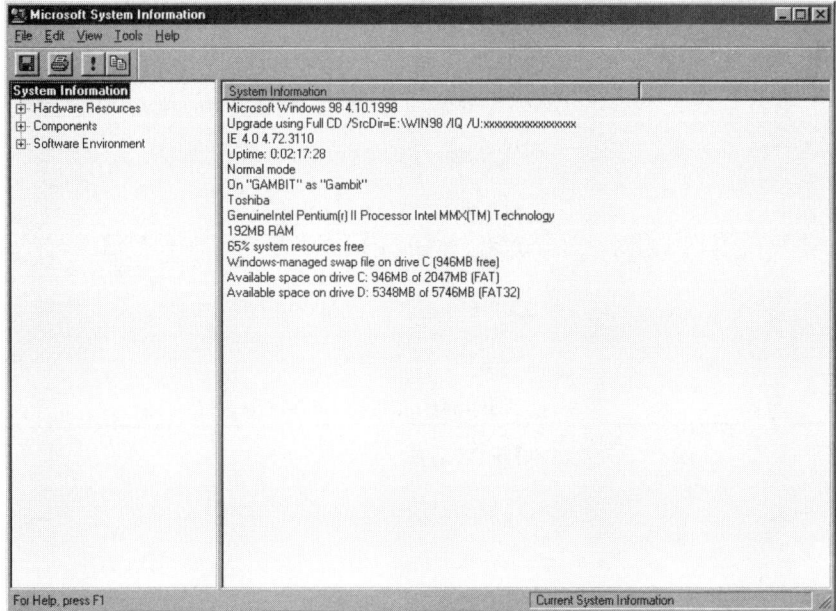

F I G U R E   16.4

The Windows
Report tool

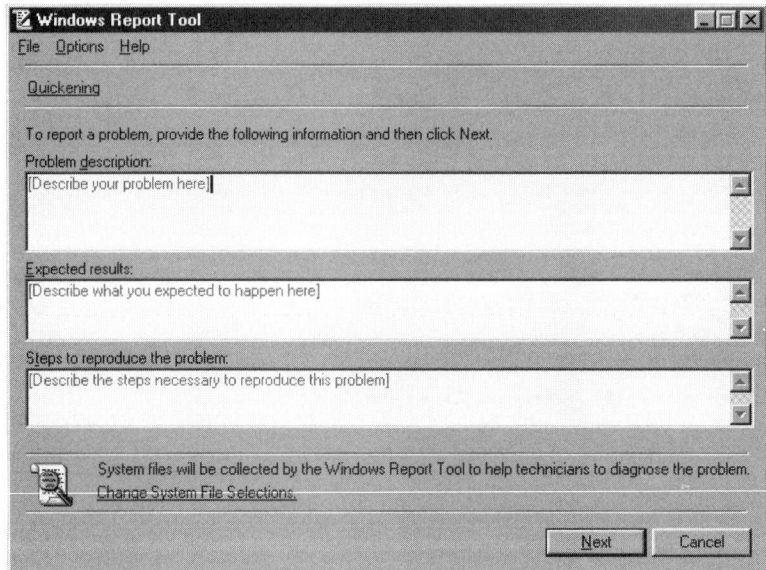

Update Wizard Uninstall

If you used the Windows Update tool to install an updated version of a patch, driver, or system tool and you are having trouble with it, you can use the Update Wizard Uninstall utility to uninstall the new version. This utility is very useful when you cannot establish your Internet connection through the Windows Update tool. The Update Wizard Uninstall utility will display the updates that have been installed on your computer. Older versions of patches, drivers, and system tools will be saved in a backup folder on your system. When you uninstall an item, the newer version is copied to the backup folder and the older version is reinstalled.

System File Checker

You can use the System File Checker tool (see Figure 16.5) to verify the integrity of your Windows 98 system files. You can also use the utility to restore files when they are corrupted, and you can use it to extract compressed files from your installation CD-ROM. The System File Checker can make backups of existing files before you overwrite them with the original files.

Microsoft Exam Objective

Tune and optimize the system in a Microsoft environment and a mixed Microsoft and NetWare environment. Tasks include:

- Optimizing the hard disk by using Disk Defragmenter and ScanDisk
- Compressing data by using DriveSpace3 and the Compression Agent
- Updating drivers and applying service packs by using Windows Update and the Signature Verification tool
- Automating tasks by using Maintenance Wizard
- Scheduling tasks by using Task Scheduler
- Checking for corrupt files and extracting files from the installation media by using the System File Checker

NOTE Disk Defragmenter, ScanDisk, Maintenance Wizard, and Task Scheduler are covered in Chapter 7. Windows Update and the Signature Verification tool are covered in Chapter 6.

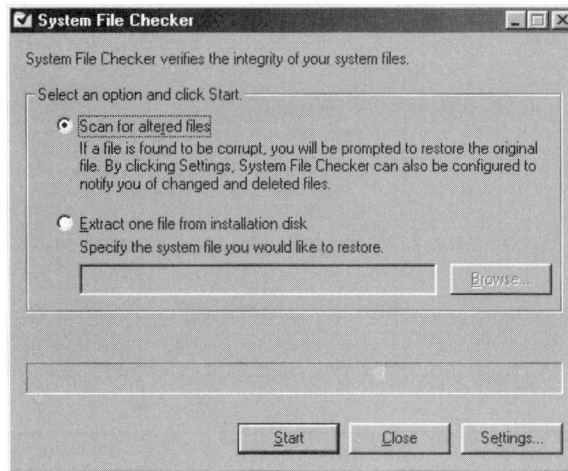

If you click the Settings button, you can now specify backup options like whether or not to always back up a system file before you overwrite it, prompt to back up, or never back up a file. You can also modify the folder in which your backups will be stored. From the Settings dialog box (see Figure 16.6), you can also specify whether or not you want to track these changes with a log file. Other options can determine whether or not the tool should check for changed and/or deleted files.

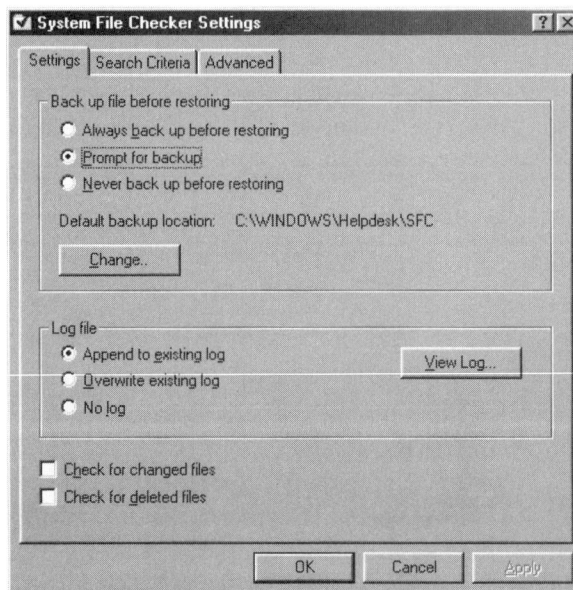

If you select the Search Criteria tab (see Figure 16.7), you can determine which system files to look for and in which folders to look for them. You can also specify different file types to search for. The Advanced tab settings are beyond the scope of this book. Essentially, the Advanced tab allows you to create a System File Checker template.

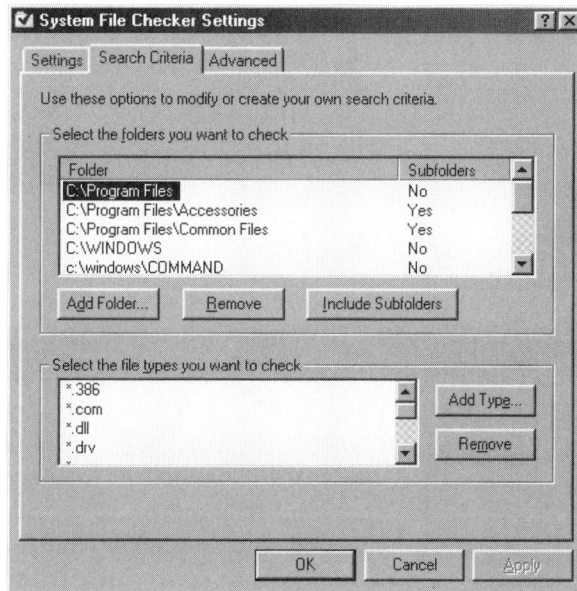

Signature Verification Tool

The Signature Verification tool (see Figure 16.8) is used to find digitally signed and unsigned files on your Windows 98 machine. When a signature has been applied to a file, you can be assured that the file has not been tampered with since it was digitally signed. To obtain a digital signature, you must work with a Certificate Authority (CA). Using the Signature Verification tool, you can:

- View the certificates

- Search for signed files

- Search for unsigned files

FIGURE 16.8

The Search Criteria tab

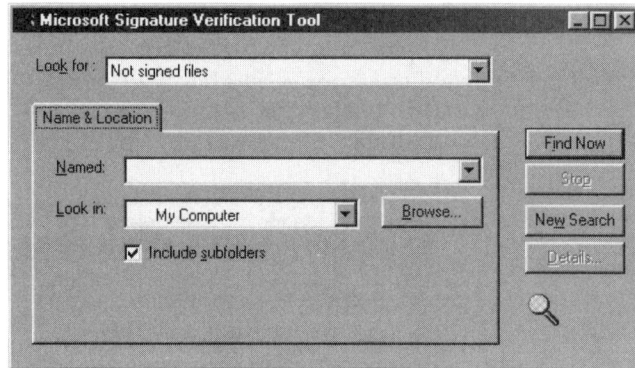

Registry Checker

As you learned earlier, there is a backup copy of both of your Registry files. These backups are named SYSTEM.DA0 and USER.DA0. The Registry Checker automatically scans your Registry. If Registry Checker finds problems in the Registry, it will automatically replace the Registry with the backup copy.

If no problems are found, the Registry Checker will determine if your Registry has already been backed up today. If it has, it will notify you that it was backed up and then ask if you would like to back it up again.

Automatic Skip Driver Agent

The Automatic Skip Driver (ASD) is used to identify failures that have caused Windows 98 to stop responding on previous startups and marks them so they are bypassed on subsequent startups. When you use ASD, you can view the devices or operations that have failed to start. With ASD you can then reenable any device that was disabled by the ASD process. Windows 98 will then try to use that device again during the next startup attempt. You can also gather additional information about the problematic device by clicking on the device and then choosing Details.

Dr. Watson

The Dr. Watson tool is used to take a snapshot of your system whenever a system-level fault occurs. Generally, it can identify the software that faulted, identify what the fault was, and then describe the cause of the error. In many cases, Dr. Watson can even diagnose the problem and offer some suggestions on how to fix it.

When you first start Dr. Watson, an icon is added to your system tray. Double-clicking the icon will invoke Dr. Watson. The tool will then take a snapshot of your system and look for any problems. Once the inspection is finished, you should get a screen similar to Figure 16.9.

F I G U R E   16.9

Dr. Watson

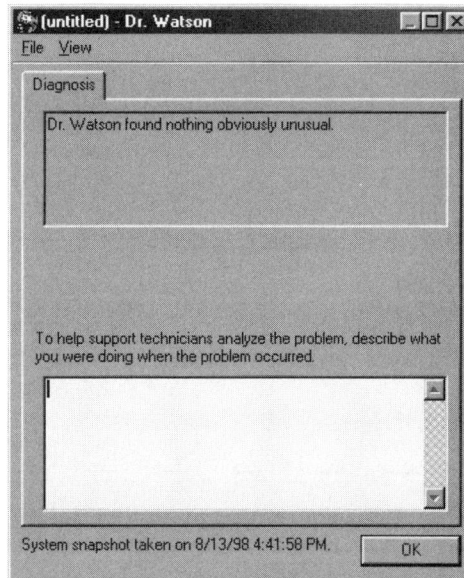

System Configuration Utility

The System Configuration utility (see Figure 16.10) can help to automate troubleshooting by walking you through the same steps that the Microsoft Technical Support people would follow to track down and diagnose problems. With the System Configuration utility, you can modify the system configuration files through an easy-to-use point-and-click interface. This saves you the time of editing the CONFIG.SYS, AUTOEXEC.BAT, MSDOS.SYS, SYSTEM.INI, and WIN.INI files by hand. You can also create backups of the current system files before you begin making changes to them. In this fashion, you can undo any modifications that you make during your troubleshooting.

F I G U R E   16.10

The System
Configuration utility

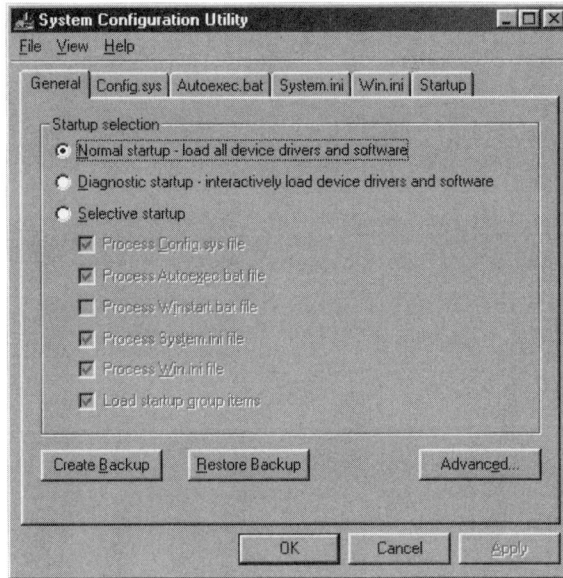

ScanDisk

ScanDisk allows you to check your hard drives for both logical and physical errors. The ScanDisk program itself (see Figure 16.11) is capable of fixing errors in most cases. It also contains options for dealing with lost clusters of data. They can be deleted or saved that specific filenames.

F I G U R E   16.11

ScanDisk utility

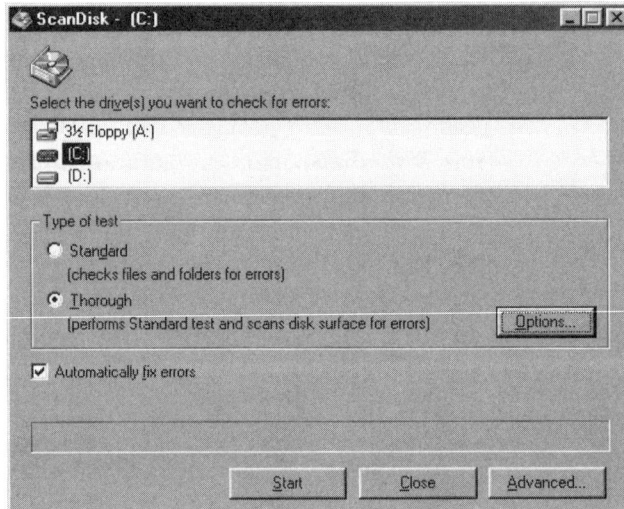

Version Conflict Manager

Microsoft Exam Objective

Diagnose and resolve installation failures. Tasks include:

- Resolve file and driver version conflicts by using Version Conflict Manager and the Microsoft System Information utility.

NOTE

The System Information utility is covered earlier in the chapter.

The Version Conflict Manager (see Figure 16.12) is used to replace older versions of files that were updated when new software was added to your system. The older versions of the software were automatically saved to a backup folder by Windows 98. If a conflict is listed, you simply need to select the version of the software you want to use from the panel in the window and then click Restore. This will replace the current version of the file with the old version of the file. The current version which is being replaced will then be saved as a backup.

FIGURE 16.12

The Version Conflict Manager

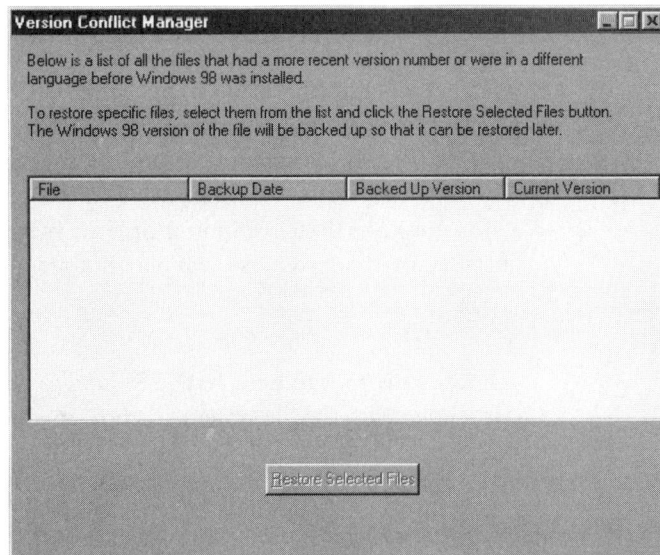

Monitoring Windows 98

To troubleshoot your system effectively, you need to know what its "normal" operation is. By monitoring your system on a regular basis, you can see how the system is working when things are going smoothly, and so you can spot possible problem areas before they become critical conditions.

The System Monitor

Windows 98 provides a powerful tool that you can use to monitor the system: the System Monitor. If you are using Windows 98 as a server, you can monitor its operations with the Net Watcher tool.

Microsoft Exam Objective   **Monitor system perfomance by using Net Watcher, System Monitor, and Resource Meter.**

NOTE   Net Watcher is discussed in Chapters 10 and 14 and the Resource Meter is discussed in Chapter 6.

As you learned, the System Monitor is a tool for tracking memory and other system resources for usage and possible problems. The following sections examine different ways to use the System Monitor's options in the file system, IPX/SPX-compatible protocol, Kernel, Memory Manager, Microsoft Client for NetWare Networks, and Microsoft Client for Microsoft Networks categories. The System Monitor options vary depending on what you have installed on the system, so you may not see all of the options described here.

File System

Choose Edit ➤ Add Item ➤ File System to access options for viewing items associated with the file system and how it is being used. You can monitor the following items:

- **Bytes Read/Second:** The number of bytes read from the file system each second.

- **Bytes Written/Second:** The number of bytes written by the file system each second.

- **Dirty Data:** The number of bytes waiting to be written to the disk. Dirty data is stored in cache blocks, so the number reported might be larger than the actual number of bytes waiting.

- **Reads/Second:** The number of read operations delivered to the file system each second.

- **Writes/Second:** The number of write operations delivered to the file system each second.

IPX/SPX-Compatible Protocol

If you are using the IPX/SPX-compatible protocol, choose Edit ➤ Add Item ➤ IPX/SPX-Compatible Protocol to view details of IPX/SPX activities. You can monitor the following items:

- **IPX Packets Lost Per Second:** The number of IPX packets received by the computer from an IPX network that were ignored.

- **IPX Packets Received Per Second:** The number of packets received by the computer from an IPX network each second.

- **IPX Packets Sent Per Second:** The number of packets sent by the computer to an IPX network each second.

- **Open Sockets:** The number of free sockets.

- **Routing Table Entries:** The number of IPX internetworking routes known.

- **SAP Table Entries:** The number of service advertisements known.

- **SPX Packets Received Per Second:** The number of packets received by the computer from an SPX network each second.

- **SPX Packets Sent Per Second:** The number of packets sent by the computer to an SPX network each second.

Kernel

Choose Edit ➤ Add Item ➤ Kernel to view details of Kernel activities. You can monitor the following items:

- **Processor Usage:** The approximate percentage of time that the processor is busy. Monitoring this setting will increase processor usage slightly.

- **Threads:** The current number of threads present in the system.

- **Virtual Machines:** The current number of virtual machines present in the system.

Memory Manager

Choose Edit ➤ Add Item ➤ Memory Manager to view memory details. Here are the memory-related items you can monitor:

- **Allocated Memory:** The total number of bytes allocated to applications and system processes. This is the sum of the Other Memory and Swap File Memory settings.

- **Discards:** The number of pages discarded from memory per second. These pages are discarded rather than swapped because their data already exists on the hard drive and the data hasn't changed.

- **Disk Cache Size:** The current size of the disk cache in bytes.

- **Free Memory:** The total amount of free physical RAM in bytes. This number is not related to Allocated Memory. If this value is zero, memory can still be allocated, depending on the free disk space available on the drive that contains the swap file.

- **Instance Faults:** The number of instance faults per second.

- **Locked Memory:** The amount of memory, in bytes, that is locked by the system, or an application, and cannot be swapped out.

- **Maximum Disk Cache Size:** The largest possible disk cache size, in bytes.

- **Minimum Disk Cache Size:** The smallest possible disk cache size, in bytes.

- **Other Memory:** The amount of allocated memory, in bytes, that cannot be stored in the swap file. This includes code from Win32 DLLs and executable files, memory-mapped files, memory that cannot be paged, and disk cache pages.

- **Page Faults:** The number of page faults per second.

- **Page-Ins:** The number of pages swapped from the page file to physical RAM per second.

- **Page-Outs:** The number of pages swapped from physical RAM to the page file per second.

- **Swap File Defective:** The number of defective bytes in the swap file. These are caused by bad sectors on the hard drive.

- **Swap File in Use:** The number of bytes currently being used by the swap file.

- **Swap File Size:** The current size of the swap file, in bytes.

- **Swappable Memory:** The number of bytes allocated from the swap file. This includes locked pages.

Microsoft Client for NetWare Networks

If the machine has the Microsoft Client for NetWare Networks installed, choose Edit ➢ Add Item ➢ Microsoft Client for NetWare Networks to view details about the NetWare network connection. You can monitor the following items:

- **Burst Packets Dropped:** The number of burst packets from this computer lost in transit.

- **Burst Receive Gap Time:** Interpacket gap for incoming traffic, in microseconds.

- **Burst Send Gap Time:** Interpacket gap for outgoing traffic, in microseconds.

- **Bytes in Cache:** The amount of data, in bytes, that is currently cached by the redirector.

- **Bytes Read Per Second:** Bytes read from the redirector per second.

- **Bytes Written Per Second:** Bytes written to the redirector per second.

- **Dirty Bytes in Cache:** The amount of dirty data, in bytes, that is currently cached by the redirector and is waiting to be written.

- **NCP Packets Dropped:** The number of regular NCP packets lost in transit.

- **Requests Pending:** The number of requests that are waiting to be processed by the server.

Microsoft Network Client

If the machine has the Microsoft Client for Microsoft Networks installed, choose Edit ➤ Add Item ➤ Microsoft Network Client to view details about the Microsoft network connection. You can monitor the following items:

- **Bytes Read Per Second:** The number of bytes read from the redirector each second.

- **Bytes Written Per Second:** The number of bytes written to the redirector each second.

- **Number of Nets:** The number of networks currently running.

- **Open Files:** The number of open files on the network.

- **Resources:** The number of resources used.

- **Sessions:** The number of sessions running.

- **Transactions Per Second:** The number of SMB transactions managed by the redirector each second.

Microsoft Network Server

If the machine has File and Printer Sharing installed for a Microsoft or NetWare network, choose Edit ➤ Add Item ➤ Microsoft Network Server to view details about the sharing connection. You can monitor the following items:

- **Buffers:** The number of buffers used by the server.

- **Bytes Read Per Second:** The total number of bytes read from a disk each second.

- **Bytes Written Per Second:** The total number of bytes written to a disk each second.

- **Bytes Per Second:** The total number of bytes read from and written to a disk each second.

- **Memory:** The total amount of memory used by the server.

- **Server Threads:** The current number of threads used by the server.

Microsoft Network Monitor Performance Data

If the machine is a Microsoft server on a network, choose Edit ➤ Add Item ➤ Microsoft Network Monitor Performance Data to view details about its performance. You can monitor the following items:

- **Mediatype Broadcasts/Sec:** Broadcast frames transmitted over the network adapter each second.

- **Mediatype Bytes/Sec:** Total number of bytes transmitted over the network adapter each second.

- **Mediatype Frames/Sec:** The total number of frames transmitted over the network adapter each second.

- **Mediatype Multicasts/Sec:** The total number of multicast frames transmitted over the network adapter each second.

If proper access privileges are present, the System Monitor can also be used over a network to monitor remote systems. You can run multiple instances side by side to compare the performance of different computers.

> **NOTE** To use the Remote System Monitor, the Microsoft Remote Registry Service must be installed and enabled. See Chapter 14 for details.

The Net Watcher

As you learned in Chapter 14, the Windows 98 Net Watcher tool allows you to create, control, and monitor remote shared resources. It can be useful for managing peer sharing in Windows 98.

Net Watcher has easy-to-use icons that give you several options:

- Add a shared resource or stop sharing a resource on a local or remote system.

- Show all shared resources, connected users, and open files.

- Close any files that users have open.

- Disconnect a user.

- Change the properties of a remote shared folder, including its share name and the access rights to the folder.

- For shared folder(s) on any remote system, find out which users are connected to the shared resource, how long they've been connected, and which files they have open.

> **NOTE** File and printer sharing services must be installed and enabled to use Net Watcher. See Chapter 14 for details.

Auditing Windows 98 with Log Files

Windows 98 has the ability to log certain items to ASCII text files. These files can be extremely useful in tracking down elusive problems. The available log files are described in the following sections.

> **TIP** Detailed information about interpreting the Windows 98 log files, including individual line-by-line breakdowns, is available in the *Windows 98 Resource Kit.*

The Boot Log

BOOTLOG.TXT is a text file that is automatically created during the first boot sequence following a successful setup. After that, Windows 98 creates this file when you choose the Logged option from the Startup menu (press and hold Ctrl during the startup process to see this menu).

This log records all devices and drivers loaded by the system. You can use this information to diagnose driver load failures by determining whether or not the driver was found and if there were driver initialization failures. For more information, see Chapter 2.

The Hardware-Detection Logs

DETLOG.TXT is a text file that contains a record of whether or not specific hardware devices were detected and identifies the parameters for each specific device. When you run the Windows 98 Setup program, a hardware-detection procedure is performed on the system. This hardware detection also takes place when you run the Add New Hardware Wizard. During this detection, DETLOG.TXT is created as each piece of hardware is successfully detected.

By using a text editor, you can view DETLOG.TXT and determine which hardware was not successfully detected, and you can attempt to manually correct the problem. For more information, see Chapter 3.

The Windows 98 file that keeps track of any hardware-detection failures is DETCRASH.LOG. This is not an ASCII file; it is a binary file and can be read only by Windows 98. If a piece of hardware crashes the detection process, a failure code is added to the file. The next time that the hardware detection is run, the file is checked, and the hardware that caused the failure is ignored. This process is continued until all hardware is either successfully detected and properly installed or ignored and bypassed. Once a completely successful detection is completed, the DETCRASH.LOG file is deleted.

The Setup Log

When you run the Windows 98 Setup program, the SETUPLOG.TXT file is created to document all successes and failures during the setup process. Similar to the procedure used during hardware detection, Windows finds where the process was interrupted, skips the step, and attempts to continue.

By using a text editor, you can review this text file to determine what errors occurred if Setup fails prior to hardware detection. See Chapter 2 for more details.

The Network Log

NETLOG.TXT is a text file similar to SETUPLOG.TXT and DETLOG .TXT. This log documents successes and failures during network component detection and installation. Like the other text file logs, NETLOG.TXT can be viewed with any text editor. Check this file if errors occur in your network setup procedures.

Optimizing Windows 98 Memory Usage

Sometimes, the problems with Windows 98 aren't so much fatal errors as they are slow performance, which could be caused by inefficient use of memory. Here are some ways that you can optimize memory usage:

- **Have only necessary programs open.** Each program you have open uses some physical RAM. By increasing the number of applications that you have open, you force Windows 98 to use paging more frequently and hinder system performance.

- **Minimize network services.** Network clients and protocols use memory even when you are not logged in to the network. By loading only the client you are currently using, and loading only necessary protocols, system performance can be improved.

- **Make wise use of system resources.** System resource heaps exist in memory. By keeping resources to a minimum, you can increase memory performance. Here are some tips for reducing the amount of system resources in use:

  - Close unnecessary applications.

  - Close unnecessary files within an application.

  - Run DOS applications at full screen rather than in a window.

  - Turn off unused application objects, such as toolbars, rulers, and status bars.

  - If you need multiple applications open, minimize them while they are not in use.

  - Turn off appearance features, such as themes or wallpaper.

- **Enable caching.** The system cache plays a very important part in system performance. Check your system BIOS to ensure that caching is properly enabled. Depending on the BIOS on your system, the cache may be called L1 cache, internal cache (built into the processor), external cache (on the motherboard), or system memory cache.

- **Empty the Clipboard.** Whenever you cut or copy text or an object, it is placed in the Clipboard for retrieval at a later time. When large items are left in the Clipboard, they use up resources. Empty the Clipboard by copying something small to overwrite the large item, or open the Clipboard Viewer and delete the contents. (The Clipboard Viewer is an accessory that you can add to Windows 98 through the Add/Remove Programs icon in the Control Panel.

- **Reboot the system.** Although Windows 98 tries to free up system resources as it can, not all applications will let go of resources, even after they have been closed. These resources should be automatically released back to Windows, but this doesn't always happen. By rebooting the system, these resources can be reclaimed by the system. In some special cases, IRQs, DMA channels, and base I/O addresses can become corrupted. In these instances, a simple reboot of the system is not enough. You must actually cycle the power on the system to regain control of these resources. Cycling the power is often referred to as "kicking" (e.g., "Yeah, I had to kick the server last night").

- **Add more memory.** The easiest way to increase the available memory in a system is to add more memory. Windows 98 will take advantage of any and all memory installed in the system. Consult your computer manufacturer for information about the correct type of memory for your system.

Optimizing the Swap File

Windows 98 creates a special file on the hard drive called a *virtual-memory swap file* or *paging file*. This file uses the space on the hard drive as virtual RAM. Some of the program code and other information are kept in physical RAM, while other information is swapped in virtual memory. When the information is needed, it is pulled back into RAM and information no longer being used is transferred to the swap file. The only noticeable indication that this process is taking place is that the hard drive light is flashing. This allows the system to run more applications than would normally be allowed by the RAM.

In Windows 3.*x*, the swap file could be temporary or permanent, but it required contiguous (nonfragmented) space on the hard drive. In Windows 98, the swap file is *dynamic*. This means that it can shrink or grow as needed by the current applications. Fragmentation of the swap file is no longer an issue.

You can change the virtual memory settings from the Performance tab of the System Control Panel. Clicking on the Virtual Memory button brings up the Virtual Memory dialog box. It's best to let Windows manage the swap file settings for you, but you can make changes if necessary. There are some things to keep in mind when making changes to the swap file settings:

- **Use the hard disk with the most free space.** The more space available on the drive, the better the swap file will perform. This will allow the file to grow as required by the current applications. Putting the swap file on a drive with limited space can cause swap file problems and lead to other abnormalities.

- **Use the drive with the fastest access,** In addition to space, you want the swap file to be on a drive with fast access time. This allows the system to page-swap information from RAM to virtual memory and back in less time, so that your system performs faster and better.

- **Use the System Monitor to track the swap file size.** As explained earlier in this chapter, one of the items you can view in the System Monitor is the size of the swap file (choose Edit ➢ Add Item ➢ Memory Manager). When this approaches the size of the amount of the free space on the drive, you will probably want to free up some space on the drive to allow the swap file complete flexibility (room to grow).

- **Defragment the drive containing the swap file.** Keep the drive with the swap file defragmented to allow the swap file to be as contiguous as possible. Although Windows 98 does not require a contiguous block on the drive, having an area available helps optimize performance.

- **Do not use a compressed drive.** Putting the swap file on a compressed drive forces the information being swapped in and out to be compressed and uncompressed, slowing system performance.

- **Do not use a network drive.** As with a compressed drive, on a network drive, the information being swapped must travel a greater distance, over hardware with a slower throughput, which hinders system performance.

WARNING Do *not* disable virtual memory. Doing this will result in drastic adverse effects on Windows 98 performance. If you are running out of disk space, moving or deleting files is a much better course of action.

Troubleshooting Applications

Application problems may occur during or after installation, while you are using the application. The following sections describe some techniques for troubleshooting various application problems.

The Task Manager

In previous versions of MS-DOS, the Ctrl+Alt+Del keyboard combination would reboot the system in the event of a lockup or program crash. In earlier versions of Windows, pressing these keys would give you the opportunity to close an application that crashed while you were in it; otherwise, your only option was to reboot, just like with DOS.

In Windows 98, as in Windows 95, Ctrl+Alt+Del brings up the Task Manager. Windows 3.*x* also had the Task Manager, which you could use to switch between applications or close applications—but only if the system was not locked up. Now you can get to it even in the event of a lockup.

The Task Manager shows which applications are open on the system and which, if any, have stopped responding. In the event that an application has stopped responding, it will have the words "Not Responding" in brackets just to the right of the application name.

One option is simply to close the application that has stopped responding. You can also try closing another application, even though it has not stopped responding, in an attempt to bring back the application that has stopped. This capability can be very helpful when you have several applications open with unsaved information. By closing unnecessary applications, or those that don't require saving, you can often avoid losing information that would have been lost in earlier operating systems.

The Task Manager can be useful at any point during installation or normal operation of an application or Windows 98 itself.

Reboot or Reinstall

If problems persist, such as lockups or crashes, they can often be corrected by simply rebooting the system. This allows memory components to rearrange, applications to reload, and resources to refresh. If this does not correct the problem, it is probably either the application or Windows 98 itself. You may need to reinstall the application or Windows 98.

Some problems with an application's installation may not become apparent until the application is used regularly. By reinstalling the application, any errors that occurred can be corrected. This procedure can also be used with Windows 98 itself if a common situation occurs in several different applications.

Troubleshooting Printing

One of the most frustrating problems is a printer that just won't print. Windows 98 has some built-in features that can help you with printer problems, and there are others options you can try as well. Here are some of the most common problems and the Windows 98 Print Troubleshooter tool. See Chapter 11 for more details about Windows 98 printing.

Microsoft ✓ *Exam* *Objective*	**Diagnose and resolve printing problems in a Microsoft environment or a mixed Microsoft and Neware environment.**

Printer Installation Problems

Here are some tips for troubleshooting problems with installing printers:

- **No printers are listed in the print box.** If nothing appears in the dialog box when you are trying to install a printer, you should verify that the printer INF file exists. The PRTUPD.INF is the built-in list of printer manufacturers and models. You may also need an updated INF file from your printer's manufacturer.

- **Setup cannot find the printer driver files.** The Add Printer Wizard will try to pull the required driver files from the Windows 98 default installation drive and directory if they are not found from an updated file. If these files cannot be found, you will be prompted to enter a path to their location. You can either enter the path to the required files or use the Browse button to search for them.

- **Copy errors occur during printer installation.** If an error occurs while the system is trying to copy files during the installation process, a dialog box is displayed with the expected source and destination paths and filenames that were being copied when the error occurred. Verify the proper locations of the files and retry the installation.

Printing Problems

There are several things you can try to resolve problems with printing. The following sections provide suggestions for troubleshooting some of the most common problems.

The Printer Will Not Print

If the printer simply won't print, here are some ways to discover what the problem is:

- Check to see that the printer is turned on, it is online, and all cables are connected correctly.

- Check to see that the printer has paper and is not jammed.

- Try turning the printer off, waiting a few seconds, and turning it back on. This will clear the printer memory buffer.

- Try printing to a file and copying the file to the printer port (local printers only).

- Try printing directly to a port without spooling. If this works, you may have run out of disk space on the drive that handles print spooling.

- Delete the printer and reinstall it in the Printers folder.

Printing Is Delayed or Slow

Here are some techniques for troubleshooting delayed or slow printing problems:

- Check to see that spooling is enabled and spooling to EMF files.

- Restart in Safe mode and try printing.

- Make sure you have plenty of room on the drive for spooling.

- Run Disk Defragmenter to create contiguous space on the drive for spooling.

- Check for available space on the disk for temporary files.

- Check for low system resources.

- Delete and reinstall the printer driver in the Printers folder.

- Make sure that TrueType fonts are being sent as outlines and not as bitmaps (check the Fonts tab of the printer's property sheet).

Print Jobs Are Garbled or Data is Missing

When your print jobs are not printing correctly, you can try the following solutions:

- Restart in Safe mode and try printing.

- There may not be enough printer memory. Try using a lower resolution or increasing memory.

- Try spooling in RAW format rather than EMF format.

- If available, try printing with a PostScript driver. If this corrects the problem, you probably have a corrupted UNIDRV.DLL. This file can be extracted from the Windows 98 CD-ROM.

- If PostScript fails, there is either a problem with the application or the GDI. Try printing from another application.

- Try printing one job at a time to avoid jobs conflicting.

Only Partial Pages Are Printed

When only part of the page is being printed, try the following techniques:

- There may not be enough printer memory. Try printing at a lower resolution or adding more memory.

- If it is a graphic, try printing it from a different document or application.

- Make sure that the font used is valid and correctly installed.

- Check the printable region of the printer by printing a test page.

- Try printing from a different document or application with the same font.

- Try printing from the same document or application with a different font.

- Enable Print TrueType as Graphics (an option on the Fonts tab of the printer's property sheet).

- Simplify the page by reducing the number of graphics or fonts.

The Print Troubleshooter

Windows 98 has a tool built in for dealing with printer trouble, called the Print Troubleshooter. You access it by selecting Start ➤ Help. When the Help dialog box appears, open the Troubleshooting book, and choose If You Have Trouble Printing. This brings up the Print Troubleshooter, as shown in Figure 16.13. You will be guided through a series of questions, each answer leading to another set of questions, that will narrow down the problem and help you find a solution.

FIGURE 16.13

The Print Troubleshooter

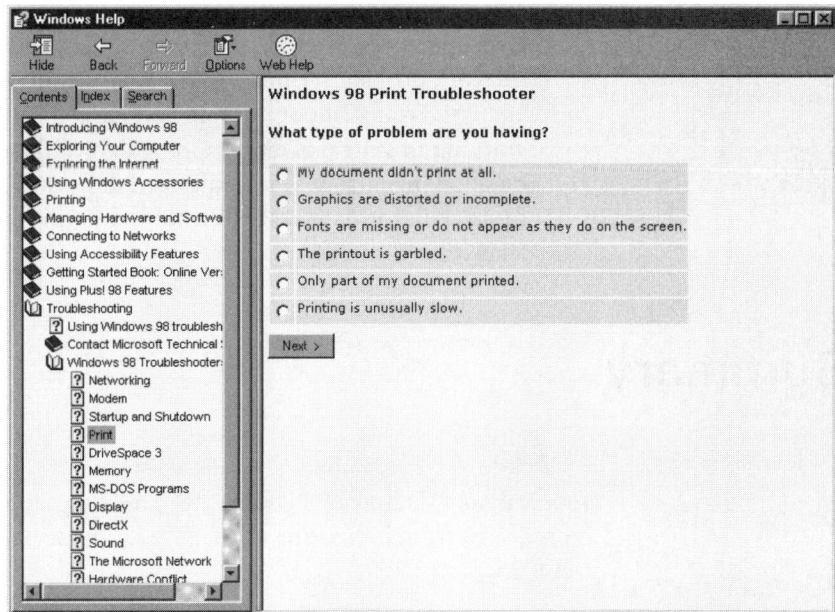

Other Troubleshooting Tips

The following are some other areas in which you may experience problems:

- **The boot process:** If the system hangs during booting, try using either the Safe mode or Step-by-Step Confirmation option from the Startup menu. This will help you to determine whether device drivers, hardware, or conflicts are causing the problem. The Windows 98 Startup disk can also be useful in troubleshooting a problem with the boot process. Try running FDISK /MBR at a command prompt from your Windows 98 Startup disk if you suspect you have a boot virus. See Chapter 4 for details about the Startup menu options, the Startup (emergency boot) disk, and other techniques for troubleshooting booting problems.

- **The file system:** The Performance tab of the System Control Panel has several options for configuring the file system that can be helpful in troubleshooting problems. You can also access these options by right-clicking the My Computer icon on the Desktop.

- **Dial-up networking:** The Help system has a guide for troubleshooting network problems, similar to the Print Troubleshooter. Select Start ➤ Help ➤ Troubleshooting ➤ If You Have Trouble Using Dial-Up Networking to start this online aid, which walks you through a series of questions to narrow down, and solve, different situations. See Chapter 15 for more information about troubleshooting modems and other problems related to dial-up connections.

Summary

As a systems engineer or administrator, you must know how to troubleshoot Windows 98 effectively. This chapter explained the general approach to troubleshooting and offered suggestions for solving common problems.

You began with the basics of diagnosing the problem, finding trouble-shooting resources, and using the Windows 98 troubleshooting tools. You then took a closer look at the System Information utility and the tools that it exposes. Next, you covered ways to avoid system problems, including monitoring the system, auditing Windows 98, optimizing Windows 98 memory usage, and optimizing the swap file. Then you reviewed trouble-shooting problems with applications, printing, the boot process, the file system, and dial-up networking. You can find more information about trouble-shooting specific problems in this book's previous chapters.

Review Questions

1. What is the first step in troubleshooting?

   A. Isolate error conditions.

   B. Find out if it is a common issue.

   C. Diagnose specific symptoms.

   D. Consult technical support resources.

2. There are many different ways that you can get help when you are having problems with Windows 98. What is the quickest form of electronic help?

   A. The Internet

   B. Online Help files

   C. BBS services

   D. 1-900 Help lines

3. You are having problems during the boot-up process of Windows 98. You decide to reboot and hold down the Ctrl key. When the Startup menu appears, you choose Safe mode boot. During a Safe mode boot, which files are bypassed? Choose all that apply.

   A. CONFIG.SYS, AUTOEXEC.BAT, and the Startup group

   B. The Registry and the Startup group

   C. The Registry, SYSTEM.INI, and WIN.INI

   D. CONFIG.SYS and AUTOEXEC.BAT

4. You have installed Windows 98 on your computer and you want to optimize your system. You want to track information like the CPU utilization and number of threads currently processing. Which application allows you to monitor a variety of system resources?

   A. Net Watcher

   B. Freecell

   C. System Monitor

   D. Remote Registry Service

5. You have shared several folders and your printer. You now want to see all of your shared resources and who is using them. Which application allows you to monitor and manage a variety of network information?

   A. Net Watcher

   B. Freecell

   C. System Monitor

   D. Remote Registry Service

6. You want to take a look at all of the protected-mode drivers that Windows 98 is attempting to load. You remember that a file is created during the Windows 98 startup process. You open the Notepad program to view this file. Which log file tracks items during the boot process?

   A. BOOTLOG.TXT

   B. DETCRASH.LOG

   C. NETLOG.TXT

   D. SETUPLOG.TXT

7. During the setup process, Windows 98 creates several different files which track hardware enumeration as well as all the things that occurred during the boot process. It also tracks successful and failed protected drivers initializations. Which of the following ASCII log files are created during Windows 98 setup?

   A. BOOTLOG.TXT

   B. DETLOG.TXT

   C. SETUPLOG.TXT

   D. All of the above

8. Windows 98 uses a swap file to virtualize memory. It does this so that your applications appear to have more RAM than is really available in your system. You can modify the way this swap file behaves. Which of the following describes the default behavior of the swap file in Windows 98?

   A. Permanent

   B. Dynamic

   C. Fixed in size

   D. None of the above

9. You swap file performance is directly tied with which hard drive attribute(s)?

   A. Access time

   B. Free space

   C. Manufacturer

   D. A and B

10. Which of the following will have the most adverse effect on system performance?

   A. Ten or more applications running

   B. Disabling the swap file

   C. Having a dual-boot configuration

   D. Installing more than two printers

11. What will pressing Ctrl+Alt+Del do?

   A. Reboot the system

   B. Automatically close the current application

   C. Bring up the online Help system

   D. Start the Task Manager

12. You have applications that don't appear to be responding properly. You decide to use the Ctrl+Alt+Del key sequence to open up the Task Manager. The Task Manager window shows you currently running applications in Windows 98. What does the Task Manager allow you to shut down?

   A. Windows 98

   B. An application that has stopped responding

   C. Any running application

   D. All of the above

13. There are lots of different things that you can do to handle problems with printing. Windows 98 provides you with an application that will walk you through the troubleshooting process for most common printer issues? What is the name of this applet?

   A. Print Troubleshooter

   B. Add New Hardware Wizard

   C. Control Panel

   D. None of the above

APPENDIX

A

Review Answers

Chapter 1

1. Your company is upgrading its computers. The choice is between Windows 98 and Windows NT. You want to support user profiles, the Registry, and 32-bit applications, but you have many DOS applications that access the video card directly. Which operating system should you choose, and why?

    A. Windows 98 because you need to allow applications to access the video card directly.

    B. Windows NT because it runs DOS applications just fine.

    C. Both A and B would work fine.

    D. Neither A nor B would work.

    Answer: A. Windows 98 allows direct access to the hardware while Windows NT does not. Because some legacy applications require direct access to the hardware, Windows 98 is the only choice that will work.

2. How many CPUs can Windows 98 support?

    A. 1

    B. 2

    C. 4

    D. Unlimited

    Answer: A. Windows 98 supports only a single CPU. In order to support multiple CPUs, you would need Windows NT.

3. Which of the following support Plug and Play? Choose all that apply.

    A. MS-DOS 6.22

    B. Windows 98

    C. Windows NT Workstation 4.0

    D. Windows NT Server 4.0

    Answer: B. Windows 98 supports Plug and Play while the others do not.

4. Which of the following support multithreaded, multitasking applications? Choose all that apply.

    A. MS-DOS 6.22

    B. Windows 98

    C. Windows NT Workstation 4.0

    D. Windows NT Server 4.0

Answer: B, C, and D. Windows 98 and all versions of Windows NT support multithreaded, multitasking applications. MS-DOS (all versions) does not.

5. Which network model has no dedicated server?

    A. Stand-alone

    B. Networked

    C. Workgroup

    D. Member of an NT Domain

Answer: C. The workgroup model supports clients and servers without a dedicated server. A stand-alone system is not networked, and a networked system may or may not be using a dedicated server. An NT domain requires an NT server set up as a domain controller.

6. In which model can Windows 98 be both a client and a server? Choose all that apply.

    A. Stand-alone

    B. Networked

    C. Workgroup

    D. Member of an NT Domain

Answer: C and D. Windows 98 can be a client, and it can act like a server in both the workgroup and domain models. The stand-alone model has no networking, and there is no such thing as just a networked model.

7. Which model would be appropriate for the home user with one computer?

   A. Stand-alone

   B. Networked

   C. Workgroup

   D. Member of an NT Domain

Answer: A. The stand-alone model is best for those with only one computer, especially home systems.

8. Which model would be most appropriate for a large company?

   A. Stand-alone

   B. Networked

   C. Workgroup

   D. Member of an NT Domain

Answer: D. A large company would normally have a Windows NT domain installed because of the added security, auditing ability, and speed that such a system provides.

9. Which model would be appropriate for a small office on a limited budget?

   A. Stand-alone

   B. Networked

   C. Workgroup

   D. Member of an NT Domain

Answer: C. A small office can successfully use the workgroup model, with Windows 98 acting as a client and server.

10. You want to upgrade to Windows 98. Which of these computers can be upgraded without any hardware additions?

   A. 486/66 CPU with 8MB of RAM and 150MB of free disk space

   B. 486/66 CPU with 16MB of RAM and 150MB of free disk space

   C. Pentium CPU with 32MB of RAM and 75MB of free disk space

   D. Pentium CPU with 64MB of RAM and 150MB of free disk space

   Answer: B, D. Windows 98 requires a 486+, at least 16MB of RAM, and at least 120MB of disk space. This means that the 486 with only 8MB of RAM and the Pentium with only 75MB of free hard drive space do not meet the specifications for Windows 98.

11. You have only Windows 98 at your office. You want to share files and folders but need as much security as possible. You want all users to be able to read the Memos folder but only the managers to be able to create new memos. How would you set up the sharing services?

   A. Use share-level security. Share the Memos folder and give Read rights to The World and Full rights to the managers group.

   B. Use share-level security. Share the Memos folder with a password for read-level access and a different password for full-level access. Give the appropriate password to the appropriate users.

   C. Use user-level security. Share the Memos folder and give Read rights to The World and Full rights to the managers group.

   D. Use user-level security. Share the Memos folder with a password for read-level access and a different password for full-level access. Give the appropriate password to the appropriate users.

   Answer: B. Even though share-level security isn't as tight as user-level security, it can still be used to secure access to resources. By sharing the Memos folder with two different passwords, one for read access and one for full access, you can allow people to have the type of access they need. User-level security requires an NT or NetWare server.

Chapter 2

1. What is a deployment guide?

    A. An automated script

    B. Part of the Uninstall process

    C. A carefully laid plan to install Windows 98

    D. Part of the DBSet file structure

    Answer: C. The deployment guide is your blueprint to the installation process. Having a well-laid plan leads to a successful installation of Windows 98.

2. What are some of the minimum hardware requirements for Windows 98? Choose all that apply.

    A. 120MB of free hard disk space

    B. 16MB of RAM

    C. Sound Blaster

    D. 14.4 baud modem

    Answer: A and B. A and B are required; C and D are optional.

3. How much disk space will you typically need to save the existing file system?

    A. 35MB

    B. 40MB

    C. 50MB

    D. 75MB

    Answer: D. The previous file systems usually take up 75MB.

4. Which version of MS-DOS is considered to be the bare basics?

A. MS-DOS 7.0

B. MS DOS 6.22

C. MS-DOS 5.0

D. MS-DOS 3.3

Answer: C. MS-DOS 5.0 is the preferred minimum.

5. If you upgrade Windows 98 to a hard disk that is compressed, how much free noncompressed space must you have?

A. 1MB

B. 3MB

C. 5MB

D. 10MB

Answer: B. You need at least 3MB of free noncompressed hard disk space to install Windows 98.

6. Windows 98 can be installed on which of the following file systems? Choose all that apply.

A. NTFS

B. FAT16

C. FAT32

D. HPFS

Answer: B and C. Windows 98 can be installed to a FAT32 drive; however, this type of file system is not compatible with Windows NT.

7. Windows 95 uses a 12-step installation process. How many steps does Windows 98 use?

A. 5

B. 8

C. 10

D. 12

Answer: A. Windows 98 follows a five-phase installation setup process.

8. The most optimized Windows 98 upgrade is from which operating system?

A. MS-DOS

B. Windows 3.*x*

C. Windows 95

D. Windows NT

Answer: C. Installing and upgrading from Windows 95 is the most optimized and efficient manner by which to upgrade Windows 98.

9. The Windows 98 setup could require the use of which of the following? Choose all that apply.

A. DR-DOS

B. HPFS

C. Protected-mode drivers

D. Real-mode drivers

Answer: C and D. However, the most correct answer is D. Windows 98 needs to have access to all drivers, and sometimes it needs the real-mode driver to maintain a connection to the network or to access files from your CD-ROM.

10. The `Setup /d` option prevents Windows 98 from doing what?

   A. Diagnosing real-mode problems

   B. Diagnosing hard-disk errors with ScanDisk

   C. Detecting virtual hard disks

   D. Detecting and using any previous version of Windows

   Answer: D. This feature is used to prevent the setup process from detecting any other version of Windows on the hard disk.

11. Which of the following processors are required for Windows 98? Choose all that apply.

   A. Pentium/60MHz

   B. 386DX/25MHz

   C. 486SX/33MHz

   D. 486DX/66MHz

   Answer: A and D. You must have a 486DX/66MHz or higher processor.

12. According to Microsoft, what is the minimum amount of RAM required to run Windows 98?

   A. 4MB

   B. 8MB

   C. 16MB

   D. 32MB

   Answer: C. Microsoft states that the answer is 16MB, but 8MB has been known to work.

13. Which of the following are needed to perform a successful installation? Choose all that apply.

   A. A bootable floppy accessible

   B. A backup of CONFIG.SYS and AUTOEXEC.BAT

   C. ScanDisk must be run on your system

   D. Defrag must be run on your system

   Answer: A, B, C, and D. All are needed for a successful installation.

14. You want to install Windows 98, but you do not want it to perform the ScanDisk or Registry check. Which of the following switches should you use?

   A. Setup /is /ir

   B. Setup /is /nr

   C. Setup /ih /ir

   D. Setup /ih /is

   Answer: B. Use these options when you are certain that there are no problems with your hard disk drive. If the Registry is functioning and you don't feel that you need to test it, use the /nr (no Registry check) switch.

15. If you want Setup to run automatically, what type of file could you use to assist in the setup process?

   A. SETUP.DAT

   B. MSBATCH.DAT

   C. SETUP.INF

   D. MSBATCH.INF

   Answer: C and D. Depending on the data you stored in these two files, you should be good to go as long as you have the proper information in an .INF file.

16. Which of the following is not one of the five setup phases?

   A. Preparing to run Windows 98 Setup

   B. Collecting information about your computer

   C. Compressing the source files on your computer

   D. Finalizing settings

   Answer: C. There are no compression options in the Windows 98 setup process. During the installation of 98 Plus, you can choose to convert to FAT32.

17. What is Wininst0.400?

   A. A file needed for the installation process

   B. A folder on the Windows 98 CD-ROM that contains the installation instructions

   C. A temporary folder created to help facilitate the setup process

   D. A permanent folder used by Internet Explorer 4

   Answer: C. It is a temporary directory used during the installation process.

18. What are the WINUNDO.DAT and WINUNDO.INI files?

   A. Compressed files stored on the Startup disk

   B. Compressed files stored on the Windows 98 CD-ROM that are used to install

   C. Hidden/read-only files stored on the local drive as a result of saving the previous file system

   D. Hidden/read-only files stored in the C:\Windows folder used to uninstall Windows 98

   Answer: C. These two files are the data from the previous file system, Windows 95 or Windows 3.*x*. If for whatever reason Windows 98 doesn't work correctly or do what you need it to, you can return to your previous operating environment.

19. Which of the following statements are correct? Choose all that apply.

A. The Startup disk contains drivers for generic CD-ROM readers.

B. The Startup disk will create a RAM drive on your system.

C. The Startup disk can be used to view files on a NTFS partition.

D. Other files can be added to the Startup disk.

Answer: A, B, and D. The Windows 98 Startup disk contains generic drivers for most CD-ROM drivers. When you boot from the Startup disk, a menu will appear asking you if you want to install the CD-ROM drivers. After you make your choice, a RAM disk is created. Files that were stored in the EBD.CAB are extracted and placed into the RAM drive. You can place additional files in this EDB.CAB file using the CABARC.EXE utility.

20. Which program can automate the Windows 98 setup process?

A. DBSetup

B. Microsoft Batch 98

C. NetSetup

D. Microsoft Information Installer

Answer: B. NetSetup was the Windows 95 utility; it no longer exists in Windows 98. DBSetup and Information Installer allow you to enhance or augment the setup process. The Microsoft Batch 98 utility allows you to create script information that answers the questions that you are prompted with during the Windows 98 installation process.

21. Which file allows you to add device drivers to the installation process?

A. DBSet

B. Microsoft Batch 98

C. APPS.INI

D. INFINST.EXE

Answer: D. INFINST.EXE allows you to add additional .INF files to install during the Windows 98 installation process.

22. BOOTDISK.BAT allows you to do which of the following?

A. Create a Startup disk for Windows 98

B. Create a Startup disk for Windows NT

C. Format the existing drive and copy the system files to it

D. Boot up with OS/2

Answer: A. This feature is for laptop users who physically swap the floppy disk drive and the CD-ROM disk drive. By executing this command, a startup disk can be created.

23. To uninstall Windows 98, which of the following must be true?

A. You did not select to Save File System during setup.

B. You selected to Save File System during setup.

C. You have a compressed drive.

D. You have a FAT32 drive.

Answer: B. In order to uninstall Windows 98, you must have saved the existing file system. Otherwise, you will not be able to use this feature.

24. To dual-boot with Windows NT, which of the following must be true? Choose all that apply.

A. The boot partition must be FAT16.

B. The boot partition must be NTFS.

C. You must install Windows 98 from MS-DOS shell while in NT.

D. You must install Windows 98 from MS-DOS from the Boot Manager menu.

Answer: A and D. Both Windows 98 and Windows NT can read data from a FAT16 file system. In order to coexist, the boot partition must be FAT16. You install Windows 98 from a MS-DOS prompt.

25. You can install Window 98 from a server using push technology if you are using which of the following? Choose all that apply.

A. Channels from Internet partners

B. Microsoft's BackOffice SMS

C. Logon Scripts

D. DBSET

Answer: B and C. Two things to help automate the installation process are SMS's BackOffice tool and using logon scripts that call a file that runs Install.

Chapter 3

1. Two modems are installed in your computer, and each one uses a separate phone line. You used the Windows NT RAS services to log in to Windows NT using PPP with multilink. While online with Windows NT, you want to send a fax from your computer, but you don't want to lose your connection. You decide to suspend one of your connections to the Windows NT server and use that modem to send your fax. When you are finished faxing, you resume your connection with the multilink. How would you rate this solution?

A. This is an excellent solution and will work.

B. This is a good solution, but you will lose your connection to your RAS session on both lines and will have to reinstate both of them.

C. This is poor solution, but it appears to work.

D. This is a poor solution and will not work as specified.

Answer: A. This is an optimal solution and meets all the criteria specified. With a multilink session, you can suspend connections and resume them without losing your link.

2. Your infrared printer is not automatically installing itself when you bring your laptop into range. You decide to manually install your infrared device. You start the Install New Hardware Wizard and choose the "Generic Infrared Serial Port or dongle device". How would you rate this solution?

A. This is an excellent solution and appears to work.

B. This is a good solution, but the Generic choice will not work with your printer.

C. This is a poor solution, but it appears to work.

D. This is a poor solution and will not work.

Answer: A. The Generic option is used for all non–Plug-and-Play devices.

3. WDM (Win32 Device Manager) is built into the operating system of Windows 98. The WDM supports which of the following features?

A. The WDM forces hardware vendors to create a single version of their hardware, but they must write platform-specific minidrivers.

B. The WDM forces hardware vendors to create a single version of their minidriver software, but they must design platform-specific versions of their hardware.

C. The WDM allows hardware vendors to create a single card that will fit into the motherboard of any computer.

D. The WDM allows hardware vendors to create a single version of their hardware and minidriver software which will run on any platform.

Answer: D. The WDM provides a specification that allows hardware vendors to create a single version of their hardware and minidrivers that can run on any WDM-compliant platform.

4. IEEE 1394 FireWire supports which of the following? Choose all that apply.

   A. Low bandwidth connections

   B. High bandwidth connections

   C. Speeds in excess of 200Mbps

   D. Speeds around 115Kbps

   Answer: B and C. The FireWire is used for high-end multimedia applications that require high bandwidth and speeds ranging from 100Mbps to 400 or more Mbps.

5. Which of the following bus architectures are supported by WDM? Choose all that apply.

   A. PCI

   B. ISA

   C. SCSI

   D. IEEE 1394 FireWire

   E. USB

   Answer: D and E. The WDM supports the emerging USB and IEEE 1394 bus architectures. These architectures are geared toward high-bandwidth connections.

6. Which of the following support an isochronous connection where you have a guaranteed rate of data transfer? Choose all that apply.

   A. PCI

   B. ISA

   C. SCSI

   D. IEEE 1394 FireWire

   E. USB

   Answer: D and E. Both IEEE 1394 and USB support isochronous connections.

7. Windows 98 has been installed on all of your office computers as well as on all of your laptop computers. You want to use power management schemes to reduce energy consumption costs and increase the lifespan of your hardware components. Which of the following are true regarding power management schemes? Choose all that apply.

   A. You can have the monitor and the hard drive turn off automatically after a predetermined amount of time.

   B. You can have either the monitor or the hard drive turn off automatically, but you can't have both of them turn off automatically.

   C. A device on standby can wake up the system if the need arises.

   D. When installed on a laptop computer, Windows 98 offers some additional options regarding battery use.

   Answer: A, C, and D.

8. Your laptop computer is currently running the Windows 98 operating system. You want to be able to view information about your system, its resources, and its configuration settings. You decide to use the Device Manager. The Device Manager can be used for which of the following? Choose all that apply.

   A. Determining the devices currently attached to your PC

   B. Determining the resources with which each device is currently configured

   C. Modifying the configuration of your devices

   D. Installing new devices on your PC

   Answer: A, B, and C. To install a new device on your PC, you should use the Add New Hardware Wizard in the Control Panel.

9. Multidisplay is an exciting new feature of Windows 98 that allows you to spread a virtual desktop across multiple monitors. Which of the following are true regarding multidisplay? Choose all that apply.

   A. All monitors involved in multidisplay must have the same resolution.

   B. The primary monitor always has an upper-left coordinate of 0,0.

   C. Every secondary display has coordinates based on the primary display.

   D. Every display's coordinates butt up against each other.

   Answer: B, C, and D. The monitors in a multidisplay do not need to have the same resolution. However, if you change resolutions, there may be space in the virtual desktop that can be used, but not seen.

10. Windows 98 supports several different bus architectures. In the past, these bus architectures required a hardware vendor to create a specialized card, a special type of socket, and cable to connect to the custom card. New emerging standards allow Windows 98 to take advantage of standard cables and sockets. Which of the following specifies a particular type of cable and socket for use as part of its bus architecture? Choose all that apply.

    A. WDM

    B. IEEE 1394 FireWire

    C. SCSI

    D. USB

    E. PCI

    Answer: B and D. WDM is not a bus architecture. It is a specification for designing new busses and devices. SCSI and PCI require you to plug a card into your system. There are several different types of SCSI interfaces and PCI interfaces.

11. Infrared technology allows you to make all kinds of connections to various hardware devices without the need of a cable. Your current Windows 98 laptop is equipped with an infrared port. Which of the following can you do with this infrared-enabled laptop? Choose all that apply.

A. Print to an infrared printer

B. Send files to an infrared-enabled computer

C. Use Direct Cable Connection software to make a network-style connection over infrared

D. RAS into Windows NT

Answer: A, B, and C. To RAS into Windows NT requires a modem connection.

12. You have a manager who uses a laptop at work and at home. She has a docking station at work with a network card but uses an external modem at home to dial into the network. How would you set up the laptop so that she can use both configurations easily?

A. Create two hardware profiles. Disable the network card for the work profile and disable the modem for the home profile.

B. Create two hardware profiles. Delete the network card driver in the home profile and delete the modem driver in the work profile.

C. Create user profiles. Disable the network card driver in the home user profile and disable the modem driver for the work profile.

D. Create two hardware profiles. Disable the network card for the home profile and disable the modem in the work profile.

Answer: D. When choosing between hardware configurations you need to create a hardware profile, not a user profile. You don't delete drivers in a profile you just disable them. You would want to disable the network card driver at home and disable the modem at work to match the hardware situation.

13. Where are hardware profiles stored?

A. The Hkey_Local_Machine Registry key.

B. The Hkey_Users Registry key.

C. CONFIG.SYS

D. The Hkey_Dyn_Data Registry key.

Answer: A. Hardware profiles are held in the Hkey_Local_Machine Registry key in the Config subkey.

Chapter 4

1. What is the first step in the Windows 98 boot process?

A. BIOS bootstrap phase

B. Master boot record and boot sector phase

C. Real-mode boot phase

D. Protected-mode boot phase

Answer: A. The BIOS bootstrap is the first phase in the boot process.

2. During what step of the boot process is VMM32.VXD loaded?

A. BIOS bootstrap phase

B. Master boot record and boot sector phase

C. Real-mode boot phase

D. Protected-mode boot phase

Answer: C. The VMM32.VXD loads during the real-mode boot phase. Once it is loaded, WIN.COM switches to protected-mode and then initializes and configures the devices listed in the VMM32.VXD file.

3. Your local PC has been upgraded from Windows 95 to Windows 98. You would like to configure changes to your boot process. Which of the following methods will allow you to configure the way in which Windows 98 boots? (Select three.)

A. Using the Startup menu

B. Editing BOOT.SYS

C. Editing IO.SYS

D. Editing MSDOS.SYS

E. Using the System Configuration utility

Answer: A, D, and E. All three of these can be used to modify the Windows 98 boots.

4. You have recently upgraded your Windows 3.*x* computer to Windows 98. When you were using Windows 3.*x*, you had no problems with your old two-speed CD-ROM player. When you boot to Windows 98, the player doesn't seem to work properly. Because you are using real-mode drivers to work with your CD-ROM, which Startup menu option should you choose to see which real-mode driver(s) might be giving you trouble?

A. Previous Version of DOS

B. Safe Mode with Network Support

C. Safe Mode

D. Step-by-Step Confirmation

Answer: D. Step-by-step confirmation allows you to see exactly which drivers and startup options are being used.

5. After the real-mode boot sequence occurs, Windows 98 begins its pro-tected-mode boot phase. You want to determine which virtual device drivers and 32-bit protected mode drivers are loaded during the startup process. Some of these drivers appear to be giving you prob-lems, but you are not sure which ones. What Startup menu option should you choose to see which protected-mode driver(s) might be giving you trouble?

   A. Logged (to create BOOTLOG.TXT)

   B. Step-by-Step Confirmation

   C. Command Prompt Only

   D. Previous Version of DOS

   Answer: A. Once your drivers have been loaded, you can edit the BOOTLOG.TXT file and look for the keyword Failure.

6. Your Windows 98 machine seems to be having all kinds of problems during the boot phase and won't start. You have recently updated sev-eral drivers on your system and are confident that these new drivers are causing the problems. You decide to do a Safe-mode boot of Win-dows 98 so that you can actually get into Windows 98 and make the appropriate changes. During a Safe-mode boot, which of the fol-lowing drivers are loaded? Choose all that apply.

   A. Mouse driver

   B. Keyboard driver

   C. Standard VGA device driver

   D. Network drivers

   Answer: A, B, and C. The network drivers are not loaded during a Safe-mode boot.

7. Windows 98 supplies you with additional startup switches when you run the WIN.COM program. You can't remember what these switches do. What can you use to find out which switches are available with WIN.COM?

   A. `Win /?`

   B. `Win /help`

C. `Win /switches`

D. `Help /Win`

Answer: A. `WIN /?` will list available switches and their usage.

8. Windows 98 has been installed on your desktop PC. Since its installation, you have installed new network drivers and new sound card drivers. Windows 98 recognizes these new drivers and allows them to be installed. A new feature of Windows 98 automatically backs up the old drivers in case you want to use them again. Which of the following utilities will allow you to specify which version of a driver (the original or a newer one that has been installed) is to be used?

   A. System Information utility

   B. System Configuration utility

   C. Version Conflict Manager

   D. MSDOS.INI

   Answer: C. The Version Conflict Manager is used to back up and restore different versions of your drivers and DLL files.

9. You can alter the boot sequence on your Windows 98 machine by making modifications to the MSDOS.SYS file, the SYSTEM.INI file, the Registry, and the WIN.INI files. You can use the Notepad program and the Regedit programs to make these modification to each file, one at a time. Which of the following Windows 98 utilities will allow you to specify which values are processed during the boot sequence from a single program?

   A. System Information utility

   B. System Configuration utility

   C. Version Conflict Manager

   D. MSDOS.INI

   Answer: B. The System Configuration utility can be used to modify entries in the MSDOS.SYS file, SYSTEM.INI, WIN.INI, and the Registry.

Chapter 5

1. What is the name of the Registry key that holds user settings?

   A. Hkey_Local_Machine

   B. Hkey_Users

   C. Hkey_Dyn_Data

   D. Hkey_Current_Config

   Answer: B. The Hkey_Users Registry key holds settings that are unique to individual users.

2. What is the name of the Registry key that holds Plug-and-Play settings?

   A. Hkey_Local_Machine

   B. Hkey_Users

   C. Hkey_Dyn_Data

   D. Hkey_Current_Config

   Answer: C. The Hkey_Dyn_Data Registry key is used to hold Plug-and-Play settings. (*Dyn* stands for dynamic which applies to Plug-and-Play hardware because the settings could change dynamically.)

3. What is the name of the Registry key that holds generic hardware information?

   A. Hkey_Local_Machine

   B. Hkey_Users

   C. Hkey_Dyn_Data

   D. Hkey_Current_Config

   Answer: D. The Hkey_Current_Config Registry key holds most (if not all) generic hardware settings.

4. What is the name of the Registry key that holds hardware profile information?

   A. Hkey_Local_Machine

   B. Hkey_Users

   C. Hkey_Dyn_Data

   D. Hkey_Current_Config

   Answer: A. The Hkey_Local_Machine Registry key holds hardware profile information in the Config subkey.

5. What is the name of the Registry file that holds system settings?

   A. USER.INI

   B. USER.DAT

   C. SYSTEM.DAT

   D. SYSTEM.INI

   Answer: C. The Registry is stored in two different physical files: the SYSTEM.DAT and the USER.DAT. They are also backed up as SYSTEM.DA0 and USER.DA0. The SYSTEM.DAT file stores system settings; the USER.DET file stores user-related settings. For example, Hkey_Local_Machine would be found in the SYSTEM.DAT. Hkey_Users would be found in the USER.DAT file.

6. What is the name of the Registry file that holds user settings?

   A. USER.INI

   B. USER.DAT

   C. SYSTEM.DAT

   D. SYSTEM.INI

   Answer: C. The Registry is stored in two different physical files: the SYSTEM.DAT and the USER.DAT. They are also backed up as SYSTEM.DA0 and USER.DA0. The SYSTEM.DAT file stores system settings; the USER.DET file stores user-related settings. For example, Hkey_Local_Machine would be found in the SYSTEM.DAT. Hkey_Users would be found in the USER.DAT file.

7. What is the name of the Registry editor for Windows 98?

   A. REGEDT32.EXE

   B. REGISTRY EDITOR.EXE

   C. REGEDIT.EXE

   D. REGISTRY.EXE

Answer: C. REGEDIT.EXE is the Registry Editor for Windows 98. REGEDT32.EXE is the Registry Editor for Windows NT. There are no such programs as REGISTRY EDITOR.EXE and REGISTRY.EXE.

8. What is the name of the real-mode Registry Checker that must be run from MS-DOS mode?

   A. REGCHECK.EXE

   B. REGCHECKW.EXE

   C. SCANREG.EXE

   D. SCANREGW.EXE

Answer: C. SCANREG.EXE is the real-mode MS-DOS version of the Registry Checker that can be used to check, back up, or restore the Registry.

9. What is the name of the protected-mode version of the Registry Checker that can be run from within Windows 98?

   A. REGCHECK.EXE

   B. REGCHECKW.EXE

   C. SCANREG.EXE

   D. SCANREGW.EXE

Answer: D. SCANREGW.EXE is the protected-mode Windows 98 version of the Registry Checker that can be used to check and back up the Registry.

10. What is the name of the backup Registry file that is automatically created by the Registry Checker?

   A. RBXXX.CAB

   B. USER.BAK

C. SYSTEM.BAK

D. REGISTRY.BAK

Answer: A. The Registry Checker saves backups of the Registry as RBXXX.CAB. Windows 95 used to keep a copy of the Registry in USER.BAK and SYSTEM.BAK, but Windows 98 doesn't do that. There has never been a REGISTRY.BAK file.

11. You need to edit the Registry on a user's computer. You want to back it up first. What Windows 98 tool should you use to back up the Registry?

A. ScanDisk

B. Disk Defragmenter

C. WALIGN.EXE

D. Registry Checker

Answer: D. The Regsitry Checker (SCANREG.EXE or SCAN-REGW.EXE) can be used to check, back up, or restore the Registry.

12. A user dual-boots Windows 98 and Windows NT. He or she wants to keep the Registries in sync so that applications will run on both operating systems. You are asked for advice. How can this be done?

A. Run Registry Checker on one system to back up the Registry, and Registry Checker on the other system to restore it.

B. Run Regedit on one system to back up only the changes in the Registry, and use Regedit to import those changes to the other operating system.

C. Run Cfgback on one operating system to make a backup, and run Regedit on the other operating system to restore the Registry.

D. Because the Registries are incompatible, you can't use any automated method to synchronize them.

Answer: D. The Registries of Windows 98 and Windows NT, although similar in appearance, are *not* the same. Copying settings from one operating system to the other may cause unexpected, fatal errors.

Chapter 6

1. Which of the following are virtual machines used in Windows 98? Choose all that apply.

    A. System VM

    B. Core VM

    C. W98 VM

    D. MS-DOS VM

    Answer: A and D. There is no such thing as a Core VM or a W98 VM.

NOTE For the next three questions, please use this scenario. You have three 16-bit applications, one 32-bit application, and two MS-DOS–based applications running.

2. If one of the 16-bit applications is hung, how many programs will be hung including the hung application?

    A. 1

    B. 2

    C. 3

    D. 5

    Answer: C. All three 16-bit application will be hung because they all share the same queue. The MS-DOS–based programs run in their own VMs and are not affected. The 32-bit application runs in its own address space and, likewise, will not be affected.

3. If one of the 32-bit applications has hung, how many programs will be hung including the hung application?

    A. 1

    B. 2

    C. 3

    D. 5

    Answer: A. Because 32-bit applications run in their own separate address space, other applications are not affected when a 32-bit application crashes.

4. If an MS-DOS application has a GPF, how many programs will be affected including the crashed MS-DOS application?

A. 1

B. 2

C. 3

D. 5

Answer: A. Only the MS-DOS program will be affected. Each MS-DOS–based program runs in its own separate, virtual machine. When one of the VMs crashes or hangs, the other VMs don't know about it.

5. You want to run a batch file to log on to a network server before your MS-DOS application runs. What is the easiest method to accomplish this?

A. Build a shortcut to the batch file and to the MS-DOS program; double-click on the batch shortcut first, and then run the MS-DOS program.

B. Go to a command prompt and run the batch file before running the MS-DOS program.

C. Add the batch file to the Batch File parameter in the property sheet for the MS-DOS program.

D. You don't need to run the batch file because Windows 98 will automatically detect that the MS-DOS program needs access to the server and will log you in.

Answer: C. Although answers A and B would work, they are overly cumbersome. Answer C is the best solution.

6. Your MS-DOS program is named FOO.EXE. You create a PIF file for your MS-DOS program. What is the name of the PIF file?

A. MS-DOS.PIF

B. PIF.EXE

C. _DEFAULT.PIF

D. FOO.PIF

Answer: D. When you create a PIF file, it takes the same name as the MS-DOS program and includes the .PIF extension.

7. In the Working parameter of an MS-DOS property sheet, you specify C:\Temp. What, if anything, will be placed in the C:\Temp directory?

   A. Output files used by your MS-DOS program

   B. The files used by Windows 98 to track program performance

   C. The .INI files used by all the Windows programs running at the same time your MS-DOS program is running

   D. Nothing

   Answer: A. Any output files generated from your MS-DOS program that do not have a specific folder assigned to them will be placed in the Working directory specified in your PIF file.

8. You are editing a document in Microsoft Word. You highlight a line of text and press Ctrl+C to copy it to the Clipboard. Suddenly your MS-DOS application starts up. What could cause this?

   A. The OLE functionality of Microsoft Word is linked to your MS-DOS program.

   B. You have chosen Ctrl+C as a shortcut for your MS-DOS–based application.

   C. Ctrl+C always starts up the last used MS-DOS program.

   D. This is a glitch in the computer system and should never happen.

   Answer: B. OLE does not link with MS-DOS–based programs, and Ctrl+C does not start the last used MS-DOS program. In general, Ctrl+C is used to copy selected information to the Windows Clipboard.

9. When you are in your MS-DOS program, you want to be able to press Alt+Enter to switch to another running application. How could you enable this feature?

   A. In the Misc tab of the MS-DOS property sheet, click on the Alt+Enter checkbox.

   B. You don't have to do anything—this functionality always exists for MS-DOS applications.

   C. This is not an available feature and can't be implemented.

   D. You must edit the Registry in order to do this.

   Answer: A. You must enable this option by editing the PIF files Miscellaneous tab and selecting the Alt+Enter option.

10. Because 16-bit code is non-reentrant, how does Windows handle multitasking procedures that require the same DLL function usage?

A. Windows employs a Win16Mutex flag to signal other programs that a particular 16-bit procedure is currently in use.

B. Windows employs a 16- and 32-Mutex flag to signal other programs that a particular procedure is currently in use.

C. Windows does not need to worry about this because it is a cooperatively multitasked environment.

D. Windows uses thunking to work with all 32-bit code instead of working with flags to signal 16-bit DLL usage.

Answer: A. There is no 32-Mutex flag in Windows because 32-bit procedures are reentrant. Windows is a preemptively multitasked environment, not a cooperatively multitasked environment.

Chapter 7

1. What is the name of the program that can fix minor errors on your hard drive?

A. Format

B. Fdisk

C. ScanDisk

D. Vcache

Answer: C. ScanDisk can fix minor errors on your disk. Format is for formatting drives, Fdisk manages disk partitions, and Vcache is a caching program.

2. What is it called when files get scattered over a hard drive?

A. Compression

B. Corruption

C. Clustering

D. Fragmentation

Answer: D. Fragmentation happens when files get scattered on a drive and are no longer contiguous.

3. What is the name of the new 32-bit caching tool of Windows 98?

A. Format

B. Fdisk

C. ScanDisk

D. Vcache

Answer: D. Vcache is the new 32-bit caching program for Windows 98.

4. Does Windows 98 include a native antivirus program?

A. Yes, but only on the CD-ROM version of Windows 98

B. Yes, but you have to pay for it before you can install it

C. Yes, but it only comes with the upgrade version

D. No

Answer: D. Windows 98 does not include an antivirus program. You will need to buy a third-party program or the Plus! pack for Windows 98, which includes McAfee's antivirus program.

5. Windows 98's Backup program can restore backups made from which operating system? Choose all that apply.

A. MS-DOS 5.0

B. MS-DOS 6.22

C. Windows 3.11

D. Windows 95

Answer: D. Windows 98 cannot restore any backups made with the backup programs from MS-DOS or Windows 3.11.

6. Is creating smaller partitions a more efficient way to format your hard drive if you have to use FAT16 partitions?

   A. Yes, because files take up less room on your disk.

   B. Yes, because the hard drive works faster.

   C. Yes, because the hard drive spins less often, saving wear and tear.

   D. No, there is no difference.

Answer: A. Using FAT16 partitions, the only way to have smaller cluster sizes is to make smaller partitions, which more efficiently use hard drive space.

7. The long filename "This is a company memo about the party for.1997.doc" would have which 8.3 name created for it?

   A. This is .doc

   B. Thisis~1.199

   C. Thisis~1.doc

   D. Thisisal.doc

Answer: C. Windows 98 takes the first six valid characters, adds a tilde (~) and a number from 1 to 9 and then the first three characters of the last extension. If the name is used again, Windows 98 takes the first five valid characters, adds a tilde (~) and a number from 10 to 99 and then the first three characters of the last extension.

8. Disabling the write-behind cache is done with which program?

   A. Control Panel ➤ System

   B. Control Panel ➤ Devices

   C. Control Panel ➤ Drives

   D. My Computer ➤ Properties of the Drive

Answer: A. Disabling the write-behind cache is done by using the System applet of the Control Panel.

9. You can restore deleted files in Windows 98 due to which program?

    A. Vcache

    B. Recycle Bin

    C. Trash Can

    D. Undelete

    Answer: B. The Recycle Bin tracks deleted files for easy undeletion.

10. Which program can be used to schedule tasks such as ScanDisk and Disk Defragmenter in Windows 98?

    A. My Computer ➤ Properties

    B. Shortcuts

    C. Scheduled Tasks

    D. The AT command

    Answer: C. Windows 98 adds Scheduled Tasks which allows you to easily schedule an application to run at a certain time.

11. How do you enable FAT32 support?

    A. Run FAT32.EXE.

    B. Run Fdisk with the /FAT32 switch.

    C. It is always enabled.

    D. Run Fdisk, and answer Yes to the Large Disk Support prompt.

    Answer: D. When you are starting FDISK, FAT32 support is enabled by answering Yes to the prompt "Do you want to enable large disk support?"

12. What is the easiest way to create tasks to do regular hard drive maintenance?

    A. Create the tasks by hand.

    B. Copy the tasks from another computer.

    C. Use the Maintenance Wizard.

    D. Use the Create Scheduled Tasks Wizard.

    Answer: C. The Maintenance Wizard can be used to quickly and easily set up drive maintenance tasks.

13. A user comes to you and says he has compressed his C: drive on his Windows 98 computer and wants to install Windows NT so that he has a dual-boot system. How can you do this?

   A. Install Windows NT normally. It will automatically set up dual-booting.

   B. Convert to FAT32, and then perform the Windows NT installation.

   C. Use FDISK to mark the partition as Other, and then install Windows NT.

   D. Decompress the drive, and then install Windows NT.

   Answer: D. Windows NT cannot see compressed or FAT32 drives. Setting the partition type to Other (which you can't do from within FDISK anyway) will not help the situation.

14. A user wants to know what is the tightest compression level she can pick. She is running Windows 98 with a FAT16 partition. What do you tell her?

   A. Hipack

   B. Ultrapack

   C. Default

   D. Compression is not supported for FAT16 partitions.

   Answer: B. Ultrapack is the highest level of compression and is not recommended for 486 or slower computers.

15. A user wants to know what is the tightest compression level he can pick. He is running Windows 98 with a FAT32 partition. What do you tell him?

   A. Hipack

   B. Ultrapack

   C. Default

   D. Compression is not supported for FAT32 partitions.

   Answer: D. FAT32 drives cannot be compressed.

16. You want to back up your drive so that it is quick to restore in case of a hard disk failure. You don't plan on doing full backups every night. What method would you choose when backing up your drive?

A. Partial

B. Incremental

C. Differential

D. Saved

Answer: C. Differential backups take longer to perform than incremental backups, but they are fast to restore. There is no such thing as partial or saved backup methods.

17. Which types of partitions can be marked active (bootable)? Choose all that apply.

A. Primary

B. Extended

C. Logical

D. Expanded

Answer: A. Only primary partitions can be marked active. There is no such thing as an expanded partition.

18. You upgraded a Windows for Workgroups computer to Windows 98. You want to minimize the space wasted on your hard drive. Which utility should you run?

A. Disk Defragmenter

B. ScanDisk

C. Fdisk

D. FAT32 Converter

Answer: D. By converting your FAT16 partition to FAT32 you minimize wasted space because of the much smaller cluster size.

19. A user comes to you and explains that she wants to uninstall Windows 98 and go back to Windows for Workgroups. She has a FAT32 partition with 1GB of free space. How can you uninstall Windows 98 without losing her data?

    A. Convert the FAT32 partition to FAT16 by using the FAT32 conversion program, and run uninstall.

    B. Run uninstall. The FAT32 partition will automatically revert to FAT16.

    C. Run Fdisk. Choose No when asked if large disk support should be enabled. Then run uninstall.

    D. Back up the data, run Fdisk, delete the partition, and create a FAT16 partition, reinstall Windows, and restore the data.

Answer: D. Microsoft doesn't supply a program that will convert from a FAT32 to a FAT16 partition, so you have to use Fdisk to delete the FAT32 partition and then create a FAT16 partition.

Chapter 8

1. Which Microsoft layer talks to the network card?

    A. Device Driver Interface

    B. Physical Driver Interface

    C. Transport Driver Interface

    D. Session Driver Interface

Answer: A. The Device Driver Interface is the layer responsible for communicating with devices and, therefore, the network card.

2. Which of the following is not a protocol that Windows 98 supports?

    A. IPX/SPX

    B. Frame0

    C. NetBEUI

    D. TCP/IP

Answer: B. There is no such thing as Frame0 protocol. Windows 98 supports TCP/IP, IPX/SPX, and NetBEUI natively.

3. Which NDIS specification was designed for Windows 98 and for Windows NT 5.0?

    A. NDIS 2.0

    B. NDIS 3.0

    C. NDIS 4.0

    D. NDIS 5.0

Answer: D. NDIS 5.0 is the new specification for drivers that will work for both Windows 98 and Windows NT.

4. Does Windows 98 support auto-reconnect for both Windows NT and NetWare environments?

    A. Yes, for both environments

    B. No, only for the Windows NT environment

    C. No, only for the NetWare environment

    D. No, for neither environment

Answer: A. Auto-reconnect is supported for both the Microsoft and NetWare clients.

5. What does UNC stand for?

    A. Universal Network Convention

    B. Universal Naming Convention

    C. Universal NetBIOS Convention

    D. Universal NetWare Convention

Answer: B. UNC stands for Universal Naming Convention. The format of a UNC is *Server**Shared resource*.

6. Microsoft servers communicate natively with which language?

    A. NCP

    B. MMP

C. BTT

D. SMB

Answer: D. Microsoft servers use SMBs (Server Message Blocks) to communicate. By installing the Microsoft Client for Microsoft you configure Windows 98 to be able to use SMB packets to communicate with Microsoft servers.

7. Can Windows 98 be both a Microsoft and a NetWare client simultaneously?

A. Yes, it can be both.

B. No, it can only function as a Microsoft client.

C. No, it can only function as a NetWare client.

D. No, it can do both but not simultaneously.

Answer: A. Windows 98 can have multiple client software installed, including software that allows it to communicate with Microsoft and NetWare servers simultaneously.

8. Can Windows 98 be both a Microsoft and NetWare server simultaneously?

A. Yes, it can be both.

B. No, it can function only as a Microsoft server.

C. No, it can function only as a NetWare server.

D. No, it can function as one or the other but not both simultaneously.

Answer: D. Windows 98 can have only one sharing service installed at a time—either the File and Printer Sharing for Microsoft or the File and Printer Sharing for NetWare.

9. Which protocols can cross routers (under normal conditions)? Choose all that apply.

   A. TCP/IP

   B. NetBEUI

   C. IPX/SPX

   D. Fast Infrared

   Answer: A and C. TCP/IP and IPX/SPX can both cross a router, while NetBEUI cannot. Fast Infrared protocol is designed for local use, from one device to another (camera to a computer, etc.).

10. What feature of Windows 98 lets you see network resources?

    A. My Computer

    B. Network Resources

    C. Network Servers

    D. Network Neighborhood

    Answer: D. Network Neighborhood lets you see servers and their shared resources.

11. Refer to Figure 8.1. You are configuring a computer with the address of 131.107.8.31. What should you enter for the default gateway?

    A. 131.107.24.1

    B. 131.107.16.1

    C. 131.107.8.1

    D. 127.0.0.1

    Answer: C. The default gateway is the address of the router that will get you out of the subnetwork. After you get out of the subnet, the router will take care of the rest of the routing of the packet.

12. Your computer has an address of 131.107.8.31. What class of address is it?

A. Class A

B. Class B

C. Class C

D. Class D

Answer: B. Because the first number is 131, it falls into the range of a class B address.

13. Your computer has an address of 131.107.8.31. What is the network address where your computer resides?

A. 131

B. 131.107

C. 131.107.8

D. 127.0.0.1

Answer: B. Because this is a class B address, the first two octets refer to the network address, leaving the last two for the node address.

14. You have a network across five routers that consists of NetWare and Windows NT servers. You also have HP printers with JetDirect cards in them. You want your clients to be able to get to the Internet. Which protocol(s) should you install? Choose all that apply.

A. DLC

B. TCP/IP

C. IPX/SPX

D. NetBEUI

Answer: A, B, and C. You need DLC to get to the JetDirect printers, TCP/IP to get to the Internet, and IPX/SPX to get to the NetWare servers. The Windows NT computers are not running NetBEUI because they wouldn't be able to see each other across the routers, so they are running either TCP/IP or IPX/SPX.

15. You have an application that uses NetBIOS computer names. The application works for computers on the local subnet, but it fails to connect to computers across the router. Which service do you need to install?

   A. DHCP

   B. DNS

   C. WINS

   D. MSNDS

Answer: C. The WINS service resolves NetBIOS names to TCP/IP addresses. WINS is necessary because NetBIOS broadcasts will not cross a router.

16. Some of your users complain that they can connect to some servers but not to others. You find that the affected users can connect to servers in their department but not to those in other departments. You are using TCP/IP. What parameter is probably set up wrong?

   A. Subnet mask

   B. Default gateway

   C. TCP/IP address

   D. DNS address

Answer: B. The default gateway tells the computer how to access remote networks. With a bad gateway address, a computer can still contact other computers in its subnetwork, but it doesn't know how to get packets out to the rest of the network.

17. You want users to be able to connect to Microsoft and NetWare servers. The Microsoft servers are using TCP/IP, and the NetWare servers are using IPX/SPX. You want TCP/IP addresses to be automatically assigned. Here is your proposed solution: Install TCP/IP and IPX on each client. Install DHCP on a fast Windows 98 computer. Configure the DHCP server to give out addresses. Does your solution work?

   A. Yes, it works perfectly.

   B. Yes, it will work after you install WINS as well.

C. Yes, it will work after you install DNS as well.

D. No, the proposed solution won't work.

Answer: D. This is a trick question. DHCP servers require a Windows NT Server computer to be installed on, not Windows NT workstation or Windows 98.

18. You want users to be able to connect to Microsoft and NetWare 4.11 servers. The Microsoft servers are using TCP/IP, and the NetWare servers are using their default protocols. You want TCP/IP addresses to be automatically assigned. Here is your proposed solution: Install TCP/IP on each client. Install DHCP on a Windows NT Server. Configure the DHCP server to give out addresses. Does your solution work?

A. Yes, it works perfectly.

B. Yes, it will work after you install WINS as well.

C. Yes, it will work after you install DNS as well.

D. No, the proposed solution won't work.

Answer: D. NetWare 4.11 servers use the IPX/SPX protocol, so the clients would need IPX/SPX installed as well as TCP/IP.

19. Which protocol is used to connect to cameras, laptops, and personal devices.

A. ATM

B. NetBEUI

C. TCP/IP

D. Fast Infrared

Answer: D. The Fast Infrared protocol is designed for personal devices such as cameras, laptops, and hand-held computers.

Chapter 9

1. When installing a network card, you may need to configure which items? Choose all that apply.

   A. Interrupt

   B. I/O port

   C. Memory address

   D. Slot number

   Answer: A, B, C, and D. The interrupt, I/O port, memory address, and slot number may need to be configured for your network card, although the interrupt and I/O are the two major settings.

2. You can use which program(s) to configure the network card?

   A. Control Panel ➤ Network ➤ Properties of the card

   B. Network Neighborhood ➤ Properties ➤ Properties of the card

   C. Control Panel ➤ Devices ➤ Properties of the card

   D. Control Panel ➤ System ➤ Device Manager ➤ Properties of the card

   Answer: D. You can examine and change the network card driver from Device Manager, which is accessed by using the System applet of the Control Panel.

3. By installing the Client for Microsoft Networks, you allow Windows 98 to understand which language?

   A. NCPs

   B. MMPs

   C. NTBs

   D. SMBs

   Answer: D. Microsoft networks use the SMB language, which a Windows 98 computer can communicate with after the Client for Microsoft is installed.

4. If Windows 98 is set up to use IPX/SPX and it cannot auto-detect a frame type, what frame will it pick?

A. No frames

B. All frames

C. Ethernet_802.2

D. Ethernet_II

Answer: C. Ethernet_802.2 is the default frame type if no frame is detected.

5. Which service allows automatic assignment of TCP/IP addresses?

A. DHCP

B. WINS

C. DNS

D. DXNP

Answer: A. DHCP (Dynamic Host Configuration Protocol) is a service that can be used to automatically assign a TCP/IP address and settings to a client when the client boots. Windows 98 can be a DHCP client, but it cannot be a DHCP server using only software from Microsoft.

6. Can NetBEUI packets cross a router?

A. Yes, always

B. Only if the router is connected to the Internet

C. Only if the router is the latest model

D. No, they can't

Answer: D. NetBEUI packets are like interoffice mail—they are small and quick because they have only a local workstation address and do not have a network address. Routers work by examining the network address and routing packets to the correct network. Because NetBEUI packets have no network address, the router does not send them through.

7. True or False: You can change your NT password from within Windows 98.

   A. True, but not your screen saver

   B. True, and also your screen saver at the same time

   C. True, and all other passwords (including NetWare)

   D. False

Answer: C. Passwords for the local Windows account, network, screensaver and other software can all be changed by using the Passwords applet of the Control Panel.

8. NetWare servers communicate using which language?

   A. SMB

   B. PPP

   C. NDS

   D. NCP

Answer: D. NCP (NetWare Core Protocol) is the language that NetWare clients and servers speak.

9. Windows 98 can communicate with which NetWare servers? Choose all that apply.

   A. 2.*x* (bindery)

   B. 3.*x* (bindery)

   C. 4.*x* (NDS)

   D. 5.*x* (NDS)

Answer: A, B, C, and D. If the correct client is installed and properly set up, Windows 98 can communicate with all of the types of NetWare servers.

10. Which clients are real-mode clients? Choose all that apply.

  A. NETX

  B. VLM

  C. Microsoft's Client for NetWare

  D. Novell's Client for Windows 95

  Answer: A and B. NETX and VLM are real-mode clients. Client for Windows and Client for NetWare are native 32-bit, protected-mode clients.

11. Which clients are true NDS clients? Choose all that apply.

  A. NETX

  B. Service for NetWare Directory Services

  C. Microsoft's Client for NetWare

  D. Novell's Client for Windows 95

  Answer: B and D. Both the Service for NetWare Directory Services (provided by Microsoft) and the Client for Windows 95 (provided by NetWare) are true NDS clients for use with NetWare 4 and 5 servers.

12. A user complains that sometimes she can connect to a certain NetWare 4.11 server but at other times the connection doesn't work. She is using Service for NetWare Directory Services. What could be the problem?

  A. The NetWare server could be out of licenses.

  B. The client and the server could be using different frame types.

  C. The client needs to install the Microsoft Client for NetWare.

  D. The client needs to install IPX/SPX.

  Answer: A and B. If the NetWare server is low on licenses, the client may be getting connected sometimes and refused other times. If the client is using a different frame type, she may be connecting to the server through a third machine that is acting as a router. If the third machine happens to be turned off, the connection fails. Service for NetWare Directory Services requires the Microsoft Client for NetWare, so it must already be present. MS-NDS also requires IPX/SPX, but you know the protocol is already installed because the connection works some of the time.

13. Your network consists of Windows 98 clients and Windows NT servers. Which networking clients do you need installed on your clients? Choose all that apply.

A. Microsoft Client for Microsoft

B. Microsoft Client for NetWare

C. Service for NetWare Directory Services

D. Microsoft Family Logon

Answer: A. In order to connect to Windows NT servers, all you need to install is a compatible protocol and the Microsoft Client for Microsoft.

14. Your network consists of Windows 98 clients and NetWare 3.12 servers. Which networking clients do you need installed on your clients? Choose all that apply.

A. Microsoft Client for Microsoft

B. Microsoft Client for NetWare

C. Service for NetWare Directory Services

D. Microsoft Family Logon

Answer: B. The Microsoft Client for NetWare allows you to connect to NetWare servers using a bindery connection, but that is all right because bindery connections are all that NetWare 3.12 servers can communicate with.

15. You have Windows NT servers running TCP/IP and NetWare servers running IPX. You are running the Client for Windows and the Client for NetWare clients. What can you do to optimize your connections?

A. Unbind TCP/IP from the NetWare client and IPX/SPX from the Windows client

B. Unbind TCP/IP from the Windows client and IPX/SPX from the NetWare client

C. Run the Network Optimization Wizard

D. Nothing, because there are no options to help optimize performance

Answer: A. By unbinding TCP/IP from the NetWare client (which won't be used because NetWare is communicating via IPX) and unbinding IPX from the Microsoft client (which isn't being used because the Windows server is communicating via TCP/IP), you may gain a slight improvement in performance, especially on slower computers without a lot of RAM.

Chapter 10

1. Which of the following are true? Choose all that apply.

   A. Windows 98 can be a client to an NT server while it is also acting as an NT server.

   B. You can set read-only rights using just share-level security.

   C. A stand-alone Windows 98 computer can use user-level security.

   D. A stand-alone Windows 98 computer can use share-level security.

   Answer: A, B, and D. Windows 98 can have multiple client software installed while it is acting as a server. Share-level security can be set for read-only rights or full control rights. A stand-alone computer can use share-level security, but it needs a logon server like Windows NT or Novell NetWare to switch to user-level security.

2. Windows 98 must use which type of security to share files on a NetWare network?

   A. Share-level security

   B. User-level security

   C. Default-level security

   D. Secure-level security

   Answer: B. In order for Windows 98 to successfully install File and Printer Sharing for NetWare, it must be configured to use user-level security based on an existing NetWare server.

3. You have a mixture of new, fast computers with lots of RAM and older computers with a minimum of RAM. All of them run Windows 98 in your peer-to-peer network. At times browsing seems slower. What can you do to help keep the speed of the browsing fast?

   A. Set the browser service to disabled on the fast computers and enabled on the slow computers.

   B. Set the browser service to automatic on the fast computers and enabled on the slow computers.

   C. Set the browser service to enabled on the fast computers and automatic on the slower computers

   D. Set the browser service to enabled on the fast computers and disabled on the slow computers.

   Answer: D. The browser service will take some overhead, which means you should run it on your fastest computers in order to make browsing as fast as possible. Setting the browser configuration to Enabled forces it to be the browser server, while the Disabled setting forces the computer to never be a browser server.

4. You have a mixture of MS-DOS, WFW, and Windows 98 computers on your NetWare network. Some of the users who have Windows 98 are allowed to share their files with the others. The people on older computers are complaining that they cannot see the Windows 98 computers. What must you enable on the Windows 98 computers?

   A. SAP

   B. RIP

   C. HTTP

   D. VMS

Answer: A. Older (non-Windows) NetWare clients see servers by the SAP advertisements the servers issue. In order for those older clients to see Windows 98 as a NetWare type of server, you need to enable SAP advertising on the Windows 98 computers.

5. Joe was sharing three folders when he switched from share-level security to user-level security. Now no one seems to be able to see the shares. What must Joe do to get the shares back?

   A. Reboot, then the shares will come back.

   B. He has to re-create all the shares because he switched security modes.

   C. The shares are still there, they are just hidden.

   D. The share are still there; however, the clients need to view them differently.

   Answer: B. When you switch from share-level to user-level (or vice versa), any shared folders or printers you have need to be reshared under the new security system.

6. Which of the following types of servers can be security providers for user-level security? Choose all that apply.

   A. Windows 98

   B. Windows NT Server

   C. Windows NT Workstation

   D. NetWare Server

   Answer: B, C, and D. Windows 98 requires some sort of server to base its user list from when switching to user-level security—either a Windows NT computer (workstation or server) or a NetWare server.

7. Sue is using default security settings on Windows 98 and is sharing office memos. She wants to be certain that the sales team can read the memos, but only the sales manager can make new memos. How can she do this?

    A. Share the folder as Full control, and mark the memos Read-only.

    B. Share the folder as Read-only, and then make a second Full control share.

    C. Share the folder as Depends On Password.

    D. Switch to user-level security.

    Answer: C. Because she is using default settings, she is using share-level security. Windows 98 cannot share a folder twice, once with one set of permissions and once with another. If the share is created as a read or full-control share, she cannot have some people with Read rights and others with Full control rights. By sharing the folder with Depends On Password, she can create a Read and Full control password (using different passwords, of course) and then give the correct password to the people that need either Read or Full control.

8. Net Watcher allows you to do which of the following? Choose all that apply.

    A. Create new shares for folders

    B. Delete shares based on folders

    C. Disconnect users from shared folders

    D. Monitor shares on remote computers

    Answer: A, B, C, and D. Net Watcher can do all of these things. Of course, you can only monitor remote computers if it has been enabled correctly.

9. Certain people should never be allowed to use a new color printer. What is the best way to secure it?

    A. Switch to user-level security and give access rights to the printer rights to the printer only to those who need it.

    B. Switch to user-level security and give everyone No Access. Then give the Print right only to the specific users and groups you want to be able to print.

C. Switch to share-level security and share the printer with a password.

D. Switch to share-level security and share the printer with Depends On Password.

Answer: A. If you give everyone No Access (answer B), the No Access right blocks them from ever getting rights even though you grant rights later.

10. Which of the following must be unique? Choose all that apply.

A. Computer name

B. Workgroup name

C. Username

D. Domain

Answer: A and D. Computer names always have to be unique in Microsoft networks. Domains should also be unique in that a single company cannot have two or more domains with the same name. Usernames are not required to be unique, although it is usually a good idea. Workgroups are a collection of associated computers that have a shared workgroup name.

11. You have three workgroups (Sales, Marketing, and Accounting) and two domains (Headquarters and Branch1). The Headquarters domain has two servers, HQ1 (the PDC) and HQ2 (the BDC). All users at your location log in to the Headquarters domain. You want your Windows 95 clients to switch to user-level security in the Headquarters domain. What do you enter for the security provider?

A. HQ1

B. HQ2

C. HQ1 or HQ2

D. Headquarters

Answer: D. When you switch to user-level security and you are basing it on a domain, you need to enter the domain name, not the server name.

12. You have three workgroups (Sales, Marketing, and Accounting) and two domains (Headquarters and Branch1). All users at your location log in to the Headquarters domain. The users from sales would like to see the computers in their sales group when they first open Network Neighborhood. How do you set their computers?

A. Have their computers be members of the Headquarters domain, and set Network Neighborhood to the Sales workgroup.

B. Have their computers be members of the Sales workgroup.

C. Have their user accounts in the Sales workgroup.

D. Have their user accounts in the Branch1 domain, and set Network Neighborhood to the Sales workgroup.

Answer: B. Because the users want to see the servers in the Sales workgroup, you should set Windows 95 to be in that workgroup. Network Neighborhood will then show all computers in the Sales workgroup at the first (default) level of Network Neighborhood. Where their accounts reside is not as important as what workgroup they are a member of when it comes to browsing resources in Network Neighborhood.

13. Your network consists of MS-DOS NetWare and Windows Microsoft clients. You want all of the clients to access your computer so that they can look at old company memos. You intend to install the following components: File and Printer Sharing for Microsoft, File and Printer Sharing for NetWare, Service for NetWare Directory Service, IPX/SPX, and TCP/IP. Will this installation fulfill the requirements?

A. Yes, all requirements are fulfilled.

B. Yes, but only if you enable SAP advertising.

C. Yes, but only if you enable the browser service.

D. No, this installation will not work.

Answer: D. You can only have one type of sharing service installed—either File and Printer Sharing for Microsoft *or* File and Printer Sharing for NetWare.

14. Your network consists of MS-DOS NetWare and Windows NetWare clients. You want all of the clients to access your computer so that they can look at old company memos. You intend to install the following components: File and Printer Sharing for NetWare, Service for NetWare Directory Service, and TCP/IP. Will this installation fulfill the requirements?

A. Yes, all requirements are fulfilled.

B. Yes, but only if you enable SAP advertising.

C. Yes, but only if you enable the browser service.

D. No, this installation will not work.

Answer: D. You need to install the IPX/SPX protocol because this is the protocol that older NetWare servers and clients use.

15. Your network consists of a domain (SALES) with a Windows NT PDC (PDC1) and a Windows NT BDC (BDC1) as well as threee application servers (UT, ID, CA). You are allowing users to share folders on their local workstations. Your domain covers three states. You want users to only see the shared resources from their state. How would you do this?

A. Make three NT groups, one for each state. Assign the appropriate users to each group, give the appropriate group rights to the appropriate computers.

B. Make three workgroups, one for each state. Assign the appropriate computers to the appropriate workgroups.

C. Name each of the computers in the state after the state (UT, ID, CA).

D. Make three workgroups and set Network Neighborhood to the preferred workgroup in the Registry.

Answer: B. By creating three workgroups and assigning computers to their respective workgroups, Network Neighborhood will show just the servers in the local workgroup when it is opened unless Entire Network is chosen.

Chapter 11

1. You have 30 Windows 98 computers installed on your network. You have an HP LaserJet IIP Plus printer attached to your local Windows 98 computer. You have shared this printer with others on the network. How can you check the status of your print queue in Windows 98? Choose all that apply.

   A. Select Start ➤ Run ➤ CheckQueue.

   B. Double-click the printer icon in the system tray.

   C. Go to the Printers folder, find your printer, and double-click it.

   D. Both A and C.

   Answer: B and C. There is no such program as CheckQueue. The easiest method is to double-click your printer icon in the system tray or from the Printers folder.

2. Windows 98 supports several methods to reference your shared resources in a networked environment. You browse the network and install the HPLaserJet printer located on the Frogger computer to your local PC. Once you have installed this Point-and-Print printer on your Desktop, how does Windows 98 reference the networked printer?

   A. Using a mapped drive letter (for example, P:)

   B. Using mapped ports (for example, LPT2:)

   C. Using a special printer reference tool (for example, MyPrinter)

   D. Using the UNC name (for example, "\\Frogger\HPPrinter").

   Answer: D. You may set up references using a mapped port; but by default, Windows 98 will use the UNC name shown in choice D.

3. Windows 98 allows several different methods for you to install a networked printer on your machine. Which of the following should you do to *install* and *configure* a printer from a Windows 98 machine? Choose all that apply.

A. Browse the network until you find the shared printer, and then double-click its icon. Do nothing else. All options will be inherited.

B. Browse the network until you find the shared printer, and then double-click its icon. You will then have to create new configuration options because they will not be inherited.

C. Drag-and-drop the shared printer icon. Do nothing else. All options will be inherited.

D. Drag-and-drop the shared printer icon, and then make your configuration changes because options will not be inherited.

Answer: A and C. Windows 98 automatically sends the current configuration settings when you install a printer using drag-and-drop or Point-and-Print.

4. Windows 98 allows several different methods for you to install a networked printer on your machine. When you install a Point-and-Print printer from a Windows NT server, which of the following must be true?

A. The NT machine will download the files as well as the current printer configurations.

B. The NT machine will download the files, but they will not have the current configuration information.

C. The NT machine will not download the files. You must manually drag-and-drop the files and then set the configurations.

D. The NT machine will not download the files. You must manually drag-and-drop the files. The files will have the current configuration.

Answer: B. Windows NT will download the original printer drivers to your Windows 98 machine. You will then have to make your own configuration changes (e.g., orientation, font, paper tray, etc.).

5. Novell does not support Point-and-Print printers by default. You are working on a Windows 98 computer that is using a Novell server for login validation. Which of the following is true about setting up Novell for Point-and-Print? Choose all that apply.

  A. You must have a bindery or NDS tree.

  B. You must be the Supervisor or equivalent.

  C. You must copy the file to the location specified by the bindery or the NDS Root object that you altered.

  D. Clients must have read permissions on the directory where the files are stored.

  Answer: A, B, C, and D. All answers are correct. You must have all of those items in order to set up Point-and-Print in a Novell environment.

6. In order for Windows 98 to actually take advantage of Point-and-Print, Windows 98 needs some information. Which of the following are required to set up a printer for Point-and-Print? Choose all that apply.

  A. The printer manufacturer's name and printer model

  B. The network that you are using

  C. The driver names

  D. The driver locations

  Answer: A, C, and D. The network that you are using is irrelevant. You must, however, know the printer type and manufacturer as well as the driver files and their location.

7. What is the maximum number of printers Windows 98 can support?

  A. 1

  B. 2

  C. 6 (LPT1, LPT2, COM1–COM4)

  D. There is no predefined maximum

  Answer: D. Ports have become virtual devices in Windows 98, and you can assign just about anything you want to any port that you create.

8. You have a printer attached to your Windows 98 machine, and it is shared across your Microsoft Windows NT network. You want to install a second printer on your computer and share that one as well. Which of the following is the best solution?

   A. Add a second parallel card to your computer. The BIOS will recognize it as LPT2, and you can now attach a second printer to your system.

   B. Use one of the SCSI adapters already on your computer and purchase a printer that can use the SCSI cable for support rather than a parallel port.

   C. If your computer supports infrared, just place a new infrared enabled printer in the computer's line of sight.

   D. Add a new parallel card to your computer that supports the ECP standard. Connect a printer that supports ECP to the new parallel port.

   Answer: D. Microsoft is really pushing the ECP technology. Printers are now available that support the ECP technology and can maximize your printing efficiency.

9. Which of the following should you check if your printer is not printing? Choose all that apply.

   A. The amount of hard disk on the computer

   B. The cable connections

   C. Whether the printer is on

   D. The \Windows\Spools directory to be sure that print jobs are being spooled properly

   Answer: A, B, C, and D. You should check all of these things. If they do not appear to be the problem, try reinstalling your printer drivers. Frequently, this will fix the problem.

10. A user complains that his print jobs come out at the wrong printer if he forgets to change the printer before he prints a job. What can you do to fix it?

A. Set the printer to offline.

B. Change the printer device type.

C. Change the default printer to the one he prints to most often.

D. Install a new local printer on his computer and set it to offline.

Answer: C. Each user should have the printer that he or she prints to most often set as his or her default printer. This is done from the Printers folder.

11. Your printer is sending you a message that it is low on toner. You have printed the first 60 pages of a 200-page document and don't want to rerun the entire print job. You decide to cancel the print job and then resubmit the print job from your application, beginning with page 60. How would you rate this solution?

A. This is an excellent solution and will work.

B. This is a good solution and will work.

C. This is a poor solution, but it appears to work.

D. This is a poor solution and will not work.

Answer: C. This will probably work. However, canceling the print job after 60 pages have already printed will most likely print any additional pages that had already been submitted to the printer. Therefore, you will print duplicate pages. An excellent solution would be to pause the printing process from the printer's Print Queue, add toner, and then resume that print job.

12. When you turn on your printer, it takes about five minutes to finish its warm up routines before it comes online. Print jobs that were submitted receive error messages. Which of the following is the best choice to alleviate this problem?

A. Set the printer to Offline and use deferred printing.

B. Increase the timeout settings in the Details tab of the printer's property sheets.

C. Change the default printer to a printer other than this one.

D. Change the spool settings to print directly to the printer in RAW format.

Answer: B. Changing the timeout settings is the best choice. You could use deferred printing, but you must turn it on and off manually.

13. Which of the following must you have to take advantage of ECP printing in Windows 98? Choose all that apply.

A. ECP-compliant printer

B. IEEE 1284-compliant cable

C. ECP card in your computer

D. ECP enabled

Answer: A, B, C, and D. You must have all of these items to use ECP printing.

14. You are low on disk space and have a large document that needs to be printed. What can you do to ensure that the document will print properly and will not generate spooling errors? Choose the best answer.

A. Set the spooler options to print after the first page has spooled.

B. Set the spooler options to print after the last page has spooled.

C. Set the spooler options to print directly to the printer.

D. You don't have to do anything. It will print normally.

Answer: C. Printing directly to the printer is the best choice. This will not use spooling. Your application will not regain control until the printing process has completed; however, your print job will not overload your hard disk.

Chapter 12

1. To make profiles work, a unique copy of which Registry file is saved?

    A. REG.DAT

    B. REGISTRY.OUT

    C. SYSTEM.DAT

    D. USER.DAT

    Answer: D. User settings are held in USER.DAT. Before profiles are enabled, everyone shares the same file. After profiles are enabled, a unique USER.DAT is created for every user.

2. Roaming profiles (with all options) are enabled. You are logged in at two computers. You add a shortcut to your Desktop and log out from the first computer. You log out of the second computer. You log in at the first, but your shortcut isn't there. Why?

    A. Your local profile is not enabled.

    B. The profile from the second computer overwrote the profile from the first.

    C. The roaming profile is cached and isn't available for immediate loading.

    D. Profiles don't track shortcuts.

    Answer: B. Roaming profiles are saved to the server when you log out of the local workstation. If you are logged in to more than one computer, the last computer you log out of will have its settings saved to the roaming profile.

3. Which of the following is required to enable roaming profiles on an NT server? Choose all that apply.

    A. Users must have a home folder.

    B. Users must use TCP/IP.

    C. Usernames must be eight characters or less.

    D. The Client for Microsoft Networks must be the default logon.

Answer: A and D. Roaming profiles on a Windows NT network require that you have a home folder assigned to the user account and that the Client for Microsoft Networks be the default client. TCP/IP is not required (any valid protocol will work) and usernames don't have to be eight characters or less.

4. Roaming profiles (with all options) are enabled. Profiles are being saved locally. They are present on the Windows NT server, but after a user logs into the domain, the profile does not always work. You set up profiles using Windows 98, but you also have Windows NT workstations in your company. What could be the cause? Choose all that apply.

   A. The time on the problematic workstations is ahead of the time of the server.

   B. The problematic workstations are not using the same protocol as the server.

   C. The problematic workstations don't have profiles enabled.

   D. The problematic workstations are NT workstations.

   Answer: A, C, and D. If the local time of the workstation is newer than the server time, and a copy of a profile exists on the local computer, the roaming profile will not be downloaded. Although you need to use the same protocol as the server, if you don't have the same protocol, you won't even be able to log in. The local workstations need to have profiles enabled in order to use roaming profiles. NT Workstation computers cannot use Windows 98 profiles.

5. You want the local profile to include the Start menu but not the Desktop. Is that possible? If so, which option do you pick?

   A. Yes, enable profiles normally (with no options picked).

   B. Yes, enable profiles with the "Include Desktop Icons…" option.

   C. Yes, enable profiles with the "Include Start Menu…" option.

   D. No, this is not possible.

   Answer: C. Profiles can be made to include both the Desktop and/or the Start Menu. By selecting only the "Include Start Menu…" selection, and not the "Include Desktop Icons…" selection, you can have the profile do just that.

6. If you are using a Windows 98 client and Windows 98 is installed in the C:\Windows folder, where are roaming profiles stored on a NetWare 3.12 network?

  A. On the local computer, in the C:\Windows folder

  B. On the local computer, in the C:\Windows\System32 folder

  C. On the NetWare server, in the Public folder

  D. On the NetWare server, in the \Mail\Userid folder

Answer: D. NetWare 2.*x* and 3.*x* servers store roaming profiles in the SYS: volume in the \Mail\Userid folder.

7. How do you make a mandatory profile?

  A. Create a new group called "Mandatory" and assign the user to the group.

  B. Check the box "Create Mandatory Profile" when initially creating the profile.

  C. Set USER.DAT to hidden.

  D. Rename the USER.DAT to USER.MAN

Answer: D. In order to make a profile into a mandatory profile, simply rename USER.DAT to USER.MAN on the server after the roaming profile is created.

8. What is required to enable roaming profiles on a NetWare 3.12 server? Choose all that apply.

  A. The IPX/SPX protocol

  B. Microsoft Client for NetWare

  C. Default Login set to Microsoft Client for NetWare

  D. Profiles enabled on the Windows 98 client

Answer: A, B, C, and D. Because NetWare 3.*x* servers use the IPX/SPX protocol, the client does too. You also need the Microsoft Client for NetWare installed and set to the default logon, as well as having profiles enabled on the client.

9. When can the same roaming profile be used on Windows NT workstations and Windows 98 clients?

    A. Never, they are incompatible.

    B. If you rename the profile to USER.NT, it will also work for Windows NT.

    C. If you place the profile in the NETLOGON share, both operating systems can use it.

    D. If you check the box "Create NT Compatible Profile" when initially setting up the profile.

    Answer: A. Profiles are incompatible between Windows 98 and Windows NT.

10. How can you disable a person's ability to enable or disable profiles?

    A. Set the security on the profile to Administrators Only.

    B. Edit the Registry and add the Admin Edit Only value.

    C. Create a system policy that blocks normal users from the Password applet.

    D. Create a system policy that blocks normal users from the Profile applet.

    Answer: C. Profiles are configured from the Password applet of the Control Panel. There are no such thing as Administrators Only, Admin Edit Only, and the Profile applet.

Chapter 13

1. The System Policy Editor is installed by which method?

    A. It is installed by default.

    B. It is installed when you perform a "Custom" installation.

    C. It is installed automatically when you log on to a Windows NT server with Administrator rights.

    D. You must install it manually.

    Answer: D. You must install the System Policy Editor manually by entering the path to the setup files. The files are contained on the CD-ROM, although they are hard to find.

2. Policies can be used to enforce restrictions based on which of the following? Choose all that apply.

   A. Users

   B. Groups

   C. Time of Logon

   D. Computers

   Answer: A, B, and D. Policies can be based on username, group membership, and computer name. You probably could write some kind of batch file to impose a restriction based on time, but that function is not part of a system policy.

3. Templates end with which extension?

   A. .TEM

   B. .FIL

   C. .ADM

   D. .POL

   Answer: C. Templates end with the .ADM extension. Once the policy file is filled out and saved, it will have the .POL extension. There are no such things as .TEM or .FIL files.

4. Policies end with which extension?

   A. .POL

   B. .ADM

   C. .DLL

   D. .SEC

   Answer: A. Policy files end with the .POL extension.

5. Group policies are not working. What steps should you check? Choose all that apply.

    A. Group policy support must be installed on every computer that will load policies based on groups.

    B. Users may not be assigned to the correct groups.

    C. The policy file should be named GROUPPOLICY.POL.

    D. The policy file should be named CONFIG.POL.

Answer: A, B, and D. Group policies require that each computer have group policy support installed, that users are assigned to the correct group, and that CONFIG.POL is the default name of the policy file.

6. Phil is a member of both the Management and Sales groups. You want the Management group to take precedence over the Sales group. How would you set this up?

    A. Make the Sales group higher in the list.

    B. Make the Management group higher in the list.

    C. You can't control it—it goes alphabetically.

    D. Set Phil's primary group to the Management group.

Answer: B. In the list of groups, those higher in the list have precedence over those lower in the list.

7. Sally and Phil share a computer. Sally will have a restriction in place, but Phil shouldn't. How should you set Phil's checkbox for that restriction?

    A. Leave it gray (default).

    B. Put a check in it.

    C. Uncheck it (make it white).

    D. Leave Phil's checkbox alone; set Sally's checkbox to gray.

Answer: C. Because Sally's policy file will set the restriction (it is checked), Phil's policy file needs to specifically uncheck (show a cleared box on) the restriction in order to override Sally's setting

8. Windows 98 looks for the policy file in which NT share by default?

   A. The NETLOGON share of all domain controllers

   B. The NETLOGON share of the primary domain controller

   C. The USERS share of all domain controllers

   D. The USERS share of the primary domain controller

   Answer: B. By default load balancing is not enabled, which means that Windows 98 looks for the policy file only on the PDC in the NETLOGON folder. Once load balancing is enabled, all controllers can be used to download the policy file.

9. Templates can be stored as which type of files? Choose all that apply.

   A. ASCII text files

   B. Compressed binary files

   C. Word (.doc) files

   D. Policy Editor (.pol) files

   Answer: A. Templates are ASCII files and can easily be added to or edited.

10. You want to enable system policies on a NetWare network. You have 3.12 servers and 4.0 servers running in Bindery Emulation. Where do you need to put the system policy file so that your clients will find it?

    A. In the PUBLIC folders of the 3.12 servers, and the POLICY folders of the 4.*x* servers

    B. In the PUBLIC folders of all of the NetWare servers

    C. In the POLICY folders of all of the NetWare servers

    D. In the POLICY folders of the 3.12 servers, and the PUBLIC folders of the 4.*x* servers

    Answer: B. When NetWare servers are set as the primary network logon servers, the policy file will be looked for in the PUBLIC folder of the SYS: volume of the NetWare servers.

11. You have a group created for your temporary employees called temp_
     users. You don't want them to be able to share their folders or
     printers. How would you set your policy file?

   A. Create a policy file that selects "Disable file sharing" and "Disable
       printer sharing" and assign it to the temp_users group.

   B. Create a policy file that selects "Disable file sharing" and "Disable
       printer sharing" and name it TEMP_USERS.POL.

   C. Edit your existing policy file. Create a new group policy for the
       temp_users group, and select the "Disable file sharing" and "Dis-
       able printer sharing" options.

   D. Edit your existing policy file. Create user policies for all of the tem-
       porary employees and select the "Disable file sharing" and
       "Disable printer sharing" options.

   Answer: C. All of the policies for the entire network are contained in
   a single file (called CONFIG.POL by default). The most efficient way
   to make a new policy for a group is to edit the existing file, make a new
   group, and restrict that group's ability. Creating policy settings for
   each individual would work, but it would be very difficult and
   inefficient.

12. You need to save your policy file on a NetWare server. What do you
     name it so that your Windows 98 clients can find it by default?

   A. CONFIG.POL

   B. NWCONFIG.POL

   C. NTCONFIG.POL

   D. 98CONFIG.POL

   Answer: A. It doesn't matter where the file is held; the default name of
   the file is still CONFIG.POL.

13. You have 10,000 clients (both Windows NT and Windows 98) in one large Windows NT domain. You have a large PDC in the central office, with a BDC in each of your 30 regional offices. Users complain that logging in from the Windows 98 clients take twice as long as logging in from the Windows NT clients. What steps do you need to take in order to speed up the login process? Choose all that apply.

   A. Make sure the policy file is on all the BDCs.

   B. Enable Manual Updates, and specify load balancing on the Windows 98 clients.

   C. Copy the policy file to the local hard drives of all of the Windows 98 clients.

   D. Set the policy file to only test for user configurations.

   Answer: A and B. Specifying load balancing will cause each Windows 98 client to look to its local controller for CONFIG.POL. You need to make sure the file exists on all BDCs before enabling load balancing.

14. Your policy file is working for the Default Computer restrictions but not for the Default User restrictions. What is probably the cause?

   A. The users are not logging into the network.

   B. The users have blank passwords.

   C. The workstations do not have File and Printer Sharing installed.

   D. The workstations do not have profiles enabled.

   Answer: D. In order for polices to work based on usernames, the Windows 98 computers must have profiles enabled. Enabling profiles allows Windows 98 to track each person by name instead of using the same settings for everyone.

Chapter 14

1. In Windows 98, remote administration is accomplished through the use of which mechanism?

   A. Named pipes

   B. RPCs

   C. IPX/SPX

   D. TCP/IP

   Answer: B. Named pipes, IPX/SPX, and TCP/IP are network protocols. RPCs are remote procedure calls. They allow one machine to ask another machine to run specified procedures.

2. You have 15 Windows 98 computers on your network. You want to remotely administer the file structure on these Windows 98 computers from your own Windows 98 computer. All of the PCs have File and Print Sharing installed, and they all have the Remote Administration option enabled from the Passwords applet in the Control Panel. Which utility do you use to administer the file structure on a remote computer?

   A. Net Watcher

   B. Remote System Monitor

   C. Administer

   D. Remote Registry Editor

   Answer: C. The Net Watcher utility allows you to monitor shared resources. The Remote System Monitor displays current statistics on a remote computer. The Remote Registry Editor is used to edit and compare the Registry on remote computers. The Administer utility is used to manage the file structure on a remote workstation.

3. You want to view which resources are shared and who is using them on computers in your Windows 98 network. All 20 Windows 98 machines have been installed with File and Printer sharing. All of them use Windows NT Server for logon validation. Share-level security has been implemented on all of the PCs, and the Remote Administration option has been enabled. Which utility can you use to view resources that are shared on your PC and who is sharing them?

   A. Net Watcher

   B. Remote System Monitor

   C. Administer

   D. Remote Registry Editor

   Answer: A. The Net Watcher utility allows you to monitor shared resources. The Remote System Monitor displays current statistics on a remote computer. The Remote Registry Editor is used to edit and compare the Registry on remote computers. The Administer utility is used to manage the file structure on a remote workstation.

4. In this scenario, all 50 computers on your network have been config- ured with Windows 98. They are using Novell NetWare 4 as a logon validation server. User-level security has been enabled on all 50 PCs, and the Remote Registry Service has been installed as well. Which utility do you use to view performance statistics on a remote workstation?

   A. Net Watcher

   B. Remote System Monitor

   C. Administer

   D. Remote Registry Editor

   Answer: B. The Net Watcher utility allows you to monitor shared resources. The Remote System Monitor displays current statistics on a remote computer. The Remote Registry Editor is used to edit and compare the Registry on remote computers. The Administer utility is used to manage the file structure on a remote workstation. Keep in mind that the Remote System Monitor and the Remote Registry Editor require user-level security on both machines and must have the Remote Registry Services installed on both machines.

5. You are attempting to modify the Registry database on a client Windows 98 machine from your administering Windows 98 machine. You have installed user-level security on both machines and have enabled remote administration from the Passwords applet in the Control Panel. You can work with the remote Net Watcher and the Administer features, but you cannot seem to get the Remote Registry Editor or the Remote System Monitor utilities to work. Which of the following could solve your problem?

A. Install Net Watcher Services

B. Install Remote Registry Services

C. Install Client Services for Remote Administration

D. Install Novell NetWare Client32 for Windows 98

Answer: B. You can deduce that the Remote Registry Services is not installed because of the following. You know that user-level security has been enabled. You also know that remote administration has been enabled because you can successfully use the Net Watcher and Administer features. Because neither the Remote System Monitor nor the Remote Registry Editor are working and you know that both of these tools require Remote Registry Services enabled on both machines, it is safe to assume that this is the cause of the problem.

6. You have 30 Windows 98 computers in your network. Each server is configured with user-level security and is gaining logon validation from a NetWare 3.12 server. You want to use some of the remote administrative utilities that come bundled with Windows 98. Which of the following utilities require user-level security on both the remote workstation and the administering workstation? Choose all that apply.

A. Net Watcher

B. Remote System Monitor

C. Administer

D. Remote Registry Editor

Answer: B and D. Both the Remote System Monitor and Remote Registry Editor require user-level security and must have the Remote Registry Services installed on both the administrating PC and the remote PC.

7. To enable remote administration of a client PC, you must first enable remote administration. From where is this accomplished?

   A. Network property sheets

   B. Add/Remove Programs icon in the Control Panel

   C. Passwords icon in the Control Panel

   D. Remote Administration icon in the Control Panel

Answer: C. To enable your PC to be remotely administered, you must first enable remote administration through the Control Panel, Passwords program.

8. Which of the following is true about Installing Remote Registry Services and your PC's performance?

   A. The 32-bit software makes your system run faster and makes access to the Registry quicker.

   B. The entire Registry will now be loaded into memory for quick access by any administering PC.

   C. The Service requires memory, CPU cycles, and hard disk space and will, therefore, slow your system down.

   D. The Service has no impact either way on your system's performance.

Answer: C. The service requires additional memory, hard disk space, and CPU cycles on both the administering PC and the remote PC. You should not install this service unless you need to remotely edit the Registry or use the Remote System Monitor.

9. You are working in a mixed Windows 98 and Novell NetWare environment. The Novell server is performing all user validation. You have installed the Remote Registry Services on all of your PCs. They are all set up with user-level security, and you have enabled File and Print Sharing. You have also shared several folders on each of your PCs. When you try to use the Remote System Monitor, it fails to allow you access. Which of the following could be the cause?

   A. You cannot use Remote System Monitor when you are being validated by a Novell server.

B. You have not yet assigned users the ability to remotely administer your computer from the Control Panel/Passwords tool.

C. Remote System Monitor is available only when both PCs are using share-level security.

D. There is no Remote System Monitor utility.

Answer: B. In order to use any of the remote administration features of Windows 98, you must enable the PC to be administered from the Remote Administration tab in the Passwords utility in the Control Panel. In addition to this, the computers must both be running user-level security and have the Remote Registry Services service installed.

10. The following tuples (sets of elements) indicate what levels of security have been assigned on the remote PC and the administrating PC. Which of the following will support the Administer option? Choose all that apply.

   A. User – Share

   B. Share – Share

   C. User – User

   D. Share – User

   Answer: B, C, and D. The Administer option requires that both PCs use a minimum of share-level security. The administrating computer must have the same level of security or more restrictive security than the remote PC.

11. The following tuples indicate what levels of security have been assigned on the remote PC and the administrating PC. Which of the following will support the Remote System Monitor option?

   A. User – Share

   B. Share – Share

   C. User – User

   D. Share – User

   Answer: C. The Remote System Monitor option requires that both PCs use a minimum of user-level security. You must also have installed the Remote Registry Services.

12. Your Windows 98 machine is currently set up with user-level security and TCP/IP. A NetWare server is providing your login validation. You have installed File and Printer Sharing for NetWare networks and have shared your printer and several folders. None of the other machines in your network have enabled remote administration. Using the Net Watcher utility, which of the following things can you accomplish?

A. Create new shares for folders

B. Delete shares based on folders

C. Disconnect users from shared folders

D. Monitor shares on remote computers

Answer: A, B, and C. The Net Watcher utility can do all of these things on the local computer. In addition, the Net Watcher utility can also monitor shared printers. Monitoring Shares on remote computers requires the proper configuration which includes enabling remote administration on each of the client PCs.

13. You have installed a new 32-bit program on your Windows 98 machine. You want to make sure that the program is operating properly, so you run the System Monitor utility. With the System Monitor running, you view the number of threads in the system. At program startup, approximately 10 threads are running. After 10 minutes, the program shows 30 threads running. You have not started any other programs during this time. Looking back through the graphic history shown in the System Monitor, you notice that the threads were steadily added. You check the System Monitor again after 30 minutes and now see that the threads have steadily continued to increase. Which of the following is true about this 32-bit program?

A. The program is running normally.

B. The program is not releasing memory properly.

C. The System Monitor cannot show this type of information.

D. The ReleaseMem Agent isn't installed on this computer.

Answer: B is correct. The program is obviously not releasing its threads properly. It is, therefore, grabbing more and more of your system resources.

14. You have been using the Remote Administration tool on your Windows 98 machine to administer other network client PCs. You have just added an additional 10 PCs to the network. You have enabled File and Printer Sharing on the 10 new PCs and have shared various folders and printers. You do have access to these shares from all of the different computers on the network. When you attempt to remotely administer the new PCs, you find that you cannot. What else do you need to do to enable remote administration of these 10 new client PCs?

A. Add a new protocol to the Network property sheets.

B. Add the Net Watcher program from the Add/Remove Programs icon in the Control Panel.

C. Enable remote administration from the Passwords icon in the Control Panel.

D. Run the Remote Administration icon in the Control Panel.

Answer: C. You enable and set the security for remote administration from the Remote Administration tab of the Passwords applet in Control Panel. There is no Remote Administration applet. The Net Watcher program only needs to be installed on the administrative computer. You can already see the new computers in the network, so adding a new protocol is not necessary.

15. You have 25 Windows 98 computers in your network. They are all currently configured to use Windows NT Server for logon validation. You want to use the Remote System Monitor to gather performance statistics on the remote computers. Which of the following must be installed in order to use Remote System Monitor?

A. Remote Registry Services on the remote PC

B. Remote Registry Services on the administrating PC

C. User-level security on the remote PC

D. User-level security on the administering PC

Answer: A, B, C, and D. The remote system monitor uses information found in the Hkey_Dyn_Data Registry key. In order to read this key, both the administering and remote PC must have Remote Registry Services installed. Using Remote Registry Services requires user-level security on both the administrating and remote PCs.

Chapter 15

1. What three network protocols are supported by Dial-Up Networking?

   A. NetBEUI

   B. PPP

   C. IPX/SPX

   D. TCP/IP

   Answer: A, C, and D. PPP is not a network protocol; it is a line protocol.

2. What can you do to increase security when using mobile computing? Choose all that apply.

   A. Utilize user-level security on the host computer.

   B. Use password encryption.

   C. Encrypt your data files when transferring them.

   D. Use a system policy.

   Answer: A, B, C, and D. All of these options help increase security.

3. A Windows 98 dial-up server can support all of the following except:

   A. Windows 98 client

   B. PPP-based client

   C. Windows NT client

   D. Macintosh client using AppleTalk

   Answer: D. Macintosh clients require Windows NT Server (not Windows 98).

4. Which dial-up line protocol is the most flexible and is the default used by Windows 98?

   A. SLIP

   B. PPP

   C. NRN NetWare Connect

   D. NT RAS

   Answer: B. PPP is the latest line protocol and is used by default by Windows 98.

5. What protocol is required in order to use Internet Explorer?

   A. TCP/IP

   B. IPX/SPX

   C. NetBEUI

   D. DLC

   Answer: A. TCP/IP is the protocol used by the Internet and, therefore, used by Internet Explorer.

6. Can Windows 98 run Internet browsers?

   A. Yes, but only Microsoft's Internet Explorer.

   B. Yes, but only if you have the latest version of Internet Explorer.

   C. Yes, it can run any Internet browser written for Windows 98.

   D. No.

   Answer: C. Windows 98 can run any browser written for it such as Netscape Navigator or Mosaic.

7. What is Active Desktop?

   A. It turns your computer into a Personal Web Server.

   B. It converts your Desktop into an ActiveX object.

   C. It converts your Desktop into HTTP objects, which means that IE is then used to manage local as well as Internet resources.

   D. It changes the Explorer to more of a file-manager type interface.

   Answer: C. The Active Desktop makes all local and remote resources appear as HTTP objects, adding flexibility at the expense of speed.

8. What do WWW servers and browsers use to communicate?

   A. DLC

   B. TCP/IP

   C. FTP

   D. HTTP

   Answer: D. HTTP (Hypertext Transfer Protocol) is the native protocol used by WWW servers and Internet browsers.

9. Which HTTP server would be the best fit for a small doctor's office intranet server?

   A. Personal Web Server on Windows 98

   B. IIS on Windows NT Server

   C. Peer Web Services on Windows NT Workstation

   D. Site Server on Windows NT Server

   Answer: A. Windows 98 running PWS makes a fine WWW server for a small office environment.

10. Which HTTP server should be used for a large, informational HTTP server?

   A. Personal Web Server

   B. IIS on Windows NT Server

   C. Peer Web Services on Windows NT Workstation

   D. Site Server on Windows NT Server

   Answer: B. IIS on Windows NT is designed for large HTTP Web sites that are mostly informational.

11. Which HTTP server should be used for a mission-critical electronic commerce server?

   A. Personal Web Server

   B. IIS on Windows NT Server

   C. Peer Web Services on Windows NT Workstation

   D. Site Server on Windows NT Server

   Answer: D. Site Server is the HTTP server for Windows NT Server. It is designed to handle a large number of transactions.

12. If you are accessing the Internet using a dial-up connection, which protocol is required? Choose all that apply.

   A. NetBEUI

   B. IPX/SPX

   C. TCP/IP

   D. DLC

   Answer: C. Even though you are using a dial-up connection, you still need to run TCP/IP to access the Internet.

13. To access the WWW sites on the Internet as a client, you need to run which type of software?

   A. An HTTP server

   B. An HTTP browser

   C. Explorer will work fine

   D. My Computer will work fine

Answer: B. An HTTP browser is required to access WWW (HTTP) sites.

14. To connect to an HTTP server running on a NetWare 3.12 server, you will need which protocol(s)? Choose all that apply.

   A. NetBEUI

   B. IPX/SPX

   C. TCP/IP

   D. DLC

Answer: C. The NetWare server, in order to be running as an HTTP server, will be using the TCP/IP protocol. The clients will also need to run TCP/IP protocol to connect to the HTTP service.

15. If you can connect to a Unix HTTP server by address, but not by name, which software program is probably at fault?

   A. WINS

   B. DNS

   C. DHCP

   D. NetBIOS

Answer: B. DNS (Domain Name Service) is the service that lets you type the friendly name of a computer and then looks up the address so the connection can be made.

16. Which type of computers can be HTTP servers? Choose all that apply.

A. Windows 98

B. Windows NT

C. NetWare

D. Unix

Answer: A, B, C, and D. All of these computers can operate as HTTP servers.

17. In order to bypass security restrictions on a local network, proxy server settings should be configured to access an intranet as which of the following?

A. Allow access to local intranet

B. Bypass proxy server for local (intranet) addresses

C. Don't allow access to local intranet

D. Bypass security for local (intranet) addresses

Answer: B. There are no actual options that correspond to A, C, or D.

18. What program comes with Windows 98 that allows you to easily edit and create Web pages?

A. Notepad

B. Word

C. FrontPage Express

D. Access

Answer: C. FrontPage Express comes with Windows 98 and allows you to quickly build simple Web sites.

19. Some users are worried about security when they access the Internet using Dial-Up Networking because they have some shared folders. What is one method can you use to help secure their system when they access the Internet?

A. Don't allow them to use Dial-Up Networking.

B. Have them use PPTP to access the Internet.

C. Have them unbind the Dial-Up Networking adapter from their File and Printer Sharing service.

D. Have them use modem compression.

Answer: C. Because they only want to be clients when using Dial-Up Networking, they can safely unbind the File and Printer Sharing service so that no one can connect to their machines via Dial-Up Networking.

20. A user wants to make a newsletter available to the entire company. What service can she install in Windows 98?

A. An Internet browser

B. IIS

C. FPNW

D. PWS

Answer: D. By installing PWS (Personal Web Server), she can share HTML files on the network. IIS (Internet Information Server) and FPNW (File and Print Services for NetWare) only run on Windows NT computers and installing a browser sets you up as a client, not as a server.

21. A user has a hard time connecting to one particular dial-up server. How can log files can be created for a dial-up session?

A. They can't be created.

B. Log files must be enabled globally for every dial-up connection.

C. Log files can be enabled individually for dial-up connections.

D. Log files are enabled by default.

Answer: C. Log files can be enabled by going to the properties of an individual dial-up Networking connection.

Chapter 16

1. What is the first step in troubleshooting?

   A. Isolate error conditions.

   B. Find out if it is a common issue.

   C. Diagnose specific symptoms.

   D. Consult technical support resources.

   Answer: C. The first step in troubleshooting is to diagnose the specific symptoms.

2. There are many different ways that you can get help when you are having problems with Windows 98. What is the quickest form of electronic help?

   A. The Internet

   B. Online Help files

   C. BBS services

   D. 1-900 Help lines

   Answer: B. The quickest form of electronic help is the online Help files. If you have an Internet connection, you may want to search the Internet next.

3. You are having problems during the boot-up process of Windows 98. You decide to reboot and hold down the Ctrl key. When the Startup menu appears, you choose Safe mode boot. During a Safe mode boot, which files are bypassed? Choose all that apply.

   A. CONFIG.SYS, AUTOEXEC.BAT, and the Startup group

   B. The Registry and the Startup group

   C. The Registry, SYSTEM.INI, and WIN.INI

   D. CONFIG.SYS and AUTOEXEC.BAT

   Answer: C and D. A Safe mode boot will bypass the CONFIG.SYS, the AUTOEXEC.BAT, the Registry, and the SYSTEM.INI and WIN.INI files.

4. You have installed Windows 98 on your computer and you want to optimize your system. You want to track information like the CPU utilization and number of threads currently processing. Which application allows you to monitor a variety of system resources?

A. Net Watcher

B. Freecell

C. System Monitor

D. Remote Registry Service

Answer: C. The System Monitor allows you to view a variety of system resources. The Net Watcher tool allows you to manage shared printers and folders. The Remote Registry Service does nothing by itself other than make the Registry of a computer available to be monitored by a properly configured and authenticated administrating computer. Freecell is a game.

5. You have shared several folders and your printer. You now want to see all of your shared resources and who is using them. Which application allows you to monitor and manage a variety of network information?

A. Net Watcher

B. Freecell

C. System Monitor

D. Remote Registry Service

Answer: A. The Net Watcher tools allows you to monitor and manage network shares. Freecell is a game. The System Monitor looks at ongoing performance statistics on your computer. The Remote Registry Service is one of the tools used to remotely administer a system's Registry.

6. You want to take a look at all of the protected-mode drivers that Windows 98 is attempting to load. You remember that a file is created during the Windows 98 startup process. You open the Notepad program to view this file. Which log file tracks items during the boot process?

A. BOOTLOG.TXT

B. DETCRASH.LOG

C. NETLOG.TXT

D. SETUPLOG.TXT

Answer: A. The BOOTLOG.TXT file tracks all protected-mode drivers that are loaded during the boot process and whether or not they were successfully loaded. The DETCRASH.LOG file is used by the Setup program during the setup of Windows 98. The NETLOG .TXT file tracks network settings. The SETUPLOG.TXT file is also used as a support file during the Windows 98 setup process.

7. During the setup process, Windows 98 creates several different files which track hardware enumeration as well as all the things that occurred during the boot process. It also tracks successful and failed protected drivers initializations. Which of the following ASCII log files are created during Windows 98 setup?

A. BOOTLOG.TXT

B. DETLOG.TXT

C. SETUPLOG.TXT

D. All of the above

Answer: D. All three of these files are created during the setup of Windows 98. The DETLOG.TXT file is used to recover after a crash during setup. The SETUPLOG.TXT file is used to show all successfully found devices and their settings. The BOOTLOG.TXT file is created upon initial bootup of your system and tracks protected-mode driver information.

8. Windows 98 uses a swap file to virtualize memory. It does this so that your applications appear to have more RAM than is really available in your system. You can modify the way this swap file behaves. Which of the following describes the default behavior of the swap file in Windows 98?

A. Permanent

B. Dynamic

C. Fixed in size

D. None of the above

Answer: B. The swap file, by default, automatically resizes itself as needed. You can, however, give it a permanent fixed size if you prefer. This is not normally suggested, but it may be useful in cases where you have a very small hard drive.

9. You swap file performance is directly tied with which hard drive attribute(s)?

A. Access time

B. Free space

C. Manufacturer

D. A and B

Answer: A. Access time directly affects the swap file performance. Free space and manufacturer may affect access time, but access time is the main culprit in hard disk speeds.

10. Which of the following will have the most adverse effect on system performance?

A. Ten or more applications running

B. Disabling the swap file

C. Having a dual-boot configuration

D. Installing more than two printers

Answer: B. Removing the swap file will have a huge negative impact on your system. The only way it won't is if you have an inordinate amount of RAM (somewhere between 512MB and 1024MB of RAM).

11. What will pressing Ctrl+Alt+Del do?

    A. Reboot the system

    B. Automatically close the current application

    C. Bring up the online Help system

    D. Start the Task Manager

    Answer: D. The Task Manager can be started using the Ctrl+Alt+Del key sequence.

12. You have applications that don't appear to be responding properly. You decide to use the Ctrl+Alt+Del key sequence to open up the Task Manager. The Task Manager window shows you currently running applications in Windows 98. What does the Task Manager allow you to shut down?

    A. Windows 98

    B. An application that has stopped responding

    C. Any running application

    D. All of the above

    Answer: D. The Task Manager allows you to stop any application whether it is running or not responding. This includes the operating system as well.

13. There are lots of different things that you can do to handle problems with printing. Windows 98 provides you with an application that will walk you through the troubleshooting process for most common printer issues? What is the name of this applet?

    A. Print Troubleshooter

    B. Add New Hardware Wizard

    C. Control Panel

    D. None of the above

    Answer: A. Many troubleshooters are available in Windows 98. A troubleshooter is a step-by-step troubleshooting process in which you answer questions presented by the troubleshooter. The troubleshooter will then suggest actions that you can take to fix the problems.

APPENDIX

B

Glossary

A

accounts

Containers for security identifiers, passwords, permissions, group associations, and preferences for each user of a system. User accounts need to be created on a NetWare or Windows NT server before a Windows 98 machine can log in as a client.

Active Desktop

Windows 98 allows you to enable the Active Desktop, which makes the desktop a programmable active window. Local resources, as well as the Internet, are all accessed via the same style of interface. The Active Desktop requires more resources that the plain desktop and should not be enabled on slower computers.

adapter

Any hardware device that allows communications to occur through physically dissimilar systems. This term usually refers to peripheral cards permanently mounted inside computers that provide an interface from the computer's bus to another media, such as a hard disk or a network.

Administer utility

A Windows 98 utility that gives an administrator access to the hard disks on a remote workstation.

Administrators

Users who are part of the Administrators group. This group has the ultimate set of security permissions. See also *Permissions*, *Groups*.

API

See *Application Programming Interface*.

Application layer

The layer of the OSI model that interfaces with user-mode programs called "applications" by providing high-level network services based on lower-level network layers. Network file systems like named pipes are an example of Application-layer software.

Application Programming Interface (API)

An application to allow transparent access to operating system or networking functions.

asynchronous data stream

In communications, the method of passing packets of information one packet at a time in a continuous stream. Communications resources that provide this can be physical (e.g., a modem) or logical (e.g., a fax service on a computer that uses the modem for transmittal and reception of faxes.)

auto-detect

The Windows 98 ability to automatically detect and install drivers for newer hardware.

B

backup browser

A computer on a Microsoft network that maintains a list of computers and services available on the network. The master browser supplies this list. The backup browser distributes the browsing service load to a workgroup or domain.

Basic Input/Output System

See *BIOS*.

bindery

A NetWare 2.*x* and 3.*x* structure that contains user accounts and permissions. NetWare 4.*x* and Netware 5.*x* replace the bindery with Novell Directory Services (NDS).

BIOS (Basic Input/Output System)

A set of routines in firmware that provides the most basic software interface drivers for hardware attached to the computer. The BIOS contains the bootstrap routine.

boot

The process of loading a computer's operating system. Booting usually occurs in multiple phases, each successively more complex, until the entire operating system and all its services are running. Also called "bootstrap." The computer's BIOS must contain the first level of booting.

bridge

A device that connects two networks of the same Data Link protocol by forwarding those packets destined for computers on the other side of the bridge. See also *router*, *Data Link layer*.

Briefcase

A Windows 98 utility that can be used to synchronize files on two computers.

browser

A computer on a Microsoft network that maintains a list of computers and services available on the network. A browser is also a piece of software that interprets HTML code and can display formatted graphics and text, thereby making finding and using information on the Internet much easier. Internet Explorer and Netscape Navigator are examples of Internet browsers.

browsing

The process of requesting the list of computers and services on a network from a browser.

bus

The type of adapter that the motherboard uses to connect any peripheral devices. Different buses include ISA, EISA, and PCI.

C

caching

A speed-optimization technique that keeps a copy of the most recently used data in a fast, high-cost, low-capacity storage device (RAM) rather than in the device upon which the actual data resides (the hard disk). Caching assumes that recently used data is likely to be used again. Fetching data from the cache is faster than fetching data from the slower, larger storage device. Most caching algorithms also copy next-most-likely-to-be-used data and perform write caching to further increase speed gains. See also *write-back caching, write-through caching.*

client

A computer on a network that subscribes to the services provided by a server.

client/server

A network architecture that dedicates certain computers called "servers" to act as service providers to computers called "clients," which users operate to perform work. Servers can be dedicated to providing one or more network services, such as file storage, shared printing, communications, e-mail service, and Web response. See also *share, peer.*

client/server application

An application that splits large applications into two components: computer-intensive processes that run on an application server and user interfaces that run on clients. Client/server applications communicate over the network through interprocess communications mechanisms.

components

Interchangeable elements of a complex software or hardware system. Windows 98 components can be added to an installed system through the Add/Remove Programs applet in the Windows 98 Control Panel.

compression

A space-optimization scheme that reduces the size (length) of a data set. Compression reduces redundancy in the data by creating symbols smaller than the data they represent and an index that defines the value of the symbols for each compressed set of data. Windows 98 comes with a built-in compression utility called DriveSpace 3.

computer name

A NetBIOS name (containing from one to fifteen characters) used to uniquely identify a computer on the network.

Control Panel

A Windows 98 software utility that controls the functions (properties) of specific operating system services through property sheets. The Registry contains the Control Panel settings on a system and/or per-user basis. The main Control Panel applets in Windows 98 include Add New Hardware, Add/Remove Programs, Date/Time, Display, Fonts, Internet, Mail and Fax, Modems, Mouse, Multimedia, Network, Passwords, Printers, and System. Some applications add other applets to the Control Panel.

cooperative multitasking

A multitasking scheme in which each process must voluntarily return on time to a central scheduling route. If any single process fails to return to the central scheduler, the computer will lock up. Both the Windows and Macintosh operating systems use this scheme. Cooperative multitasking is supported by Windows 98 for backward compatibility with 16-bit applications. Preemptive multitasking is the newer method of multitasking that both Windows 98 and Windows NT use.

D

Data Link layer

In the OSI model, the layer that provides the digital interconnection of network devices and the software that directly operates these devices, such as network interface adapters.

database

A related set of data organized by type and purpose. The term also can include the application software that manipulates the data. The Windows 98 Registry is a database.

Desktop

The Windows 98 GUI (graphical user interface). Windows 98 boots directly to the Desktop, which includes the taskbar. Documents, folders, and short-cuts to printers can be stored directly on the Desktop.

DNS

See *Dynamic Host Configuration Protocol*.

dial-up connections

Data Link layer digital connections made via modems over regular telephone lines. Refers to temporary digital connections, as opposed to leased tele-phone lines, which provide permanent connections.

Dial-Up Networking (DUN)

A Windows 98 feature that allows the system to use a modem to connect to a network using telephone lines. The modem acts like a slow network card.

Direct Cable Connection

A Windows 98 feature that allows the connection of two Windows 98 machines (a host and a guest) directly through a null-modem cable. With Direct Cable Connection, files can be copied back and forth between the machines or the network can be connected through the host machine.

DLL

See *dynamic-link library*.

DNS

See *Domain Name Service*.

domain

In Microsoft networks, an arrangement of client and server computers, referenced by a specific name, that share a single security permissions database. On the Internet, a domain is a named collection of hosts and subdomains, registered with a unique name by the InterNIC (the agency responsible for assigning IP addresses).

domain name

The textual identifier of a specific Internet host. Domain names are in the form *server.organization.type* (for example, `www.microsoft.com`) and are resolved to Internet addresses by domain name servers.

domain name server

An Internet host dedicated to the function of translating fully qualified domain names into IP addresses. For example, when a user types `www.microsoft.com`, the DNS server resolves the friendly name into the actual TCP/IP address, which is then used to make the connection. DNS services come with Windows NT. Windows 98 can be a DNS client but not a DNS server.

Domain Name Service (DNS)

The TCP/IP network service that translates textual Internet network addresses into numerical Internet network addresses.

driver

A program that provides a software interface to a hardware device.

dual-booting

The process of booting to another operating system while Windows 98 is installed. The other operating system can be a previous version of MS-DOS or Windows, or Windows NT. Note that FAT16 partitions have to be used if you want both operating systems to see the same partitions.

Dynamic Data Exchange (DDE)

A method of interprocess communications within the Microsoft Windows operating systems. When two or more applications that support DDE are running at the same time, they can exchange data and commands.

Dynamic Host Configuration Protocol (DHCP)

A method of automatically assigning IP addresses to client computers on a network. DHCP services are included with Windows NT Server. Windows 98 can be a DHCP client but not a server.

dynamic link library (DLL)

A library of modular functions that can be used by many programs simultaneously. The three main components of the Windows 98 operating system are implemented as DLLs: the Kernel (KERNEL32.DLL and KERNEL.DLL), User (USER32.DLL and USER.DLL), and GDI (GDI32.DLL and GDI.DLL). Hundreds of functions are stored within DLLs.

E

Easter Egg

A mini-application built into many applications, usually to display information about the developers. Easter Eggs are usually not documented and are revealed by going through a series of oftentimes odd procedures.

ECP

See *Extended Capabilities Port*.

EISA

See *Extended Industry Standard Architecture*.

electronic mail (e-mail)

A type of client/server application that provides a routed, stored-message service between any two user e-mail accounts. E-mail accounts are not the same as user accounts, but a one-to-one relationship usually exists between them. Because all modern computers can attach to the Internet, users can send e-mail over the Internet to any location that has telephone or wireless digital service.

emergency repair disk

A floppy disk that contains critical Registry information about a Windows 98 installation, also called a Startup disk. With an emergency repair disk, a Windows 98 installation can be salvaged using the Restore option when re-installing from CD-ROM. This disk can be created during Windows 98 setup or later through the Add/Remove Programs applet of the Control Panel.

encryption

The process of obscuring information by modifying it according to a mathematical function known only to the intended recipient. Encryption secures information being transmitted over nonsecure or untrusted media.

environment variables

Variables, such as the search path, that contain information available to programs and batch files about the current operating system environment.

Ethernet

The most popular Data Link layer standard for local area networking. Ethernet implements the carrier sense multiple access with collision detection (CSMA/CD) method of arbitrating multiple computer access to the same network. This standard supports the use of Ethernet over any type of media, including wireless broadcast. Standard Ethernet operates at 10Mbps (megabits per second). Fast Ethernet operates at 100Mbps.

Exchange

See *Microsoft Exchange*.

Explorer

See *Windows Explorer*.

Extended Capabilities Port (ECP)

A Windows 98 feature that allows you to add printer cards to your PC. The additional cards become ECPs and can be used to attach a printer.

Extended Industry Standard Architecture (EISA)

An architecture that provides 32-bit bus access. EISA is compatible with 8-bit and 16-bit ISA.

extranet

A secured wide area network between two or more companies that uses the Internet for packet transfer. For example, a manufacturing company may use an extranet and allow its clients to connect to the Web page to fill out orders. Extranets are not meant for the public to access.

F

FAT32

A FAT (file allocation table) format that overcomes some of the limitations of the original FAT but loses backward capability with some older disk utilities. The OSR2 version of Windows 95 and Windows 98 are the only operating systems that support FAT32.

File Allocation Table (FAT)

The file system used by MS-DOS and available to other operating systems such as Windows (all variations), OS/2, and Macintosh. FAT has become something of a mass-storage compatibility standard because of its simplicity and wide availability. FAT has few fault-tolerance features and can become corrupted through normal use over time.

File and Printer Sharing

A Windows 98 feature that allows Windows 98 to act as a server. When File and Printer Sharing is installed, other computers can connect to the machine and copy files or print to a printer.

file attributes

Bits that show the status of a file (such as archived, hidden, and read-only) and are stored along with the name and location of a file in a directory entry. Operating systems use file attributes to help in implementing such services as sharing, compression, and security.

file system

A software component that manages the storage of files on a mass-storage device by providing services that can create, read, write, and delete files. File systems impose an ordered database of files, called volumes, on the mass-storage device. Volumes use hierarchies of directories to organize files.

File Transfer Protocol (FTP)

A simple Internet protocol that transfers complete files from an FTP server to a client running the FTP client. FTP provides a simple method of transferring files between computers, but it cannot perform browsing functions. You must know the URL of the FTP server to which you want to attach.

folder

A directory in Windows 98.

frame type

The main parameter of the IPX/SPX protocol. Different frame types can be run on networks. For example, Ethernet has four possible frame types; Token Ring has two possible frame types.

FTP

See *File Transfer Protocol.*

G

gateway

A computer that serves as a router, a format translator, or a security filter for an entire network.

GDI

See *graphical device interface.*

General Protection Fault (GPF)

A General Protection Fault occurs when a program violates the integrity of the system. This often happens when a program tries to access memory that is not part of its memory address space. A GPF is a defense mechanism employed by the operating system.

graphical device interface (GDI)

The programming interface and graphical services provided to Win32 for programs to interact with graphical devices such as the screen and printer.

graphical user interface (GUI)

A computer shell program that represents mass storage devices, directories, and files as graphical objects on a screen. A cursor driven by a pointing device such as a mouse manipulates the objects. Typically, icons that can be opened into windows that show the data contained by the object represent the objects.

group

A security entity to which users can be assigned membership for the purpose of applying the broad set of group permissions to the user. By managing permissions for groups and assigning users to groups, rather than assigning permissions to users, security administrators can keep coherent control of very large security environments.

GUI

See *graphical user interface.*

H

hardware detection

The Windows 98 ability to automatically find new hardware. An element of Plug and Play.

hardware profiles

Used to manage portable computers that have different configurations. For example, laptops may have two different hardware profiles (configurations): one for docked and one for undocked.

home directory

A directory that stores user's personal files and programs.

home page

The default page returned by an HTTP server when an URL containing no specific document is requested.

host

An Internet server. Hosts are constantly connected to the Internet.

HTML

See *Hypertext Markup Language*.

HTTP

See *Hypertext Transfer Protocol*.

hyperlink

A link in text or graphics files that has a Web address embedded within it. By clicking on the link, users can jump to another Web address. A hyperlink is usually a different color than the rest of the Web page.

Hypertext Markup Language (HTML)

A textual data format that identifies sections of a document as headers, lists, hypertext links, and so on. HTML is the data format used on the World Wide Web for the publication of Web pages. See also *Hypertext Transfer Protocol.*

Hypertext Transfer Protocol (HTTP)

An Internet protocol that transfers HTML documents over the Internet and responds to context changes that happen when a user clicks on a hypertext link. See also *Hypertext Markup Language, World Wide Web.*

IDE (Integrated Drive Electronics)

A simple mass-storage device interconnection bus that can handle no more than two attached devices. IDE devices are similar to but less expensive than SCSI devices.

Industry Standard Architecture (ISA)

The design standard for 16-bit Intel-compatible motherboards and peripheral buses. The 32/64-bit PCI bus standard is replacing the ISA standard. Adapters and interface cards must conform to the bus standard(s) used by the motherboard in order to be used with a computer.

Integrated Services Digital Network (ISDN)

A direct, digital dial-up PSTN (public-switched telephone network) Data Link layer connection that operates at 64KB per channel over regular twisted-pair cable between a subscriber site and a PSTN central office. ISDN provides twice the data rate of the fastest modems per channel. Up to 24 channels can be multiplexed over two twisted pairs.

Internet

A voluntarily interconnected global network of computers based upon the TCP/IP protocol suite. TCP/IP was originally developed by the U.S. Department of Defense's Advanced Research Projects Agency to facilitate the interconnection of military networks and was provided free to universities. The obvious utility of worldwide digital network connectivity and the availability of free complex networking software developed at universities doing military research attracted other universities, research institutions, private organizations, businesses, and finally the individual home user. The Internet is now available to all current commercial computing platforms.

Internet Explorer

See *Microsoft Internet Explorer*.

Internet Protocol (IP)

The Network layer protocol upon which the Internet is based. IP provides a simple, connectionless packet exchange. Other protocols such as UDP or TCP use IP to perform their connection-oriented or guaranteed-delivery services. See also *TCP/IP*.

Internet service provider (ISP)

A company that provides dial-up connections to the Internet.

Internetwork Packet Exchange (IPX)

The network protocol developed by Novell for its NetWare products. IPX is a routable, connection-oriented protocol similar to IP; however, it is much easier to manage and has lower communication overhead. The term IPX can also refer to the family of protocols that includes the SPX (Synchronous Packet Exchange) Transport layer protocol.

InterNIC

The agency that is responsible for assigning IP addresses. InterNIC also maintains the naming of Web pages or the domain name (e.g., www.sybex.com).

interprocess communications (IPC)

A generic term describing any manner of client/server communication protocol, specifically those operating in the Session, Presentation, and Application layers of the OSI model. IPC mechanisms provide a method for the client and server to trade information. See also *named pipe, remote procedure calls, NetBIOS*.

interrupt request (IRQ)

A hardware signal from a peripheral device to the microprocessor indicating that it has I/O (input/output) traffic to send. If the microprocessor is not running a more important service, it will interrupt its current activity and handle the interrupt request. IBM PCs have 16 levels of interrupt request lines. Each device must have a unique interrupt request line.

intranet

A privately owned network based on the TCP/IP protocol suite.

IP

See *Internet Protocol*.

IP address

A four-byte (32-bit) number that uniquely identifies a computer on an IP internetwork. An example would be 131.107.2.200. InterNIC assigns the first bytes of Internet IP addresses and administers them in hierarchies. Huge organizations like the government or top-level ISPs have class A addresses, large organizations and most ISPs have class B addresses, and small companies have class C addresses. In a class A address, InterNIC assigns the first byte, and the owning organization assigns the remaining three bytes. In a class B address, InterNIC or the higher-level ISP assigns the first two bytes, and the organization assigns the remaining two bytes. In a class C address, InterNIC or the higher-level ISP assigns the first three bytes, and the organization assigns the remaining byte. Organizations not attached to the Internet are free to assign IP addresses as they please.

IPC

See *interprocess communications*.

IPX

See *Internetwork Packet Exchange*.

IRQ

See *interrupt request*.

ISA

See *Industry Standard Architecture*.

ISDN

See *Integrated Services Digital Network*.

ISP

See *Internet service provider*.

K

kernel

The core process of a preemptive operating system, consisting of a multitasking scheduler and the basic services that provide security. Depending on the operating system, other services such as virtual memory drivers may be built into the kernel. The kernel is responsible for managing the scheduling of threads and processes.

L

LAN Manager

The Microsoft brand of a network product jointly developed by IBM and Microsoft that provided an early client/server environment. LAN Manager/ Server was eclipsed by NetWare, but it was the genesis of many important protocols and IPC mechanisms used today, such as NetBIOS, named pipes, and NetBEUI. Portions of this product exist today in OS/2 Warp Server. See also *interprocess communications*.

LFN

See *long filenames*.

local user profile

A user profile that is stored only on the local computer. If a user logs on to one computer, makes changes to the environment, and then logs on to another computer, the changes from the first computer are not reflected on the second computer.

logging

The process of recording information about activities and errors in the operating system. Usually the more events you log, the more overhead it takes. Bad logon attempts and critical errors with Windows NT or applications are events which are logged frequently.

logon

The process of being authenticated by a Windows NT server. Windows 98 can also provide a logon into a NetWare network or into a local list of users and passwords.

logon script

Command files that automate the logon process by performing utility functions such as attaching to additional server resources or automatically running different programs based upon the user account that logged in. Logon scripts can be run by both NetWare and Windows NT servers.

long filename (LFN)

A filename longer than the eight characters plus three-character extension allowed by MS-DOS. In Windows 98 (and NT), filenames can contain up to 255 characters.

M

MAC layer

See *Media Access Control (MAC) layer*.

mandatory user profile

A user profile that is created by an administrator and saved with a special extension (.MAN) so that the user cannot modify the profile in any way. Mandatory user profiles can be assigned to a single user or a group of users.

MAPI

See *Messaging Application Programming Interface*.

master boot record (MBR)

Contains the pointer to the machine's boot files. After the BIOS bootstrap, the system loads the MBR and the partition table of the bootable drive and executes the MBR.

master browser

The computer on a network that maintains a list of computers and services available on the network and distributes the list to other browsers. The master browser may also promote potential browsers to browsers. See also *backup browser*.

MBR

See *master boot record*.

Media Access Control (MAC) layer

The MAC layer is an implementation and enhanced specification of the Data Link layer of the OSI model. It consists of the driver for the network interface card. This layer helps watch for errors in the transmission and conversion of signals.

Messaging Application Programming Interface (MAPI)

A messaging application standard developed by Microsoft to allow for interaction between an application and various message service providers.

metafile

In Windows, a file with a .WMF extension that contains a collection of internal commands that Windows 98 uses to render graphics to the screen.

microprocessor

An integrated semiconductor circuit designed to automatically perform lists of logical and arithmetic operations. Modern microprocessors independently manage memory pools and support multiple instruction lists called "threads." Microprocessors are also capable of responding to interrupt requests from peripherals and include onboard support for complex floating-point arithmetic. Microprocessors must have instructions when they are first powered on. These instructions are contained in nonvolatile firmware called a "BIOS."

Microsoft Client for Microsoft Networks

Software that allows Windows 98 to be a client on a Microsoft network. Installing the Client for Microsoft allows Windows 98 to communicate with Microsoft servers, including LAN Manager, Windows NT, and Windows 98 computers that have the File and Printer Sharing for Microsoft service installed.

Microsoft Client for NetWare Networks

Software that allows Windows 98 to be a client on a NetWare network.

Microsoft Exchange

Microsoft's messaging application. Exchange implements Microsoft's Mail Application Programming Interface (MAPI) as well as other messaging protocols (such as POP, SNMP, and faxing) to provide a flexible message composition and reception service.

Microsoft Fax

Software that allows a fax modem to send and/or receive faxes.

Microsoft Internet Explorer

A World Wide Web browser produced by Microsoft and included with versions of Windows 98 and Windows NT 4.0.

Microsoft Service for Netware Directory Service (MS-NDS)

The MS-NDS service allows Windows 98 to connect to NetWare servers that use NDS (NetWare 4.x, 5.x). MS-NDS must be used in conjunction with the Microsoft Client for NetWare.

MIDI

See *Musical Instrument Digital Interface.*

minidriver

A driver from a manufacturer that, combined with Microsoft's universal driver, provides full functionality.

module

A software component of a modular operating system that provides a certain defined service. Modules can be installed or removed depending upon the service requirements of the software running on the computer. Modules allow operating systems and applications to be customized to fit the needs of the user.

multiprocessing

Using two or more processors simultaneously to perform a computing task. Depending on the operating system, processing may be done asymmetrically, wherein certain processors are assigned certain threads independent of the load they create, or symmetrically, wherein threads are dynamically assigned to processors according to an equitable scheduling scheme. The term usually describes a multiprocessing capacity built into the computer at a hardware level in that the computer itself supports more than one processor. However, multiprocessing can also be applied to network computing applications achieved through interprocess communications mechanisms. Client/server applications are, in fact, examples of multiprocessing. Although Windows NT supports multiple processors, Windows 98 does not.

multitasking

The capacity of an operating system to rapidly switch among threads of execution. Multitasking allows processor time to be divided among threads as if each thread ran on its own slower processor. Multitasking operating systems allow two or more applications to run at the same time and can provide a greater degree of service to applications than single-tasking operating systems like MS-DOS. See also *multiprocessing, multithreaded.*

multithreaded

Refers to programs that have more than one chain of execution, therefore relying on the services of a multitasking or multiprocessing operating system to operate. Multiple chains of execution allow programs to simultaneously perform more than one task. In multitasking computers, multithreading is merely a convenience used to make programs run smoother and free the program from the burden of switching between tasks itself. On multiprocessing computers, multithreading allows the processing burden of the program to be spread across many processors. Programs that are not multithreaded cannot take advantage of multiple processors in a computer. Windows 98, as well as Windows NT, supports *multithreaded applications*.

Musical Instrument Digital Interface (MIDI)

A serial interface standard that allows you to connect musical instruments to the computer.

N

named pipe

An interprocess communications mechanism that is implemented as a file system service, allowing programs to be modified to run on it without using a proprietary application programming interface. Named pipes were developed to support more robust client/server communications than those allowed by the simpler NetBIOS.

NCP

See *NetWare Core Protocol*.

NDIS

See *Network Driver Interface Specification*.

NDS

See *Novell Directory Services*.

Net Watcher

A built-in Windows 98 interactive tool for creating, controlling, and monitoring remote shared resources.

NetBEUI (NetBIOS Extended User Interface)

A simple Network layer transport developed to support NetBIOS installations. NetBEUI is not routable, and so it is not appropriate for larger networks. NetBEUI is the fastest transport protocol available for Windows 98, although its use is limited.

NetBIOS (Network Basic Input/Output System)

A client/server interprocess communications service developed by IBM in the early 1980s. NetBIOS presents a relatively primitive mechanism for communication in client/server applications, but its widespread acceptance and availability across most operating systems make it a logical choice for simple network applications. Many of the network interprocess communications mechanisms in Windows 98 are implemented over NetBIOS.

NetBIOS Extended User Interface

See *NetBEUI*.

NetBIOS over TCP/IP (NetBT)

A network service that implements NetBIOS over the TCP/IP protocol stack.

NetDDE

See *Network Dynamic Data Exchange*.

NetWare

A popular network operating system developed by Novell in the early 1980s. NetWare is a cooperative, multitasking, highly optimized, dedicated-server network operating system that has client support for most major operating systems. Recent versions of NetWare include graphical client tools for management from client stations and pre-emptive multitasking. The latest release includes a native IP protocol.

NetWare Core Protocol (NCP)

The language that NetWare servers use to communicate. A Windows 98 machine with the Microsoft Client for NetWare Networks software installed can communicate with NetWare servers.

Network Basic Input/Output System

See *NetBIOS*.

Network Driver Interface Specification (NDIS)

A Microsoft specification to which network adapter drivers must conform in order to work with Microsoft network operating systems. NDIS provides a many-to-many binding between network adapter drivers and transport protocols.

Network Dynamic Data Exchange (NetDDE)

An interprocess communications mechanism developed by Microsoft to support the distribution of DDE applications over a network.

network interface card (NIC)

A Physical layer adapter device that allows a computer to connect to and communicate over a local area network. See also *Ethernet*, *Token Ring*.

Network layer

The layer of the OSI model that creates a communication path between two computers via routed packets. Transport protocols implement both the Network layer and the Transport layer of the OSI model. IP is a Network layer service.

network operating system (NOS)

A computer operating system specifically designed to optimize a computer's ability to respond to service requests. Servers run network operating systems. Windows NT Server and NetWare are both network operating systems.

New Technology File System (NTFS)

A secure, transaction-oriented file system developed for Windows NT that incorporates the Windows NT security model for assigning permissions and shares. NTFS is optimized for hard drives larger than 500MB and requires too much overhead to be used on hard disk drives smaller than 50MB. Windows 95 cannot read or write to an NTFS partition.

nonbrowser

A computer on a network that will not maintain a list of other computers and services on the network. See also *browser*, *browsing*.

Novell Directory Services (NDS)

In NetWare, a distributed hierarchy of network services such as servers, shared volumes, and printers. NetWare implements NDS as a directory structure with elaborate security and administration mechanisms. (Formerly called NetWare Directory Services; name change came with NetWare 5.)

NTFS

See *New Technology File System*.

O

object

Almost anything in Windows 98. In Microsoft's object-oriented approach to the Windows 98 interface, files, folders, printers, programs, the Desktop itself, hard drives, the monitor, the keyboard, and so on are considered objects. The characteristics of an object are controlled by that object's properties.

Object Linking and Embedding (OLE)

A mechanism that allows Microsoft Windows applications to include each other's creations, such as a graphics image or a spreadsheet, in files. An OLE object incorporated in a document can be edited or modified by the program that created it; the user can double-click that object to invoke its originating program.

ODI (Open Data-Link Interface) real-mode drivers

Novell's older standard for drivers used to install network cards. For Windows 98, these drivers are loaded from the AUTOEXEC.BAT file. ODI drivers include LSL, NE2000, IPXODI, VLM, or NETX. (ODI is similar to Microsoft's NDIS specification.)

Open Graphics Language (OpenGL)

A standard interface for the presentation of two- and three-dimensional visual data.

Open Systems Interconnect model

See *OSI model*.

OpenGL

See *Open Graphics Language*.

operating system (OS)

A collection of services that form a foundation upon which applications run. Operating systems may be simple I/O (input/output) service providers with a command shell, such as MS-DOS, or they may be sophisticated, preemptive, multitasking, multithreaded applications platforms like Windows 98.

optimization

Any effort to reduce the workload on a hardware component by eliminating, obviating, or reducing the amount of work required of the hardware component through any means. For instance, file caching is an optimization that reduces the workload of a hard disk drive.

OSI (Open Systems Interconnect) model

A model for network component interoperability developed by the International Standards Organization (ISO) to promote cross-vendor compatibility of hardware and software network systems. The OSI model splits the process of networking into seven distinct services: Physical layer, Data Link layer, Network layer, Transport layer, Session layer, Presentation layer, and Application layer. Each layer uses the services of the layer below to provide its service to the layer above.

OSR2

The latest releases of Windows 95, also called the B version. This version includes all the patches to the original version of Windows 95, plus additional features such as FAT32.

P

packet

A piece of information that is exchanged between computers. A packet usually contains the source and destination addresses, as well as the actual data being exchanged.

page fault

Occurs when there is a call for a data page that is not in physical memory (RAM). When the system has a page fault, it is reading information from hard disk rather than memory. Excessive page faulting can result in poor overall performance. See also *thrashing*.

page file

See *swap file*.

paging

The process of transferring some data pages out to a swap file before the physical RAM becomes full. Also called demand paging.

partition

A section of a hard disk that can contain an independent file system volume. Partitions can be used to keep multiple operating systems and file systems on the same hard disk.

PCI

See *Peripheral Connection Interface*.

PDC

See *primary domain controller*.

peer

A networked computer that both shares resources with other computers and accesses the shared resources of other computers. A non-dedicated server. See also *client*.

peer-to-peer

A networking or type of messaging system in which each computer can be both a client and a server. In Windows 98, this type of sharing can be configured and used by end users without a special server configuration.

Peripheral Connection Interface (PCI)

A high-speed, 32/64-bit bus interface developed by Intel and widely accepted as the successor to the 16-bit ISA interface. PCI devices support I/O (input/output) throughput about 40 times faster than the ISA bus.

permissions

Assignments of levels of access to a resource made to groups or users. Administrators can assign permissions to allow any level of access, such as read only, read/write, or delete, by controlling the ability of users to initiate object services. Permissions are used to assign rights to users in a Microsoft or NetWare network when user-level security is being used in Windows 98.

Personal Web Server (PWS)

A Web server component for Windows 98. PWS can enable Windows 98 to act as a full-service Web server.

Physical layer

In the OSI model, the cables, connectors, and connection ports of a network. The passive physical components required to create a network.

PIF

See *Program Information File*.

Plug and Play

The technology that allows installation of Plug-and-Play hardware into a Windows 98 system without needing to configure the hardware or the computer system. When a new Plug-and-Play device is added, Windows 98 will automatically detect and configure the device.

Point-and-Print

A Windows 98 method used to install driver files for a networked printer by dragging the Point-and-Print printer icon from the networked PC to the Printers folder. Documents can be printed to networking printers by simply dragging and dropping them onto the printer icon.

Point-to-Point Protocol (PPP)

A Data Link layer transport that performs over point-to-point network connections such as serial or modem lines. PPP can negotiate any transport protocol used by both systems involved in the link and can automatically assign IP, DNS, and gateway addresses when used with TCP/IP.

Point-to-Point Tunneling Protocol (PPTP)

Protocol used to create secure connections between private networks through the public Internet or an ISP. Using the PPTP protocol a virtual private network (VPN) can be established. Sometimes VPN is used synonymously with PPTP although they are separate items.

policy

See *system policy*.

Policy Editor

See *System Policy Editor*.

post office

A central location for storage of e-mail messages. This storage can be on a workstation's hard drive or on a network server.

PPP

See *Point-to-Point Protocol.*

PPTP

See *Point-to-Point Tunneling Protocol.*

preemptive multitasking

A multitasking implementation in which an interrupt routine in the kernel manages the scheduling of processor time among running threads. The threads themselves do not need to support multitasking in any way because the microprocessor will preempt the thread with an interrupt, save its state, update all thread priorities according to its scheduling algorithm, and pass control to the highest priority thread awaiting execution. Because of the preemptive nature, a thread that crashes will not affect the operation of other executing threads. Windows 98 supports preemptive multitasking.

Preferences

Characteristics of user accounts on a server, such as password, profile location, home directory, and logon script.

Presentation layer

The layer of the OSI model that converts and, if necessary, translates information between the Session and Application layers.

primary domain controller (PDC)

The domain server in a Windows NT system that contains the master copy of the security, computer, and user accounts databases and that can authenticate workstations. The PDC can replicate its databases to one or more backup domain controllers. The PDC is usually also the master browser for the domain.

print driver

The software that understands a specific print device's command set. Each print device has an associated print driver.

Print Provider Interface (PPI)

A modular interface with interchangeable components that allows third-party vendors to seamlessly integrate network print drivers into Windows 98.

print queue

A folder where print jobs are held until they are printed.

print server

A computer on which the printers in a network are defined. When a user sends a job to a network printer, it is actually sent to the print server first.

print spooler

A directory or folder on the print server that actually stores the print jobs until they can be printed. The print server and print spooler should have enough hard disk space to hold all of the print jobs that could be pending at any given time.

process

A running program containing one or more threads. A process encapsulates the protected memory and environment for its threads.

processor

A circuit designed to automatically perform lists of logical and arithmetic operations. Unlike microprocessors, processors may be designed from discrete components rather than be a monolithic integrated circuit.

program

A list of processor instructions designed to perform a certain function. A running program is called a process. A package of one or more programs and attendant data designed to meet a certain application is called software.

Program Information File (PIF)

A file that allows MS-DOS–based programs to coexist with Windows programs. A PIF is a configuration header file for the MS-DOS virtual machine.

Programming Interfaces

Interprocess communications mechanisms that provide certain high-level services to running processes. Programming interfaces may provide network communication, graphical presentation, or any other type of software service.

property

A characteristic of a Windows 98 object. Properties include a wide variety of attributes that can be examined and changed. For example, changing the wallpaper on the Desktop is done through the Desktop's properties; swapping the left and right mouse buttons is done through the mouse's properties.

protected mode

The Windows 98 32-bit mode of operation, which offers superior performance, protection, and security compared with real mode. Protected mode requires a 386-compatible CPU and an operating system that supports it. Protected-mode commands are executed in extended or XMS memory.

protocol

An established communication method that the parties involved understand. Protocols provide a context in which to interpret communicated information. Computer protocols are rules used by communicating devices and software services to format data in a way that all participants understand. See also *transport protocol*.

Proxy Server

A service that provides WWW caching, firewall protection, and protocol conversion services. Proxy Server 2.0 for Windows NT is Microsoft's current premier proxy server. Clients can be configured to take advantage of a proxy server's functions, or they may use a proxy server without even realizing it.

PSTN

See *Public-Switched Telephone Network*.

Public-Switched Telephone Network (PSTN)

A global network of interconnected digital and analog communication links originally designed to support voice communication between any two points in the world, but quickly adapted to handle digital data traffic when the computer revolution occurred. In addition to its traditional voice support role, the PSTN now functions as the Physical layer of the Internet (in the OS model architecture) by providing dial-up and leased lines for the interconnections.

R

RAS

See *Remote Access Service*.

real mode

The older, Windows 16-bit mode of operation. Windows 3.*x* and MS-DOS 6.*x* are written to 16-bit standards. Real-mode commands execute in conventional memory below the 1MB barrier. See also *protected mode*.

Recycle Bin

The Windows 98 utility that keeps track of deleted files and allows users to recover them.

redirector

A software service that redirects user file I/O (input/output) requests over the network. The redirector can go either to local resources or to a NetWare, Windows NT, or other network server.

Reduced Instruction Set Computer (RISC)

A microprocessor technology that implements fewer and more primitive instructions than typical microprocessors and can, therefore, be implemented quickly with the most modern semiconductor technology and speeds. Programs written for RISC microprocessors require more instructions (longer programs) to perform the same tasks as normal microprocessors, but they are capable of a greater degree of optimization and usually run faster.

Registry

A database of settings required and maintained by Windows 98 and its components. The Registry contains all the configuration information used by the computer. It is stored as a hierarchical structure and is made up of keys, hives, and value entries. You can use the Registry Editor (REGEDT32 command) to change these settings.

Remote Access Service (RAS)

A service that allows network connections to be established over telephone lines with modems or digital adapters. The computer initiating the connection is called the RAS client; the answering computer is called the RAS host. (DUN replaced RAS.) See also *Public-Switched Telephone Network*, *DUN*.

remote procedure call (RPC)

A network interprocess communications mechanism that allows an application to be distributed among many computers on the same network.

Remoteboot

A service that starts diskless workstations over a network.

resource

Any useful service, such as a shared network directory or a printer. See also *share*.

RIP

See *Routing Information Protocol*.

RISC

See *Reduced Instruction Set Computer*.

roaming user profile

A user profile that is stored and configured to be downloaded from a server. Roaming user profiles allow users to access their profile from any location on the network.

router

A Network layer device that moves packets between networks. Routers provide internetwork connectivity.

Routing Information Protocol (RIP)

A protocol within the TCP/IP protocol suite that allows routers to exchange routing information with other routers. A variant of RIP also exists for the IPX/SPX protocol suite.

RPC

See *remote procedure calls.*

S

Safe mode

A boot mode that bypasses loading the Registry, CONFIG.SYS, and AUTOEXEC.BAT files. It does not load any network functionality or protected-mode drivers. Safe mode starts Windows 98 in standard VGA and loads HIMEM.SYS, IFSHLP.SYS, and the PATH statement from MSDOS.SYS.

SAP

See *Service Advertisement Protocol.*

ScanDisk

A program that looks for errors on the hard disk. ScanDisk can find and fix errors in folders or files.

scheduling

The process of determining which threads should be executed according to their priority and other factors. See also *preemptive multitasking.*

SCSI

See *Small Computer Systems Interface*.

search engine

A Web site dedicated to responding to requests for specific information, searching massive locally stored databases of Web pages, and responding with the URLs of pages that fit the search phrase.

security

Measures taken to secure a system against accidental or intentional loss, usually in the form of accountability procedures and use restriction.

Serial Line Internet Protocol (SLIP)

An implementation of the IP protocol over serial lines. SLIP has been obviated by PPP.

server

A computer dedicated to servicing requests for resources from other computers on a network. Servers typically run network operating systems such as Windows NT Server or NetWare. See also *client/server*.

Service Advertising Protocol (SAP)

A NetWare packet, broadcast from the server every 60 seconds, that contains the server name and the shared resources it has. Windows 98 can also generate a SAP so that NetWare clients will see the Windows 98 machine as a NetWare server.

Session layer

The layer of the OSI model dedicated to maintaining a bidirectional communication connection between two computers. The Session layer uses the services of the Transport layer to provide this service.

share

A resource, such as a directory or printer, shared by a server or a peer on a network.

share-level security

The default level of security used in Windows 98 (and Windows for Work-groups). Share-level security is based on passwords assigned to shared resources. See also *user-level security*.

shell

The user interface of an operating system; the shell launches applications and manages file systems.

shortcut

A special instruction, or pointer, to launch an object (program, file, printer, and so on) with Windows 98. Shortcuts are usually stored on the Desktop, but they can be stored in folders as well. Deleting or editing a shortcut does not affect the original object. Shortcuts are identified with an .LNK extension.

Simple Message Blocks (SMB)

The language Microsoft servers use to communicate on a network.

Simple Network Management Protocol (SNMP)

An Internet protocol that manages network hardware such as routers, switches, servers, and clients from a single client on the network.

SLIP

See *Serial Line Internet Protocol*.

slow link

Networking across telephone lines rather than over a standard network cable. Modem connections to a network are considered slow links because they generally run between 14,400 to 28,800bps on an analog modem and up to 128,800bps on a digital modem using ISDN (Integrated Services Digital Network) connections. A network cable can run between 4.2 million to 10 million bps, or 65 to 200 times faster than a modem connection.

Small Computer Systems Interface (SCSI)

A high-speed, parallel-bus interface that connects hard disk drives, CD-ROM drives, tape drives, and many other peripherals to a computer. SCSI (pronounced "scuzzy") is the mass-storage connection standard among all computers except IBM compatibles, which may use SCSI or IDE.

SMB

See *Simple Message Blocks*.

SNMP

See *Simple Network Management Protocol*.

spooler

A service that buffers output to a low-speed device, such as a printer, so the software outputting to the device is not tied up waiting for it.

Startup disk

A bootable floppy disk with Windows 98 startup files that can be used to boot or troubleshoot a Windows 98 machine. Windows 98 can create a Startup disk during Windows 98 installation, or later, through the Add/Remove Programs applet in the Control Panel.

subnet mask

The role of the subnet mask is to determine if a request is going to local resources or outside to a remote resource. A number is mathematically applied to IP addresses to determine which IP addresses are a part of the same subnetwork as the computer applying the subnet mask.

swap file

The virtual memory file on a hard disk containing the memory pages that have been moved out to disk to increase available RAM.

System Monitor

A Windows 98 utility that monitors system parameters and statistics. For example, the System Monitor can be used to monitor virtual machine usage, page faults, and threads.

system policy

A method used to control what a user can do and the user's environment. System policies can be applied to a specific user, a group, a computer, or all users. System policies work by overwriting current settings in the Windows 98 Registry with the system policy settings. For Windows 98, system policies are created through the System Policy Editor. In Windows NT, policies affect restrictions on password use and rights assignment and determine which events will be recorded in the Security log.

System Policy Editor

A Windows 98 utility used to create system policies. This program is not installed by default; it must be installed from the Windows 98 CD-ROM.

T

TAPI

See *Telephony Application Program Interface*.

Task Manager

A Windows 98 application that allows users to view and close running processes. The Task Manager can also be used to view CPU and memory statistics. Press Ctrl+Alt+Del to launch the Task Manager.

taskbar

The gray bar at the bottom of the Windows 98 screen, which replaces the Task Manager of previous versions of Windows. The taskbar holds buttons that represent running programs as well as the Start menu button. It is used to switch between running programs and to open the Start menu.

TCP

See *Transmission Control Protocol.*

TCP/IP

See *Transmission Control Protocol/Internet Protocol.*

Telephony Application Program Interface (TAPI)

A standard way for programs to interact with the telephony functionality in Windows 98.

templates

ASCII files with an .ADM extension used to create Windows 98 system policies. Entries in a template correspond to subkeys and values in the Registry.

thrashing

Excessive page faults. This can occur when RAM runs low, and programs and data are paged out to the hard disk. Thrashing can often be eliminated by adding more memory or by using fewer applications at one time.

thread

A list of instructions running in a computer to perform a certain task. Each thread runs in the context of a process, which embodies the protected memory space and the environment of the threads. Multithreaded processes can perform more than one task at the same time. See also *multitasking.*

throughput

The measure of information flow through a system in a specific time frame, usually one second. For instance, 28.8Kbps is the throughput of a modem: 28.8 kilobits per second can be transmitted.

Token Ring

A Data Link layer standard for local-area networking. Token Ring implements the token-passing method of arbitrating multiple-computer access to the same network. Token Ring operates at either 4 or 16 megabits per second (Mbps).

Transmission Control Protocol (TCP)

A Transport layer protocol that implements guaranteed packet delivery using the IP Protocol. See also *Transmission Control Protocol/Internet Protocol.*

Transmission Control Protocol/Internet Protocol (TCP/IP)

A suite of network protocols upon which the global Internet is based. TCP/IP is a general term that can refer either to the TCP and IP protocols used together or to the complete set of Internet protocols.

Transport layer

The OSI model layer responsible for the guaranteed serial delivery of packets between two computers over an internetwork. TCP is the Transport layer protocol for the TCP/IP transport protocol.

transport protocol

A service that delivers discrete packets of information between any two computers in a network. Transport protocols may operate at the Data Link, Network, Transport, or Session layers of the OSI model. Higher-level, connection-oriented services are built upon transport protocols.

U

UNC

See *Universal Naming Convention.*

Uniform Resource Locator (URL)

An Internet standard naming convention for identifying resources available via various TCP/IP application protocols. For example, `http://www.microsoft .com` is the URL for Microsoft's World Wide Web server site; `ftp:// gateway.dec.com` is a popular FTP site. A URL allows easy hypertext references to a particular resource from within a document or mail message.

universal driver

A driver written by Microsoft that contains the bulk of the code that makes up the entire driver. A universal driver, such as a printer driver or the Unimodem driver, is used in conjunction with a minidriver, supplied by the manufacturer.

Universal Naming Convention (UNC)

A multivendor, multiplatform convention for identifying shared resources on a network. The format for a UNC is \\Server\Shared Resource. For example, to connect a network drive, you can issue the command NET USE T: \\SERVER\NETLOGON. This would map the T: to the NETLOGON share of the server called SERVER.

Unix

A multitasking, kernel-based operating system developed at AT&T in the early 1970s and provided (originally) free to universities as a research operating system. Because of its availability and ability to scale down to microprocessor-based computers, Unix became the standard operating system of the Internet and is the closest approximation to a universal operating system that exists. Most computers can run some variant of the Unix operating system.

URL

See *Uniform Resource Locator*.

user-level security

A level of security that allows Windows 98 to share its resources by granting rights to existing users and groups from an existing Windows NT or NetWare server. User-level security is preferred over share-level security because rights can be assigned to specific users and/or groups. User-level security requires an existing server such as Windows NT or NetWare in order to function. When a client makes a request, the request is passed through to the server, which then authenticates it and passes it back to the Windows 98 computer. See also *share-level security*.

user profile

A method used to save each user's Desktop configuration. See also *local user profile*, *mandatory user profile*, *roaming profile*.

username

A user's account name in a logon-authenticated system. See also *security*.

V

Vcache

A protected-mode hard drive caching program that is integrated into Windows 98.

VCOMM

A Windows 98 driver that communicates with the serial ports and modems.

virtual machine (VM)

A method used by Windows 98 to fool programs into thinking that they have exclusive access to all system hardware. Virtual machines run in Ring 3 of the Windows 98 system architecture and use a message-passing technique to access memory and hardware. Two types of virtual machines exist in Windows 98: a System VM and multiple MS-DOS VMs. All Windows-based programs run in the System VM. Each MS-DOS–based program runs in its own MS-DOS VM.

virtual memory

A kernel service that stores memory pages not currently in use on a mass-storage device to free up the memory occupied for other uses. Virtual memory hides the memory-swapping process from applications and higher-level services. See also *swap file*.

VM

See *virtual machine*.

volume

A collection of data indexed by directories containing files and referred to by a drive letter. Volumes are normally contained in a single partition, but volume sets and stripe sets extend a single volume across multiple partitions. NetWare servers always have a volume called SYS where the system files are stored. Windows NT can also use a volume or stripe set. Windows 98 does not use volumes.

W

Web browser

An application that makes HTTP requests and formats the resultant HTML documents for the users. Most Web browsers understand all standard Internet protocols.

Web page

Any HTML document on an HTTP server.

Win16

The set of application services provided by the 16-bit versions of Microsoft Windows: Windows 3.1 and Windows for Workgroups 3.11.

Win32

The set of application services provided by the 32-bit versions of Microsoft Windows: Windows 95/98 and Windows NT.

Windows 3.11 for Workgroups

The current 16-bit version of Windows for less-powerful, Intel-based personal computers. Windows for Workgroups (WFW) was replaced by Windows 95, but it is still in use in many companies. The primary limitations of WFW are that it is limited to 16-bit applications and does not support long filenames. WFW can be both a Microsoft and NetWare client, and it can also share its files on the network.

Windows 95

The 32-bit operating system from Microsoft that emphasizes compatibility over security. Windows 95 was released in August of 1995. The current version is called OSR2 or Windows95B. Windows 98 replaced Windows 95 in July 1998.

Windows 98

The current 32-bit version of Microsoft Windows for medium-range, Intel-based personal computers. This system includes peer-networking services, Internet support, and strong support for older DOS applications and peripherals. Windows 98 also includes support for FAT32, support for the latest hardware, and various enhancements to the interface including better integration with the Internet.

Windows Explorer

The default shell for Windows 98 and Windows NT 4.0. Explorer implements the more flexible Desktop object paradigm rather than the Program Manager paradigm used in earlier versions of Windows.

Windows Internet Name Service (WINS)

A network service for Microsoft networks that provides Windows computers with Internet numbers for specified NetBIOS names, facilitating browsing and intercommunication over TCP/IP networks.

Windows NT

The current high-level 32-bit version of Microsoft Windows for powerful Intel or Alpha-based computers. Windows NT was designed with security in mind. Windows NT requires a secured logon into the operating system and doesn't allow any applications to have direct access to the hardware. The current version of Window NT is 4.0, with 5.0 scheduled for some time in 1999. Windows NT Workstation is designed to be a client on a network, but it can still have up to ten connections into the system at any given time. Windows NT Server is designed to be a network server.

WINS

See *Windows Internet Name Service.*

workgroup

In Microsoft networks, a collection of related computers, such as a department, that don't require the uniform security and coordination of a domain. Workgroups are characterized by a small group of computers under decentralized management as opposed to the centralized management that domains use.

World Wide Web (WWW)

A collection of Internet servers providing hypertext-formatted documents for Internet clients running Web browsers. The World Wide Web provided the first easy-to-use graphical interface for the Internet and is largely responsible for the Internet's explosive growth.

write-back caching

A caching optimization technique wherein data written by applications is cached until the cache is full or until a subsequent write operation overwrites the cached data. Write-back caching can significantly reduce the write operations because many write operations are subsequently obviated by new information. Data in the write-back cache is also available for subsequent reads. If something happens to prevent the cache from writing data to the application, the cache data will be lost. See also *write-through caching*.

write-through caching

A caching optimization technique wherein data written to applications is kept in a cache for subsequent rereading. Unlike write-back caching, write-through caching immediately writes the data to the application and is, therefore, less optimal but more secure.

WWW

See *World Wide Web*.

X

X.25

A standard that defines packet-switching networks.

Index

Note to the Reader: Throughout this index **boldfaced** page numbers indicate primary discussions of a topic. *Italicized* page numbers indicate illustrations.

G

X

Z

MCSE CORE REQUIREMENT STUDY GUIDES FROM NETWORK PRESS

Sybex's Network Press presents updated and expanded second editions of the definitive study guides for MCSE candidates.

STUDY GUIDES FOR THE MICROSOFT CERTIFIED SYSTEMS ENGINEER EXAMS

MCSE ELECTIVE STUDY GUIDES FROM NETWORK PRESS®

ybex's Network Press expands the definitive study guide series for MCSE candidates.

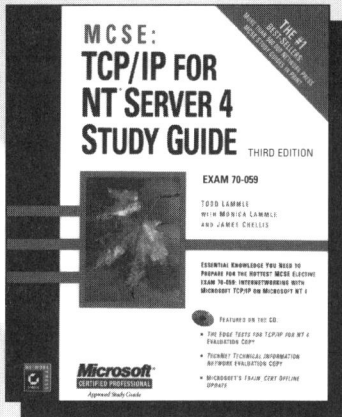

MCSE:
TCP/IP FOR
NT SERVER 4
STUDY GUIDE THIRD EDITION

EXAM 70-059

TODD LAMMLE
WITH MONICA LAMMLE
AND JAMES CHELLIS

ISBN: 0-7821-2224-8
688pp; 7¹/₂" x 9"; Hardcover
$49.99

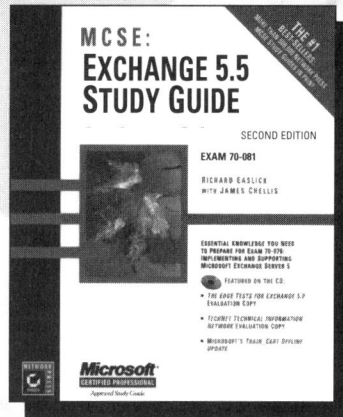

MCSE:
EXCHANGE 5.5
STUDY GUIDE

SECOND EDITION

EXAM 70-081

RICHARD EASLICK
WITH JAMES CHELLIS

ISBN: 0-7821-2261-2
848pp; 7¹/₂" x 9"; Hardcover
$49.99

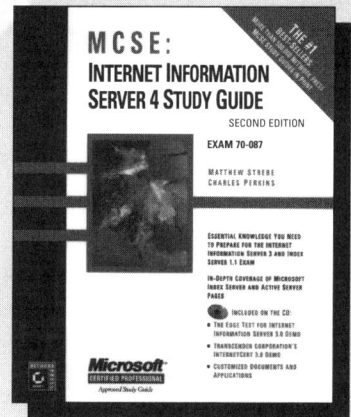

MCSE:
INTERNET INFORMATION
SERVER 4 STUDY GUIDE

SECOND EDITION

EXAM 70-087

MATTHEW STREBE
CHARLES PERKINS

ISBN: 0-7821-2248-5
704pp; 7¹/₂" x 9"; Hardcover
$49.99

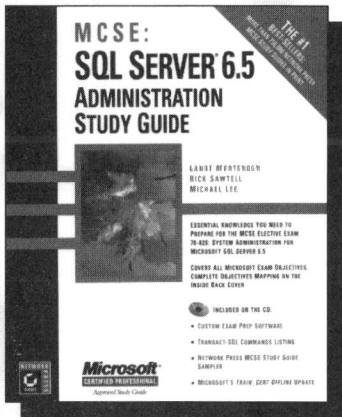

MCSE:
SQL SERVER 6.5
ADMINISTRATION
STUDY GUIDE

ISBN: 0-7821-2172-1
672pp; 7¹/₂" x 9"; Hardcover
$49.99

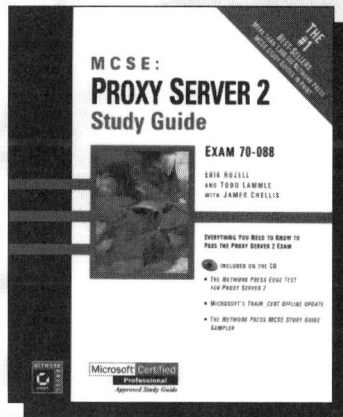

MCSE:
PROXY SERVER 2
Study Guide

EXAM 70-088

ERIK ROZELL
AND TODD LAMMLE
WITH JAMES CHELLIS

ISBN: 0-7821-2194-2
576pp; 7¹/₂" x 9"; Hardcover
$49.99

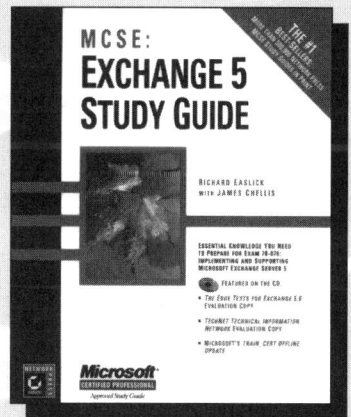

MCSE:
EXCHANGE 5
STUDY GUIDE

RICHARD EASLICK
WITH JAMES CHELLIS

ISBN: 0-7821-1967-0
656pp; 7¹/₂" x 9"; Hardcover
$49.99

Microsoft® Certified
Professional
Approved Study Guide

NETWORK PRESS®
SYBEX

STUDY GUIDES FOR THE MICROSOFT CERTIFIED SYSTEMS ENGINEER EXAMS

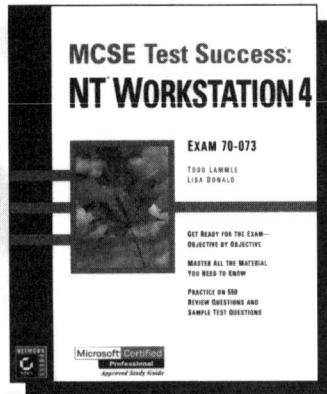

MCSE: Windows 98 Study Guide

Official Microsoft Objectives for Exam 70-098: Implementing and Supporting Windows® 98

Objective	Page
PLANNING	
Develop an appropriate implementation model for specific requirements in a Microsoft environment or a mixed Microsoft and NetWare environment. Considerations include choosing the appropriate file system and planning a workgroup.	9, 263
Develop a security strategy in a Microsoft environment or a mixed Microsoft and NetWare environment. Strategies include system policies, user profiles, file and printer sharing, and share-level access control or user-level access control.	355, 426, 444
INSTALLATION AND CONFIGURATION	
Install Windows 98. Installation options include automated Windows setup, New, Upgrade, Uninstall, and dual-boot combination with Microsoft Windows NT.	16, 26, 44, 49, 58, 66
Configure Windows 98 server components. Server components include Microsoft Personal Web Server 4.0 and Dial-Up Networking server.	524, 534
Install and configure the network components of Windows 98 in a Microsoft environment or a mixed Microsoft and NetWare environment. Network components include Client for Microsoft Networks, Client for NetWare Networks, network adapters, File and Printer Sharing for Microsoft Networks, File and Printer Sharing for NetWare Networks, Service for NetWare Directory Services (NDS), asynchronous transfer mode (ATM), virtual private networking and PPTP, and Browse Master.	276, 299, 322, 323, 335, 355, 359, 373, 375, 523
Install and configure network protocols in a Microsoft environment or a mixed Microsoft and NetWare environment. Protocols include NetBEUI, IPX/SPX-compatible protocol, IP, TCP/IP, Microsoft DLC, and Fast Infrared.	277, 285, 293, 295, 296, 298
Install and configure hardware devices in a Microsoft environment or a mixed Microsoft and NetWare environment. Hardware devices include modems, printers, Universal Serial Bus (USB), multiple display support, IEEE 1394 FireWire, Infrared Data Association (IrDA), multilink, and power management scheme.	80, 82, 84, 85, 87, 89, 92, 395, 500, 501
Install and configure Microsoft Backup.	236
CONFIGURING AND MANAGING RESOURCE ACCESS	
Assign access permissions for shared folders in a Microsoft environment or a mixed Microsoft and NetWare environment. Methods include passwords, user permissions, and group permissions.	357
Create, share, and monitor resources. Resources include remote computers and network printers.	369, 476
Set up user environments by using user profiles and system policies.	427, 447
Back up data and the Registry and restore data and the Registry.	149, 236

NOTE Exam objectives are subject to change at any time without prior notice and at Microsoft's sole discretion. Please visit Microsoft's Training & Certification Web site (www.microsoft.com/Train_Cert) for the most current listing of exam objectives.